RESEARCHERS

The following researchers have contributed to the 'Researcher reflections' features within the book, sharing their own experiences of undertaking qualitative research.

Mats Alvesson works at Lund University, Sweden and University of Queensland, Australia. He does research on organizations, working life, identity, gender, knowledge work and leadership. He has published many books and articles on the reflexive and creative aspects of methodology, including *Reflexive methodology* (with K. Sköldberg), *Interpreting interviews* and *Qualitative research and theory development* (with D. Kärreman) (all Sage).

Sue Anthony works at Western University, Ontario, Canada and has been a nurse for thirty years, the last sixteen in academia, where she has held administrative and teaching positions. Her teaching includes paediatric/family health and professional development. Her research involves the teaching–learning process and interprofessional education. Family, sports, quilting and the arts keep her professional life in balance.

Amy Bender is an Assistant Professor of nursing at the University of Toronto, Canada. Her research focuses on the mental health dimensions of tuberculosis, and she gives specific attention to notions of psychosocial wellbeing and identity. She approaches her research from a global health perspective that is influenced by health geography, post-colonialism, and public health ethics, and through critical qualitative methodologies.

J. Patrick Biddix is Associate Professor in the Department of Educational Leadership and Policy Studies at The University of Tennessee, Knoxville, USA. He teaches courses in postsecondary administration and research design and methodology. Dr Biddix's research interests include student engagement, research design, technology use and student affairs administration.

Carlos Calderón (PhD, MD, MA Sociology, MPH) is a Senior Consultant at the Health Center of Alza–San Sebastián (Spain) in the Basque Health Service-Osakidetza. He also serves as member of the Primary Care Research Unit of Gipuzkoa. He has worked and lectured widely on qualitative health research and he is particularly interested in its practical and methodological development in primary care.

Susan E. Chase is Professor of Sociology at the University of Tulsa, USA. She is author of *Learning to speak, learning to listen: How diversity works on campus*; *Ambiguous empowerment, the work narratives of women school superintendents*, and co-author of *Mothers and children: Feminist analyses and personal narratives*.

Sara M. Childers is Assistant Professor of Research Methodology in the College of Education at the University of Alabama, USA. She received her doctorate in Social and Cultural Foundations of Education from the Ohio State University. Her research focuses on qualitative methodologies including sociocultural policy analysis, educational anthropology, and feminist, critical race and post-structural theories.

Sebnem Cilesiz is an Assistant Professor of cultural foundations, technology, and qualitative inquiry in the School of Educational Policy and Leadership at The Ohio State University, USA. Her research interests include social and cultural contexts of technology use and qualitative research methodology. Her previous work has been published in the *American Educational Research Journal*, *Educational Technology, Research and Development* and *Qualitative Inquiry*.

Simon Cooper is a Nurse Educator at Monash University, Australia with an interest in emergency care and teamwork. Originally trained as a quantitative researcher, his work has expanded to include qualitative and mixed methods approaches that capture the richness and quality of experiences in the emergency field.

Madeleine Duncan MScOT, DPhil (Psychology) is an Associate Professor in the Department of Health and Rehabilitation Sciences, University of Cape Town, South Africa. Committed to the advancement of contextually relevant occupational therapy education and practice in a developing country, her service, research and publication interests focus on undergraduate teaching and learning, the impact of chronic and structural poverty on humans as occupational beings and psychiatric disability.

Colleen Fisher is an Associate Professor in the School of Population Health at the University of Western Australia where she teaches qualitative research at undergraduate and postgraduate levels and has supervised numerous Masters and PhD students. Her main research interest is women's health generally and family and domestic violence specifically.

Bent Flyvbjerg is the first BT Professor and Founding Chair of Major Programme Management at Oxford University's Saïd Business School. He was twice a Visiting Fulbright Scholar to the USA, where he did research at UCLA, UC Berkeley and Harvard. His books and articles have been translated into eighteen languages.

As Professor of Professional Education in the Centre for Medical Education at Queen Mary, University of London, **Della Freeth** works alongside a wide range of health professionals to research and promote the conditions necessary to support high-quality learning in workplaces, simulated environments and classrooms. She has particular interests in education that supports patient safety; learning through simulated professional practice and interprofessional collaboration. Recently, she has been studying aspects of safety culture in hospital teams and also examining healthcare practitioners' transitions from initial qualification through the first two years of professional practice.

Karri Holley is Associate Professor of Higher Education at the University of Alabama, USA. She received her PhD from the University of Southern California. Her research interests include graduate education, interdisciplinarity, organizational change and qualitative inquiry. She formerly served as a Peace Corps volunteer in Ukraine.

Adrian Holliday is a Professor of Applied Linguistics at Canterbury Christ Church University, UK, in the Department of Language Studies, where he coordinates doctoral research in international English language education and intercultural issues. He is also Head of the Graduate School and Research Office and directs the university research degrees programme. He has published widely in the critical sociology of TESOL, qualitative research methodology and intercultural communication.

Alecia Jackson holds a PhD in Language Education from The University of Georgia, USA where she also obtained a Women's Studies Graduate Certificate and a Qualitative Studies Graduate Certificate. She teaches educational research at the master's, specialist's and doctoral levels in the College of Education at Appalachian State University.

Dr Jackson's research interests bring feminist and post-structural theories of power, knowledge, language and subjectivity to bear on a range of overlapping topics: deconstructions of narrative and voice, cultural studies of schooling (with an emphasis on the rural) and qualitative method in the post-modern. She has publications in the *International Journal of Qualitative Studies in Education*, *Qualitative Inquiry*, the *International Review of Qualitative Research*, and *Qualitative Research*. Her co-edited book *Voice in qualitative inquiry* (with colleague Lisa Mazzei) was published in September 2008 by Routledge Press and *Thinking with theory in qualitative research: Using epistemological frameworks in the production of meaning*, also co-authored with Mazzei, was published by Routledge Press in 2011.

Lisa A. Mazzei is Associate Professor, Doctoral Program in Leadership Studies, Gonzaga University, USA. She is also Visiting Research Fellow at the Education and Social Research Institute, Manchester Metropolitan University, UK. She is co-editor with Alecia Y. Jackson of *Voice in qualitative inquiry* (Routledge), co-author with Alecia Y. Jackson of *Thinking with theory in qualitative research* (Routledge), and author of *Inhabited silence in qualitative research*.

Robin Jarrett is a sociologist and Professor in the Departments of Human and Community Development and African American Studies at the University of Illinois at Urbana-Champaign, USA. She is an urban ethnographer and uses a repertoire of qualitative methods (interviews, participant observation, neighbourhood observations, photo documents and geographic information systems) in her work. Her research focuses on the resilient coping strategies of low-income, African American families.

Elizabeth A. Jones is Professor and Director of the Doctoral Program in the School of Education at Holy Family University, Philadelphia, USA. She conducts research on student learning and assessment. She has published articles on the assessment of general education and critical thinking as well as assessment of the first-year experience.

George Kamberelis is the Wyoming Excellence in Higher Education Endowed Chair in Literacy Education at the University of Wyoming, USA. He teaches and conducts research on critical social theory, philosophical foundations of inquiry, interpretive research methods and literacy learning in school and community settings.

Magdalena Kazubowski-Houston is Assistant Professor of Anthropology at Wilfrid Laurier University, Canada, where her research focuses on performance and experimental ethnography. Her book, *Staging strife* (2010), is co-winner of the 2011 International Congress of Qualitative Inquiry Outstanding Qualitative Book Award and the Canadian Association for Theatre Research Ann Saddlemyer Book Prize.

Dr Hok Bun Ku obtained his PhD from the department of anthropology and sociology at SOAS, University of London, in 1999. In 2001, he joined the Hong Kong Polytechnic University and began to advocate participatory research methodology. He has been involved in China's rural development for about fifteen years and has written extensively on topics related to rural community development, cultural politics, participatory design, social exclusion and marginality, and social work education.

Dr Aaron M. Kuntz is an Assistant Professor in Educational Studies at the University of Alabama, USA. His research interests include critical geography, academic citizenship and activism, materialist methodologies and critical inquiry.

Guillaume Latzko-Toth is an Assistant Professor in the Department of Information and Communication at Université Laval (Quebec City, Canada). He holds a PhD in Communication from Université du Québec à Montréal, where he is still active as a member of the Laboratory on Computer-mediated Communication (LabCMO) within the Interuniversity Research Center on Science and Technology (CIRST).

Eric Laurier is a Senior Lecturer in Geography and Interaction at the University of Edinburgh, UK. He has been the principal investigator on Economic and Social Research Council-funded research projects on cafe life, car travel and film editing.

Dr Shosh Leshem was a visiting Lecturer at Anglia Ruskin University, UK, for eight years. She worked with doctoral candidates, supervisors and examiners and conducted research on the nature of doctorateness. She is currently Head of Teacher Education Faculty at Oranim, Academic College of Education, Israel, and lectures at Haifa University.

Eric Margolis is a Sociologist and Associate Professor in the Hugh Downs School of Human Communication at Arizona State University. He is President of the International Visual Sociology Association. His scholarly interests have included the politics and hidden curricula of higher education, visual research methods in general and visual ethnography in particular.

Matt Mawer is a Research Assistant in Psychology at Coventry University, UK and is undertaking a PhD at the Learning Innovation Applied Research Group. His doctoral research explores students' perspectives on the educational use of virtual worlds in UK higher education. Matt's academic interests are multidisciplinary and span educational technology, forensic psychology, the sociology of virtual spaces, social research methods and philosophy.

Roland Mitchell is an Associate Professor in the Department of Educational Theory Policy and Practice at Louisiana State University, USA. He is the Program Leader for Higher Education Administration and Co-Director of the Curriculum Theory Project. He has a BA in History from Fisk University, an MEd in Higher Education from Vanderbilt University, and a PhD in Educational Research from The University of Alabama.

Betsy Palmer is an Associate Professor of Adult and Higher Education and Educational Research and Statistics at Montana State University, USA. She conducts research on college student outcomes and university teaching, particularly focused on student epistemology, non-traditional pedagogies and multicultural education. She recently expanded her research agenda to include a focus on the intersection of education and economic development in Nepal.

Mary Romero is Professor of Justice Studies and Social Inquiry at Arizona State University, USA. She received the American Sociology American Section on Race and Ethnicity Minorities 2009 Founder's Award and the Society for the Study of Social Problems' Lee Founders Award 2004. She is the author of *Maid in the U.S.A.* and *The maid's daughter: Living inside and outside the American dream.*

Jerry Rosiek is Associate Professor of Education Studies at the University of Oregon, USA where he teaches courses on the cultural foundations of education and qualitative research methodology. He is also affiliated faculty in the Department of Philosophy and the Department of Ethnic Studies. His empirical scholarship focuses on teacher knowledge and the ways teachers learn from their classroom experience. His research has experimented with the use of narrative modes of representation, narrative inquiry, and most recently theatrical representations of educational research. His writing has appeared in several major journals including *Harvard Educational Review*, *Education Theory*, *Educational Researcher*, *Qualitative Inquiry*, *Curriculum Inquiry*, *Educational Psychologist* and the *Journal of Teacher Education*.

Johnny Saldaña, Professor of Theatre at Arizona State University, USA is the author of several books including *Drama of color*, *Longitudinal qualitative research: Analyzing change through time*, *Fundamentals of qualitative research*, *Ethnodrama: An anthology of reality theatre*, *Ethnotheatre: Research from page to stage*, and *The coding manual for qualitative researchers*.

Jörgen Sandberg is Professor in Management and Organization Studies at the University of Queensland, Australia. His research interests include competence and learning in organizations, leadership, practice-based theories, qualitative research methods and the philosophical underpinnings of organizational research.

Ian Shaw is Professor of Social Work at University of York, UK. Founder and co-editor of *Qualitative social work*, his next book is a back-catalogue of essays from his career (*Practice and research*, Ashgate: 2012). He is researching networks in social work research, and the intertwined emergence historically of social work and sociology.

Elizabeth Adams St. Pierre is Professor of Language and Literacy Education and Affiliated Professor of both the Qualitative Research Program and the Women's Studies Institute at the University of Georgia, USA. She focuses on post-structural theories of language and subjectivity and, currently, on a critique of both scientifically based research and conventional qualitative research methodology.

Robert Thornberg, PhD, is Associate Professor of Education at Linköping University, Sweden. His current research is on school bullying as a social process as well as from the perspectives of the students. His second line of research is on school rules and morality in everyday school life.

Gemma Tombs is an educational researcher at Coventry University, UK. Her research interests are centred around virtual worlds, practitioner perspectives and the socio-political culture of higher education. She is also currently finishing a PhD in virtual world pedagogy, utilizing a case study methodology. Additionally, Gemma is keenly interested in the developing role of social media in education and the ways in which these might influence research methodologies. In her spare time she enjoys ice skating, card-making and web design.

Professor Emeritus **Vernon Trafford** worked in the Business School and Education Faculty at Anglia Ruskin University, UK, establishing the DBA and EdD professional doctorates. Supervision and examination of theses plus attending over 100 doctoral vivas have provided ten years of insider-research into the nature of doctorateness.

Elizabeth Vitullo is the Director of Masters Programs at West Virginia University's College of Business and Economics, USA. She completed her PhD in Education and MBA at West Virginia University. Elizabeth is responsible for the assurance of learning for graduate programmes at the college and is an adjunct professor in the Entrepreneurship Program.

Marcus Weaver-Hightower is Associate Professor of Educational Foundations and Research, University of North Dakota. His research focuses on boys and masculinity, food politics and the politics and sociology of education. He the author of *The politics of policy in boys' education: Getting boys 'Right'* and other articles and collections.

Dr Katherine Wimpenny is a Research Fellow at Coventry University, UK and has a background in occupational therapy. Katherine has been involved in applied research in health and social care for the past nine years and is experienced in the use of participatory approaches and working collaboratively with a range of stake holder groups. She currently supervises five PhD students using a range of qualitative research methodologies.

Gina Wisker is Head of the Centre for Learning and Teaching, and Professor of Higher Education and Contemporary Literature at the University of Brighton, UK, where she also teaches undergraduate literature, supervises postgraduates and runs writing courses . Gina is editor of the SEDA journal *Innovations in Education and Teaching International* and an ex chair of the Heads of Educational Development Group. She enjoys travelling to work with colleagues in South Africa, Australia, New Zealand, Ireland, Iraq and Saudi Arabia and tries to balance that with living in both Cambridge and Brighton. Gina's second edition of *The good supervisor* (Palgrave Macmillan) was published in May 2012.

FIGURES

TABLES

INTRODUCTION

Context: Two students chatting by the photocopier late one September morning:

Graham: Sorry, nearly finished; I just need to copy different parts from all these books for my research course this term.

Sally: Oh, OK. What's the course?

Graham: Introduction to qualitative research. No idea what it is about really, but I am trying to avoid buying all five required text books . . . I'm broke, and sometimes I think Wikipedia's more helpful than the texts anyway.

Sally: Yeah, I agree. Sounds like a course I need to do, though. I just did some qualitative surveys and the odd interview for a course project, but my grade on my first draft of the paper wasn't great, so I think maybe I need to change my approach. I'm not sure what I should do instead, though.

Graham: My lecturer keeps talking about a 'conceptual framework' and a 'researcher's lens'. No idea what those are, but I think they must be important.

Sally: Well, maybe you could help me because my lecturer's comments on my paper said that my interpretive lens wasn't clear, so I guess you are right that it is important, whatever it is.

Graham: Yes certainly, I'll help you, if you'll help me figure out what research approach I need to use to answer my research question!

Many readers will find this story familiar, as there are a number of complexities associated with qualitative research. In particular, the story illustrates challenges and choices associated with research approaches, conflicting or confusing terminology, and the necessity of having multiple texts for novice researchers. These are issues that we have attempted to address with this text.

THE CHALLENGE OF COUNTLESS CHOICES

For many people in academic life, research is a challenge, whether they are new or experienced in their research fields. Part of the challenge is due to the range of approaches and methods available, and it is not always a straightforward decision when deciding which one to choose. With the rapid development of qualitative research in particular, there has been a startling increase in the number of ways to carry out a study. Given what seems like an endless array of choices, for many researchers, the following seem to be the options:

- read sporadically, pick something and hope it will work,
- read everything and find something that looks like it will work, or
- ignore everything and just do some interviews.

These tactics, however, undercut the intentional nature of qualitative research and can thus lead to bad research. Researchers instead should be aware of the choices they will face and approach them with some degree of intentionality.

To address the challenge of myriad research choices and researchers' need to know about them, in this book we outline the essential choices qualitative researchers face when designing and implementing a qualitative study. These choices range from positioning oneself theoretically, to framing the study, working with an existing research approach, collecting and working with data. We present a conceptual model of these choices, which illustrates the fact that each choice affects the next, and attempts to provide a balance across various perspectives as well as to offer some down to earth practical advice about where to begin, suggesting how and what particular approaches work best in given contexts and situations, as well as providing some warnings against the 'just setting off and hoping' approach.

THE CHALLENGE OF NUMEROUS TEXTS

There are many fine texts that address various issues in qualitative research and we have cited many of them throughout this book. These books often choose a specific topic related to qualitative research to address, whether research design, interviewing, data analysis or other. We believe that these books are essential for the field inquiry as we are struggling to come to grips with what the field really is. They provide much needed depth that helps researchers to focus on these specific topics and the issues that attend them.

We also believe, however, that the array of quality texts can be challenging for novice researchers, who most often are seeking a broad introduction to and overview of critical issues and choices, as well as for teachers who are attempting to provide students with a first exposure to qualitative research. Indeed, we have at times found ourselves teaching an introductory course while drawing from at least five different texts (when we would have liked just one but simply could not find one that addressed what we see as the most critical issues for new researchers to consider).

For this reason, we saw space for a text that provides readers with a breadth approach to the field; one that highlights key choice moments and provides practical advice about making them and then carrying on with the study. Thus in many ways this book is born out of our own struggles as researchers to find a textbook that deals with a sufficient range of issues in one tome. It is our attempt to highlight the most critical choices that new researchers face, providing a breadth of exposure to attending ideas and issues.

THE CHALLENGE OF ASSORTED TERMINOLOGY

We are researchers and writers who are acutely aware of the issues in terminology related to qualitative research. Indeed, it seems to us that scholars use many different terms to portray similar aspects of the research process. Moreover, we believe that 'English' across the Atlantic divide has served to divide scholars by a seemingly common language, which in actuality has many differences in terminology as well as inference. This discrepancy has led to the likelihood of qualitative scholars' misinterpretation and misunderstanding of each other.

Indeed, as we set about writing this text, we often began a section by using the same terms, thinking we were talking about the same thing, only to realise later that we were talking about completely different things. It has been important to us to avoid jargon and overly complicated terms in the writing when possible, striving instead to explain complex concepts in plain English, but without oversimplifying them. We have attempted to draw out and explain concepts, then, in what we believe is an accessible way and to provide illustrations, examples and a range of reflections from expert researchers from around the globe that allow for demonstrating their complexity.

THIS BOOK IN BRIEF

For the many years we have known each other, we have discussed and debated issues related to qualitative research. This book is both a reflection and continuance of our debates and discussions. The text stems from our desire to share 'really useful knowledge' as well as practical examples and tales from experience, with an intent toward being both helpful and encouraging. From our own perspectives, it stems too from the struggles we have encountered in our own research as well as in explaining differences in approaches to others when teaching or mentoring research. Our vision for this text has been to create a book that supports researchers who are seeking to do sound qualitative research: research that is philosophically informed, located in an appropriate approach, well designed, competently analyzed and interpreted and that produces trustworthy findings. We have striven to accomplish this in a text that is laid out in seven parts.

In Part 1 of this book, 'Considering perspectives', we provide introductory information about qualitative research as a field of inquiry, about the philosophies that underpin it and about the choices a researcher faces when designing and doing qualitative research. It is in this section, in Chapter 3, that we provide our conceptual model of research choices. In Part 2 of this text, 'Acknowledging a position', we describe an array of philosophical and personal positions that a qualitative researcher may assume and articulate. In Part 3, 'Framing the study', we describe a range of issues, from choosing a phenomenon to study, to writing good research questions, to developing a literature review as well as a theoretical or conceptual framework. In Part 4, 'Choosing a research approach', we provide overviews of ten research approaches that we find many qualitative researchers choose to take up. In Part 5, 'Collecting data', we describe issues related to collecting data, such as choosing a site and participants to gaining ethical approval. We also describe ways to approach fieldwork as well as specific data collection techniques, including interviews, focus groups, observations and document collection. In Part 6, 'Working with data and findings', we describe techniques for data coding, analysis and interpretation. We also describe issues in and techniques for ensuring the quality of a study. Finally, in Part 7, 'Writing about the research', we describe the ways in which qualitative researchers establish their voices and positions in the text, as well as the ways in which they may go about writing the research report.

In writing this book, we grappled not only with ideas and issues but also with the language, and at times with each other, in order to come to mutual understanding and consensus. Putting this textbook together, then, has been very much a space of debate for both of us as we have sought to appreciate and challenge common usage of terms and accepted understandings of theories, concepts, myths and legends from earlier texts in this field. We believe – and hope – that this text will provide clear and helpful guidance for academics and students alike.

Maggi Savin-Baden   Claire Howell Major

 Please see the corresponding section of your Interactive Textbook for an interview with Professor Maggi Savin-Baden.

ACKNOWLEDGEMENTS

Many people have supported the production of this text and have worked tirelessly to support us in this large undertaking. We therefore wish to thank Cathy Tombs and Sonia Lal for their editorial work in checking the manuscript and references, Katherine Wimpenny for her supportive reflections, Christine Sinclair for her critical comments on a number of chapters, Stephanie Blackmon for editorial work on several chapters, and all the reviewers who commented on the text during the writing process. We also are grateful to the University of Alabama executive EdD Cohort 5 who provided useful insights as we 'tried out' various ideas from the text with them.

We are grateful too to all our colleagues around the world who have provided interesting and insightful researcher reflections throughout the book.

Our final and heartfelt thanks go to John Savin-Baden for the detailed checking and critical comments – as well as much needed humour – during the final phases of the completion of the manuscript.

VISUAL TOUR OF *QUALITATIVE RESEARCH: THE ESSENTIAL GUIDE TO THEORY AND PRACTICE*

PEDAGOGICAL FEATURES

Qualitative Research offers an array of pedagogical features specifically designed to enhance your teaching and learning experience.

Marginal definitions of key terms

Difficult terminology is defined both within the margins of the text and in a comprehensive glossary at the end of the book. This reinforces students' knowledge and understanding of key qualitative research terminology.

Tips boxes

These useful boxes guide students through the more difficult concepts of qualitative research, making challenging topics accessible and easy to digest.

Researcher reflections boxes

Hands-on, practical examples run throughout the book to help students relate theory to practice. In addition, unique and exclusive Researcher reflections boxes provide real-life examples from expert researchers around the globe, bringing the subject to life.

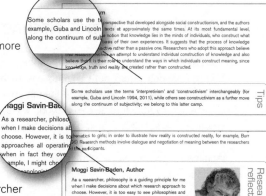

Further reading

Each chapter concludes with an annotated list of important scholarly books and articles relevant to the topic at hand. These key resources guide independent study and provide a useful point of departure for students wishing to develop their studies.

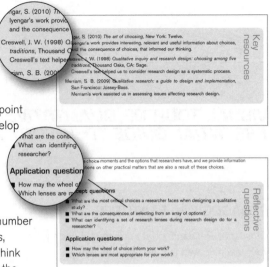

End of chapter reflective questions

At the end of each chapter there are a number of key concept and application questions, encouraging students to reflect on and think critically about the material presented in the chapter. These can be used to promote class discussion or as assignable homework tasks.

Figures, tables and diagrams

The book contains a wealth of supporting figures, diagrams and tables to help students visualise processes described in the text.

VISUAL TOUR OF THE INTERACTIVE TEXTBOOK

You can access your Interactive eTextbook at home, on campus or on the move*. Your eTextbook offers note sharing and highlighting functionality, as well as exclusive interactive content to enhance your learning experience. The notes you make on your Interactive eTextbook will synchronise with all other versions, creating a personalised version that you can access wherever and whenever you need it. Throughout the text you will see icons in the margin where further multimedia resources are available via your Interactive eTextbook. These include:

    additional case study abstracts relating to the chapter at hand

    audio and video

Unique to *Qualitative Research: the essential guide to theory and practice*

Student resources

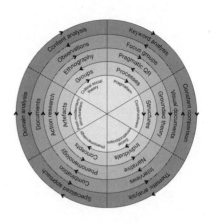

- Video introduction to the book and author team
- Exclusive chapters on 'planning and managing your writing' and on 'publishing qualitative research'
- A fully interactive 'Wheel of Research Choices', complete with video and audio resources, guiding you through the decisions involved in choosing your own approach to qualitative research
- Additional case study abstracts, providing further examples of the concepts included in the book
- Informative links to *relevant journals*, *conferences*, *special interest groups* and *online resources* for the qualitative researcher.

Instructor resources

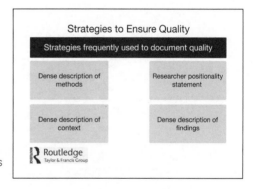

- Comprehensive lesson plans for each chapter, including ideas for:
  o   Lectures
  o   Class activities
  o   Discussions
  o   Homework
  o   Group activities
  o   Class assessments
- There is also a complete set of PowerPoint slides to accompany each chapter.

Many of these exciting interactive teaching and learning resources are also available for instructors to download from the following site: www.routledge.com/9780415674782

BookShelf* will provide access to your eTextbook either online or as a download via your PC, Mac (OS X 10.6>), iPad, iPhone, iPod Touch (iOS 3.2>), Android app or Amazon Kindle Fire.

Considering perspectives

PART ONE

Chapter 1

Qualitative research

INTRODUCTION

Social researchers work in a number of disciplines, such as sociology, psychology and anthropology, and professional fields, such as education, business and the health professions. These researchers face a range of increasingly complicated questions and issues and, therefore, strive to choose the best approaches for investigating these complexities. Such researchers tend to adopt research methods that are compatible with their ideas about the world and the nature of **knowledge** and social reality.

Some scholars approach social research from a positivist or post-positivist **paradigm** and typically a quantitative perspective, while others approach it from a paradigm more common to qualitative research, such as critical social theory, pragmatism, phenomenology, post-critical/post-structural, constructionism or constructivism. Indeed, there is considerable conflict amongst researchers about the best ways to view and investigate social phenomena, which some researchers have called 'the paradigm debates' (for example, Klenke 2008). However, more and more social researchers are choosing to use qualitative research, pairing it with their choice of paradigm, and thus it has emerged from these debates as an increasingly important way in which social researchers carry out their work.

The field of qualitative inquiry has continued to evolve since early twentieth century debates about whether post-positivism was an appropriate paradigm for social research. Now, researchers, who would in the past have had no choices about how to view and carry out research, are at times faced with an overwhelming number of them. As a result of these choices, taking up qualitative research is not straightforward and requires that a researcher has world views, central goals and questions that are sympathetic to and compatible with a qualitative approach. Therefore, knowing the essential features and elements of the approach is critical for someone considering conducting a qualitative study. In this chapter, we consider the ways in which questions about how to explore human experience have changed. We also discuss the alternatives that exist for doing social research that are associated with a qualitative perspective and consider the questions of 'what are the origins of qualitative research?', 'what is qualitative research?' and 'what are the key characteristics of qualitative research?'.

Knowledge

The body of 'truths', information or awareness that humans have acquired or constructed

Paradigm

A belief system or world view that guides the researcher and the research process (Guba and Lincoln 1994)

WICKED PROBLEMS AND WICKED CONSTRAINTS

Social research has roots in both sociology and statistics, and social researchers originally drew upon a positivist philosophy to guide their work. Positivists see the world in terms of

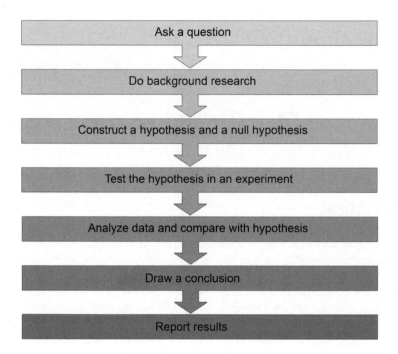

Figure 1.1 The scientific method

cause-and-effect relationships and believe that by making assumptions (hypotheses) and then testing them, it will be possible to prove what is true. Positivists favour quantitative methods, since they allow for the collection of factual data, and so the methods, and how knowledge is gained, are critical. Central to the positivist position of prediction and control is the experiment, or the idea that it is possible to find a solution or develop a law by manipulating the variables that affect the subject of study. Positivists, then, place faith in quantification and upon the idea that using the correct techniques will provide correct answers, and thus they are concerned about ensuring that measurements produced are consistent and accurate. The researcher does not directly interact with the people they are studying, because interaction would risk influencing their behaviour. In short, positivism is founded upon scientific methods and experiments. The scientific method is depicted in Figure 1.1.

The dominance of the positivist perspective on social research led people to assume that all research should be carried out based upon on a model of natural sciences, aimed at providing clear and unambiguous causes of certain social phenomena. This dominance also led some to assume that there was a correlation between social phenomena and their causes and others to believe positivist research to be inadequate to explain how people live, view the world and effect change, since it is largely inappropriate for such a task (Ryan 2006).

Early social researchers tended to take up the objective stance of positivism in order to focus on the natural world and to examine relationships between variables (Ryan 2006). They often used natural science approaches, such as controlled experiments, in which they attempted to isolate small samples of people from their social contexts and rely upon comparison and classification for analysis, applying statistical tests to determine statistical significance. For early social researchers, then, objectives were clear, rules were straightforward and research goals

The legacy of positivism

While most contemporary qualitative researchers do not assume a positivist stance, positivism maintains a strong presence, as some qualitative researchers still use terms related to it, such as validity and reliability (see Chapter 30).

Significance and statistical significance

When researchers use the term 'significance', they tend to mean statistical significance, which is different from the typical definition of significance.

Tips

and paths were linear. For decades, social research remained entrenched in its positivistic paradigm; indeed, many social researchers still operate from this perspective. (For additional information about positivism, see Chapter 2.)

In time, however, some researchers began to view knowledge in a different way. Instead of seeing their responsibility as the quest for 'truth' or 'reality' that could be measured objectively, researchers began seeking to understand human knowledge and experience. Indeed, individuals by nature, some scholars argued, experienced the world qualitatively. Leading American educationalist and philosopher Dewey explained:

> The world in which we immediately live, that in which we strive, succeed, and are defeated is pre-eminently a qualitative world. What we act for, suffer, and enjoy are things in their qualitative determinations ... it is safe at the outset to refer simply to [qualitative thought as that] which has to do with objects involved in the concerns and issues of living.
>
> (Dewey 1931)

The way in which individuals experience the world directly influences the way in which they think about it: 'This [qualitative] world forms the field of characteristic modes of thinking, characteristic in that thought is definitely regulated by qualitative considerations' (Dewey 1931). Indeed, some researchers began to consider conscious thought as a qualitative act. In practice, individuals sense and perceive an object, event or phenomenon and then bring it to a conscious level, thus conscious thought, which is influenced by the world in which we live and is qualitative in nature. Kestenbaum (1977), for example, called this process one of qualification and argued that it is through the dialectic of the self and the world that meaning comes into being. Thus, experience and thought are inextricably linked and individuals experience both life and conscious thought qualitatively. At times, social researchers seek to understand that experience of life.

We suggest that all of these components make social research an exploration of wicked problems. Wicked problems are messy, circular or aggressive; they have no single right solution. In contrast, tame problems, such as math problems or puzzles, tend to have a single, correct answer (Higgs and Cherry 2009; Rittel and Webber 1973). The increase of wicked problems led to the need for new ways of conceptualizing them.

Significance
Importance; being worthy of attention

Statistical significance
A result from a statistical analysis that is unlikely to have occurred by chance

Validity
Determines whether the research truly measures what it was intended to measure or how truthful the research results are

Reliability
Reliability is ensuring that experiments can be repeated to measure the same thing again accurately

Given the growing complexity of the human condition and research problems, researchers in the 1920s and 1930s began to consider the constraints of quantitative research methods to be too tight for answering important questions about the qualities that humans experience and that shape their thoughts and actions. Dewey, for example, pointed out that:

> The propositions significant in physical science are oblivious of qualitative considerations as such; they deal with 'primary qualities' in distinction from secondary and tertiary; in actual treatment, moreover, these primary qualities are not qualities but relations.
>
> (Dewey 1931)

Wicked problems then also led to the need for new ways of conducting social research.

ORIGINS OF CONTEMPORARY QUALITATIVE INQUIRY

While some scholars trace the origins of qualitative research back several centuries (for example, Vidich and Lyman 2000), many trace it to this period of conceptualizing ways to address wicked problems that arose in the early twentieth century. The constraints of the scientific method inhibited many twentieth century scholars. Eventually, beginning around the late 1960s, scholars became forcefully critical of social research that used natural science as a model, arguing that the two were incompatible since 'the most challenging themes and theoretically exciting questions are not reached by the logico-deductive scientific method. Instead they are reached by a process that resembles artistic imagination' (Ryan 2006: 17).

Prompted by the need to solve both questions involving the subjective mind and criticisms of existing methods, mid and late century scholars began to seek new ways of carrying out social research that emphasized that knowledge is not neutral. Instead, it was considered that divisions between objectivity and subjectivity at times were socially and intersubjectively constructed (Ryan 2006). Scholars had different ways of viewing the world and thus thought different methods were best for conducting research (Bryman 2004). In addition, these critics believed that dualistic thinking (black/white, right/wrong) was inadequate but, rather, multiplicity and complexity were hallmarks of humanity (Ryan 2006). Gaining ground in the 1960s, interpretivist and constructivist researchers began to perceive that research should be holistic rather than reductionist. Thus, much social science research today is carried out from a range of philosophical perspectives, which we describe in Chapters 2 and 4.

Starting in the late 1960s, new approaches emerged, suggesting that 'the personal is political, that the subjective is a valid form of knowledge ... and that all people are capable of naming their own world and constructing knowledge' (Ryan 2006: 17). Researchers saw that individuals were aware of themselves and their relationship to others. They also believed that people made deliberate choices about how to behave in different situations. This argument centred on the fact that society does not exist in an objective, observable form; rather, it is experienced subjectively because individuals give it meaning by the way they behave. Individuals, then, create and recreate a sense of the social system. Facts about behaviour may be established but those facts are always context bound and do not apply to all people at all times in all situations.

Qualitative researchers generally do not test for cause and effect but rather seek to learn because they believe that the social world is different from the natural world. They tend to believe that, when studying individuals, the best that researchers can do is learn about, describe and explain them from the perceptions of those involved. Qualitative researchers seek the perspective provided by the whole picture and assert that values, passion and politics are important in this research. Such research requires patience, honesty, courage, persistence, imagination, sympathy and self-discipline, as well as a view of researchers as people who conduct research amongst other people and learn with them, rather than conduct research on them (Reason and Rowan 1981). These perspectives have led qualitative social researchers to lean toward collecting qualitative data and using methods such as unstructured interviews and participant observation.

Given the emergence and growth of the field over time, it is little wonder that scholars debate the precise origins of qualitative research. The key questions of the debate revolve around both its disciplinary and historical origins, as well as whether it truly represents a fundamentally new way of thinking or a potent way to react against and reshape the scientific method. Some scholars see a revolution of sorts, while others see an evolution over time that has led us to the current vision of qualitative research. We believe that these are compatible perspectives and that qualitative research was a revolution in thinking and approach that has evolved over time.

Revolution

Some scholars argue that qualitative research is a revolution in thinking about social research (for example, Lincoln and Guba 1990), marking what Kuhn referred to as a 'paradigm shift' (Kuhn 1970). What such an argument suggests in essence is that theoretical ideas and technical procedures, which are rooted in language and terminology, fundamentally change. In this way, the rise of qualitative research was:

> A quiet methodological revolution ... in the social sciences ... . Where only statistics, experimental designs, and survey research once stood, researchers have opened up ethnography, unstructured interviewing, textual analysis, and historical studies. Rather than 'doing science' scholars are now experimenting with the boundaries of interpretation ... to understand more fully the relationship of the researcher to the research. In various disciplines in various guises, this implicit critique of the traditional world view of science and quantitative methods is taking place. All of these trends have fallen under the rubric of 'qualitative research'.
>
> (Denzin and Lincoln 1994: ix)

Evolution

While qualitative research emerged as a reaction against quantitative approaches and may be viewed as a revolution, the field of inquiry has grown and changed over time. Indeed, some scholars (for example, Vidich and Lyman 2000) trace the origins of qualitative social methods to the fifteenth and sixteenth centuries, with the emergence of descriptive ethnography that examined early explorers' voyages to new places and their encounters with other cultures. Most scholars, however, place the origins of the current and more structured form of qualitative social research in the twentieth century. Many of these scholars also point specifically to the 1960s as the time that the current form of qualitative research emerged, with the pragmatist development of symbolic interactionism (Becker *et al.* 1961) (see Chapter 11) and grounded theory (Glaser and Strauss 1967) (see Chapter 12).

Denzin and Lincoln (1994) fell somewhere between the two historical approaches (the long view and the shorter view) and described the development of qualitative research in terms of five phases or moments, starting in the early twentieth century. They pointed out that, although the emergence of each phase can be historically located, each continues to influence and be present in research practice across the world. Below is a summary of their account of the different moments or phases of the emergence and development of qualitative inquiry.

First moment: the traditional phase (1900–1940s)

In this moment, researchers drew upon pragmatic understandings of reality. They relied upon accounts of field experiences, sought to provide 'valid, reliable, and objective interpretations' (Denzin and Lincoln 1994: 7) and developed written accounts that attempted to depict reality.

Second moment: the modern phase (1950s–1970s)

As in the first moment, researchers presented accounts of work in the field, and added marginalized and other voices, although continuing to seek to establish rigour in similar ways to quantitative approaches. Denzin and Lincoln refer to the 1960s as 'the golden age of rigorous qualitative analysis' (1998: 17).

Third moment: blurred genres (1970–1986)

In this moment, post-positivist, naturalistic/interpretive and constructivist perspectives emerged that blurred the boundaries between the social sciences and the humanities. In this moment, researchers took up diverse strategies and techniques, including narrative, phenomenological and hermeneutic approaches. This moment is the one in which the researcher is considered a 'bricoleur' who borrows from many disciplines to design and implement a study as well as to report the findings to an audience.

Fourth moment: crises of representation (mid 1980s–1990)

In this moment, the blurring of genres problematized the writing of research. The researcher's identity and power as constructor of the text was acknowledged, so the direct link between lived experience and the text was open to challenge. In turn, issues of validity, reliability and generalizability arose, so research became difficult to evaluate and its authority was questioned.

Fifth moment: the post-modern period of experimental ethnography (1990–1995)

In this moment, researchers attempted to grapple with the crises of the post-modern era, searching for different ways to represent the 'other'. Grand narratives and 'distant observers' were abandoned in favour of action-based and activist research and local, small-scale theories. Other evaluative criteria were sought, including moral and critical perspectives. Table 1.1 summarizes Denzin and Lincoln's five moments.

By the time a decade had elapsed, Denzin and Lincoln (2005) had identified a triple crisis of representation, legitimation and praxis that began occurring during the fifth moment and continues within social sciences today:

- Representation: Inability of qualitative researchers to present in writing the lived experiences of participants.
- Legitimation: What warrants researcher attention and why (really about quality, 'how are qualitative studies to be evaluated in the contemporary, post-structural movement?')
- Praxis: 'Is it possible to effect change in the world if society is only and always a text?' (2005: 20). If the results of research are just a text, how can we change the world ... ?

Table 1.1 Major moments in qualitative research (a summary of Denzin and Lincoln 1994)

Moment	Philosophical perspective	Researcher role	Methods	Analysis	Quality	Write up	Key authors
1. Traditional (1900–1940s)	Positivism	Lone	Fieldwork		Validity and reliability	'Objective' colonizing accounts intended to create a museum-like picture of culture studied (Denzin and Lincoln 1994: 7)	Malinowski (1967)
2. Modern (1950s–1970s)	Post-positivism	Cultural romantic	Participant observation and open-ended and semi-structured interviewing	Constant comparison emerged	Internal and external validity	Scientific article	Becker et al. (1961)
3. Blurred genres (social sciences and humanities) (1970s–1986)	Full complement of positions for qualitative researchers (including symbolic interactionism, constructivism, interpretivism, critical theory, structuralism)	Researcher is considered a 'bricoleur'	Wide range of approaches, including grounded theory, case study and historical biographic, ethnographic, action and clinical research	Semiotics, hermeneutics	Thick description	Divers genres, documentaries, parables, theoretical treatises; 'the essay as an art form was replacing the scientific article' (Denzin and Lincoln 1994: 18)	Geertz (1973; 1983)
4. Crises of representation (mid 1980s–1990)	Pattern and interpretive theories more common; critical theory, feminist theory, and epistemologies of colour competed for attention	Questioned authority of the researcher	Realist and experimental ethnographies	Fieldwork and writing blur; writing as form of analysis	Questioned ways of demonstrating quality	Different view of 'text', including memoirs, experimental ethnographies	Stoller and Olkes (1987)
5. Post-modern period of experimental ethnography (1990–1995)	Critical theory, feminist theory and epistemologies of colour continued to compete for attention	Blurred; supporting participation through co-authoring with members of groups that were traditionally silenced	Action, participatory and activist research		Objectivity abandoned	Write up of local, small-scale theories	Ellis and Bochner (1996); Fine et al. (2000)

In this work, they argued that this triple crisis created an additional three moments, which we summarize in the following paragraphs.

Sixth moment: post-experimental inquiry (1995–2000)

In this moment, researchers undertook new ways of expressing lived experience, such as poetry, literary forms, autobiography, visual and performative approaches. They also abandoned the idea of the researcher as the arbiter of the truth. Rather, cooperation and collaboration that blur the lines between researcher and research are required throughout the research process. This moment also saw a growth of action, participatory and activist research.

Seventh moment: the methodologically contested present (2000–2004)

In this moment, demands for evidence-based approaches to practice and knowledge, using objectivist models and experimental techniques, led to questioning the value of qualitative research. This moment represented a backlash to the growth of qualitative research, or at least to the extreme post-modernist positions, and was an expression of more contemporary conservatism.

Eighth moment: the fractured future (2005–?)

The fractured future is a moment in which qualitative researchers confront the methodological backlash and revisit the demands of moral discourse, and the sacred and critical conversations about the diversity of human life, including experiences of freedom and control in a global society.

Liquid evolution

Instead of identifying the sixth, seventh and eighth moments as separate, as Denzin and Lincoln suggest, we see the fifth moment as extending to the present and the three later moments simply as developments that have occurred within the fifth moment. These changes represent the maturing of a field that has done more than merely react against positivist research (as three separate moments); instead, the field has expanded by adopting new approaches and then developed and refined these. What has occurred simply are waves of change.

In Table 1.2 we show how our 'further developments' represent the evolution of approaches that occurred in response to each of the three crisis areas.

Some researchers have argued that what has occurred over this hundred-year timeframe is not a paradigm shift, as Denzin and Lincoln suggest, and that to position it as such under-emphasizes some complexities and nuances (for example, Atkinson 1995; Thorne *et al.* 1999). Others see it as the emergence, development and refinement of a method of inquiry (for example, Higgs and Cherry 2009). What scholars agree upon is that the scientific method is no longer the only means to approach social research; qualitative research now stands with it as a field of inquiry.

WHAT IS QUALITATIVE RESEARCH TODAY?

There is no one commonly agreed upon definition of qualitative research today. Some scholars in this area of inquiry, however, have offered the following:

Table 1.2 Further developments in moment 5 (adapted from Denzin and Lincoln 2005)

Development	Representation	Legitimation	Praxis
Post-experimental inquiry (1995–2000)	Publication outlets for social science scholarship expressed in drama, performative, visual, multimedia and conversational modes		
Methodologically contested present (2000–2004)		Search for consensus on how to decide which articles to publish	
The fractured future (2005–?)			Increased demands, largely politically driven, for research aimed at addressing problems of education, poverty and society

Qualitative research is an umbrella cross- and interdisciplinary term, unifying very diverse methods with often contracting assumptions, which defies simple definitions.

(Gabrielian 1999: 178)

Qualitative research is a form of social inquiry that focuses on the way people interpret and make sense of their experiences and the world in which they live. A number of different approaches exist within the wider framework of this type of research, but most of these have the same aim: to understand the social reality of individuals, groups and cultures. Researchers use qualitative approaches to explore the behavior, perspectives and experiences of the people they study. The basis of qualitative research lies in the interpretive approach to social reality.

(Holloway 1997: 2)

Qualitative research, also called naturalistic inquiry, developed within the social and human sciences and refers to theories on interpretation (hermeneutics) and human experience (phenomenology). They include various strategies for systematic collection, organization and interpretation of textual material obtained while talking with people or through observation. The aim of such research is to investigate the meaning of social phenomena as experienced by the people themselves.

(Malterud 2001a: 398).

What is apparent in all of these definitions is the notion of variety and choice. There is no one single way to approach qualitative research but, rather, as evident in these definitions, there are a number of 'diverse methods', 'different approaches' and 'various strategies'. We define qualitative research simply as social research that is aimed at investigating the way in which people make sense of their ideas and experiences.

QUALITATIVE RESEARCH CHARACTERISTICS

While there is great diversity in the field of qualitative inquiry, there are several shared assumptions that are common to many qualitative research approaches (as suggested by several scholars, including Lincoln and Guba 1985; Bryman 2008; Onwuegbuzie and Leech 2005). We describe shared characteristics in the following paragraphs, noting that, although shared, the way in which these characteristics play out across various qualitative research approaches necessarily differs, which is why it is important for researchers to acknowledge the ways in which their research approaches address these characteristics.

Qualitative research is situated within a given world view or philosophy. There are many different views of the world, the nature of knowledge and the nature of reality, which are at times referred to as paradigms. (We describe the origins of the paradigms more fully in Chapter 2 and their belief structures more fully in Chapter 4.) As qualitative research has matured as a field, researchers have both situated their work within one of the many different philosophies and also been increasingly intentional in describing that philosophy and its influence on their subsequent choices.

Tips

Philosophy and qualitative research

All researchers have world views, and they have ideas about the nature of reality and knowledge. These views often are associated with different philosophies/philosophical views; see Chapters 2 and 4. While some do not acknowledge a given philosophy, their work is influenced by their world view. Qualitative researchers have begun to articulate these world views so as to be more intentional and transparent about their work.

Qualitative research has a more or less subjective and personal orientation. Qualitative researchers acknowledge that all research is inherently subjective. The decisions that a researcher makes, from what to study to what the research questions will be, from site selection to participant selection, all necessarily bound the research in specific ways. In short, researchers make decisions about what will be included and excluded in their study; these then determine the form of the study. An important part of any form of subsequent publication is the acknowledgement of the selection decisions that occurred and an indication of how these decisions contributed to the uniqueness of the research.

The research focuses on an emic perspective or the views of the people and their perceptions, meanings and interpretations. Qualitative researchers focus on understanding people and their circumstances, and they consider how people see the world and make meaning of it. Qualitative research helps researchers to understand individuals, cultures and other phenomena rather than

Qualitative research has an 'emic' perspective (describing behaviour or beliefs that are meaningful to the participant) which leads to choices in determining what might be meaningful for a participant. **Quantitative research** has an 'etic' perspective (describing behaviour or belief of an observer).

to analyze relationships between variables or to test cause-and-effect relationships. Qualitative researchers tend to view external reality as a symbolic representation of individual views and perspectives. Researchers often describe their views of reality and the nature of knowledge, and thus how they believe they may come to know the views of their participants (see Chapter 4).

Researchers acknowledge multiple constructed realities. Qualitative researchers often believe that individuals have different perceptions of reality and that at least to some degree they construct realities. Individuals then attribute meaning to events, concepts and situations, which is what researchers seek to understand. The 'truth' is not out there merely waiting to be discovered. Qualitative researchers tend to describe how they understand and come to know the 'reality' or 'realities' of their participants (see Chapter 4).

Qualitative research occurs in natural settings of people whose experiences are the object of exploration. Qualitative researchers tend to examine phenomena in their natural settings, often striving to interpret these phenomena in context. In qualitative research, where and when the research takes place is a critical factor of the research itself. Understanding the context is critical to understanding the meanings that individuals communicate. Qualitative researchers look for deep meaning about local settings in context and at a particular time. They tend to give voice to how they have made choices about their participants, the places they inhabit and how this influences their research.

The researcher is the primary instrument of data collection, so research is necessarily 'value bound'. The researcher's motivations for conducting the research are crucial (Schratz and Walker 1995). Qualitative researchers acknowledge the subjectivity of the social world. They believe that their values are evident in the ways in which the researcher asks questions and interprets results. As Reason and Rowan (1981: xi) explained, 'Qualitative research has many different approaches to enable us to understand the variety of human actions and experience and to recognize that research cannot be value-free'. Researchers describe their own views, positions and biases and how these influence their choices as researchers (see Chapter 4).

The researcher must show respect for the participants, acting ethically toward them and, where appropriate, engage participants as co-researchers. Qualitative researchers attempt to assume a non-judgmental, yet empathetic, stance toward participants and are bound by an ethical code to treat them with respect and dignity. Participants are integral to the study, rather than merely part of an experiment. There is a sense of collaborating with people rather than treating them as subjects. Therefore, researchers acknowledge the ways in which they see participant roles and their reasons for deciding how participants are involved in the research.

The research process changes both the investigator and the subject/participant. The researcher/researched relationship is an interesting one, as some researchers believe that it is important to retain some distance (Patton 1990). However, others believe that self-disclosure can deepen a relationship and create opportunities for sharing ideas and information. Researchers tend to acknowledge their beliefs and how they influence their choices about relationships with participants. Whatever distance a researcher seeks, almost all acknowledge that, in qualitative research, the researcher and research are interdependent and they change and are changed by each other.

The location of the research philosophy and justification of the research strategy demonstrate congruence between the philosophical and methodological stance. Although it is possible to talk about qualitative research as if it were a singular approach with clearly bounded characteristics, it comprises many different and diverse approaches, which require researchers to make choices, whether conscious or unconscious ones. While there are several philosophical perspectives from which qualitative researchers operate (see Chapters 2 and 4) and there is a range of research approaches (see Part 4), researchers acknowledge that it is imperative that there be a good fit between the two. Ensuring congruence requires a careful consideration of the views of the nature of knowledge and being, and the best ways to uncover those views.

Researchers are immersed in the setting. Researchers tend to spend extended and extensive time in a research setting. The length of in-field time is necessary for gaining adequate data. Doing so is necessary for understanding the world of the participants, which in turn is necessary for understanding the meanings that they communicate. Researchers must make choices about how long it will take them to accomplish understanding, and they tend to be explicit about this choice when describing the research.

Researcher reflections

Claire Howell Major, Author

While in graduate school, I made a clear and conscious choice to become a qualitative researcher. My educational background was in English literature, and when I decided to pursue a doctoral degree in higher education, I found that the skills that I had developed as a humanities scholar were immediately applicable to the study of the social world. Moreover, my beliefs and interests were compatible with qualitative research. I wanted to engage with a philosophy, understand individual experiences, and conduct research in a natural setting. I also had experience interviewing individuals, am comfortable with ambiguity, and enjoy writing, and thus it seemed to me that I had appropriate skills for qualitative research as well. The choice to become a qualitative researcher, then, seemed a natural one.

Data come from multiple sources. Data collection involves fieldwork: going out to collect data from people, places of work, homes and cultures. Data tend to include interview transcripts, field notes, documents and personal reflections, and researchers must make decisions about what kind of data to gather. The data are 'soft' in that they are rich in descriptions of people, places and conversations and are not easily handled by statistical procedure. Data collection, therefore, involves looking, asking, noting, describing, listening and interpreting.

Data have primacy. Qualitative researchers tend to believe that data are central to meaning and the final manuscript. Theoretical ideas tend to come from the data themselves and can in turn help to uncover essence of phenomena or to modify existing theories. Researchers necessarily choose which data are the most significant and influential and typically are conscious of this when reporting findings. Thus data, meaning and findings are inextricably linked.

Analysis and interpretation occur from the beginning of the study and are inductive processes. There is a range of strategies that qualitative researchers use for analysis and interpretation and the number and sophistication of these is increasing, which requires researchers to make choices about the best analytic tools for them. Researchers tend to move from the specific to the general or from the data to the description or theory. Such movement is inductive rather than deductive and demonstrates the primacy of the data. Qualitative researchers often rely upon analogy and metaphor for analysis and interpretation. The researcher typically is concerned with process rather than just outcomes of analysis and typically gives voice to this concern and the final choices.

There is an acknowledged pursuit of quality, which may differ according to beliefs and research strategy. The term 'validity' comes from quantitative research and, while it remained in use for some years, eventually researchers turned to other views of quality, such as 'trustworthiness', requiring researchers to make decisions about their views of what quality is and how they may ensure it. There are many practical challenges for ensuring that studies using qualitative approaches are sound (see Chapter 30).

While there is a pursuit of simplicity and elegance in the written report of the research, researchers rely upon thick description to convey meaning. Data tend to appear in the manuscript in the form of rich, thick description. Leading sociologist Geertz (1973) popularized the notion of thick description while describing his approach to ethnography, although Ryle (1971) was the originator of the term. Ryle believed that the concept of culture was critical in social science research and thus worthy of attention. Geertz's description of his concept involved explanation of the context as well as the importance of interpretation. Geertz's definition of thick description involved observation of social life captured through dense descriptions, which thereby allowed for generalization and interpretation. Denzin argued that thick description:

> does more than record what a person is doing. It goes beyond mere fact and surface appearances. It presents detail, context, emotion and the webs of social relationships that join persons to one another. Thick description evokes emotionality and self-feelings. It inserts history into experience. It establishes the significance of an experience, or the sequence of events, for the person or persons in question. In thick description, the voices, feelings, actions and meanings of interacting individuals are heard.
>
> (Denzin 1989b: 83)

Thick description is not just reporting detail but instead demands interpretation that goes beyond meaning and motivations, and so there are a number of ways in which researchers may accomplish thick description. It is critical both for ensuring quality and for making the narrative compelling, and researchers must decide what 'rich, thick description' means for them and their work.

We believe it is important to acknowledge that qualitative research characteristics stand in sharp contrast to quantitative ones. In particular, a comparison of these characteristics demonstrates the complexities that adopting a qualitative study necessarily entails, owing to the many choices that researchers face when designing and carrying out a qualitative study. These are summarized in Table 1.3.

Table 1.3 Comparison of quantitative and qualitative characteristics

	Quantitative	*Qualitative*
Guiding philosophy	Positivistic	Several options
Orientation	Objective/impersonal	Subjective/personal
Perspective	Etic	Emic
Focus	Single reality	Multiple realities
Setting	Controlled	Uncontrolled, natural environment
Instrument	Survey/test	Researcher as instrument
Distance	Objective outsider	Involved participant
Method	Prescribed by design	Variable
Data	Single source	Multiple sources
Analytic process	Deductive/reductionist	Inductive/holistic
Quality	Fixed	Variable
Report characteristics	Concise, numerical	Rich, descriptive, verbal

While qualitative researchers have a range of philosophies to guide their work from which they may choose, the quantitative philosophical choice is either positivism or post-positivism. Qualitative research is subjective and personal, which introduces several questions about the level of subjectivity involved, while quantitative is objective and impersonal. Qualitative research has an emic perspective, while quantitative has ... and so on.

Qualitative researchers seek to uncover multiple realities, while quantitative researchers seek only a single reality, the setting is natural and this lack of control can lead to complexities in research approach; quantitative research has a controlled setting. In qualitative research, the researcher is a human instrument with many potential biases that should be considered, while in quantitative research, the instrument is a test or experiment that may be validated.

CONCLUSION

Qualitative research embodies a unique approach that can help researchers answer wicked questions about human action and experience. As the field has grown, there are several characteristics that have established qualitative research as a field of inquiry in its own right. As this field of qualitative inquiry continues to grow and evolve, it is likely to become increasingly diverse. As a result of this growth, qualitative researchers, particularly novice ones, need guidance in making sense of a growing number of choices available when designing and carrying out a qualitative study.

Reflective questions

Concept questions

- In considering the emergence of qualitative research, what were the most significant changes from the quantitative perspective?
- What features do the different definitions of qualitative research share and how do they differ?
- What characteristics of qualitative research are the most appealing to you?

Application questions

- Is qualitative research a good fit for what you want to accomplish in your research? Why or why not?
- What features of qualitative research are the most appealing to you? Which are the least appealing?

Bryman, A. (2004) *Quantity and quality in social research*, London: Routledge.
In chapter 1, Bryman suggests that the tension between interpretivist and positivist perspectives is based upon political debate about the nature, importance and facility of different research methods. This book, particularly this chapter, helped us broadly to consider the differences in qualitative and quantitative traditions.

Denzin, N. K. and Lincoln, Y. S. (eds) (2005) *The Sage handbook of qualitative research*, Thousand Oaks, CA: Sage.
The introduction to this text provides a good overview of the qualitative research moments which we have summarized in this chapter.

Dewey, J. (1931) *Philosophy and civilization*, New York: Minton Balch. Chapters 'Qualitative Thought' and 'Affective Thought', 93–125.
This early text provided us with a useful way of thinking about thought itself as a qualitative endeavour.

Higgs, J. and Cherry, N. (2009) Doing qualitative research on practice. *In*: J. Higgs, D. Horsfall and C. Grace (eds) *Writing qualitative research on practice*. Rotterdam, The Netherlands: Sense Publishers.
Higgs and Cherry's chapter sparked the idea of wicked problems and they articulated well the need for a roadmap for making decisions in qualitative research.

Key resources

Chapter 2

A brief history of philosophical perspectives

INTRODUCTION

Contemporary qualitative research has evolved since the early twentieth century and, over the past 100 years, qualitative researchers from a range of disciplines have adopted different philosophical perspectives to guide their work. Without philosophical underpinning, technique can become an empty process. Understanding the origins of and circumstances under which different philosophies developed can help researchers to ascertain which philosophies are most compatible with their own, which in turn can help them to make better research choices and ultimately do better research.

In this chapter, we provide a brief history of key Western philosophies that researchers draw upon. We begin with a brief discussion of positivism and post-positivism to show how these philosophies differ from those most frequently used by qualitative researchers today. Then we turn to a discussion of the philosophies that qualitative researchers frequently use to guide their work. We present this history by grouping related ideas and philosophical schools of thought together, rather than by proceeding in strict chronological order, although we consider the importance of chronology both across and within philosophical traditions. Moreover, while we describe these philosophies as distinct from each other in order to provide clarity, we note that the philosophies and philosophers actually had great influence upon each other, through many related ideas. Thus, there are many interconnections and interrelations between the different schools of philosophical thought, and the lines we have drawn in order to provide a concise overview of different ideas are actually blurred in many instances; at times we point out important bridges between ideas.

Philosophy

The term philosophy, broadly conceived, means the study of both knowledge and the nature of reality and existence. Qualitative researchers tend to choose from interpretive, constructivist and critical philosophical stances

POSITIVISM AND POST-POSITIVISM: PHILOSOPHIES TYPICALLY UNDERPINNING QUANTITATIVE RESEARCH

As we indicated in Chapter 1, most quantitative research is done under the rubric of positivism and post-positivism. These philosophies have a long history in natural science and, as we noted in Chapter 1, have had an enduring presence in social research.

Positivism

Positivism is a research paradigm associated with natural sciences that holds that positive knowledge is based upon natural phenomena, their properties and relations as verified by science. Knowledge, then, is something that is to be discovered, rather than something that. is produced by humans, and researchers gain knowledge by identifying facts. Positivists value objectivity, rationality, neutrality and 'truth' and seek to reduce knowledge to abstract and universal principles. The paradigm suggests reduction rather than holism. Two forms are particularly prominent for social researchers: Comtean positivism and logical positivism.

Comtean positivism

Comtean positivism is based on the work of French philosopher Auguste Comte (1968–1970), who argued that the scientific method may be used to study all human activities, including morals. Comte believed that science should be focused on objectively determined observable phenomena and that science should be focused on measuring what one may observe. As Ritzer and Goodman (2007) indicated, Comte argued for three phases through which the human being and the human mind developed:

> The theological stage is dominated by a search for the essential nature of things and people come to believe that all phenomena are created and influenced by gods and supernatural forces. The metaphysical stage is a transitional stage in which mysterious, abstract forces (e.g. nature) replace supernatural forces as the powers that explain the workings of the world. The positivist stage is the last and highest stage in Comte's work. In this stage, people search for invariant laws that govern all of the phenomena of the world.
>
> (Ritzer and Goodman 2007: 85)

Comte also argued that scientific claims are predictive and in his sociology work he applied observation and experimentation approaches. In practice, he believed that persistent social problems could be understood through application of certain hierarchical rules.

Logical positivism

Logical positivism, also called logical **empiricism**, emerged predominantly from a group of scientists and philosophers in Vienna in the early twentieth century, who were against **metaphysics** (the underlying idea is that it is possible to examine what can be asserted about anything that exists just because of its existence and not because of any special qualities it possesses). They argued that something is only meaningful if it may be seen or measured. The Vienna circle, led by German philosopher and physicist Schlick (1918), met weekly from 1924 to 1936 to discuss problems in the **philosophy** of science. Thus, the central argument of logical positivism is the rejection of statements about ethics and aesthetics since they are unverifiable. The group argued, then, that 'great unanswerable questions' about issues such as God and freedom, and cause and effect, were unanswerable because they were not seen as genuine questions at all.

Post-positivism

The limitations of the positivist perspective and methods concerned many scholars. A group of critics emerged that challenged the very structures of positivism, although they still retained some of their beliefs, including the perspective of realism.

Empiricism

A philosophy about the nature of knowledge that suggests that experience, especially of the senses, is the only source of knowledge. This term is closely related to positivism, and at times the terms are used interchangeably

Metaphysics

A branch of philosophy concerned with explaining the fundamental nature of being. Metaphysics attempts to answer two questions: 'What is there?' and 'What is it like?'

Tips

Post-positivism is a term that scholars have used, and at times misused, in many different ways in literature about qualitative research. Although some scholars use the term interchangeably with qualitative research (for example, Ryan 2006, 'post-positivist research'), others use it to mean early qualitative research, such as early versions of grounded theory (for example, Urquhart 2001). Still other scholars use it to mean an adaptation of positivism (for example, Guba and Lincoln 1994; 2005). Some of these scholars with this latter view have suggested that, while post-positivists typically use modified experimental designs aimed at falsification of hypotheses, they may also use qualitative methods (Guba and Lincoln 2005).

As we see it, the first view (that all qualitative research is done within a post-positivist paradigm) is inaccurate, since relatively little of contemporary qualitative research is truly post-positivist; indeed, much of it is done from one of the six paradigms we outline below. We believe that the second view (that early modern qualitative research was done within a post-positivist paradigm) is inaccurate and that much of this early work could be more accurately categorized within the paradigm of pragmatism, and particularly symbolic interactionism (see below) – although we do acknowledge that some very early forms of qualitative research, such as early ethnography, were post-positive. Finally, we believe that the latter view is the most accurate and that post-positivism is simply a reaction to positivism; it is 'post' (after) positivism, yet post-positivists retain some positivist perspectives such as the view that reality exists and may be discovered (although imperfectly known) through logical processes. Moreover, we believe that when post-positivists use qualitative techniques, they often do so simply as an 'add on' to quantitative studies rather than for the sake of qualitative inquiry in its own right.

They also believed in objectivity, seeing their findings as probably or most likely true. These scholars often are referred to as post-positivists.

Amongst the most famous post-positivists is Austrian scientist Popper (1959), who questioned the way science verified its claims. He explored the relationship between scientific belief and the guarantees for such beliefs and argued that the essence of science was the extent to which it could be refuted, suggesting that scientific claims and assumptions needed to be subject to strong criticism. The consequence of this exploration was his argument that what is true is not shown to be the case by proving it is true but, instead, criticizing the 'truth' that has been discovered. His work was also important in that he distinguished between three world views (Popper 1972: 143):

■ World 1: comprising physical and material objects.
■ World 2: a subjective world of mind and contents.
■ World 3: entities that are the products of minds but exist separately, such as books.

Popper's work has been influential, especially his position that no human views are fully correct and that all should be evaluated. Stressing this point, he said: 'But if you are interested in the problem which I tried to solve by my tentative assertion, you may help me by criticizing it as severely as you can' (Popper 1968: 27). Popper (1959) also argued that scientific knowledge claims can never be proven or fully justified; they can only be refuted, stating that:

Table 2.1 Overview of positivist and post-positivist philosophers

Positivist traditions	Post-positivist traditions
Comtean positivism Comte (1798–1857) Logical positivism Schlick (1882–1936)	Critical rationalism Popper (1902–1994) Critical realism Bhaskar (1944–)

everybody interested in science must be interested in world 3 objects. A physical scientist, to start with, may be interested mainly in world 1 objects – say crystals and X-rays. But very soon he must realize how much depends on our interpretations of the facts, that is, on our theories and on world 3 objects. Similarly a historian of science, or a philosopher interested in science, must be largely a student of world 3 objects.

(Popper 1968: 183)

Popper is seen by many, including himself, as the one who prompted the 'demise' of positivism (Popper 1968). Post-positivist approaches, however, had several limitations for social researchers, as they retained many of the aspects of positivism, including basic views of reality and ways of gaining knowledge. A comparison of these approaches can be seen in Table 2.1.

An additional development of post-positivism is found in the work of Bhaskar (1989), who developed a now widely used philosophical position called 'critical realism'. His approach emphasizes the rational: the bridge between science and philosophy that neither fully embraces positivism nor on the other hand post-modernism. His ideas suggest that work can be both critical and not shy away from the notion of objectivity, which he believes can motivate social change.

OVERVIEW OF PHILOSOPHIES UNDERPINNING QUALITATIVE TRADITIONS

In attempting to classify contemporary social research studies, Guba and Lincoln (1994) identified what they deemed the four main paradigms social researchers used. In their consideration, Guba and Lincoln outlined two paradigms that quantitative researchers frequently adopt: positivism and post-positivism; and two more frequently adopted by qualitative researchers: critical theory and constructivism. They later added a 'participatory' paradigm to these four (Guba and Lincoln 2005). We believe that in this early and ground-breaking work, Guba and Lincoln began an important conversation about the schools of philosophical thought that underpin most modern or contemporary qualitative research. Our view differs from theirs somewhat, however, in that we find that the following are several different philosophies that qualitative researchers work within: critical social theory, pragmatism, phenomenology, post-modernism/structuralism, social constructionism and constructivism. We discuss the differences in how those in these traditions view realities and the nature of knowledge more fully in Chapter 4. Here, we provide a historical context for the different traditions and philosophies.

OVERVIEW OF PHILOSOPHIES THAT UNDERPIN QUALITATIVE RESEARCH

Critical social theory

A philosophy that emerged from the work of German philosophers and economists during the early 1900s that investigates power relationships and aims for transformation (scholars sometimes call it transformational research). Key beliefs are:

- Researchers should question and examine power structures.
- People should participate as equals in discussion about the pursuit of truth.
- Ideologies inform and affect research.

Pragmatism

A philosophy that emerged from the work of American philosophers in the early 1800s that focuses on observation of natural behaviour in a natural context. Key beliefs are:

- Research should reconcile theory and practice.
- It should be done in a natural context.
- Research approaches are eclectic and designed based upon the circumstance.

Phenomenology

An interpretive philosophy that emerged from German philosophers in the late 1800s and early 1900s that focuses on human experience. Key beliefs are:

- Research should involve a search for deeper meaning.
- Researchers should seek to uncover meaning before participants categorize it.
- Researchers should bracket their experiences (see Chapter 14 for information about bracketing).

Post-modernism/structural

An interpretive philosophy that emerged from the work of French literary critics during the 1960s. The focus is on the text and subtext and their deeper meanings. Key beliefs are:

- The text exists and is a thing to be interpreted.
- Even when examining underlying structures, researcher biases still exist.
- Language and society are governing systems that researchers should examine.

Social constructionism

A philosophy that emerged from the work of Austrian-American and German sociologists during the mid-1900s, that focuses on interpretation of subjective meaning and shared knowledge that is developed through interaction. Key beliefs are:

- Researchers should focus on how knowledge develops as a social construction.
- Research centres on dialogue and negotiation.

continued

Constructivism

A philosophy that emerged from the work of Russian psychologists during the mid-1900s, which suggests that individuals make and socially construct their own meaning. Key beliefs are:

■ Researchers should search for individually constructed meaning.

■ Researchers should seek to understand the way meanings are constructed; truth is a result of perspective and therefore knowledge and truth are created rather than discovered.

Critical social theory

Given that many qualitative researchers hold a strong interest in social justice and transformation, many of them adopt a critical social theory paradigm. The common belief systems that critical social theorists hold are that research should involve an interrogation of existing power structures and seek to transform the lives of those who are oppressed by these structures. This paradigm initially emerged with the work of German economists, specifically through the work of Karl Marx.

Tips

There are two types of critical theory: critical social theory, as we describe here, and post-modern critical theory, which we describe in our section on post-modern and post-structural theories.

Origins: Marxism

Marx sparked the development of the field now known as critical theory. Originally interested in philosophy, Marx later turned his attention to economics and politics, although even his later works maintained points of contact with contemporary philosophical debates. Marx's theory of history, historical materialism, suggested that all societies make progress by rising and falling through class struggle, which he believed culminates in communism. His work focused on transformation and he suggested that social theorists and underprivileged people alike should strive for revolution and for social change. Marx focused on the notion of 'critique' and, as a result, has been called the first user of the critical method in social sciences, a field that his ideas helped to found.

The Frankfurt School

The Frankfurt School is an informal title that refers to a group of philosophers that began in the early 1900s, associated with the Institute of Social Research at the University of Frankfurt am Main. The school initially comprised dissident Marxists who believed that Marx's followers had become too narrow in their ideas; later it became a school of neo-Marxists, who followed interdisciplinary social theory. Key researchers and philosophers in this tradition were German philosophy/sociology theorists such as Benjamin, Horkheimer, Adorno, Marcuse and Habermas, the latter of whom was a student of Adorno and Horkheimer. These theorists initially attempted to explain why Marx's prediction of a mid-nineteenth socialist revolution did not occur (they decided it was due to Marx's underestimation of the extent to which workers' false consciousness could be exploited to maintain the status quo). The early writers and philosophers in this perspective opposed what they saw as traditional theory such as positivism and quantitative and observational methods; they argued instead for a move away from the idea that facts existed 'out there'. Horkheimer, an early and leading figure in the Frankfurt School, argued that critical theory 'has as its object human beings as producers of their own historical form of life' (Horkheimer 1993: 21). For Horkheimer, a capitalist society needed to become more democratic, so that 'all conditions of social life that are controllable by human beings depend on real consensus' (Horkheimer 1982: 249–50). One of their most important arguments stated that positivist approaches merely reinforced the status quo rather than challenged it. Thus, the Frankfurt School theorists set out to illustrate that it was difficult, probably impossible, to generalize easily from experience, because of the way in which research is designed by the researcher. They argued that critical theory should be aimed at change and emancipation through enlightenment.

Some of the works of Frankfurt School members were written while they were in exile in the United States, during which time they shifted their emphasis of critical theory from a critique of capitalism to a critique of Western Civilization. They argued for an examination of power and domination in the world generally. For example, these theorists pointed out that the role of observer in a social setting could not be ignored as some kind of external participant. They also were responsible for some of the first accounts that unpacked the influence of mass culture and communication in the control of culture and society.

Another development in critical theory emerged from the ideas of more recent theorists such as Habermas, also a German philosopher/sociologist, who was particularly critical of Marxist positivism which he believed was writ large in Marx's work (Agger 1991). Habermas believed that the stances taken by Horkheimer and Adorno were too pessimistic, and instead argued for the importance of valuing the public sphere, where people participated as equals in discussion about the pursuit of truth and the common good. He believed that it was important to make a distinction between knowledge gained from self-reflection and knowledge gained from causal analysis and technique, and in this way he reconstructed historical materialism. Habermas marks a shift in critical social theory away from German idealism and towards American pragmatism (Agger 1991). Habermas also criticized hermeneutics (described later in this chapter) for not seeing the hermeneutic dimensions of critical theory.

Pragmatism

Pragmatism developed in the late 1800s, as the group of sociology scholars who founded the Metaphysical Club at Johns Hopkins University, USA, engaged in discussion that was opposed to the European metaphysical tradition. This group challenged the notion of traditional empiricism and instead turned their focus on the subjective experience of the social world. They believed this world should be researched by the methods most appropriate for the research question and that this research should be carried out in a natural context. Pragmatism evolved over time and several different forms of pragmatism are still in use by social researchers today. Those forms of pragmatism that have proved enduring for social researchers are classical pragmatism, 'Chicago School' interactionism and neopragmatism.

Classical pragmatism

Classical pragmatism is a movement that was founded by Americans Peirce and James at Johns Hopkins University, USA (Outhwaite 2009). Other contributors to the classic pragmatic school included the American educator and philosopher, Dewey, and philosopher, novelist and poet, Santayana. The basic idea of this form of pragmatism is that the meaning of conceptions should be sought in their practical applications. The tenets of pragmatism also suggest that the function of thought is to guide action and that truth should be tested based upon the practical consequences of that 'truth'.

Interactionism and the Chicago School

Sociologist scholars at the Chicago School in the 1930s developed a new approach to research that emphasized the importance of the social and interactional nature of reality, as opposed to genetic and personal characteristics. Such information must be interpreted by a researcher, who necessarily has biases. These researchers investigated urban environments with ethnographic approaches, with an emphasis on fieldwork and interviewing. American sociologist, Thomas, and Polish-American sociologist, Znaniecki, for example, studied Polish letters from a ghetto in Chicago in order to examine an insider's perspectives of immigrant life (Thomas and Znaniecki 1927). American sociologist, Park, who originally was a journalist and sent his students to be observers of city life, was also a leading figure in the Chicago School (Faris 1967). These qualitative researchers argued that the emphasis should be upon understanding people and situations, rather than upon measuring observably defined facts. These researchers, along with American philosopher, sociologist and psychologist, Mead (1928), and American sociologist, Blumer (1969), developed symbolic interactionism as a school of thought interested in the subjective experiences of people, which would later serve as the basis for social constructivism.

Neopragmatism and neoclassical pragmatism

Pragmatism received renewed attention in the late twentieth century. In particular, American philosopher, Rorty, who is perceived by some as a deconstructionist scholar (see section below on post-critical/post-structuralism for additional information about deconstructionism), developed his own brand of pragmatism: neopragmatism. His account considered scientific methods as contingent vocabularies which scholars adopted or abandoned based upon social convention. Rorty believed that people are aware of this contingency of vocabulary, that ideas of representation stood in between the mind and the world, and he envisioned a post-philosophical culture (Rorty 1979).

Neoclassical pragmatism has revived the work of Peirce, James and Dewey, including Haack, an American professor of philosophy and law, who has taken up classical pragmatic approaches. In particular, feminist philosophers have taken classical pragmatism as a source of feminist theories and there are many important links between pragmatism and feminism (Duran 2001; Keith 1999; Whipps 2004). Among the features these feminist scholars point to as appealing are criticism of the positivist method; giving priority to political, cultural and social issues; linking dominant discourses with domination; and striving for links between theory and praxis.

Phenomenology

Phenomenology is interpretive philosophy that emerged from the work of German philosophers during the late 1800s and early 1900s. The phenomenon of interest is the human experience, which researchers sought to uncover before individuals categorized it, so that the essence of the experience could be uncovered. Many phenomenologists share the belief that a researcher's experience cannot be untangled from the participant experience; so researchers should consider and bracket their experiences (see Chapter 14).

Tips

Interpretivism is a term that has many meanings among different qualitative researchers. Some researchers use the term 'interpretivist research' to mean all qualitative research, since the researcher is an interpreter of the social world. Others see interpretivism as a select group of philosophies that include pragmatism, phenomenology and hermeneutics, and post-critical/post-structuralism; we are most sympathetic to the latter description.

Classical phenomenology

Phenomenology's origins lie in the early twentieth century, with the work of Husserl, a German philosopher and mathematician often called the father of phenomenology (Polkinghorne 1983), and his colleagues. Husserl criticized psychology for using objective scientific methods to study human issues and suggested instead examination of the way people lived in the world. His arguments to some extent stood against the Cartesian model in which the mind and body were seen as separate and distinct entities as suggested by others (for example, Descartes 1979/1641). Concerned that natural sciences were only attending to external physical stimuli, Husserl viewed the central structure of an experience as its intentionality, which is always directed towards an object that is not itself conscious. Husserl, then, wanted to examine life just as it is experienced and, in this way, his philosophy was realist phenomenology.

Hermeneutics

Hermeneutics is a discipline that initially focused on the interpretations of texts, particularly legal and biblical ones. At a fundamental level it is the art of interpretation. In the mid-nineteenth century, Dilthey, a German historian, psychologist, sociologist and hermeneutic philosopher, noted that the subject matter investigated by natural scientists is different from that examined by social scientists, and that facts and values could not be separated. In particular he argued for the importance of having a sound foundation in the human sciences (*Geisteswissenschaften*). Dilthey (1900/1996) also argued for the importance of the logical underpinning for the human sciences but believed that lived experience itself did not provide self-understanding.

Philosophical hermeneutics (that is tied closely to existential phenomenology) is a theory of knowledge attributed to German philosopher, Heidegger. Heidegger considered the conditions necessary for symbolic communication and moved beyond to consider the question of human life and existence. He also suggested that meaning should be mediated and understood, and therefore that language is central to understanding. Heidegger worked with Husserl but rejected Husserl's view and instead focused on the situated meaning of an individual in the world. Uncovering situated meaning involves interrogation into conditions for symbolic interaction. It also recognizes the historicity of human understanding and sees ideas as nested in historical, linguistic and cultural horizons of meaning. Heidegger later departed from hermeneutics and moved toward a more post-structural position. Ricœur, a French philosopher, combined phenomenological description with hermeneutic interpretation, thus bridging the gap between phenomenology and hermeneutics.

Post-modernism/structuralism

French literary critics developed several different forms of post-structuralism during the 1960s that are related to hermeneutics, given their emphasis on the text and interpretation of deep linguistic structure. We highlight here two prominent forms used for qualitative research: post-modern critical theory and post-structuralism. Individuals who adopt post-modernism and post-structuralism approaches share a belief that language itself is a governing system that researchers should examine, since it provides evidence of meaning.

Post-modernism

One of the most explicit post-modernists was French philosopher, Lyotard, who rejected grand narratives, such as Marxism, that attempted to explain the world in patterns of interrelationships (Agger 1991). He believed that it was impossible to argue for the use of grand narratives about the world but that it was possible to tell stories from the perspectives of individuals and plural social groups. Another influential post-modernist was Foucault, a French philosopher, who believed that knowledge must be traced to different discourses/practices that framed the knowledge formulated from within them. In particular, Foucault focused on the exploration of power and institutions as sites of power for managing and controlling humanity (Foucault 1979), such as asylums, prisons and hospitals. Drawing from linguistic theory, French philosopher and literary critic, Barthes, suggested the unit of a city as a discourse, rather than an individual, and French sociologist, Baudrillard, suggested that consumer society commodities have a 'sign value' that people desire. He believed that reality was increasingly simulated for people. Post-modernists are concerned with the demise of the subject, the end of the author and the impossibility of truth.

Post-structuralism

Post-structuralism is a broad term for a loose amalgamation of literary theories originating in France in the 1960s. Post-structuralist philosophers shared a common stand against structuralism: the belief that people are shaped by sociological, psychological and linguistic structures over which they have little, if any, control. Post-structuralists believe that even in an examination of underlying structures, biases exist since people are formed though their cultures and the systems in which they live. Post-structuralists argue for a subtext, or next level of meaning, and that this subtext is what constitutes reality. Early post-structuralism developed from the work of Saussure, a linguist who examined the impact of linguistic structures. Derrida, also a post-structuralist philosopher, argued that language is not transparent but derives meaning and connection with others. He also argued for a methodology of textual reading called **deconstructionism**, which has become one of the most significant post-structuralist approaches to literary criticism.

    His method stood in opposition to what was then common, textual objectivism, but his texts are difficult to fathom, since they neither offer a clear position, nor have a sense of being about everything (for example, Derrida 1986; 1988). Kristeva, a philosopher and literary critic, is an important feminist post-structuralist, who along with Lacan, in the area of psychoanalysis, and Barthes in literary studies,

Deconstructionism

A form of criticism (usually of literature or art) that seeks to expose hidden contradictions in a work by delving below its surface meaning; it is often associated with post-structuralism used forms of rhetorical analysis to deconstruct and question the nature of taken-for-grated concepts such as the body, the self and issues such as gender, power and resistance.

Post-structuralist ideas have been highly influential in qualitative research, in helping to stand against the ready acceptance of boundaries in relation to gender, age, class and race, when reading or writing research. An example of a text that has sought to take an explicit post-structuralist stance was edited by McCarthy *et al.* (2007), who sought to write about new ways of undertaking textual, post-colonial, post-structural and political economic approaches to research.

Tips

Post-modernity, post-modernism and post-modern are terms that are used inconsistently in the literature. What we mean when we use these terms is the following.

■ Post-modernity: the post-modern era, the time after modernity (as suggested by Lyotard 1979). We note that some scholars, such as Giddens (1992), believe we are in a period of later modernity rather than post-modernity.
■ Post-modernism: the post-modern condition, or belief systems characteristic of the post-modern era. The post-modern condition is characterized by a shift in attitude and position within humanity (as suggested by Foucault 1979 and Nicholson 1990), which ultimately has led to movements such as feminism, gay rights, racial equality movements.
■ Post-modern critical theorists: a group of French literary critics, many of whom are also associated with post-structural theories.

Post modernism (what we call post-modern critical theory) and post-structuralism are often treated as interchangeable terms. While there is overlap, post-modernists take a stance towards the state of the world, the period that is following the modernist period, whereas post-structuralists explicitly seek to deconstruct structures and systems that are seen to normalize people and ignore subtext. Foucault and Barthes may be claimed by either camp, and indeed both often are.

Social constructionism

American historian and philosopher Kuhn (1962) argued, controversially at the time, that science and thus scientific knowledge is socially and culturally constructed, just as much as it is in other disciplines. He suggested that scientific knowledge is not cumulative and, at times, theories, views and perspectives simply change. An example of such a shift is the Ptolemaic solar system, which was replaced by the Copernican system. Drawing upon social science ideas (specifically political science notions of revolution) in considering the application to natural sciences which he deemed culturally constructed, Kuhn described a process of scientific revolution or paradigm shift. When these anomalies become an issue and are questioned, new theories emerge, eventually causing a crisis. The crisis requires extraordinary research, which then develops a new paradigm. The new paradigm, or belief system, is a revolution. Thus, Kuhn documented how knowledge is socially and culturally constructed and ultimately changed and transformed.

While considering social construction of knowledge at a field rather than individual level, Kuhn's ideas interestingly led to a shift in thinking about how individuals construct knowledge, or their social realities, with each other in a form of shared reality and knowledge. Austrian-American sociologist, Berger, and German sociologist, Luckmann's, book *The social construction of reality* (1966) introduced the term social construction into the social science vocabulary. The idea of social constructionism is that individuals construct social meaning, and their own shared realities, through interacting with each other (Gergen and Gergen 1991). Several scholars suggest that cultural influences (such as custom, religion, language) play an important part in the way that individuals construct knowledge through interacting with each other (for example, Dougiamas 1998; Cole and Wertsch 1996).

Researchers who share this philosophy tend to explore the way in which people and society construct meaning in particular areas of interest (for example, mental health, prejudice, teaching mathematics to girls; in order to illustrate how reality is constructed reality, for example, Burr 1995). Research methods involve dialogue and negotiation of meaning between the researchers and the participants.

Maggi Savin-Baden, Author

As a researcher, philosophy is a guiding principle for me when I make decisions about which research approach to choose. However, it is too easy to see philosophies and approaches all operating in isolation from one another, when in fact they overlap and inform each other. For example, I might choose to do a case study located in a phenomenologist philosophy, or a constructivist philosophy. These two case studies look different, and require different research approaches and ways of working with participants and their data. In Chapter 4, we provide additional information about how philosophy guides research.

Researcher reflections

Constructivism

Constructivism is a perspective that developed alongside social constructionism, and philosophers representing these paradigms published seminal texts at approximately the same times. At its most fundamental level, constructivism is the notion that knowledge lies in the minds of individuals, who construct what they know on the basis of their own experiences. It suggests that the process of knowledge construction is an active rather than a passive one. Researchers who adopt this approach believe that research involves an attempt to understand individual construction of knowledge and also believe that it is their role to understand the ways in which individuals construct meaning, since knowledge, truth and reality are created rather than constructed.

Some scholars use the terms 'interpretivism' and 'constructivism' interchangeably (for example, Guba *et al.*, 2011), while others see constructivism as a further move along the continuum of subjectivity; we belong to this latter camp.

Tips

CONSTRUCTIVISM APPLIED TO LEARNING THEORY

Example

Constructivism is a cognitive theory developed by Piaget (1951; 1969), a Swiss philosopher and psychologist, rather than a philosophy in its own right. Based on work with children, Piaget asserted that the learner constructs knowledge. Similarly, American psychologists, Ausubel *et al.* (1978) argued that individuals will interpret new information by contextualizing, both in terms of prior knowledge and shared perspectives. Therefore, individuals' existing cognitive structures are the primary influence on meaningful learning. In practice, meaningful learning will only occur in relation to previously learned relevant concepts. Early constructivism is a theory that suggests that individuals construct their own unique meaning in order to learn. Piagetian constructivism, however, suggests objectivity – constructs may be validated through experimentation.

There is much confusion in the literature between the epistemological philosophy of social constructionism and an educational theory of the same name. Constructionism, a learning theory developed by one of Piaget's students, Papert, suggests that learning occurs best when constructing an object 'whether a sand castle on the beach or a theory of the universe' (Papert 1990: 1). Papert believed that, by constructing something that other people would see and possibly critique, students were more likely to become intensely caught up in learning. However, it was through this process of construction that such involvement would prompt them to become highly motivated and they would endeavour to problem solve and learn competently.

Constructionism is an extension of constructivism in that the individual as the constructor and builder of knowledge and meaning. Constructionism builds on this by suggesting that as people learn, they need to express this so that their teachers can understand their meaning-making process in order to enhance it. For example, Papert argued:

> We understand 'constructionism' as including, but going beyond, what Piaget would call 'constructivism.' The word with the v expresses the theory that knowledge is built by the learner, not supplied by the teacher. The word with the n expresses the further idea that this happens especially felicitously when the learner is engaged in the construction of something external or at least shareable ... a sand castle, a machine, a computer program, a book. This leads us to a model using a cycle of internalization of what is outside, then externalization of what is inside and so on.
>
> (Papert 1990: 3)

This education theory is different, however, from the social constructionist philosophy (Berger and Luckmann 1966). Social constructionist philosophy suggests that there is shared knowledge and reality that individuals negotiate with each other; social constructionism educational theory suggests that individuals learn for themselves by working with others.

BLURRED BOUNDARIES, BORDER CROSSINGS AND PHILOSOPHICAL MASHUPS

We recognize that the way in which we have presented this brief history may indicate that philosophies are divided neatly into their silos and that philosophers fit squarely within a certain philosophical camp. Such neat divisions are not always, or even often, the case. There are many blurred boundaries between what counts as one philosophical school and what counts as another. Divisions between phenomenological and constructivist traditions are murky, as are divisions between these two and some of the critical traditions. Within traditions, the divisions between post-modernism and post-structuralism are particularly blurry, as often it is virtually impossible to tell the difference between the two or to make sharp distinctions between their philosophers; such is the case when a philosophical tradition explicitly defies classification and definitions. There are at times blurred boundaries between hermeneutics and post-structuralism, as another example, both of which are concerned with interpretation of the text.

As we have indicated throughout this chapter, many of these philosophers cannot be neatly located into any one tradition (for example, Rorty: considered a pragmatist by some and a post-modern or post-structural deconstructionist by others). Indeed, many philosophers have phases (for instance, Foucault attended to several different foci over time) and shift between traditions effortlessly in their quest to find the nature of knowledge (for example, Heidegger's work in hermeneutics prior to his work in post-structural criticism). We term these philosophers 'border crossers'. Border crossing happens to single individuals as well as groups with common interests who work across philosophies. Feminists, then, are border crossers, as they defy neat classification into any one paradigmatic or philosophical camp. While many scholars link feminists to critical theory because of their interest in transformation (for example, Denzin and Lincoln 2011), feminists have adopted a range of other paradigms such as pragmatism, post-modern critical theory and post-structuralism, in order to guide their work.

Moreover, many of the scholars bring together philosophical traditions in unique and interesting ways. Ricœur's use of phenomenological description and hermeneutic interpretation is a prime example of what we have in mind with the notion of a **philosophical mashup**, as it set the stage for using one philosophy's focus on experience and another's focus on interpretation, in order to explore meaning. Post-modern post-structuralism is another good example of a mashup, as it brings together ideas from critical social theory and considers them in light of the challenges wrought by post-modern perspectives when applied to literary texts and structures.

We agree that much of the time philosophy is a tricky discipline to navigate; indeed, 'philosophy is a walk on the slippery rocks' (Brickell 2002) and we acknowledge that often these blurred boundaries, border crossings and mashups lead to new insights and perspectives. Our intention in this chapter was to provide some general context, so that researchers can begin to understand the interconnected and at times virtually incomprehensible group of ideas that, and philosophers who, have been concerned with the nature of knowledge.

Philosophical mashups

We define philosophical mashups as the integration of two different philosophies, often within a single study. We encourage novice researchers to be aware of philosophical mashups in principle, so that they can recognize these mashups when they occur. However, we believe it is best initially for new researchers to identify, stay within and fully comprehend one philosophical tradition, before trying a mashup themselves

Table 2.2 Overview of philosophers associated with the different paradigms

Critical social theory	Pragmatism	Phenomenology	Post-modernism and Post-structuralism	Constructionism	Constructivism
German philosophers/ economists	American philosophers/ educators/sociologists	German philosophers	French literary critics	Austrian-American and German sociologists	Swiss and German-American psychologists
To transform social realities	To describe behaviour in natural contexts	To explain experience in the world	To uncover the essence of meaning in texts	To understand socially constructed realities	To understand constructed realities
Marxism	*Classic pragmatism*	*Realist phenomenology*			
Marx (1818–1883)	Peirce (1839–1914)	Husserl (1859–1938)			
	James (1842–1910)				
	Dewey (1859–1952)				
	Santayana (1863–1952)				
	Chicago School				
	Mead (1863–1931)				
	Znaniecki (1882–1958)				
	Thomas (1863–1947)	Scheler (1874–1928)			
Critical social theory		*Existential/hermeneutics*			
Horkheimer (1895–1973)		Heidegger (1889–1976)			

Frankfurt School

Benjamin (1892–1940)

Marcuse (1898–1979)

Adorno (1903–1969)

Piaget (1896–1980)

Blumer (1900–1987)

Gadamer (1900–2002)

Merleau-Ponty (1908–1961)

Ricœur (1913–2005)

Post-modernism/ post-structuralism

Barthes (1915–1980)

von Glasersfeld (1917–2010)

Lyotard (1924–1998)

Foucault (1926–1984)

Luckmann (1927–)

Habermas (1929–)

Baudrillard (1929–2007)

Berger (1929–)

Derrida (1930–2004)

Neopragmatism

Rorty (1931–2007)

Gergen (1935–)

Neoclassical pragmatism

Haack (1945–)

CONCLUSION

In this chapter, we have provided an overview of the primary philosophies that qualitative researchers tend to use to underpin their work. There are a number of different yet interconnected views; the differences between them lie in the alternative views of realities, the way that they may be known and the purposes of social research. Table 2.2 depicts the history of the different philosophical traditions that underpin qualitative research. We suggest that qualitative researchers come to grips with their own philosophical positions, and we provide guidance for doing this in Chapter 4.

Reflective questions

Concept questions

■ In considering the way that each of the philosophies has evolved over time, which do you believe have made the most significant changes from their original positions?
■ Which of the positions has changed the least?
■ Which of the traditions seemed most like a reaction against positivism and post-positivism?
■ Which of the philosophies seemed the most revolutionary?

Application questions

■ How can knowing about the history of philosophies help you in your work as a qualitative researcher?
■ Which of the different philosophers has a message that can help you with your research?

Key resources

Schwandt, T. A. (2000) Three epistemological stances for qualitative inquiry: Interpretivism, hermeneutics and social constructionism. In: N. K. Denzin and Y. S. Lincoln (eds) *Handbook of qualitative research (2nd edn.)*. Newbury Park, CA: Sage.
This book chapter provided an interesting overview of interpretivism, hermeneutics and social constructionism, and it contained some brief historical information, leading us to the belief that more context would be helpful to situate the different philosophies.

Agger, B. (1991) Critical theory, poststructuralism, post-modernism: Their sociological relevance. *Annual Review of Sociology*, 17, 105–31.
This article provided a useful overview of some of the theoretical contributions of critical theory, post-structuralism and post-modernism.

Chapter 3

Research choices and lenses

INTRODUCTION

Researchers face many **choices** when designing and implementing a study, ranging from who or what to study to where and how they will report the results. The choices researchers make range from complex ones required to frame and design a study to simple ones that involve matters of administrative concern. They may thrive on having a sufficient number of choices, yet at the same time, having too many choices or an ill-defined set of choices can be overwhelming and leave some unable to make a selection necessary to move forward. When researchers do make choices, they do not always do so rationally or even consciously; invariably their final choices stem from their values and beliefs. Researchers do not always make these conscious or unconscious research choices with full information available. In addition, the demands of undertaking a research project can mean that researchers make choices for speed or convenience rather than from a well-thought through selection.

Choice
An act of making a selection among options

Choosing
A process of examining available options and making a decision about the best amongst them, given a particular set of circumstances

If they consider their options consciously and carefully, however, researchers may better understand their biases and the underlying reasons for the choices they make and, as a result, make better choices. In this chapter, we identify some of the choices that researchers face and discuss the implications of making a selection from among them. We also present a conceptual model for thinking through the interrelation of essential choices, as well as describe how this model works to create a set of lenses through which a researcher may view data.

Choosing is a process of examining available options and making a decision about the best amongst them, given a particular set of circumstances.

THE GROWING NUMBER OF CHOICES IN QUALITATIVE RESEARCH

Qualitative research is a developing field of inquiry, which continues to attract the interest of academics and practitioners working in diverse fields from around the world. There are many varieties of paradigms, perspectives, approaches and methods. Researchers and reviewers are receptive to many different ways of designing and conducting a study, which provides them with much choice as they design and implement their studies. This vast landscape both gives latitude and also encourages individuality, creativity and experimentation in qualitative research studies. Many view such diversity and the number of choices that this brings as a great strength:

> Qualitative research is increasingly regarded as a powerful and credible tool for revealing and understanding the human world. The rich range of qualitative research approaches is one of its great strengths. It provides multiple ways of understanding the inherent complexity and variability of human behaviour and experience.
>
> (Higgs and Cherry 2009: 8)

For others, however, the large variety of qualitative research approaches is a weakness since it can lead to questions of how to go about qualitative research, which can be overwhelming for both new and seasoned researchers, while such diversity also leads to different views about what counts as knowledge or as 'important', 'good' or 'ethical' research. Issues such as these can lead to confusion among researchers and reviewers and a general lack of credibility for the field. Indeed, Denzin and Lincoln argue that 'an embarrassment of choices now characterizes the field of qualitative research' (Denzin and Lincoln 2005: 20).

We agree that there are more choices in qualitative research than ever before. However, we disagree that they are an embarrassment; they simply reflect a range of views, perspectives and ideas about the best ways for different researchers to investigate particular phenomena. Indeed, as we see it, the number of choices allow for freedom, creativity and play. Moreover, it seems that any effort to restrict choices could compromise the very freedom that qualitative researchers have always sought.

For first-time qualitative researchers, trying to make sense of the full range of options can be a difficult task, which is only made more difficult because of the confusing, overlapping and sometimes inconsistent terminology that is used. Researchers should be aware of the options available to them so that they may make good choices from among the available options. Finding clear and usable road maps of the terrain, which outline specific choices and the options that then result, can be the first step in a successful research journey.

CHOICE MOMENTS

'Choice moments' are points in time during that researchers must make a choice that will ultimately influence multiple choices thereafter, which sets a course of action into motion. These moments are critical points in the design of any research project. Ensuring that they are correct ultimately enhances the design and outcomes of research. We believe there are five 'essential choice moments' in the research design process, during which all qualitative researchers ultimately choose from a similar set of options. Their choices consequently affect each essential choice moment thereafter. In addition to these 'essential choice moments', researchers have 'complementary choice moments', which allow them to make their studies unique. They can choose from unlimited options and, in making these choices, they tailor their studies, making them personalized and unique. We summarize these choice moments, described in the remainder of this book, in Table 3.1.

When presented with options at each of these moments, we believe that researchers make choices based upon a mixture of logic and intuition. Thinking through these moments and the array of choices they have to consider, however, allows for sound planning and refinement of the research design. Being able to consider critical moments of choice and the attending options and consequences, then, provides researchers with a decision-making framework that can allow them to do better research. Achieving congruence from choice to choice can allow for the development of sound research plans.

Table 3.1 Essential choice moments in qualitative research

Category	Essential choice moments	Complementary choice moments
Inhabiting a position	Philosophical stance (Chapter 4)	Personal stance, positionality and reflexivity (Chapter 5)
Framing the study	The 'who' or 'what' of study (Chapter 6)	Research questions (Chapter 7) Literature review (Chapter 8) Theoretical and conceptual frameworks (Chapter 9)
Using a research approach	*Basic approaches:* • Case studies (Chapter 10) • Pragmatic qualitative research (Chapter 11) • Grounded theory (Chapter 12) • Ethnography (Chapter 13) • Phenomenology (Chapter 14) • Narrative approaches (Chapter 15) • Action research (Chapter 16)	*Families of approaches:* • Collaborative approaches (Chapter 17) • Evaluation (Chapter 18) • Arts-based approaches (Chapter 19)
Collecting data	*Data collection methods*: • Interviews (Chapter 23) • Focus groups (Chapter 24) • Observation (Chapter 25) • Documents (Chapter 26)	Time, place and participants (Chapter 20) Ethics and ethical approval (Chapter 21) Fieldwork (Chapter 22)
Working with data	*Analytical strategy*: • Data analysis (Chapter 28)	Data handling and coding (Chapter 27) Data interpretation (Chapter 29) Quality (Chapter 30)
Writing about the research		Researcher voice (Chapter 31) The research report (Chapter 32)

Claire Howell Major, Author

When I design a study, I begin by asking myself the basic questions of 'what do I want to know?' and 'what is the best way to find that out?'. I then think through the issues, what we have termed here 'choice moments' and ask myself whether the choices I am planning make sense at a basic level. I think about whether the research phenomenon that I have chosen to study makes sense given my philosophical framework. I consider whether the research approach makes sense given the phenomenon. I think through issues of data collection and analysis to ensure that my choices have been congruent. When working with students on dissertations, I ask them to think through similar questions and issues.

Researcher reflections

INHABITING A POSITION

Qualitative researchers have become increasingly more conscious about their world views and about their own positions in the research. We believe that the vast majority of qualitative researchers today identify with a given philosophical position and that they tailor their studies, making them specific through adopting personal stances, positionality and reflexivity that are complementary to the essential choice of philosophical stance. We provide additional information about these choice moments in the following sections.

Essential choice moment: choosing a philosophical position

One of the first choice moments that researchers face is to determine how they will position themselves philosophically, which requires them to consider how they view the nature of knowledge, as well as how they believe that they may best obtain knowledge, whether they make these considerations intentionally or unintentionally. The world views with which they identify are underpinned by philosophies that inform research practice. We suggest that six research paradigms or philosophies guide most qualitative studies: critical social theory, pragmatism, phenomenology, post-modernism and post-structuralism, constructionism and constructivism (see Chapters 2 and 4 for additional information about each philosophy). *Critical social theory* (Horkheimer and Adorno 1972) as a philosophical perspective suggests that there is a reality that has been created and shaped by a range of forces, including social, race, class and gender, that individuals, including the researcher, take for granted but which must be explored more fully. *Pragmatism* (for example, Rorty 1979) does not require adherence to a particular philosophical position about the nature of reality and knowledge, but instead implies that a researcher will take a practical view when attempting to problem solve and to link theory and practice through the research process. Phenomenology suggests that social reality resides with the individual and that it may be uncovered through unpacking the essence of individual experiences (Polkinghorne 1983). *Post-modern critical theory and post-structuralism* as positions imply that there are layers of meaning and that it is important to discover the subtext of the structures, such as text and language, which may be perpetuated through generations (for example, Derrida 1986; 1988). *Social constructionism* suggests that individuals construct reality with each other, that knowledge is relational and that it may be uncovered by examining interactions and meaning making between and among individuals (Berger and Luckmann 1966). *Constructivism* suggests that individuals create their own realities and that it is those that researchers must explore (Piaget 1951).

Complementary choice moment: personal stance, positionality and reflexivity

In addition to these general philosophical positions from which most researchers choose, the researcher comes to a study with a set of beliefs about the world, a position that we term *personal research stance* (see Chapter 5). In a given study, researchers choose how they will position themselves in relationship to the research, the researched and the research context. They tend also to select from a range of strategies to ensure that they have considered their own influence on the research during their investigations (see Chapter 31).

FRAMING THE STUDY

Researchers go about framing their studies in a number of different ways. The essential choice moment related to framing is the choice of a phenomenon to study. Tailoring the study and making it more specific and unique involves choosing a topic and question, reviewing literature, choosing conceptual or theoretical frameworks and giving attention to ethical considerations.

Essential choice moment: choosing the phenomenon to study

Some qualitative researchers choose to investigate individuals and, in particular, are interested in their attitudes and perspectives. Other researchers choose to study groups, and qualitative researchers seem to be frequently drawn to choose cultures and subcultures as a research phenomenon. Alternatively, some researchers examine structures, whether organizational, social or linguistic. Other researchers select processes, a category in which we also include actions and events. Some researchers study complex concepts, such as love, hate or care, to get at their essential features and elements. Artefacts, particularly those that have cultural significance such as art, pottery or even video games, also have served as the phenomena of some qualitative studies. Having begun the design process the researcher must then decide in detail how such data will be collected.

CONGRUENCE BETWEEN PHILOSOPHY AND PHENOMENON

A student planning a dissertation study identified himself as a critical theorist. He decided to investigate a cultural group to try to understand their perceptions of their experiences.

Another student who was working on a dissertation decided she was a critical social theorist. She wanted to explore participant experiences of wealth inequality in her country. She did not, however, wish to transform the situation or to encourage participants to transform it themselves. Ultimately she realized that critical social theory was not a good fit for her and that a more interpretive philosophy, such as phenomenology or post-structuralism, would better reflect her approach.

Example

Complementary choice moments: research questions, literature reviews and theoretical and conceptual frameworks

Choosing a research question (see Chapter 7) requires coming to grips with what is at the heart of the study, what a researcher *really* wants to know. Reviewing literature (see Chapter 8) and presenting it to set the stage for a study requires the researcher to choose from the available body of literature. In order to accomplish this, researchers must make inclusion and exclusion decisions based upon a variety of issues such as fit for the study and quality of the research or theoretical work. Choosing a conceptual or theoretical framework (Chapter 9) requires careful reading and finding a good match of concepts and theories for the study at hand. It requires a researcher to choose to use one, the other or both, and to make decisions about which concepts and theories are most apt.

CHOOSING A RESEARCH APPROACH

For decades in most social science fields, qualitative research was considered synonymous with either ethnographic research or grounded theory, or it was considered to be a single monolithic approach. These views no longer hold true. Even since the publication of Creswell's (1998) classic text *Qualitative inquiry and research design: Choosing among five traditions*, the number, breadth and varieties of approaches have grown. Although researchers refer to these by a number of different names, we simply refer to them as research approaches.

METHODOLOGY, RESEARCH APPROACH AND METHODS

Methodology

The standard or dictionary definition of the word methodology is the study or analysis of the principles of research methods, rules or postulates. Methodology is a theoretical analysis of the methods and principles appropriate to a field of study or other branch of knowledge. It is this definition of methodology that we adopt in this text. Some researchers, however, have used the term methodology as a substitute for the term research approach (for example, case study or ethnography), some have used it as a substitute for the term methods (what they are actually planning to do during the study, such as methods of data collection) and some researchers also use it as a substitution for the philosophical traditions that undergird their work. While these other uses appear frequently in the literature, we believe that the standard definition is the most accurate.

Research approach

We define research approach as the particular kind of qualitative research study undertaken, such as ethnography or phenomenology. Some researchers call these approaches research strategies, research designs or research traditions.

Methods

We define methods as the particular steps or processes taken during a study.

Essential choice moment: research approach

Most qualitative researchers today conduct case studies (Merriam 1998; Yin 1994). A case study (see Chapter 10) is an approach that involves focusing on a specific and bounded 'case'. Case study researchers use a range of research approaches to direct their methods (we present the primary and specific methods they use in Chapters 11–16). Pragmatic qualitative research (Caelli *et al.* 2003) requires a practical approach to research questions and an eclectic set of methods that fits the unique needs of the study (Chapter 11). Grounded theory (Glaser and Strauss 1967) is an approach in which the researcher develops a theory about the human experience that is grounded in data (Chapter 12). In ethnography (Atkinson and Hammersley 1994), researchers seek to explore and understand group experiences (Chapter 13). Phenomenology (Husserl 1962/1977) requires researchers to interpret how several individuals experience an occurrence, event or concept; it is concerned with the structures of consciousness (Chapter 14). Researchers using a narrative approach (Chapter 15) rely upon narratives or stories to understand individual human experience (Clandinin and Connelly 2000). In action research (Chapter 16) (Lewin 1946), researchers and participants examine a problem, implement a solution and evaluate the results. Participatory action research and related approaches (Kemmis and McTaggart 2005) are newer forms of action research that have an emancipatory aspect and come from a more constructivist (and at times post-structural) position.

In addition to these primary research approaches, researchers can draw upon other approaches that may contain overtones of the primary approaches. Some researchers choose, for example, to engage in collaborative or co-inquirer approaches (Chapter 17), in which they strive to break down the barriers between research and practice and between researcher and researched. Other researchers might use qualitative approaches for the purposes of evaluation (Chapter 18) (Patton 2001), which moves beyond solving problems to rendering judgment about a practice, programme or organization. Qualitative researchers may also choose arts-based inquiry (Chapter 19) by employing art such as photographs, pottery and other media to understand the human condition (Barone and Eisner 2011).

We acknowledge that these are not the only qualitative research approaches a researcher might choose; we have selected for inclusion those that are in our opinion most frequently discussed and adopted. Adopting a research approach that fits with the research paradigm at the outset of the project will make the research design stronger, and doing so will enable a researcher to develop a clear argument for the approach and methods he or she has adopted.

CONGRUENCE BETWEEN PARADIGM, PHENOMENON AND RESEARCH APPROACH

Example

We recently reviewed an article abstract for potential inclusion in an edited book we were planning. The author suggested that she was planning to use an interpretive approach. She was planning a virtual ethnography to investigate individual experiences of XDA developers (people who hack cell phones). Thus her paradigm, phenomenon and research approach were well matched.

A colleague of ours recently examined a PhD dissertation and found that the student had argued that he was using hermeneutics as the paradigm for his research into examining individuals' experiences, but he had designed the study using survey methods. The student was unable to defend his use of hermeneutics, as this philosophy did not fit with the survey approach (that tends to be carried out from a post-positivist position as we indicate in Chapters 2 and 4). So the student had to reconsider his philosophical position, his phenomenon and his approach to find a path that allowed for congruence among the three.

COLLECTING DATA

A researcher also faces the choice of what data to collect and how to go about fieldwork. The essential choice associated with this choice moment is choosing the kind of data to collect. The complementary choice involves choosing time, place and participants (Chapter 20), ethics and ethical approval (Chapter 21) and type of fieldwork (Chapter 22).

Essential choice moment: choosing a data collection method

Just as the number of research approaches has grown, so too have the number of ways in which a researcher collects data. Many, if not most, qualitative researchers choose interviews as a method of data collection. Interviewing typically involves developing a set of procedures and questions, which often are semi-structured in form, and then talking with a number of individuals in depth. Researchers may also choose to do *focus group interviews*, which involve asking questions of a group and prompting discussion amongst the group members. *Observations* have always been a mainstay of qualitative research; researchers in many of the research traditions, including grounded theory, ethnography and case study have decisions to make about how directly involved with a site to be when conducting them. *Document and visual artefact reviews* are detailed lists of items created by organizations or participants that have become an increasingly important method of data collection. Many, if not most, researchers use a *combination* of these approaches, differing in the degrees of emphasis that they place on each, as well as the ways in which they are carried out. Data collection is a complex process that should not be taken lightly. Each approach requires thoughtful preparation, time and attention, as well as reflection. We discuss data collection approaches more fully in Part 5 of this book.

Example

CONGRUENCE BETWEEN PHENOMENON AND DATA COLLECTION

A student recently decided to do a study investigating the influence of globalization on folk craft, with a focus on quilt makers in the southern USA. The student decided to use a combination of interviews and artefacts (quilts) as data.

A student wanted to investigate the experiences of production line workers and considered relying solely on observations. The student eventually came to the realization that to truly understand their experiences, particularly from the perspective of an interpretivist researcher, it would be necessary to talk with them as well; she ultimately decided she would need to interview them as well and also decided to add focus groups (we describe what focus groups can add to data collection in Chapter 24).

Complementary choice moment: time, place and participants, ethics and fieldwork

Complementary choices related to collecting data include determining who participants will be as well as where and when to conduct the study (Chapter 20). A researcher would also be advised to ensure that their ethical practices go beyond the minimum ethical board approval required, moving instead toward ensuring an ethical design, excellent treatment of individuals, transparency of products, and plausibility of products (Chapter 21). In addition, researchers must consider the ways in which they will carry out fieldwork, deciding what role for example they will take in the research (Chapter 22).

WORKING WITH DATA

There are several considerations when working with data. The first is which analytic strategy to adopt to make meanings of findings. Additionally, a researcher should consider how to move beyond analysis toward interpretation. Finally, a researcher should consider how to ensure the quality of his or her findings.

Essential choice moment: choosing an analytical strategy

Data analysis frequently receives short shrift in qualitative research. The notion that there is more than one way to do data analysis in qualitative research receives even less. Many believe that 'constant comparison', an approach used widely in grounded theory research, is the only way to analyze data. We suggest, however, that the researcher has many approaches from which to choose (see also Leech and Onwuegbuzie 2007; Bernard and Ryan 2010) and so is able to draw upon a range of primary analytic methods that tend to be best suited to those data collection methods that create verbatim transcriptions. In a *keyword analysis*, for example, a researcher searches out existing text for participant use of specific words in context. The researcher focuses upon the words themselves and notes frequently repeated words, unusual words and words used in context with other words. In *content analysis*, the researcher focuses upon the content itself and keeps a numeric tally of the words that are used. So the frequency of usage is the subject of interest and analysis. Through the process of *constant comparison*, a researcher codes text for words or phrases that stand out while constantly comparing codes with each other in the search for concepts and themes. In *domain analysis*, the researcher looks for specific categories of relations (for example, *x* is a kind of *y* or alternately *x* is a subset of *y*). *Thematic analysis* involves reading and rereading text and searching holistically for themes. The last three, constant comparison, domain analysis and thematic analysis, also work with data gathered through methods that are textual but not verbatim.

There are many specialized methods of data analysis and these require considerable study and guidance to use effectively. They include: *heuristic/phenomenological analysis*, *ethnographic analysis*, *narrative analysis*, *discourse analysis*, *hermeneutical analysis*, *semiotic analysis*, *event analysis and analytic induction*. Many of these are associated with a specific research tradition and thus a specific form of data collection (for example, someone employing phenomenography might choose to do phenomenological interviews and then phenomenological analysis,

---

CONGRUENCE OF ANALYTIC APPROACH

Example

A student known to us recently decided to do a grounded theory study using constant comparison as the approach to data analysis. As we note in the chapter on grounded theory, this analytic approach was developed along with the grounded theory method and thus is a strong choice.

Another student, who adopted a post-structuralist philosophical stance, decided to use a case study to investigate linguistic structures of participants at his site. The student wanted to use thematic analysis, however, as the analytic approach. We advised that domain analysis or the advanced method of discourse analysis would be a more appropriate selection for considering the linguistic structures of participants.

and someone employing ethnography might do ethnographic interviews and then ethnographic analysis, and so on). Non-textual data, such as artefacts, tend to be paired with a modified form of content analysis or semiotic analysis. We describe each of these analytic approaches more fully in Chapters 27 and 28 of this book.

Complementary choice moment: interpretation and quality

In addition to using a specific approach to analyzing data, researchers are faced with a range of options about how to go about interpretation (Chapter 29) and there is no one-size-fits-all approach. Indeed, as the researcher is the instrument of data interpretation, it is fully dependent on that person and his or her beliefs about interpretation. There are however, a number of strategies that a researcher may use to help facilitate interpretations, which we describe in Chapter 29. There also are many ways of ensuring quality (Chapter 30), from how a researcher will conceptualize it to how quality is operationalized and strategized.

A QUALITATIVE RESEARCHER'S WHEEL OF RESEARCH CHOICES

We have created a conceptual model that depicts the way in which each of the essential choice moments work together to create a 'qualitative researcher's Wheel of Research Choices'. The Wheel comprises a set of five rings, representing the five moments. Each ring is divided into six sectors. *The first ring* illustrates the choice of a research paradigm: pragmatism, constructivism, social constructionism, phenomenology, post-modernism/structuralism and critical social theory. The researcher's choice of paradigm consequently influences not only the second ring but also the entire research process. *The second ring* represents the choice of a research phenomenon: individuals, groups, structures, concepts, processes and artefacts. This selection is influenced by the preceding selection and it influences each decision that comes after it. *The third ring* represents selection of a qualitative research approach: pragmatic qualitative research, grounded theory, narrative, phenomenology, ethnography, or action research. The selection is influenced by the preceding choice of paradigm and phenomenon, and it consequently influences each subsequent choice. *The fourth ring* represents the choice of a data collection approach: interviews, focus groups, observation, documents, visual documents and a combination. Again, choices before influence and after are influenced by this selection. The analytical strategy is *the fifth ring* on the Wheel: keyword analysis, content analysis, constant comparison, domain analysis, thematic analysis, and specialized approach. All choices are inherently interconnected. In Figure 3.1 we show such choices, which are separated by rings and spokes, our qualitative researcher's Wheel of Research Choices.

Even though it is fixed on the printed page, we intend the model to be dynamic rather than static, since we do not intend for the rings of the Wheel to be locked; instead, they may spin as the arrows indicate, allowing for the creation of unique combinations. While the number of possible combinations may seem daunting, certain combinations of paradigms, phenomena, approaches, data collection methods and analytical strategies are more natural fits than others. While there are no 'wrong' combinations necessarily, often there are 'better' combinations for which it is possible to create a strong rationale for selection. See the chapters on various approaches (Part 4) for some common combinations.

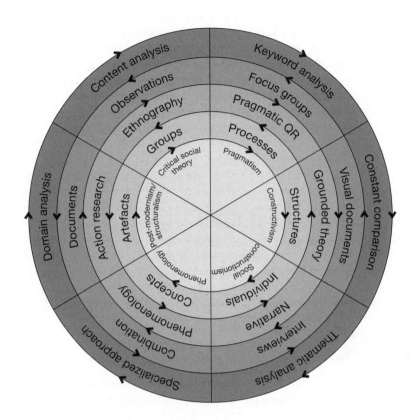

Figure 3.1 Qualitative researcher's Wheel of Research Choices

USING THE WHEEL OF RESEARCH CHOICES TO SELECT A SET OF RESEARCH LENSES

The qualitative researcher's Wheel of Research Choices can help researchers to identify and articulate the different lenses through which they are viewing their research.

The research lens

Qualitative researchers often use the term 'research lens' when talking about their work. Unfortunately, there is a general lack of agreement among researchers about what exactly may serve as a research lens, which makes the concept of 'the research lens' seem at best mysterious and at worst a vague and unhelpful construct. Indeed, the literature does not provide a definitive answer to the question of what may serve as a lens. Some scholars seem to view qualitative research itself as a unique research lens (Dooley 2007). Others scholars see the selection of a philosophical paradigm as the lens (Marshall 2001). Yet others see the selection of a specific theory to serve as a theoretical framework as the research lens (Creswell 2007).

As we see it, a lens is something that both facilitates and influences perception, evaluation and understanding. We believe that the lack of an agreed definition of a research lens stems from the fact that any of these lenses clearly can help a researcher focus and determine what is really important in the research. Indeed, we believe that all of them do. We define a research lens as *a mental model that helps researchers to clarify the focus of the investigation*. It makes meaning easier to see, determines what is and is not included in a given view and eases decisions about what is and is not important. Thus, a research lens helps researchers to interpret data (see Chapter 29).

A set of lenses

We believe that qualitative researchers tend to use a number of different research lenses — philosophical, personal, theoretical and strategic — to understand the phenomena they choose to investigate. We also assert that using multiple lenses can allow researchers to more clearly understand different aspects of the phenomena. Like different schema, each of these lenses leads a researcher to focus on certain things, while ignoring others (Ancona *et al.* 1999). While a single lens in isolation cannot form a very sharp image, when combined, these simple lenses create a more complex, multilayered set of lenses, which ultimately enable the researcher to have a sharper image of data and thus lead to better interpretation. A lens set then *is a complex combination of several different lenses*. Each lens offers its own set of variables and relationships, its own view of specific phenomena and its own set of parameters to guide researcher thinking.

The Wheel of Research Choices and research lenses

The selections that researchers ultimately make at choice moments serve as a separate example of the often invoked but rarely illustrated research lens, which help researchers to focus on and highlight different aspects of the phenomena being examined. The *paradigm lens*, for example, helps researchers to focus on what reality is and how they may know it. The *research phenomena lens* assists researchers to think about what or who is really important to the study. The *research approach lens* enables researchers to consider how individual approaches may focus on different understandings of everyday lived experiences or unique happenings or occurrences. The *data collection lens* helps researchers to focus on the ways in which they can best gather information to answer their research questions, avoid collecting data that will serve no purpose and treat data for the unique characteristics that they possess. The *analytic lens* enables researchers to focus on (multiple) methods of deconstructing and reconstructing data, assisting them to see what is important in the data, which ultimately leads to better interpretations and evaluation of findings.

Using the Wheel of Research Choices can allow researchers to develop a set of five lenses through which to view data. In practice, the researcher creates a wedge on the Wheel that serves as a guide or plan for the particular study. This wedge or set of lenses will hopefully be the best or a good fit, through compatible selections having been made by the researcher at the five choice moments. We illustrate how this works in Figure 3.2.

These choices that a researcher makes in creating such a lens have meaning. 'I am a critical social theorist', 'I am an ethnographer', 'I am an examiner of groups', 'I am a participant-observer', and 'I am an ethnographic analyst', are statements that show who a researcher is, what he or she deems important, what he or she actually does during the research process, and how he or she sees the world and the collected data. When a researcher says, for example, 'I am a critical social theory researcher', that provides information and meaning that tells a listener where the researcher is coming from and how he or she is positioning himself/herself. 'I am an

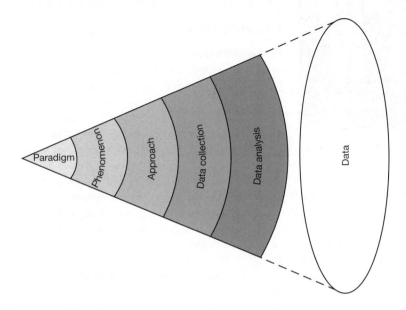

Figure 3.2 Set of lenses

ethnographer' has meaning to the researcher as an individual, to colleagues and to an audience of a published study about how the researcher views the world. Such statements are indicative of deeply held beliefs evident in the paradigms most often associated with them, but they also are indicative of patterns and methods that the individual is likely to adopt when carrying out research. 'I am an examiner of groups' says something about what the researcher views as important as well: group daily lived experiences. 'I am a participant-observer' has meaning, as does 'I am an interviewer'. It conveys meaning about how the researcher obtains information that says something about what he or she values. 'I am a data analyst who uses ethnographic analysis' illustrates how the researcher uncovers what is important, how he or she manipulates data. Each of these choices work together to construct a unique qualitative study that is tailored to answer a specific research question, and they serve as a guide for interpretation of data. Thus, the choice may be combined to create a complex lens that can help researchers better understand human experience. As researchers refine their lenses, they permeate their research methods. Through using them, researchers become the creators of meaning, using symbols and stories to represent what they see through their various lenses.

Some researchers hone in on specific parts of their lenses. We believe that when they do this, the philosophical perspectives are embedded in their research approaches. Mary Romero demonstrates this in her following researcher reflection.

CONCLUSION

Researchers make choices throughout the research process, whether intentionally or unintentionally, that ultimately create their research lenses. While choices may be complex and even at times occur at a subconscious level, as we see it, researchers have a duty to be as intentional as possible about this process, in order to make the best selections from among the options, or alternately to invent new ones.

Mary Romero, Arizona State University, USA

Narrating life as the maid's daughter

For the past decade, various social scientists have thrown the word 'lens' around quite a bit. It is usually meant as a synonym for ideological or standpoint position, as in 'I approach this study through the lens of critical theory'. A maximum close-up lens is frequently employed by ethnomethodologists and microethnographers, who examine small bits of symbolic interaction whereby society is 'accomplished'. The wide angle lenses of 'mainstream' research seek to understand social relations in large statistical studies. In my own case, I used a less macro lens than the micro-ethnographers and a form of 'stop action photography' to analyze the everyday rituals of power relations, identity and resistance. The life story approach allowed me to capture enduring interactions, continuity as well as changes occurring over time. In my life history of Olivia, I interviewed one Chicana over a twenty-year span; she was the daughter of a live-in domestic worker in a gated Los Angeles community.

Unit of analysis

The specific element that the researcher will be able to say something about at the end of the study; the unit then drives the analysis (see Chapter 6)

In my first book, *Maid in the U.S.A.*, the **unit of analysis** had been the employer's home, without a comparable examination of employees' families. Rarely has the dilemma of 'women's work' been examined from the child's view-point. What does it mean when working mothers are too tired to spend quality time with their children at the end of day? How does the child interpret 'work obligations' that extend into family time? How does their mother's occupation shape the way that children are treated by their employers and the larger community? These are all questions concerning mothers caring for their employers' children and cleaning their houses – raised from the position of employees' children.

My narrative conveys the ways that children learn their own status in various social settings, and come to recognize social class/racial/ethnic/gender and other expectations as they cross borders from one social group to another. After reflecting on her life and understanding the present from those experiences, Olivia never wavered on the specific incidents that revealed tensions and contradictions. However, her stories became more nuanced and complex in representing the paternalistic relationship used by her mother's employers, as they sought to make her "one of the family", and with her own mom, who sometimes seemed more concerned with the employer's children than with Olivia.

After our first interview in Austin, Texas, I did not imagine decades of interviewing and writing about Olivia. I interviewed her more or less every year over a twenty-year span. A life narrative told over a period of time is never straightforward and always quite messy. However, I am glad that it did take me almost two and half decades to finish the project because otherwise I would not have seen Olivia grow from a recent college graduate to become a well-respected consultant who blended the Mexican immigrant community into her professional life, embraced her lessons and social capital accrued as 'the maid's daughter', and established an unbreakable bond with her mother. Her mother lives with her now, and they blend parenting styles in raising Olivia's two children. After two decades of interviewing, I found myself listening to the voice and emotions of a woman who had gained new perspectives and had no regrets in her life but had become very content with her life as a consultant, daughter and mother.

The maid's daughter: Living inside and outside the American dream
NYU Press, 2011

Although the Wheel of Research Choices simplifies the choices that researchers will make in qualitative design and thus could be said to 'normalize' and striate the relationships between paradigm, phenomenon, approach, data collection and analysis, we suggest that understanding the complexity and availability of different choices at the outset can equip researchers to understand in depth their own stances as researchers, the values that underpin their research and the issues they believe to be important in a piece of research. Indeed, we believe that choices researchers make during essential choice moments ultimately create a set of researcher lenses, through which they interpret data.

Whatever choices a researcher makes, we believe that it is his or her responsibility to provide a strong rationale for these choices. Information, logic and intuition should guide the choices, and sharing information with an intended audience about how and why the choices were made is imperative. Throughout the remainder of this book, we provide additional information about each of these choice moments and the options that researchers have, and we provide information about implications on other practical matters that are also a result of these choices.

Concept questions

- What are the most critical choices a researcher faces when designing a qualitative study?
- What are the consequences of selecting from an array of options?
- What can identifying a set of research lenses during research design do for a researcher?

Application questions

- How may the Wheel of Research Choices inform your work?
- Which lenses are most appropriate for your work?

Reflective questions

Iyengar, S. (2010) *The art of choosing*, New York: Twelve.
Iyengar's work provides interesting, relevant and useful information about choices, and the consequence of choices, that informed our thinking.

Creswell, J. W. (1998) *Qualitative inquiry and research design: Choosing among five traditions*, Thousand Oaks, CA: Sage.
Creswell's text helped us to consider research design as a systematic process.

Merriam, S. B. (2009) *Qualitative research: A guide to design and implementation*, San Francisco, CA: Jossey-Bass.
Merriam's work assisted us in assessing issues affecting research design.

Key resources

Acknowledging a position

PART TWO

Chapter 4

Philosophical stance

INTRODUCTION

Qualitative researchers share many similar views and values but they disagree on many issues as well. Qualitative researchers tend to believe, for example, that the social world is distinct from the natural one and, as such, researchers should learn about it by exploring that world, rather than by way of cause-and-effect tests that seek to examine an objective reality. Furthermore, qualitative researchers value the human experience, and they tend to believe in the transparency of researcher role, pursue knowledge in uncontrolled and natural environments and typically use inductive analytic processes. They generally value the holistic, the unique and the specific. Qualitative researchers are divided, however, in many ways in their views about realities, knowledge and how knowledge may best be obtained; in short, they have different philosophies and different views about how to use these philosophies during the research process. These differences are important, since the question of 'how to research' necessarily is a philosophical one.

To guide their views and ultimately their work, qualitative researchers often articulate a philosophical stance that helps them make their assumptions more explicit, to the researchers themselves and to potential readers. Researchers position themselves in relation to their philosophies, whether consciously or unconsciously, as they determine how to undertake a given study. In this chapter, we argue for the importance of being explicit about the choice of philosophies that underpin the research. In this chapter, we define the terms epistemology and ontology and consider different approaches to research methods. We outline the different paradigms that contemporary qualitative researchers often draw upon to guide their philosophical positions, specifically critical social theory, pragmatism, phenomenology, post-modern critical theory and post-structuralism, constructionism and constructivism. Finally, we argue that the choice of a paradigm influences all other choices that a researcher makes during a qualitative study. Being aware of their philosophical views, articulating and owning them, then, can inform and improve researchers' choices and help them carry out better research.

DEFINITION OF PHILOSOPHICAL STANCE

Being able to identify a theory of knowledge, a set of guidelines by which they may decide whether and how they may know a social phenomenon, and a set of principles about how they will demonstrate that knowledge, is an indispensable part of qualitative research. In order to accomplish these goals, researchers should understand and articulate their views of social reality and what they count as knowledge or evidence related to the social world. Philosophy can support researchers by providing principles that can guide researchers when procedural information fails to address a particular issue. Investigating their philosophies and understanding how these philosophies affect them requires researchers to consider the underlying assumptions that they use to make sense of their work.

A philosophical stance suggests a view of reality and knowledge that in turn informs researcher perspectives, approaches and methods. It also clarifies a set of assumptions that enables researchers to be clear about the reasons they have chosen a particular research design (Trede and Higgs 2009: 17). A researcher's philosophical stance also guides that researcher's actions and behaviours during the implementation of a study; it indeed influences what will be discovered. A philosophical stance, however, is not simply a tool. Rather, a philosophical stance is *a philosophically informed view about reality, knowledge and ways to gain knowledge that serves as a guide for a particular study; it is a guiding perspective about the nature of truth and human behaviour and thus is the very foundation for research.*

Rosiek explains the importance of identifying a philosophical position (see facing page).

Choosing a philosophical stance requires researchers to come to an understanding of what they believe counts as knowledge and how that knowledge may be uncovered. It requires 'critical thinking, of a more or less systematic kind about the general nature of the world (metaphysics or theory of existence), the justification of belief (epistemology or theory of knowledge), and the conduct of life (ethics or theory of value)' (Honderich 1995: 666). Indeed, choosing a philosophical stance requires qualitative researchers to determine what kind of researchers they are specifically.

It is often evident when researchers have considered the philosophical underpinnings of their work, as they tend to come across as knowledgeable and believable, providing an assurance of trust to the reader. Some researchers, however, fail to ponder philosophical issues related to their research, which 'implies that they either find philosophic questions as non-relevant in their research settings or they take their own philosophic position as self-evident and known' (Eriksson and Kovalainen 2008: 11). Failure to consider and disclose belief systems can have repercussions, such as faulty research processes or unbelievable findings. At other times, while researchers will indicate a philosophical position: 'I am this' or 'I am that', they do not put their philosophical stance into practice in their research design, which can defeat the purpose of having and articulating a philosophical perspective.

Example

Identifying and articulating a philosophical stance

A researcher may argue with peers that knowledge is political and that power should be examined in research, but neither recognize the importance of acknowledging a critical social theory base or other compatible philosophy nor what that means for research questions and the research approach.

Thus, researchers should identify and articulate a philosophical stance. There are a number of concepts that researchers consider when they identify a philosophical stance, such as views of reality, views of knowledge and views of the ways in which knowledge should be discovered; ultimately, a philosophical paradigm guides the researcher's philosophical position. In Table 4.1 we offer a brief overview of the key concepts related to philosophical stance, along with examples from different philosophical perspectives, and we follow the overview with a fuller description in the remainder of the chapter.

Jerry Rosiek, University of Oregon, USA

The role of philosophy in qualitative research methodology

The first thing I tell students in their first course on qualitative research methodology is that there is no such thing as a 'qualitative' research method. 'Qualitative' is a word given to a wide array of research practices that share one main characteristic: they do not focus on the interpretation of quantitative data. Beyond that, the word 'qualitative' doesn't tell us much about a study's research design, its main phenomenon of interest or its underlying assumptions about inquiry. We are better served by describing our research in terms of the theoretical frameworks that inform it. Philosophical frameworks specify the assumptions that organize our research.

At the most basic level are questions about ontology: what aspects of reality do we think are worth examining? For example, a cultural ethnographer considers patterns of cultural and social influence to be the most important things to examine in her inquiry. A psychologist using phenomenological methods, however, may consider individual cognitive and affective experience to be the most important things to attend to in her studies.

At another level are questions about epistemology: what counts as knowledge in our modes of inquiry? For example, an ethnographer using a post-positivist epistemology would consider it necessary to design a study that would be replicable by another researcher. This would require developing procedures for data collection and analysis that minimized the influence of her personal experiences on her conclusions. It would also likely inspire the author to write using third-person descriptive prose. An ethnographer influenced by post-structuralist conceptions of knowledge, however, would consider it impossible to bracket out the influences of her identity and experience. This would lead her to refrain from claims of interpretive certainty. It would also likely inspire the author to write using first-person descriptive prose as a way of being transparent that the interpretations being offered do not aspire to transcendent authority.

Finally, there are questions about ideology or the teleology of research: what explicit and implicit purposes does it serve? An ethnographer influenced by critical theory would consider it necessary to interrogate the way her research sustains social stratification by reproducing certain kinds of expertise at the expense of the empowerment of working class persons. A narrative inquirer influenced by pragmatism would look for the validity of a narrative description, not in how accurately it describes a scene but in how effectively the narrative transforms the experiences of people involved in the research.

This is why we should lead with an account of the philosophical influences when describing our research. If a student tells me they are doing a 'qualitative' study on gender in elementary schools, I do not really know what her research will look like. But if she tells me that she is doing a cultural ethnography of the influence of gender on elementary student experiences, using post-structuralist theory to frame her knowledge claims and pragmatism to inform her ethical responsibility to ameliorate gender bias in the school in which she works, then I have a much clearer idea of what kind of work she will be doing.

Researcher reflections

Table 4.1 Key concepts related to philosophical stance

Perspectives	*Example of perspectives from different philosophical traditions*	
Ontological views (philosophies that address the nature of reality)	Realism	Reality exists and humans may (at times imperfectly) know it; objectivism is directly connected to realism (the notion that there is an objective reality)
	Idealism	Reality is fundamentally mental, mentally constructed or otherwise immaterial; subjectivism is directly connected to this view (the notion that reality is mentally and subjectively constructed)
Epistemological views (philosophies that address the nature of knowledge)	Empiricism	Knowledge develops through sensory perception (quantitative)
	Rationalism	Knowledge develops through reason (usually quantitative)
	Historicism	Knowledge develops in context, such as historical period, geographic place and local culture
	Instrumentalism	Knowledge develops from matching theory with observed phenomena
	Experientialism	Knowledge develops through experience. Reality is constantly changing
	Structuralism	Knowledge is embedded in higher mental, linguistic, social, cultural structures; a way of overcoming the problematic conception of 'man'
	Existentialism	Knowledge begins with the human mind but there is a recognition that human knowledge is limited and fallible
Research perspective (positions on the nature of research)	Objectivity	Research is unbiased, impartial and based upon facts
	Subjectivity	Research is always personal and based upon the researcher's values and perceptions
	Intersubjectivity	Research is mutual and co-arises from the engagement of interdependent individuals
Paradigms (philosophical perspective that guides ontological, epistemological, and methodological perspectives)	Positivism	Positive knowledge exists and is based upon natural phenomena, their properties and relations and may be discovered through the scientific method (quantitative)
	Post-positivism	Positive knowledge exists but is imperfectly understandable, and it may be uncovered through falsification (quantitative primarily)
	Critical social theory	Positive knowledge exists and may be discovered through historical approaches
	Pragmatism	Reality exists for individuals, but knowledge is contextually contingent; knowledge may be discovered by examining the usefulness of theory in practice
	Phenomenology	Reality and knowledge reside in the mind, as the individual perceives and experiences it, and knowledge may be discovered by exploring human experiences
	Post-critical/ structuralism	Reality exists and knowledge may be found deeply embedded in structures; a later view is that human agency is problematic since there is no unified truth but rather many truths and systems, and such systems impose linguistic codes and structures. Examining codes and structures can help researchers uncover knowledge
	Constructionism	Reality and knowledge are socially constructed; knowledge may be gained by examining the ways in which individuals co-create knowledge
	Constructivism	Reality and knowledge reside in the minds of individuals. Knowledge may be uncovered by unpacking individual experiences

Some scholars, post-modernists in particular, argue that ontology (views of reality) and epistemology (views of knowledge) are one and the same. We agree that there is certainly considerable overlap and, as we have mentioned in this chapter, we see them as inextricably linked. At the same time, however, we note that some scholars suggest that treating views of reality and views of knowledge as the same concept is problematic. For the sake of clarity and to highlight the distinctions between the different branches of philosophy, in this chapter we have defined ontology and epistemology separately.

VIEWS OF REALITY

When qualitative researchers undertake a study, their views about what counts as 'reality' necessarily influence what they do during the course of their work. Views about reality also influence how they view their findings, whether they acknowledge or even are aware of such influence. Ontology, a branch of metaphysics, is a philosophical term that addresses questions of the nature of reality, what the real world is and what exists in it (Flew 1984). Ontology also addresses questions of whether social entities are or should be viewed as entities that exist in a reality that is external to social actors or whether, alternatively, they are social constructions that arise from the perceptions and actions of others (Bryman and Bell 2003: 19). Moreover, ontology addresses ideas about the relationships between people, society and the world, and as such 'ontological assumptions embrace all theories and methodological positions' (Eriksson and Kovalainen 2008: 13).

Ontological questions for social researchers include the following:

■ What is real?
■ What can be known about it?

Two ontological positions are seen in realism, an objective perspective, and idealism, a subjective perspective. Realism suggests that there is an objective external and knowable reality that exists independent of individual means of apprehending it. There are objects in the world that have inherent properties. This perspective suggests that reality is a matter of the physical universe that is external to human experience, and so the physical world is a separate reality from perception and the mind (MacKay 1997); therefore, realists acknowledge a 'social reality' in addition to a 'physical reality'. Some realists/objectivists believe that perception may be distorted, but realists tend to criticize idealistic/subjectivist stances as extreme. Idealism is the view that suggests reality is subjective and is constructed by individuals and groups. This ontological perspective suggests that knowledge is the meaning that research participants assign to their lives; it is a product of their minds and may be gained by learning about the knowledge that they hold (Schuh and Barab 2008). Qualitative researchers occupy different points along the continuum that exists between realism and objectivism.

> **Tips**
>
> Some scholars mention relativism as an ontological perspective, but we find that very few researchers claim to have a relativist ontology, arguably because relativism does not have a clear definition and thus can mean anything and everything goes, which can lead to criticism.

VIEWS OF KNOWLEDGE

knowledge

The body of 'truths', information or awareness that humans have acquired or constructed

Researchers also consider their views of knowledge as well as their views of how **knowledge** may be uncovered. More and more often, researchers are interrogating their views of knowledge and then articulating them for an intended audience. Epistemology is a branch of philosophy concerned with knowledge and how it may be known (Honderich 1995). Epistemology comprises theories of knowing and the relationship between the researcher and the researched, and serves as a guide to developing understanding of the phenomenon under study. Epistemologies are constrained by ontologies (Guba and Lincoln 1994; 2005).

> **Tips**
>
> Key epistemological questions
>
> ■ What is knowledge?
> ■ To what extent may knowledge be gained?
> ■ To what extent does knowledge represent 'reality'?
> ■ What is the relationship between the knower and what could be known?

Qualitative researchers have moved away from empiricism and rationalism as epistemological positions. Instead, they draw from a different set of philosophical perspectives to drive their epistemological positions. Some operate from a perspective of historicism (or historical realism), for example, while others draw upon notions of experientialism. Others have drawn from or reacted against structuralism, while others have operated out of views of knowledge that most closely approximate existentialist perspectives.

VIEWS TOWARD THE NATURE OF RESEARCH: OBJECTIVISM, SUBJECTIVISM AND INTERSUBJECTIVITY

Qualitative researcher views of ontology and epistemology necessarily influence researchers' views of research approach and ultimately how they carry out their studies:

> When we enter the world of formal scholarship, it is essential that we examine the foundations of our thinking. When we do this, we discover that there exist alternative answers to each foundational question. Two scholars who hold different beliefs on ontology and epistemology may be interested in examining the same phenomenon, but their beliefs will lead them to set up their studies differently because of their different views of evidence, analysis, and the purpose of research.
>
> (Potter 1996: 35–6)

Figure 4.1 Objectivism and subjectivism on a continuum

Social researchers, then, approach their work from different places, notably taking an approach that is either objective, intersubjective or subjective. Objectivism and subjectivism may be thought of as existing on a continuum at opposite ends from each other, with intersubjectivity falling somewhere in between, as we depict in Figure 4.1.

Qualitative researchers fall at different points along the continuum (Holden and Lynch 2004). An objectivist position towards research assumes that there is an external reality that may be known and that the researcher maintains a detached, objective position. Most quantitative researchers adopt an objectivist position and draw upon positivism and post-positivism to guide their work. A subjectivist position towards research assumes that reality is constructed by individuals and that the subject and researcher should be actively involved. Somewhere between objectivity and subjectivity lies a closely related concept: intersubjectivity. Intersubjectivity is mutual agreement, generally among a small group of people, about what is real.

These different views have challenges when the positions are seen as too discrete. As Bateson suggests:

> The word 'objective' becomes, of course, quite quietly obsolete; and the world subjective, which normally confines you within your skin, disappears as well ... The world is no longer 'out there' in quite the way it used to be ... There is a combining or marriage between an objectivity that is passive to the outside world and a creative subjectivity, neither pure solipsism nor its opposite ... Somewhere between these two is a region where you are partly blown by the winds of reality and partly an artist creating a composite out of inner and outer events.
>
> (Bateson 1978: 244–5)

Yet they are useful concepts for helping researchers to understand the basic assumptions about research that they might use to guide their work.

PARADIGMS

Qualitative researchers often use philosophical **paradigms** to help locate themselves and their studies by adopting a given paradigm to guide their ontological, epistemological and research perspectives. The six paradigms that we believe qualitative researchers adopt most often are critical social theory, pragmatism, phenomenology, post-modernism and post-structuralism, constructionism and constructivism (we also describe these in Chapters 2 and 3).

These paradigms indicate several core assumptions that are interrelated and mutually supportive of each other (Lombardo 1987; Reber 1995). We offer additional brief descriptions of these differences in the following few paragraphs. We follow these descriptions with a summary table indicating the position of the different approaches along a continuum.

paradigm
A paradigm is a belief system or worldview that guides the researcher and the research process (Guba and Lincoln 1994)

Critical social theory

Critical social theory means many different things to many different people, but the unifying idea is that all knowledge is political and that research should be aimed at eliminating social injustice, particularly related to ethnicity, gender, sexual orientation, disability and other marginalized groups (MacKenzie and Knipe 2006). The aim of this research is to bring about social transformation. Thus, critical social theorists focus on the idea of the world as it should be. The critical social theorist view of reality is related to the influences of power and authority, as well as to how political, historical and socio-economic forces influence the lives of people (Trede and Higgs 2009). Critical social theorists also argue that some societal groups are privileged over others and that oppression is widespread and varied.

Critical social theorists recognize that knowledge is not value free. Rather, they see knowledge as a self-reflective understanding and theoretical explanation. Thus, critical social theorists seek to understand the ideologies that inform and affect both their research and their own stances, in an effort to gain knowledge while simultaneously striving to reduce systems of domination and increase autonomy of research participants.

Critical social theorists see research as essentially an exploration of social and cultural power and believe that values and facts cannot be isolated from one another. Rather, 'inquiry needs to be intertwined with politics and a political agenda' (Creswell 2003: 9) and contain an agenda for active reform 'that may change the lives of the participants, the institutions in which individuals work or live, and the researcher's life' (Creswell 2003: 9–10). Research methods tend to involve collaboration and seek to avoid discrimination (MacKenzie and Knipe 2006). Critical social theorists consider all the different facts that are imposed upon others in terms of views, values and beliefs and the ways these affect research. Research based in critical social theory at times is called transformational research. Researchers often draw upon action research as an approach.

Pragmatism

Pragmatism is a philosophical tradition that asserts that truth may be interpreted in terms of the practical effects of what is believed and, in particular, the usefulness of these effects. The underlying idea is that the truth of an idea is dependent upon its workability; ideas or principles are true in so far as they work. For the pragmatist, reality is a process or an experience. Early pragmatists focused on what adaptive purposes justify the existence of the mind. Neopragmatist, Rorty, argues that pragmatism does not require an ontology, but rather sees the truth is 'in William James' phrase, what is good for *us* to believe' (Rorty 1991: 22, emphasis in the original).

Pragmatism is based upon the idea that the subject of the human world is a completely different enterprise from the natural world and thus must be known differently. Knowledge is equivalent to the consequences of interaction (Schuh and Barab 2008). Again, neopragmatist Rorty (1991) argues that pragmatism does not require a specific epistemological perspective. Pragmatism is therefore an experience-centred philosophy that emphasizes change.

The purpose of pragmatic qualitative research is to link theory and practice. Pragmatists believe that knowledge may be gained through a variety of methods. Pragmatists reject 'the scientific notion that social inquiry was able to access the 'truth' about the real world solely by virtue of a single scientific method' (Mertens 2005: 26). The way pragmatists accomplish their purposes is to extract theory from practice and then to apply it back to practice. Pragmatist researchers focus on the 'what' and 'how' of the research problem (Creswell 2003: 11). Pragmatic research places 'the research problem as central and applies all approaches to understanding the problem' (Creswell 2003: 11). With the research question as 'central', the researcher chooses data collection and analysis methods that are most likely to provide insights into the question, without any loyalty to a specific research approach, thus allowing for eclectic approaches to research that are necessary to answer the research questions (Tashakkori and Teddlie 2003; Somekh and Lewin 2005). Indeed, pragmatists emphasize the importance of trying different methods and then evaluating them based upon their effectiveness. Therefore, good research is a trial-and-error process. Pragmatists then gauge the meaning of theories or beliefs by the success of their practical applications. Pragmatism offers a practical and matter-of-fact approach to assessing situations or solving problems, and some adopt this perspective when carrying out pragmatic qualitative research. Some pragmatic researchers also conduct ethnographies or narrative research.

Phenomenology

Phenomenologists see reality as a product of the mind, the world of ideas (van Manen 1997). Meaning is shaped through individual experiences of the world. It is human action that is meaningful (Schwandt 2000). Reality is not something that is viewed as separate from the individual (Valle *et al.* 1989). As Laverty (2003: 4) suggests, 'the 'life world' is understood as what we experience pre-reflectively, without resorting to categorization or conceptualization, and quite often includes what is taken for granted or those things that are common sense'. Understanding is necessarily biased because it is grounded in individual perceptions and an event or experience. It is also biased because of the researcher's experience of history and traditions. Indeed, since traditions 'shape what we are and how we understand the world, the attempt to step outside them would be like trying to step outside of our own skins' (Gallagher 1992: 87). Coming to understand reality as human experience then requires engagement of biases. Understanding is always bound up with language and thus the 'text' (Schwandt 2000).

To understand the social world, it is necessary to understand the meanings of that action (Schwandt 1994). Phenomenologists are concerned with understanding how the everyday intersubjective world is constituted (Schwandt 2000). Meaning also is contextual, so interpretation must consider the context. Phenomenology requires the study of conscious experience, as it is experienced from a first-person point of view. The goal is to 'reconstruct the genesis of the objective meanings of action in the intersubjective communication of individuals in the social life-world' (Outhwaite 1975: 91). Knowledge is uncovered through systematic reflection on the structures of consciousness and phenomena that appear in acts of consciousness.

While a philosophy originally, phenomenology also became associated with a method. Phenomenology is concerned with developing objective processes to interpret those things typically considered subjective. Phenomenology is carried out in order to understand 'the world of human experience' (Cohen and Manion 1994: 36); therefore, phenomenological researchers seek to understand participants' conscious views of the situation under study whilst also recognising the influence of their preconsciousness, their background and experiences, on the research. The starting point is a first-person perspective and the approach involves attempting to describe the essential features and elements of a given experience.

Post-modern critical theory and post-structuralism

Post-structuralism has been called post-hermeneutic, in large part owing to its emphasis on language and on the text. Post-structural researchers are interested in investigating individual and social relationships and, like hermeneutists, they are interested in the self as a construct and how these constructs are formed through language; like post-modern critical theorists, however, they are interested in more than interpretation and instead how these structures gain meaning through relations of power. Thus, they have a strong emphasis on investigating discourse, which indicates power–knowledge relationships.

Post-modern critical researchers and post-structuralists believe that there is no unified reality, but rather multiple and individual realities. While hermeneutists seek to understand and interpret those realities, as conveyed through language between and among individuals, post-structuralists maintain that systems, such as structural systems, are fictitious and cannot be trusted to provide meaning or order. Post-structuralists also believe that structures always become unstable or decentralized. Their work is concerned with power structures and hegemonies and how they maintain structures and enforce hierarchy.

Their research approaches involve a close examination of language. Research may be done by an examination of text, rhetoric or discourse, for example through narrative inquiry and discourse or domain analysis. Researchers seek to bring the interpretations of both participants and themselves into the work. The researcher strives to remain open to the attitudes, beliefs and values of participants. Research usually involves a small number of participants in a search for deep understanding and detail.

Constructionism

The notion of social construction has led to a shift in thinking about the constructed nature of knowledge. Social constructionists take a pluralist position, suggesting critical reflection on 'truths' as individuals construct shared experiences of them. Social constructionists argue that instead of focusing on the mind (the cognitive approach), it is important to recognize that the world is shared. The argument is that the world is produced and understood through interchanges between people and shared objects and activities. Constructionists believe that hidden or private phenomena such as emotions gain their meaning through social settings and practice, and are therefore socially constructed. Constructionists argue that reality is not entirely external and independent of individual conceptions of the world and therefore signs and systems play an important part in the social construction of reality as individuals make and experience meaning together.

Social constructivists believe that knowledge and the knower are interdependent and embedded within history, context, culture, language and experience. The social constructivist believes that groups construct knowledge by creating a culture of shared artefacts with shared meanings. They value local knowledge constructed between people who are actively engaged in its creation – participatory or relational knowing. Constructionists believe that:

> The conception of knowledge as a 'mirror of reality' is replaced by the conception of the 'social construction of reality' where the focus is on the interpretation and negotiation of the meaning of the world.
>
> (Kvale 1996: 41)

Social constructionist research involves a focus on dialogue and negotiation. The goal is to understand shared and co-constructed realities. Constructionists believe that the researcher cannot maintain a detached or objective position, and they believe that both the researcher and the subject should actively collaborate in the meaning-making process. Thus, researchers and participants are co-constructors of knowledge rather than conveyors and receivers of it. Knowledge emerges through dialogue and negotiation and, in research, this means that the dialogue between researchers and participants is critical. Socially constructed knowledge can be transforming for participants and researchers (Etherington 2009). In practice, this means that researchers seek to capture participants' perspectives but the researchers' interpretations of participants' views need to be understood and verified by those involved in the research. The main approach researchers use is asking participants, whether individuals or groups, to describe their social constructions and the way that they have arrived at their construction of knowledge. The researcher tends to be a full participant in the research process. Thus, social constructionist researchers often draw upon approaches such as narrative inquiry.

Constructivism

Constructivism is based upon the notion that reality is a product of one's own creation. Constructivism suggests that all 'knowledge is a compilation of human-made constructions' (Raskin 2002: 4), so constructivists believe that reality is an internal construction where individuals assign meaning to experiences and ideas. Constructivists also tend to believe that 'reality' cannot be separated from knowledge of it, so subjectivity and objectivity are in a sense united. Truth is a result of perspective and therefore knowledge and truth are created rather than discovered. Some who operate within this paradigm see the mind as a space for acquiring, storing and retrieving information but, in the main, knowledge is not seen in the constructivist tradition as independent of the knower; it is something that is useful for attaining goals. This means that individuals invent concepts, models and schemes in order to make sense of their experiences and to test and modify these constructions when they have new experiences (Schwandt 2000). In this way, individual knowledge claims and their subsequent evaluation take place within an individual's framework for viewing and describing the world (Schwandt 2000). Constructivists in general believe that the only thing that they may come to know is people's constructions of their own realities and therefore research emphasizes gaining data concerning how individuals construct knowledge (Jonassen 1991: 10).

Constructivists doing research seek to understand the way meanings are constructed and to apprehend how such meanings are presented and used though language and action. Constructivists generally do not begin with a theory but instead 'generate or inductively develop a theory or pattern of meanings' (Creswell 2003: 9) throughout the research process. They use a range of approaches to seek individuals' reconstructions of their realities, and might use data collection methods such as interviews, narratives and new or existing artefacts that express individuals' ideas and experiences.

COMPARISON OF PHILOSOPHIES

Drawing upon the ideas of a number of researchers and theorists (Holden and Lynch 2004; Hussey and Hussey 1997; Burrell and Morgan 1979; Morgan and Smircich 1980), we offer our comparison of the epistemological, ontological and research perspectives of these different paradigms in Table 4.2, overleaf.

Table 4.2 Comparison of perspectives in different paradigms

Research approaches →	Objective		Intersubjective			Subjective
	Critical social theory	Pragmatism	Phenomenology	Post-critical and post-structuralism	Social constructionism	Constructivism
Ontological assumptions (reality)	Reality is socially constructed through power relationships	Reality is that which is practical	Reality is an individual's interpretation of experience	Reality is what is passed on through symbolic discourse	Reality is socially constructed	Reality is an individual's mental construction
	Realism →				→	*Idealism*
Epistemological assumptions (how to gain knowledge)	Knowledge is gained by co-construction of critical consciousness	Knowledge is derived from observation of interaction among a group of individuals and artefacts in their environment	Knowledge is derived from the interpretation of individual experiences	Knowledge may be gained through the deconstruction of social products, including language, media, institutions, etc.	Knowledge is constructed through dialogue and negotiation	Knowledge is constructed by the researcher and not discovered in the world
	Positivism →				→	*Anti-positivism*
Purpose (of the research)	To study systems, process and change for the purpose of transformation	To test theories in practice	To develop phenomenological insight	To understand patterns of symbolic discourse	To aid in the unpacking and creation of social reality	To understand individuals
	Universal →				→	*Local*
Methods (how to gain knowledge)	Structural/historical insights	Observation of subject in context	Close examination and interpretation of individual experience	Deconstruction of text/meaning/structures	Individual and collective reconstructions	Individual reconstructions
	Nomothetic →				→	*Ideographic*
Researcher perspective	Transformative intellectual	Interested observer	Self-aware translator	Decoder	Passionate participant	Meaning maker
	Removed →				→	*Involved*

USING A PHILOSOPHICAL STANCE DURING RESEARCH: ORIENTATION TOWARD STANCE

While it may or may not be easy to identify a philosophical stance, knowing what to do with it during research design and implementation is an important challenge. We argue that simply espousing a philosophically informed stance and stating a position towards it is insufficient to drive sound research decisions or to ensure quality research. Choosing both the philosophical stance and the orientation towards it at the outset of a research project is important. We believe that researchers may choose to adopt one of several different orientations, which we describe in the following paragraphs, drawing ideas from the works of Green 2007; Green and Caracelli 1997; Tashakkori and Teddlie 2003; Niglas 2000. In our view, some of the orientations are more appropriate for qualitative research than others; in particular, those that retain the assumptions of the different philosophies in practice, and we indicate our beliefs in our descriptions.

Purist orientation

Those who occupy a purist orientation believe that only one philosophical approach is appropriate for social inquiry. They believe that different paradigms/philosophies have different and incommensurable assumptions. They also believe that paradigms should guide all methodological decisions. In particular, those who adopt a purist stance believe that the stance necessarily influences the choice of who or what a researcher will study (see Chapter 6), which will in turn influence the selection of a research approach (Chapters 10–19), the selection of data collection approaches (Chapters 23–26) and finally the analytical approach(es) to be selected (Chapters 27 and 28). They also believe that the researcher should acknowledge a philosophical stance and provide a strong rationale for the position selected.

Situationalist orientation

Those who adopt a situationalist orientation believe that different philosophies should be applied to different situations and contexts. So, a researcher should adopt the approach that is best suited for the given research topic, question, context, and so on. These researchers retain the purist perspective that the philosophical stance guides the remaining decisions, including how to frame the study, what research approach to select and how to collect and treat data. The researcher who relies upon the ontological, epistemological and methodological assumptions of a philosophical paradigm simply adopts a philosophy based upon the needs of the study.

Congruence-with-theory orientation

Those who occupy the congruent theory position believe that a substantive theory serves as a theoretical framework (see Chapter 9) and thus guides most methodological decisions. This theory needs to be congruent with the researcher's paradigm and thus the researcher believes that the philosophical assumptions regarding reality, knowledge, methods and values of the philosophical stance must be respected. The philosophical assumptions still guide practical decisions in the research, yet they complement the theoretical framework and research context.

Blended philosophies orientation

Those who occupy a blended philosophies orientation believe that ontology, epistemology and methods are different considerations, which can and should be easily mixed and matched, based upon the researcher's views. As Reichardt and Cook suggest:

> All the attributes which ... make up the paradigms are logically interdependent ... The attributes themselves are not logically linked to one another ... [So] there is nothing to stop the researcher, except perhaps tradition, from mixing and matching the attributes from the two paradigms to achieve the combination which is most appropriate for the research problem and setting at hand.
>
> Reichardt and Cook (1979: 18)

This orientation is appealing because it allows such latitude and freedom, yet it can trivialize beliefs and assumptions and undervalue the ways in which they guide what counts in qualitative research (Green 2007).

A-paradigmatic orientation

Those who espouse an a-paradigmatic orientation believe that applying philosophies to research is impractical, and so completely oppose those who adopt a purist approach. They believe that stating orientations about ontology and epistemology a priori impinges on the creativity of the researcher and imposes preconceptions about the findings. While we acknowledge that this is a position that some researchers espouse and hold, in practice we do not believe that it is possible to operate in a complete philosophical void. It is instead our view that, whether qualitative researchers acknowledge it or not, they have philosophical perspectives that are compatible with the six theories we have identified or alternatively hold a different philosophy that we have not included in this book. Thus, we suggest that rather than selecting an a-paradigmatic approach, it is more beneficial to adopt a blended or situational position. Pragmatism also can be a good philosophical option as it allows more leeway in views of how to carry out research.

Philosophical stance and positionality statement

Researchers frequently acknowledge philosophical stance, along with personal stance, in a positionality statement (see Chapter 5). This statement is an opportunity for a researcher to suggest how both philosophical and personal stances influenced the research design, process and products.

CONCLUSION

In this chapter, we have examined a number of philosophies that may inform a qualitative researcher's identification of a philosophical stance, considering their ontological, epistemological and research perspectives. We have also indicated that there are a number of ways that researchers position themselves in relation to their stances. If taken as a driving force of a given study, as the base of the researcher's lens, then a researcher's philosophical stance can have a profound influence on the quality of the work, no matter whether it is assumed from a purist, situationalist or complementary theory approach. When designing a qualitative study, a researcher should choose a stance and make sure that other aspects of the research are congruent with it.

Concept questions

- What is the purpose of identifying a philosophical stance?
- How may a researcher's philosophical stance inform the research process?
- Is it important for researchers to acknowledge a position toward the philosophy they have adopted? Why or why not?
- What are the consequences of not identifying a philosophical stance?

Application questions

- What stance makes the most sense to you?
- Which stance are you likely to adopt for your next study?

Reflective questions

We found several sources to be critical in the development of this chapter.

Bryman, A. (2004) *Quantity and quality in social research*, London: Routledge.
In chapter 1 Bryman suggests that the tension between interpretivist and positivist perspectives is based upon political debate about the nature, importance and facility of different research methods. This book, particularly this chapter, helped us consider the differences in qualitative and quantitative paradigms broadly.

Snape, D. and Spencer, L. (2003) Foundations of qualitative research. *In*: J. Ritchie and J. Lewis (eds) *Qualitative research practice: A guide for social science researchers.* London: Sage.
Snape and Spencer define the concept of epistemological stance, framing it around two primary paradigms: positivist and interpretivist. This helped us move from thinking about paradigms (as framework) to stance (as world view).

Guba, E. G. and Lincoln, Y. S. (1994) Competing paradigms in qualitative research. *In*: N. K. Denzin and Y. S. Lincoln (eds) *Handbook of qualitative research*. Thousand Oaks, CA: Sage.

Guba, E. G. and Lincoln, Y. S. (2005) Paradigmatic controversies, contradictions, and emerging confluences. *In*: N. K. Denzin and Y. S. Lincoln (eds) *The SAGE handbook of qualitative research (3rd edn.)*. Thousand Oaks, CA: Sage.
Lincoln and Guba's chapters helped us think about the epistemological and ontological positions of those with different research stances.

Key resources

Chapter 5

Personal stance, positionality and reflexivity

INTRODUCTION

Research supervisors and reviewers often encourage researchers to 'assume a stance', 'articulate positionality' or 'document reflexivity' and for good reason. Indeed, qualitative researchers should know and be able to articulate who they are and what they believe personally, so that they may understand and acknowledge how these factors in turn influence the research. Rarely, however, do supervisors and reviewers explain how to do these things well, which is problematic, since it is challenging for researchers to articulate personal perspectives in a way that is both meaningful and a seamless part of the research process. In this chapter, we explain the concepts of researcher stance, positionality and reflexivity, demonstrating how they are related and even interconnected concepts. We suggest ways of ensuring that researchers choose to address these concepts both in the research design and in the way they undertake and present the research.

PERSONAL STANCE

A personal stance is a position taken towards an issue that is derived from a person's beliefs and views about the world. It reflects deeply held attitudes and concerns about what is important. A person may assume a personal stance on a range of issues. Susan may be a feminist, for example. Simon may be pro-abortion. Jennifer may be a proponent of social justice. All of these are personal stances and reflect an individual's values and priorities. These stances, then, reflect people's core values, which are derived from a range of personal characteristics (such as culture, upbringing, political views, occupation, race and gender). Personal stance is not static but tends to change, move and grow as people's views about life, culture and identity shift; thus, stance is something individuals 'have' as well as something that they 'construct'.

The influence of stance on research

Researchers' personal stances affect their research in myriad ways, from the ways that they choose to go about research to whether they will undertake a given study. It is easy, however, for researchers to forget about the influence of personal stance on research. The following examples further illustrate this point.

INFLUENCE OF PERSONAL STANCE ON RESEARCH

Mike, a white male, grew up in a large city. Mike valued group experiences and was less concerned about individuals; thus, he believed that the overall meaning of the group experience was more important than personal qualities or individuality of those he interviewed. When referring to individuals, Mike simply used a number, which he considered to be a source from which to build theory through a process of aggregation of individual experiences.

Rachel was a therapist, a caregiver by nature and by profession, whose belief in the centrality of people's stories in the research and the need for these stories to be heard, led her to adopt a narrative approach to research.

Betty, a member of an underrepresented ethnic group, grew up in a rural community which had a strong tradition of art and music. Along with her strong sense of self belief, she felt the importance of her cultural roots and the value of arts in research, which led her to use story telling mechanisms along with pictures and poems as ways of representing her data.

John, who is a pacifist, refused to carry out studies funded by the Government's Ministry of Defence.

Example

Although these perspectives only offer a small snapshot of the influence of personal stance on research, they do raise some interesting questions about how much of the research is the researcher. How much of the research, for example, is related to researcher interests, their experiences, beliefs and personal positions? Such questions can help researchers to consider where they stand in the research process, what they believe is important and ultimately how their stance influences the design, analysis and writing of the research. Thus, when addressing the issue of stance, researchers also should consider the ways in which their stances affect the choices they make about which research approaches to adopt.

When researchers consider the issue of personal stance, some of the following questions are worthy of their attention:

■ What is your race/class/gender/age? How do those factors influence how you experience the world and view research?
■ What are the issues you find the most important? How does that influence your view of research?
■ In what ways has your education affected the way you think about research?
■ What other life experiences have influenced the way that you think about your research?

Contemplating the answers to even a few questions such as these can help researchers to identify their stances towards particular issues and to explore and unpack issues related to stance. Such questions are important because they enable researchers to interrogate their deeply held beliefs that become apparent in undertaking research. The answers to these questions are individual to each researcher and, importantly, they can help researchers to point out and clarify their personal stances. For example, the questions highlight beliefs about the influence of background, self-belief and education, and what needs to be researched. These, along with issues such as religious beliefs, political views, sexual orientation, (dis)ability, and so on, could all be important or relevant to a given study.

The relationship between stance and bias

At a fundamental level, personal stance can affect researcher views about research context and participants, a process that is connected inherently to the notion of bias. Bias is a preconception about a thing, person or group. It means that a researcher holds a preferential perspective at the expense of (possibly equally valid) alternatives. Bias can cloud researchers' judgment and lead them to see what they expect or want to see, which may or may not be what the data suggest. In short, the concept of bias highlights the apparent dangers of the adage: *You ain't gonna learn what you don't want to know* (Adams and Sardiello 2000).

Table 5.1 Comparison of stance and bias

Stance	Bias
A personal stance is a researcher's position towards an issue that is derived from that person's beliefs and views about the world.	Bias is a preconception or preference that limits one's ability to consider alternatives.
Researchers' personal stances reflect their deeply held attitudes, opinions and concerns about what is important, which in turn influences their research decisions, such as what topic they take up, who they include in their studies and how they will collect and analyze data.	In research, ignoring bias could mean failing to recognize one's preconceptions and the influence these have on how researchers unintentionally influence research, such as how they frame questions, interact with participants and view data.

In qualitative research, bias often is considered to be negative and something to be removed, although some researchers believe this to be impossible. Becker argues that research is always conducted from someone's point of view (Becker 1967). Accusations of bias in qualitative research are common, as if bias is something researchers should seek to avoid entirely. For other qualitative researchers, the question of bias is not so clear. Indeed, at times researchers seek to clarify, interrogate and at times embrace, rather than exclude, their biases. Gitlin *et al.* claim that 'the question is not whether the data are biased; the question is whose interests are served by the bias' (Gitlin *et al.* 1989: 245). This implies that research *should* be biased in favour of serving one group rather than another (Hammersley and Gomm 1997). Alternatively, qualitative researchers may seek to develop a better set of biases.

Tips

Researchers should be prepared to engage with biases – the researcher's own biases as well as those of the participants.

Understanding the concept of bias in qualitative research requires researchers to explore their views of reality and knowledge (see Chapter 4). Investigating bias may best be done through an exploration and acknowledgement of world views as well as personal perceptions. As Malterud (2001b: 484) suggests 'Preconceptions are not the same as bias, unless the researcher fails to mention them'.

RESEARCHER POSITIONALITY

Positionality emanates from personal stance. Positionality, however, is more narrowly defined than researcher stance in that it reflects the position the researcher has chosen to adopt *within* a given research study. Making positionality clear can provide the reader with the ability to determine whether preconceptions have unnecessarily influenced the results. Positionality means acknowledging and allowing a researcher to have a place in the work. Thus, to examine researcher positionality it is critical to locate researchers. Locating researchers requires that they continually interrogate their biases, beliefs, stances and perspectives. Doing so can be a challenge, since the process does not involve a formulaic pronouncement of a particular positioned identity, such as one associated with class, gender and race, but rather a close and personal examination and open description of how the researcher influences the research and vice versa. Acknowledging positionality may be accomplished in three primary ways: locating the researcher in relation to the subject, participants, and research context and process.

Locating the researcher in relation to the subject

Locating the researcher in relation to the subject involves directly acknowledging personal positions related to the particular subject or issue that have the potential to influence the research. It requires a transparent process of articulating a personal stance and acknowledging how this stance sets the parameters for the study. A researcher's views, interests and experiences typically set the selection of a topic; this selection privileges what will and will not receive researcher attention. A research question, again driven by researcher interest, further sets the boundaries for the study and identifies what will and will not be given scholarly time and attention. A researcher's selection of databases to identify suitable literature, typically done based upon what is conventional for the discipline, is an example of the way in which the researcher's 'file drawer' further binds the research to their own and/or disciplinary perspectives. In qualitative research, the key is to be aware of and acknowledge the ways in which researcher stance is directly related to what will be researched.

Locating the researcher in relation to the participants

Another issue related to positionality is the way in which researchers locate themselves in relation to the participants. Deciding how to go about this task requires researchers to consider how they view themselves as well as how others view them. Indeed, often individuals may be unaware of how they have constructed and others have constructed their identities, and researchers are no exception. We illustrate this idea from the incident in the USA, where a famous professor and author, who also is an African American, returned home from an overseas trip only to find the front door stuck. He broke into his house, his only means of entry. He was arrested because of this; he accused the police of arresting him because of his race. Ropers-Huilman and Winters described this incident and suggested that it illustrates the issue of bias in societies and the consequences of biases for marginalized groups.

The authors suggest that this example illustrates the notion of the ways in which individuals and groups construct identities:

> This situation demonstrated how identities are constructed both internally (our constructions of ourselves) as well as externally (others' constructions of our identities), and of how those identities and constructions can bring to light larger social systems. 'Who we are' as manifest

RACE AND BIAS

In July 2009 Professor Henry Louis Gates, Jr. of Harvard University was arrested at his home after police were alerted by an emergency telephone call of a possible break-in. While the details of this situation were much debated, the arresting officer Sergeant James Crowley claims that Gates was disorderly, and Gates claims that Crowley profiled him because of his race. United States President Barack Obama initially made his own judgment on the events of that day, and then after public concern about his comments, invited those involved to the White House to discuss the situation over beer and pretzels ... Gates' official statement, released from his legal counsel, states that he was returning from a trip to China, only to find that his front door did not open because it had been damaged. Gates and the taxi driver who had driven him home from the airport successfully forced open the front door. An officer arrived shortly thereafter and asked Gates to step outside. When Gates eventually complied, he was placed under arrest ... The charges were dropped shortly after Gates' arrest but the case continued to draw national and international attention. Notably, after delivering a press conference on healthcare reform, President Obama took questions from the Press. A reporter asked his thoughts on the arrest of Professor Gates and Obama commented that, while he didn't know all the details, he believed that the police force had 'acted stupidly' in the arrest (Obama, 'News conference', 22 July 2009). Obama's comment, and not the content of his policy speech, made the news and late-night satire rounds for a few days. Obama expressed regret over the 'acted stupidly' comment and invited Crowley and Gates to have beer with him and Vice President Joe Biden on one of the White House lawns. This invitation resulted in a gathering of men in suits to discuss racism over beer and pretzels in the backyard of the White House, one of the most culturally recognizable symbols of power.

(Ropers-Huilman and Winters 2011: 43–4)

in relationships with others and with cultural structures and institutions is not necessarily who we think we are, since these external narratives about what constitutes intelligibility affect how we can be known and understood in the world (Loseke 2007). The selves and identities that we might believe to be the most authentic and comfortable to perform are not unitary (Montoya 2003).

(Ropers-Huilman and Winters 2011: 43–4)

Thus, when locating themselves in relation to the participants, researchers should consider how participants' perspectives of themselves and others shape cultural contexts and in turn examine their own positions in a way that is reflexive. Yet doing these things can be exceedingly complicated. In Salmon's helpful example of this point, she examined the idea of her personal stance in relation to those of the participants during a talk she was giving, thereby showing one way in which researchers and participants may explore the co-construction of identity.

Example

LOCATING THE RESEARCHER IN RELATION TO THE PARTICIPANTS

Salmon said:

I asked all the participants to attend to their perception of me, as a particular person standing in front of them. What kind of person, on this preliminary acquaintance, did I seem to be? I invited them to note down, for their eyes only, what kind of person, provisionally, they would define me as being. Then I asked them to think about these perceptions as referring to their own personal stance towards me.

(Salmon 1989: 231)

Locating the researcher in relation to the research context and process

Social science scholars have given attention over time to the influence of the researcher on the research. This attention is warranted, since the researcher is the individual entering the site and interacting with participants as well as the one who will develop a unique interpretation of a data set (Johnson 1999); research necessarily will influence and be influenced by the research context. Locating the researcher's influence in a study requires 'an awareness of the researcher's contribution to the construction of meanings throughout the research process, and an acknowledgment of the impossibility of remaining outside of one's subject matter while conducting research' (Willig 2001: 10). In addition, it urges us 'to explore the ways in which a researcher's involvement with a particular study influences, acts upon and informs such research' (Nightingale and Cromby 1999: 228).

Researchers may consider their influence in various phases of the study and explain that process in the final written product. The process requires consideration of how to choose an area for study, design the study and then collect, analyze and ultimately interpret data (Jensen and Allen 1996; Major and Savin-Baden 2010a and 2010b; Willig 2001). It also requires consideration as to how the research has in turn shaped the researcher. This critical part of the research process allows researchers to reflect on their roles and their responsibilities as subjective and engaged observers, translators and participants.

THE POSITIONALITY STATEMENT

Many researchers seek to convey their positionalities to the reader by way of a positionality statement and, increasingly, researchers are including a positionality statement in their theses, dissertations or articles. Such a statement can help readers to see how researchers have located themselves. When they are well done, they can be useful in communicating the level to which the research was undertaken honestly, plausibly and effectively (see Chapter 30). We offer on page 74 two examples of positionality statements.

In some instances, positionality statements have become almost sterile and, at times, they add little to and may in fact detract from the overall research. In the Tips box on page 75, we articulate how positionality statements can go wrong and provide suggestions for writing a strong positionality statement.

POSITIONALITY STATEMENT

Lana's positionality: As a South African who grew up in the apartheid era, and is now experiencing the transition of our society, I appreciate how the powerful influence of government and political party politics penetrate personal domains, such as religion, relationships and work. It is unnecessary to make a case for the roles of power and privilege as social determinants that shape almost every dimension of people's lives. The issue that should be raised is how seldom such influences are recognized as a pertinent factor in research. Health research in South Africa rarely took into account the political and/or social forces that might have influenced the questions asked and the answers constructed. For example, very little research explores why persons with psychiatric disability have remained on the margins of society and, in fact, the disability movement. Instead, the tendency is to limit the focus of research by excluding issues situated in the macro context. The absence of political power and will, required to bring about change, has been ignored – and was something that I found deeply troublesome.

(van Niekerk and Savin-Baden 2011: 29)

POSITIONALITY STATEMENT

Becca's positionality: Whilst I believed gaining an understanding of the course approval process (the focus of my study) would cohere and be guided through a social constructionist lens, I wanted to ensure that I did not simply provide an account of how a course became approved. Yet I still held questions linked to the dynamics between those involved in approval, in which some groups were 'seemingly' in a privileged position to decide what was to constitute approval or accreditation. As Knafo (2008: 3) observes, it is one thing to say that an institution is socially constructed, but it does not answer the question of 'how' it is being constructed. As I perceived it, each approval event was unique, yet opened multiple interpretations depending on where one stood. I wanted to know why things had come to be this way, and what action or ways of thinking sustain current practice. I realized I sought to do more than describe the realities of participants. Subsequently, I also identified myself with Kincheloe and McLaren's (2005) definition of a critical researcher as someone who was seeking ways to irritate sources of power and provide insights into what is considered as certain ... I was to realize that in following an interest in narrative inquiry there was to be no straight answer. Owing to the nature of the theoretical perspectives guiding the research, I found myself in 'borderland spaces' (Clandinin and Rosiek 2007). I took from the above exploration that it was only through 'standing aside of the map' and being able to reflect on the wider context in which this study and myself are situated that the choices available in designing the research would become more accessible.

(Khanna 2011: 56 and 60)

A weak positionality statement simply states researcher demographic characteristics or potential relationship to participants and the research site, while intimating that the researcher has attended to them with efforts toward ensuring quality (see Chapter 30).

A strong positionality statement typically includes a description of:

■ the researcher's lenses (see Chapter 3)
■ *relevant* researcher beliefs
■ the potential influences that are relevant to the study, such as physical characteristics, position (nationality, education level, etc.) and self-presentation
■ the position a researcher has chosen to take up within a given study, in relation to participants and the research context
■ concerns about the researcher's influence in the research process.

Tips

REFLECTION AND REFLEXIVITY

Two concepts that often are conflated in qualitative research are the notions of reflection and reflexivity. Qualitative researchers not only should engage in reflection but also move beyond reflection to reflexivity.

Reflection

Debates proliferate about what reflection is, how it is used and the ways in which it develops and emerges in different people at different times. At a fundamental and definitional level, reflection is the turning back or illumination of something. When thinking about reflection as a mental process, it involves a process of consideration and meditation, of turning thoughts back upon themselves. For qualitative researchers, reflection involves thought and meditation about processes and products associated with a study. The question of how to reflect is a complicated one, and it involves a consideration of individual capacity for reflection (Boud *et al.* 1985).

Reflection may happen at different times during a research study. Boud *et al.* (1993) have suggested that it is possible to target reflection in three ways, which are informative for qualitative researchers. First, reflecting in advance is *prospective* reflection; it involves deep thinking about design, planning and methods. Second, reflecting immediately is *spective* reflection, involving the capture of thoughts and ideas on the spot, such as during fieldwork through field notes. Third, reflecting on past events is termed *retrospective* reflection and can include a consideration of what could have been different; hindsight is a wonderful thing.

Reflection may also happen at different levels. Mezirow's (1981) account is one of the best and most useful descriptions of the different types of reflection, each representing a deeper level of reflection over the preceding one. His account has endured over time and is an important tool for qualitative researchers. We summarize his classification of types in Table 5.2.

Mezirow (1981) argued that everyone has constructions of reality that are dependent upon reinforcement from various sources in the sociocultural world. Reflection is vital to ensure that researcher perspectives are transformed, and it is part of an emancipatory process of becoming critically aware of how and why social and cultural assumptions have constrained researchers' views of themselves. For qualitative researchers, this process links reflection to philosophical as well as personal stance. Mezirow described such emancipatory learning as that which involves an interest in self-knowledge and in gaining personal insights through critical self-awareness.

Table 5.2 Adaptation of Mezirow's (1981: 12–13) seven types of reflection for qualitative researchers

Mezirow's type	Our example of its application in research practice
1 *Basic reflection* is an awareness of a specific perception, meaning or behaviour	Researchers' consideration of the meaning of finding to the research
2 *Affective reflection* is an awareness of feelings in relation to the specific perception, meaning or behaviour	Researchers' consideration of their feelings about the meaning of the finding
3 *Discriminant reflection* seeks to assess the validity of awareness	Researchers' consideration of whether what they see and feel is accurate
4 *Judgmental reflection* is an awareness of the value judgments being made	Researchers' awareness of the values and biases they bring to the research and how these are influencing their judgments
5 *Conceptual reflection* is an assessment of how adequate the concepts are that are being used to make an accurate judgment	Researchers' consideration of whether, given the weight of the evidence, findings fall into the category of: – substantiated – likely – plausible – possible
6 *Psychic reflection* is reflection on the way judgments are normally made	Researchers' consideration of the processes of arriving at judgments
7 *Theoretical reflection* is an awareness of the strengths and weaknesses of the approach to perceptions	Researchers' consideration of the efficacy of the processes of arriving at judgments

Reflexivity

Reflexivity is a process that helps researchers to consider their position and influence during the study, and it also helps them to know how they have constructed and even sometimes imposed meanings on the research process. Reflexivity is 'self-critical sympathetic introspection and the self-conscious *analytical* scrutiny of the self as researcher. Indeed reflexivity is critical to the conduct of fieldwork; it induces self-discovery' (England 1994: 244). Reflexivity helps the researcher to consider that it is not possible to remain outside the subject or process of the research and look in; rather, the researcher is both integral and integrated into the research.

Liminal

A threshold or a sense of being on a threshold in an in between space

Liminality

A state of being in between two positions, so that there a sense of being a 'transitional being' (Turner 1967) for which confusion and ambiguity becomes the norm

The move from reflection to reflexivity is a subtle one for qualitative researchers. Mezirow (1991) argued that it is at the points at which individual constructions of reality are no longer reinforced by the forces of the sociocultural world that researchers begin to move from a state or position of reflection towards reflexivity. Thus, we suggest that a move from reflection to reflexivity requires a reflective space that has a sense of being betwixt and between about it, a sense of **liminality** that means being in a period of transition, often on the way to a new or different space, since:

The **liminal** qualities of reflective spaces generally seem to emerge at the points where there are moves away from reflection towards reflexivity. This is because reflective spaces are interstitial spaces, spaces at the margins, zones of revelation and movements towards understanding. To be in a position of trans-formational reflective space is reflexive, because it prompts an examination of beliefs, values and identity.

(Savin-Baden 2004: 69)

Many authors have attempted to categorize various types of reflexivity. Willig (2001) suggests that there are two types of reflexivity: personal and epistemological. Finlay (2002) identifies five types: reflexivity as introspection, as intersubjective reflection, as mutual collaboration, as social critique and as discursive deconstruction. May (1998 and 1999) describes two types of reflexivity: endogenous and referential reflexivity. We summarize these types in Table 5.3.

As researchers, it is often easy to concentrate on research methods, ways of doing interviews, types of sampling, forms of validity and sometimes even ways of being reflexive; so that, rather than researcher values becoming explicit, instead they become obscured by a sort of procedural nature that creeps into the research process. We suggest that reflexivity is about working with people and sharing perspectives in the process of doing research.

Table 5.3 Types of reflexivity

Types of reflexivity	Key features
Personal reflexivity Willig (2001)	This is a process where researcher values, experiences and beliefs shape the research. A consideration of how the research has in turn shaped the researcher is critical.
Epistemological reflexivity Willig (2001)	This involves exploring how the researcher's belief system has shaped research design as well as the interpretation of findings.
Reflexivity as introspection Finlay (2002)	Here the researcher uses personal reflection as a form of self-revelation to gain in-depth meanings and insights about the research.
Reflexivity as inter-subjective reflection Finlay (2002)	This form encourages researchers to examine meaning making in and through the research relationship and the ways this is negotiated between researcher and researched.
Reflexivity as mutual collaboration Finlay (2002)	In this type, researchers see participants as co-inquirers and encourage reflexivity in participants, who are part of the research throughout data collection, analysis and interpretation.
Reflexivity as social critique Finlay (2002)	Here, the focus is on managing the power imbalance between the researchers and the participants, whilst also acknowledging the importance of shifting researcher–participant positions.
Reflexivity as discursive deconstruction Finlay (2002)	In this type, the researcher explores ambiguity and the way language is used and how this impacts on presentation. For example, researchers here would explore how they and participants presented themselves and how text was used and not used in particular ways.
Endogenous reflexivity May (1998; 1999)	This type of reflexivity is the way in which particular communities construct their reality; for example, understanding not only who but also how they are viewed by others; therefore, researchers should be aware of how they might be viewed by participants in the research.
Referential reflexivity May (1998; 1999)	This is the exploration of knowledge that is generated as a result of having the routines in social life disrupted by sudden changes in social conditions or everyday routines.

Researcher reflections

Mats Alvesson, Lund University, Stockholm

Reflexive methodology

Reflexivity can be broadly defined to mean an understanding of the knowledge-making enterprise, including a considera-tion of the subjective, institutional, social and political processes whereby research is conducted and knowledge is produced. The researcher is part of the social world that is studied and this calls for exploration and self-examination.

The recent interest in reflexivity has been linked to the influence of post-modernism and post-structuralism, whose insights have drawn attention to the problematic nature of research, the dubious position of the researcher, the crisis of representation, the constructive nature of language, as well as an admission of the fact that there is no 'one best way' of conducting either theoretical or empirical work. Reflexivity is about dealing with a sense of uncertainty and crisis in social research.

There are different uses of reflexivity or reflection which typically draw attention to the complex relationship between processes of knowledge production and the various contexts of such processes as well as the involvement of the knowledge producer. There are reasons to de-emphasize the knowledge producer as an individual and pay more attention to how social forces, like cultural and academically accepted truths and conventions, affect research and at worst lead to our established frameworks and dominating vocabularies defining most of the research results a priori. Briefly, in Alvesson and Sköldberg (2009), reflexive methodology means that serious attention is paid to the way different kinds of linguistic, social, political and theoretical elements are woven together in the process of knowledge development, during which empirical material is constructed, interpreted and written.

Reflective research, as we define it, has two basic characteristics: careful interpretation and reflection. The first implies that all references – trivial and non-trivial – to empirical data are the *results of interpretation*. Thus, the idea that data have an *unequivocal* or unproblematic relationship to anything outside the empirical material is rejected on principle. Interpretation comes to the forefront of the research work. This calls for awareness of the theoretical assumptions, the importance of language and pre-understanding, all of which constitute major determinants of the interpretation. The second element, reflection, turns attention 'inwards' towards the person of the researcher and his/her social belongingness and broader framework, associated with the relevant research community, society as a whole, intellectual and cultural traditions. Systematic reflection on several different levels can endow the interpretation with a quality that makes empirical research of value. Reflection can, in the context of empirical research, be defined as the *interpretation of interpretation* and the launching of critical self-exploration of one's own interpretations of empirical material (including its construction). Reflection can mean that we consistently consider various basic dimensions behind and in the work of interpretation, by means of which this can be qualified. One can ask: how come that we tend to see phenomena in this way? Use this vocabulary? Or even better: What in hell am I doing?

In order to facilitate this, a (loose) structure for reflexive methodology can be used. In Alvesson and Sköldberg (2009) we suggest that researchers work with four levels or four positions and try to compare and confront these. The four levels are:

continued

1. The empirical or data-near level, where one works inductively to treat data by collecting and processing them in a way that aims to mirror the phenomena under study, often based on classifications and sortings. Here, the emphasis is to carefully and in detail, with justice to social reality, diligently work with data in a way that guarantees reliability.

2. The hermeneutic level, where all material is carefully, but also imaginatively scrutinized in order to go beneath and beyond the surface, searching for hidden meanings or aspects that escape a codification and sorting logic. The researcher uses pre-understanding and intuition and does not see data as speaking for themselves, if only properly processed.

3. The critical level, where one tries to take a more sceptical view on both the empirical material and the used classification, categories and interpretations produced and investigate how dominant ideologies, institutions, interests and identities are at work. What may appear to be innocent, neutral and conventional is viewed as potentially being about domination and social arbitrariness and should be challenged rather than reproduced. Dominating research interest and vocabularies are met with suspicion and a partisan view is taken.

4. The level of researcher text authority. The fourth level addresses how the researcher produces research results in textual format that typically claim to offer a credible, coherent, superior and robust delivery and points at how this can be opened up with various conventional modes of persuasion being in operation, accompanied by an awareness of the freezing elements in the text, which thereby encourages alternative interpretations. Also, the critical level, often aspiring to expose domination and effort liberating knowledge results, is questioned for how it produced superior critical insights.

The overall idea is that through considering these four levels or positions of interpretation and playing these out against each other, the research process and results can be more thoughtful, better grounded in terms of careful interpretation and more creative in terms of results. Perspective shifting and confrontation between perspectives/lines of thinking are viewed as key for reflexivity and for more interesting research.

Thus, in reflective empirical research, the centre of gravity is shifted from the handling of empirical material towards, as far as possible, a consideration of the perceptual, cognitive, theoretical, linguistic, (inter)textual, political and cultural circumstances that form the backdrop to – as well as impregnate – the interpretations. These circumstances make the interpretations possible but, to a varying degree, they also mean that research becomes in part a naïve and unconscious undertaking. For example, it is difficult, if not by definition impossible, for the researchers to clarify the taken-for-granted assumptions and blind spots in their own social culture, research community and language.

Empirical material – interpretations referring to 'reality' – remains important, but we must proceed with care and reflection, pondering a good deal more upon what the empirical material means, and why we make just these particular interpretations, before forming any opinions of 'reality' as such. The research process constitutes a (re)construction of the social reality in which researchers both interact with the agents researched and, actively interpreting, continually create images for themselves and for others: images which selectively highlight certain claims as to how conditions and processes – experiences, situations, relations – can be understood, thus suppressing alternative interpretations.

We describe reflexivity further in Chapter 31; however, some strategies for maintaining reflexivity include:

- keeping a field diary
- noting reflections that occur into digital story
- writing biographical accounts of the participants
- drawing data maps
- free writing ideas, biases and feelings of troublesomeness
- using poetry or the art of creative writing to represent researcher biases and stances.

Challenges with reflexivity

Reflexivity has become a common and almost expected practice. Greenbank, for example, argues that:

> Users of both quantitative and qualitative methods all need to recognize the influence of values on the research process. . . . The inclusion of reflexive accounts and the acknowledgement that educational research cannot be value-free should be included in all forms of research . . . researchers who do not include a reflexive account should be criticised.
>
> (Greenbank 2003: 798)

One of the difficulties with the conception of reflexivity is that researchers themselves value it variably. As a concept, reflexivity is deeply embedded in both researcher perceptions of self and of the world, which ultimately are connected to personal stance. Thus, when engaging with reflexivity, there is a sense that qualitative researchers are located in an interrupted world, and where they stand and how they interpret the world constantly changes and moves in and out of focus. This means that reflexivity must be central to all qualitative work.

Reflexivity has critics and has been criticized as part of 'cultural geography's fragmenting, reflexive self-obsession' (Peach 2002: 252). Kobayashi (2003: 347–8) 'struggled' over the 'reflexive turn', concerned that it is 'actually a privileged and self-indulgent focus on the self' that is at odds with philosophies such as feminism and anti-racism. Thus, reflexivity should be connected to a wider purpose or it is of little value to the research (Kobayashi 2003).

RELATIONSHIP BETWEEN STANCE, POSITIONALITY AND REFLEXIVITY

Since the interrelationship between researcher stance, positionality and reflexivity is difficult to separate and articulate, we offer Figure 5.1 to illustrate this interconnectedness.

We provide an example of one person's views and their influence on her work on pages 81–82.

We encourage researchers to articulate their personal stances, positionalities and plans for reflexivity in a given study, in a way that makes sense within the research context.

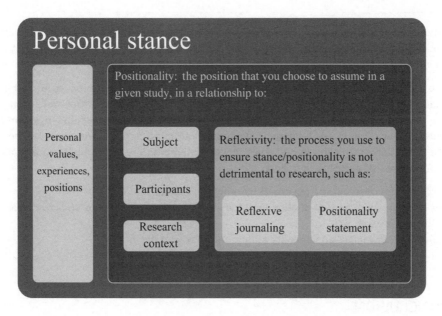

Figure 5.1 Interrelationship between researcher stance, positionality and reflexivity

RELATIONSHIP OF PERSONAL STANCE, POSITIONALITY AND REFLEXIVITY

Julia was brought up in a religious family and attended religious services at least twice weekly throughout her childhood and early adult life. Her moral convictions were largely driven by religious texts and related literature, which also guided her views of right and wrong. As a young college student, she participated in a faith-based organization and, as a part of this group, she spent time volunteering in the community.

As a new graduate student, for her first assignment on a quantitative research course, Julia undertook a study of college students' perceptions of plagiarism. In order to do so, Julia surveyed 100 first-year college students; many of whom admitted on the survey both that they had cheated and (to her surprise) indicated a religious affiliation. Julia found that the data she had collected helped her to understand that many more students than she had imagined were cheating, but the data did not help her understand people's values and experiences better. She wondered how students could reconcile religious beliefs, particularly the importance of always telling the truth, with such flagrant dishonesty.

Later in her academic career, Julia decided to use narrative inquiry to hear people's stories about cheating in college but, despite being a student herself, she found it challenging to accept other students' willingness to plagiarize in order to get better grades. She felt that, despite her best efforts to avoid bias, she was judging them. She wondered if her feelings were evident to the other students and, if so, whether that was influencing their willingness to share their stories with her. She asked them to describe her as a researcher, and they all shared that she seemed friendly and

Example

continued

concerned about the issue; none suggested that they were disinclined to share with her, and their willingness to tell her tales of their cheating led her to believe that if they were inhibited in any way, it was not disruptive to the study.

She worked hard to acknowledge her biases to herself and to try to locate herself in relation to the other students so that, even if she did not accept what they were doing, she did accept them as her peers. She tried to understand how they saw the world and to convey that in her findings. Julia kept a journal of her personal thoughts and she described her biases in her positionality statement. She later published a book about stories of cheating in college life.

Personal stance: ideology governed by religious tenets.
Positionality: an opponent of cheating studying it, a student peer, and an active agent in the research site.
Reflexivity strategies: positionality statement, research diary.

CONCLUSION

Understanding researchers' views and perspectives reflects deep-seated beliefs and values. Researcher beliefs and values affect the way research is designed, planned, undertaken and written up. As a result, it is important for researchers to understand themselves and their stances, so that they come to know the ways in which stances influence the research lens adopted. Qualitative researchers need to understand themselves since this affects the research and its processes – far more than often is realized. Yet the self-reflection needs to be purposeful, otherwise it risks being self-indulgent.

Reflective questions

Concept questions

- How does stance influence a researcher?
- Why is it important to acknowledge stance?
- How may reflexivity enhance a qualitative study?
- How may a researcher balance bias and honesty in research?

Application questions

- How would you describe your core values?
- How do you think your values and individual characteristics could influence your research?

Several resources were key in shaping this chapter, including the following.

Malterud, K. (2001b) Qualitative research: Standards, challenges and guidelines. *The Lancet*, 358, 483–8.

This article covers reflexivity. In particular, pages 483–4 suggest that researcher background and position will affect several key areas, including focus, methods, findings uncovered and the way in which conclusions are communicated; this fits well with our conception of how each choice a researcher makes influences the next.

Lincoln, Y. S. and Guba, E. G. (1985) *Naturalistic inquiry*, Newbury Park, CA: Sage.

Lincoln and Guba both discuss reflexivity and several strategies for ensuring it, which influenced our inclusion of strategies.

Peach, C. (2002) Social geography: New religion and ethnoburbs – contrasts with cultural geography. *Progress in Human Geography*, 26 (2), 252–60.

We found Peach's article to be particularly useful for reminding us that reflexivity for reflexivity's sake is futile; it must be done in order to improve the research or it amounts to something akin to navel gazing.

Key resources

Framing the study

PART THREE

Chapter 6

The 'who' or 'what' of study

INTRODUCTION

Choosing 'who' or 'what' to study is one of the most important decisions that researchers will make, since what they will investigate determines what the **research question** will be, which data will be collected and how analysis will be undertaken. Ultimately then, the selection of 'who' or 'what' to study determines what a researcher will discover. At times, however, it can be challenging for researchers to clarify exactly what they will study, as well as keep to their research plan throughout their research timescale, which can compromise study methods as well as findings. In this chapter, we describe the concept of a phenomenon of study and provide an overview of the various phenomena to which many qualitative researchers have given their attention and thus foregrounded in their work. Throughout the course of the chapter, we provide examples of various phenomena in published studies.

Research question
An interrogative sentence that highlights the phenomenon to be studied and indicates what the researcher wishes to know about it

PHENOMENON OF STUDY

A phenomenon is an appearance or immediate object of awareness in experience. It is a thing as it appears to and is constructed by the mind, as distinguished from a noumenon, or thing-in-itself. The phenomenon of the study is literally what the study is about. Patton states:

> *The key issue in selecting and making decisions about the appropriate [phenomenon] is to decide what it is you want to be able to say something about at the end of the study.* Do you want to have findings about individuals, families, groups, or some other [phenomenon]? (Emphasis in the original)
>
> (Patton 2002: 229)

This statement intimates the importance of selecting an appropriate and intended 'who' or 'what' to guide other decisions throughout the research process, since it will influence data collection as well as analysis.

At times, researchers confuse the phenomenon of the study with other aspects of the study that are related to it. In particular, the phenomenon of study is not the same as the participants, the latter of which is the 'who' or 'what' from which the researcher obtains data (quantitative researchers at times use the term *unit of observation* instead of study participants). We discuss

Tips

The term phenomenon of the study is related to what quantitative researchers refer to as the 'unit of analysis' (Altman and Bland 1997), a term which indicates that the central entity of the study is dependent upon what analysis will be done. For example, if a researcher examines individual performance in a classroom, the individual is the unit of analysis because data from individuals will be analyzed. If several classrooms are examined together, the group/class is the unit of analysis because student data will be analyzed at the aggregate level.

Although some qualitative researchers use the term unit of analysis, more frequently they use the term 'phenomenon of study' to describe the 'who' or 'what' they are studying, arguably because what they are studying is not tied to statistical analysis; because the term is more applicable in a subjectivist approach to research than unit, which means an entity (that is, something that exists or the fact of existence) that is part of a larger whole; and because of a general unwillingness to refer to people (whether individuals or groups) as units.

Moreover, the term unit of analysis has been applied many different ways in qualitative research, which makes its use problematic as its meaning is not always immediately evident. Unit of analysis could mean any of the following:

- The general subject of the study (classroom, programme, organization, person, group, community, state, nation, and so on) (Mertens 1998; Patton 2002).
- The specific or unique 'case' (Yin 2002; Jenner and Titscher 2000) examined.
- The chunk of text, such as interviews, abstracted text, individual words, that will be analyzed (Downe-Wamboldt 1992; Feeley and Gottlieb 1998; Weber 1990); this usage is most frequently associated with discourse and textual/content analysis. Related terms include content or coding unit (Baxter 1991), an idea unit (Kovach 1991) and a textual unit (Krippendorff 1980).

study participants further in Chapter 20. In addition, researchers sometimes confuse the phenomenon with the data they will collect or alternatively with how they will parcel data for analysis. We clarify the differences between these concepts in Figure 6.1.

Researchers should make clear distinctions between: (i) the phenomenon of study, (ii) the people or places from which data will be collected, and (iii) the data that will be collected. While these concepts are closely connected, they are not the same.

PHENOMENA IN QUALITATIVE RESEARCH

Qualitative researchers choose to study a number of different phenomena. Many qualitative researchers, for example, investigate people and cultures, since doing so fits more naturally into their philosophical stances. Some of these researchers choose to study individual perceptions, while others choose to study cultural groups and behaviours of members in natural settings. Various researchers study larger organizations such as universities, businesses and governments, in order to examine organizational structures, while other researchers choose to study the family unit and consider aspects of it such as marriage, divorce or children. Others consider social justice issues and concepts, such as race, class and gender, and how these issues affect opportunities and relationships. A number of researchers consider social movements, such as women's rights or social protests. Researchers might even choose to study an object or artefact,

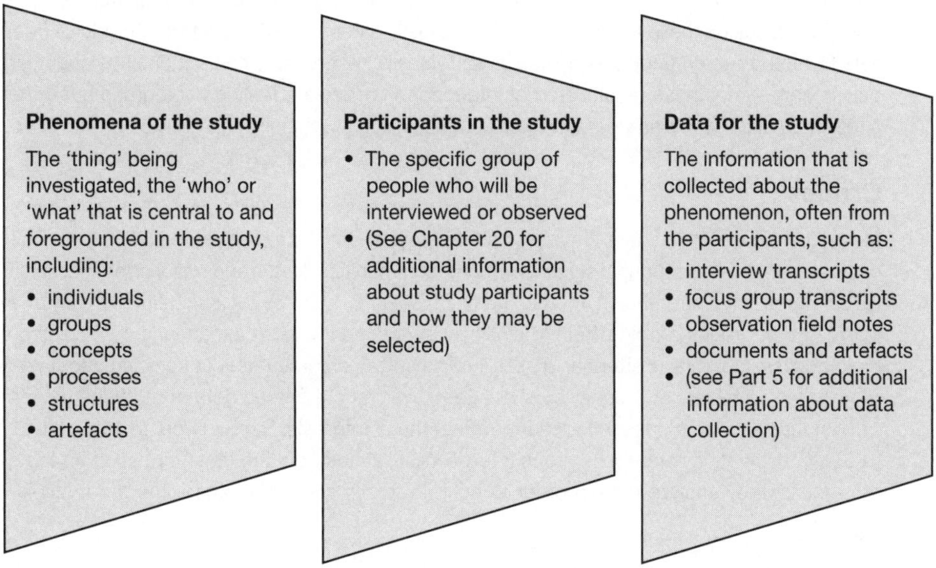

Phenomena of the study

The 'thing' being investigated, the 'who' or 'what' that is central to and foregrounded in the study, including:

- individuals
- groups
- concepts
- processes
- structures
- artefacts

Participants in the study

- The specific group of people who will be interviewed or observed
- (See Chapter 20 for additional information about study participants and how they may be selected)

Data for the study

The information that is collected about the phenomenon, often from the participants, such as:

- interview transcripts
- focus group transcripts
- observation field notes
- documents and artefacts
- (see Part 5 for additional information about data collection)

Figure 6.1 Phenomena of study and related aspects

considering its cultural production and dissemination, such as the production of jeans or their transformation into cultural symbols.

In thinking about the phenomena to which qualitative researchers most often give their attention, we have identified the following broad categories: individuals, groups, structures, concepts, processes and artefacts. Our list is by no means intended to be exhaustive. Rather, it is intended to provide an overview of the kinds of things researchers can and do study, along with a consideration of the implications of choosing one or several of them to study.

Individuals

Individuals are the phenomenon that qualitative researchers most often choose to investigate. Individuals include individual students, lecturers, administrators, managers, programme participants, doctors, nurses, patients, clients, workers, mothers, children, and so forth. Researchers frequently

---

INDIVIDUALS AS PHENOMENON

Burns and Bell (2011) considered the development of individual teachers' professional identity. Their phenomenon was individuals with dyslexia working in tertiary education. The researchers used narrative research to understand professional teacher identities. While the phenomenon was the individual, they reported results in aggregate. In particular, they found that individuals constructed several professional teacher identities that were closely linked to each teacher's perception of their dyslexia. The researchers also found that experience of dyslexia was a positive element in each identity.

Example

are interested in an individual's perspectives, attitudes and experiences, and thus research questions focus on these topics. Researchers usually gather data directly from individuals (Merriam 1998), often through one-to-one interviews. Typically, researchers present findings about individuals in aggregate; these results are not intended to portray the feelings of a group but rather are a reporting of what the individuals have in common, such as what they similarly think, feel or believe.

Groups

Many qualitative researchers choose to study groups. Groups may include cultures, subcultures, cultural groups, ethnic groups, neighbourhoods, communities, states and nations. Indeed, qualitative researchers often are drawn to the study of specific cultures or subcultures. They may be interested in groups ranging from 'a small tribal community in an exotic land or a classroom in middle-class suburbia' (Fetterman 1998: 1). They often are interested in knowing about patterns of knowledge, beliefs and behaviours or alternatively about shared sets of attitudes (D'Andrade 1992); thus, research questions tend to reflect these interests. Researchers tend to collect data through observations and focus group interviews, all aimed at gathering information on the group as a focus; they analyze data in order to be able to say something about the group itself.

Example

GROUP AS PHENOMENON

Swanson (2009) conducted a critical ethnography investigating the emergent, American, upper-middle-class 'soccer mom'. Drawing upon Bourdieu's theories of social class differentiation and class reproduction, Swanson analyzed class-based identity politics in contemporary suburban America. The articles focused on the women, as a group, who are driven by upper-middle-class habitus.

Concepts

A researcher might also choose to study a concept as the phenomenon of interest (Moustakas 1994). Concepts include ideas, notions and theories. Examples of concepts are 'care', 'love', 'hope', or 'success'.

Example

CONCEPT AS PHENOMENON

Elliott and Olver (2009) sought to investigate hope in persons who are terminally ill. As part of a study on end-of-life decision making, the researchers asked cancer patients, believed to be within weeks of their death, to talk about hope. They identified three versions of hope, each of which connected hope and life: identified-hope as essential to, and for, life; hope, life, death and others; and hope/s changing during (or in) life.

A research question is designed to illicit information about the concept, such as what the concept means; what its basic structures, features or elements are. Data often are collected through interviews, to arrive at the meaning that individuals make of the phenomenon. When a concept is the phenomenon of investigation, it means that the researcher is interested in the concept itself, so findings describe the concept. Fisher provides a reflection of her selection of a phenomenon.

Dr Colleen Fisher, University of Western Australia, Australia

I have undertaken research into many facets of domestic violence and have attempted to make a contribution to knowledge in terms of understanding this issue and its impact – on individuals, structures (such as families and communities) and how it is reflected in policy. Identifying the phenomenon of study is vital at the outset of research in such a complex area because any research project could, potentially, identify any of the above. By way of an example, I have recently completed a pragmatic qualitative study examining domestic violence in African refugee background communities post-settlement in Perth, Australia. Data analysis for the study was informed by Crenshaw's 1994 concept of intersectionality. Specifically, in this study I was interested in understanding what participants perceived as constituting domestic violence and its impact at various levels: individuals, families, communities and settlement. Hence, the focus of the study was firmly on the issue and, as such, I identified domestic violence (a concept) as the phenomenon of study. Had my phenomenon of study been for example, individuals, then my focus would be on individuals and how they responded to the violence, rather than its impact on them. My collected data would have included information in much more depth on what they did to mitigate its effects, their support seeking behaviours and attitudes towards its perpetration, rather than a focus on, and foregrounding of, the issue. Hence, the identification of my phenomenon of study as a concept (domestic violence) had implications for the data I collected and that were available for analysis and interpretation.

When I was conceptualizing the study, two words were important in informing my thinking – 'impact' and 'response'. Since I was interested in understanding domestic violence in these communities, its 'impact' forms part of this understanding. This logically foregrounded the issue of domestic violence and facilitated my identification of it as the phenomenon of study. Had I been interested in saying something about individuals, families, communities or settlement, understanding their 'responses to' domestic violence would have foregrounded them and rendered the issue itself secondary. Although this is a nuance rather than a stark difference, its importance cannot be overstated. Had I identified my phenomenon of study as either individuals, families, community or settlement then my research question would be worded in terms of the 'response' of individuals or these structures to the issue rather than its 'impact'. Therefore, identification of the concept – domestic violence – as the phenomenon of study for this study had fundamental implications for the actual research question, as well as data collection, analysis and interpretation.

Identification of the phenomenon of study, however, is not always straightforward. When I'm supervising postgraduate research students I have found that having them verbalize what they actually want to know about makes the identification of the phenomenon of study easier.

Researcher reflections

Socialization

Socialization is a process by which individuals acquire the habits, beliefs and accumulated knowledge of society through education and training for membership in a group or organization

Processes

Qualitative researchers also study processes or actions. Examples of processes or actions are **socialization**, matriculation, childbirth, recovery or the civil rights movement.

Example

PROCESS AS PHENOMENON

Gardner (2010) studied socialization during the doctoral student experience. In particular, she was interested in the issue of attrition in doctoral education, which, she suggests, researchers often attribute to poor or inappropriate socialization. In particular, Gardner considered socialization of doctoral students within specific disciplinary and institutional contexts. She found that the doctoral experience is centralized within the discipline and that the department and institutional context and culture uniquely influence the student experience.

Researcher reflections

Claire Howell Major, Author

I recently served as the chair of Cindy's dissertation committee. Cindy was a great student: hardworking and motivated. We spent what seemed like ages talking about the phenomenon of her study. She wanted to examine internationalization efforts at a given campus. Initially, it seemed as if she wanted to learn about how one campus's internationalization efforts influenced the campus culture and vice versa. During our conversations, however, it became apparent that, while she was interested in campus culture, it was not what she really wanted to know about. What she really wanted to know about was internationalization itself, what it meant at a given campus and how it happened in a day-to-day manner. The difference might seem subtle but it influenced her research questions, her data collection approach and her analytic approach. It was ultimately a very different study than the one she initially thought she would undertake.

As the phenomenon of study, the researcher would strive to understand the process itself. A research question could be how students experience a given process, such as socialization or home schooling. Data could be collected in a variety of ways, depending upon the phenomenon, including interviews, focus groups, observations, documents and artefacts.

Biddix reflects upon the process of identifying a phenomenon, in particular a process.

Structures

Many qualitative researchers have taken a 'structure' as a phenomenon of investigation. Some of these researchers have chosen to study an *organizational structure*. Organizational structures include governments, corporations, social networks, universities, schools, hospitals, programmes and projects. A researcher might ask for example how an organizational structure is related to

Identifying the phenomenon of study, J. Patrick Biddix, The University of Tennessee, USA

Women, technology or something else?

If the research question guides the study, then what guides the research question? The challenge of identifying the central phenomenon can be more complex than researchers, at all levels of experience, think. I like to visualize a research problem as a dartboard. My training has given me darts (strategies of inquiry) and the ability to aim at a target (research problem). However, at times it is difficult to see the bull's eye (phenomenon) and much less to hit it.

Consider an example from a study I completed on women leaders and the use of technology for college activism (Biddix 2010). Previous research and communications theory suggested that women and men approached the use of technology differently as a means of recruiting students to activist involvement. Men tended to see technology use as a tool for reaching the maximum number of students with the hope that some would respond, while women tended to favour the relational aspects of connecting individually with others to foster involvement. So, I had a viable research problem but what was the central phenomenon?

Technology was a candidate, given that ultimately I wanted to know how women used communications to reach others. Women were also a possibility since studying women's practices may lead me to an understanding of how they viewed the leadership activities of recruiting and engaging others. If this had been a quantitative design, I would have my unit of analysis – technology use by women; however, the purpose of this study was to understand women's approaches at getting others involved and keeping them engaged. Activism just happened to be the activity, but it could be any type of involvement. Technology just happened to be a means. I struggled with this for some time before coming to the realization that *the process was the phenomenon*, not the women or the tools they used. Identifying this bull's eye meant I needed to shift my aim to hit it – interviews with questions about technology use and leadership activities would hit the target, but leave the bull's eye unmarked. Realizing that the study was about the process helped me to see that I needed to shift my interview questions and to add document analysis (for example, participant shared emails, discussion board posts, websites and online marketing materials). This gave me the precision I needed to get much closer to the centre of the target.

Identifying the central phenomenon is a critical thinking exercise for me. Since I think best when I have a visual aid, I have found it most helpful to use a large whiteboard to develop my study. This allows me to begin with the problem and visually work toward identifying an assessable and appropriate unit of analysis. This is fundamental work that infuses all aspects of qualitative inquiry and can dramatically shift the previous evidence, theoretical framework and strategies of inquiry that guide, inform and ultimately build toward our understanding of a problem.

prestige. In addition to studying organizational structures, some researchers have chosen to study *social structures*. Such structures include social institutions such as marriage and family. It is the structure itself that is of interest. A research question could focus on family compositions that are different to the traditional nuclear family. In addition to organizational and social structures, a researcher might also choose to examine *discourse structures*. In doing so, a researcher may consider lexical items (the structure of individual words); various structures such as clauses, sentences or paragraphs, or whole discourses. In so doing, the researcher makes distinctions between 'local' and 'global' structures of discourse, with the former the smaller units and the latter the entire discourse. A research question could focus on discourse structures between employers and employees. When a structure is the phenomenon, data are collected in a variety of ways, such as interviews, focus groups, observations and documents and artefacts. The purpose of the analysis, however, is to uncover information about the structure itself.

ORGANIZATIONAL STRUCTURE AS PHENOMENON

Example

Holligan (2011) examined research cultures in university education departments. The purpose of the study was to explore and describe characteristics of research-intensive university education departments in the UK, particularly those attempting to achieve high rankings, with the aim of contributing to knowledge about academic labour. Data were analyzed to consider the structure of the organization, rather than experiences of individuals.

Artefacts

Some researchers choose to study artefacts as the phenomenon of study. Such artefacts might include paintings, films, architecture, apparel, pottery, sculpture, photographs, prints, drawings, tapestry and rugs. Researchers who study artefacts typically are interested in the lifecycle of the object or the use and meaning of the object in its cultural context. A researcher might be interested in the cultural production of a tennis shoe, or ask the following question: how have advertising and celebrities made Nike shoes into cultural icons? A researcher could choose a range of data collection approaches and probably would be drawn to documents or artefacts as data; with the Nike example, data might include advertisements featuring celebrities promoting the products, or even photographs of them wearing the shoes in their lives and professions. The analysis then centres on the artefacts themselves.

ARTEFACT AS PHENOMENON

Example

Whitmore and Laurich (2010) considered the question of what features of the physical environment in video game arcades lead children to become so engaged. They analyzed physical space in video game arcades and participants' positions within them, to explore student-designed learning spaces. Their qualitative analysis of the arcade space revealed three learning principles: clustering and collaborating, inverting traditional structures of power, and reconstituting access and ownership. The authors argued that understanding the physical space in video arcades offers principles of design to advance opportunities for students' and teachers' literacy learning and identity formation.

RESEARCH TRADITIONS AND RESEARCH PHENOMENA

Just as different research paradigms drive the selection of research traditions, so too do research traditions drive the selection of research phenomena, as we described in Chapter 2. This is by necessity, as some phenomena are more natural fits with different traditions than others. Creswell (1998) and Merriam (1998) have offered examples of how different qualitative traditions tend to suit different phenomena. Drawing upon their work, we suggest that the following are the most common pairings of traditions and phenomena, in Table 6.1.

Table 6.1 Common pairings of traditions and phenomena

Approach	Phenomena
Pragmatic	Structures or processes
Grounded theory	Concept or phenomena; group
Case study	Case (individual, group, organization, other)
Phenomenology	Concepts or processes
Ethnography	Groups
Action research	Structures or processes
Narrative	Individuals
Arts based	Artefacts
Collaboration	Structures, processes, groups
Evaluation	Structures or processes

These approaches and phenomena have paired naturally together, as we have demonstrated in some of the examples in this text. The Burns and Bell (2011) study that examined teacher identity drew upon narrative inquiry. The Swanson (2009) study of the soccer moms used an ethnographic approach. Holligan's (2011) research on university structure used a basic approach. We do not intend to suggest that other pairings are not possible; these are simply the ones we have seen most frequently in the literature.

The choice of a phenomenon of the study in turn guides many choices researchers face later. Identifying the phenomenon helps a researcher determine from whom or what data will be collected (see Part 5). Identifying the phenomenon of study also determines much of what will and will not count as relevant information in a study, which helps a researcher during data analysis (see Chapter 28). The phenomenon of the study serves as another level of the lens that the researcher uses to help guide interpretations.

It is imperative to correctly identify the phenomenon of study early in the study's development; early time spent overcoming any significant challenges to correct identification will result in much time being saved later in the study. Failing to identify a clear phenomenon can lead to faulty interpretations that can invalidate the effort altogether. It is critical to be clear on the selection and to have and provide a good rationale for the choice.

CHALLENGES OF IDENTIFYING A PHENOMENON OF STUDY

Choosing a phenomenon to study seems like an easy task but is more complicated than it first appears. At times, it is difficult to tell the difference between the phenomenon under study and the person from whom data will be collected. Qualitative researchers frequently suggest that they will investigate the 'influence' of one thing on another, and it can be difficult to tell at times which is the phenomenon under investigation, the influence or influenced.

While many qualitative researchers say they are investigating the 'influence' or 'impact' of something, this is not entirely accurate in most cases. Many (particularly quantitative) researchers argue that, to truly measure influence or impact, it is necessary to carry out an experimental study, in which participants are randomly selected and assigned to control and treatment groups. Others, such as Yin (1984), suggest that it is possible to conduct explanatory case studies exploring influences of variables upon each other. We believe that what many qualitative researchers attempt to do is to account for people's perspectives on the influence or impact of something in their lives. Even so, qualitative researchers would do well to make a stronger effort to make that distinction clear in writing about their research questions. Someone writing for a journal that publishes quantitative as well as qualitative studies or who has a quantitative researcher on a doctoral committee may simply wish to avoid using the terms 'influence' or 'impact'.

Most often, it is what is being influenced that is of interest. By way of example, Holley and Taylor (2009) undertook a study investigating perspectives of the influence of online degree programmes on undergraduate student socialization. In this case, as it is in most, the phenomenon of study is what is influenced or, in this case, socialization; it is what the researchers are interested in learning and saying something about. Finally, it can be challenging at times to differentiate between the phenomenon of investigation and the data themselves. We illustrate this point in the following study by Banning (2000).

BANNING (2000)

Banning undertook an ethnographic case study to illustrate the use of campus artefacts, in this case 'automobile bumper stickers', to assist in the understanding of campus culture and subcultures. The author categorized bumper stickers by thematic content as well as by campus groups associated with assigned parking lots. Banning was able to make statements both about how cultural values differed between campus groups and concerning apparent conflicts with campus values.

While Banning collected and examined bumper stickers as cultural artefacts, the phenomenon of study was the campus culture. He was not studying an artefact; rather, he was studying a group/culture.

PRACTICAL ADVICE FOR CHOOSING THE PHENOMENON OF STUDY

Researchers should attempt to identify the phenomenon of study early in the research process, as it will influence everything else about the study, particularly what data will be collected and deemed important. For example, a researcher should be clear on the phenomenon of study when collecting data, because it will determine what counts as data and what does not. When analyzing data, the phenomenon will influence what is important and what is not. When writing about the research, the phenomenon will influence what is reported and what is not. Thus it is critical to both find a phenomenon and then maintain focus on it.

A researcher should avoid choosing more than one phenomenon of study if possible, unless there is strong justification for mixing. It may be possible to explain choosing different phenomena from different categories, but doing so would require complex theory, which can be challenging to employ. When studying groups, a researcher should also avoid the 'ecological fallacy', which means assuming that something learned at group level applies to an individual. For example, something that might be true for a group of 'wealthy people' may not be true of a 'wealthy individual'.

CONCLUSION

The phenomena that a qualitative researcher might study are numerous. The key is to home in on the exact phenomenon of study, since doing so drives future decisions and ultimately shapes the researcher's lens and the specific study being undertaken. In this chapter, we have considered several different categories of phenomena and how selecting one of them influences research decisions. We hope that this information will enable qualitative researchers to make good choices about 'who' or 'what' to study. The decision about which phenomenon to study tends to happen concurrently or just prior to the process of setting the research topic and question, which we describe in the next chapter. If the phenomenon is not clear, unfortunately the result is almost certainly bad research.

Concept questions

■ Are there other phenomena of study beyond those described here that are worthy of attention?
■ Which is the most common phenomenon of qualitative research studies? Why is that the case?
■ What is the difference between the phenomenon of the study and participants in the study?

Application questions

■ As a researcher, which phenomenon of study do you find most compelling?
■ How would you justify a selection of this phenomenon? (What is research-worthy about this particular phenomenon)?
■ Which phenomenon would be the most challenging for you to investigate? Why?
■ How would you ensure that the phenomenon you select fits with the research tradition you are planning to adopt?

Reflective questions

Key resources

For some reason, the phenomenon of study is not given as much attention in qualitative texts as it is in quantitative ones. In developing this chapter, we found the following chapters to be particularly informative:

Patton, M. Q. (2002) *Qualitative research and evaluation methods (3rd edn.)*, Thousand Oaks, CA: Sage.
This book contained one of the better descriptions of 'unit of analysis' that we could find in a qualitative text. Although still brief, it provides good information about this concept and its importance to a given study.

Tellis, W. (1997) Introduction to case study. *The Qualitative Report*, 3 (2).
This article had a useful discussion about different units of analysis adopted in case study research; this review informed our selection of main categories of units of analysis.

Graneheim, U. H. and Lundman, B. (2004) Qualitative content analysis in nursing research: Concepts, procedures and measures to achieve trustworthiness. *Nursing Today*, 24, 105–12.
This article indicated several different ways that the term 'unit of analysis' has been used in qualitative research, which led us to our belief that we need to be more careful about this term and distinct in describing what it is we mean; this led us in turn to our selection of the term 'phenomenon of study' to distinguish this concept from the chunk of text that will be considered during analysis.

Creswell, J. W. (1998) *Qualitative inquiry and research design: Choosing among five traditions*, Thousand Oaks, CA: Sage.
This book has a brief section on differentiating the traditions by phenomena. This provides useful information about some of the traditions and their attending phenomena.

Chapter 7

Research questions

INTRODUCTION

Social science researchers come from a variety of **subject** areas to investigate an array of research topics and do so for differing reasons, which range from describing the human experiences of a phenomenon to generating theory. Being able to articulate an investigable question that captures the **topic** and the **purpose** of the research is critical to the research endeavour. Good research questions, however, do not magically appear; researchers must carefully formulate them in order to accomplish their purposes. Few scholarly sources provide guidelines for framing research questions. In this chapter, we discuss the reasons why research questions are important, indicate traditional ways for formatting questions and articulate some of factors that guide the development of research questions. We also describe new ideas about methodologically sound ways to develop questions. Throughout the chapter, we attempt to provide specific guidance about and concrete examples for developing strong research questions.

Subject
The general field or area

Topic
The specific matter of interest

Purpose
What the research will accomplish, what its intent is

DESCRIPTION OF RESEARCH QUESTIONS

Research questions are interrogative sentences that highlight the phenomenon to be studied and indicate what the researcher wishes to know about it. They make a formal statement about the goal of the study, identifying clearly what the researcher intends to learn. Research questions summarize what is unknown that requires further exploration. They require a clear, focused and concise question that forms the centre of the research. Research questions also require framing through the philosophical and personal lenses of the researcher (see Chapters 4 and 5). Moreover, research questions require framing aimed at developing an understanding of the central phenomenon under investigation (see Chapter 6).

THE NEED FOR GOOD RESEARCH QUESTIONS

Researchers undertake studies for a variety of reasons. One common factor that unites qualitative researchers is that they all hope to develop interesting studies that lead to vital findings. Strong research questions can highlight important research problems, resolve controversies and perhaps challenge conventional assumptions that can make studies interesting (Alvesson and Sandberg 2011; Abbott 2004; Bruner 1996; Davis 1986). As Sandberg and Alvesson (2011: 24), whose work is featured in our 'researcher reflections' in this chapter, suggest: 'if we do not pose innovative research questions, it is less likely that our research efforts will generate interesting and significant theories'. Researchers also hope to develop influential studies. There are many factors that contribute to how interesting and influential written reports are perceived to be, including how timely the topic and how well-read the publication. Beyond those factors, however, is the fact that studies are considered interesting and influential if they challenge current assumptions (Black 2000; Hargens 2000; Sandberg and Alvesson 2011).

Another uniting factor is that qualitative researchers expect to produce studies of quality that are both rigorous and plausible. At a fundamental level, the choice of research question is crucial to the rest of the research, since the pursuit of knowledge through a qualitative study ultimately begins with the framing of a research question, a process that has been given some attention in qualitative research texts (see Creswell 1998). A research study is only as good as the research questions posed, with Flick (2006) suggesting that the research question is what drives the research. Silverman (2001: 77) suggests that research questions organize the product and give it direction, delimit or bound the problem, keep the researcher focused, point to methods required and provide a framework for writing the research manuscript. For these reasons, it is critical for researchers to work diligently to develop strong questions and scholars tend to agree that qualitative studies should seek to answer clearly stated and important research questions (Frankel and Devers 2000).

STEPS IN THE PROCESS OF DEVELOPING RESEARCH QUESTIONS

Most research methods texts suggest that researchers should follow a specific process when developing research questions (see Merriam 1998; Creswell 1994; 1998). It is, in our view, an incomplete perspective on how researchers actually develop research questions, but the process is indeed useful in helping to explain how different concepts work together, many of which researchers seek to describe in introductions to their studies. The basic idea is that researchers choose a subject area, a topic, a problem and a purpose; after these four selections they will then be ready to formulate the research question.

Choose the subject

The common view is that a researcher's field naturally sets the boundaries for the knowledge area, and most researchers work within a particular knowledge area throughout their careers. The subject area of the chosen research is where the researcher will spend their time.

Identify the topic

The research topic is a specific category or unit of the subject. One key to identifying a good topic is ensuring that it can hold a researcher's interest as well as the interest of the intended audience. Defining the topic too broadly may mean that it is too unwieldy to be useful or meaningful. On the other hand, defining the topic too narrowly may mean that it is impossible to generate anything interesting or meaningful. The following example indicates the difficulties of finding a good balance.

DEFINING THE TOPIC

It might be tempting to identify a topic that is all encompassing, such as 'student experiences of learning'. Defining the topic this way provides a range of opportunities and potential directions in which to go; however, while this might make a good subject area, as a topic it will not be manageable. While 'student experiences of learning' might be too broad a topic to manage, something like 'mature students learning in evening classes in Birmingham' might be too narrow to generate sufficient data.

Identify a research problem

Upon identification of a specific research topic, the next step is to identify a research problem, which is intended to further solidify the direction of the study. The research problem should stress the rationale for studying the topic, making clear why it is worthy of investigation. Research problems may come from a range of sources, including life experiences, previous research, theory and practical issues in the field. The problem could be a problem of practice or of research. It could be set up as an extension of what other researchers have found or as filling a gap or eliminating a deficiency in existing literature. Dissertations, theses and published studies often contain a formal 'statement of the problem' and the problem explicitly indicates a dearth of research in a particular area or a gap in the knowledge base that needs to be filled.

Define the research purpose

The term 'research purpose' is a bit murky in social science literature, with definitions of the research purpose at times actually using the term 'purpose' in the definition, as evident in the following definition for example: 'The purpose statement should provide a specific and accurate synopsis of the overall purpose of the study' (Locke *et al.* 1987: 5). There are several key goals or purposes often found in qualitative research studies, as noted by Ritchie and Lewis (2003):

- contextual: describes the form or nature of what exists
- explanatory: examines the reasons for, or associations between, what exists
- generative: aids the development of theories, strategies or actions
- evaluative: is done for the purpose of assessment, measurement, or evaluation
- ideological: is done for the purpose of advancing an ideological position.

What the 'purpose of the study' has generally come to mean within social science research contexts, however, is a basic synopsis of the study, outlining one of the above key goals.

Sometimes researchers conflate purpose and rationale in social science research, but at other times they make a clear distinction between the purpose (synopsis) and rationale (the reason for doing the study). What is important is for a researcher to give both aspects consideration, whether reporting them separately or together.

Creswell (1998) provides a template for a purpose statement that a researcher may adapt:

Example

A TEMPLATE FOR A PURPOSE STATEMENT

(Adapted from Creswell 1998: 96)

The purpose of this _____ (biographical, phenomenological, grounded theory, ethnographic, case) study is (was? will be?) to _____ (contextualize? explain? develop? evaluate?) the _____ (topic of the study) for _____ (phenomenon of the study: a person? processes? groups?). At this stage in the research, the _____ (central concept being studied) will be generally defined as _____ (provide a general definition of the central concept).

Craft different levels of questions

In qualitative research, there tends to be an overarching or *primary question*, or at most two, and there may also be *sub-questions* associated with the primary questions. Creswell recommends starting with one overarching question and having no more than seven total questions. We believe that having too many sub-questions is a distraction. It is often better to have one or two clear questions that are easy to explain to someone, and we would recommend only having as many as four in special circumstances. In qualitative research, the research question requires reliance on inductive logic; it is not stated as the research hypothesis. Research questions are designed from inference and observation, and tend to start with 'what' or 'how'. A good qualitative research question should be open rather than closed, exploratory rather than explanatory, focused on meaning, and a single phenomenon or concept, related to a specific research tradition, answerable, and worth answering (Creswell 1998).

Tips

Writing qualitative research questions (Creswell 1998):

■ Begin with words such as 'how' or 'what'.

■ Tailor the wording to the purpose:
  − use 'what happened?' for description
  − ask 'what was the meaning to people of what happened?' or 'how did participants experience it?' for understanding
  − ask 'what happened over time?' to explore the process over time.

■ Explain what you are attempting to 'discover', 'explore', 'identify' or 'describe'.

■ Avoid words such as relate, influence, impact, cause and effect.

Components in the process of identifying research questions

The different components of the tasks involved in determining the focus of the study are related, and move from general to specific. We offer examples of a research subject, topic, problem, purpose and question in Table 7.1.

Table 7.1 Examples of a research subject, topic, problem, purpose and question

Subject	Teaching in higher education
Topic	Online learning
Problem	Lack of lecturer acceptance of online courses
Purpose	To explore lecturer perceptions of the quality of online learning
Question	How do lecturers describe the quality of their online courses?

SOURCES OF RESEARCH QUESTIONS

While it is comforting to consider it possible to follow a formulaic process to develop a research question, the process does not explain the source of research questions. Researchers come to research questions on their own terms and through a variety of different avenues. We argue that researchers should be reflective about the sources of their research questions and take as much ownership as possible in developing them. We provide Figure 7.1 to show possible sources of research questions.

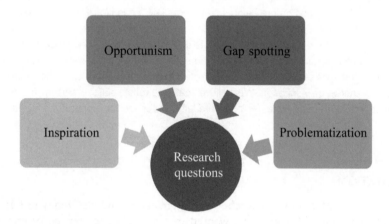

Figure 7.1 Sources of research questions

Inspiration

Many researchers develop a research question based upon their intrinsic interests. Willis and Smith (2000: 6), for example, suggest that researchers 'make sure they are asking questions which they find "natural" and are about something they find important and interesting. They need to have … a "feel" for the kind of inquiry they will need to pursue'. It is typical for a researcher's intrinsic interests and biases to drive this decision. Inspiration can lead researchers to 'aha' moments that provide ideas about the kinds of questions that they might be interested in investigating, but 'inspiration' is a 'fuzzy' word that has an unclear definition and an even more unclear operation. American inventor Thomas Edison is credited with the saying 'success is 10%

inspiration and 90% perspiration'. We think this general idea largely holds true for developing good research questions; while inspiration is important, it cannot occur without hard work accompanying it.

By way of example, Meyer and Land (2006) provide insight into how an 'aha' moment can happen, or at least the preconditions that are necessary for it to occur. While working with a team of researchers investigating student learning, they began to realize that they had discovered a new way of understanding how and why students became stuck in learning. They found that there were particular concepts (they called these threshold concepts) that students often do not grasp; these are concepts in a subject that are conceptually difficult. Understanding these concepts, however, is a necessary condition for further learning to occur. They offer the example of a cook who comes to realize that understanding the concept in physics of heat transfer as a function of temperature gradient is key to the chef's art. 'Imagine', they write 'that you have just poured two identical cups of tea; you want to cool down one as quickly as possible, you add milk to the first cup immediately, wait a few minutes and then add milk to the second'. It is easy to believe that the first cup will be the cooler, but it is the second because 'in the initial stages of cooling it is hotter than the first cup with the milk in it and it therefore loses more heat because of the steeper temperature gradient' (Meyer and Land 2006: 3). Such a shift in understanding, they argue, is going over the threshold into new forms of understanding; it is irreversible and necessary – it is an 'aha' moment.

For researchers, the subject of investigation has many threshold concepts that are necessary for the researcher to grasp before being able to formulate a question. Researchers must consider the subject from several angles, and read both related theory and other research studies to fully engage and understand the subject's concepts at a threshold level. The process of moving over the threshold of basic understanding within the subject of investigation then leads to being able to formulate the research question. The push across the threshold can often come from an unexpected source of inspiration. We believe that inspiration plays a part in the development of all research questions, whether they are also influenced by opportunism, gap spotting, problematization or other factors.

Example

INSPIRATION

George had completed his comprehensive examination and was ready to begin his dissertation research. He knew he wanted to study the experiences of immigrant women working in residence in domestic jobs for wealthy native born citizens, but did not know what his research questions should be. For months George struggled, worrying he would never start, never mind complete, the dissertation. Despite reading everything he could about immigrant employees, watching documentaries and talking the possibilities through with his research supervisor, nothing seemed to help. One day in a pub with his friends, his 'aha' moment came as he watched the interaction between two people working behind the bar, a white immigrant from Poland and a black American. It was then that he knew that he was most interested in the interrelationships that developed between the employee and employer and framed his question around that aspect:

How do immigrant workers and employees negotiate the balance of professional and personal relationships?

Opportunism

While many scholars see opportunistic research negatively, the cold hard truth is that there are a number of opportunistic avenues that provide scholars with sources of inspiration, support and potential dissemination outlets for their work. Trede and Higgs (2009), for example, note that interests may be driven extrinsically; for instance, with an eye toward publication or obtaining funding. Grant funding agencies, whether they be governmental, charitable or foundational, may choose to support research in a given area. If researchers choose to pursue these funding opportunities, they must be sure that the funder's values are compatible with their own personal stances (see Chapter 5) and that they will not be compromising the integrity of their work. Often, however, such funding sources provide both inspiration for research questions through their requests for proposals and financial support to allow scholars to pursue research that otherwise might be unattainable. Similarly, journal calls for submissions to regular or special issues can provide ideas about questions that might be worthy of investigation. We do not recommend that opportunism be the only factor influencing development of research questions, but we acknowledge the reality that it has the possibility of sparking research ideas and directions.

OPPORTUNISM

Wanda focused primarily on rural community colleges as her research setting. When a private foundation announced a new research programme that funded studies seeking to examine factors of student retention in rural community colleges, the call was a strong match for her research interests. Indeed, the foundation's focus on online education spurred her to consider the relationship between the digital divide (poor rural families that did not have access to technology) and retention. She thus framed her research question as follows:

- **How do rural community college students experience online courses?**
- **What factors of online learning do students perceive as barriers or opportunities for their learning?**

Example

Gap spotting

One way that some researchers go about developing research questions is what Alvesson and Sandberg (2011) and Sandberg and Alvesson (2011) call gap spotting. These researchers carry out a review of the literature in their identified purpose/problem area, identify the gaps in the literature and then set about developing research questions. Barrett and Walsham (2004) carried out an investigation of a three-year period of journal articles (52 articles) in that they identified the most common ways researchers identify research questions, which they frame around the concept of gap spotting, or seeing an opportunity during a review of existing literature (see Chapter 8). They indicate three key ways of gap spotting: confusion spotting, neglect spotting and application spotting.

Confusion spotting

This form of gap spotting means seeing competing explanations in the literature and crafting a question that can address the contradictions. We believe that many confusion spotting opportunities present themselves in quantitative literature, in which competing findings are not uncommon (for example, one researcher finds significant differences whereas another finds no significant differences). These may be opportunities for qualitative researchers to further probe why these differences might exist.

Neglect spotting

This form of gap spotting involves finding an overlooked or under-researched (lacking empirical support) area. Since qualitative research is a relatively new field and human social problems seem boundless, there are many opportunities available for developing questions in non- or under-researched areas.

Application spotting

This form of gap spotting involves finding a way to extend and complement existing literature. Often, syntheses of literature, such as meta-analysis, systematic reviews and qualitative synthesis, involve integration of information that can provide new ways forward. Typically, published studies suggest ways forward in their suggestions for future research.

Example

GAP SPOTTING

Dana was having a difficult time developing a research question on the subject of funding for non-profit organizations. She conducted a thorough review of the literature and carefully examined the 'suggestions for future research' sections in current publications and dissertations, in order to find ways to extend the literature. She stumbled upon several quantitative studies, which suggested that future research should explore public perceptions of different funding opportunities for non-profit organizations. She framed her research questions around these suggestions:

■ **What are public perceptions of how non-profit organizations should be funded and how are such perceptions perceived by the organizations themselves?**

However, Alvesson and Sandberg (2011) and Sandberg and Alvesson (2011) suggest that researchers should move beyond gap spotting toward a methodology of problematizing the research questions.

Problematization

Alvesson and Sandberg (2011) describe their views of development of good research questions in Table 7.2.

Researchers use a range of techniques for identifying research questions that range in levels of intentionality on their part from less intentional waiting for inspiration or seeking out

Table 7.2 The development of good research questions with high problemization

Aim of the problematization methodology

Generating novel research questions through a dialectical interrogation of one's own familiar position, other stances and the literature area targeted for challenging

A typology of assumptions open for problematization

In house:	*Root metaphor:*	*Paradigm:*	*Ideology:*	*Field:*
Assumptions that exist within a specific school of thought	Broader images of a particular subject matter underlying existing literature	Ontological, epistemological, and methodological assumptions underlying existing literature	Political-, moral- and gender-related assumptions underlying existing literature	Assumptions about a specific subject matter that are shared across different theoretical schools

Principles for identifying and challenging assumptions

Identify a domain of literature:	*Identify and articulate assumptions:*	*Evaluate articulated assumptions:*	*Develop alternative assumptions:*	*Relate assumptions to audience:*	*Evaluate alternative assumptions:*
What main bodies of literature and key text make up the domain?	What major assumptions underlie the literature within the identified domain?	Are the identified assumptions worthy to be challenged?	What alternative assumptions can be developed?	What major audiences hold the challenged assumptions?	Are alternative assumptions likely to generate a theory that will be regarded as interesting by the audiences targeted?

existing opportunities to the more intentional efforts to identify gaps or confusion in the literature. Some researchers are able to move to a different level of intentionality when crafting questions that is beyond gap spotting. They are able to look at existing studies and rather than seeking gaps instead problematize it. In short, they seek to challenge conventional wisdom and common assumptions, not only through argument but by crafting questions that can provide answers as to whether their challenges are correct. Alvesson and Sandberg (2011) call this approach problematization of research questions, which they describe in the following researcher reflection.

WHEN TO DEVELOP RESEARCH QUESTIONS

Some researchers develop their research questions first, prior to selecting a research tradition to work within. Other researchers choose to begin research prior to developing specific questions and instead identify them later in the process. Still other researchers choose a research approach (see Chapters 10–19) first and then frame research questions that work within it appropriately. Whichever path is taken, researchers sometimes find themselves writing, rewriting, reframing and reformulating their research questions during a study. If one does so, it will probably be necessary to work with the ethics review board (see Chapter 21) to ensure that the reformulated questions are within the ethical guidelines of the original study.

Mats Alvesson and Jörgen Sandberg,
University of Queensland, Australia

*Constructing research questions: doing
interesting research*

A fundamental step in all theory development is the formulation of carefully grounded research questions. One could
even say that good questions might be as valuable and
sometimes even more valuable than answers. Questions
may open up, encourage reflection and trigger intellectual
activity. Answers may lead to the opposite: to rest and
closure. Good research questions, however, are just not out
there but need to be created and formulated.

While several factors influence the development of
research questions (such as researcher's curiosity, research
funding, publication opportunities, interests from practitioners, fashion and fieldwork experience), in this text we
concentrate on one core aspect, namely, how researchers
can construct research questions from *existing literature*
that will lead to the development of interesting and influential theories.

One established way of constructing research questions from existing literature
within social science appears to be *gap spotting*. It is by identifying or constructing
gaps in existing literature that need to be filled that most social scientist researchers
formulate their research questions and develop their theories. However, a core
characteristic of interesting and influential research is not gap filling for its own sake
but challenging assumptions underlying existing theories in a field in some significant
new way(s).

Generating research questions through *problematization*, in the sense of identifying
and challenging the assumptions underlying existing theories, therefore appears to be
a central ingredient in the development of more interesting and influential theories.
Problematization means taking something that is commonly seen as good or natural
and turning it into something problematic. For example, rather than seeing leadership
as leaders leading followers, one may ask who, if anyone, is leading who, in a
manager–subordinate relationship? Similarly, rather than asking what students learn,
one could ask why do they learn so little?

Problematizing the assumptions underlying existing literature enables you to open
up and reframe them in other ways and then point at something calling for a new
understanding. Against a dominant assumption one can, if lucky, come up with a good
counter-assumption, offering a starting point for an innovative research project. Rather
than follow the implications of existing studies, one goes, in some respects, against
them. We see the research question quite broadly. It is not only the stated objective,
indicating the specific intended delivery of results, but includes the broader framing of
the study; that is, its overall direction, its line of reasoning, based on a set of assumptions
and 'truths' already inscribed into the discourse guiding the inquiry. The research
question and the way it is addressed need to incorporate reflexivity and articulation
and explicit questioning of where the chosen research approach comes from, where
it is heading and what may be problematic about it. All this should lead to something
challenging and innovative, in relationship to what is already known – and in particular
assumed. The research question then gives the major input, frames the research and
provides direction setting and is, thus, a key element of the research process.

PROBLEMATIZATION

Stephen knew the literature on tutor experiences of problem-based learning inside and out. Most of it focused on the locus of tutor control and how comfortable tutors were with sharing or relinquishing control. George had even read a qualitative research synthesis on the topic (Major and Savin-Baden 2010b; Savin-Baden and Major 2007). Stephen, however, thought that while the issue of control was important, it was potentially overlooking some broader issues of how tutors experience teaching with problem-based learning. In particular, he thought the issue of control ultimately was bound up in teacher identity and, thus, he constructed the following research question:

■ How do tutors teaching using problem-based learning construct their identities as teachers?

Example

RESEARCH QUESTIONS IN DIFFERENT RESEARCH APPROACHES

Researchers working in the different research traditions tend to frame questions in different ways. In Table 7.3, we provide sample research questions related to the topic of online learning as they could look across different research approaches (that we describe in Part 4 of this book).

Table 7.3 Sample research questions from different research approaches

Approach	Sample question
Pragmatic qualitative research	What do online teachers see as the incentives and barriers of teaching online?
Grounded theory	What explains (how can we theorize) instructor online teaching behaviour?
Phenomenology	What is the essence of online teaching?
Ethnography	How might distance learning teachers' online personas be described and understood?
Narrative inquiry	How would an individual teaching online convey his or her online life story?
Action research	How can the interests and needs of distance learning teachers inform and change teaching practice?
Collaborative inquiry	How do teachers learn with and through others in distance learning programmes?
Evaluative inquiry	How effective is the online programme at helping students develop content knowledge?
Arts-based inquiry	How do instructors use student developed graphic art as an evaluation method?

Tips

Researchers have different opinions about how many times and where research questions appear in a paper or dissertation. Often, they appear both at the end of the introduction and again in the approaches or method section of a research report; at other times they appear only once, in the methods section of the paper. If they appear in more than one place, the researcher should take care that the questions are exactly the same in both places to avoid potential confusion.

Tips

Considering the research questions

Researchers may consider not only whether they *can* answer the research question but also whether they *should*. We offer further thoughts on several critical issues in the following paragraphs.

Is the research important?

There are several issues related to the significance of the question: why the issue is important, why the reader should care, and what a solution to the problem will achieve, such as filling a gap in the literature or informing policy and practice. The question should either matter to the intended or to the people who matter to them. A researcher should clearly spell out who will benefit from the results of the research, and beneficiaries may include the intended audience, practitioners, researchers, policy makers, or other stakeholders (such as parents, patients . . .).

Does it advance knowledge?

A qualitative research study should advance knowledge in a given field or across multiple fields. It may advance knowledge for knowledge's sake, extend a prior line or web of knowledge, or advance a field's theory. A researcher undertaking a qualitative study should consider the ways in which the project contributes to the field. As we note in Chapter 21, some scholars also consider this issue to be an ethical one.

Does it contribute to practice?

While some qualitative researchers undertake studies simply for the purpose of advancing knowledge, a growing number of researchers are beginning to consider the question of how research might contribute to improved practices. In particular, the evidence-based policy and practice movement that is now well established in health professions, education and other fields, has led to an interest in using qualitative research in addition to quantitative research, in order to improve policy and practice. Researchers should consider the question of whether they wish to accomplish this goal or not. If so, then this goal becomes an essential part of the planning project.

CONCLUSION

In this chapter, we have highlighted the importance of developing good and interesting research questions, suggesting that research will only be as good as the question that drives it. We have suggested that there are multiple ways in which researchers can develop questions, from waiting for inspiration to taking action by problematizing existing literature. We acknowledge that writing research questions is not easy, but we suggest that it is an activity that deserves careful and considered attention.

Concept questions

- What are the most common sources of research questions?
- What is the process for developing a research question?

Application questions

- What will be the source(s) of your research questions?
- How will you convey to a reader the way in which you developed your research question?

Reflective questions

Alvesson, M. and Sandberg, J. (2013) *Constructing research questions*, London: Sage.

Alvesson, M. and Sandberg, J. (2011) Generating research questions through problematization. *Academy of Management Review*, 36 (2), 247–71.

Sandberg, J. and Alvesson, M. (2011) Ways of constructing research questions: Gap-spotting or problematization? *Organization*, 18 (1), 23–44.
Alvesson and Sandberg's articles helped us to consider that the typically outlined process of developing a research question does not explain how to source it; their works also helped us to see the importance of moving beyond gap spotting to being more intentional in the development of research questions.

Creswell, J. W. (1998/2007) *Qualitative inquiry and research design: Choosing among five traditions*, Thousand Oaks, CA: Sage.
This text provided good information about the process of developing a research question. Creswell's text includes useful information about the relationship between topic, problem and research question. Both the template for purpose statement and our Table 7.1 are based upon his text.

Key resources

Chapter 8

Literature review

INTRODUCTION

The literature review is a part of the research process that has challenged many scholars over time. Scholars face choices about whether, how and when to do a literature review. In this chapter, we consider the literature review in the context of a qualitative research study. We begin by defining what we mean by a literature review and by describing why we believe that producing one of good quality is important. We provide advice about how to develop a literature review that is broad, deep and critical. Finally, we describe processes for searching for as well as managing and organizing literature.

THE PURPOSE OF A LITERATURE REVIEW

While the term 'literature review' has held varied meanings in different contexts over time, in this chapter we generally describe the kind of literature review that is intended to establish context for a qualitative research study. This type of literature review should contain critical analysis of previous research studies, and sometimes non-research-based literature, on the topic of investigation (Hart 1998). The research literature review is something more than a descriptive cataloguing of findings and evidence, since a researcher also needs to provide an analytical argument and draw conclusions. Rather than being an exhaustive and unstructured summary, it enables researchers to focus on and use the literature in the field. It engages with theories and establishes them in relation to the current work. Some view the literature review as a 'synthesis' of the literature on a topic (Pan 2009: 1). The process of carrying out a literature review can help a researcher to develop research questions, as we described in Chapter 7, and it may provide context and foundations for the later findings produced by the study. It will be important to highlight any context and foundations when writing up the literature review.

CHARACTERISTICS OF A GOOD LITERATURE REVIEW

Over time, many researchers have become discontent with a traditional literature review, which has led to scholarly consideration of what constitutes an effective review. We believe there are several characteristics that are hallmarks of a good literature review in qualitative research, which also are beginning to appear in a body of work aimed at describing the synthesis of previously

In order to accomplish these goals, a researcher should seek to answer the following questions when conducting a literature review:

■ What do we already know about the proposed topic?
■ Has anyone else ever conducted the same study?
■ Has anyone else even conducted a similar study?
■ How is the work situated when compared with completed works?
■ What do we still need to know about the proposed topic?
■ Why is this research worth doing in the light of other research already completed?
■ What assumptions about the topic are apparent in the literature?

Tips

published qualitative studies (see Major and Savin-Baden 2010; Dixon-Woods *et al.* 2006; Sandelowski and Barroso 2007; Thorne *et al.* 2004b; Gough and Elbourne 2002; Doyle 2003).

A good literature review is one which is conducted in an organized manner. It makes the processes undertaken for search and selection of studies clear to the reader. It relies upon sound, documented evidence from high-quality sources. It indicates how sources were selected as well as how they were excluded. A good literature review goes beyond summary to both criticality and drawing connections and conclusions. Such a review makes clear the connection between the proposed study and research already completed. A good literature review is structured logically and provides accurate references.

Taking a critical stance towards the literature also is an important component of the review, because it not only sets the context of the piece of research being undertaken, but also locates the work in a critical way. A researcher should move away from just describing and documenting the available literature and instead offer a critique of what has been undertaken already. Doing so means engaging with the literature that demonstrates the researcher has:

1. [Demonstrated] a comprehensive coverage of the field being studied and has a secure command of that literature;
2. Shown breadth of contextual understanding of the disciplines(s) that are appropriate to your study;
3. Successfully critiqued the various established positions and traditions in those disciplines;
4. Engaged critically with other significant work in your field;
5. Drawn on literature with a focus that is different from the main viewpoints(s) in your research and explained the relevance of that literature;
6. [Found] a balance between delineating an area of debate and advocating a particular approach.

(Trafford and Leshem 2008: 73)

Thus, a critical stance towards the literature requires that a researcher examines whether the available literature has ingrained ideas that have gone unchallenged, faults in his or her arguments, contradictory positions, poor data sets, inadequate analysis or flawed conclusions. Trafford explains this idea in the following researcher reflection.

Vernon Trafford, Professor Emeritus, Anglia Ruskin University, UK

Reviewing the literature or developing theoretical perspectives?

Many dissertations and doctoral theses have a chapter called 'literature review'. But reading such chapters is often disappointing or even confusing. If the chapter title contains '*search*' instead of '*review*' then what authors were searching for or found is seldom apparent (Trafford and Leshem 2008: 87).

Such problems originate from two oversights. First, the criteria that guided the review/search are inadequately explained. Second, the conclusions from the review/search are often not explicit. These oversights are apparent in other forms of academic writing which Hart (1998: 1) describes as being '. . . thinly disguised annotated bibliographies'.

So, why is reviewing/searching the literature handled in this way? Perhaps authors have not appreciated its centrality to the research process. If so, then neither has the role of literature been recognized as an ever-growing accessible body of knowledge that is a foundation for understanding past research. As Wheeler (2005: 95) neatly observes, 'Reviewing the literature provides the researcher with information about what others have learned about the topic and places it in the context of what others in the field are thinking and doing'. Reviews therefore link previous and current thinking into an explainable perspective.

Researchers use theoretical perspectives on a topic to inform/guide/shape the development of conceptual framework(s) and their research design. Clearly, connections between these components depend on the type of research design that is adopted, and readers expect authors to explain the connection in a sentence, paragraph or chapter. Readers will then recognize that authors understand the connection between the corpus of their topic and the research process itself. In this way, authors demonstrate episteme and are thinking like researchers (Perkins 2006: 43). Thus, undertaking a literature review is a scholarly quest to arrive at theoretical perspectives on a topic.

Engaging with literature will display depth of thinking and understanding of theories that introduce higher-level meaning to research topics. However, engagement involves summarizing, synthesizing and analyzing cited sources to arrive at conclusions that legitimize a scholarly view of the topic (Trafford and Leshem 2008: 75–8). Conversely, the absence of engagement with literature indicates that an author's understanding is neither deep nor explicit despite '*searching*' or '*reviewing*' that literature. Therefore, authors are expected to act as judges of literature rather than being advocates for particular schools of thought or perspectives.

Developing a theoretical perspective that integrates reading, thinking and writing as a process gives authors academic authority to design, undertake and draw conclusions from their research. A literature review is therefore a technical means to a scholarly end via theoretical perspectives.

WHEN TO DO A LITERATURE REVIEW

Whether and when to conduct a literature review is an interesting question. There is a range of opinions about the answer to it. The standard approach to the literature review is to conduct it prior to undertaking the research (Cronin *et al.* 2008). The idea is that it is important for new research to build upon the foundation that has been laid out in prior research. Others believe that the literature review should occur *during the research process*. These scholars argue that depending on the research tradition, previewing other work may bias thinking, as doing so could influence reading for themes; Glaser and Holton (2004) indeed argued that, when doing a grounded theory (GT) study, literature should be integrated into the process of data analysis naturally:

> Instead, GT treats the literature as another source of data to be integrated into the constant comparative analysis process once the core category, its properties and related categories have emerged and the basic conceptual development is well underway. The pre study literature review of QDA is a waste of time and a derailing of relevance for the GT Study
>
> (Glaser and Holton 2004)

Glaser and Holton do encourage readers to engage in related literature throughout their studies. Some researchers believe that the literature review should be completed *after the research has been completed*. These scholars advocate waiting until after conducting the research to carry out the review (Silverman 2005). This view is based upon the idea that one may waste effort without knowing what literature will actually be relevant. Some scholars believe that a literature review should *not be done at all*. Strauss and Corbin (1998) suggest that conducting a full traditional literature review is unnecessary:

> To begin with, let us assure our readers that there is no need to review all of the literature in the field beforehand, as is frequently done by analysts using other research approaches. It is impossible to know prior to the investigation what the salient problems will be or what theoretical concepts will emerge. ... It is not unusual for students to become enamored with a previous study (or studies) either before or during their own investigations, so much so that they are nearly paralyzed in an analytic sense. It is not until they are able to let go and put trust in their abilities to generate knowledge that they finally are able to make discoveries of their own.
>
> (Strauss and Corbin 1998: 49)

Strauss and Corbin do not suggest ignoring prior research completely; rather, they suggest that a traditional review need not be done and that indeed the prior research can count as part of the data.

Most researchers will not want to avoid the research literature review altogether. It is most common to consult prior research before beginning the approach, as it allows the researcher to determine what has been done previously and to advance the field of inquiry in question. This is the approach that we advocate under most circumstances, although Chapter 12 on grounded theory provides a different perspective on this issue.

STEPS IN CONDUCTING A RESEARCH LITERATURE REVIEW

For conducting a systematic and rigorous research review, there are several key stages in the process, which we overview in Figure 8.1 and describe more fully in the remaining sections of this chapter.

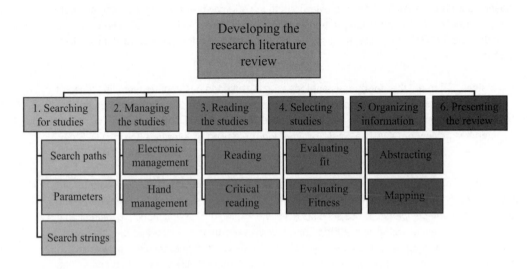

Figure 8.1 Stages in writing a research literature review

Searching for studies

Searching for studies is a critical element of the literature review process (Dixon-Woods *et al*. 2006). What is important in this phase is determining the ways or paths to follow, limiting the search parameters and determining the search strings. We describe these steps in the following paragraphs.

Identifying search paths

Databases are the quickest way to begin a search for studies. They provide quick access, often to full text articles, of large numbers of studies. The selection of specific databases can lead to a 'file drawer bias' meaning that one will return information based upon the database selected. The following are databases frequently used in social science and professional research: Academic Search, ERIC, Google Scholar, Cochrane, IngentaConnect, JSTOR, PsycINFO(r), Sociofile, Social Science Citation Index, Dissertation Abstracts, and PubMed.

In addition to searching databases, there are several additional steps in the search process that are critical:

■   *Ancestry searching/citation searching*: combing through bibliographies of relevant articles to find the studies that they have cited.

- *Hand searching*: reviewing tables of contents of key relevant journals.
- *Raiding*: reviewing archives of listservs and other relevant mailing lists.
- *Expert polling*: asking tutors and colleagues for suggestions.
- *Popular polling*: reviewing popular sources such as magazines and newspapers to determine whether they have cited relevant sources.
- *Random firing*: random trial of search terms in search engine of choice to determine whether any additional 'hits' are returned.

Despite best efforts to do exhaustive searching, it is difficult to locate every relevant publication in existence. Current indexing systems of massive amounts of information simply will not allow it. The researcher's responsibility is to design and execute a search that yields the most relevant literature possible.

Limiting search parameters

Whether searching by database or by some other method, one has opportunities to limit the search to make it more immediately relevant to the study. There are several key ways to make this limitation: type of paper, publication outlet and date of publication.

Type of paper

There are several types of scholarly papers frequently used in social sciences. Among these are empirical research reports, evaluation reports, research reviews/syntheses, descriptive reports, essays and opinions. In writing a literature review, it is important to plan to review existing research, as that is one of the most important ways to determine what gaps need to be filled. One may opt to include other types of papers as well; if so, it is important not only to determine which of these to include in the literature review but also to explain the rationale for this selection and to make it clear throughout the document which type of study is included. Many new researchers make the mistake of presenting all types of papers as if they are research reports. They may say for example, 'Shulman (1986) found', when actually Shulman's article was a theoretical piece rather than an empirical research study, so there were no 'findings' per se. This kind of error should be avoided and can be eliminated by being more precise with language. It would be accurate to say Shulman theorized, postulated or argued.

Claire Howell Major, Author

Researcher reflections

In my roles as journal editor and dissertation chair, as well as lecturer in a regularly offered literature review course, I often work with new researchers. I find that one of the greatest challenges for them is to distinguish between different types of literature. I often advise that they begin the process by treating them separately: most specifically by starting with the empirical research prior to tackling anything else. If they have a good rationale for including other types of literature, I encourage them to organize them into separate categories initially, one for empirical studies, one for theoretical pieces, one for scholarly essays and so forth. This process helps researchers become more familiar with the different types of literature, and even if they choose to combine them and work more thematically later, they have gained a better understanding of the types of papers they are including.

In Table 8.1, we provide descriptions of different scholarly paper types as well as sample verbs, which researchers can use when presenting work from these different types of papers, to make clear distinctions among them.

Table 8.1 Types of scholarly papers in social science research

Paper type	Description of contents	Verbs
Empirical research reports	Presents findings that have been gathered in order to answer a research question	Found, discovered, examined
Evaluation reports	Presents an overview of an assessment done of a programme, institution or other	Judged, appraised, ranked
Research reviews/ syntheses	Integrates information from several or many research or evaluation reports	Generated, integrated, built, combined, produced
Conceptual/theoretical papers	Presents a new concept or theory or describes existing theories or concepts associated with the topic	Theorized, proposed, hypothesized
Descriptive reports	Describes an event, programme, institution or other	Summarized, described, named, defined
Essays	Presents an argument and supports it with evidence	Argued, believed, suggested
Opinions	Presents an author's view of an issue	Stated, told, estimated

Publication outlet

In addition to the consideration of what kind of scholarly paper to include, another key consideration is what kind of publication outlet to include, whether peer reviewed articles or **grey literature**. Peer reviewed studies are considered the industry 'gold standard' since they have been subjected to a process to ensure quality, although different journals have different standards for this process, with some being more rigorous than others. There are good arguments for also including grey literature, so that coverage of all available evidence is achieved. There are an increasing number of publications that are only available on the Internet, such as self-published articles and online encyclopaedias. Researchers should consider carefully whether to use these publications, since they often are not perceived as having the same weight or value as publications in other formats, although their acceptance is growing.

Grey literature

Comprises unpublished studies, such as conference presentations and dissertations

Books are mostly not peer reviewed in the same way as articles, so are mostly considered to carry less weight. However, at times, both whole books and individual book chapters have been peer reviewed, either in their own right or because they are (edited) collections of past research articles. Researchers should be explicit about which types of publications they are including, which they are excluding, and why. In Table 8.2 we provide descriptions of the various types of social science publications.

Table 8.2 ...olic.

Source	Description
Peer reviewed journal	A scholarly journal that publishes research reports, book reviews and other scholarly papers. An author submits a manuscript, which is then sent to two or more expert reviewers without the author's identification. These reviewers critique the paper anonymously and make suggestions to the journal editor about whether the paper should be published.
Non-peer reviewed journal	A journal that publishes scholarly papers but does not subject them to the peer review process.
Magazine	A periodical containing articles, pictures or other features of interest to a specific audience. The articles that magazines publish tend to be more descriptive or essay type than those in journals. The magazine may or may not be peer reviewed; there are many prestigious magazines in social science fields.
Book	A lengthy document prepared by an expert on a specific topic and published by a university press or commercial publisher. A book may or may not be peer reviewed.
Scholarly monographs	In this case, we consider a monograph as a book-length research report prepared by an expert. It typically is peer reviewed.
Book and monograph chapters	Book and monograph chapters are written by experts and may be a research report or other type of publication.
Grey literature	Government reports, white papers, dissertations, conference papers and other papers not available through commercial means.
Internet resources	Papers that exist only in Internet form.

Date of publication

A good argument exists to limit the literature review to the most current work possible. The argument goes that older studies may not be as relevant, since they necessarily have been conducted in different social and cultural contexts, which change over time. Newer research should have been built upon this older foundational work and thus should have advanced the line of work. It is not uncommon to limit a search to work conducted in the past five to ten years. Another common way to limit by date is to determine a turning point or pivotal moment in which research changed dramatically.

LIMITING BY DATE

Research on distance learning prior to 1998 was most likely to be investigating education conducted through television. The late 1990s marked a turning point in the development of the personal computer and commercial learning management systems, so later work will invariably be investigating online learning. Thus, distance education research changed dramatically during that time.

Example

However, it is important that when using date as a consideration, researchers should not exclude seminal or watershed studies that have driven the development of field, simply because they are older.

Developing search strings

Selection of search strings necessarily alters the studies that one returns. These search terms should be clear and focused. A useful way to start is to pose a short general research question that the study should help answer. Brainstorming a list of topics that are related to this general question would be a useful next step.

We offer the following example.

Example

SEARCH STRINGS

■ **Question: how do students describe the problem-based learning experience in medical school?**
■ **Brainstormed list of search strings: medical school, problem-based learning, medical students, medical school curricula.**

Turning these from a list into search terms that return useful study titles can feel like a process of divination. A good place to start is with the database programme and turning to a thesaurus to find the 'descriptors' that match these most closely. Descriptors can help return a more refined and perhaps precise set of studies. The next step is to enter these terms as 'key terms' rather than descriptors, which will allow broadening of the search. During the search phase, researchers should strive not only to find the appropriate search terms but also to use Boolean logic effectively. Most databases allow a researcher to use connectors to extend or limit a search. The search commands in Table 8.3 could be used to return articles about learning.

Table 8.3 Search commands

Command	Function	Example
AND	Searches for articles that include all keywords	Learning AND outcomes (includes articles with both terms)
OR	Searches for articles that include any of the keywords	Learning OR outcomes (includes articles with either term)
NOT	Excludes articles with specific keyword	Learning NOT Service (excludes service learning articles)

When conducting an advanced search, parentheses may be used to extend or limit the search. For example: *education AND (school OR college)* – this combination allows a search for information about education schools or education colleges.

Managing the studies

Before beginning the search, it is important to plan how to manage the studies that will be discovered. Doing so will help avoid unnecessary backtracking and repeating steps, or worse still, from losing forever an article that later seems essential to the review. Managing the studies is a necessary part of the research process.

There are many existing computing applications that can help manage citations, which are particularly useful when conducting large reviews or working on a body of work over an extended time. When working with these tools, typically one enters a full citation. These tools usually work with an existing word processing programme that generates a reference list automatically for a paper. Some of these tools allow for capturing citations from online searches. Some of these bibliographic management programs are available through libraries, such as Refworks (www.ref works.com); others are available for commercial purchase, such as Endnote (www.endnote.com); and many word processors, such as Microsoft Word, have bibliographic management tools as well.

While reference management systems can be useful, they are not essential, as it is possible to manage citations by hand. Some scholars choose to maintain full references (for example, author/s, date, title, journal, volume, issue, page numbers) for each source in a box file or on disk. Scholars who prefer this kind of system stress the importance of being able to hand-manage how the material is stored and retrieved.

Reading the studies

There are two main ways to read an article: reading for the general idea (reading on the face) and reading critically. We recommend beginning with the former and moving to the latter, when appropriate.

Reading for the general idea of the article

Most social science research studies follow a similar format that helps with the ease of reading and understanding. This format normally contains most or all of these sections in this rough order: abstract and introduction, literature review, method(ology), findings, data analysis, discussion and conclusion, followed by references, appendices and any notes and acknowledgements. Sometimes a long introduction might also include the literature review and methodology. Sometimes the findings and data analysis may be intertwined. On a first general read, the reader should try to attain a general sense of what information is presented in each of these sections. The author should also begin to make some assessment of quality, and consider issues such as: what were its strengths, its weaknesses, and did the author accomplish his or her purpose?

Reading for the general idea:

- Read the abstract and the conclusion first to get a general sense of the article.
- Grade the reading so that difficult or complex looking articles are considered first when one is fresh and the simpler articles when one becomes tired.
- Do not be put off by difficult words or phrases. Look up the terms and scribble them in the margin of the article so that, upon re-reading, it will make sense.
- Try reading and discussing an article with a friend, which might stimulate thinking about it.
- Do not worry if it is difficult to understand on first reading. Not understanding an article does not mean one is thick or stupid. Inaccessibility is more likely to be due to the points being put across in an overly complex way.

Tips

Critical reading

Critical reading of the works means including critique of the articles read for the study as an essential part of the research literature review. When reading, strive to think. Do not take whatever an author says or finds as a given. Rather, read from the position of being an unconvinced thinker. Be critical. Another critical question is how this bias might influence the study (for example, development of questions, selection of a sample, interpretation of findings, and so forth).

Questions for reading and reviewing qualitative studies

While the role of the literature review is not merely to summarize each piece of literature, it is important for researchers to engage with the research they select in a critical way. The notion of suggesting a set of universal indicators of quality of qualitative research is fraught with difficulties. Yet there are clearly aspects of research that make one study strong while another is considered weaker.

Researcher reflections

Claire Howell Major, Author

I find that new researchers have difficulty in accepting that not all research is of equal quality. Just because an article appears in a journal does not necessarily mean that it is good and without flaw. Below we have offered some suggestions on reading for quality.

For this reason, we offer Table 8.4: general guidelines that a researcher may adapt and use to review an article, compiled from a range of sources, including Britten *et al.* (1995); Creswell (1998; 2007); Elder and Miller (1995); Giacomini and Cook (2000); Hammersley (1990); Lincoln and Guba (1985); Mays and Pope (2000a; 2000b); Miles and Huberman (1994); Patton (1999); Popay *et al.* (1998); Yardley (2000).

Selecting studies

The goal of a research literature review is to include as many relevant quantitative and qualitative studies as possible. Studies are included and excluded from literature reviews for a number of reasons. Among the most common and arguably most important is fit with the proposed study. Another common and important consideration is the article's fitness for inclusion; quite simply, it is a question of whether the article is worthy of mention.

Table 8.4 Questions for evaluating a qualitative study

Clear focus
- Is the topic of the research clearly identified?
- Is it a significant topic?
- Is the purpose of the research clearly articulated?

Adequate grounding
- Is the research connected to prior research?
  - Does the researcher use prior research either before or after data collection to connect the work to prior knowledge?
  - Does the researcher indicate how the research corresponds with or advances current knowledge?
- Is the research connected to theory?
  - Is the study theoretically positioned?
  - Is the theory clear, insightful and appropriate?
  - Is there an alternative theory that would be a better choice?
  - Is the theory actually a theory?

Research question
- Is the central question (phenomenon, culture, event, or other) clearly described?
- Has the researcher identified a well-defined question?
- Is the question interesting and important?

Research tradition
- Is a rigorous tradition indicated and validated?
- Does the tradition match the question?
- Is the tradition the best approach for answering the question?

Site and sample
- Was the site of the study described?
- Were the participants a reasonable group to select?
- Were an appropriate number of participants selected?
- Were they selected in a reasonable way?
- Were sound measures used to ensure confidentiality?

Data
- What data were used?
- Were they clearly described?
- Are the data sources free from obvious bias?
- Are there potentially better sources of data?
- How were data collected?
- Were sufficient data collected to support rich thick description?
- Was sufficient time spent in the field?
- Were appropriate procedures used to record and transcribe data?

Data analysis
- How were data analyzed?
- Were the methods clearly described?
- Were the methods selected the best ones?
- Was the researcher systematic in the data analysis process?
- Did the data support the analysis?

Results
- Were results communicated clearly and succinctly?
- Do the findings make sense?
- Do the results answer the questions?
- Were data cited effectively?
- Are participants represented fairly and sensitively in the report?
- Are the conclusions convincing?
- Were appropriate caveats indicated?
- Are there alternative explanations for the results?
- Were findings verified?

Rigour
- Were approaches to validity or trustworthiness described?
- Does the researcher provide a plan to minimize potential bias?
- Has the researcher given sufficient detail to determine whether findings or methods might be generalizable?

Overall
- Did the researcher articulate decisions throughout the process?
- Did the researcher provide good rationale for those decisions?
- Is the study of practical or theoretical importance?

Fit

Once scholars have developed as exhaustive a list of references as possible, they will want to screen those references for applicability to their studies, as not everything returned, particularly through database searching, will be applicable. Practical screening questions could include the following:

1. Is it written in a language that is on a par with the current study?
2. Does it seem immediately relevant to the study when scanning the title or abstract?
3. Does it add something of value to the review?

Tips

Keep a running list of articles that are determined to be irrelevant to the study, along with a notation of why they were excluded. This will help to avoid rereading articles multiple times to remember why you discarded them in the first place.

Fitness

While it is important that the article is a good fit for the study, it is also critical that it is itself a fit article. Not all literature is of equal quality and, while weaker works may have something to contribute, those that are fatally flawed should be excluded. We offer the following considerations for inclusion:

- *Originality of the work*: the works included should be original and have something new to contribute. It is not uncommon for an author to reuse ideas, information and findings, and publish essentially the same study or information under a different title. Work to include only those studies that make an original contribution to the review, or alternatively at least note when the information is redundant because it has already been published elsewhere.
- *Quality of the analytical argument*: we believe that all writing is argument and that even research papers begin with arguments about why and how the study should be done. The argument should be considered for how it fits or challenges the existing literature.
- *Quality of the information and evidence cited in the work*: the works included in the literature review should contain accurate information, both facts and, if used, examples and other anecdotal information.
- *Quality of the conclusions*: conclusions of the works included in the review should be clear and should flow directly from the evidence presented. They should not come as a complete surprise to the reader.
- *Structural quality*: the pieces one includes in the literature review should have structural integrity. They should be organized logically and evidence quality of writing and clarity of assumptions.
- *Quality of references cited*: the references cited in the works included should be of high quality. They should include citations from leaders in the field and publications from highly regarded journals.
- *Quality of publication outlet*: the publication outlet should be a legitimate and accurate source, preferably that has demonstrated longevity (it has a good historical track record) and impact (highly cited).

Organizing the information

Upon locating scholarly works that fit the research topic, it is time to begin extracting relevant information from them. This determines the structure of the literature review. It is worth considering that if the literature review is 10,000 words, it could be structured around four to five themes that emerge across the literature located. This means one may have approximately 2,000 words per section, which means each section can reasonably review eight articles. Developing a spreadsheet is ideal for this purpose. Consider extracting the information that we demonstrate in Table 8.5.

Table 8.5 Extracting information

	Article 1	Article 2	Article 3	Article 4	Article 5	And so on...
Topic						
Research question						
Research tradition						
Sample/participants						
Setting						
Methods						
Data collection						
Data analysis						
Notion of validity						
Key findings						

Once information has been extracted from the studies, the findings should be examined to determine key themes or concepts. This is done through a simple process of translating findings into each other, as we demonstrate in Figure 8.2.

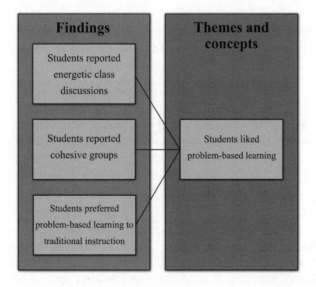

Figure 8.2 Translation of findings to central concepts

Mapping

Once findings have been translated, it is possible to begin a literature review map, which will help to organize thoughts about the works. To map, it is important to identify and group key findings into key themes or concepts. Themes may then be mapped in one of several different ways.

Matrix

A matrix (see Table 8.6) is a graphic organizer that allows documentation of which themes are contained in which articles. The horizontal axis is used to list the article, while the vertical axis is used to list the theme. Marks are then used to document presence of a theme in a given article.

Table 8.6 Using a matrix to map literature

	Theme 1	Theme 2	Theme 3	Theme 4	Theme 5
Article 1				•	
Article 2		•			
Article 3		•		•	
Article 4	•				
Article 5				•	•

Concept map

A concept map (see Figure 8.3) is a diagram that resembles a web. Nodes are used to represent the main themes and concepts in the literature and ties are used to demonstrate connections between them.

Hierarchy literature review map

A hierarchy literature review map (see Figure 8.4) allows for mapping subordinate relationships between concepts and themes that may not otherwise be apparent.

Flow chart

A flow chart (see Figure 8.5) allows depiction of information in a chronological sequence. In our example of problem-based learning in a medical school, for example, problem-based learning evolved over time, so it is possible to consider outcomes in the different models that developed in stages.

Venn diagram

A Venn diagram (see Figure 8.6) is used to illustrate when two concepts have overlapping characteristics. In our problem-based learning example, it is conceivable that outcomes of problem-based learning in medical school would have been the topic of both theoretical papers and empirical research papers. Some common ground between these two is likely; thus, a Venn diagram may be an appropriate mapping tool.

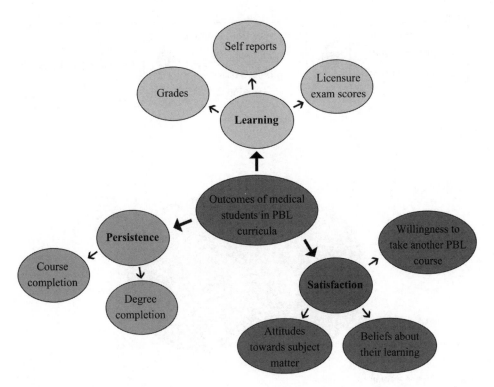

Figure 8.3 Literature review concept map

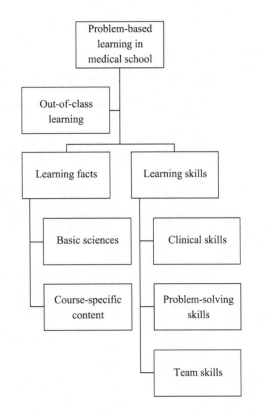

Figure 8.4 Hierarchy literature review map

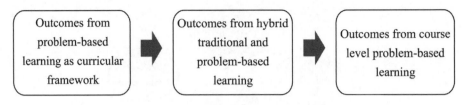

Figure 8.5 Flow chart

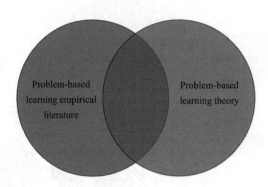

Figure 8.6 Venn diagram

Table 8.7 Format of the review (adapted from Carnwell and Daly 2001; Cronin *et al.* 2008)

Approach	Description	Advantages and disadvantages	Useful mapping tool
Dividing by themes or categories	Distinct themes developed from findings of existing literature	Most common approach and most accepted. Requires critical thinking and critical review. Allows for integration of ideas and avoidance of potential redundancy. May be challenging to make clear what is empirical research and what is not.	Matrix; concept map; hierarchy map
Dividing empirical literature and theoretical literature into two different sections	Empirical and theoretical literature are discussed separately	Allows for clear and different treatment of different types of literature. May lead author towards description and away from criticality; may introduce redundancy when treating themes.	Venn diagram
Presenting it chronologically	Literature divided by time period	Shows development of a topic over time, clearly documenting a line of progression in work. May be dull to read and probably increases the odds of redundancy of ideas.	Flow chart

Presenting the research literature review

The literature review map may serve as a guide for the way in which the literature review will be presented. The format of a research review in a social science or professional field may vary. In Table 8.7, we present some of the main ways that a literature review may be organized.

Whatever the format, a literature review should be lively and engaging; it should not be a boring section that encourages a reader to skim or pass over it entirely. Instead, it should capture the reader's attention, provide relevant information and instil a desire to know more about a particular area of research. Indeed a literature review should tell the story of the literature.

CONCLUSION

Writing the literature review is not an easy process. When done well, reviewing prior research is just as rigorous an activity as conducting original research. It takes sustained effort, perseverance, tenacity and plain old intelligence. When it is a critical part of the research design, a good literature review serves as an integral and iterative process involved in focusing a research study. It provides a reader with confidence that the research has been built upon a prior store of knowledge and that the researcher has made the necessary preparations to carry out his or her current study.

Concept questions

- Why is doing an effective literature review important?
- When might one choose not to do a traditional literature review?
- What are the central features of a literature review for a research study?

Application questions

- How will you identify the literature to include in your review?
- What search strings are likely to produce the articles you need?
- How will you evaluate the articles for fit and quality?
- How will you organize the articles?
- How will you present them in writing?
- When will you conduct a literature review for your study?
- How will you ensure that it is critical?

Reflective questions

Key resources

Hart, C. (1998) *Doing a literature review: Releasing the social science imagination*, London: Sage.
This book provides a solid overview of writing literature reviews; the information about mapping literature sources is particularly useful.

Cronin, P., Ryan, F. and Coughlan, M. (2008) Undertaking a literature review: A step-by-step approach. *British Journal of Nursing*, 17 (1), 38–43.
This article is good for informing thinking about the ways to carry out a literature review.

Major, C. H. and Savin-Baden, M. (2010a). *An introduction to qualitative research synthesis: Managing the information explosion in social science research*, London: Routledge.
Our own work on qualitative research synthesis informed this chapter, particularly the search for and evaluation of articles for inclusion in the study.

Chapter 9

Theoretical and conceptual frameworks

INTRODUCTION

There is a range of views about the use of theories and concepts in qualitative research. Both qualitative and quantitative researchers place varying degrees of emphasis on the use of theories and concepts: some choose to use less formal theories and concepts for their research; some opt to use theories and concepts in ways that differ from traditional norms and a few choose to forgo the application of theories and concepts to their work completely. Perhaps because of these disparate views and practices, social science research studies at times have been criticized for lacking a sound theoretical and conceptual foundation. Admittedly, the use of theories and concepts in qualitative research is a complex issue, and researchers rarely are provided with much guidance about whether, when, where, and how to use them. This chapter provides key definitions of theories and concepts, debates competing perspectives on each and explores the role that both of these frameworks play in qualitative research. It goes on to apply these ideas to practice, presenting the nuts and bolts of developing and using theoretical and conceptual frameworks within a qualitative study.

CONFUSIONS IN TERMINOLOGY: THEORETICAL AND CONCEPTUAL FRAMEWORKS

The terms 'theoretical framework' and 'conceptual framework' appear frequently in published social science studies, and there appears to be some general confusion about the difference between the two, with good reason. At times, researchers seem to use the terms almost interchangeably. At other times, researchers seem to make sharp distinctions between the two; sometimes they use one or the other in their studies, sometimes both and sometimes neither. The competing opinions about the difference between a theoretical framework and a conceptual framework, coupled with a lack of a clear distinction in the literature, makes understanding either term and putting either concept in to practice a challenge. Indeed, in reading through many social science studies, it would appear that the notion of having some kind of theoretical or conceptual framework may have become lost, overlooked or misunderstood. Recent research, for example, has indicated that many PhD candidates struggle with the idea of conceptual frameworks:

> Their difficulty arose despite the sessions/tutorials that many had previously received elsewhere 'on research' ... The majority of candidates could identify concepts and relate

them to their intended research design and research process. However, despite clarifying research questions and 'reading around-their-subject', one-third of candidates still had problems in visualising concepts within a framework.

(Leshem and Trafford 2007: 93)

Such difficulty intimates that the lack of understanding of conceptual frameworks is having a long-term influence on the quality of qualitative studies in general. For this reason, researchers need clear ideas about conceptual or theoretical frameworks, and whether and how one or both should be applied.

WHAT IS A THEORY?

A theory, as we see it, is an effort to explain, predict and master a phenomenon, such as a relationship, event or behaviour. Reeves *et al.* (2008), for example, define a theory as 'an organized, coherent, and systematic articulation of a set of issues that are communicated as a meaningful whole'. Hitchcock and Hughes (1995) also state the following of theory:

> Theory is seen as being concerned with the development of systematic construction of knowledge of the social world. In doing this theory employs the use of concepts, systems, models, structures, beliefs and ideas, hypotheses (theories) in order to make statements about particular times of actions, events or activities, so as to make analyses of their causes, consequences, and processes.

(Hitchcock and Hughes 1995: 20–1)

Strauss and Corbin (1994: 278) similarly suggest that 'theory consists of plausible relationship produced among concepts or sets of concepts'. Theories, then, are attempts to construct models that describe and explain 'reality'.

Theories generally are developed deductively, following from an empirically informed act of creativity, and then are verified empirically, a process which results in an on-going and cyclical process of deduction and induction (Reeves *et al.* 2008). Ary *et al.* (1990) suggest that the following are essential elements of a theory:

- It should aid understanding of observed phenomena by explaining them in the simplest form possible (*principle of parsimony*).
- It should fit cleanly with observed facts and with established principles.
- It should be inherently testable and verifiable.
- It should imply further investigations and predict new discoveries.

A theory is useful because it enables generalizations to be made about observations and consists of an interrelated, coherent set of ideas and models (Camp 2000).

What kinds of theories exist?

Theories may fit into one of three primary categories: grand, middle range and substantive theories. *Grand theories* are used to explain major categories of phenomena and are more common in the natural sciences than in the social sciences. An example of a grand theory is Wilson's (1998) theory of the unity of knowledge. *Middle-range theories* fall somewhere below grand theories in a hierarchy and tend to describe a specific phenomenon. Middle-range theory is sometimes referred to as *formal theory*. Merton's theory of a reference group (having a group by which to compare oneself) is an example of middle-range theory (Merton and Kendall 1946). *Substantive/ practice theories* offer explanations in a restricted setting and are limited in scope (such as emergency room care), often being expressed as propositions or hypotheses. Narrow typologies and classification systems may also be considered substantive theory.

Social science researchers tend to use middle-range theories and substantive theories, and grounded theory researchers tend to seek to develop substantive theories.

How do quantitative and qualitative researchers see theory differently?

While there is general agreement as to the nature of a theory and its general categories, as might be expected, quantitative and qualitative researchers have tended to define and use theory differently. The primary difference seems to be in the way in which theory is used to understand or explain key variables or concepts.

Theory according to quantitative researchers

Quantitative researchers tend to see theory as a documentation of relationships between variables of interest (Camp 2000). Creswell (1994) suggested that quantitative research involves 'an inquiry into a social or human problem, based on testing a theory composed of variables, measured with numbers, and analyzed with statistical procedures, in order to determine whether the predictive generalisations of the theory hold true' (1994: 2). He noted that the relationships among variables are typically stated in terms of magnitude and direction, thus providing 'overarching explanation for how and why one would expect the independent variable to explain or predict the dependent variable' (1994: 82–3). Quantitative researchers, then, tend to use a theory to develop hypotheses about relationships between variables, for the purpose of predicting and explaining phenomena (for example, Kerlinger 1979; Ary *et al.* 1990; Best and Kahn 1993).

Theory according to qualitative researchers

Qualitative researchers often see theory as something that researchers do during data collection and analysis, so theory for the qualitative researcher does not predict relationship between variables (Camp 2000). According to Merriam (1998), unlike in quantitative research, hypotheses are always tentative in qualitative research and are developed through use of a constant comparative analysis of data. Hypotheses emerge, according to her, simultaneously with the collection and analysis of data, rather than being stated in advance of data collection as occurs in quantitative research. Merriam described this view of the role of theory when she wrote that 'Thinking about data theorising is a step toward developing a theory that explains some aspect of educational practice and allows a researcher to draw inferences about future activity' (Merriam 1998: 188). She defines theorizing as 'the cognitive process of discovering or manipulating abstract categories and the relationships among those categories' (1998: 188). Theory, then, explains the relationship between categories rather than predicts them. What researchers should consider is whether they will test theories, use theories to guide data analysis or generate theory.

What is a theoretical framework?

Marshall and Rossman (1989/1995: 24) used the term 'theoretical frame' to describe the use of theory in qualitative research, and this term has been applied increasingly to the ways in which specific theories are applied in social science research. The authors argue that the theoretical frame 'provides the conceptual grounding of a study. It is built upon a combination of tacit (experience-based) theory and formal (literature-based) theory and serves to inform researcher's assumptions and guide his or her questions about the research setting' (1989: 24). Merriam (1998), for example, defines a theoretical framework as a 'lens through which [the researcher] view[s] the world' (1998: 45). Within the context of qualitative research, a framework is a structure that is intended as a guide for thinking about the research subject and as an interpretive lens through which to view data. In our view, a theoretical framework is a theory that works with the philosophical lens in a complementary theory way, which we described in Chapter 4. We illustrate the interconnection between philosophy and complementary theory in Figure 9.1.

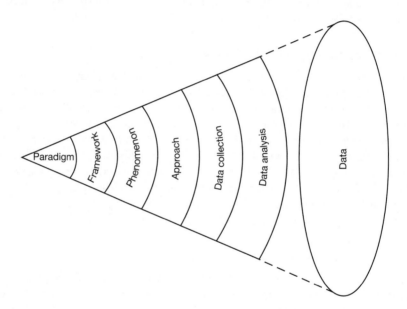

Figure 9.1 The philosophy and theory lens

In the researcher reflection, Childers explains how she uses a theoretical framework as a complementary theory (see Chapter 4) to her philosophical position.

Sara M. Childers, Assistant Professor of Research Methodology, University of Alabama, USA

As discussed in this book, there are multiple ways in which theory can be utilized to frame a study. In my own work, I have found that theoretical frameworks are useful when they provide explanatory power, or help me to better articulate, the phenomena I am witnessing and experiencing as I conduct my research. I think some considerations are in order as we think through which lenses are most appropriate for our work.

Appropriate theoretical frameworks: where's the fire
As students begin to situate themselves paradigmatically and philosophically outside positivism, these positions often seem overwhelming. One of the best ways to reorient oneself is to read widely and pay attention to those social and philosophical orientations that both align with the way you read the world and also inspire your thinking. The social theories then that comprise these orientations also provide researchers with theoretical lenses for analyzing data.

Owing to my early training in feminist theory and research, my exposure to critical and post-structural philosophies and social theories was extensive. I found in reading the theories of feminists, critical race theorists and post-structuralists that their work 'set me on fire', galvanized my thinking and helped me to make sense of my perceptions of the world. Their theoretical frameworks for understanding power, knowledge, race/gender/class, difference and social materiality became analytic tools for analysis.

Explanatory power, fit and critique
While theoretical frameworks can be indispensable to data analysis, they can also be dangerous when researchers try to force the fit between lens and data. When a theoretical framework is adopted prior to entering the field site it is imperative that the framework 'earn its keep'. And if it does not, we must seek out other theoretical frameworks that offer explanatory power to describe what we are witnessing in the data.

I conducted an eighteen-month ethnographic case study of a high-achieving, high-poverty, predominantly black college-preparatory high school in Central Ohio. The preliminary research that included policy and document analysis, pre-pilot interviewing and casual observation pointed me towards an a priori hunch that it could serve as a critical case study of how one school was successful in circumventing the No Child Left Behind (NCLB) policy through practices of curriculum and instruction that went against the grain of 'teaching to the test'. Through the course of data collection, my hunch earned its keep and the theoretical frameworks of Michel Foucault, through which I had become accustomed to thinking about relations between power and knowledge, earned their keep as well by providing explanatory power for analyzing how policy comes to be practiced in a high-achieving school.

At the same time though, I also witnessed an internal racial segregation of students across the curriculum where African American students were concentrated in the basic college prep level courses, while advanced placement and international baccalaureate courses were predominantly white. Foucault's theories were not adequate to address

continued

the racial stratification across the curriculum. I turned to critical race theory because it provided the explanatory power lacking in post-structural theories inattention to race and also offered a language through which I could frame the material effects of this stratification on students.

Together, critical race theory and post-structural theory provided generative co-critique and were constitutive of the larger analysis that resulted where both success and failure were engaged in coming to understand how race continues to matter, even in our best schools.

Researcher reflections

Claire Howell Major, Author

In teaching a course on reading research in higher education, I held a session on theoretical frameworks. I presented definitions of theoretical frameworks and how they might be applied. To demonstrate how a qualitative researcher uses a theoretical framework, I described some of my work on lecturer experiences of teaching online (Major 2010). For the research, I used qualitative meta-synthesis as my research approach (see Major and Savin-Baden 2010). To illustrate my point about theoretical frameworks, I presented students with a quotation and asked them what it meant.

I then told the students about my theoretical framework, which involved change theory related to technology. In particular, I relied upon Zuboff (1984), who conceptualizes change in the *nature and character of jobs* that using technology creates. Zuboff asserted that computer-based technologies are not neutral. Rather, technology imposes as well as produces new patterns of information and social relations. Technology may 'automate', replacing human labour and physical motions, so leading to dull jobs with lack of meaning. It also may 'informate', replacing human contact with collecting information and data but potentially leading to more stimulating, challenging work and greater job satisfaction. In its ability to 'informate', Zuboff suggests that information technology displaces sensory or expressive relationships with objects or persons, and replaces them with the technological interface. Thus, the sensory- or expressive-based skills diminish, while new skills develop, in order to allow the effective management of the new interface, so as to harness the full power of the technological tool. I then asked students to use this theoretical framework and examine the data again.

The students felt that the theoretical framework provided them with guidance for thinking about the data. It helped them focus on a specific aspect of what the lecturers in question were verbalizing, in this case, lecturers' experiences as teachers in an online environment. It made them think about what the lecturers were saying in ways that had not occurred to them before, specifically about how the technology could informate or automate their work as teachers. The difficulty of using a framework can result in it imposing meanings on the data, without really examining them in-depth and exploring the subtext of what was being said. The disadvantage then of using a theory in this way is that data analysis can be simplified into easy categories too quickly that just fit almost too readily with the chosen theory. For a specific example of the student interpretation of a quotation with and without the theoretical framework, see Table 9.1.

Table 9.1 Student responses to the question posed in author reflections

Quote	Sample student responses	Student reading with framework as lens
I think it has added some excitement to teaching, some new challenges. Teaching is not a new concept, it has been around for hundreds of years. People have learned what works and what doesn't work. Then all of a sudden with computers and technology, a new avenue has been opened for us. This offers a new mode of teaching for us we are not familiar with. Because you are an effective teacher in the classroom does not mean you are an effective teacher in this mode. There are new issues, new challenges, new tools to bring to this. (Coppola *et al.* 2002: 185)	Technology is cutting edge. Technology can improve teaching and learning. This teacher likes technology.	Technology changed the teaching job and made it more exciting. This tutor member's efforts were most closely aligned with 'informating'.
Things are much more structured and perhaps rigid than they are in a regular course. When I teach a course, oftentimes I find topics and readings and things of interest the day before I teach. I read a book, I read a new journal article, I would see something in the paper. I bring that into class. And I modify and adjust my syllabus accordingly. In an online environment, I have to make decisions about what to teach, what to talk about, what content to cover 6 months in advance, without knowing the audience, without knowing their specific needs, without being able to react to what's coming from the class. (Conceição 2006: 35)	This is a late adopter. This teacher isn't thinking that he could post this on a discussion board. This teacher doesn't like technology.	This tutor member found that the job was more dull and boring. The job was changed in a way that made him feel it was more automated.

WHAT IS A CONCEPT?

A concept is a general idea generated from specific instances, which frequently is part of a theory or model. At its base level, it is a unit of meaning that tends to signify something. Chinn and Jacobs (1983: 200) define a concept as: 'A complex mental formulation of an object, property or event that is derived from individual perception and experience'. Meleis (1991: 12) defines a concept as: 'A label used to describe a phenomenon or a group of phenomena'. McKenna (1997) argues that concepts are labels that give meaning and enable an individual to categorize and interpret a phenomenon. For example, the concept 'bird' brings to mind qualities that eagles, jays and robins all share. Concepts are thought to derive from experiences, from which they may be compared to other concepts (a bird is in some ways like a butterfly), reflected upon (what makes a bird a bird?) or abstracted (a dog is not a bird). A concept can call to mind or conjure an image; for example, the phrase 'don't think of a black cat' immediately calls to mind the image of a black cat. Thus, a concept is an abstract signifier of something else. As Cohen *et al.* (2000: 13) suggest:

> Concepts express generalizations from particulars – anger, achievement, alienation, velocity, intelligence, democracy. Examining these examples more closely, we see that each word is representing an idea: more accurately, a concept is a relationship between the word (or symbol) and an idea or conception. Whoever we are and whatever we do, we all make use of concepts. ... Concepts enable us to impose some sort of meaning on the world; through them reality is given sense, order and coherence. They are the means by which we are able to come to terms with our experience. The more we have, the more sense data we can pick up and the surer will be our perceptual (and cognitive) grasp of whatever is 'out there'.
>
> (Cohen *et al.* 2000: 13)

What is a conceptual framework?

A conceptual framework is a collection of general but related concepts from the literature that serve as partial background for the study and that support the need for investigating the research question. They are deemed by many researchers as a key part of research design (Miles and Huberman 1994; Robson 2002; Maxwell 2005).

Miles and Huberman (1994: 20) defined a conceptual framework as 'the current version of the researcher's map of the territory being investigated'. Likewise, Rudestam and Newton suggest that:

> A conceptual framework, which is simply a less developed form of a theory, consists of statements that link abstract concepts to empirical data. Theories and conceptual frameworks are developed to account for or describe abstract phenomena that occur under similar conditions.
>
> (Rudestam and Newton 1992: 6)

Weaver-Hart (1988) defines a conceptual framework as: 'A structure for organizing and supporting ideas; a mechanism for systematically arranging abstractions; sometimes revolutionary or original, and usually rigid' (1988: 11).

While we believe these are reasonable starting points, we suggest that a conceptual framework is more likely to relate to the focus of the study, is broader and more far reaching and can guide the design of an entire study. Smyth (2004) defines a conceptual framework as 'a set of broad ideas and principles taken from relevant fields of enquiry and used to structure a subsequent presentation'. We describe a conceptual framework as *a model for thinking that is the direct result of a systematic process of reviewing and synthesizing information from a related body of knowledge that provides the intellectual underpinning to guide the development and conduct of an empirical research study*. In practice, this means that the framework guides each step of the process, as in Table 9.2 on the facing page.

We suggest that what is useful about having a conceptual framework is that it helps the researcher to answer questions about the study in terms of:

■ In what ways did the literature inform the study?
■ How did the literature read affect the ways the study was designed?
■ What research approaches were considered?
■ Which research approach was chosen and why?
■ How did the tradition chosen inform the ways data were collected, analyzed and presented?

A researcher needs to consider the conceptual set to determine whether it offers new directions, and to consider how what is being done or learned may contradict what the theory or set would suggest. Smyth (2004) describes her experience with using a conceptual framework.

> In my case, the conceptual framework became the heart of the study as the research gained momentum. It increasingly scaffolded, strengthened and kept my research on track by:
>
> ■ Providing clear links from the literature to the research goals and questions
> ■ Informing the research design
> ■ Providing reference points for discussion of literature, methodology and analysis of data
> ■ Contributing to the trustworthiness of the study (Goetz and LeCompte, 1984).
>
> (Smyth 2004: 167)

Table 9.2 A map for using a conceptual framework to design research (adapted from Savin-Baden 2010: 133)

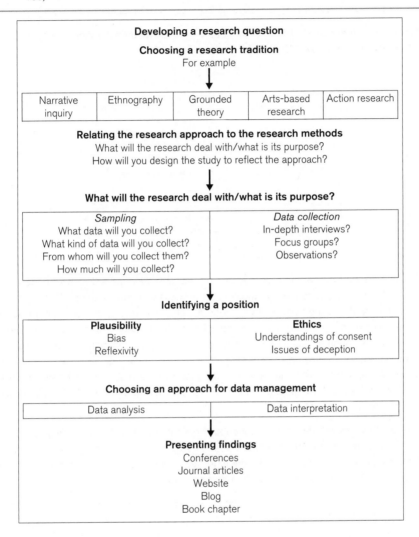

Conceptual frameworks have drawbacks as well. Smyth offers the following cautions about conceptual frameworks:

> Firstly, the framework is a construction of knowledge bounded by the life-world experiences of the person developing it and should not be attributed a power that it does not have. Secondly, the nature of a conceptual framework means that it consciously, or unconsciously informs thought and practice by increasing personal sensitivity to notice particular occurrences so this must be accounted for (Mason and Waywood 1996). Thirdly, no researcher can expect that all data will be analyzed using the framework without the risk of limiting the results from the investigation.
>
> (Smyth 2004: 168)

We provide a concrete example of a conceptual framework in Figure 9.2.

Marshall and Rossman (1999) offer the following model and description of a conceptual framework from Benbow (1994: 28–29), see Figure 4.1:

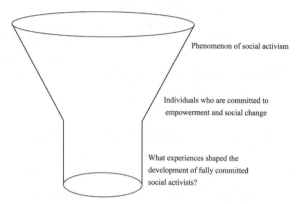

Phenomenon of social activism

Individuals who are committed to empowerment and social change

What experiences shaped the development of fully committed social activists?

'The large end of the funnel represents the general conceptual focus – the issue of social activism and its role in ameliorating oppressive circumstances. Midway down the funnel, the focus narrows to a concern with individuals who have demonstrated and lived an intense commitment to social causes. An alternative choice at this point would have been to focus on social movements as group phenomena rather than on individuals whose lived experiences embody social consciousness. The small end of the conceptual funnel focuses even more closely on a research question (or set of questions) about how life experiences helped shape and develop a lifelong, intensive commitment to social activism'.

Thus Benbow used three related concepts from the literature base: – social activism, individuals committed to social causes, and life experiences of committed individuals – to serve as the conceptual frame for the study, so driving the selection of many research choices, such as the research question and participants.

Figure 9.2 Conceptual funnel

COMPARING THEORETICAL AND CONCEPTUAL FRAMEWORKS

Theoretical and conceptual frameworks have some similar features. They both serve as tools for the researcher to help guide their studies, particularly the interpretation of data. The following researcher reflection from Leshem illustrates the benefits of theoretical and conceptual frameworks.

Yet there are clear differences between a theoretical framework and conceptual framework. Namely, a theory helps to structure an explanation of a phenomenon and so a theoretical framework is used largely as complementary to a philosophical framework (see Chapter 4) and intends to serve as an explanation of the findings and to help drive the interpretation. A concept

Dr Shosh Leshem, Oranim, Academic College of Education and Haifa University, Israel

Developing conceptual or theoretical frameworks?

Research reviewers place importance on the significance of conceptualization. Evidence also suggests that a research report without a conceptual framework is unlikely to exhibit scholarship. Thus, engaging with conceptual frameworks is an essential prerequisite of solid research. However, research conducted by Leshem and Trafford (2007) suggested that researchers frequently are uncertain about both what constitutes a conceptual framework and how it can be applied within the research process. Confusion also arises from the fact that the terms 'theoretical perspectives', 'conceptual frameworks' and 'theoretical frameworks' are sometimes used interchangeably in texts on research.

Theoretical perspectives provide views, approaches and arguments on the research issue that originate in the literature and the corpus of the topic. They identify and confirm the foundation for a gap in knowledge. They then define the research topic by delimiting the research through stating what is included or excluded from the investigation. The justifications for such choices are found within the perspectives themselves. Thus, theoretical perspectives provide a lens outwards from the literature.

In contrast, theoretical frameworks and conceptual frameworks serve different purposes. They are tangible foundations to act on and 'tools for researchers to use' (Weaver-Hart 1988). They provide ways of linking theoretical perspectives with the act of research. Thus, they serve similar functions within the research process.

Research texts use a variety of metaphors as bridges between theoretical perspectives and the act of research. They all relate to the notion of conceptual frameworks and theoretical frameworks. They both fulfil an integrating function between theories that explain the research issue and provide a scaffold within which strategies for the research design can be determined and the fieldwork undertaken (Leshem and Trafford 2007). They also shape the research conclusions by emphasizing the conceptual significance of evidence. Conceptual frameworks and theoretical frameworks therefore have a linking function between the paradigm of the research topic and the paradigm of the research process.

Conceptual and theoretical frameworks introduce order and cohesion both in the thinking and writing process. They are the signposts that run through the thesis as a conceptual thread (Trafford and Leshem 2008: 24), to show interconnectedness between stages and components of the research. They provide answers to the 'why' questions of the research process that demonstrate depth, rigour and a high level of conceptualization. Thus, they are essential prerequisites to research since they both serve the same function in the planning and conduct of serious high-level research.

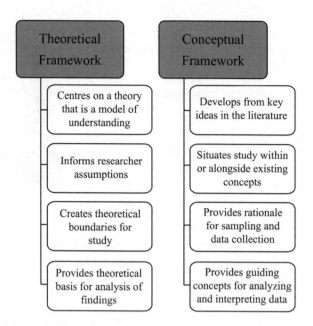

Figure 9.3 Comparison of theoretical and conceptual frameworks

is a key idea, generally taken from the literature, that can guide study design. We offer additional details comparing and contrasting theoretical and conceptual frameworks in Figure 9.3.

ONE, BOTH OR NEITHER?

Social scientists are more frequently being called to both elaborate and prove their reliance upon theories and concepts in their work. Increasingly, journals and conferences are requiring inclusion of a theoretical or conceptual framing section and, often, dissertation and thesis advisors and committee members are calling for the same. Professional preference in some countries and in some fields appears to favour including a theoretical or conceptual framework (or both) in a qualitative research study.

The underlying notion behind the drive to use theories and concepts to frame research is that doing so should allow for a more rigorous and robust study. May puts it this way:

> The idea of theory, or the ability to interpret and understand the findings of research within a conceptual framework which makes 'sense' of the data, is the mark of a discipline whose aim is the systematic study of particular phenomena. ... Theory informs our thinking which, in turn, assists us in making research decisions and sense of the world around us.
>
> (May 1993: 20)

The trend seems to suggest that theoretical and conceptual frameworks will be worth a researcher's consideration.

Whether to use one or the other, both or neither depends upon the purpose of the study and the availability of supporting work. Some research topics have been the subject of much investigation and thus there are a range of concepts and theories from which to draw. Others may not have been as well researched but will still possess related concepts and theories that can be of good use. In such cases, researchers may wish to choose to use both theoretical and conceptual frameworks.

> Theoretical and conceptual frameworks may be used well together in a study. A researcher may, for example, draw key concepts from the literature that inform the choice of a phenomenon of study and selection of participants (see Chapter 6) and then use a specific theory to guide data analysis. Typically, the researcher presents the conceptual framework first and concludes the review of research, concepts and theories with the choice of a theory to frame data interpretation.

Tips

On the other hand, some scholars believe that using theories and concepts to frame research goes against the very purpose of qualitative research and moreover stifles researcher creativity. Such researchers may believe that theories and concepts should not be applied a priori. The argument is that doing so predetermines study findings, prevents new information from developing, and limits creativity (Thomas 1997). Those researchers who are against the application of theory or concepts contend that they should be the result, outcome or product of research. For example, pragmatic researchers may not take up a theoretical or conceptual framework on the grounds that they are guided simply by the best way to answer a question and that they want to gauge the efficacy of results by application to practice rather than theory. Moreover, pragmatic researchers taking up grounded theory in particular wish to generate new theory, not explore existing theory. Instead, these researchers believe that data can and should be used to develop new substantive theories. Another situation arises with specific research topics, for which it is difficult to find an existing body of supporting concepts or theories, and in these cases researchers justifiably choose not to bend concepts and theories inappropriately just to say that they have used them.

It is a legitimate stance to take to choose not to apply a theoretical or conceptual framework. However, we think whether to take up a theoretical or conceptual framework should be a conscious and purposeful decision. A researcher, then, should determine whether or not to use a theoretical or conceptual framework or both, provide a strong rationale for this decision and make it apparent that it is a clear choice when writing about a study. Researchers who use theory or concepts, however, need not feel constrained by them; rather, researchers may be guided by them, whether in designing their research, explaining data or refuting an existing theory. The important part is to make good use of theories and concepts in the research.

HOW TO FIND THEORIES AND CONCEPTS

Finding a theory or concept to help guide a study is a daunting task. While many concepts and theories exist, finding those that are compatible with the research topic and question can be a challenge. The process generally takes several trials before the ideal theory or concepts are found. We have found the following approaches to be most beneficial.

Examine what theories and concepts others have drawn upon

When reviewing literature related to a specific topic, a researcher will find a range of related studies. Carefully abstracting information from these studies, as we suggested in Chapter 8, provides ready access to a list of theories that others have either used to frame their own studies or developed in their own research. These can be a rich vein of theories and concepts from which to draw. As we noted earlier in this chapter, however, not all researchers have paid as much heed as others to the use of theory concepts, so it is possible that one may not find as many as desired. Alternatively, it may not be possible to find an exact fit for the intended study.

Ask mentors for suggestions

Mentors, particularly experts in the field, can be a great source of information about theories and concepts that have been used over time in a particular area. Moreover, they may simply have come across theories and concepts in reading and reviewing articles, dissertations and theses. Checking with mentors often can yield several potential sources for theoretical or conceptual frameworks. Doing so can also provide a researcher with the opportunity to 'try out' the theory with a critical thinker, who can critique its application.

Use a search engine

Search engines, such as Google, can be surprisingly good at yielding theories and concepts that are applicable. It takes a good list of search terms, patience and a lot of trial and error for this to yield an appropriate theory or concept but sometimes it is possible to hit gold in this way. The process, much like turning up articles for a literature review (Chapter 8) involves identifying good search terms and trying several different combinations.

HOW TO PRESENT A THEORETICAL OR CONCEPTUAL FRAMEWORK IN A QUALITATIVE STUDY

Many researchers have questions about how to present a framework in the study and about the degree to which it should be explored. It is a complicated question but the answer is that the framework needs to be presented with clarity and with sufficient detail to allow a reader to make a judgment about its applicability its use. We offer several suggestions that we see as key to introducing the framework and to acknowledging the role it will play in the research.

Introduce the framework clearly and early

It is important to provide a clear indication of the framework. Generally, a phrase such as the following is used: 'Moore's transactional distance theory (1972) served as a theoretical framework for my study' or 'The following five concepts from the existing literature served as my conceptual

Tips

In social science papers, theoretical and conceptual frameworks typically are introduced at the end of the literature review section.

framework . . .'. This technique provides a reader with immediate grounding about the framework being applied.

Identify the essential features and elements of the framework

After specifying the framework to be used, it is critical to describe its most important components. These should distinguish it from other theories or concepts and make clear the particular components that are driving the work. This approach also allows a researcher the opportunity to explain his or her perspective about what the framework means.

Illustrate the framework, if possible by means of a diagram

Many researchers have developed figures or models to represent their theories. If possible, it is a good idea to include the author's diagram. If not, researchers may consider developing a diagram of the theory of their own, as doing so can illustrate how they view theory and thus inform readers about how it is being used. Concept maps are often used to demonstrate the relationships within conceptual frameworks; examples of a concept map can be found in Chapter 8.

Explain the role that the framework will play in the research

It should be clear whether the components of the framework will help guide design, frame the interpretations or be used in another way. The researcher should make a clear acknowledgement of the components that will be applied, as it is possible to apply only part of a theory if appropriate. It is also imperative to explain in what way(s) the theory or conceptual set were used. Making direct links from the different elements to explain their use is essential.

Provide a rationale for application of the framework

Some frameworks simply seem to work better than others in serving as a lens and some seem just plain wrong for the case at hand. For this reason, we believe it is critical for a researcher to provide some rationale that the theoretical or conceptual framework both makes sense and is useful in the way it is intended. Providing a rationale for the selection also allows a reader a chance to evaluate the researcher's choice of a lens.

Cite main proponents of the framework, if appropriate

A good way to give credence to a framework is to cite others who have used it successfully. Citing proponents can also demonstrate how the framework has been used, and in what contexts, over time. It can also document the development of a body of research based upon the framework, which can help position a study. Moreover, it can help build the case for the current study from a theoretical perspective; it can demonstrate how the current study may extend or build theory.

Support the exposition of the framework by ideas from other experts, if warranted

At times, it can be useful to describe other theories and concepts that are related to the one being applied. This approach can demonstrate relationships between critical issues in a field. It can also help to situate the theory within a broader knowledge base, which can clarify its role in the current study. It is important to proceed with caution, however, as including too many 'related' ideas can create confusion.

Reiterate the framework

After explaining the framework, it can be important to restate how it will be used in the work, particularly if lengthy or complex analysis of the framework and its uses in the field or discipline is required. This strategy can help the reader best appreciate the particular practical application that is intended for the framework, before preparing to learn about what is next, typically the study methods.

CONCLUSION

Despite being heavily debated, theories and concepts have a crucial role to play in qualitative research. In this chapter, we have defined, compared and exemplified theoretical and conceptual frameworks in order to demystify these two important terms. We have explored the reasons for and against the use of each to show that ultimately, whether and how a researcher chooses to employ a theoretical or conceptual framework requires a strong rationale and explanation of the decision. We have also presented some of the nuts and bolts of finding, developing and using conceptual and theoretical frameworks in order that students can actively apply these theories to practice.

Tips

In some research studies in which a theoretical or conceptual framework ostensibly is employed, it is left, hanging, at the end of the literature review section. It seems as if some researchers just give a perfunctory nod toward including one but then never really do anything with it. If researchers choose to adopt one, the other, both, or neither, they should make these choices clear as well as the ways in which, if any, they have employed them.

Reflective questions

Concept questions

■ What is the difference between a theoretical and conceptual framework?
■ What can a theoretical framework do for a researcher? A conceptual framework?
■ Should one, both or neither be employed in a given study?

Application questions

■ Is a conceptual or theoretical framework (or both) the best approach for your study?
■ How will you identify it/them?
■ Is the framework a natural fit with the topic?
■ Does the framework naturally follow from the literature reviewed?
■ Is it the clearest avenue available for understanding the research question under investigation?
■ Are the assumptions described succinctly and logically so that the framework seems coherent?
■ Does the framework accomplish a clear and distinct purpose in the study?
■ Does the framework seem related to the findings?
■ Does the framework serve to help explain the findings?

Camp, W. G. (2000) Formulating and evaluating theoretical frameworks for career and technical education research. *Journal of Vocational Education Research*, 26 (1), 4–25.

Camp's article is one of the best we have found on using theoretical frameworks in qualitative research. It provides solid information of what theory is and what it means in different traditions.

Leshem, S. and Trafford, V. (2007) Overlooking the conceptual framework. *Innovations in Education and Teaching International*, 44 (1), 93–105.

Leshem and Trafford's article was particularly influential to us in considering what it means to the field to overlook conceptual frameworks.

Smyth, R. (2004) Exploring the usefulness of a conceptual framework as a research tool: A researcher's reflections. *Issues in Educational Research*, 14 (2), 167–80.

We found Smyth's article to be an engaging one on this topic, particularly in her descriptions about her personal efforts in grappling with a conceptual framework; she provides a strong example of her own framework (that we would suggest is a theoretical rather than conceptual frame).

Key resources

Choosing a research approach

PART FOUR

Chapter 10

Case study

INTRODUCTION

During the last few decades, **case** studies have been the approach of choice for a growing number of qualitative researchers. The growth of interest in and use of this approach in large part is due to the flexibility of case studies and what they offer research by way of framing in-depth examinations of a subject of the study. With the rapid rise in the use of case study approaches by qualitative researchers, however, there has been attending imprecision in the literature about what a case study is and how one might be carried out. We begin this chapter by exploring early definitions of case study and then we introduce more recent conceptualizations. We offer information about when a case study might be a good choice, highlighting advantages and disadvantages of the approach. We move to providing information necessary for designing a case study. In the latter section of the chapter, we identify some practical issues involved in its use and provide an example of case study research.

Case
The bounded case

ORIGINS OF CASE STUDY RESEARCH

Many scholars (for example, Healy 1947) trace the origins of case study approaches to Le Play, a French sociologist and economist who, in 1829, used case study in his statistical work in examining the economic conditions of the working class, particularly family budgets (Le Play 1879). In Le Play's work, clear post-positive origins of case study research are evident. Case study research also may be traced to the works of the early American pragmatists and the Chicago School interactionists in the early 1900s. Case study was introduced into the field of education by education scholars Yin (1984) and Stake (1995), the latter of whom also used case study in educational evaluation. Both approached case study from a pragmatic position, asserting the importance of subjective creation of meaning, whilst not outright rejecting some acceptance of objectivity. By the late 1990s, the approach had gained further ground, with Creswell (1998) and Merriam (1988; 2009) both identifying case study as one of the primary research traditions employed in qualitative research, especially in professional fields such as education and health (Merriam 1988).

DESCRIPTION AND PURPOSE OF CASE STUDY

There is a decided lack of clarity in the literature about what a case study is, due in part to imprecision in terminology and in part to disagreements by scholars. One view is that the term case study simply means the way in which the case is delimited (Stake 2005). The second view is that a case study is a specific approach to research, as indicated by several scholars such as Creswell (2007). A third is that a case study is the final product or narrative of a qualitative study. The difference in perspectives matters because they influence the ways in which a researcher goes about conducting a study. If, for example, researchers define case study simply as a case, they risk minimizing conflating qualitative research and case study research and so might not attend to the differences between case studies and more extensive/broader forms of qualitative research. If on the other hand researchers characterize it as a method in its own right, they could misjudge the importance of pairing it with a specific research approach and end up making imprudent methodological decisions and resulting poor research. Similarly, if they frame it as simply a form of reporting, they risk missing the importance of bounding a case and selecting sound methods necessary for carrying out the study. We offer a fourth alternative to this polarizing debate, which is that a case study is none of these three extremes but rather it is all of them.

Case study method
The approach to data collection and analysis

Case narrative
The written description of the case

We believe this perspective is critical; researchers need to understand the three views and how they work together in order to be able to do case studies well. In short, researchers must understand the concepts of the case, **case study methods** (and how they differ from other qualitative methods) and the **case narrative**. Indeed, all of these are necessary for doing a case study well:

> Case studies are not easy to do (some of our best friends are presently trapped inside case studies, trying to get out. Almost none will escape unscathed).
>
> (Adelman *et al.* 1980: 52)

Case study as 'the case'

When some researchers refer to a 'case study', what they actually mean is what exactly they intend to study. A 'case' for them, then, is a particular situation or instance that the researchers will investigate, such as a school, doctor's surgery or shopping mall. Adelman *et al.* (1980: 48) describe case study as: 'an umbrella term for a family of research methods having in common the decision to focus on enquiry around an instance', with the 'instance' being the 'case'. The 'case' that is selected is what defines a relationship between parts of systems and wholes. Adelman *et al.* suggest that:

> Case study research always involves 'the study of an instance in action.' Yet lying behind the concept 'instance' lurk problems concerning the relationship of the 'instance' to the 'class' from which it is drawn.
>
> (Adelman *et al.* 1980: 49)

A case could also be an individual, such as a professional or a single child. Put more simply, case study is essentially about where to draw the boundaries around a study – 'what is the case?' and 'what is it a case of?'. In this conception of case study research, the case is deemed to be necessarily bounded. It is easy to assume that constructing boundaries around a case is a fairly straightforward process. However, it has become increasingly acknowledged in the case study literature that boundaries cannot easily be predicted or managed because case study research moves between the general and the particular. Yet there are some suggestions about how to bind a case, for example by time and place (Creswell 2003), time and activity (Stake 1978) and by definition and context.

Qualitative research and case studies are not synonymous. Rather, the line that marks the barrier between what is a case study and what is not is crossed at the point where intensive studies of cases are not possible. That is, it is no longer a case study when there are simply too many extant cases for intensive study. In this way, then, the line between what is a case study and what is not is highly permeable (Sandelowski *et al.* 2011).

Tips

Case study as research approach

Some researchers consider a case study to be an approach to research rather than simply the way that researchers delimit their studies. Such researchers suggest that it is a unique form of qualitative research. Indeed, Creswell (1998) designates case study as a unique research approach when he juxtaposed it with biography, ethnography, phenomenology, and grounded theory. It is less than clear how these researchers position case study methodologically. Yin (1994: 13), for example, simply suggests that 'A case study is an empirical inquiry that investigates a contemporary phenomenon within its real-life context, especially when the boundaries between phenomenology and context are not clearly evident'.

While case study researchers may use qualitative data, quantitative data or both, for the purposes of this chapter we are using 'case study' as a term to mean case study that draws upon qualitative data.

Case study as the written manuscript

Some researchers use the term 'case study' to describe the written product of a qualitative study, regardless of the research approach. Wolcott (1992: 36) suggests that the case study is 'an end-product of field-oriented research'. The case study report typically contains a description of the following:

- the nature of the case itself
- the historical background of the case
- the physical setting in which the case is bounded
- other important contexts, such as economic, political and legal ones that influence the cases
- other cases through which the case may be recognized
- the informants through whom the case may be known (Stake 2002).

Case study as a combination of the case, the research approach and the research report

When doing a qualitative case study, all three of the aspects we have described are critical components of the whole and so a researcher must attend to all of them. With a case study, there is a case, a case study approach (drawing upon other research approaches) and a case presentation. These necessarily work together in a coherent fashion in case study research. Thus, as we see it, a 'case study' is an approach to research that focuses on a specific 'case'. It employs 'case study research methods' that draw upon other research approaches. When cast as case studies, the other approaches are generally more holistic, particularistic, contextual, descriptive and concrete (a process that we describe later in this chapter) than they would be when applied to more extensive (rather than intensive) study of a given phenomena. All of this is then documented in a contextualized 'case report'.

Characteristics of case studies

Merriam (1988) and Yin (1994) outline a number of essential features of a case study that support our characterization of case studies. A case study tends to be *bounded*, which means that it is focused and intensive as well as narrow in scope. It also means that the case has clear boundaries or limiters. If a case is bounded, then there should be a finite number of people who might be interviewed, a finite number of documents to be reviewed or a finite number of observations that might be made. If the capacity for data collection seems unlimited, most researchers would consider the study to not qualify as a case study; again this is where the distinction between what is and what is not a case study happens. A case study also is *holistic*, meaning that it seeks to describe the whole of the case as well as the relationships of the parts to the case. A case study is *particularistic*, in that it focuses on the specific rather than the general. It is *contextual*, in that it is necessary to give an accounting of the context whether historical, political, cultural or other, in order to understand the case. It is *concrete* in descriptions in order to convey meaning about the case to the reader.

TYPES OF CASE STUDY RESEARCH

A number of researchers have described a range of 'types' of case study (for example Eisenhardt 1989; Merriam 1988; Stake 2005; Yin 1993). We believe that the types they identify may be classified by purpose, discipline and research approach, as we describe in Table 10.1, and see them, then, as different choices that case study researchers face during the selection process, and we describe this view after we present the types found in the literature about case studies.

Types by purpose

Six different types of case study that appear in the literature highlight choices related to the purpose of the study. The types that often appear in the literature are exploration, description, instrumentation (in this instance for refining theory), interpretation, explanation and evaluation.

Exploratory case study (Yin)

In these studies, researchers undertake exploratory fieldwork and data collection before deciding upon and defining research questions. This type of case study may be done simply for exploration or it may be done as an early phase of a larger study (the latter is sometimes referred to as

Table 10.1 Choice and options in case study research

Choice	Options
Purpose	Exploratory Descriptive Instrumental Interpretive Explanatory Evaluative
Disciplinary norms	Anthropologic/ethnographic Historical Psychological Sociological Educational
Research approach	Pragmatic qualitative research Grounded theory Ethnography Phenomenology Narrative Action research

pilot case study). Exploration is important when the researcher initially recognizes the difficulties of case selection. Such difficulties may be addressed by then exploring the population in order to select the best cases that will yield the most useful data. This type of case study enables recognition of complexity of cases before data collection. The disadvantage of this type is that mistakes made in earlier fieldwork may compromise later data collection.

Descriptive case study (Yin)

The descriptive case study involves a detailed account of the subject of study. There is some disagreement about the role of theory in this type of case study. Merriam (1988) suggests that descriptive case studies do not use theory to guide the research or interpretations but rather stop at description. However, we find that some researchers doing descriptive case studies choose to rely upon a theoretical framework to guide their descriptions. This type of case study lends itself to detailed and rich description of the context and case, but may lack appropriate theoretical grounding.

Instrumental case study (Stake)

This type of case study allows researchers to refine a theory about a given instance. The case is then used to support the researcher's understanding and the exploration of the case is used to improve the understanding of the case. For example, Becker *et al.* (1977) studied the student culture in medical schools to confirm and improve their understanding of this culture. The advantage of this type of case study is that it helps to confirm theories and ideas, while the disadvantage is that seeking confirmation of a theory can result in unquestioned assumptions about it.

Interpretive case study (Merriam)

Interpretive case study seeks to develop conceptual categories or theories. This type of case study moves past description to the translation of key concepts and the development of theories about the subject under investigation. It differs from the instrumental purpose in that it does not simply seek to refine existing theories but instead seeks first-hand construction of theory, so it is a matter of degree. This type of case study requires data gathering for the explicit function of theorizing and it presents findings in depth and with thick description. Interpretative case study fits well with the philosophical positions of many qualitative researchers and allows for interpretation of meaning; moreover, it allows researchers to strive to develop theory. However, the goal of interpretation can lead researchers to overgeneralize about findings and interpretations.

Explanatory case study (Yin)

Researchers use this type of case study when they want to explain something or to find a cause-and-effect relationship. Some scholars believe that qualitative research cannot determine cause-and-effect relationships but Yin suggests that they can. This type of case study aims to make explicit a problem or pattern of difficulties that is recurrent and in the main relates to a given context. In some studies, pattern matching is used in order to make sense of complex cases and situations; when pattern matching is used, patterns are located and organized into pattern languages. In the original work by Alexander (Alexander 1979; Alexander *et al.* 1977), he argues that patterns can be seen as normative. Yet we would suggest this view is misplaced, since people are always located in contexts that have at their heart issues of structure, power, agency and control, which will affect and change environments and patterns. This type of case study can help a researcher to make sense of complex cases, although it can lead to researchers ignoring context.

Evaluative case study (Yin)

Researchers use this type of case study when they want to move beyond description to judging the merit or worth of a case. This type of case study is often used in organizations, including educational and health-related organizations. The advantage of this type of case study is that it can help to explain real-life interventions that are too complex for survey research. The disadvantage is that it assumes a cause-and-effect relationship that can be explained, where none may exist.

Types by discipline

Case studies also are classified at times along the lines of disciplinary norms. Both Merriam and Stenhouse describe several different disciplinary case study types, which in our view highlight the choices that researchers face regarding disciplinary norms that they will follow.

Anthropologic case study (Merriam)

This disciplinary case study is more than an intensive, holistic description and analysis of a social unit or phenomenon. It is a sociocultural analysis and interpretation of the unit of study. Such a case study could, for example, focus on the culture of a given organization or institution. This type of case study provides an in-depth examination of one cultural setting. The disadvantage is that it can be too narrow and insufficiently explanatory.

Historical case study (Merriam)

This type of case study presents a holistic description and analysis of a specific case from a historical perspective. It relies upon historiographical methods and heavily on primary source material. Historical case study has tended to describe institutions, programmes and practices as they have evolved over time. This type of case study takes context into account effectively but it can tend toward excessive description.

Psychological case study (Merriam)

This type of case study requires focus on an individual as a way to investigate some aspect(s) of human behaviour. It relies upon concepts and theories from psychology to guide the research. This type provides in-depth data of one person that may be applicable to others (see for example Freud's self-analysis in the 1890s) but sometimes it can be difficult to generalize from one human case.

Sociological case study (Merriam)

This type of case study attends to the constructs of society and socialization in studying phenomena. It draws upon sociological theory and methods. This approach heightens awareness of the effect of social structures in a case, although it requires sound sociological understanding that may be beyond the expertise of the researcher.

Educational case study (Stenhouse and others)

This type of case study emerged from the work of researchers such as Stenhouse (1988), Adelman *et al.* (1980) and Simons (1980), who undertook case study research in schools in the 1970s. Much of their work focused on the biographies of those involved in the case study of the school. These forms of case study are often strongly based in narrative whilst often crossing the border into evaluation. This approach has been used to help to develop educational theory and understanding, although sometimes at the expense of ignoring social theory and evaluative judgment.

Types by research approach

This third classification of case study by method often is overlooked in texts about qualitative research, even though an examination of published studies yields evidence of ethnographic case study, phenomenological case study and the like. We believe this omission is in part due to the fact that many researchers have started to view case study as a methodology in its own right, a notion with which we disagree. When researchers consider case study as an approach, we believe they pair it, whether intentionally or unintentionally, with one of the research approaches we describe in this section of the book.

We argue that case study researchers most often adopt methods from pragmatic qualitative research (see Chapter 11), grounded theory (see Chapter 12), ethnography (see Chapter 13), phenomenology (see Chapter 14), narrative inquiry (see Chapter 15), and action research (see Chapter 16). There are also fewer instances of collaborative case studies (see Chapter 17), evaluative case studies (see Chapter 18) and arts-based case studies (see Chapter 19).

We demonstrate these choices in Table 10.2, p. 158, which also references the chapters where additional information about the methods may be found.

When a case study is blended with one of these methods it creates an altered and synergistic version of the approach, making the approach, for example, more holistic, particularistic, contextual, descriptive and concrete. An overview of case study types is given in Table 10.3, p. 159.

Table 10.2 Case study research approaches

Approach / Disciplinary origins*	Common research paradigms (Chapters 2 and 4)	Common phenomenon of interest (Chapter 6)	Common data collection methods (Chapters 23–26)	Common analytical strategies (Chapters 27 and 28)
Pragmatic qualitative research (Chapter 11)				
Professional fields	Pragmatism	Individuals Structures Processes	Interviews Documents Observation	Constant comparison Keyword analysis or Thematic analysis
Grounded theory (Chapter 12)				
Sociology	Pragmatism; Post-modernism; Post-structuralism Constructivism	Concepts Structures Processes	Interviews Observation Documents	Constant comparison
Ethnography (Chapter 13)				
Anthropology	Post-positivism Critical theory Pragmatism Post-structuralism Constructionism Constructivism	Groups	Interviews Observation Documents	Ethnographic analysis Ethnographic content analysis
Phenomenology (Chapter 14)				
Philosophy	Phenomenology Constructivism	Concepts	Interviews Observation Documents	Phenomenological analysis Interpretive phenomeno-logical analysis
Narrative approaches (Chapter 15)				
Humanities (history and literary criticism) and sociology	Critical social theory Pragmatism Post-structuralism Constructionism Constructivism	Individuals Groups	Interviews Documents	Thematic analysis Narrative analysis Discourse analysis Semiotic analysis
Action research (Chapter 16)				
Psychology; education	Post-positivism Critical social theory Pragmatism Post-modernism Post-structuralism Constructionism Constructivism	Structures Processes	Interviews Observation Documents	Thematic analysis
Collaborative approaches (Chapter 17)				
Psychology; education	Critical social theory Social constructionism Constructivism	Structures Processes	Interviews Observation Documents	Content analysis Thematic analysis Interpretive interactionism
Evaluation (Chapter 18)				
Education	Post-positivism Pragmatism	Structures Processes	Interviews Observation Documents	Content analysis Thematic analysis Interpretive interactionism
Arts-based approaches (Chapter 19)				
Arts and humanities	Critical Social constructionism	Cultural artefacts and individuals	Interviews Observation Documents	Content analysis Thematic analysis Interpretive interactionism

* See chapter associated with specific approach.

Table 10.3 An overview of the different case study types

Type	Focus	Key features
Exploratory (Yin)	To gain initial insight into a subject not well understood (contextual)	Undertakes fieldwork and data collection prior to definition of the research questions and hypotheses. Seeks to gain initial insight into a subject not well understood (contextual).
Descriptive (Yin)	To present a detailed account of the subject of study (contextual)	Focuses on background information. Typically does not require being guided by hypotheses or developing them. Presents a detailed account of the subject of study (contextual).
Instrumental (Stake)	To gain understanding that can help to confirm or refine an existing theory	Refines a theory about a given instance. The case is then used to support the researcher's understanding and the exploration of the case, helping to confirm or refine an existing theory.
Interpretive (Merriam)	To analyze, interpret or theorize (generative)	Moves beyond description to developing a set of concepts or theories that can help to explain.
Explanatory (Yin)	To clarify relationships between variables (explanatory)	Explains reasons for or associations between what exists.
Evaluative (Yin)	To judge the merits or worth of the subject of study (evaluative)	Moves beyond description to judgement.
Anthropological/ ethnographic (Merriam)	To understand and describe the everyday life of cultural groups	Seeks to provide a real appraisal of everyday life of given cultural group. Analyzes and interprets the unit of study socioculturally.
Historical (Merriam)	To use primary materials to create a chronological account of an event	Uses primary materials to create a chronological account of an event. Examines and analyzes a historical case with the benefit of hindsight.
Psychological (Merriam)	To employ theories and techniques from psychology to explore problems	Focuses on investigation of aspects of human behaviour using psychological concepts and ideas.
Sociological (Merriam)	To employ theories from sociology to explore constructs of society	Examines constructs of society and socialization and seeks to describe and understand social context.
Educational (Stenhouse)	To employ theories from a range of fields in investigating educational programmes and practices	Focuses on understanding educational action and their impact on students, teachers and institutions.
Pragmatic qualitative research	In-depth descriptive examination of individual experiences	Attempts to cull general information through interviews and other data collection approaches.
Grounded theory	Development of theory about the case	Gathers information from a range of sources, from prior literature to interviews and observations; relies upon field notes. Seeks to develop theory.
Ethnography	Deep description of group experiences	Seeks to gather information through prolonged exposure in the field. Deep description of group experiences.
Phenomenology	Understanding of the concept or phenomenon under study	Seeks to gather information through a process of considering researcher and participant perceptions.
Narrative	Holistic examination of individuals' lived experiences	Seeks to gather data from interviews and documents to tell the stories of individuals.
Action research	To improve an environment	Seeks to gather data including documents, interviews and focus groups, for the purpose of improvement.

DESIGNING AND DOING CASE STUDY

Identifying the 'case'

The design phase for undertaking a case study involves the following processes:

- defining the case
- bounding the case
- deciding whether to use single or multiple cases.

Defining the case

Defining the case is refining the research questions, problem or activity that is the object of study, so that the researcher has made some clear decisions about what is to be studied and how such a study should be undertaken (see Chapters 6 and 7).

Bounding the case

Bounding the case is defining what constitutes the boundaries of the case, such as whether it is a project, school or programme. For example, researchers may want to study schools located in geographical areas of poverty; they will need to identify the type of school, the geographical areas and the definition of poverty (see Chapter 6).

Deciding whether to use single or multiple cases

Single cases offer the opportunity to provide a more in-depth analysis of the case and can explore unique/extreme, typical or longitudinal cases more effectively, most often from a single site. Multiple cases offer the opportunity to replicate the study and can be perceived as offering stronger evidence in support of the findings, often from multiple sites. Multiple case study designs are expected to be able to demonstrate similarities, rather than be a collection of unconnected cases. Thus, if no similar cases are discovered, the researcher must either widen the multiple design or adopt a single-case approach. Yin (1994) asserted that case study results must be applicable to a theory, rather than a specific population. An example of a collective study about universities is illustrated in Table 10.4.

Table 10.4 Collective case study of universities

Types	Public	Private
Size	Up to 20,000 students	Over 20,000 students
Location	Urban	Rural
Dominant disciplines	Science	Arts

Selecting what is to be studied within the case

This involves assessing how and from where participants will be selected, according to the type of case study being used. For example, an ethnographic study may study one school (a case) over a long period of time, whereas a narrative case study may access stories of poverty across several schools (see next section).

Choosing the research approach

While most authors view the individual case study types as distinctive and the ways of categorizing them as separate, as we have argued, we view the three 'different' categories (purpose, discipline and approach) as critically and inseparably interrelated. As we see it, a researcher should consider not only the purpose of the case study but also how it will be situated within a disciplinary context, as well as what research approach will be employed.

Thus, when conducting a case study, researchers choose a purpose, a disciplinary norm and a research approach. We provide an example of this interrelation as a process of choosing among options at three different levels as illustrated in Figure 10.1.

Case study researchers will want to ensure that they have a clear purpose in mind and identify a clear disciplinary perspective. Moreover, they will want to make a sound choice of research approaches that will best enable them to answer their research questions (see Chapters 6 and 7). Selecting from the various approaches can allow researchers to take many different paths. A researcher might for example undertake an exploratory sociological study with a grounded theory research approach. Another might undertake a description of an educational institution using pragmatic qualitative approach. In Figure 10.2 we demonstrate how these various aspects could be linked together to design a case study.

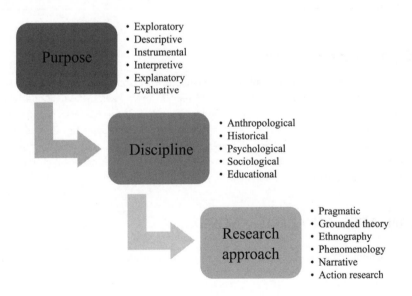

Figure 10.1 Case study research approach

Greg is a PhD candidate in the field of educational research. Greg decided that he wanted to do a life history of a kidnapping survivor. Thus, Greg's intent was to be descriptive and to provide a historical and chronological history of M. He will use life-history research methods, relying heavily on sources such as in-depth interviewing and the author's personal letters and diaries. If he pursues this path, his case study design will look something like this:

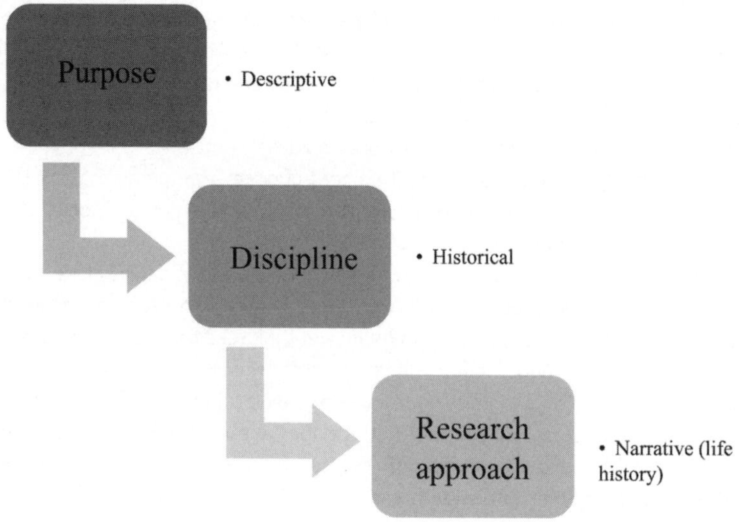

Figure 10.2 An example of a case study design

Writing the case narrative

Researchers use many writing conventions (see Chapter 31) when deciding how to write up a case study. They also use a variety of formats to report their research (see Chapter 32). The forms and formats they often use are influenced by research philosophical stance and the norms of the research approach chosen. What is consistent across these reports, however, is that there typically is a 'case narrative' or a description of the case itself and how it is bounded. In the example on page 163, Harris and Hartley provide a narrative of their case, which they refer to as a 'witch hunting process' that happened at a single university site.

ADVANTAGES AND CHALLENGES

There are several advantages as well as challenges to case study research, as we indicate in this section.

Advantages of case study research

Case study research has a number of distinct advantages, making it an appealing choice for many researchers.

CASE NARRATIVE

(Harris and Hartley 2011)

The case presented here describes a witch hunt at Crucible University, a small, private faith-based college. The crisis came to a head after it was learned that Crucible's president agreed to an alteration in the grade point average of a star athlete, which allowed him to continue to play. This action spurred a subsequent confrontation by a group of influential senior faculty members who were deeply concerned about this precedent and its effect on academic integrity.

A deeper examination of events, however, reveals that the incident exposed long-standing tensions that had developed at the institution regarding its future direction. The case describes the formation and details the responses of two influential ideological camps, both of which sought to root out the cause of the institution's ill fortune by demonizing and neutralizing the other. Each group was influenced by a larger organizational culture, one that valued the faith-based mission of the institution and its claim to uphold and advance the highest standards of ethical behaviour. However, the two factions came to very different opinions about how to best accomplish this and advance the interests of the institution moving forward. The resulting escalation demonstrates how poisonous invective and rigid dogmatism can damage even the most well-meaning academic community.

Crucible came to our attention when a colleague who worked at the institution happened to relate some of the details of the impending crisis to one of us (Harris). Neither of us had any prior relationship with the university. While our contact was of great help assisting us negotiate access with administrators and faculty leaders, he was not a key player in the events. Initially, our intent was to create a brief case that might be used for instructional purposes. We quickly became convinced, however, that we had uncovered what Patton (1990: 169) describes as an 'information-rich' case.

Example

It is flexible

Case study is flexible. Researchers employing a case study may have a number of different research goals, such as description or evaluation. They also may approach the study from a range of different philosophical positions, such as constructivism or interpretivism. Moreover, case study tends to draw from a range of research approaches, such as ethnography or grounded theory.

It allows for depth of investigation

Case study emphasizes detailed contextual analysis of a limited number of events or conditions and their relationships. Merriam (1988) suggests that this makes them particularistic, meaning that they focus on a particular phenomenon. A case study may be used to document multiple perspectives, while also acknowledging and presenting diverse points of view, which Merriam suggests makes them holistic.

It is thorough

One of the advantages cited for case study research is its uniqueness, its capacity for understanding complexity in particular contexts (Simons 1996: 225). A key strength of the case study method involves using multiple sources and techniques in the data gathering process (as exemplified by Stake 1995). The researcher determines in advance what evidence to gather and what analysis techniques to use with the data to answer the research questions. Evidence may include observation, interview and negotiation. The case study format allows for presentation with rich, thick description.

It is responsive

Case study can be flexible, responsive and not necessarily time and approach dependent. Case study can be used to notice, describe and document the processes of change as they occur and unfold. It is particularly useful for providing solutions to problems.

It has wide appeal

Case study can be written in a variety of ways and used for a variety of audiences. The use of narrative reporting tends to be widely accessible. As Merriam (1988) suggests, case study is heuristic, meaning that it illuminates readers' understanding about the subject of study. Thus, through reading another's case study a researcher can see what counts as best practice or see what to do or avoid in a similar situation.

The challenges of case study research

There have been many criticisms of case study research and, whilst we would not agree with all of them, we acknowledge that challenges with the approach exist. Walker (1983) suggested three concerns of doing case study, in terms that it:

- can be viewed as an invasive intrusion in subjects' lives
- can lead to a simplistic and incorrect world view, and
- is an approach through which it is possible to harm those who are constantly changing practices.

We add the following concerns to this list:

- dependence on a single case
- the boundedness of a case
- the eclectic nature of case study.

Dependence on a single case

The focus on the particular and the use of intrinsic case study are seen by some researchers as being too narrow. However, authors such as Stake have argued that this dependence on a single case is important for theory building. When adopting case study of whatever type, it must be remembered that initial planning is important, in order to ensure that the correct single or multiple case(s) are selected, so that research objectives are met and the study is successful.

If multiple cases are selected, Hamel *et al.* (1993) contended that researchers must not fall into the trap of considering their research to be a macroscopic study, since even if as many as 100 cases are used, they should all have been selected on the basis of similarities.

The boundedness of a case

One of the difficulties with case study research is the question of the 'bounded' case. The boundaries of the case in some forms of case study are seen as relatively straightforward. Stake, for example, suggested that it is possible to recognize features that make some 'a case'. He argues that both boundedness and behaviour patterns are central to understanding the case. However, it has become increasingly acknowledged that boundaries cannot always easily be predicted or managed. This is because case study research moves between the general and the particular.

The eclectic nature of case study

Case study is in the main not seen as a specific approach and therefore case study cannot be located on a methodological spectrum. This can be problematic, since mixing diverse approaches within the context of a case study can result in a messy incoherent research project. As case study is seen as eclectic, it draws from a wide range of approaches.

Flyvbjerg addresses some of the concerns of case study research by identifying several misconceptions about them and refuting them.

Professor Bent Flyvbjerg, University of Oxford, UK

Five misunderstandings about case study research, corrected

Bent Flyvbjerg is author of *Making social science matter: Why social inquiry fails and how it can succeed again*, which explains the importance of the 'power of example' and of narrative, that is, of case study research, to the health and impact of social science in the academy and society.

The following five misunderstandings about the case study systematically undermine the credibility and use of the method. The five misunderstandings constitute the conventional view, or orthodoxy, of the case study. As can be seen, theory, reliability, and validity are at issue: in other words, the very status of the case study as a research method. The five misunderstandings are corrected one by one in order to clear the ground for a use of case study research in the social sciences that is based on understanding instead of misunderstanding.

Misunderstanding no. 1: General theoretical knowledge is more valuable than concrete case knowledge.

Correction no. 1: Predictive theories and universals cannot be found in the study of human affairs. Concrete case knowledge is therefore more valuable than the vain search for predictive theories and universals.

continued

Misunderstanding no. 2: One cannot generalize on the basis of an individual case; therefore, the case study cannot contribute to scientific development.

Correction no. 2: One can often generalize on the basis of a single case and the case study may be central to scientific development via generalization as supplement or alternative to other methods. But formal generalization is overvalued as a source of scientific development, whereas 'the force of example' and transferability are underestimated.

Misunderstanding no. 3: The case study is most useful for generating hypotheses, that is, in the first stage of a total research process, while other methods are more suitable for hypotheses testing and theory building.

Correction no. 3: The case study is useful for both generating and testing of hypotheses but is not limited to these research activities alone.

Misunderstanding no. 4: The case study contains a bias toward verification: that is, a tendency to confirm the researcher's preconceived notions.

Correction no. 4: The case study contains no greater bias toward verification of the researcher's preconceived notions than other methods of inquiry. On the contrary, experience indicates that the case study contains a greater bias toward falsification of preconceived notions than toward verification.

Misunderstanding no. 5: It is often difficult to summarize and develop general propositions and theories on the basis of specific case studies.

Correction no. 5: It is correct that summarizing case studies is often difficult, especially as concerns case process. It is less correct as regards case outcomes. The problems in summarizing case studies, however, are due more often to the properties of the reality studied than to the case study as a research method. Often, it is not desirable to summarize and generalize case studies. Good studies should be read as narratives in their entirety.

Read more in:

Flyvbjerg, B. (2006) Five misunderstandings about case study research. *Qualitative Inquiry*, 12 (2), 219–45.

Flyvbjerg, B. (2001) *Making social science matter: Why social inquiry fails and how it can succeed again*, Cambridge, UK: Cambridge University Press.

EXAMPLE OF A CASE STUDY

In the following researcher reflection, Sue Anthony describes her work with case studies.

Sue Anthony, Western University, Ontario, Canada

Having explored the historic use of case study in an integrative review (see Anthony and Jack 2009), I chose case study methodology as the research approach in my doctoral dissertation to explore the phenomenon of nurse educators' experience with interprofessional education in the real-life context (Yin 2009) of academia. Choosing a multiple case design was deliberate so as to enhance robustness of the study findings. A hallmark of case study methodology is generation of data from multiple sources. This feature brought richness, breadth, and depth to individual and cross-case analyses. Embarking on case study research requires a significant time commitment. However, this worthwhile and rewarding research approach results in significant, robust, and relevant outcomes. My dissertation is described below in the following text.

Nursing is a primary partner on the interprofessional team, yet there is minimal empirical evidence of nurse educators as architects of interprofessional education. Feminist post-structuralism (FPS) guided an exploration of nursing's engagement in interprofessional education (IPE) using Yin's (2009) case study methodology. A multiple case design investigated the following research questions: what are the antecedents of nursing's engagement in IPE; how are nurse educators/nursing faculty engaged in IPE; how does gender impact nursing's involvement in IPE development and implementation; and how is nursing's IPE engagement impacted by contextual factors (such as social, political, historic) inherent in the broader health professional and academic contexts? Nine propositions guided the study, including: interprofessional education has not made its way into the mainstream of baccalaureate nursing curriculum; faculty may not be knowledgeable about or have opportunities to engage in IPE; historically, the nursing profession has struggled to establish itself as an autonomous and independent discipline; nursing's relationship with medicine has evolved from a history grounded in patriarchy, dominance and conceptualized as 'power over' (Falk Rafael 1996); increasingly, nursing is simultaneously acknowledging itself and being recognized as an academic discipline, with its own knowledge and power base; IPE will require nursing to work collaboratively and interdependently rather than subjugating its discipline-specific knowledge and power; baccalaureate curriculum development is recorded in committee minutes and represented by course and other academic documents; nursing students' IPE involvement is reported in the literature, yet few nurse scholars are published authors of research on development and implementation of IPE in nursing education; nurse scholars' representation as architects of IPE curriculum development and implementation is minimal.

Three individual cases were bounded by Ontario, English language university sites of four-year baccalaureate nursing programmes, full- and part-time nursing and health

Researcher reflections

continued

professional faculty and time frame June 2008 to June 2009. Data were generated from documents, archival records, individual and focus group interviews, field notes, non-participant observation and a demographic questionnaire. Individual case reports resulted from an editorial style analysis that linked study propositions to research questions and from examination of rival explanations for data-derived emergent themes and patterns. In the cross-case analysis, the research questions were answered and then interpreted through FPS tenets including language, discourse, subjectivity and power. Findings indicate that despite value held for IPE, nursing's IPE engagement is minimal, inconsistent and diverse in the presence of discrepant, uncertain understandings of the term interprofessional. The cross-case analysis outcome speaks principally of nursing's general experience in the academy with IPE engagement seemingly providing the vehicle to convey messages of enduring concern and tension inherent in this experience. Prominent concepts uncovered included: nurse academic, professional subjectivity and professional identity; historic, hegemonic discourses of women, nurse, and nursing's relationship with medicine impact nursing's professional subjectivity such that nurse academics' sense of professional self and professional confidence are viewed as antecedents to nursing's IPE engagement. Consequently, nurse academics must negotiate professional identities as they move between practice and academic roots while navigating historic roots circumscribed by hegemonic discourses of women, nurse and newer discourses surrounding nursing's academic role.

CONCLUSION

Case study research is a research approach that examines the relationship between people and structures, in which they work, live and learn; it acknowledges that the dynamics of interaction must be the starting point for research. A detailed case study can enable the fleshing out or expansion of an existing theory or challenge it, provide a specific new theory from a unique population or answer specific questions posed by diverse stakeholders. Researchers should consider multiple aspects of case study, including purpose, disciplinary perspective and research approaches and give ample time to planning a case study. Doing case study offers the potential to be more traditional in approach or more cutting edge in methodological choices, making this a truly flexible research approach.

Reflective questions

Concept questions

- What is a case study?
- What are the advantages of using case study?
- What are some of the common misunderstandings about case study?

Application questions

- What configuration of a case study would best fit your research?
- How transferrable do you think the findings of a particular case can be?

Simons, H. (2009) *Case study research in practice*, London: Sage.
  This is a comprehensive and accessible text book that explains case study and its different types well.

Merriam, S.B. (1988) *Case study research in education*, San Francisco, CA: Jossey Bass.
  This is one of the most frequently used books on case studies, with good reason. It is an accessible text with plenty of examples.

Stake, R. (2010) *Qualitative research: Studying how things work*, New York: Guilford.
  This text provides more traditional views on case study, especially that cases should be clearly bounded.

Flyvbjerg, B. (2011) Case study research. *In*: N. K. Denzin and Y. S. Lincoln (eds) *The SAGE handbook of qualitative research*. London: Sage.
  This chapter provides an up-to-date and down-to-earth exploration of some of the challenges of using case study approaches.

Chapter 11

Pragmatic qualitative research

INTRODUCTION

Qualitative researchers today draw from a range of research philosophies and adopt a range of approaches to qualitative research, including grounded theory, phenomenology, ethnography, and so forth. There are times during which, however, what the situation calls for is a more practical approach to answering a research question that allows for an eclectic set of methods. Particularly in professional fields, a more **pragmatic** approach to qualitative research may well be best-suited for providing the descriptive information that can inform professional practices. Unfortunately, however, few clear descriptions of this widely used approach exist. In this chapter, we discuss and describe pragmatic qualitative research, an approach that researchers can and should take up when the situation demands it.

Pragmatic
Concerned with practical results

ORIGINS OF PRAGMATIC QUALITATIVE RESEARCH

Pragmatic qualitative research has a long history in this field of inquiry, as it is grounded in the ideas and approaches of the early pragmatists in the 1930s, such as the Chicago School interactionists (see Chapter 2). Initially, those who used the approach took a realist stance (see Chapter 4) and believed in an objective reality that could be (imperfectly) understood, realising that the social world is more subjective than the natural world. Early researchers sought to observe human behaviour and experiences as they occurred in natural settings. As different views of the researcher role and participant views of reality emerged, researchers have adopted a number of views about the nature of reality and knowledge, in response to the ways in which philosophy guides research. Moreover, researchers over time have adopted a range of data collection approaches, such as interviewing, in addition to direct observation. The approach has taken hold particularly in professional fields such as health, business and education, and is now one of the most widely used qualitative approaches in these fields (Sandelowski 2000; Neergaard *et al.* 2009).

DESCRIPTION AND PURPOSE OF PRAGMATIC QUALITATIVE RESEARCH

Growth in the number of qualitative research approaches has led to a seemingly united quest for 'epistemological credibility' (Thorne *et al.* 1997: 170). This quest ultimately has urged some researchers to engage in 'methodological acrobatics' (Sandelowski 2000: 334), where they feel obliged to call their work grounded theory, ethnography, phenomenology or narrative inquiry, when in fact it is not. Often, these studies are in fact pragmatic qualitative research.

Pragmatic qualitative research is just what its name implies: *an approach that draws upon the most sensible and practical methods available in order to answer a given research question.* Researchers using this approach seek 'to discover and understand a phenomenon, a process or the perspectives and worldviews of the people involved' (Merriam 1998: 11). Pragmatic studies 'offer a comprehensive summary of an event' in the everyday terms of those events' (Sandelowski 2000: 336). Rather than having a goal of thick description (such as in ethnography), theory development (grounded theory) or interpretive understanding of experience (phenomenology), pragmatic qualitative research aims for a description of an experience or event as interpreted by the researcher (Neergaard *et al.* 2009).

While pragmatic qualitative research is widely used, it is relatively unacknowledged. This is arguably owing to a reluctance of researchers to 'own up' to adopting a plainer and 'less sexy' method (that is, an important method that fails to capture attention it deserves) coupled with 'tyranny of method' (Sandelowski 2000: 334), in which some designs unfortunately and inappropriately are viewed as lower on the qualitative research design hierarchy of goodness. This kind of posing and posturing (Wolcott 1992), however, has negative implications for the field of qualitative inquiry. It adds, for example, to conflicting and ambiguous terminology and as a result less clear research designs associated with the different research approaches (Neergaard *et al.* 2009). Indeed:

> A confusing state of affairs exists whereby studies are called narrative, even though they may include nothing more than minimally structured, open-ended interviews; phenomenologic, even though they may include nothing more than reports of the 'subjective' experiences of participants; or ethnographic, even though they may including nothing more than participants in different ethnic groups.
>
> (Sandelowski 2000: 334).

Moreover, these trends toward methodological acrobatics have led to a neglect of the many benefits of a more pragmatic approach to qualitative research. Pragmatic qualitative research is important in many professional fields, in which it is employed with great frequency. It is not an easy approach or one to be taken lightly. Indeed, 'there is nothing trivial or easy about getting the facts, and the meanings participants give to those facts, right and then conveying them in a coherent and useful manner' (Sandelowski 2000: 336).

Researchers may take up pragmatic qualitative research when they want to provide a descriptive account from an interpretive perspective and believe that no other research approach (such as grounded theory, ethnography, phenomenology, narrative) presents a better approach for examining a particular research topic and question in the specific setting. Pragmatic qualitative research should be adopted when a researcher desires an eclectic and unique approach to understanding a phenomenon or event.

TYPES OF PRAGMATIC QUALITATIVE RESEARCH

While the approach is so eclectic that it is difficult to identify what is the main approach and what are its variations, there are different perspectives about how to carry out pragmatic qualitative research. Thorne *et al.* (1997), for example, described a new approach in nursing research, 'interpretive description', and suggested that the approach is noncategorical and highly interpretive; interpretive description requires an explication of theoretical influence as well as an analytical framework that situates the interpretation. Sandelowski (2000: 335) responded to Thorne *et al.*'s description with her conception of a '*basic or fundamental* qualitative description' used to describe what she sees as categorical, less interpretive and less abstract research, done for the purpose of providing a descriptive summary of the data. As she sees it, researchers do not move as far from or into their data, nor do they require a conceptual or abstract rendering of the data. Another qualitative scholar in the field of education, Merriam (1998), used the term 'basic' or 'generic qualitative approach' to apply to some studies in education that took a pragmatic approach to research. She suggests that these studies draw from concepts, models and theories, most often from education, psychology or sociology. Although she indicates the application of a theoretical framework and results that appear in the form of patterns, categories or factors, her explanation of the approach seems to argue for a more descriptive and low-inference approach. Our view of pragmatic qualitative research, as we have described it in this chapter, falls somewhere between the non-categorical purely interpretive approach described by Thorne *et al.* and the categorical purely descriptive approach described by Merriam and Sandelowski. We illustrate the forms along an objective to subjective continuum in the following Figure 11.1.

Pragmatic qualitative research, as we see it, marks the meeting point of description and interpretation, in which description involves presentation of facts, feelings and experiences in the everyday language of participants, as interpreted by the researcher. However, researchers may choose to adopt a more objective or more subjective approach than we have described in this chapter.

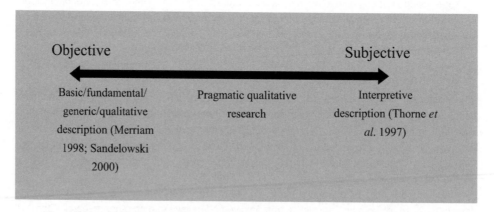

Figure 11.1 The objective–subjective continuum of pragmatic qualitative research

DESIGNING AND DOING PRAGMATIC QUALITATIVE RESEARCH

By the very nature of the approach, there is no one right way to do a pragmatic qualitative research study. Caelli *et al.* suggest, however, that pragmatic qualitative research studies:

> exhibit some or all of the characteristics of qualitative endeavor but rather than focusing the study through the lens of a known methodology they seek to do one of two things: either they combine several methodologies or approaches, or claim no particular methodological viewpoint at all. Generally, the focus of the study is on understanding an experience or an event . . .
>
> (Caelli *et al.* 2003: 2)

While many researchers have used pragmatic qualitative research, then, documented guidelines for this approach are lacking in the literature. It is critical, however, for those using pragmatic qualitative research to ensure that their research is methodologically sound and their practices rigorous.

When using pragmatic qualitative research, the researcher faces essential choices about philosophical and personal position, framing the study, collecting data, working with data and writing about the results. In the next few paragraphs, we provide an overview of the choices researchers who use pragmatic qualitative research often make. We follow this description by a summary of these common choices in Table 11.1 on page 177. This table provides links to other parts and chapters in this book where we provide fuller descriptions and practical advice for doing qualitative research.

Philosophical and personal positioning

Several of the scholars who describe pragmatic qualitative research consider it to be 'a-paradigmatic' (for example, Merriam 1998) (see Chapter 4). We believe, however, that researchers who adopt this approach, consciously or unconsciously, align with a pragmatic philosophical paradigm. They adopt general beliefs of naturalists/pragmatists, such as an open orientation to what they are studying, and strive for unobtrusive observation in a natural setting. They also, like pragmatists, fall somewhere between realists and idealists and typically take up a situational or blended-philosophies orientation, (in which they describe how pragmatism and their theoretical frameworks work together and thus guide the research process; Rawnsley 1998; King 1995; Guba and Lincoln 1994; Harding 1987).

Pragmatism and *pragmatic qualitative research* are not synonymous. Pragmatism is a philosophy (see Chapters 2 and 4) and pragmatic qualitative research is a specific research approach. A researcher who chooses to use pragmatic qualitative research as an approach may well take up pragmatism as a paradigm, as it is a flexible perspective. Researchers who adopt pragmatism as a philosophical paradigm, however, also choose a range of other research approaches, such as grounded theory, ethnography, narrative research and action research.

Tips

Focus of the study (see Part 3)

As we explain in Chapter 6, there are many different phenomena of investigation from which researchers may choose when undertaking a qualitative study. Many of these kinds of questions, in their very articulation, suggest a particular research approach. Pragmatic qualitative researchers have chosen many different phenomena of interest (see Chapter 6), including for example individuals, structures and processes (the latter of which includes actions and events). In framing a study, researchers seek to demonstrate congruence between the phenomenon and research questions (see Chapter 7) and pragmatic research. Caelli *et al.* (2003) also argue that researchers who employ pragmatic qualitative research should make their disciplinary affiliations clear, identify what led them to the research question and articulate assumptions they have made about the topic. Pragmatic qualitative researchers also tend to produce and describe literature reviews comprehensively (see Chapter 8). Literature reviews, then, typically include quantitative as well as qualitative studies. Researchers at times adopt theoretical frameworks (see Chapter 9) to guide the development of the research design, but they do not always use them to frame interpretation of data (Merriam 1998).

Research approach (see Part 4)

There is no one pragmatic research design that serves as a map for guiding a study. Rather, researchers take an eclectic approach to the research, depending on what is most beneficial to the study. They draw upon a range of other methods to complement pragmatic research, which some researchers have described as having a 'cast', or overtone. Thus, those using pragmatic qualitative research may choose to conduct their studies so that they have a grounded theory, phenomenological, ethnographic, narrative, or other casts.

Tips

Blending is common in several qualitative research approaches: Charmaz (1990) for example, described grounded theory studies as having a 'phenomenological cast' and Sandelowski *et al.* (1992) described their grounded theory work as having a 'phenomenological and narrative cast'.

See Chapters 10 and 12–19 for descriptions of other research approaches that may be used to support pragmatic qualitative research. Some researchers who use mixed methods take up pragmatic qualitative research when carrying out the qualitative part of their research, as does Cooper, who provides a researcher reflection on page 179.

Data collection (see Part 5)

When researchers have not relied on one of the traditional qualitative approaches (such as ethnography, case study, grounded theory), they often provide insufficient information about their approaches to data collection and leave the reader to speculate about what has gone on, by piecing the information together from clues provided in the study. A researcher employing pragmatic qualitative research has a unique duty to provide information about the methods that he or she has undertaken and a rationale for them. For this reason, assurance of ethics in study design and presentation of products are critical to this approach. Sampling seems to be done to gain perspectives from many different types of participants. Cooper and Endacott (2007), for example, suggest that gaining maximum variation could be a good way to sample for pragmatic qualitative research (see Chapter 20). Fieldwork (see Chapter 22) tends to involve note taking, often during semi-structured interviewing, focus group interviews and observations (see Chapters 23–25); at times, researchers also use documents as data (Chapter 26). Many scholars recommend articulating decisions about methods when using pragmatic qualitative research (for example, Sandelowski 2000; Neergaard *et al.* 2009).

Working with data and findings (see Part 6)

There is not an abundance of literature describing a specific approach to data analysis in pragmatic qualitative research. Cooper and Endacott (2007) suggest that inductive approaches are ideally suited for pragmatic qualitative research. They describe three general steps as follows:

■ Reduce and display data: researchers independently read and re-read the transcripts (giving attention to their preconceived ideas); then they independently identify key categories and chart them appropriately.
■ Draw conclusions: researchers identify category clusters and indicate relationships within the data. This step enables development of overarching themes and sub-themes.
■ Confirm the results: researchers weigh the evidence and make contrasts and comparisons.

We simply suggest that it is critical for the researcher to select an analytical approach carefully, probably from one of the basic analytical approaches such as constant comparison, keyword or thematic analysis (see Chapters 27 and 28). Similarly, there are no strong guides for interpretation, although Sandelowski (2000: 335) suggests that interpretation is low-inference and thus results in easier consensus among researchers. We provide an example of her description of such low-inference interpretation in the following example.

PRAGMATIC INTERPRETATION

(Sandelowski 2000: 335)

Even though one researcher may feature the feelings and a second researcher the events a woman reported in an interview, both researchers will likely agree that, for example, the woman stated several times that she was angry and that she stated that her mother died one day after she herself learned that she had breast cancer. In the case of the two researchers describing ostensibly the same scene, one researcher might feature the spatial arrangement in a room, while the second researcher will feature the social interactions. But both researchers ought to agree with each other's descriptions as accurate renderings of the scene.

Example

In terms of quality in pragmatic qualitative research, the researcher tends to take a position of striving for validity and in particular seek descriptive validity or an accurate accounting of the meanings with which participants would agree. They employ a range of strategies for ensuring validity, such as member checking and peer examination of codes, themes and findings (see Chapter 30).

Writing (see Part 7)

As there is no one way to approach a study using a pragmatic qualitative approach, the burden not only of making sound decisions about what to do but also the burden of clearly communicating those decisions to a reader rests with the researcher. Writing tends to be concise and straightforward (see Chapter 31). Researchers typically report findings in the standard social science research report (see Chapter 32).

Summary of choices when doing and designing pragmatic qualitative research

In Table 11.1, we highlight key choices that researchers using pragmatic qualitative research commonly make. Our intent is not to say how the approach must be done but rather to provide a description of the way that we have most often seen it in the literature. Thus, this table is intended to serve as a general guide that researchers may consider when they design and do their own pragmatic qualitative studies.

ADVANTAGES AND CHALLENGES OF PRAGMATIC QUALITATIVE RESEARCH

There are many advantages to pragmatic qualitative research, particularly for practitioners in fields such as business, education and health care. There are also, however, some disadvantages and challenges associated with the approach.

Advantages of pragmatic qualitative research

There are a number of distinct advantages of pragmatic qualitative research, which largely are related to the flexibility that the approach provides to researchers.

Pragmatic research does not require philosophical or theoretical orthodoxy. With a pragmatic qualitative approach, researchers either attempt to remain philosophically neutral (that is, a-paradigmatic, see Chapter 4) or alternatively and more appropriately to describe their own philosophical orientations, during which they articulate a purist or situational, pragmatic perspective (see Chapter 4), or a combination of assumptions from various philosophies, in a blended philosophies orientation (see Chapter 4). They may also choose to use a theoretical framework (see Chapter 9), as Merriam suggests, in a complementary theory approach (see Chapter 4).

The approach does not require methodological orthodoxy. While qualitative researchers suggest that there is flexibility among different approaches, they have over time come to realize that certain approaches possess key characteristics and conventions. In a study employing pragmatic qualitative research, however, researchers have the freedom to mix and match approaches that are appropriate for answering the question. Indeed, researchers who use this approach have great flexibility; they often propose their own guidelines and approaches (Caelli *et al.* 2003).

Pragmatic qualitative research is becoming increasingly common (Caelli *et al.* 2003). As this approach is becoming more common and even popular, the approach is gaining acceptance within the qualitative research community, particularly in the professions (Sandelowski 2000). As the approach becomes better articulated, this trend is likely to continue.

Table 11.1 Designing pragmatic qualitative research

Design	Specifics in pragmatic qualitative research	Chapter
Philosophical origins	Pragmatic origins	2
Philosophical stance	Outsider looking in	4
Personal stance	Low degree of disclosure of positionality in final report	5
Who or what of study	Varied: often individuals, structures and processes	6
Research topic and question	Practical and often related to practice	7
Literature review	Typically comprehensive and all inclusive	8
Theoretical or conceptual framework	Can be applied to guide research design and more infrequently for interpretation of data	9
Time, place, participants	Shorter duration in field than other approaches, such as ethnography	
	Done in natural environment	
	Purposeful sampling, frequently maximum variation	20
Ethics	Ethical design, treatment of individuals, processes, and presentation of products important; particular emphasis on design and processes	21
Fieldwork	Note taking during interviews	22
Data collection methods	Many forms possible, including various combinations of:	
	– semi-structured interviews with individuals or focus groups – observations in context – review of documents or other pertinent materials	23–26
Data handling	Basic and descriptive coding of information	27
Analysis	Qualitative content analysis using modifiable coding systems that correspond to the data collected	28
Interpretation	Stay close to the data – low-level interpretation	29
Quality	View of quality, quality criterion and strategies to ensure quality important; particular emphasis on strategies	30
Researcher voice	External observer and reporter	31
Report	Description of the data organized in a way that 'fits' the data (chronologically by topic, by relevance, etc.)	32

There are instances in which it is desirable to be able to do a study quickly, particularly when practitioners need information to improve practice immediately. In the case of doctors, nurses and educators, there are times during which practitioners need information immediately in order to make good professional decisions. Indeed, in the cases of health professions, answers to research questions indeed could be a matter of life and death. In these instances, an in-depth ethnographic study may not be feasible in the timeframe available (although it might provide a good follow up study). A pragmatic qualitative study can provide initial answers to questions in a timely fashion.

Doing a pragmatic qualitative study can circumvent criticisms of qualitative researchers who review manuscripts and proposals. In many cases, reviewers are unable to agree upon a manuscript because of conflicting opinions about the particular paradigm or research tradition being drawn upon. When this happens, it can leave a researcher who has attempted a particular tradition in a difficult situation. Researchers who have designed their own qualitative approach may not face such criticisms of whether they have followed the 'proper' approach.

Challenges of pragmatic qualitative research

Many of the advantages of pragmatic qualitative research are simultaneously disadvantages as well.

A pragmatic qualitative study may be viewed as less theoretically or philosophically rigorous than another tradition. Since some who adopt this approach choose to do so from an a-paradigmatic orientation (see Chapter 4), a pragmatic qualitative study could be viewed by some as less theoretically grounded. Indeed, some researchers have described negatively the practice of description rather than interpretation, from a philosophically or theoretically informed perspective. Thorne *et al.* (1997: 170) suggested that description in qualitative research is the 'crudest form of inquiry'. We, however, assert that pragmatism is a philosophy and so, given the approach's origins and current practices, it can be philosophically informed. We also assert that the research may be carried out with a philosophical orientation other than a-paradigmatic, such as from a blended or complementary theory orientation (see Chapter 4).

There is no commonly accepted and understood approach or method. While many researchers have attempted pragmatic qualitative research, there has yet to emerge a common understanding of what pragmatic qualitative research is or how to do it. Until at least some common understanding of the approach and its methods emerges, it will not be as readily accepted as it might be if it were widely recognized by a single term. It is not currently possible, for example, to shorthand methods sections in any meaningful way; researchers writing about pragmatic studies must include lengthy descriptions of methods.

The approach has negative connotations. While many scholars are doing pragmatic qualitative research under a number of different terms, many of these terms can be viewed as negative. 'Basic' may be viewed as simple, 'generic' as plain, and 'non-categorical' even has a negative prefix, which implies a lack of precision or indecision on the part of the researcher. Because it signals its philosophical origins, its aim toward practicality and a sensible approach to research, we prefer the term pragmatic qualitative research to any of the others currently in use.

Some view the approach as an 'easy' or fast way to go about qualitative research. Not all qualitative studies have been created equally. In fact, some studies that their researchers call qualitative research are simply dreadful. Many of these have proceeded without naming a specific research approach and some have lumped such research together with pragmatic qualitative research. There is, however, a distinct difference between bad qualitative research and pragmatic qualitative research. A researcher should approach a pragmatic qualitative study in a systematic and rigorous way and strive to communicate that effort to a potential audience; we provided some guidance for how to do that in the section on 'designing and doing pragmatic qualitative research' above.

There are no clear standards for evaluating pragmatic qualitative research. In part owing to a lack of acceptance about what pragmatic qualitative research is and in part due to a lack of agreement as to what counts as quality in qualitative research, the guidelines for ensuring quality in pragmatic qualitative research are fuzzy at best. So, while readers and reviewers may not impose inappropriate standards, they often do not have a clear sense of how to evaluate the approach, which can lead to challenges in acceptance of the work.

EXAMPLE OF PRAGMATIC QUALITATIVE RESEARCH

Simon Cooper offers a reflection about his uses with pragmatic qualitative research, which he has called 'basic qualitative research'.

Dr Simon Cooper, Campus Head School of Nursing and Midwifery (Berwick), Monash University, Australia

Pragmatic qualitative research in the health professions

In our previous work, my colleagues and I described pragmatic qualitative research approaches as generic or descriptive approaches (Cooper and Endacott 2007). Working with this type of approach, we have undertaken several studies with nurses, doctors and paramedics.

We have, for example, followed a theme of research examining the management of deteriorating patients. In all studies, we have adopted mixed-methods approaches with a pragmatic qualitative phase. In Endacott *et al.* (2011), we examined registered nurses' ability ($n = 34$) to manage deteriorating patients in a simulated setting and included participant reflective interviews whilst reviewing video records of performance. The aim was to capture participants' rationale for their actions. We identified four themes that indicate a variety of participant performance outcomes:

1. Exhausting autonomous decision-making (complete patient assessment and correct actions).
2. Misinterpreting the evidence (complete assessment but incorrect actions).
3. Conditioned response (incomplete assessment but correct actions).
4. Missed cues (incomplete assessment and incorrect actions).

We concluded that reflective review and video performance analysis revealed insights into decision making that were not available from quantitative ratings of performance.

In a study of interprofessional education (IPE), we also used a mixed-methods approach aiming to identify the effects of interprofessional resuscitation skills teaching with nursing and medical students ($n = 53$) with a particular focus on attitudes, teamwork and performance. In the pragmatic qualitative research phase, we not only incorporated five focus groups to explore students' attitudes identifying broad support for IPE with perceived benefits for communication and teamwork but we also considered concerns over hierarchical issues, professional identity and the timing of IPE episodes. Subject to some limitations, we concluded that clinically realistic IPE episodes based on shared learning outcomes do have positive benefits.

In a third qualitative study (Cooper 2005), we used individual and focus group interviews ($n = 44$) with UK ambulance staff and stakeholders in order to develop an understanding of the current and future system of ambulance training. Emergent themes included concerns around entry level requirements, a desire for a higher education curriculum, valid and reliable assessment methods, supportive mentorship, professional

Researcher reflections

continued

development requirements and a desire for IPE. In conclusion, we identified the transient nature of ambulance training in an emerging profession and the desire for cultural and organizational changes.

Pragmatic qualitative approaches have enabled us to capture the richness within the data without the formal constraints of other qualitative approaches, such as ethnography or phenomenology. Such approaches answer the question 'how many' and also give an insight into the 'why'.

CONCLUSION

In this chapter, we have advanced the idea of pragmatic qualitative research. We have articulated ways of doing and designing pragmatic qualitative research. These are intended as general guidelines to allow a researcher some structure when undertaking pragmatic qualitative research. We believe that this approach is gaining in acceptance and popularity, particularly in applied disciplines, and with good reason. It provides a meaningful way to interpret processes and events and to report the findings to individuals who need them. Pragmatic qualitative research, however, is not easy. To do it well requires critical thinking and planning, appropriate selection of research tools and strong interviewing, observation, and writing skills.

Reflective questions

Concept questions

■ What is pragmatic qualitative research?
■ What makes a pragmatic qualitative approach different from other qualitative approaches?

Application questions

■ How useful is pragmatic qualitative research for your study?
■ What would be the key advantages of undertaking a pragmatic qualitative study?
■ What would be the challenges for you?

Key resources

Sandelowski, M. (2000) Focus on research methods: Whatever happened to qualitative description? *Research in Nursing & Health*, 23, 334–40.
Sandelowski's response to Thorne *et al.* (1997) provided a strong case for descriptive qualitative research, as well as useful consideration of Thorne's version of interpretive description and her own, which provided useful explanation and also helped us to consider that our view of pragmatic qualitative research is something between these two approaches.

Caelli, K., Ray, L. and Mill, J. (2003) 'Clear as mud': Toward greater clarity in generic qualitative research. *International Journal of Qualitative Methods*, 2 (2), 1–13.
In this article, the authors describe the notion of 'generic' qualitative research and

provide some important information about the key elements. Although we do not prefer the term 'generic' or 'basic' research, as we have indicated in this chapter, the article provides useful information about an approach that we believe is frequently used but all too often overlooked in qualitative texts.

Cooper, S. and Endacott, R. (2007) Generic qualitative research: A design for qualitative research in emergency care? *Emergency Medicine Journal*, 24 (12), 816–19.
In this article, Cooper and Endacott provide useful information about 'generic qualitative research'. Again, while we prefer the term pragmatic, in part because we think it is clearer and has fewer negative connotations, the authors provide useful examples of 'best practices' in this research approach that does not conform to traditional methods employed in other approaches such as grounded theory or phenomenology.

continued

Chapter 12

Grounded theory

INTRODUCTION

Grounded theory is a research approach that explicitly intends to develop theory from the study of cases. It was one of the earliest forms of a qualitative research approach that marked a sharp distinction between a natural science and a social science view of conducting research. In this chapter, we describe grounded theory in the forms that qualitative researchers tend to adopt. We consider the interrelated processes involved in conducting a grounded theory study and explain the practical tenets required to carry out such a study. We suggest that a number of different types of grounded theory have emerged over the years. Finally, we consider advantages as well as criticisms of the approach.

ORIGINS OF GROUNDED THEORY

While the intellectual origins of this work may be traced to pragmatism and symbolic interactionism, American sociologists, Glaser and Strauss, formally developed the grounded theory approach and made it popular with the publication of *The discovery of grounded theory* in 1967. In this text, they outlined a basic process of gathering data and using it to generate theory through an inductive process. Their work had a profound influence on social science research and, even today, some people think that grounded theory and qualitative research are one and the same.

While many grounded theorists continue to hold an a-paradigmatic approach (Chapter 4) to data analysis and interpretation (or the notion that grounded theory is in itself a paradigm), a modified approach articulated by Strauss and Corbin (1990) opened up the possibility for grounded theory researchers to work from other paradigms, as we describe in our section on 'forms of grounded theory' later in this chapter. While this opening up has been viewed by many as a positive thing, it also has been viewed by some as a drift from the core method to a state of methodological morass. Cutliffe, for example, argues:

> While Glaser and Strauss acknowledged then that it was entirely appropriate for the methodology to evolve and develop, some of the studies that claim to be based on grounded theory methodology share little methodological similarity, and at times, bear only a passing resemblance to Glaserian grounded theory.

(Cutliffe 2005: 421)

Cutliffe highlights the idea that the dissimilarities within the various approaches are problematic and emphasizes that researchers who claim to be doing grounded theory are not always in fact doing so. Bryant and Charmaz (2007: 11) suggest that there is a 'family of methods claiming the GTM [Grounded Theory Method] mantle' that bear 'family resemblances' or similarities, rather than a distinct group of methods that share clear and precise common attributes. Thus, what is and what is not grounded theory is hotly contested.

DESCRIPTION AND PURPOSE OF GROUNDED THEORY

Grounded theory at a fundamental level is a research approach that focuses on interaction, action and processes. It has the overt purpose of generating theory from empirical data by use of inductive analysis called constant comparison of data. Participants in a grounded theory study each report many incidents, creating a total set of several hundred incidents. Researchers develop a theory from these incidents that explains the phenomenon under investigation. Rather than using a philosophical position or theoretical or conceptual framework, grounded theory research strives to develop a hypothesis directly from the data.

We situate grounded theory as a qualitative research approach, although we know that others (such as Glaser and Strauss) view it as a theoretical position or paradigm, while others still (such as Lincoln and Guba) view it more as a method of data analysis. Grounded theory does have some characteristics that make it more practical than a philosophical position, as well as some that make it more in keeping with a research approach than strictly a method of data analysis. Thus, we use the term grounded theory to refer to a qualitative research approach that is undertaken for the purpose of generating a theory to explain a process (or other phenomenon of study). Grounded theory has an implicit aim of developing probabilities, not through statistical methods but rather through an examination of relationship between concepts (Glaser 1998). Even so, grounded theory is not a strictly qualitative method, since it includes any kind of data, including quantitative data, and even other research studies as data (Glaser 2001; 2003). The approach as we see it, however, is inherently qualitative, in its focus on narrative rather than numerical data and in its approach toward building rather than testing theory.

Grounded theory allows the researcher to engage in a step-by-step, systematic procedure, to formulate a hypothesis based upon concepts and to test this hypothesis by constantly comparing cases. Researchers should choose grounded theory when they hope to generate a theory through inductive and deductive reasoning that can explain a process, action or interaction, regardless of time and place. Researchers who want to stay close to the data and who do not necessarily seek 'truth' but rather a conception about what is taking place in a particular situation will benefit from a grounded theory approach.

TYPES OF GROUNDED THEORY

While many researchers still hold to classic grounded theory methods which we describe in this chapter, several different forms of grounded theory have emerged over time. The variations for the most part have developed out of differences in philosophical perspectives (see Chapter 4). In particular, many of these researchers criticize the tenets of classic grounded theory as being too positivist or post-positivist in its leaning. They argue for the need to develop theory from data but believe that other philosophies are better suited for this work. We present some of these in the following paragraphs and summarize them in a table at the end of this section.

Classic grounded theory

Glaser and Strauss developed this approach together in 1967. The primary focus of the approach is on generation of theory. The researchers stressed the importance of relying upon the data and for allowing codes to develop from data themselves. The researchers stress the use of field notes as the primary data collection method as well as the use of memoing. 'All is data', including related literature, is a continuing refrain in writings about classic grounded theory. We describe this form of grounded theory more fully below in the 'Designing and doing grounded theory' section of this chapter.

Modified grounded theory

While Glaser and Strauss developed the grounded theory approach together, they later disagreed about how the approach should be conceived and carried out, which led to further publications by the two and considerable crossfire between them. Strauss published *Qualitative analysis for social scientists* (1987) and Strauss and Corbin wrote in *Basics of qualitative research: Grounded theory procedures and techniques* (1990). These works laid out an approach which some have called modified grounded theory. Glaser responded to these publications in his 1992 work in a strong rebuke that proceeded chapter by chapter to illustrate differences between the original and intended approach. While Glaser's approach seeks to conceptualize places and people through a wholly emergent and inductive design, Strauss described a systematic approach that could well involve use of a **coding paradigm**.

Coding paradigm

A generic structure used to guide coding (see Chapter 27)

Thus, as Kelle (2005: 407) suggested, it is possible to view Glaser's and Strauss's later works as attempts to further refine their concept of theoretical sensitivity in regards to coding. In particular, Strauss advocates using a theory of action to build a frame from which a theory may emerge. Glaser argued strongly against this idea (Glaser 1992), even though he had proposed a similar concept previously: 'theoretical codes' that 'may relate to each other as hypotheses' may 'be integrated into a theory' and these could be used to conceptualize incidents in the data (Glaser 1978: 72). Kelle suggests that the controversy between Glaser and Strauss really amounts to whether the researcher should use a well-defined 'coding paradigm' or a fund of 'coding families', or not, and whether these theoretical codes should be employed as they emerge, in the same way that substantive codes can be.

Constructivist grounded theory

Charmaz (2006: 187) introduced a constructivist orientation to grounded theory analysis, in which researchers and participants construct their own realities (Berger and Luckmann 1966). In doing so, the researcher must acknowledge that their own interpretations of the phenomenon of study are in themselves constructions. She describes the process as follows:

> Constructivist inquiry starts with the experience and asks how members construct it. To the best of their ability, constructivists enter the phenomenon, gain multiple views of it, and locate it in its web of connections and constraints ... As such, Constructivism 'assumes the relativism of multiple social realities, recognizes the mutual creation of knowledge by the viewer and the viewed, and aims toward interpretive understandings of subjects' meanings.
>
> (Charmaz 2000: 510)

Charmaz (2000) argues that classic grounded theory methods view the discovery of categories inherent in data, observed in an external world by a neutral observer, as the driver or theory. She argues that such a position is no longer feasible given the 'interpretive turn' (Denzin and Lincoln 1998) in qualitative social scientific research. Rather, she posits a constructivist stance from which she argues: 'we can view grounded theories as products of emergent processes that occur through interaction. Researchers construct their respective products from the fabric of the interactions, both witnessed and lived' (Charmaz 2006: 178).

Constructivist grounded theory is essentially a flexible approach to undertaking grounded theory in which it is recognized that the world of social research is ever changing. In terms of practical application, Charmaz assumes that data and theories are not discovered. Instead, they are constructed by the researcher and participants; such constructions also include theorizing about the world. Scholars who advocate this form of grounded theory suggest that the researcher and the researched are co-producers of data, and that it is important for researchers to immerse themselves in the data in order to embed the participant data in both the findings and the final research outcome. The researcher's writing also should represent and evoke participants' experiences. What is perhaps most helpful about this form of grounded theory is that it offers a means of both analyzing participants' data and presenting it in the final report in ways that earlier forms of grounded theory did not necessarily do.

Post-modern grounded theory

In a post-modern take on grounded theory, Clarke relies upon the model of modified grounded theory but situates it within a post-modern perspective, primarily through different forms of data analysis. Post-modernism is difficult to define and capture, as it covers a range of literature and disciplines from cultural studies to architecture, cinema to education. Post-modernism is not a unified position or set of concepts but rather is seen by many as a contested space. Thus, post-modernism is an umbrella term that has been used by many philosophers and theorists to distinguish between the modern and post-modern era (Lyotard 1979; Featherstone 1991). However, authors such as Foucault (1979) do not see post-modernism as an era but, instead, argue it to be a shift in attitude and position within humanity. Clarke (2005), after Castellani (1999), described grounded theory with an explicit focus on issues of power, making a link between the work of the Chicago symbolic interactionism school and Foucauldian work on discourse and power. Clarke (2005: 52) states that '*If action is at the heart of Strauss's project and power at the heart of Foucault's work, they meet in related conceptualizations of practices as fundamental processes of action and change*' (emphasis added). Clarke indicates that concepts of practice, including discourse and power regimes (Foucault) as well as social worlds and negotiated orders (Strauss), are not equivalent but instead are related (Vasconcelos 2007). Both Foucault and Strauss, then, emphasized discourse as being constituted through interaction (Clarke 2005). Strauss viewed social worlds as '*universes of discourse*', while Foucault placed discourse far more explicitly in the framework of power: he characterized discourses as being affected '*by disciplining practices that produce subjects/subjectivities through surveillance, examination, and various technologies of the self*' often through the influence or the imposition of social groups (Clarke 2005: 54; Vasconcelos 2007).

In terms of the suggestion for mixing grounded theory and post-modernism, Clarke employs several types of visual strategies for displaying results from data analysis, which resemble concept maps in form (see Chapters 8 and 27). The maps she outlines are as follows:

1. Situational maps that lay out the major human, nonhuman, discursive, and other elements in the research situation of concern and provoke analyses of relations among them;
2. Social worlds/arena maps that lay out the collective actors, key nonhuman elements, and the arena(s) of commitment within which they are engaged in ongoing negotiations or interpretations of the situation;
3. Positional maps that lay out the major positions taken, and not taken in data vis-à-vis particular discursive axes of variation and difference, concern, and controversy surrounding complicated issues in the situation.

(Clarke 2003: 554)

(See Chapter 27 for other forms of data display.)

Post-modern grounded theory is regarded by some (Schwandt 1994) as being located in constructivism. Annells (1996) points out that this positioning is problematic for two reasons: first, that grounded theory has roots in symbolic interactionism and second because the notion of theory construction in grounded theory does not fit well with a post-modern stance. We agree with this perspective, since the diversity across the post-modern field has meant that rather than locating post-modernism as an era or position, it is often referred to as the post-modern condition, in which the decentring of knowledge, the lack of fixed reference points, rapid change and uncertainty are common. These conditions would seem to be a problematic fit with the notion of grounding theory.

Discursive grounded theory

This type of grounded theory focuses on analyzing aspects of discourse when examining phenomena. Discursive grounded theory is proposed by McCreaddie and Payne (2010) as a useful addition to existing research approaches. This approach was developed by the authors to explore spontaneous humour in healthcare settings. While their original intent was to use constructivist grounded theory, they found that they needed to adopt more of a discourse-based approach to understand the phenomena. They began by identifying the phenomenon of humour broadly and then developed interpretative and illustrative frameworks to understand it further, which comprised:

■ open coding
■ aspects of discursive psychology
■ various theories and theoretical frameworks.

The discursive features of this approach are exemplified in their explanation below:

Discursive features were coming to the fore in line by line open coding because of the use of naturally occurring interactions. A participant uttering 'we' instead of 'I' (footing) or using a deontic modality (e.g. 'to have to') to describe their experience are examples of specific discursive features identified in the data. Second, it was also apparent that the humour identified needed to be collated in a more meaningful way to enable each humour excerpt (and humour excerpts across different interactions), to be compared and contrasted.

(McCreaddie and Payne 2010: 784)

What is apparent is that this approach seeks to combine grounded theory with critical discourse analysis and conversational analysis in a broadly constructivist stance. However, it is likely to be

Table 12.1 Types of grounded theory

Type	Commonly adapted paradigms	Focus	Key features
Classic grounded theory Glaser and Strauss (1967)	Pragmatism	Generation of theory	Reliance upon data Codes come from data themselves Use of memoing 'All is data', including related literature
Modified grounded theory Strauss (1987) Strauss and Corbin (1990)	Pragmatism	Generation of theory	Adoption of many classic grounded theory tenets but less focused upon emergent design and allowing for the use of existing coding schemes
Constructivist grounded theory Charmaz (2000; 2006)	Constructivism	Generation of theory with participant data as central	Adoption of modified grounded theory methods but allowance for the notion that individuals construct their own realities
Post-modern grounded theory Clarke (2003; 2005)	Post-modernism	Mapping and generating theory	Adoption of modified constructivist grounded theory methods with situational mapping employed
Discursive grounded theory McCreaddie and Payne (2010)	Post-structuralism	Mapping, generating and deconstructing theory	Adoption of modified grounded methods with a focus on language interaction and discourse

an approach that first requires strong familiarity with forms of analysis such as critical discourse analysis.

In Table 12.1, we provide a summary of these different types of grounded theory.

DESIGNING AND DOING GROUNDED THEORY

When using grounded theory, the researcher faces essential choices about philosophical and personal position, framing the study, collecting data, working with data and writing about the results. In the next few paragraphs, we provide an overview of the choices researchers who use grounded theory, particularly classic grounded theory, often make. We follow this description by a summary of these common choices in Table 12.2. This table provides links to other parts and chapters in this book where we provide fuller descriptions and practical advice for doing qualitative research.

Philosophical and personal positioning

The classic grounded theory researcher most often takes a pragmatist paradigm when undertaking a study and, in particular, symbolic interactionism (see Chapter 2) has had a major influence on this research approach. Grounded theory researchers have developed other forms of grounded theory that have occupied a range of philosophical positions, including pragmatism, post-modernism, post-structuralism, and constructivism (see the 'Types of grounded theory' section).

The researcher seeks to understand the essence of what is happening in the situation as well as to consider how the participants work within the situation. The process requires researchers to continually question themselves: What is going on? What problems do the participants have? How are they trying to solve them?

Focus of the study (see Part 3)

According to Glaser (1978), the main goal of the grounded theory method is to discover the basic social process(es); that is, 'the theoretical reflections and summarizations of the patterned, systematic uniformity flows of social life which people go through, and which can be conceptually "captured" and further understood through the construction of basic social process theories' (1978: 100). The phenomena that researchers investigate then tend to be structures, processes or concepts associated with human behaviour.

Tips

Grounded theory shares some common features with phenomenology, in that researchers employing both are trying to understand the human experience. In grounded theory, however, the researcher strives to develop a theory about that experience, something that explains the experience and how it occurs in a natural setting, while, in phenomenology, the researcher seeks to describe the very essence of the experience, the deep categories and structures of it before individuals categorize it.

Classic grounded theory holds that doing an initial formal literature review causes the researcher to be desensitized to the data and rather to rely on borrowed concepts, so in classic grounded theory there is typically no pre-research literature review. According to classic grounded theory principles, the researcher should instead access literature during data collection and coding, and this literature is considered to be additional data to code and compare to prior codes and categories. Other forms of grounded theory suggest reviewing research ahead of time, at least in related areas. Researchers typically do not apply a conceptual or theoretical framework since they are trying to generate new theory, rather than explore existing concepts or theories.

Data collection

Researchers using grounded theory place a high importance on ethics (as do most qualitative researchers) and consider ethics from design to treatment of individuals, to processes, to presentation of products. Grounded theory researchers place special emphasis on ethics in study design, focusing on adherence to the structures of the approach or alternately justifying breaking away from there. They also place particular emphasis on ethics of the processes inherent in grounded theory and ethical research (see Chapter 21).

'All is data' is a core feature of grounded theory. This phrase indicates that data include everything related to the topic the researcher encounters when engaging in the research study. Grounded theory follows a fairly standard process of data collection, which is relatively simple and direct and which is intended to bring about understanding of a situation. Grounded theory researchers frequently collect data through observation, formal or informal interviews and focus groups. Data collection methods are considered to be emergent, just as theory developed in the process is emergent (see Chapters 23–26). All collection methods are considered valid; data then may include anything that helps the researcher develop concepts which in turn lead to emerging theory. 'Anything' might include other research, newspaper articles, discussion boards, blog postings, lectures, seminars, television shows, and so on. Interviewing is a common method of data collection. Some grounded theory researchers believe that recording while interviewing is a waste of time; others use more typical approaches to interviewing and transcription. After each data collection phase, the researcher notes key issues in extensive field notes (see Chapter 22). Glaser (1998) suggests that the researcher should not talk about the theory prior to writing it up. Doing so, he believes, drains the researcher's motivational energy. Talking about the theory tends to garner praise or criticism from the listener, either of which can diminish the researcher's motivational drive to write memos that can further develop and refine the theory. According to Glaser, any conversations about the emerging theory should be limited to people who are likely to assist researchers, and unlikely to influence their judgment.

Working with data and findings

The researcher's aim is to understand the research situation and to discover theory implicit in the data. Theory is said to 'emerge' from the data. This distinction between 'emergence and forcing', as Glaser identifies it, is fundamental to understanding the grounded theory method. As Glaser suggests, 'grounded theory is multivariate. It happens sequentially, subsequently, simultaneously, serendipitously, and scheduled' (Glaser 2004). Quality concerns focus on whether the theory fits the data.

Key phases in treating data are coding, memoing and sorting. *Coding* is the process of noticing, naming and labelling. Grounded theory coding is fairly informal compared to coding in other research approaches. In grounded theory, coding is generally done for broad concepts and as new concepts arise. Data already coded are not necessarily re-coded based upon the new descriptions. Grounded theorists do at times use code lists to keep a running record of codes. Grounded theory coding may occur in four phases: open coding, axial coding, selective coding and memoing or theoretical coding (see Chapter 27). *Memoing* is 'the core stage of grounded theory methodology' (Glaser 1998). Memos are relatively short notes that the researcher develops while engaging with data. In memos, the researcher indicates thoughts about the names of concepts and their relationships to each other (see Chapter 27). *Sorting* is reading and re-reading notes in order to uncover categories and their interrelationships through a comparative and inductive process. In this phase of grounded theory, the researcher sorts memos into common groupings. So, during the coding phase the researcher breaks data apart into smaller chunks then, during the sorting phase, the chunks are put back together (see Chapter 27). During sorting, new ideas are recorded as new memos, which at times means that memos are written about memos. This process continues until a point of theoretical **saturation** is reached. This process is called 'constant comparison' (see Chapter 28). Through the process of sorting, the researcher generates a data-driven theory that should explain the primary **incident** under examination. This phase requires integrating theory by moving from core and related concepts to developing a hypothesis to explain participant concerns. When all of the data points fit the hypothesis, the researcher has finalized the theory. The theory must not be forced but should emerge during constant comparison.

Saturation

Saturation is a point at which no new themes are being uncovered

Incident

In grounded theory, an incident is a selection of the data, whether a word, line or paragraph, that the researcher has labelled

Strauss and Corbin (1990: 78) provide the following brief example of grounded theory construction.

Example

Text fragment: **'Pain relief is a major problem when you have arthritis. Sometimes, the pain is worse than other times, but when it gets really bad, whew! It hurts so bad, you don't want to get out of bed. You don't feel like doing anything. Any relief you get from drugs that you take is only temporary or partial'.**

Grounded theory-building: **'One thing that is being discussed here is PAIN. One of the properties of pain is INTENSITY: it varies from a little to a lot. (When is it a lot and when is it little?) When it hurts a lot, there are consequences: don't want to get out of bed, don't feel like doing things (what are other things you don't do when in pain?). In order to solve this problem, you need PAIN RELIEF. One AGENT OF PAIN RELIEF is drugs (what are other members of this category?). Pain relief has a certain DURATION (could be temporary), and EFFECTIVENESS (could be partial)'.**

Pain is the phenomenon of interest, arthritis is the causal condition, taking drugs is the action strategy, and pain relief is the consequence of the action.

The grounded theory researcher has different methods of documenting quality, validity and rigour; more than most other researchers undertaking qualitative approaches. They place particular importance on the view of quality (see Chapter 30). Glaser and Strauss argue that in grounded theory, validity is inherent in the constant interrogation of evidence to continually refine the emergent theory. Data, then, drive validity. Validity is judged by the following criterion (Glaser and Strauss 1967; Glaser 1978; 1998).

- Fit: how well concepts fit the incidents; fit also relies on how thorough a job the researcher did of constant comparison
- Relevance: the real concerns of participants based on what captures their attention, rather than just the attention of academics
- Workability: the usefulness of the theory in explaining the phenomenon or incident being studied
- Modifiability: the ability for the theory to be modified when new and relevant data are considered and compared.

For additional information about validity as we describe it, see Chapter 30.

Writing

While writing up can be done from the first point of data collection and then throughout the process, these reports are generally initial reports. Grounded theory researchers generally begin to write up their memos more formally following the sorting phase, at which time the theory is nearly finalized. Final report writing does not occur until all categories relate to the core variable and to each other. It is during rewriting that relevant literature is introduced to the narrative in order to situate the new theory within a scholarly context. Formal writing for publication may be thought of as part of collegial communication (Strauss and Corbin 1998), which provides sufficient evidence so that the reader understands the conceptual work involved (Glaser 1978). The final report tends to be in the form of a set of hypotheses, which emphasizes the relationship between concepts, rather than a more traditional report of findings, although it does generally contain narrative as well as tables or figures (see Chapters 31 and 32).

Summary of choices when designing and doing grounded theory

In Table 12.2, we highlight key choices that researchers using grounded theory commonly make. Our intent is not to say how the approach must be done but rather to provide a description of the way that we have most often seen it in the literature. Thus, Table 12.2 is intended to serve as a general guide that researchers may consider when they design and do their own grounded theory studies.

Table 12.2 Designing grounded theory

Design	Specifics	Chapter
Philosophical origins	Pragmatic origins; later forms varied	2
Philosophical stance	Often outsider looking in	4
Personal stance	Low degree of disclosure of positionality in final report (unless using a later form)	5
Who or what of study	Concepts, structures, processes	6
Research questions	Research questions are constructed to allow for generation of theory	7
Literature review	Not always completed ahead of time; literature may count as data	8
Theoretical/conceptual framework	Typically not used; goal is to generate theory, not test it	9
Time/place/participants	Length of time in field varies by project	
	Done in natural environment	
	Purposeful sampling, frequently maximum variation	20
Ethics	Ethical design, treatment of individuals, processes, and presentation of products important; particular emphasis on design and processes	21
Fieldwork	Extensive field notes taken throughout process	22
Data collection methods	Various combinations of the following are possible:	23–26
	– Semi-structured interviews with individuals or focus groups – Observations in context – Review of documents or other pertinent materials	
	Everything counts as data	
Data handling	Open, axial and selective coding	27
Analysis	Constant comparison	28
Interpretation	Highly interpretive	29
Quality	View of quality, quality criterion and strategies to ensure quality important; particular emphasis on view and criterion	30
Researcher voice	External observer and reporter	31
Report	Data reported organized around new substantive theory	32

ADVANTAGES AND CHALLENGES OF GROUNDED THEORY

The process of grounded theory is an inductive one, which fits with the aims of many qualitative researchers. It takes as its focus human behaviour, thus grounding findings in participants' lived experiences, also congruent to many qualitative researchers' goals. Grounded theory has the unique advantage of seeking to develop hypotheses and theories to explain what is happening in a given situation.

Criticism of grounded theory centres on what is produced from analysis; the question is whether the product truly rises to the level of theory (Thomas and James 2006). In addition, critics suggest that one may never truly feel free of preconceptions that influence collection and analysis of data, which Glaser and Strauss argues is necessary. Thomas and James (2006) also argue that grounded theory is formulaic, which goes against creative interpretation that some believe is critical to qualitative inquiry. It is also possible to take issue with grounded theory on the grounds that it can only account for participants' views of what is happening in a particular situation; on the other hand, some scholars would argue that the participants' views are all that can or should be sought in a qualitative approach.

Example

In the following researcher reflection, Thornberg offers his thoughts about using grounded theory (GT) with pragmatic qualitative research, which he has called 'basic qualitative research'.

Researcher reflections

Robert Thornberg, Linköping University, Sweden

While the family tree of GT is rooted in pragmatism, constructivist grounded theorists also work from a constructivist stance. This later version of GT provides systematic and rigorous but flexible guidelines. Data are seen as constructed by the researchers as a result of their interactions with their field and its participants. The main focus in GT is on interaction, meaning, and social processes.

We conducted a constructivist GT study on school bullying. The aim was to investigate how individuals, who had been victims of school bullying, perceived their bullying experiences and how these had affected them, as well as to generate a grounded theory of being a victim of bullying at school. Twenty-one participants (age range 17–34 years) were qualitatively interviewed. The participants were asked to talked about (a) their victimization experiences of school bullying, from the very start to the end; (b) their thoughts, feelings and actions regarding the bullying they had experienced; and (c) their perceptions of how their bullying experiences had affected them during and after the bullying period. Each interview was transcribed. Coding started directly as we gathered and transcribed interview data. During this ongoing interplay between interviewing and coding, insights, hunches and questions were evoked, which in turn guided our continuing data gathering. Hence, theoretical sampling resulted in adding new questions in the interview guide during the research process.

Initial coding was the first coding step, with an open mind and close reading of the data. During the next step of coding – focused coding – the most significant and frequent initial codes were compared to each other to synthesize the large amounts of data into more elaborated categories. 'Victimizing' was identified as the core concept, as well as a set of other focused codes; these now delimited and guided the coding work. During the theoretical coding, we compared the data and our constructed codes and categories with a huge set of theoretical codes (that is, underlying logics that could be found in pre-existing theories) in order to relate our constructed concepts to each other as hypotheses to be integrated into a theory. Memos were written during the research process. We came up with a grounded theory of victimizing in school bullying. The path through victimizing involved four phases: (a) initial attacks, (b) double victimizing, (c) bullying exit, and (d) after-effects of bullying. The concept of double victimizing (covering the main bullying period) refers to an interplay and cycling process between external victimizing and internal victimizing. Acts of harassment were repeatedly directed at the victims from their social environment at school – a social process that constructed and repeatedly confirmed their victim role. A main theme was stigmatizing by being labelled as different. This external victimizing affected the victims and initiated an internal victimizing, which meant that they incorporated the socially constructed victim image, and thought, felt, and acted upon this image. Initial victimizing consists of a sense of not fitting in, distrusting others, self-protecting, self-doubting, self-blaming and resignation. The analysis also revealed a lingering internal victimizing many years afterwards. Hence, even if the bullying had ended, the internal victimizing continued, which in turn created psychosocial problems or maladjustments for the participants.

continued

CONCLUSION

Whatever the type of grounded theory adopted, it is important to remember that the philosophical roots of this approach are in critical realism. As a result, matching grounded theory with other stances and philosophies can result in imprecise application of the method, if the researcher is not aware of the complexities of interlacing different approaches and philosophies. In this chapter, we have described grounded theory as an approach that developed in the late 1960s and which has had a profound influence on social science research. We have considered the various forms of the approach that have developed over time. In addition, we have described issues and challenges concerning its use. A researcher considering using the approach should evaluate whether the approach can achieve the specific research goals required and, if so, whether the advantages outweigh the disadvantages of the situation at hand.

Reflective questions

Concept questions

- What is the purpose of grounded theory?
- How does that purpose differ from other qualitative approaches?
- What are the key steps in the process?
- How has grounded theory evolved over time?

Application questions

- Is your goal to generate theory?
- Which form of grounded theory is most suited to your work?
- When using grounded theory, how will you collect data?

Key resources

Glaser, B. G. and Strauss, A. L. (1967) *Discovery of grounded theory: Strategies for qualitative research*, New York: Aldine de Gruyter.

This classic text helped us to understand the creator's original conception of this research approach. It outlines in detail important concepts and issues and provides practical guidance on how to use it.

Strauss, A. L. and Corbin, J. (1990) *Basics of qualitative research: Grounded theory procedures and techniques*, Newbury Park, CA: Sage.

We also found Strauss and Corbin's follow up to Glaser and Strauss to be essential for our understanding of how at least one form of grounded theory evolved from the original.

Charmaz, K. (2000) Grounded theory: Objectivist and constructivist methods. *In*: N. K. Denzin and Y. S. Lincoln (eds) *Handbook of qualitative research (2nd edn.)*. London: Sage.

Charmaz, K. (2005) *Grounded theory: Methods for the 21st century*, London: Sage

Charmaz, K. (2006) *Constructing grounded theory: A practical guide through qualitative analysis*, London: Sage.

Charmaz's work in constructivist grounded theory has been critical in a further evolution of this method of inquiry. Matching constructivist philosophy with grounded theory methods has given the approach and researchers who use it a new way forward.

Chapter 13

Ethnography

INTRODUCTION

Ethnography is a broad research approach that has evolved since it was first used in anthropology and, today, there are many different types of ethnography. The places and spaces in which researchers have conducted ethnographies over time have mostly changed, moving from the exotic to the local and familiar. From a specific method through which researchers sought to understand tribes and cultures, ethnography has evolved into a broad and inclusive approach that comprises many varieties, such as virtual ethnography and auto-ethnography. In this chapter, we present some of the origins and key features of ethnography. We next describe how researchers generally design and do ethnographic studies. We then present several different types that researchers have adopted. Finally, we describe the advantages and disadvantages to adopting ethnography as an approach.

ORIGINS OF ETHNOGRAPHY

Much of qualitative research traces its origins to ethnography, as it was one of the first qualitative research methods used. Early ethnography emerged from anthropological studies that sought to understand other cultures, countries and ways of life and dates at least as far back as the 1700s (Vidich and Lyman 2000). Primary forms of ethnography focused on hand-collection of data by an anthropologist and the provision of an in-depth description of the setting from which these data were collected. Western anthropologists used early ethnography to explore, understand and tell the stories of marginalized people (Vidich and Lyman 2000). There has been considerable criticism of this kind of ethnography that focused on difference, thereby implying that Western values and practices were somehow better than those of other cultures. Such criticism stemmed around the origins of ethnography as an approach of studying the 'other', in many cases indigenous populations (Vidich and Lyman 2000).

During the 1900s, Malinowski's study of the social life of islanders in the Trobriand islands (Malinowski 1922/1984) and Mead's Samoan study concerning adolescence, childbearing and the influence of culture on personality (Mead 1928) drew attention to ethnography. Such early versions positioned the approach as pragmatic in its stance; researchers sought to interpret the lived experiences of a cultural group. Malinowski argued, for example, in his seminal text *Argonauts of the Western Pacific* (1922/1984):

[Ethnography has a] goal, of which an Ethnographer should never lose sight. This goal is, briefly, to grasp the native's point of view, his relation to life, to realize his vision of his world. We have to study man, and we must study what concerns him most intimately, that is, the hold life has on him. In each culture, the values are slightly different; people aspire after different aims, follow different impulses, yearn after a different form of happiness. In each culture, we find different institutions in which man pursues his life-interest, different customs by which he satisfies his aspirations, different codes of law and morality which reward his virtues or punish his defections. To study the institutions, customs, and codes or to study the behaviour and mentality without the subjective desire of feeling by what these people live, of realising the substance of their happiness — is, in my opinion, to miss the greatest reward which we can hope to obtain from the study of man.

Malinowski (1922/1984: 25)

Early versions of more contemporary ethnography were influenced by the pragmatic sociologists of the Chicago School in the 1930s and 1940s. These interpretive interactionists, along with educationalists such as Dewey, argued against the positivist stances of natural scientists and, instead, sought to combine the scientific study of human behaviours with observational approaches. This shift in the use of ethnography enabled it to be seen as an approach that had more utilitarian value, and was less focused on the 'other' than early forms of ethnography. The result was that ethnography began to be adopted in more local settings than earlier studies and be used to study marginalized and underrepresented groups locally, such as the homeless.

Along with the growth of the approach over time have come questions concerning how the conduct of ethnography can be developed, widened and improved. For example, a collection of papers entitled *Writing culture* (Clifford and Marcus 1986) highlighted two major issues: the crises of legitimacy and representation. The crisis of 'legitimacy' addressed the issue of whether ethnographers should measure the legitimacy of an action by the norms generated by their own world view or by those stemming from the cultural norms, beliefs and practices of the studied culture. The crisis of 'representation' centred on how ethnographers actually interpreted and then presented the individuals and groups they were researching. At about the same time, Geertz (1988) began to argue that anthropological writings should be seen as fiction, since they were crafted and shaped by their authors and were not truly representative of the cultures studied. This argument launched further criticism about the value and values of the method. Despite such criticism, there are still many researchers who value this 'slice of life', 'really real' approach to research.

DESCRIPTION AND PURPOSE OF ETHNOGRAPHY

The term ethnography comes from the Greek, *ethnos*, and is translated as 'folk'. Ethnography is the study of people, cultures and values. It is an approach that aims to create an understanding of those being studied. There are many different views about what counts as ethnography but, broadly speaking, it is an approach that requires intensive fieldwork to gain a detailed and comprehensive view of a social group and its setting. In order to undertake such studies, ethnographers spend time, often years, in the culture, trying to understand its ways, customs and hierarchies. An ethnographic study usually is presented as a written document that portrays a people group with a clear explanation of where the boundaries of that culture begin and end. Thus, ethnographic accounts would necessarily include descriptions of the geography, history, subsistence, infrastructures, kinship and language of a culture. Key characteristics of the approach are as follows:

■ *Focus on everyday life rather than the unusual or peculiar* – the researcher does not want to examine issues that are unusual but instead seeks to understand what is 'normal' within a context. For example, what would a normal day be like for a group of homeless people who live under the railway arches near the River Thames in London?

■ *Immersion of the researcher in a particular field or setting* – researchers spend time with those they are studying. For example, they might choose to live as a homeless person, sleeping out at night and experiencing the poverty and deprivation of a homeless group.

■ *Engagement in the setting for an extended period of time* – the duration of their experiences are lengthy; for example, a researcher might live with a population for months or years.

■ *Use of participant observation as a primary method* – the idea is that through participating in the community it is possible to come to understand it better. Thus by living and working with a group of medical students it should be possible to understand how they become inducted into the medical profession.

■ *In-depth and unstructured data collection* – the researcher uses these data to undertake comprehensive interpretations of meaning and actions of those observed.

■ *Presentation of findings from the participants' point of view* – the researcher traditionally attempts to understand and articulate a particular culture from the perspectives of its members.

Researchers use ethnography when the study of a group will help understand a larger issue or when the researcher wants a day-to-day picture of a particular group. Ethnography also is something that researchers choose when they want to study the everyday lived experiences of a cultural group. It is an appropriate choice when someone wants to search for meaning by way of examining cultural norms. In practice, traditional ethnography is now difficult to undertake, since the extended time and in-depth field work required to carry out traditional ethnography is not a luxury that many researchers have in the twenty-first century.

Ethnography requires in-depth long term study and therefore researchers should be aware of knowing they can choose it only when:

■ access is possible and regular
■ study is allowed of a group's general or specific type of behaviour, religious practice or other observable trait.

Tips

TYPES OF ETHNOGRAPHY

Since ethnography is an approach focusing in-depth on a particular context or group of people, it invariably involves researchers taking themselves away from their own routines of everyday life to observe and study other cultures and settings. While in-depth longitudinal immersion was common in the early days of ethnography (as can be observed in the film *Gorillas in the Mist*) this is not often the case now. For example, studying the playground games of eight-year-olds in practice might mean gaining access to several schools and spending a number of weeks observing children at play. Yet even this is not always possible in the context of small-scale case studies that may last only a few months.

Many researchers now choose to take up more modern forms of ethnography that have emerged since the early versions; these allow more flexibility in approach (Van Maanen 1996). Among the modern forms of ethnography are realist ethnography, critical ethnography, auto-ethnography, duo-ethnography, ethnodrama/performance ethnography, virtual ethnography and cognitive ethnography. Researchers still able to use traditional ethnographic approaches now often refer to their work as 'cultural ethnography', as opposed to simply 'ethnography', so differentiating their work from the later forms.

We outline some of the new ethnographic approaches in Table 13.1 on page 206, and provide further information about each form in the following paragraphs.

Realist ethnography

Realist ethnography, at times called critical realist ethnography, is based upon the ontological perspective of critical realism (see Chapter 2). Critical realism involves the idea that there is an objective reality and so it is possible to know the world as it really is, even if that knowledge is imperfect. Realist ethnography tends to use a post-positivist view toward research and focus on the issue of social structures and ask questions like:

■ Are there such things as social structures?
■ Is it possible to use ethnographic methods to examine those structures and their relationships with social action?

Those in the field of realist ethnography argue that the philosophy of science provides a sound basis for moving ethnography beyond the examination of specific social instances, in order to examine the general structural context of those instances. In realist ethnography, it is the participants' views that are the starting point for the research, with a recognition that human action is both supported and constrained by social structures. However, any human action is seen within this approach as either reproducing or transforming the structures in which those actions occur. This type of ethnography tends to stand in isolation from other forms of ethnography, as it takes a positivist or post-positivist approach, arguing for the need to:

■ Write all research reports in the past tense, using the third person.
■ Present all data in an objective manner without any personal slant, so portraying that the researcher has been only a detached observer, rather than unavoidably a member of the social group whilst being immersed in the culture.
■ Reproduce participants' voices only by edited quotes with total editorial control.

Realist ethnography is used to explore the relationship between structure (the rules and resources that guide and govern society) and agency (human action). A realist approach to ethnography aims not only to describe events but also to explain them, by identifying the influence of structural factors on human agency. Explanation also focuses on how agency maintains or transforms these structures.

Giddens (1984) sees structure and agency as issues that mutually affect one another. He refers to human interaction with structures as a system of norms, which he describes as structuration.

For example, Bhaskar has argued:

In their conscious human activity, [people] for the most part unconsciously reproduce (or occasionally, transform) the structures that govern their substantive activities of production. Thus people do not marry to reproduce the nuclear family, or work to reproduce the capitalist economy. But it is nevertheless the unintended consequence (and inexorable result) of, as it is also the necessary condition for their activity.

(Bhaskar 1989: 80)

Bhaskar argues that whilst individuals may not consider that their life choices reproduce social structures, they in fact do so; therefore the researcher's role is to both unpack the value-ladened-ness of society and choice and the ways in which structures affect and influence our lives.

However, Hammersley has argued that there are difficulties with this approach, he explains:

in context of critical social science today, critical realism is distinctive in putting forward a clear rationale for how evaluative conclusions can be derived directly from research evidence, such that social scientists can present evaluative and prescriptive conclusions as validated by their work. In other words, critical realism offers a rationale for being 'critical'. However, I have shown that neither of the two arguments making up this rationale is convincing. Of course, establishing this does not automatically undercut the project of critical social science, but it weakens it considerably, as against the alternative prospect of a social science committed solely to producing factual conclusions. Moreover, there are other reasons why we should reject the 'critical' project. One of the most important is that the simultaneous attempt both to produce knowledge and to bring about social change of some kind (or, for that matter, to preserve the status quo) is liable considerably to increase the danger of bias.

(Hammersley 2009: 7)

REALIST ETHNOGRAPHY

Leca and Naccache (2006) demonstrate that realist ethnographers tend to focus not only on describing events but also on explaining them, through the process of identifying the influence of structural factors on human agency. In their study, Leca and Naccache presented an institutional analysis which considered the influences of both actors' actions and the institutional structures in which they worked. They identified that these influences were critical when applied to institutional entre-preneurship strategies. They began the study by observing connections between phenomena and then identifying how connections occurred. The next step was to adopt a hypothetical model involving structures and causal powers, and then subject that proposed explanation to empirical scrutiny. As in this example, those adopting this approach begin by explaining and seeking to understand structures, then focus on how agency maintains or transforms them.

Example

Critical ethnography

This form of ethnography is political, as its focus is on challenging the existing status quo of political, social and other structures, by researching the struggles of those weak and powerless against them, with the overall aim of then seeking to change society. It is based on critical theory (see Chapter 2), which is a social theory oriented toward critiquing and changing society 'to liberate human beings from the circumstances that enslave them' (Horkheimer 1982: 244). Like cultural ethnography, those who adopt this approach acknowledge that all research is value laden, while asking strongly political questions that are designed to challenge and interrupt the status quo, such as 'Why is it so?'.

Critical ethnography tends to explore general social issues such as poverty, racism, sexism and inequality. Researchers using critical ethnography often collaborate with participants and are aware of their biases and interpretations. Madison suggests that a critical ethnographer needs to ask questions:

1. How do we reflect upon and evaluate our own purpose, intentions and frames of analysis as researchers?
2. How do we predict consequences or evaluate our own potential to do harm?
3. How do we create and maintain a dialogue of collaboration in our research projects between ourselves and others?
4. How is the specificity of the local story relevant to the broader meanings and operations of the human condition?
5. How – in what location or through what intervention – will our work make the greatest contribution to equity, freedom, and justice?

(Madison 2005: 6)

Many critical ethnography researchers adopt this approach because of their need to take a stance against merely descriptive anthropological studies of the marginalized. Instead, they have created a particular approach that acknowledges such research is value laden and which, as Foley has argued,

> generates the knowledge needed to foster a democratic society and a critical citizenry. In the Gramscian (Gramsci 1971) or Freirean (Freire 1973) formulations, such knowledge production is part of a long dialogic consciousness-raising process. Such knowledge production should have an 'emancipatory intent' (Habermas, 1971) or a 'catalytic validity' (Lather, 1991) that challenges the status quo in some way.

(Foley 2002: 472)

Critical ethnographers use a variety of methods, but what is central is the idea of exploring everyday life and cultural reality. These practices mean that researchers undertake in-depth fieldwork over a period of time (for example a year or more). What is central to critical ethnography is the recognition that the researcher must be highly reflexive whilst recognizing both the value-ladened-ness of research and that only a partial view can ever be offered.

Post-structural ethnography

While practices of realist ethnography often characterize methods in terms of techniques like direct observation, immersion in the field and the researcher as research instrument, post-structural

> **CRITICAL ETHNOGRAPHY**
>
> Baumbusch (2010) provides an example of critical ethnographic research carried out by a novice researcher, highlighting the challenges it presented. The study used critical ethnography in long-term residential care and Baumbusch describes the challenges faced in navigating issues of trust in the researcher/participant relationship and managing power relations. What is particularly useful is that the study describes both how the researcher considered and managed issues of power and developed criteria for trustworthiness.

accounts of ethnography are infused with 'theory and the broader philosophical questions of knowing and being' (Youdell 2006: 59). Knowledge is seen as fragmented and contradictory, and many theoretical questions are left unresolved and unresolvable. As Popoviciu *et al.* (2006) suggest, the task of the 'post-structuralist ethnographer is to recognize the (politically led) narratives that enmesh how we locate and identify those subject to the research' (2006: 405). As Van Maanen suggests, the writing of ethnography informed by post-structural or feminism typically is an attempt to draw an audience into an unfamiliar story world. The audience should as far as possible be able to see, hear, and feel as the researcher saw, heard, and felt. Van Maanen (1998) asserts that it attempts to present a multivocal view of the culture, one that is clearly responsible to ethical treatment of participants.

Auto-ethnography

Auto ethnography is a form of autobiographical narrative that explores the writer's own experience of life. It is an approach in which the researcher/subject draws upon his or her experience, story and self-narrative to examine and connect with the social context. Thus, they tend to come largely from a social constructivist paradigm. Auto-ethnography is an approach to research and writing that seeks to describe and systematically analyze (graphy) personal experience (auto) in order to understand cultural experience (ethno) (Ellis 2004). In practice, this research is written in the first person and features dialogue and self-stories.

Auto-ethnography generally is an approach in which researchers draw upon their experiences, stories and self-narratives to examine and connect with the social context. It is a form of self-narrative that places the self within a social context and includes methods of research and writing that combine autobiography and ethnography. Auto-ethnography is an approach that links personal and cultural issues within a context (Reed-Danahay 1997). In reality, a researcher who uses auto-ethnography writes in the first person and features dialogue and self stories. The idea is that a researcher uses his or her own experiences as the only primary data, interpreting his or her self as a member of a culture and placing his or her self in the world and cultural context, in relation to others. This approach is both a research process and a research product. Data collection in auto-ethnography requires:

- chronicling the past
- undertaking an inventory of the self
- using approaches that enable visualizing the self
- undertaking self-observation
- collecting self-reflective data.

According to the focus of what is being studied, these stories may contain more or less dialogue, thoughts, reflections and emotions. Auto-ethnographers use their own experiences to consider and examine interactions between their self and others. By their very nature, auto-ethnographers, through the process of writing themselves into their own work, are diametrically opposed to more traditional and objectively scientific approaches, where researchers' views, reflections and voices are expected to be minimal or non-existent. Thus as Ellingson and Ellis argue, 'whether we call a work an autoethnography or an ethnography depends as much on the claims made by authors as anything else' (Ellingson and Ellis 2008: 449).

An auto-ethnographer approaches their research with the view that they belong to an under-privileged or otherwise disadvantaged class. As a researcher they therefore seek to unpack, examine and disrupt the power they see as being imposed on their self to their disadvantage. In practice, they disrupt power and practice through telling their own stories, which they may view as an alternative to studying the (exotic) 'other'; rather they study themselves. An example of this would be to reject what they would see as the subjugation that occurs when being studied by a white, male, heterosexual upper class, able and Christian researcher (Denzin *et al.* 2008).

Duo-ethnography

An extension of auto-ethnography is duo-ethnography, which is based in the same tradition as auto-ethnography and uses the same methods. Duo-ethnography is based on the idea that more is learned about a situation or context by discussing it (Ellis 2009) than by reflecting on it alone. Like auto-ethnography, duo-ethnography examines the impact of structures and forces on the story, thereby seeking to understand issues of power and control that impact on someone's experience.

Duo-ethnography, like auto-ethnography, seeks to explore the autobiographical and cultural influences that have shaped beliefs, decisions and so on. However, its focus is on reflexivity through sharing the story with another.

Tips

Duo-ethnography requires one or sometimes two conversation partners and focuses on personal topics and stories, such as:

■ What was it that appealed to you about being a doctor?
■ What do you consider to be your strengths and weaknesses as a doctor?
■ Share some memorable stories from your time as a medical student.
■ What were your best and worst times during your own school experience?
■ What do you consider to be your most important beliefs, and the most important influences on you, in becoming the type of doctor you will or want to be?

Some researchers see the overriding reliance on self as the primary research subject in auto- and duo-ethnography as challenging but not necessarily self-indulgent (Holt 2003). Other related examples of the pitfalls of these approaches include:

■ overwhelming reliance on self as the main data instrument
■ overuse of narration as the main approach to data collection, exacerbated by (un)reliability of non-corroborated personal memories, complicated by where factual recollections end and interpretations begin

- poor/non-existent ethical permissions in relation to other individuals mentioned in self-narratives.

These two narrative approaches tend to be highly personalized. The difficulty with both of these methods is a tendency to be overly descriptive, which is probably because researchers have difficulty in standing back from themselves, in order to interpret their own stories and examine what may be complex and possible painful truths about themselves.

Performance ethnography and ethnodrama

Performance ethnography is a broad descriptor for a number of performative methods used by qualitative researchers. It was developed originally to examine the political nature of practice by Conquergood (2002), who argued that performance should be seen as stories 'to open the space between analysis and action ... and to pull the pin on the binary opposition between theory and practice' (2002: 145). Ethnotheatre involves in particular dramatic staging of social research. Ethnodrama is an approach developed and drawn from 'ethnography' and 'drama', coined by the anthropologist Turner (1982: 100). Ethnodrama is used when researchers believe that dramatic art form is the best way to both research and represent something that is an exploration of the human condition. We suggest there is strong overlap and overplay between ethnotheatre and ethnodrama. Perhaps the best explanation of both is provided by Saldaña:

> Ethnotheatre consists of 'the traditional craft and artistic techniques of theatre production to mount for an audience a live performance event of research participants' experiences and/or the researcher's interpretations of data'.
>
> (Saldaña 2005: 1)

> Ethnodrama consists of 'dramatized, significant selections of narrative collected through interviews, participant observation, field notes, journal entries, and/or print and media artifacts such as diaries, television broadcasts, newspaper articles, and court proceedings'.
>
> (Saldaña 2005: 2)

In practice, this approach involves writing and presenting monologues and dialogues and the scripted adaptation and dramatization of qualitative studies.

ETHNODRAMA

An example of ethnodrama is the work of Nimmon (2007), who undertook a study into linguistic barriers when trying to access health information. The results were presented as an ethnodrama to challenge the audience about issues that are normally hidden and silenced.

Example

Virtual ethnography

The work of Hine (2000) in virtual ethnography has been seminal in terms of seeking to understand, from a sociological perspective, what people do on the Internet. Hine suggests that it is important to examine online actions and spaces at face value and not merely assume that it is possible to understand what is or might be significant or meaningful. Virtual ethnography is:

> ethnography of, in and through the virtual – we learn about the Internet by immersing ourselves in it and conducting our ethnography using it, as well as talking with people about it, watching them use it and seeing it manifest in other social settings.
>
> (Hine 2000: 10)

Hine suggests the following principles of virtual ethnography:

1. Virtual ethnography examines how people use the Internet, and what it means to them as an important (sub) culture, or merely as a sometimes useful addition to their everyday life in terms of being just a cultural artefact.
2. When studying it as an important (sub) culture, intense immersion is probably the best research method, in order to replicate the actions of regular users, and to communicate with those users via the Internet itself. Intense immersion is more likely to take the form of daily and weekly immersion at particular timeslots, rather than typical long term immersion for whole days or weeks at a time.
3. When studying it as a mere cultural artefact, it may be useful to identify occasional users by visiting Internet cafes, libraries and the like, which are used by a high proportion of non-computer owners, so that contact with and observation of such users can be made.
4. As with much research, the initial posing and subsequent refining of your research question will take you in particular virtual and real directions. It is important to be wary of delineating firm boundaries between the real and the virtual, as important data may be missed or discarded as a result. How virtually and physically mobile might you wish to be? To faithfully use virtual ethnography, and to collect the 'right' amount of data, you should be considering following connecting paths on the Internet more than visiting a set number of physical field sites.
5. Finally, virtual ethnography has more likelihood than most other research methods of taking you in unexpected directions, so it is best to have an 'adaptable' mindset throughout your research period.

(adapted from Hine 2000)

Cognitive ethnography

The origins of cognitive ethnography can be seen in the work of Hutchins (1995), who employed anthropological methods in cognitive science to understand how knowledge is constructed and used (Williams 2006). This ethnographic approach has developed further from arguments such as those posed by Leander and McKim (2003), who indicated the need to move beyond place-based ethnography. The central idea lies in combining online and offline ethnographic approaches. The term cognitive ethnography now signals research that examines cognitive processes that affect online activity.

Cognitive ethnography explores the cognitive processes that contribute to activities occurring online, which will be influenced by what else is currently happening offline, such as world news, and cultural, social and individual contexts (Hollan *et al.* 2000). Hine (2007) argues that this approach is a 'methodological response to **e-science** that builds on ethnographic traditions for understanding scientific practice'. An illustration of the ways in which cognitive science and ethnography have been linked is in the use of e-science.

e-science
is the activity of undertaking large-scale science projects through distributed global collaborations enabled by the Internet, which require access to very large data collections and large scale computing resources

Thus, cognitive ethnography seeks to combine science and meaning making within the same approach. Such immersion will result in the researchers feeling 'in' or 'part of' a virtual environment as they become absorbed or deeply involved. As mentioned earlier, immersion is a complex concept. If immersive research is to take place effectively, it requires the in-depth engagement of physical senses and mental processes with the environment, in order to understand the types of interaction, emotion, embodiment and technology involved. This approach therefore moves beyond just collecting interviews and watching what people do 'in world'. The focus is to become completely immersed, so that the researcher experiences a collision of being researcher, researched and participant.

DESIGNING AND DOING ETHNOGRAPHY

When using ethnography, the researcher faces essential choices about philosophical and personal position, framing the study, collecting data, working with data and writing about the results. In the next few paragraphs, we provide an overview of the choices researchers who use ethnography often make. We follow this description by a summary of these common choices in Table 13.2 on p. 208.

Philosophical and personal positioning

Early twentieth century scholars who used ethnography originally adopted a pragmatic philosophical stance, and tended to try to 'enter' the site and observe it from the inside (see Chapter 2). As we have indicated, there are now many different types of ethnography and researchers can accordingly choose from a number of varied philosophical positions. For example, ethnography from the vantage point of critical social theory is an increasingly popular approach to understanding cultures. Many researchers who operate from a constructivist or constructionist approach also have adopted ethnography (see Chapter 4).

Focus of the study

The phenomenon of interest in ethnography is the group (see Chapter 6) and research questions signal what it is that the researcher wishes to understand about that group. Modern day ethnographers tend to engage with literature and produce full literature reviews (Chapter 8), and they often adopt theoretical frameworks to guide their interpretations of culture (Chapter 9).

Data collection

Researchers tend to use ethnographic fieldwork and may choose an outsider or insider and outsider stance (see Chapter 22). They often use participant observations and in-depth interviewing; they take extensive field notes (see Chapter 22), which are a hallmark of ethnographic

Table 13.1 Types of ethnography

Type	Commonly adapted paradigms	Focus	Key features
Realist ethnography	Critical realism	Explores the relationship between structure (the rules that guide and govern society) and agency (human action).	Describes and explains events, by identifying the influence of structural factors on human agency.
Critical ethnography	Critical social theory	Challenges the existing status quo of political, social and other structures, by researching the struggles of those weak and powerless.	Reflects upon researcher purpose, intentions and frames of analysis as researchers. Ensures that research contributes to equity, freedom and justice.
Post-structural ethnography	Post-structural and feminist theory	Considers broader questions related to knowing and being.	Brings together theory and research practice, seeking to allow for multiple voices.
Auto-ethnography	Constructivism/ constructionism	Draws upon their experiences, stories and self-narratives to examine and connect with the social context.	Uses researchers' own experiences to consider and examine interactions between their self and others.
Duo-ethnography	Constructivism/ constructionism	Seeks to explore the autobiographical and cultural influences that have shaped beliefs and decisions, through conversing with another.	Use of researcher's own experiences in conversation with another to examine interactions between him or her self and others.
Ethnodrama/ performance ethnography	Constructivism/ constructionism/ critical social theory	Use of dramatic art form to both research and represent something that is an exploration of the human condition.	Collecting data through interviews and observation, and writing and performing drama to represent the data in critical and challenging ways.
Virtual ethnography	Constructivism/ constructionism	Exploration of online actions and online spaces in order to understand what people do on the Internet.	Boundaries, especially between the virtual and the real, are not taken for granted. It is a process of intermittent engagement, rather than long-term immersion.
Cognitive ethnography	Constructivism	Combining online and offline ethnographic approaches.	Examines the cognitive processes occurring online that are influenced by offline activities.

work. Perhaps one of the greatest challenges in ethnography is the ethical one, partly because inevitably researchers become so involved in the subject culture, and ethnographic researchers tend to place particular importance on respect to individuals (see Chapter 21).

Working with data and findings

Ethnographers tend to take up ethnographic analysis or ethnographic content analysis (see Chapter 28). They use a range of approaches to establish quality in their studies. Richardson (2000: 254) provides five criteria that researchers might find useful in terms of critiquing ethnography:

1. *Substantive contribution*: 'Does the piece contribute to our understanding of social-life?'
2. *Aesthetic merit*: 'Does this piece succeed aesthetically?'
3. *Reflexivity*: 'How did the author come to write this text ... Is there adequate self-awareness and self-exposure for the reader to make judgments about the (imposed) point of view?'
4. *Impact*: 'Does this affect me? Emotionally? Intellectually? Does it move me'?
5. *Expresses a reality*: 'Does it seem "true" – a credible account of a cultural, social, individual or communal sense of the "real"?'

Writing

The written report is termed an 'ethnography' as we have indicated. The report may take the standard written form or may be represented through more creative means such as drama (see Chapter 32). Representation centres on the ability of the researcher to represent correctly, honestly and fully the researched group or individuals, through the collected data, to address the research question. An important question is 'whose voice is being heard?'. The answer requires clarifying whether the voices/views expressed are the general group opinion, the vested interest of a powerful leader, the downtrodden plea of a weak group member or whether they are from outside those researched, such as the researcher or a stakeholder (see Chapter 31).

Summary of choices when designing and doing ethnography

In Table 13.2 on page 208, we highlight key choices that researchers using ethnography commonly make. Our intent is not to say how the approach must be done but rather to provide a description of the way that we have most often seen it in the literature. Thus, this table is intended to serve as a general guide that researchers may consider when they design and do their own ethnographic studies. This table provides links to other parts and chapters in this book, where we provide fuller descriptions and practical advice for doing qualitative research.

ADVANTAGES AND CHALLENGES OF ETHNOGRAPHY

There are many advantages and challenges when using ethnography. Some of the advantages are as follows:

- *The research can provide extensive and in-depth findings about human behaviour* – as a result of this the research can evolve and explore new lines of inquiry over a number of months and years.
- *The study can be longitudinal* – ongoing research means that the research design can be flexible and emergent.

Table 13.2 Designing ethnography

Design	Specifics	Chapter
Philosophical stance	Critical theory, pragmatism, critical realism, post-modernism	4
Personal stance	High degrees of disclosure of positionality in final report	5
Who or what of study	Groups	6
Research questions	Focus on understanding the group	7
Literature review	Comprehensive and all inclusive	8
Theoretical/conceptual framework	Can be applied to guide research design but not typically imposed upon interpretation of data	9
Time/place/participants	Long duration in the field	20
	Done in natural environment	
	Purposeful sampling, frequently maximum variation	
Ethics	Ethical design, treatment of individuals, processes, and presentation of products important; particular emphasis on respect of individuals	21
Fieldwork	Ethnographic fieldwork, field notes, journals	22
Data collection	Unstructured observations in context	23–26
	Unstructured and informal interviewing	
	Review of documents or other pertinent materials	
Coding	Modifiable coding systems that correspond to the data collected	27
Analysis	Ethnographic analysis; ethnographic content analysis	28
Interpretation	High level of inference in interpretation	29
Quality	View of quality, quality criterion and strategies to ensure quality important; particular emphasis on view and criterion	30
Researcher voice	External observer and reporter	31
Report	Description of the data organized to tell a story of the participants	32

- *Research findings are plausible because of the methods used* – participant observation allows confirmation of participants' behaviour, not merely espoused behaviour that is often found when using interviews and questionnaires.
- *People are best studied in their natural environment* – and ethnography provides a much more comprehensive perspective of the user and their environment than other forms of research.

The challenges of ethnographic research make it much less popular than other approaches and it is not an approach we believe should be adopted lightly:

- *In general, ethnography only examines one culture, setting or organization* – this means that conclusions are not easily generalizable to other contexts.
- *Ethnographic research is simply hard to do* – observation can take months and years and therefore in the main is not compatible with other academic demands such as studying and teaching. Furthermore, since ethnography focuses mainly on observations about what the

participants were doing, saying or feeling, these can be misinterpreted or misrepresented by the researcher's own cultural bias or ignorance.

■ *Translating field notes into data suitable for analysis is complex and troublesome* – this takes considerable time and produces a large data set that often takes further considerable time to analyze and interpret.

■ *Ethnography tends to be expensive* – since it takes time to plan and gain access, it is then long term and in-depth, and the research site can be at an (expensive) distance.

Many of these advantages and difficulties depend upon the form of ethnography that the researcher adopts.

EXAMPLE

In the following Researcher reflections, Latzko-Toth describes his work with virtual ethnography and in the second, Kazubowski-Houston shares information about her work in performance ethnography.

Guillaume Latzko-Toth, Université Laval, Québec, Canada

Asynchronous (online) ethnography: a tale of two Internet relay chat networks

My first research on Internet relay chat (IRC) was about a local group of online chat adepts. It was an almost conventional ethnography, except for online observation and chat sessions transcripts analysis. As I was getting a deeper understanding of IRC, I was impressed by the richness of this digital microcosm in constant transformation and by the fact that users played an active role in its evolution. For my doctoral research on communication technology, I wanted to understand how it evolved from a very basic program to a vast constellation of sociotechnical networks. But because IRC development started twenty years before my research took place and people involved in it were scattered around the world, I turned to the tools of virtual ethnography.

Along with documents analysis (including official websites, technical protocols, source code of early IRC software) and online textual interviews (synchronous, asynchronous, hybrid) with actors of IRC development, a key component of my research methods was what, for want of a better word, could be called 'asynchronous online ethnography': the observation, description and analysis of the past social life of an online group, based on archived traces of digitally mediated interactions. Besides Usenet newsgroups, I analyzed archives of public and private mailing lists used by IRC 'operators'. I used the sensitizing concept of critical moment as a heuristic tool to explore the corpus of electronic discussions and spot controversies and turning points in the evolution of two major networks (EFnet and Undernet) from 1990 to 2001. The interviews, open discussions which took place synchronously (on IRC, via instant

Researcher reflections

continued

messaging, and so on) and/or asynchronously (by email, Facebook) were done concurrently with the discourse analysis, to validate and refine my interpretations.

A thorny aspect of the research was citing. Because my research had a historical dimension, it seemed necessary to give proper credit to people for their contributions, either under their real name or under their usual IRC pseudonym (nickname). For software code, it was simple since the names are made public in credit files. For verbal contributions to debates and sociotechnical decisions, which are an important aspect of the co-construction of artefacts, I had to balance between protecting privacy and protecting publicity. Some mailing lists weren't public and in the heat of a debate people may say things in a way they would not be comfortable with if it were published in another context and accessible to a broader readership. But I was concerned that mentioning a person's real name in some cases and a nickname in other occasions would destroy the coherence of an individual's identity and trajectory and make the story less intelligible for the reader. Moreover, using nicknames may mask gender information, in a context of underrepresentation of women in historical accounts of information technology innovation. That led me to adopt a pragmatic, modulated approach. I cited real names for notoriously public e-lists. For non-public lists, I asked for permission to use real names when it seemed important, otherwise I used the usual IRC nickname so as to introduce a certain amount of 'friction' or simply kept the words anonymous.

Researcher reflections

Photograph by Shawn Kazubowski-Houston

Magdalena Kazubowski-Houston, Wilfrid Laurier University, Ontario, Canada

My work is situated in the context of performance-centred ethnography that both employs theatre performance as an ethnographic research methodology and studies it as a product that emerges out of the research process. My research has explored the challenges of theatre employed as a form of ethnographic participant observation by analyzing a politically charged theatre performance undertaken with a group of Roma (gypsy) women and non-Roma actors in Poland. My book, *Staging strife: Lessons from performing ethnography with Polish Roma women* (2010), discusses the ways in which the power struggles over representation in rehearsals between the Roma women, the actors and me as the ethnographer complicated the collaborative, empowering and politicizing objectives of the project. I attempt to provide a frank account of the difficult moral and ethical decisions I was compelled to make throughout the course of the project, as conflicts and struggles between ethnographer and research participant still remain to be addressed in qualitative research literature (Kazubowski-Houston 2011b). I reveal how the shifting contexts of the field, competing personal and professional agendas and my own inability to stay above the power games threatened to derail the theatre production. By interrogating power relations within my own ethnographic process, my hope is to contribute to the literature on ethnographic uses of reflexivity and contemporary critiques of collaboration.

My most recent ethnographic work with Polish Roma elders examines dramatic storytelling as an ethnographic research methodology in the study of aging. In particular, it concerns itself with how the liminality of fiction in the context of non-public and non-collective dramatic storytelling can afford a space for the safer expression of knowledge for research participants from marginalized communities. While competing agendas, politics of representation and concerns over confidentiality and anonymity can compromise participant expression in performance and collaborative ethnography projects, I explore how dramatic storytelling that is not intended for public performance, and involves research participants individually, rather than collectively, can facilitate the construction of ethnographic knowledge about topics that participants might be less willing to discuss in a research context. Expanding upon Conquergood's notion of shared emotional knowledge, I also inquire into the ways in which non-public, non-collective dramatic storytelling can facilitate a bidirectional research process, wherein the ethnographer and research participants seek empathic and cognitive understandings of each other's worlds.

Finally, I have also studied physical theatre as a form of ethnographic research. Specifically, I have examined the ways in which the moving body, in the context of performance ethnography, can be politicizing for the research participants, the ethnographer and audience members. Building on Brecht's concept of theatre as a form of social critique and action, Mienczakowski's notion of empathy as a strategy for social intervention, and recent literature in cognitive science and neurophysiology, I have analyzed the politicizing potential of improvisation through the notion of 'bodily contagion' – the potential of the body-in-motion to kinaesthetically impact another body. At the centre of my analysis are the ways in which the interplay between movement, experience, emotion and interpretation during improvisation can constitute a form of 'transformative kinesis' in performance-centred research (Kazubowski-Houston 2011a).

continued

CONCLUSION

Ethnography has come a long way from its beginnings in cultural anthropology and Chicago School sociology. Many scholars now consider it to be a qualitative, cultural interpretation. Ethnographers are expected to produce what Geertz referred to as 'webs of significance' (Geertz 1973: 5) and not merely what group A believes about racism or how tribe B organizes adolescent initiation into adulthood. In addition, there are many different approaches to ethnography and the choice often depends on the context being studied. What is important to remember about ethnography is that it involves in-depth study, not just grabbing a few interviews before exiting the site to resume normal daily life, analyze and write up. Ethnography is a complex, long term commitment to work with participants. It cannot be done quickly or badly if it is to be viable, honest, representative and ethical.

Reflective questions

Concept questions

■ How possible do you think it is to undertake ethnography at undergraduate or Masters' level?
■ What are the main changes that have taken place in the use of ethnography since it was first developed through anthropology?
■ What are the key disadvantages of this approach?

Application questions

■ Would ethnography be a suitable approach for your study?
■ Which type of ethnography holds the most appeal?

Key resources

Atkinson, P. and Hammersley, M. (1994) Ethnography and participant observation. *In*: N. K. Denzin and Y. S. Lincoln (eds) *Handbook of qualitative research*. Thousand Oaks, CA: Sage.
A clear and accessible chapter that outlines the challenges of using this approach.

Hammersley, M. and Atkinson, P. (2007) *Ethnography: Principles in practice (3rd edn.)*, London: Routledge.
An expansion of the chapter above with good examples and practical tips.

Hine, C. (2000) *Virtual ethnography*, London: Sage.
An explanation of virtual ethnography that is accessible, up to the minute and thought provoking.

Chapter 14

Phenomenology

INTRODUCTION

Many qualitative researchers are interested in exploring human experiences and some of them seek to understand the nature of the experience itself. These researchers often are guided by the philosophical perspectives of Husserl or Heidegger (see Chapter 2). In this chapter, we describe phenomenology, a research approach that allows for investigating the human experience at a fundamental level, seeking the essence of lived experiences as it is for several individuals; in short, phenomenologists want to know about the very structures of consciousness (Polkinghorne 1989). We also explore different forms of studying lived experiences that have emerged from or away from phenomenology, including transcendental phenomenology, hermeneutic phenomenology and phenomenography. Finally, we discuss the advantages and disadvantages of phenomenology as an approach.

ORIGINS

In phenomenology, philosophy and method are inextricably linked; thus, the origins of phenomenology should be traced back to the philosophies of Husserl and later Heidegger. Phenomenology was founded by Husserl (1907/1964), who argued that consciousness was an important concept and proposed the study of lived experience or the life world. Husserl criticized psychology for trying to use objective scientific methods to study human issues. He founded phenomenology on the basis that what needed to be examined was the way people lived in the world, rather than the world being seen as a separate entity from the person. He argued that life world is what individuals experience pre-reflectively, before humans categorize or conceptualize an experience. His arguments to some extent stood against the **Cartesian** model in which the mind and body were seen as separate and distinct entities.

Descartes (1979/1641) accepted that there was some interaction between body and mind but believed there was not a substantial connection between them. In contrast, however, Husserl believed that it was only possible for the conscious mind to engage with the world since it was already part of it.

Heidegger worked with Husserl and at first adopted this form of phenomenology but later shifted his position, arguing for a more holistic stance towards understanding humanity. While Husserl focused on understanding phenomena, such as how people perceived and thought about the world, Heidegger focused on

Cartesian
Those things that are of or related to René Descartes, his mathematical methods, or his philosophy, especially in regards to an emphasis on logical analysis and mechanistic interpretation of physical nature

dasein, the mode of being human. So, while Husserl concentrated on comprehending phenomena, Heidegger focused on understanding what it meant to be human. The disagreement in Husserl's and Heidegger's stances is perhaps best captured in the view of bracketing. The idea of bracketing is where the researcher brackets off their preconceptions in order to see phenomena without being influenced by past experiences. Husserl believed it was necessary to bracket off the world and suspend judgment in order to see phenomena clearly. Heidegger however, argued against any difference between the person and their experiences and saw them as coexisting. He saw bracketing as being impossible, as it was not possible to stand outside experience (Heidegger 1927/1962).

Table 14.1 Comparison of phenomenology of Husserl and Heidegger

	Husserl	*Heidegger*
Stance	Begins with pre-reflection	Acknowledges pre-reflection has occurred
Focus	Study of phenomena as they appeared through consciousness	Understanding the situated meaning of a human in the world
Method	The researcher describes as accurately as possible the phenomenon, refraining from any pre-given framework but remaining true to the facts	The researcher seeks to describe and understand phenomena
View of the person	Knowers in the world	Creatures of fate in an alien world
Bracketing	Seeing things as they are through intuition	Not possible as one cannot stand outside pre-reflections
Position of researcher	Required to use self-reflection to become aware of biases in order to bracket them	Required to use self-reflection to realise how biases may be embedded in the process of interpretation
Data analysis	Describes structure of experience. Locates organizing principles that elucidates the life world	Seeks to understand historical meaning of experiences and the impact of this on individuals and society

The phenomenology of Heidegger was carried forward by others such as Gadamer and Merleau-Ponty. Gadamer (1960/1975) shifted the work of Heidegger into a more practical realm. He argued that having developed a procedure for understanding human experience it was important to have a means of clarifying the conditions under which understanding took place. Merleau-Ponty (1964/1998) focused specifically on the phenomenology of the body. He argued that 'being embodied' was the main way of understanding the world but he argued that embodiment was not restricted to our own bodies; we also unite with others and other things. Merleau-Ponty saw this as perception; we are both perceivers and perceived. Thus, 'the "touching subject" passes over to the rank of the touched, descends into the things' (1964/1998: 169). So, whereas positivists and post-positivists (see Chapter 2) saw being objective as a possibility, phenomenologists saw human subjects not as detached from the world but as part of it; thus, objectivity was untenable.

DESCRIPTION AND PURPOSE OF PHENOMENOLOGY

Phenomenology is a research approach that attempts to uncover what several participants who experience a phenomenon have in common (Creswell 2007). The intent is to reduce the experiences to a description of a universal essence or the very nature or essence of the thing (van Manen 1990: 177). As Owen suggests:

> Phenomenology is primarily a study of essences (definitive reflective acts) and the meanings of exemplary cases, to find the possibilities for objective thought. Seeing essences is primarily about attending to the sensual experience of that which appears. Secondly it involves naming the definitive whatness of any object, and hence, is about the categories for naming. For instance, sciences are built on the essences, categories and boundaries they draw up, which define legitimate academic discourse.
>
> (Owen 1994: 19)

Phenomenologists seek not only to uncover what individuals experience but also how they experience the phenomenon. The phenomenon is typically a concept, such as love, care, hate, anger, beauty, neglect. Phenomenological researchers may investigate the phenomenon in its outward form, which includes objects and actions, as well as in its inward form, which includes thoughts, images and feelings.

While most phenomenological researchers have followed in the footsteps of either Husserl or Heidegger, what is common across these perspectives is the study of lived experiences of individuals, which they view as conscious experiences (van Manen 1990), an effort to work without presuppositions (Stewart and Mickunas 1990) and a refusal of subject–object dichotomy (Stewart and Mickunas 1990). A particular phenomenon that several individuals experience is the focus, which is to be understood in phenomenology in terms of the way it presents itself to the consciousness of the person who encounters them. A precise meaning is given to 'experience' which refers to individual experience of ordinary things. In addition, in phenomenology, the idea of consciousness enjoys a privileged status; therefore, it is important to acknowledge consciousness rather than ignore it.

Giorgi (1989) outlines four central features of the approach which can be seen across all types of phenomenological methods. First, the research is rigorously descriptive. Second, it uses phenomenological reductions. Third, it explores the intentional relationship between people and situations. Fourth, the essences or structures are revealed through the use of imaginative variation.

Spiegelberg (1960) outlines three steps researchers undertake when doing phenomenology of whatever type:

1. Intuiting: Experiencing or recalling the phenomenon. 'Hold' it in your awareness, or live in it, be involved in it; dwell in it or on it.

2. Analyzing: Examine the phenomenon, by examining

   - The pieces, parts, in the spatial sense;
   - The episodes and sequences, in the temporal sense;
   - The qualities and dimensions of the phenomenon;
   - Settings, environments, surroundings;
   - The prerequisites and consequences in time;
   - The perspectives or approaches one can take;
   - Cores or foci and fringes or horizons;
   - The appearing and disappearing of the phenomena;
   - The clarity of the phenomenon.

   It should be investigated in their outward forms; objects, actions and others and in their inward forms; thoughts, images and feelings.

3.   Describing: Write down your description. Write it as if the reader had never had the experience. Guide them through your intuiting and analyzing.

(summarized from Spiegelberg 1960: 659)

Perhaps the most important thing to understand about this approach is that phenomenology always means appreciating what the phenomenon means to the person, just as he or she sees and experiences it. Researchers would choose to use this approach when they wanted to understand the essence of someone's experience, understand consciousness and understand the essential features of someone's experience of a particular phenomenon. The overarching principles of this approach are:

- phenomenological reduction
- description
- the search for essence.

Phenomenological reduction

Phenomenological reduction requires bracketing previous knowledge in order to take a fresh view of something and to see whatever is being researched 'as it is'. The idea of bracketing is not to empty oneself of all past experience but, instead, to put aside ideas, knowledge and thought related to the phenomenon under study so that they are not influential. The idea here is by doing so the researcher will see the phenomenon without previous interpretations interfering.

Description

Description is the way language is used to communicate the phenomenon to others. Merleau-Ponty (1962/1945) highlighted the differences between description, on the one hand, and explanation and construction on the other. We discuss these differences further in the chapters on data analysis and data interpretation. However, in phenomenology the idea of construction would mean departing from what is present and going 'behind' the phenomenon, which would be seen as a departure from a strict phenomenological approach.

The search for essence

Free imaginative variation

This is when researchers believe they have a sense of the essential characteristic of a phenomenon and then ask themselves what they can change without losing the phenomenon. The researcher changes this aspect of it and evaluates what alteration then takes place

This is where the researcher presents the meaning and context of the phenomenon to the wider research community. However, in order to do this, Husserl suggests that the researcher needs to seek the essence of the phenomenon being studied by using a method he calls **free imaginative variation**. In practice this actually means that the researcher freely alters some aspect of the phenomenon being studied and then evaluates what change has taken place.

Qualitative researchers frequently use phenomenology as a research approach. They have used it to investigate a range of phenomena from individual experiences of hospital care to individuals' experiences of anger, neglect, hope and joy. The approach has wide appeal in many social science and professional fields, including sociology, psychology, health sciences and education (Creswell 2007).

TYPES OF PHENOMENOLOGY

While researchers necessarily undertake phenomenology in a variety of ways, we see three primary types of phenomenology. These are as follows: transcendental phenomenology, hermeneutic phenomenology and phenomenography, that latter of which is a variation that is receiving increasing attention in the field of education. We describe these in the following paragraphs and provide a summary table at the end of the section.

Transcendental phenomenology

As we mentioned in the section on origins of phenomenology above, Husserl studied phenomena through exploring consciousness; he believed that by studying intentionality it would be possible to locate how people built their knowledge of reality. Intentionality is important; the idea that consciousness is always directed towards an object that is not itself conscious. Husserl borrowed this idea from Brentano (1874), who defined intentionality as the idea that what makes the mind different from things is that mental acts are always directed at something beyond themselves. What this means is that consciousness is relational so that objects are not spatial entities; therefore, the meaning of being a subject implies a relationship with an object, and to be an object means being related to it subjectively. Key components of Husserl's phenomenology are:

- *Intentionality*: the idea that the mind is directed towards the object of study.
- *Essences*: the descriptive study of subjective processes. To seek the essence of the phenomenon the researcher changes some aspect of the phenomenon being studied and then sees what change has taken place.
- *Bracketing*: the researcher must bracket out the world and personal biases in order to understand the essences of the phenomena being studied.

Moustakas (1994) drew on Husserl, arguing for transcendental phenomenology where meaning is central and data collection is undertaken for the purpose of explicating human experience. Fundamental to his perspective is the notion of bracketing, during which researchers set aside their experiences as much as possible to try to understand the phenomenon under investigation from a fresh perspective. The steps in Moustakas's (1994) approach (also Creswell 2007: 60–2) are as follows. Researchers:

- consider whether the problem is suited to a phenomenological approach (that is, it is important to understand several individuals' common or shared experiences)
- identify a common phenomenon of interest to study (such as beauty, hope, care, anger)
- articulate the philosophical assumptions of phenomenology (that is, rejection of objective/subjective distinction, view of conscious experience directed toward an object)
- bracket out their experiences of the phenomenon
- collect data from individuals who have experienced the phenomenon (interviews, observations, journals, conversations)
- ask two primary and general questions: what have you experienced in terms of the phenomenon? What contexts or situations have typically influenced or affected your experiences of the phenomenon? (other questions may be asked)
- analyze the data by highlighting significant segments and developing clusters of meanings into themes

- write descriptions of what the individual participants experienced and how the context and setting influenced what the participants experienced
- write about their own experiences and how the context and situations have influenced them
- and write a composite description of the 'essence' of the phenomenon for all participants.

Hermeneutic phenomenology

Although originally Heidegger took up Husserl's work, he did not essentially agree with his stance and so developed hermeneutic phenomenology. As we described in the 'Origins' section of this chapter, the basis of Heidegger's work was that he believed consciousness could not be seen as separate from the world since it was part of people's experience. He argued that a person's background influenced the way they saw the world, so it was important to take this background influence into account. Thus in hermeneutic phenomenology the focus is on shedding light on taken for granted experiences that then enable researchers to create meaning and develop understanding. Central to Heidegger's work was the hermeneutic circle, whereby the researcher's interpretations move from seeking to understand a particular component of experience to developing a sense of the whole, and then back again to examining a further component, in an iterative cycle. Such a process enables the researcher to engage at an increasingly deeper understanding of the phenomena being studied.

van Manen (1990), who drew upon Heidegger, has argued that the purpose of phenomenology is the interpretation of a text or a study in history in order to gain understanding. He has also developed a helpful guide to hermeneutic phenomenology which provides a structure for undertaking phenomenological research around six research activities:

1. Turning to a phenomenon which seriously interests us and commits us to the world;
2. Investigating experience as we live it rather than as we conceptualise it;
3. Reflecting on the essential themes which characterise the phenomenon;
4. Describing the phenomenon through the art of writing and rewriting;
5. Maintaining a strong and oriented pedagogical relation to the phenomenon;
6. Balancing the research context by considering the parts and the whole.

(van Manen 1990: 30–1)

A variation: phenomenography

Phenomenography can be traced to Heidegger's phenomenology, although it was initially developed to understand the phenomena of teaching and learning in a coherent way. The approaches are linked, however, by their focus on relational, experiential, contextual and qualitative perspectives. Unlike phenomenology, researchers do not seek to describe things as they are but, instead, attempt to characterize how things appear to people. Phenomenography is 'the empirical study of the differing ways in which people experience, perceive, apprehend, understand, conceptualise various phenomena in and aspects of the world around us. The words experience, perceive ... etc., are used interchangeably' (Marton 1994). It is an approach that investigates the qualitatively different ways in which people experience something or think about something.

The origins of the approach may be traced back to a group of educationalists at the Department of Education, University of Gothenburg, Sweden, in the 1970s, who developed the approach to answer questions about thinking in learning, in particular how learning took place in formal settings. These researchers initially had relied upon traditional research methods and creating artificial situations, such as using structured free recall, to understand the way students read prose. However, having realized the limitations of these initial approaches, they instead began to ask students to read excerpts from text books and then tell the researchers what they understood from that reading, and how they went about the task. Having transcribed the interviews, researchers found that students reading the same text understood in qualitatively different ways. After undertaking further studies in this area, the researchers concluded that if students had qualitatively different understandings of written materials and if these understandings could be classified, then this approach could in turn be used to classify other differences that people experience. These seminal studies not only brought about a new research approach, but also brought to the fore differences in students' approaches to learning (such as deep and surface approaches to learning, holist and aerialist approaches) that have since been accepted throughout higher education.

The assumptions then underlying this approach are that there are only a finite number of ways of understanding a phenomenon. Phenomenographic research seeks to locate variation in experience. It is not then merely concerned with the way that phenomena are experienced or, indeed, with abstract ideas, thoughts and perceptions that are seen as separate concepts from one another. Instead, it is concerned with the relationship between humans and the world

USING PHENOMENOGRAPHY

Trigwell *et al.* (1999) used phenomenography to analyze the experiences of lecturers teaching in higher education. Initially they sought to describe circumstances of two qualitatively different approaches to teaching that they thought affected the quality of student learning. Prosser and Trigwell interviewed twenty-four lecturers, analyzed the transcripts of the interviews and developed a map or model of teachers' conceptions of teaching and learning (Trigwell *et al.* 1994; Prosser *et al.* 1994). Their findings provided both examples of approaches to teaching and conceptions of teaching and learning. Below is an exemplar from one part of their study that illustrated the categories of teachers' conceptions of teaching and learning that they developed, which shows how general and generalizable these categories are:

Approaches to teaching

Approach A: A teacher-focused strategy with the intention of transmitting information to students.

Approach B: A teacher-focused strategy with the intention that students acquire the concepts of the discipline.

Approach C: A teacher/student interaction strategy with the intention that students acquire the concepts of the discipline.

Approach D: A student-focused strategy aimed at students developing their conceptions.

Approach E: A student-focused strategy aimed at students changing their conceptions.

(Prosser and Trigwell, 1999: 58)

Prosser and Trigwell argued that such an analysis may enable lecturers to account for the diversity in the experience of different students in distinct contexts with diverse teachers.

Example

they inhabit. As a result, phenomenographers do not make statements about the world as it is, but seek to understand people's conceptions of the world.

This is an approach that has had a strong impact on teaching and learning research in higher education, particularly in Europe and Australia. However, it presents a number of challenges to the researcher:

- a tendency to overstructure and decontextualize data
- the assumption that conceptions can be generalized and are not necessarily personal qualities
- the generation of categories from interview data in which context and individuals are separated
- the use of variation and comparison of conception
- the limits of applicability across disciplines and fields and instead strong links to a single field (education)
- the inherent assumption that by both understanding student conceptions and earmarking discrepancies in their thinking, that improvement can follow.

The three types of phenomenology are summarized in Table 14.2.

Table 14.2 Types of phenomenology

Type	Commonly adapted paradigms	Focus	Key features
Transcendental	Pragmatism	• Study of phenomena as they appear through consciousness	• Seeking the essence of the phenomenon by changing an aspect of it and then evaluating that change
Hermeneutic	Interpretivism	• To understand the situated meaning of a human in the world	• Understanding phenomena • Interpreting data • Using self-reflection
Phenomenography	Constructivism	• Understanding differing ways in which people experience and apprehend various phenomena of the world	• Uncovering differences in understanding • Locating socially significant ways of thinking shared across a particular group • Understanding conception of the world

DESIGNING AND DOING PHENOMENOLOGY

When using phenomenological research, the researcher faces essential choices about philosophical and personal position, framing the study, collecting data, working with data and writing about the results. In the next few paragraphs, we provide an overview of the choices researchers who use phenomenological research often make. We follow this description by a summary of these common choices in Table 14.3 provides links to other parts and chapters in this book where we provide fuller descriptions and practical advice for doing qualitative research.

Philosophical and personal positioning

In phenomenology, philosophy and method are inextricably linked. The researcher draws upon the philosophy of phenomenology (see Chapters 2 and 4) and often identifies as either transcendental or hermeneutic. The researcher spends time in the written report detailing this perspective; the level of personal disclosure depends upon whether the individual chooses to bracket out experiences or use them in interpretation.

Focus of the study

Phenomenological researchers tend to study concepts in order to understand the essence of their meaning to individuals (see Chapter 6) and research questions focus on gaining information about the essence of experience (see Chapter 7). Literature reviews often occur early in the study schedule (see Chapter 8). Because the essence of experience is so central and is to be uncovered before it is categorized, researchers do not tend to use a theoretical or conceptual framework to guide interpretation of data; doing so could impose presuppositions on the meaning of the experiences.

Data collection

Phenomenological researchers collect data in many ways but what is central to data collection is the phenomenological interview (see Chapter 23). This interview typically involves an unstructured approach with an unforced flow of questions. It is often seen as a collaborative approach, which is intended to evoke both a colourful description of the phenomenon as well as empathetic understanding of ways in which individuals experience phenomena. Seidman suggests that the phenomenological interview:

> provides access to the context of people's behavior and thereby provides a way for researchers to understand the meaning of that behavior. A basic assumption in in-depth interviewing research is that the meaning people make of their experience affects the way they carry out that experience …. Interviewing allows us to put behavior in context and provides access to understanding their action.
>
> (Seidman 1998: 4)

Documents, such as diaries or journals (see Chapter 26), and participant observation may also be used (see Chapter 25). Ethical standards are of great importance, as they generally are for qualitative researchers, and phenomenologists consider ethics from a design, participant, process, and product perspective; they give particular importance to ethical treatment of individuals and how they are portrayed in the written product (see Chapter 21).

Working with data and findings

This research approach requires seeing what the phenomenon means to the person, just as he or she sees and experiences it. Researchers following Husserl and Heidegger have different approaches to data analysis and interpretation. Transcendental phenomenologists might employ heuristic analysis, while hermeneutic ones might choose interpretive phenomenological analysis (see Chapter 28). Phenomenologists consider quality from the view of it, the criterion for it and the strategies used to achieve it; of particular focus is the view of quality, with emphasis given on a more interpretive perspective than validity and a move toward trustworthiness or plausibility.

Writing

Writing requires communicating the structure of the concrete, lived experience from the perspective of the discipline when it is applied to the data. Giorgi (1997: 239) suggests that a researcher should always try to obtain a single structure (for all of the subjects in the study) whilst not specifically forcing data into a single structure. He explains: 'if a study is conducted with five subjects, the results could be a single structure or five structures — one for each subject — or any number between'. The writing is intended to convey the information to potential readers. In particular, phenomenologists strive to communicate the essence of the experience itself, evoking understanding and empathy on the part of the reader (see Chapter 31).

Table 14.3 Designing phenomenological research

Design	Specifics	Chapter
Philosophical stance	Phenomenology; philosophy is exceedingly important in this approach	4
Personal stance	High to medium degree of disclosure of positionality in final report	5
Who or what of study	Concepts and occasionally processes; essences of how individuals experience them	6
Research topic and question	Related to understanding how individuals collectively experience a phenomenon	7
Literature review	Comprehensive and all inclusive	8
Theoretical/conceptual framework	Not typically employed on interpretation of data since the essence is to be the experience	9
Time/place/participants	Involves working with participants, preferably in context so that they may be considered together as part of meaning	20
Ethics	Ethical design, treatment of individuals, processes, and presentation of products important; particular emphasis on respect of individuals and presentation of products	21
Fieldwork	Note taking during interviews	22

Data collection methods	Methods include some combination of the following:
	    – unstructured, phenomenological interviews with individuals
	    – observations in context
	    – review of documents (such as journals or diaries) or other pertinent materials
		23–26

Data handling	Basic and descriptive coding of information for themes	27
Analysis	Phenomenological analysis, interpretive phenomenological analysis	28
Interpretation	Close to the data — but moderate levels of interpretation	29
Quality	View of quality, quality criterion and strategies to ensure quality important; particular emphasis on view of quality	30
Researcher voice	External observer and reporter of essences	31
Report	Reporting typically done by theme; often intended to evoke emotional response in reader to simulate the experience	32

Summary of choices when designing and doing phenomenology

In Table 14.3, we highlight key choices that researchers using phenomenology commonly make. Our intent is not to say how the approach must be done but rather to provide a description of the way that we have most often seen it in the literature. Thus, this table is intended to serve as a general guide that researchers may consider when they design and do their own phenomenological studies.

ADVANTAGES AND CHALLENGES OF PHENOMENOLOGY

Phenomenology assumes that knowledge is rooted in experience. This approach allows for intentionally gaining understanding of the lived experience of others as it is. It allows for investigation topics usually regarded as subjective: consciousness and the content of conscious experiences such as judgments, perceptions and emotions. It is a flexible approach, which means that it can be used across disciplines and fields as well as across topics.

There are some challenges with the approach, however. There can, for example, be a tendency to ignore the context of the research and the circumstances in which data are collected. The approach tends to objectify and structure data, which in turn takes data away from the perspectives of participants and the value of experience as it is lived and spoken about.

EXAMPLE

Cilesiz provides a researcher reflection on an example of her phenomenology research.

Sebnem Cilesiz, The Ohio State University

A phenomenological exemplar

This is a brief description of a phenomenological study I conducted on adolescents' experiences of educational computer use at Internet cafés in Turkey. Internet cafés constitute a leisure context in which adolescents use computers and the Internet with virtually full autonomy over their activities. Although Internet cafés hold significant educational potential as informal learning environments, no prior research had investigated educational experiences at Internet cafés.

I used a phenomenological framework and methodology, specifically transcendental phenomenology developed by Husserl. Phenomenological research aims to uncover the essence of the experience of a phenomenon, which refers to the condition or quality that makes an experience what it is and without which an experience would not be what it is; essence can be uncovered through its manifestations in individuals' experiences. The purpose of my study was to understand and describe the phenomenon of educational computer use at Internet cafés in depth and arrive at the essence of adolescents' experiences with this phenomenon.

My research sites were the two largest Internet cafés in an urban area in Western Turkey with a population of about 250,000, where Internet cafés are prevalent among adolescents. I recruited six adolescent high school students who had significant and regular experiences of using computers educationally at Internet cafés as participants. I collected the data through a series of three in-depth phenomenological interviews with each participant. The first interview covered participants' overall experiences of

Researcher reflections

continued

the phenomenon and its history up to the present time; the second interview focused on the details of significant experiences and participants' feelings about them; the third interview consisted of open reflection on the meaning of experiences and on the previous two interviews.

I analyzed the data using phenomenal analysis, which included identifying common textures and structures of the experience, writing individual textural and structural descriptions for each participant, writing composite textural and structural descriptions and, consequently, providing a detailed description of the essence of the experience of the phenomenon in a textural–structural synthesis. In short, this essence involves building identities as educational computer users that distinguish adolescents from those not using computers educationally, by engaging in activities perceived to have current or future utility, in an environment with a structure that is essentially unlike school. I derived a number of conclusions from these results, including that Internet cafés facilitate identity development of adolescents and that minimal structure and a high degree of autonomy are important for adolescents' choosing to use computers educationally in a leisure setting.

Phenomenological studies are demanding as they require in-depth understanding of the philosophical underpinnings and the nature of multiple interviews. The level of reflection required necessitates a fairly high level of commitment from study participants. The analysis process is complex and involves writing multiple narratives for each participant, as well as for the group. However, I believe that the effort made conducting phenomenological research is well spent because phenomenological studies have the potential to make unique contributions to educational research.

CONCLUSION

In this chapter, we have discussed the ways in which researchers make sense of the lived experiences of individuals. There are indeed variations in the ways that researchers undertake this work. What is notable in their approaches is a conscious effort to make sense of the essence of the human experience. This desire, so central to what it means to be human, is what makes these approaches so appealing to such a wide range of researchers.

Reflective questions

Concept questions

■ How might a phenomenological study differ if it was undertaken using Heidegger rather than Husserl as a guiding philosophical approach?
■ How might bracketing help or hinder a study?
■ What are the advantages of phenomenography?

Application questions

■ Is your topic suitable for a phenomenological investigation?
■ What challenges might you experience were you to undertake such an investigation?

van Manen, M. (1990) *Researching lived experience: Human science for an action sensitive pedagogy*, Albany, NY: State University of New York Press.
This offers practical advice and clear insights into undertaking phenomenology.

Finlay, L. (2011) *Phenomenology for therapists*, Oxford: Wiley-Blackwell.
Despite being billed as a book for therapists, this covers the main issues related to the theory and practice of phenomenology and is a basic and accessible guide.

Marton, F. (1994) Phenomenography. *In*: T. Husén and T. N. Postlethwaite (eds) *The international encyclopedia of education (2nd edn.)*. Oxford: Pergamon.
This offers a clear description and rationale for phenomenography.

Creswell, J. W. (2007) *Qualitative inquiry and research design: Choosing among five approaches (2nd edn.)*, Thousand Oaks, CA: Sage.
This text offers useful summaries of transcendental and hermeneutic phenomenology.

Key resources

Chapter 15

Narrative approaches

INTRODUCTION

Narrative approaches allow researchers to pursue the goal of studying the human experience, and such approaches range in form and kind from traditional narrative approaches, such as life history and biography, to emerging approaches such as digital storytelling. Researchers who have adopted narrative approaches in particular look at the meaning in stories, arguing that people create themselves and reality through narrative. We begin this chapter by presenting the background to narrative approaches and then explore various forms of narrative approaches, such as life history and life course research, biography and autobiography, suggesting contexts in which these may be used. Finally, we describe advantages and disadvantages of narrative research and also provide an example of one researcher's approach to narrative inquiry.

ORIGINS OF NARRATIVE APPROACHES

Narrative has a long history in the human experience. Barthes, for example, argues that:

> Narrative is present in myth, legend, fable, tale, novella, epic, history, tragedy, drama, comedy, mime, painting ... stained glass windows, cinema, comics, news items, conversation ... narrative is present in every age, every place, every society; it begins with the very history of mankind ... It is simply there, like life itself.
>
> (Barthes 1977: 251)

Early narratives appeared in religious texts. Dawn (2010) argues that a great deal of Western culture is built on stories or ideas that come from the Bible and the diverse narrative styles that appear in it. Dawn (2010) shows how the stories have become enmeshed in Western culture, using examples such as the biblical stories of Adam and Eve, the ten plagues of Egypt and the Prodigal Son, and explains how such narratives have influenced everyone from Shakespeare to Monty Python.

There are many theories about narratives. Many researchers view Aristotle's *Poetics*, for example, as a form of narrative theory in which Aristotle described the rudiments of dramatic texts. Whilst there have been many discussions about the relationship between narrative and philosophy (for example, Lawrence-Lightfoot and Davis 1997), others have argued that narrative inquiry is more accurately located as an approach that emerged from Levi-Strauss's analysis of myths (Manning and Cullum-Swan 1994).

Narrative as an approach to research clearly has been a mainstay in religious as well as humanities research for centuries and, thus, originally had a hermeneutic philosophical leaning. There is evidence of narrative research in social research methods from other paradigms as well. The biographical interpretive method was developed by German sociologists, for example, to produce accounts of the lives of Holocaust survivors and Nazi soldiers (Wengraf 2001). Other authors such as Riessman (1993) have sought to tell stories from the point of view of how people see their actions of past experiences, whereas Richardson (1997) has started from a methodological stance in focusing on particular mechanisms for undertaking narratives. We argue then, that the wide range of narrative approaches now used in social research have emerged from the fields of anthropology, psychology and studies of experiences in education, as well as humanities, and have been driven by many who adhere to a social constructionist position. Moving beyond these origins, many critical, post-modernist/poststructuralist researchers have taken up narrative approaches using their own unique philosophical lenses. The central point is that people's lives are storied and researchers re-present them in storied ways, regardless of the particular medium.

DESCRIPTION AND PURPOSE OF NARRATIVE APPROACHES

There is a range of views in the literature about what narrative approaches are, and the result is confusion in terminology that in our view is hindering the further development of narrative approaches. We believe that by making sense of the different perspectives, researchers wishing to undertake narrative inquiries may best position their work. As we see it, researchers should be aware of the chief views that appear in the literature in order to be better able to craft their own research approach: narrative theory as a way of understanding the human experience, narrative as data, narrative as a specific method and narrative as a research product. Thus, the central concern in any narrative approach is that the process of telling the story as well as the product, the story itself, is important.

Narrative theory as a way of understanding the human experience

The theory behind narrative approaches in social research may be traced to the work of scholars such Dewey, Geertz and Bruner. Dewey suggested that life is education (Dewey 1938), a key view of many narrative researchers. He emphasized the human capacity to reconstruct experience and thus make meaning of it. Geertz (1973) argued that narratives are stories about ourselves and are central components of most cultures. Bruner stated that 'to narrate' derives from both 'telling' (*narrare*) and 'knowing in some particular way' (*gnarus*); the two tangled beyond sorting (Bruner 2002: 27). Narrative requires recounting events to construct *with* the reader a particular way of 'knowing about', which, as Martin (2008) suggested, moves towards meaning making. Bruner (1990) also believed that narrative is a process of meaning making, particularly when encountering unusual events or issues. Bruner (1986) suggested that narrative knowledge (as opposed to a paradigmatic mode of thought) is created and constructed through the stories of lived experiences and their meanings. Polkinghorne (1995), in turn, suggested that narrative is one of the operations of the realm of meaning and therefore the examination of this realm would aid in the understanding of narrative:

> narrative meaning is one type of meaning produced by the mental realm. It principally works to draw together human actions and the events that affect human beings, and not

relationships among inanimate objects. Narrative creates its meaning by noting the contributions that actions and events make to a particular outcome and then configures these parts into a whole episode.

(Polkinghorne 1995: 6)

The underlying idea is that people make meaning through narrative; narrative in this sense is thought itself. Narrative knowledge helps make sense of the ambiguity of human lives.

Narrative as data

Some researchers see narrative as data that may be interpreted. Frye's work during the 1950s, for example:

> sought to describe literary and mythological systems, creating conceptual maps for understanding texts and textual production. Further, Frye (1957) asserted that narratives were not the invention of isolated artists; rather, authors unconsciously draw upon the long tradition of stories across generations and genres. In this way, Frye's work privileges the narrative construct and offers a connection across writers, texts and genres.

(Colyar and Holley 2010: 71)

To Frye, then, narrative is text that may be analyzed and described using categories or constructs (Colyar and Holley 2010). This notion of narrative as data can also be seen in the way data are analyzed in methods such as critical discourse analysis and event narratives, such as those described by Labov (Labov and Waletsky 1967). Labov's research was undertaken in South Harlem in the 1960s and 1970s, and examined spoken event narratives. These stories have what Labov termed a general structure that includes abstract, orientation, complicating action, evaluation, resolution and coda. The abstract, of which there is sometimes more than one, describes what the story is about. The orientation sets the scene. Complicating action tells us 'what happens next', and is, for Labov, the element that defines talk as 'narrative'.

Example

STRUCTURE OF A STORY

Thus, a story told by someone going to a party might look like this:

- **I had a terrible time getting here (abstract)**
- **I set off two hours ago, and I only live a couple of miles away (orientation)**
- **I had booked a taxi and waited ages before I rang to check if it was coming and when I did they told me I still had to wait another 15 minutes (complicating action)**
- **I became so worried I thought you'd think I wasn't coming (evaluation)**
- **Anyway I am here now (resolution)**
- **Next time I will give you a ring so you know what is going on (coda).**

Other theorists, such as Halliday and Matthiessen (2004), in the theory of systemic functional linguistics, imply that choice is inherent in the use of language; that is, not that this is conscious but, for example, if one is using 'I' one is not using 'we'. Further, speakers are somewhat constrained by what the language and register require of them. However, others such as Hoey

(2006) suggest that choice is not unproblematic, arguing that individuals do not choose but are primed to use language in particular ways.

Narrative as a research approach

Narrative theory can be used to inform the decisions researchers make about their texts. Indeed, some researchers, such as Hendry (2010), suggest that all research is narrative and argues:

> Resituating all research as narrative, as opposed to characterizing narrative as one particular form of inquiry, provides a critical space for rethinking research beyond current dualisms and bifurcations that create boundaries that limit the capacity for dialogue across diverse epistemologies ... narrative is not a method, but rather a process of meaning making that encompasses 3 major spheres of inquiry: the scientific (physical), the symbolic (human experience) and the sacred (metaphysical).
>
> (Hendry 2010: 72)

Yet others see narrative research as a group of related social research approaches. Narrative approaches generally focus on developing understanding through an exploration of story, interpretation and discourse (Leggo 2008). Barone has argued that traditional research seeks to unpack and understand the real state of the world, whereas narrative seeks to depict peoples' experiences and in doing so provide 'a degree of interpretive space' (Barone 2001: 150). Clandinin and Connelly (2000), who contend that they founded narrative inquiry as a research approach, maintain that:

> Narrative inquiry is a way of understanding experience. It is collaboration between researcher and participants, over time, in a place or series of places, and in social interaction with milieus. An inquirer enters this matrix in the midst and progresses in this same spirit, concluding the inquiry still in the midst of living and telling, reliving and retelling, the stories of the experience that make up people's lives, both individual and social. Simply stated ... narrative inquiry is stories lived and told.
>
> (Clandinin and Connelly 2000: 20)

Clandinin and Connelly (2000) believe that people's lives are full of stories and that much dialogue is story related, so researchers in this area seek to tell stories of these people's lives and then to present them as narratives of experience. Narrative approaches are also valuable for gaining data in areas where it may be difficult to gain them using other methods, such as undertaking a study into the history of prejudice, where storytelling is central to understanding.

Narrative as a research product

Denzin has argued that 'much, if not all, qualitative and ethnographic writing is a narrative production ...' (Denzin 1997: 4). He further suggests that:

> Language and speech do not mirror experience: They create experience and in the process of creation constantly transform and defer that which is being described. The meanings of a subject's statements are, therefore, always in motion.
>
> (Denzin 1997: 5)

The idea is that all qualitative research manuscripts themselves are narrative. Denzin suggests that the writing of narratives poses particular complexities because of the presence of four paired terms in any social text. These are:

(a) The 'real' and its representation in the text
(b) The text and the author
(c) Lived experience and its textual representations
(d) The subject and his or her intentional meanings.

(Denzin 1997: 5)

Characteristics of the narrative product

Narrative approaches may use plots and characters in order to draw the reader into the story, and, as Bruner argues, most narrative 'involves an Agent who Acts [character] to achieve a Goal [plot] in a recognisable Setting [context] by use of a certain Means [plot]' (Bruner 1996: 94). Bullough and Pinnegar (2001) make a distinction between *story* and *plot*, in that they see a story as a sequence of events narrated in a linear, chronological order; a telling of events. A plot, on the other hand, is a sequence of events that are organized to engage the reader emotionally.

Some researchers argue that narratives are structured with a beginning, a middle and an end, held together by some kind of plot and resolution (for example Sarbin 1986). However, we suggest that narratives do not always have a plot or structured storyline, but are often interruptions of reflection in a storied life. Storied lives may have unplanned interruptions such as an unexpected illness that may disrupt identities, thus changing the story and the storied-ness of lives.

Example

WAYS OF MAPPING STORIES

For example, the work of authors such as Sparkes (2009) provides alternative ways of understanding and mapping stories. In their study, Sparkes and Smith (2005) explored the narrative of a disabled man shared with different audiences over time. They located four types of response: depression-therapy restitution stories; break-through restitution stories; social model stories; and solace stories. Such work does not seek to promote one response over another but to explore issues and generate dialogue.

Considering potential interruptions in lives in many ways highlights the importance of realising that storytelling is a political act, one in which 'tellability' is central, as Norrick points out:

Some events bear too little significance (for this teller, this setting, these listeners) to reach the lower-bounding threshold of tellability, while others are so intimate (so frightening) that they lie outside the range of the tellable in the current context. Similarly, one narrative rendering of an event may fail to bring out its significance (humour, strangeness), and thus fail to reach the threshold of tellability, while another telling might render the event so frightening (intimate) that the story is no longer tellable. Hence, the more strange (salacious, frightening) an event (or a narrative rendering of it) is, the more tellable the story becomes, seen from the lower-bounding side, but the less tellable it becomes, seen from the upper-bounding side due to the potential transgressions of taboos.

(Norrick 2005: 327)

What we mean by narrative approaches

We are sympathetic to all the views of narrative and, as such, we define narrative approaches as *the way in which researchers conceive, capture and convey the stories and experiences of individuals*. Such stories often are co-constructed between researcher and participants, as a means of capturing and presenting the ways in which participants made meaning of their experiences. Narrative approaches are underpinned by narrative theory in which it is suggested that humans make meaning through narrative. Narrative approaches focus on collecting narratives, because the point of collecting stories is to understand the experiences and the way they are told, seeking clarity about both the events that have unfolded and the meaning that participants have made of them. Narrative approaches are theory, process, data and product combined to create a unique form of inquiry.

There are many different ways to undertake narrative approaches but we suggest that there are some key characteristics that are common to most narrative approaches as well. For example, there is a strong focus on the story of the individual and, therefore, data analysis, interpretation, reinterpretation and representation involve considerations of the perspectives and meanings of the participant via the process of storytelling by the researcher. When undertaking narrative approaches, the researcher listens to participants' stories, acknowledges the mutual construction of the research relationship (both researcher and participant have a voice with which to tell their stories), and seeks to remember that people tell and retell their stories, both during the first and any subsequent interviews. Their stories change and grow over time as their perspectives shift and move. We offer several additional common characteristics in the remainder of this section.

Focus on the individual

Those adopting narrative approaches tend to focus on the stories of a single participant or a few participants, considering them as individuals, rather than investigating the stories of a larger group. The idea is to allow space for the voices of individuals who might not otherwise be heard (Creswell 2007).

Use of stories

Narrative approaches need there to be a focus on the 'story' for both data and presentation. Stories tend to have context, characters, plot, place, turning points and resolutions. Researchers examine and use these conventions when presenting the story, often foregrounding the experiences of the participants, at times at the expense of more conventional manuscript formats (see Chapter 32 on the research report).

Flexibility

Participant stories and meanings change in the telling. This aspect of narrative approaches requires that researchers remain flexible, acknowledging that research questions and purposes may change as the inquiry progresses (Clandinin and Connelly 2000).

Focus on writing

Creswell (2007) suggests that narrative is a literary form of qualitative research and as such demands a special emphasis on writing. In addition to the conventions of stories (character, plot, context), metaphors, images and other literary constructs are used to convey complex and multi-layered meanings.

A researcher may choose a narrative approach when a story can act as a verifying mechanism, or as a means of confirming or defending truths. Researchers also adopt narrative approaches to understand the truth being shared through objects and photographs, and other story forms. Narrative approaches may also be employed as a means of sharing difficult truths or life events, and presented and understood through an object as part of the story. A researcher may also choose a narrative approach to unpack issues of control.

> For example, in professional education, stories from practice can promote the idea that a given story represents what it means to be a good nurse or excellent teacher. Kim and Latta (2010) reflected on their own journey as teachers when editing a special journal issue on narrative approaches:
>
> > We each recall encountering narrative inquiry as an empowering form for our voices as practicing teachers. Form, as a narrative way of knowing, elicited stories of values, beliefs, and feelings, regarding our teaching experiences. These values, beliefs, and feelings intersecting with students, contexts, and subject matter, comprised the stuff (Elbaz, 1991) of teaching we negotiated daily in our classrooms. Narrative inquiry attended to how each of us engaged such stuff in creating and recreating learning situations alongside our students.
> >
> > (Kim and Latta 2010: 69)

Researchers often collect stories and then retell them on behalf of the participants, partly by collating different people's stories and also by interpreting them and restating them in particular ways. Whilst this is part of the narrative approach, researchers should consider how their own stories and stances affect the way they tell and retell stories.

TYPES OF NARRATIVE APPROACHES

We suggest that there is a spectrum of narrative approaches, from those that have a strong stance about the need to justify these approaches (such as Clandinin and Huber 2010) to those who believe narratives should be reflexive and almost psychotherapeutic. For us, the notion that narrative approaches need to begin with justification is misplaced, since it seems to reflect a need to validate and normalize the processes of storytelling, so they are seen as 'reliable', yet we find the psychotherapeutic extreme also troubling, as it can bring into question the ethics of the relationship between the researcher and the researched (for example, whether the researcher has adequate training and whether theres a power differential in the relationship). We believe that what is really important in narrative research is an understanding by the researcher and the researched of the telling and retelling of the stories and the way in which they are located within the philosophical framework of the research as a whole.

Narrative approaches comprise a family of approaches and thus researchers need to position themselves so that stories can be analyzed effectively in the context of the given approach. While there are many narrative approaches, we next present four different varieties of narrative research that we have seen used frequently in social research:

■ life course research
■ life history research
■ biography and autobiography
■ digital storytelling.

Life course research

This approach involves studying a particular stage of life, which can begin at birth for studying the early years but could equally well start at age seventy or eighty for studying aspects of old age. As a concept, a life course is defined as 'a sequence of socially defined events and roles that the individual enacts over time' (Giele and Elder 1998: 22). There are a number of different ways of undertaking life course research but it is usual to explore life course over time.

This is a useful approach but drawbacks can include a tendency to focus on time and critical events too closely, as well as a tendency to ignore the national or global context by focusing too much on the individual.

CHILD OF OUR TIME

A UK example of this approach is being undertaken by Professor Lord Robert Winston, who started a life course study with babies born in the year 2000 (Livingstone 2005). The study continues and is presented on BBC television at regular intervals. The focus in this approach is in examining how chronological age, relationships, changes and common life transitions shape people over the course of their life. In practice, researchers using this method focus on the study of:

■ **cohorts: people born at the same historical time who experience given changes within a culture; for example, the removal of the Berlin Wall or the revoking of apartheid laws in South Africa**
■ **transitions: changes in role or status**
■ **trajectories: long term patterns of stability**
■ **life events: significant events which involve a change and often lasting consequence, such as marriage or job loss**
■ **turning points: a life event that produces a shift in the life course trajectory.**

Example

Life history research

This approach involves exploration of someone's life history, with a focus on the series of events that make up an individual's life. Researchers who undertake life history often focus on people's stories as insiders within a particular setting. The stories of participants are used to inform and transform historical analysis. It is an approach in which the researcher does not just describe situations but tries to explain them, to see the world through the eyes of people involved in particular events. Life history research seeks to invite other people into someone's personal history. What is important about this type of narrative approach is its strong focus on personal history, so that it highlights prejudice, misplaced norms and assumptions. Life history is seen as an approach that provides a link between personal and social worlds.

COMPOSING A LIFE

Bateson's (1990) book, *Composing a life*, portrays life history accounts by focusing on the lives of five women researchers. She presents themes across the stories that include 'unfolding stories', 'improvizations' and 'rethinking achievement'. Bateson explained how, by looking back across these five women's lives, research and professional activities, it was possible to see how they had positioned, located and created their lives.

Biography and autobiography

A biography is an account of one's life that is told by another, whereas an autobiography is a history told by the individual him or herself. Biography and autobiography explore, at an in-depth level, personal and social views and values. What is important in these biographical approaches is that the research participant is seen as the person who is the 'sense maker', in relation to her own data and the construction of his or her own identity within the story, which is different from biography and life course history in which the researcher tells the story. The researcher therefore needs to consider the reasons for choosing a particular area of study and to examine the social, cultural and personal stories that connect them to the research they are undertaking. In the Belenky example, we show how researchers developed a new form of biography to meet their research needs.

The personal knowledge and understandings of the researcher is therefore always at the forefront of the researcher's mind throughout the research and writing process.

WOMEN'S WAYS OF KNOWING

Belenky *et al.* (1986) used biographical methods to explore diverse women's perspectives and identified five categories of 'ways of knowing' characterized by a spiral. The research sought to understand the ways that women see reality, described it from five different perspectives and from this drew conclusions about the way women see truth, knowledge and authority. These are:

- *silence*, a position in which women experience themselves as mindless and voiceless and subject to the whims of external authority
- *received knowledge*, a perspective from which women conceive themselves as capable of receiving, even reproducing, knowledge from the all-knowing external authorities but not capable of creating knowledge on their own
- *subjective knowledge*, a perspective from which truth and knowledge are seen as personal, private and subjectively known or intuited
- *procedural knowledge*, a position in which women are invested in learning and applying objective procedures for obtaining and communicating knowledge
- *constructed knowledge*, a position in which women view all knowledge as contextual, experience themselves as creators of knowledge, and value both subjective and objective strategies for knowing.

The use of autobiography as a research method is predominantly located in the work of Bruner (2004), who argued that stories about our lives are essentially our autobiographies. Autobiography is a narrative about a person's life that is written by the person. However, authors such as Evans (2005) argue that much of autobiography, whether in research or in the media, is merely about self-justification.

Digital storytelling

This approach builds on traditional storytelling and is combined with digital technology (see for example, www.storycenter.org/index.html). A digital story is usually short, often presented in the first person and is video narrative created through a combination of voice, music and still and moving images. One way of creating a digital story is to use the freely downloadable software, Microsoft Photo Story. What is useful about this narrative form is that it can be created by anyone who has a desire to document life experience, ideas or feelings through the use of digital media. However, as Burgess (2006) points out, with the changes in world literacy practices in terms of how media are used, it is important to consider that the use of media for research have ethical and methodological implications, as well as unresolved tensions around issues such as agency and value. Burgess (2006) used the example of digital storytelling to explore the participatory cultural studies approach to research. The advantages of it are that it is low tech, accessible, user generated and requires minimal training. Digital storytelling involves asking participants to present their point of view using images.

- Is a written story more fixed than a digital story?
- Is the notion of showing a story, as well as or instead of telling it, important?

The use of digital stories requires researchers to consider the use of their voice, their choice of music, the way the story is paced and presented, and so on. The disadvantage of this approach is that what is presented in general is straight story. In order to use this approach effectively for qualitative research you would need to:

- Decide on the type of narrative approach you want to use, such as biography or narrative approaches.
- Ask participants to create their own stories.
- Obtain the digital stories from the participants.
- Analyze the stories using a narrative analysis framework, such as interactional analysis or performance analysis.

A summary of the types of narrative approaches

Narrative approaches tend to transcend a number of different approaches and traditions, such as biography, autobiography, life history and life course research, and digital story telling summarized in Table 15.1.

Table 15.1 Comparison of narrative approaches

Type	Commonly adapted paradigms	Focus	Key features	Link to discipline
Life history research	Constructionism	Discursive and dialogic presentation of story	Sharing personal history	Anthropology Education
Life course research	Pragmatism Interpretivism	Explanatory story	Mapping life event in quantitative and qualitative ways	Medicine Health
Biography and autobiography	Ethnography Interpretivism	Development of dialogic and collaborative story	Sharing and reflecting on situations	History Sociology
Digital storytelling	Interpretivism	Presentation of interactive story	Use of creative media to challenge perspectives	Health Sciences Education Arts

DESIGNING AND DOING NARRATIVE RESEARCH

When using narrative research, the researcher faces essential choices about philosophical and personal position, framing the study, collecting data, working with data and writing about the results. In the next few paragraphs, we provide an overview of the choices researchers who use narrative research often make. We follow this description by a summary of these common choices in Table 15.2 on page 239. This table provides links to other parts and chapters in this book where we provide fuller descriptions and practical advice for doing qualitative research.

Philosophical and personal positioning

Researchers assume a range of philosophical stances, and there are particular issues that need to be considered when using narrative approaches. For example, positionality is important because researchers need to position themselves both within the interview and the data analysis as part of the story. Positionality is vital because data are analyzed through shared sense making and story construction between researcher and participant. Not to share stories raises questions about how plausible and honest the researcher is really being in the narration process (see Chapter 5).

Focus of the study

The focus of the study is also a key consideration in narrative approaches (see Chapter 6). Almost always, the focus of the study is the individual or a small group of individuals. This is one research approach in which the focus of the study and the person(s) from whom data typically are collected are the same.

Data collection

Data collection is a design issue in narrative approaches. Always focusing on gathering stories, data may be collected in a variety of ways, including stories, journals, field notes, letters, conversations, interviews, family stories, photos (and other artefacts) and life experiences (see

Part 5). Researchers should ask questions within their interviews that enable people to tell their stories and then use a framework such as RITES, a heuristic method for interpreting narratives suggested by Leggo (2008: 6–7):

Step one: *Read*
   The researcher reads the whole narrative to gain a general sense of the story.

Step two: *Interrogate*
   The researcher asks some basic questions: Who? What? Where? When? Why? How? So what?

Step three: *Thematize*
   The researcher reads the narrative again with a focus on a theme, and spells out the parts of the story which relate to the theme.

Step four: *Expand*
   The researcher expands on the theme by reflectively and imaginatively drawing connections and proposing possible meanings.

Step five: *Summarize*
   The researcher summarizes the theme in a general statement or two in order to indicate clearly what is learned from the narrative.

Ethics are a critical issue in narrative research as well. Narrative researchers consider several issues, such as ethical design, treatment of individuals, processes and presentation of products important. They place particular emphasis on respect of individuals and transparency of process (see Chapter 21).

Working with data and findings

There are many different approaches to working with data narratives, and researchers using narrative often draw from theories from communications and literature for examining narratives. Symbolic convergence theory, for example, developed by Bormann (1972) from Bales's (1970) studies of small group dynamics, has been used by researchers to examine symbols or symbolic terminology. Symbolic convergence theory is based on the belief that communication creates reality. Through the consistent use of symbols, forms of communication are created that are particular to a community, such as a gymnast raising their arm to indicate they are ready to demonstrate, or particular colloquialisms that are developed and used in sign language. Early texts then tended to create narrative and stories which shared universal elements that transcended disciplines. Riessman (1993: 18) argues that such structures are the 'weight bearing walls' that hold texts together.

Symbolic convergence theory is often used in the context of rhetorical criticism. Rhetorical criticism is a critical approach for considering narrative, that helps researchers both to understand the way in which information and narratives are projected and to distinguish the characters, plots and storylines that are at play within the story. Rhetorical criticism requires a consideration of symbolic artefacts (including words, phrases, images, gestures, performances, texts, films, and 'discourse' in general) to discover how, and how well, they work: how they instruct, inform, entertain, move, arouse, perform, convince and, in general, persuade their audience, including whether and how they might improve their audience. In short, rhetorical criticism seeks to understand how symbols act on people. Thus, it is the process of investigating and exploring acts and artefacts though systematic analysis, and understanding the use and meaning of symbols, whether symbols of speech or symbolic representations. This form of criticism is thus concerned with the analysis and interpretations of meanings expressed in rhetorical artefacts (Foss 1989).

In addition to using theories and critical approaches to guide their work, those who use narrative research tend to use analytic approaches such as thematic analysis. They often also choose discourse analysis, narrative analysis or semiotic analysis.

Another issue in design is that there are unique ways of ensuring quality (see Chapter 30). Researchers consider several issues such as the view of quality, quality criteria and strategies to ensure quality important; they place particular emphasis on view of quality and criteria. The researcher needs to ensure the following:

- *The story is authentic*: People tell stories based on what they believe and/or wish to portray about themselves. Whether they believe it or fake it, what they say tells the researcher something about the perceptions and values they possess.
- *The story is 'real'*: Whilst it is possible to spend considerable time discussing what counts as real, what narrative approaches do offer is an opportunity for the researcher to discover information participants themselves may not realize. By analyzing and interpreting data, researchers uncover hidden values and views and bring them to the surface, making them explicit.
- *It is clear who 'owns' the story*: The story is shared but it does change and move as it is shared, reflected on and retold over time. However, often the researchers do tend to impose meaning, but such meanings need to be shared and negotiated with participants. Yet the researcher too is a participant, and therefore their story is also part of the research story, but more often it is kept in the background.
- *Decisions have been made in advance about how stories are analyzed and managed*: It is important to ensure, as a researcher, that there is clarity about whether an analysis of stories is being undertaken or the process of narrative analysis is being used (see Chapter 28). Within the narrative tradition, Polkinghorne built on Bruner's classification, in order to draw a clear distinction between (a) analysis of narratives and (b) narrative analysis. Analysis of narratives refers to studies in which the data consist of narratives that are then analyzed to produce categories. Narrative analysis refers to 'studies whose data consist of actions, events, and happenings but whose analysis produces stories' (Polkinghorne 1995: 6).
- *Participants' voices are heard not lost*: The difficulty with transcribing the story, and then presenting it either as a powerful description or as an interpretation with quotations from the participants, is that there is often a sense that the narrative is told 'for' the participant. The best way to manage this is to share the transcripts and re-storytelling early in the research, and to include discussions and reflections that have occurred between participant and researcher.

Writing

When writing, researchers should consider how they will re-present the narrative. Researchers must also consider who they are as characters in the narrative, what level of distance they will strive to maintain, and whether they will present the stories and words of the participants directly or indirectly (see Chapter 31).

Table 15.2 Designing narrative research

Design	Specifics	Chapter
Philosophical stance	Critical theory, post-structuralism, constructionism, constructivism	4
Personal stance	High level of disclosure	5
Who or what of study	Individuals and sometimes groups	6
Research questions	Focus on understanding experiences of individuals	7
Literature review	Often used; at times interspersed with the story	8
Theoretical/conceptual framework	Often used; at times related within the story	9
Time/place/participants	Typically in the natural settings of individuals	20
Ethics	Ethical design, treatment of individuals, processes, and presentation of products important; particular emphasis on respect of individuals and transparency of process	21
Fieldwork	Collaborative, often verbatim note taking	22
Data collection methods	Semi-structured, unstructured or informal interviews; narrative interviews; texts, storytelling	23–26
Data handling	Coding and drawing out of concepts	27
Analysis	Thematic	28
Interpretation	High levels of inference	29
Quality	View of quality, quality criteria and strategies to ensure quality important; particular emphasis on view of quality and criteria	30
Researcher voice	At times backgrounded to the participant, at times collaborative voices and at times, researcher voice and participant voice the same	31
Report	Traditional report or presentation through story	32

Summary of choices when designing and doing narrative research

In Table 15.2, we highlight key choices that researchers using narrative research commonly make. Our intent is not to say how the approach must be done but rather to provide a description of the way that we have most often seen it in the literature. Thus, this table is intended to serve as a general guide that researchers may consider when they design and do their own narrative studies.

ADVANTAGES AND CHALLENGES OF NARRATIVE APPROACHES

There are a number of advantages to choosing narrative approaches. It is, for example, relatively easy to encourage people to tell stories, since most people are content to share a story about themselves. Their stories provide unique information about how they have interpreted events and how their values have guided them in decisions that they have made. Through the telling of their stories, it is possible to see how individuals construct and reconstruct identity. Gaining in-depth data (thick description) is possible because it often occurs naturally when events are narrated by participants. Moreover, it is possible to gain in-depth meaning and reflection because participants are content to reveal themselves in stories, and to reflect on their accounts at a

Researcher
reflections

Susan E. Chase, University of Tulsa, Oklahoma, USA

My book, *Learning to speak, learning to listen: How diversity works on campus* (2010) is a qualitative study of undergraduates' engagement with diversity issues at the predominantly white City University (a pseudonym).

The principles of narrative inquiry informed my study from start to finish. As I conducted interviews with individual students of different backgrounds and with groups of students in a range of campus organizations, I invited them to tell their stories about what they had learned about diversity at City University (CU) and how diversity issues were addressed on campus. Later, as I listened to the interview tapes, I analyzed each individual's and each group's specific ways of narrating self and events.

I found patterns across the interviews, which suggested that the students' stories reflected the narrative environment on campus. To get a broader perspective on that environment, I conducted interviews with faculty members and administrators, and I did content analyses of CU's student newspaper, student government minutes, calendar of events, and undergraduate course schedule. Together, the interview data and the content analyses led me to characterize CU's narrative environment as one in which diversity is on the table and in which race is the most contentious issue. Three diversity discourses vied for attention on campus – social justice; abstract inclusion ('we are all human and we are all diverse'); and political difference ('liberals silence conservatives on campus').

Within this contentious narrative terrain, I found that some students learned to speak out about racial injustice. For example, Kia, a Hmong American, narrated her transformation from an uninvolved freshman to a campus activist who spoke with a quiet voice of authority. Rachelle, an African American, narrated her transformation from a freshman whose anger alienated others to a campus activist who used her voice to inspire others. At a critical moment, a group of mostly African American and Asian American students staged an innovative campus protest that succeeded in bringing about changes on campus.

Within the same contentious narrative terrain, some students learned to listen to those whose social locations differed from theirs. For example, Melanie learned to recognize her white privilege as she listened to the painful stories of students like Kia and Rachelle at weekend-long race conferences and other race-related events. And a group of white student activists, who had been meeting for years to explore racial issues, used their listening skills to support their peers during the campus protest.

Narrative inquiry, as a methodology, led me to highlight the complexity of narrative reality at CU. On the one hand, students' narrative practices were strongly influenced by the narrative environment. The campus protest, for example, might not have been possible or might not have been successful on another campus. On the other hand, students' narrative practices *shaped* the narrative environment, as the students' protest clearly did.

later date as well. People tend not to hide truths when telling their stories and, if they attempt to do so, it usually becomes apparent through data interpretation. Knowledge is interesting and brings together complex understandings about a person.

While narratives have much to offer, there also are some challenges to consider when determining whether to take them up. Stories can be difficult to interpret in terms of the relationship between the story told in the interview and the story retold in the presentation of data. A researcher must make decisions about story ownership, and how the story will be interpreted and reinterpreted; this becomes complicated if participants disagree with the presentation or if they wish to include data that may cause them more harm than they understand. Researchers in narrative approaches must be prepared to protect their participants – sometimes from themselves. Yet disagreement between participant (narrator) and listener (researcher) can add depth of understanding – or at least highlight potential misinterpretation, which might not otherwise be discerned. Another challenge is that it is often difficult to decide the relationship between the narrative account, the interpretation and the retold story. Finally, the negotiation of data interpretation and presentation of data can be continually troublesome.

CONCLUSION

Narrative approaches are varied but what is central to them all is the sense that stories reveal much about social and cultural contexts as well as about humans making meanings. What these approaches have at their heart is the belief in the importance of the storied-ness of lives: the idea that individuals live lives and construct meaning with, in and through stories. However, apart from approaches such as life course research, there is generally not a sense that stories have a beginning, middle and end. Instead stories are seen as complex, multifaceted and evolving, even as they are told and retold.

Concept questions

- Who writes or records the story?
- To whom does the story belong?
- How much of a life is recorded or presented? (for example, life history)
- Who provides the story?
- How are stories agreed?
- How are stories presented and represented?

Application questions

- Is narrative enquiry a good approach for our study?
- Which of the narrative approaches hold the most appeal for you? Why?

Reflective questions

Key resources

Clandinin, D. J. (ed.) (2007) *Handbook of narrative inquiry: Mapping a methodology*, Thousand Oaks, CA: Sage.
An overview of narrative approaches, with chapters which cover most areas.

Hartley, J. and McWilliam, K. (eds) (2009) *Story circle: Digital storytelling around the world*, Chichester, Oxford: Wiley-Blackwell.
A useful and thought-provoking book on digital storytelling, which covers a huge number of different forms of the genre.

Hendry, P. (2010) Narrative as inquiry. *The Journal of Educational Research*, 103 (2), 72–80.
A thought-provoking overview of many of the issues in narrative approaches; an article that deals with the origins and complexity of the approach.

Chapter 16

Action Research

INTRODUCTION

Action Research has a long history in social science research and, while there has been some debate in the literature about whether it is uniquely a qualitative method, we believe that the lack of clarity on this point is due largely to confusion about the method's philosophical and disciplinary origins. Both Action Research and Participatory Action Research (PAR), regardless of the model, align more closely in philosophical underpinnings and approach with a qualitative research tradition than a quantitative one, and we note that researchers who undertake the approach most often do so from a qualitative rather than quantitative perspective. Action research is a part of the qualitative tradition in its own right, with its own history, place and application in the field of qualitative inquiry. In this chapter, we describe action research, outlining the origins of the approach as well as its processes and principles. As with most qualitative traditions, there are variations in the way that it is constructed and employed, and unlike some of the other traditions, these variations mean that action research employs, and at times crosses, a number of philosophical paradigms. Finally, we discuss the advantages and disadvantages of the approach.

ORIGINS OF ACTION RESEARCH

The precise origin of action research is somewhat murky, although much of the approach's history can be linked to specific movements in the field of education. McKernan (1996) argues that action research has been evolving for more than a century and that literature documents 'clearly and convincingly that action research is a root derivative of the scientific method, reaching back to the Science in Education movement of the late nineteenth century' (McKernan 1991: 8). This movement sought to apply the scientific method to education (for example, Bain 1897; Boone 1904; Buckingham 1876). In addition, experimentalist and progressive educational work was carried out by educators such as Dewey, who believed that professional educators should be involved in community problem solving, and apply 'the inductive scientific method of problem solving as a logic for the solution of problems in such fields as aesthetics, philosophy, psychology and education' (McKernan 1991: 8). Early roots of action research may also be seen, as McKernan (1991) suggests, in the work of a number of early social reformers in the early twentieth century (for example, Native American advocate, Collier 1945; social psychologists, Lippitt and Radke 1946; educator, Corey 1953).

Most authors, however, place the origination of action research with Lewin, a German-American social psychologist, who is often dubbed the 'father' of action research (see, for example, Kemmis and McTaggart 1988; Zuber-Skerritt 1996; Holter and Schwartz-Barcott 1993; O'Brien 2001; Dickens and Watkins 1999). As a transformational Marxist, Lewin was concerned with social problems, particularly religious and racial prejudice, which he paired with a deep interest in change theory; with these in mind, Lewin developed a research approach in order to understand and facilitate change in community action programmes in the 1940s. Lewin (1946) is said by some to have coined the term 'action research' in his paper titled 'Action research and minority problems'. Lewin argued that:

> The research needed for social practice can best be characterized as research for social management or social engineering. It is a type of action-research, a comparative research on the conditions and effects of various forms of social action, and research leading to social action. Research that produces nothing but books will not suffice.
>
> (Lewin 1948: 206)

When using action research, Lewin generally focused on organizations. During the 1950s and 1960s, building on Lewin's work, researchers used action research to study industry. During this time, researchers at the Massachusetts Institute of Technology (MIT) in the USA and the Tavistock Institute in the UK were committed to the approach (McKernan 1991; Masters 1995; Rapaport 1970). In the 1970s and 1980s, although it had fallen out of favour in some fields, in large part due to the growing practice of separating theory and practice, action research gained a following in education, within the teacher-researcher movement, with the work of Stenhouse (1975). Stenhouse believed that teaching should be based upon research (McKernan 1991: 11) and teacher-researcher projects of note were the Ford Teaching Project and the Classroom Action Research Network (Masters 1995). Notable during this time was the work of Elliott (1991), who used action research for the professional development of teachers and was influential in the way action research was defined and developed. The models of action research he employed were based on the work of Lewin; however, they were not as participatory as Lewin had intended. For example, although practitioners undertook the research and data gathering, on the whole, theory development was carried out by the academic researchers. The reality was that power and control was not devolved completely to the practitioners, which some objected to on the grounds that it functionally was autocratic evaluation, whereby academics would legitimate public policy in exchange for compliance with the recommendations of the evaluation (see, for example, MacDonald 1974).

Elliott argued that action research had more potential and that it could improve 'practice by developing the practitioner's capacity for discrimination and judgment in particular, complex, human situations. It unifies inquiry, the improvement of performance and the development of persons in their professional role' (Elliott 1991: 52). Elliott's aims, then, were to improve practice and the understanding of practice through a combination of systematic reflection and strategic innovation to improve practice rather than produce knowledge. In practice, it may be argued that Elliott's move suggested a stronger leaning toward participatory approaches to action research.

Action research has evolved in several different ways and, in particular, a strand of participatory action research has captured the attention of many scholars. Reason and Rowan (1981), for example, sought to develop approaches that would provide insights into how knowledge is created and/or understood through working with people and not 'doing' research on them. These participatory approaches also built upon the critical pedagogy of Freire (1970), Fals-Borda (1992) and Frideres (1992: 3–4), particularly in their development work in low income countries.

Thus, examples of participatory action approaches can be seen in Torres's work with disempowered groups in Colombia, Freire's work in Brazil, Mahatma Ghandi in India and Nyerere's in Tanzania (Fals-Borda 1991; 2001). These contextually based approaches seek to help people within particular timeframes and locations become more familiar with and aware of the constraints that prevent them from participating fully in their communities and enable them to take action to eliminate or minimize those constraints. The work of authors such as Kemmis have further expanded the number of action research approaches (Kemmis and McTaggart 2005).

DESCRIPTION AND PURPOSE OF ACTION RESEARCH

While there is no one universally agreed upon definition of action research, leaders in this research approach have made several attempts to provide insight into the essence of the approach. We offer the following examples of their definitions.

- Action research is a form of collective self-reflective enquiry undertaken by participants in social situations in order to improve the rationality and justice of their own social or educational practices, as well as their understanding of those practices and the situations in which the practices are carried out ... The approach is only action research when it is collaborative, although it is important to realize that action research of the group is achieved through the critically examined action of individual group members (Kemmis and McTaggart 1988: 5–6).
- Action research is a framework for inquiry that 'seeks to bring together action and reflection, theory and practice, in participation with others, in the pursuit of practical solutions to issues of pressing concern to people' (Reason and Bradbury 2006: 1).
- Action research concerns action, and transforming people's practices (as well as their understandings of their practices and the conditions under which they practise) (Kemmis 2010: 417).

Considering these ideas together, we define action research as *a method of qualitative research the purpose of which is to engage in problem solving through a cyclical process of thinking, acting, data gathering and reflection*. Action research at its heart is about changing and improving practice and understanding of practice through a combination of systematic reflection and strategic innovation. It requires that participants be empowered and stresses the importance of leading social change. In most cases, action research also contains a knowledge creation element, so that understanding and theory are created through practice.

Action research is a useful tool for researchers who want to solve real world problems. It should be taken up when they want to examine a practical situation, make a change and explore the consequences of that change. The argument for action research is that all researchers should see themselves as researchers of practice, so that theories can be validated through practice. As McTaggart explains:

> Individual Action Researchers change themselves, they support others in their own efforts to change, and together they work to change institutions and society. Through critique of these efforts to change, in the slogan made famous by the environment movement, participatory Action Researchers 'think globally, act locally'.

> (McTaggart 1991: 175)

We suggest that researchers should consider the following questions when undertaking action research:

- What is the concern?
- Why are those involved concerned?
- How might the situation be mapped and understood?
- What can be done?
- What should be done?
- How will data be collected?
- How may conclusions be checked to ensure that they are reasonably fair?
- How will the significance of the action be presented and explained?
- How has change taken place?
- What practices still need to be examined and possibly changed?

TYPES OF ACTION RESEARCH

Many scholars have attempted to classify the various action research traditions (see, for example, Crooks 1988; Gardner 1974; Holter and Schwartz-Barcott 1993; McKernan 1991; Masters 1995; McCutcheon and Jurg 1990; Park 1993; Small 1995; Srivastva and Cooperrider 1986). Considering their categorizations together, we see the following primary forms:

- traditional/post-positivist
- practical/pragmatic
- responsive/constructivist
- transformative/social constructionist
- emancipatory/critical.

Traditional/post-positivist

Early advocates of this form of action research used the scientific method for structured problem solving (see, for example, Lippitt and Radke 1946; Lewin 1947; Corey 1953; Taba and Noel 1957). Thus, the origins of the approach, coupled with its penchant for describing reality, give rise to its philosophical basis. In traditional action research, the researcher identified the problem, articulated an intervention and then involved the practitioner (Holter and Schwartz-Barcott 1993). The approach, often, is to use a theoretical framework to explore the outcomes of a particular intervention in a given case. The goal of this approach, then, is predictive knowledge and refinement of theories. This form of action research is intended to develop more efficient and effective practice and it promotes personal participation. The process is deductive and often requires **validation** of instruments (Holter and Schwartz-Barcott 1993). Lundeberg *et al.*'s (2003) study is a form of traditional action research. In it, the authors employed a theoretical framework, technological pedagogical content knowledge (Mishra and Koehler 2006), to explore the outcomes of teachers engaging in action research as a part of a sponsored project.

Validation

In educational research, validation refers to the process of ensuring that the instrument in question will gather the information that it intends to gather (see Chapter 30 for additional information about validity)

Practical/pragmatic

In a practical action research project, researchers and practitioners work together to identify the primary problems as well as their underlying causes and possible interventions (Holter and Schwartz-Barcott 1993: 301). They seek to define the problem after dialogue, through reaching a mutual understanding. The design of this approach is more flexible than in the positivist paradigm. McKernan (1991: 20) indicates that practical action research promotes human interpretation, interactive communication, deliberation, negotiation and detailed description, while reducing measurement and control (Masters 1995). As McKernan suggests, 'The goal of practical Action Researchers is understanding practice and solving immediate problems' (McKernan 1991: 20).

Heinze's (2008) study of blended learning is an example of an action research project conducted from an interpretivist, and, we think, pragmatic perspective.

Responsive/constructivist

The responsive constructivist model of action research may be seen in a form known as Action Training and Research (ATR). This model progressed from the work of Lewin and Rodgers, being developed by Gardner (1974). Gardner felt that individual and group actions become self reinforcing, as a status quo becomes the norm. At times, disruptive behaviour can become the norm, such as trying to undermine the work of others to make oneself appear more competent. ATR is intended to help members of an organization become more aware of their own actions and the resulting consequences, as they strive to keep output maximized. ATR recognizes that each individual constructs his or her own reality and that for change to occur, all members of an organization should strive to reveal, clarify, discuss and refine their own constructs, collaboratively. ATR is organic, collaborative and change oriented, and requires self-discovery, at both an individual and organizational level. Employees must be involved in all phases of the process. The difference between ATR and other forms of action research lies in the recognition of constructed reality, as well as upon the fact that this approach requires a learning contract.

Transformative/social constructionist

Transformative/social constructionist action research emerged from work such as co-operative inquiry, as defined by Reason and Rowan (1981), and sought a clearer focus on the needs of those participants involved in the research process than earlier approaches had done. More recently, authors such as Ramsden (2003), Price (2001) and Brydon-Miller and Maguire (2009) have drawn strongly on authors such as Mezirow (2000), arguing that this approach combines transformative learning with high level participation. The underlying assumption is that transformative learning is central to the action research process. Such a research approach can:

- provide insights into how knowledge is created and/or understood, in terms of propositional knowledge, practical knowing and experiential knowing or knowing by encounter with patients
- locate and delineate 'thought-worlds' or unique interpretative repertoires of the participants involved in learning and teaching
- explore the extent to which particular approaches to teaching and disciplinary differences help or hinder learning in health and medical settings
- delineate the likely socio-political impact of such learning on the higher education community through exploration of virtuality, veracity and values (Atkinson and Burden 2007).

Emancipatory/critical

The emancipatory model of action research has its roots in Marxian 'dialectical materialism' and Antonio Gramsci's notions of practice. It also builds, however, upon the critical pedagogy put forward by scholars such as Freire (1970), Fals-Borda (1992) and Frideres (1992: 3–4), particularly in their development work in low income countries. Thus, the approach has roots in critical social theory as well as post-modern critical theory. In Australia, Carr and Kemmis (1986) called for more 'critical' and 'emancipatory' action research. Thus, a new generation of action research emerged via the link between transformative action research and critical emancipatory processes. This approach focuses on emancipation and overcoming power imbalances. Emancipatory action research 'promotes emancipatory praxis in the participating practitioners; that is, it promotes a critical consciousness which exhibits itself in political as well as practical action to promote change.' (Grundy 1987: 154). Researchers using this approach tend to have two goals. The first goal is to link theory and practice in order to explain and resolve the problem. The second is to enable practitioners to identify and make explicit their problems by raising their collective consciousness (Holter and Schwartz-Barcott 1993: 302). A related approach, feminist action research, strives for social transformation through an advocacy process for marginalized groups.

Participatory Action Research

Participatory Action Research is a method of intervention, development and change that is conducted within communities and groups and that involves examining an issue systematically from the perspectives and experiences of the community members most affected by that issue. The approach focuses on the effects of the researcher's actions within a participatory community. Participatory action research has been carried out from both transformative and emancipatory philosophical perspectives, as well as from post-modern and post-structural perspectives but authors such as Kemmis and McTaggart (2005), who have been highly influential in its development, see it as an all-embracing methodology. They view participatory action research, then, as both a means of carrying out research and also a philosophical stance towards research.

Participatory action research seeks to help people, within a particular timeframe and location, become more aware of the constraints that prevent them from fully participating in their communities. The research approach is conducted with people as opposed to on people. This approach challenges the notion that legitimate knowledge only lies with the privileged experts and their dominant knowledge. Instead, participatory action research asserts that knowledge should be developed in collaboration with local expert knowledge and the voices of the 'knowers'. Negotiated **participation** and the development of shared understanding of practice are central to this method. This means engaging people as active participants in the research process and it results in practical outcomes related to the work and learning of the participants.

Participation

Taking part, sharing something, often in a group who are involved in shaping and implementing research

Researchers use participatory action research to generate knowledge to inform action. Participatory action research seeks to bring about empowering benefits and has often been used to support both social transformation in developing countries and the promotion of human rights activism (Kemmis and McTaggart 2005). Researchers have used it in cross-cultural contexts and it also has potential for spanning the boundaries of research into virtual and real-world studies, and exploring the extent to which they converge and diverge (for example, Wallerstein and Duran 2003).

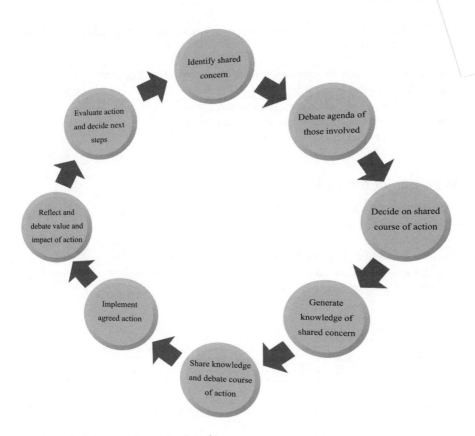

Figure 16.1 Participatory action research cycle

The process of PAR involves examining an issue systematically from the perspectives and lived experiences of the community members most affected by that issue. PAR involves:

- focusing on the agenda of participants
- using self-reflective cycles
- developing shared quality criteria to ensure validity
- generating knowledge and understanding.

A participatory action research project will therefore include elements in the cycle shown in Figure 16.1, which may be varied according to the context of the study and those involved.

Wimpenny (2010: 93) suggests a number of key elements require attention during participatory action research processes to continually question the level of participation achieved:

- relocation of power: primary researcher responsibilities
- development of a sound dialectic
- generation of knowledge and understanding
- development of shared quality criteria to ensure validity.

This work reflects Lewin's (1946) early work in which he argued that people are more likely to test out new practices when they participate actively in developing agreed strategies.

McTaggart's questions, summarized below, are a useful starting point for evaluating participatory action research:

■ How does a specific case exemplify participatory action research?
■ What does this example tell us about the criteria we might use to judge claims that an endeavour is participatory action research?
■ What contributions has this example made to the improvement of practice, the social situation of participants and others involved?

(McTaggart 1991: 169)

Comparison of the types

In Table 16.1 we provide a side-by-side comparison of the essential features and elements of the five types of action research.

Thus, the five models vary in their underlying assumptions about the nature of reality and the purpose of research. Everything else extends from those philosophical perspectives which guide the methods that will be taken up, the relationships between the researcher and the participants and the methods used to carry out the study.

Table 16.1 Types of action research

Type	Commonly adapted paradigms	Focus	Key features	Discipline
Traditional	Post-positivism	Technical validation, refinement, deduction	Seek to discover laws underlying reality Events explained in terms of real causes and simultaneous effects	Natural science
Practical	Pragmatism	Mutual understanding, new theory, inductive	Explains what occurs and the meaning people make of phenomena Understanding sought through interactions with context and own cognitive structure	History and hermeneutics
Responsive	Constructivism	Sharing of personal constructions in order to reach shared understanding	Events are understood in terms of the ways they are socially constructed Understanding, exploring and challenging power and control, while ensuring change for the better	Education, psychology
Transformative	Social constructionism	Transformation and freedom through learning	Exploration and deconstruction of power structures through learning Change management through transformative learning and action	Education
Emancipatory/ participatory action research	Critical social theory; post-modernism; post-structuralism	Mutual emancipation, validation, refinement, new theory, inductive, deductive	Uncover and understand what constrains equity and supports hegemony to free oneself of false assumptions Events are understood in terms of social and economic hindrances to true equity	Education, sociology, social policy

DESIGNING AND DOING ACTION RESEARCH

When using action research, the researcher faces essential choices about philosophical and personal position, framing the study, collecting data, working with data and writing about the results. In the next few paragraphs, we provide an overview the choices researchers who use action research often make. We follow this description by a summary of these common choices in table form. This table provides links to other parts and chapters in this book where we provide fuller descriptions and practical advice for doing qualitative research.

Philosophical and personal positioning

As we have indicated in the discussion of the types of action research, the philosophical and personal positioning researchers adopt differs greatly according to the different forms of action research. They take up a number of different philosophies including post-positivism, pragmatism, critical social theory, post-modernism and post-structuralism, constructionism and constructivism (see Chapters 2 and 4). They range in perspective but all focus on the concept of transformation, which is why this approach is often referred to as transformational research.

Focus of the study

Action researchers very often focus on structures and processes (see Chapter 6), associated with programmes, most often for the purpose of improving them. They typically engage with the existing literature prior to beginning their studies and develop full literature reviews (see Chapter 8). They may choose to adopt a theoretical framework (see Chapter 9) but it is not essential that they do so and, indeed, many action researchers prefer to stay close to data and participants' perspectives.

Data collection

Action research is a method based on cycles of action and reflection and therefore the data collection methods used within it tend to be flexible and emergent. While Small (1995) suggests that action research lacks prescribed methods, several scholars, including Lewin, have set out to describe the general processes which can provide researchers with good models for designing an action research study. Since Lewin's original model, many more have been developed. Elliott's approach, for example, marked a move away from the importance and centrality of stakeholders and a shift towards the notion of improvement of performance and professional development. It still involved the analysis of a situation in order to improve it (Elliott 1991), but Elliott viewed any production of knowledge as secondary to the improvement of practice. There are many other action research cycles (for example, Kemmis 1980; Elliott 1991) and we synthesize these in the ten-stage model shown in Figure 16.2 overleaf.

This ten-stage cycle allows for more reflection and interpretation than other models and enables those involved to examine in-depth the change that has been implemented and the influence of those involved. In each phase, different activities are likely to take place. In the *identify* phase, it is important to outline both the focus and the scope of the research and the problem or question to be examined. In the *reflect, plan, decide* and *implement action* phases, the researcher is likely to be collecting data and seeking the views of those involved as well. Data may include a combination of interviews, observations or documents (see Chapters 23–26). In the *discuss, reflect*

Figure 16.2 Action research cycle

and *interpret* phases, stakeholders discuss the change and what are the influences. As the researcher travels around the cycle, further data may be collected and more in-depth analysis occurs.

Working with data and findings

Because of the iterative nature of the process, data are gathered throughout the ten-stage cycle. The researcher and the stakeholders discuss them and, thus, data analysis and interpretation happen throughout the process. Researchers may analyze data through constant comparison or other basic analytic approaches and share information with the stakeholder. As there are differing types of action research, researchers must necessarily spend time articulating their views of quality (that differ according to philosophical paradigm) and then choosing strategies that support them (see Chapter 30).

Writing

The writing approach varies widely by researcher. In the traditional approach to action research that we have discussed so far, the writing tends to be more objective and from a third-person perspective while, in other approaches, researchers take a more subjective path and write from a first-person perspective (see Chapter 31). Action researchers often adopt the typical research report format that may be shared with stakeholders (see Chapter 32). However, those who are operating from a more constructionist or constructivist approach may choose to adopt more creative perspectives in writing about the results.

Summary of choices when designing and doing action research

In Table 16.2, we highlight key choices that researchers commonly make using action research. Our intent is not to say how the approach must be done but rather to provide a description of the way that we have most often seen it in the literature. Thus, this table is intended to serve as a general guide that researchers may consider when they design and do their own action research studies.

Table 16.2 Designing action research

Design	Specifics	Chapter
Philosophical stance	Post-positivism, critical social theory, pragmatism, post-modernism, post-structuralism constructionism, constructivism	4
Personal stance	Medium to high level of disclosure, dependent upon the type adopted	5
Who or what of study	Structures and processes (groups and individuals)	6
Research questions	Focus on the practical and problem solving	7
Literature review	Full literature review typically tends to be done ahead of time	8
Theoretical/conceptual framework	May be used, but not always, since the focus is on exploring the practical	9
Time/place/participants	Typically conducted at a single local site and involving participants in the research	20
Ethics	Ethical design, treatment of individuals, processes and presentation of products important; particular emphasis on ethical treatment of individuals	21
Fieldwork	Collaborative, interview notes and field notes	22
Data collection methods	Structured and semi-structured interviewing, exploratory, clinical or storyline focus groups; observations, texts	23–26
Data handling	Coding of notes common	27
Analysis	Often constant comparison or thematic analysis	28
Interpretation	Low levels of inference as researchers attempt to stay close to participant meaning	29
Quality	View of quality, quality criterion and strategies to ensure quality important; particular emphasis on view and strategies	30
Researcher voice	Ranges from outsider to insider voice, depending upon type	31
Report	Standard research report typically used	32

ADVANTAGES AND CHALLENGES OF ACTION RESEARCH

There are many advantages to using action research. Perhaps the most evident is the way in which it helps those working to manage and implement the change processes to work closely together. This means that there is a focus on ensuring that all voices are heard and communication is maximized. In particular the advantages of action research are that:

- Research is undertaken with an issue at its heart, which helps to ensure that it is relevant to those involved and connected to issues and concerns in daily life, such as how teachers might improve relationships with parents in the school playground.
- It can improve communication between not only the researchers and participants but also those who are affected by the change process on a broader scale; for example, in a university change may affect both lecturing staff and students as well as catering staff and administrators.
- It can help researchers and practitioners change and develop through the process; for example, often, through action research, those involved learn about themselves and their colleagues.
- It can promote collegiality and sharing practices amongst practitioners who may not usually work together or understand each other's work. For example, nurses and physiotherapists working together to change referral practices will come to know each other's work and practices better.
- It encourages participants and researchers to reflect on their own practice as well as enabling them to compare and reflect on how they practice compared with others.

However, there are also some challenges, perhaps the most obvious of which is that Lewin gave very little guidance about how it is to be undertaken and implemented, which is possibly why there are now so many different approaches. The result for novice researchers is that it is difficult to decide which form to adopt. In many forms of action research, it is not the practitioners who implement the change, build theory and write up the research, but external participants such as academics. The question is to what extent this fulfils the principle to which Lewin aspired, and whether in fact action research has just became a form of evaluation to then be used to direct specific action. Thus, many of the challenges of action research relate to structure, power and control.

- Action research can be seen as a structured plan of action rather than an iterative cycle of change and reflection.
- If too much focus is placed on technical action within an action research project, then the results tend to be focussed on targets and outcomes, rather than on ensuring everyone is supporting the change and owning the action research.
- In some forms of action research, where the researchers design the action plan for the practitioners (rather than with them), there is a danger that there will be little ownership by the practitioners and this in turn will affect the degree to which change is 'owned', implemented and really possible.
- It is important to ensure that all voices can be heard and pay attention to the 'position' of those who are participating and what this means in terms of what they wish to present and change. It is possible that the participants' stated position that they want to change may simply present as the dominant discourse and blot out more subtle differences of opinion that also exist.

The findings of the study should thus be shared openly, which in turn shows respect by validating the experience of the participants. Naturally this openness should be reflected later in the presentation and write-up of findings.

EXAMPLE OF ACTION RESEARCH

In the following researcher reflection, Dr Ben Hok Bun Ku explains his work in action research.

Dr Ben Hok Bun Ku, Hong Kong Polytechnic University, China

Hok Bun Ku advocates the interdisciplinary participatory action research methodology. He has been involved in China's rural development for about fifteen years by adopting action research.

One of his representative projects was conducted in an ethnic minority village in Yunnan province of China. When the project was first commenced in 2001, Ku and his research team found that despite governmental efforts of rural reform, China's rapid integration into the global capitalist economy has in fact made the rural poor more vulnerable, suffering from not only financial hardships but also other forms of deprivation such as the loss of cultural identity. Acknowledging such rural predicaments, in 2005, inspired by the idea of fair trade, a cross-disciplinary action research project aiming at overcoming rural poverty by preserving and developing indigenous cultural artefacts and crafts for ethnic minorities was carried out in the village. The project encouraged local villagers to use local materials and indigenous craftsmanship to produce ethnic arts and crafts for sale in urban markets, thus generating not only cash income but also a sense of renewed pride and identity, leading to stronger community participation in local culture preservation and greater resilience to the erosion of traditional community life brought on by global socio-economic forces.

After five years in development, this action research project is moving towards the intended goals of building the capacity and enhancing the financial situation of local women. The most gratifying achievements are the establishment of a core group of committed and motivated women who are keen to develop the project, the increased sense of solidarity and social cohesion among the local villagers, and the growth of confidence and pride. Through this highly participative and empowering process, many villagers have regained their sense of control over their own destiny and have developed a much stronger sense of identification with their cultural heritage.

The one major lesson the team learned from working with the women's group in the village was that what was needed in the village was not a mere increase in local economic production but something more fundamental and more sustainable – capacity building and empowerment. They found that the process of capacity building and empowerment did not take place only through individual but also via collective pathways. What is also significant about the experience of the women is that they have shown the special place of cultural tradition in development, especially in terms of providing cultural pride, identity and existential meanings; all are considered foundational attributes upon which social development is built.

This example of working with local women in rural China has been published in two journal articles (Ku 2011; Ku and Ip 2011).

Approaches that enable collective investigation and analysis of experience by those involved are the most appropriate, since it is recognized in PAR that knowledge is socially constructed and embedded. Madeleine Duncan provides an example of PAR in this researcher reflection.

Researcher reflections

Professor Madeleine Duncan, University of Cape Town, South Africa

Direct links between occupational therapy and the radical work of 'best case' participatory action research scenarios are seldom obvious. Grandmothers Against Poverty and Aids (GAPA) is a transformative social process in an informal human settlement on the outskirts of Cape Town, South Africa, that was ignited by a gerontologist, an occupational therapist and a few grandmothers during the late 1990s (Brodrick and Mandisa 2005). Through community based participatory action, more participants started joining GAPA, growing it into a robust non-profit organization over a period of ten years. The GAPA elders continue to impact the fabric of a community characterized by structural violence by using action reflection processes. In this context, a critical research stance was required when the professional researchers first made contact with the community; one that contested notions of 'empowerment' and 'participation' as being potentially colonizing and oppressive. People cannot be empowered by an external agency. It happens when people, as co-researchers, take ownership of their personal and collective development processes. Action research premised on empowerment is not about the researcher giving the community a 'helping hand'; championing on their behalf; stirring things up to see what people do to act on their own behalf or enabling things to happen without guiding the activities of co-researchers (Goodley and Parker 2000). It involves action and intense practical–theoretical reflection by everyone concerned on the methods that will make desired social change possible. Inclusion and participation are always mediated by the distribution of power and should not be held up as ideal outcomes. The very notion of participation is problematic because it assumes there is a common good or that communities are harmonious and driven by consensus. A critical research stance will recognize that people may have very good reasons not to participate because they have different, even opposing, political values and visions (Cooke and Kothari 2001).

Figure 16.3 Dialogue and productivity in community action

Informed consent for use of information about Grandmothers Against Poverty and Aids was obtained from the Director, Ms Vivienne Budasa.

CONCLUSION

In this chapter, we have presented an overview of action research as a qualitative approach to solving social problems. We have described the background of this approach as well as the epistemological underpinnings of the primary approach and its variations. We have provided examples of varied action research studies. We argue that what is important about action research of whatever model is that research is seen as a space and place of change. What is at the heart of action research is that voices are heard and change happens; not just for those seeking the change, but also for those researchers facilitating the project as well.

Concept questions

- Which model of action research was the most influential in the development of the approach and why?
- Is action research better suited to some disciplines and fields than others? Why or why not?

Application questions

- Would action research be a useful approach to you?
- How might you employ action research?
- What advantages and disadvantages would participatory action research have for your study?

Reflective questions

Masters, J. (1995) The history of action research. *In*: I. Hughes (ed.) *Action research electronic reader*, Sydney: The University of Sydney.
This article provided us with a useful history of action research, tracing the disciplinary origins as well as the philosophical ones.

McCutcheon, G. and Jurg, B. (1990) Alternative perspectives on action research. *Theory into Practice*, 24 (3), 144–51.
This article provided a useful overview of three models of action research: post-positive, interpretive and critical, which helped to shape our thinking about the three models we selected.

Savin-Baden, M. and Wimpenny, K. (2007) Exploring and implementing participatory action research. *Journal of Geography in Higher Education*, 31 (2), 331–43.
Some of the information we include about participatory action research in this chapter was adapted from this article.

Key resources

Chapter 17

Collaborative approaches

INTRODUCTION

Since the emergence of action research there has been an increasing interest in collaborative approaches to research. While action researchers have posited the idea that research can lead to constructive change and even empowerment for individuals, many scholars have believed that they have not gone far enough in breaking down the barriers between research and practice and between the researcher and the researched. This belief has led to the development of several strategies in which individuals work as co-inquirers to examine issues of mutual interest. The number of collaborative approaches has increased over time, which, in turn, has led advocates of these approaches in many and varied directions. In this chapter, we describe a number of these approaches that we believe centre firmly on a collaborative process between researcher and participants. Collaborative approaches focus highly on cooperative and collaborative working in order to bring about action and change. The chapter explores new approaches such as cooperative and collaborative inquiry, followed by more structured approaches of appreciative inquiry and deliberative inquiry.

ORIGINS OF COLLABORATIVE APPROACHES

Cooperative inquiry which is sometime used interchangeably with collaborative inquiry was developed by Heron (1971; 1981) and extended by Reason (1988; 2002; Reason and Heron 1995; Heron and Reason 2006). The initial idea was that communities of inquiry could come together to explore issues of mutual interest. Collaborative approaches largely draw upon social constructionist philosophies as exemplified by Gergen (2001: 810), who suggested that it was not possible to stand outside one's traditions and still communicate effectively.

DESCRIPTION AND PURPOSE OF COLLABORATIVE APPROACHES

Collaboration
Sharing the work between individuals who then come together to solve or manage a problem

The central premise of all these approaches is that legitimate knowledge is not just located with the privileged experts and their dominant knowledge; knowledge needs to be developed in **collaboration** with local expert knowledge and the voices of the 'knowers' (for example, Reason and Bradbury 2006). Knowing is a product of people coming together to 'share experiences through a dynamic process of action, reflection and collective investigation' (Gaventa and Cornwall 2001: 74). Kidd and Kral (2005: 187) sum up collaborative approaches as 'understanding, mutual involvement, change, and a process that promotes personal growth, and in the main are seen as both a research approach and a philosophy of life, which often prompts a deep emotional engagement with the research, its processes, its findings and outcomes'.

The process requires that those who are directly affected by the research problem must participate in the research process.

Collaborative approaches focus on the process of change that usually emanates from within a group of people, or organization. What is central to the use of the approaches is that it is the people who initiate and guide the change rather than those researching it. When adopting collaborative approaches, it is often but not always the case that the focus of change is only related to the community who want the change to take place. However, these approaches should and do change all those involved in the project. This change will occur more effectively if all involved are aware of their stances, in relation to both power and control, and also their (for example) Western, gendered, racial capitalist perspectives. Change is most likely to happen collaboratively. Change is a complex process and undertaking change with others has consequences that may not be recognized at the outset of the project. Within the change process, trust between those involved must be at the heart of the research project.

These approaches have at their core concepts such as collaboration and **cooperation**. Accordingly, in these approaches, there is a focus on acknowledging that individuals need to understand their own constructs and a recognition that there is a necessity to have a clear focus on the needs of those participants involved in the research process.

Cooperation
Mutual engagement of participants in a coordinated effort to solve the problem together

TYPES OF COLLABORATIVE APPROACHES

This section describes some of the key forms of collaborative approaches. The originators of these collaborative approaches have created and developed them in an attempt to move away from early notions of research that were less participative and more researcher guided. The collaborative approaches we discuss in the chapter are:

- cooperative inquiry
- collaborative inquiry
- appreciative inquiry
- deliberative inquiry.

Cooperative inquiry

This approach emphasizes the importance for everyone involved in the research process to be part of the decision making process related to the research (Heron 1996). The initial starting point for cooperative inquiry is undertaking a project with those who share similar concerns and, thus, the researcher works with and seeks to understand the participants' world in order to examine and explore issues. Cooperative inquiry is an approach where those doing the research and those contributing to the research are equal and both share in the thinking that goes into the project. Both researchers and participants design and manage the research project from start to finish.

In this approach, both researchers and participants work together to understand how change might take place, and all those involved decide together which questions are to be examined and what resources might be used (for example, De Venney-Tiernan *et al.* 1994; Heron and Reason 1997). The main idea behind this approach is that researchers and participants learn together and from one another about the issues under study; an example of this is Guha *et al.*'s (2011) study of children engaged in cooperative inquiry when designing technology. Cooperative inquiry centres on the idea of a research cycle that focuses on different forms of knowledge:

■   propositional knowledge (understanding facts and truths)
■   practical knowledge (understanding what works in reality)
■   experiential knowledge (gaining understanding though feedback)
■   presentational knowledge (the process through which we develop practices).

These four kinds of knowledge are used to shape the research process of cooperative inquiry, which tends to develop as follows:

Phase 1:   This phase determines the research focus and approach to be adopted, focusing mainly on understanding facts and truths.

Phase 2:   This first cycle of action is where those involved begin to explore and trial the actions, observe whether such actions meet the criteria, agree the format of the first phase and then record what has taken place.

Phase 3:   The second action phase is where exploration takes place about the consequences of action. For those involved this phase can result in heightened awareness of other issues and therefore result in new areas of actions and exploration to be included in the design of the study.

Phase 4:   This is the third cycle of action, where those involved in the research reflect on what has taken place to date during data collection and then decisions are made about how to proceed next. This phase may mean that further cycles of action are undertaken and further data are collected.

Examples of collaborative approaches can be seen in two particular studies: Traylen (1994) used cooperative inquiry to examine hidden agendas with health visitors and Treleaven (1994) used collaborative inquiry with women as part of their staff development.

Collaborative inquiry

The main theorist associated with collaborative inquiry is Torbert (1981; 2001), who argued that research takes place in the context of everyday life. In this approach data are not seen as 'secondary', in the sense of a researcher recoding or taking account of someone else's view. Instead data are re-collected amidst life. This means that data are seen as part of an integral to how we see, act and reflect on what we are doing. In practice this means that collaborative inquiry involves significant personal development as the researcher needs to:

■   reflect on his or her own behaviour in action
■   act in a way that encourages those also involved in the research process to reflect on their behaviour in action.

Collaborative inquiry is an approach that sees research as part of everyday life and therefore all our actions are also areas of inquiry. Collaborative inquiry demands that those involved in the research need to use explicit shared reflection methods about their own perspectives as well as their views about the collective dream and mission. Much of this approach focuses on the idea of transformation – both of the researchers involved and of the organization in which it is taking place.

In order to use collaborative inquiry, the researcher needs to use four types of conversation. The ways in which these can be used relate to and demonstrate peoples' experience, and enable them to cultivate forms of speech that clarify these four forms of conversation, are shown in Table 17.1.

Table 17.1 Torbert's four dimensions of conversation

Form of conversation	Territories of experience
Framing	Naming the assumptions behind the conversation
Advocacy	Suggesting a course of action
Illustration	Illustrating the suggested course of action
Inquiry	Inviting those listening to respond

The overarching argument of this approach is that in research and practice unilateral control must not be adopted, but instead research should be seen as 'experiments in practice', which involves the study of self and others.

When using collaborative inquiry:

■ Researcher activities must be included as data.
■ Research design and activities may change as the research occurs.
■ Interruptions are not irrelevant but are part of the research process.
■ Conflict between different views of reality is to be expected and valued.
■ Knowledge that is unique is as valuable as that which is generalizable.

Tips

Collaborative inquiry is a complex and demanding approach to research and in many ways although it is innovative and aspirational, it is also problematic and in some ways quite utopian. This, in many ways, is a step beyond participatory action research, and the level of collaboration needed means that all those involved must be highly committed to this kind of research practice; otherwise the project is likely to fail. An example of the values and complexity of using this approach can be seen in Flaskerud and Nyamathi's (2000) work in which low income Latina women in a nutrition programme in Los Angeles designed the programme itself and then guided both its evaluation and its dissemination of results.

Appreciative inquiry

Appreciative inquiry emerged from the Department of Organizational Behavior at Case Western Reserve University, Ohio, USA. It is an approach that is based in the social constructionist paradigm and draws strongly on the work of authors such as Gergen (1978; 2009). It was started by

Cooperrider in the 1980s and developed by Cooperrider and Srivastva (1987) to complement action research but with a more positive stance. The authors argued that action research had largely failed to be used effectively to bring about transformation or change valued in an organization. This was, they suggested, because action research was a problem-focused approach to inquiry that concentrated on what was wrong, rather than an appreciation of what was valuable and taken for granted in an organization. Appreciative inquiry was argued by these authors to be a research tradition that was seen to be more collaborative than action research and as a result more likely to produce change. Appreciative inquiry is based on the idea that inquiring in positive and appreciative ways will result in change towards what is beneficial within an organization. The notion of appreciation comes from the idea that:

> Just as we cannot prove the proposition that organising is a problem to be solved, so, too, we cannot prove in any rational, analytical, or empirical way that organising is a miracle to be embraced.
>
> (Cooperrider and Srivastva 1987: 165)

Inquiry into organizational life, Cooperrider and Srivastva (1987) argue, should have four characteristics. What is at the heart of this approach is the perspective that this method should be:

1. *Appreciative*: it examines what is positive in the organization and uses what is positive as the beginning of future growth and development.
2. *Applicable*: the idea is that this kind of inquiry is not utopian but, instead, seeks and explores best practice and ideas, in order to build on them in terms of considering what might be possible in the future. This approach then focuses on what has actually worked well and uses these foci as starting points for building for the future.
3. *Provocative*: it is an approach that encourages people to take risks and imagine the future order; to not only redesign their organization but also implement such a redesign to bring it about. The idea is that by recognizing and appreciating what is good and already in existence those involved are confident enough to suggest alternative futures.
4. *Collaborative*: in many ways, appreciative inquiry can be seen as a form of collaborative inquiry because it involves the whole organization. The view is taken in this approach that all voices must be heard and that all contributions must be valued.

Appreciative inquiry should be used when an organization wants to appreciate its own best practices. An organization can use its appreciative inquiry research findings to ensure that positive and effective practices become standard across the whole organization. Della Freeth provides a researcher reflection on appreciative inquiry on the facing page.

The starting point for an appreciative inquiry is the exploration of a constructive topic that is seen as being valuable to the organization or which is an area that the given organization wishes to understand more deeply or improve further. It is important that the whole organization is involved in the following iterative 'four-D' cycle, as presented in Figure 17.1 on page 264.

In practice this means:

Discover

In the *discovery* phase, the focus is on discerning what gives life to the organization and what enables it to function at its best. Here people are asked to talk to one another, often via structured interviews.

Professor Della Freeth, Queen Mary, University of London, UK

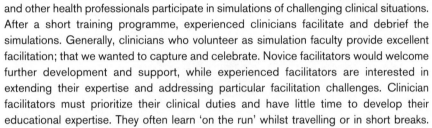

Supporting accomplished facilitation: using appreciative inquiry to support the development learning resources for clinical simulation faculty

The focus of this study, funded by the London Deanery's Supporting Technology-enhanced Learning Initiative (STeLI), was education to support patient safety. Increasingly, doctors and other health professionals participate in simulations of challenging clinical situations. After a short training programme, experienced clinicians facilitate and debrief the simulations. Generally, clinicians who volunteer as simulation faculty provide excellent facilitation; that we wanted to capture and celebrate. Novice facilitators would welcome further development and support, while experienced facilitators are interested in extending their expertise and addressing particular facilitation challenges. Clinician facilitators must prioritize their clinical duties and have little time to develop their educational expertise. They often learn 'on the run' whilst travelling or in short breaks.

We used appreciative inquiry with junior doctors and faculty in clinical simulation centres in London. Data were collected through video recordings of debriefing; appreciative semi-structured interviews with junior doctors and simulation faculty. The interviews focused mainly on debriefing and questions were phrased appreciatively, for example (to trainees) 'What do you feel are the factors that can create the most positive debrief?' or (to facilitators) 'Please describe a high point of your debriefing work and how it made you feel' (followed by probes to understand the context and behaviours of those present).

Data were then analyzed using inductive analysis guided by appreciative questions; for example: 'What do I see that is good about what is going on here?' and 'What, if it occurred more often, could improve the quality of these learning encounters?' What we found were many examples of accomplished facilitation promoting high quality learning interactions. We also identified some areas of facilitation where we thought educational insights could help facilitators to develop their practice. These were developed as web-based learning materials that included video clips and excerpts from audio narratives. We chose a format of 'bite-sized' educational input on a wide range of topics to stimulate learning and reflection 'on the run'. Giving supportive and critical feedback, developing reflection, asking evaluative questions, clean language and underpinning educational theories are some examples of the topics included.

Reflection

Appreciative inquiry is an organizational development process rather than a research methodology or educational development approach; so we had to think carefully about how it could support and inform our research and educational development. It worked at three levels, particularly informing: interview data collection, video data analysis and the design of the learning materials.

Focusing on the positive does not mean that you don't notice things that are not going well, but it forces you to attend to how people successfully address or work around difficulties.

Current learning resources may be found at http://simulation.londondeanery.ac.uk/educational-resources/supporting-accomplised-facilitation-and-improving (periodic extensions and updates are anticipated).

Figure 17.1 Appreciative inquiry cycle

Questions to use in the discovery phase include:

- What do you value most about this organization?
- What are the best practices in this organization?
- What do you value about your colleagues?
- Can you recount a time in your organization when you felt excited and engaged?
- What were the things that made this a great experience?
- What do you value most about your role in the organization?
- What are your greatest hopes for this organization?

In this phase, the aim is to locate what inspires and energizes people in their work and to find positive views and perspectives that illustrate ultimate experiences. The idea in appreciative inquiry is to use a positive approach to change management and organizational development, which is often not adopted in other approaches, where the process begins with analysis of the problem(s) as a first step.

Dream

In the *dream* phase, people are brought together in a large meeting in order to reflect on the positive and exciting experiences they have experienced, as recalled and recounted in the discovery phase of the inquiry. The idea in this phase is that people not only reflect on the past but also dream about future possibilities, in order to consider future plans and actions.

Design

In the *design* phase, a small team is identified to withdraw from their regular daily work life, in order to design ways of creating the organization dreamed in the meeting. This team is expected to develop new company structures and operating practices, to support the ideas that emerged in the dream phase. In this phase, there is a shift away from idea generalization towards formulating ways of creating what it could or should be.

Destiny

In the last *destiny* phase, changes are put into practice in order to ensure that the development and processes implemented are sustained over a period of time, so that they become an established part of the organization's operation and can in turn be 'discovered' when the next appreciative inquiry of the organization occurs. So, in practice, the four-D cycle is an iterative process whereby the last phase leads back into the first and the process of appreciative inquiry continues. Further details of practical applications can also be found in Cooperrider *et al.* (2008) and Watkins and Mohr (2001). The Prokop *et al.* study described here is an example.

Appreciative inquiry: a study of AI as an approach for researching child welfare research in Saskatchewan Aboriginal communities (summarized from Prokop *et al.* 2007: 1–2)

The research focus was to engage First Nations communities in articulating the values and community practices that promote child, youth and family wellbeing and prevent child maltreatment, and to consider how deficiencies in programmes and services might be overcome.

The research team developed positive questions such as:

- What positive programs, events and activities are happening in this community to help children and families in a healthy way?
- What makes these programs and activities good for children and families?

Researchers introduced themselves to the communities using the traditional protocols and created a written partnership agreement with the leadership. The findings emphasized the importance of cultural heritage, spirituality, community events and knowledge (education and knowing a native language). Thus, it was realized that activities and programmes that strengthened cultural identity, celebrated families and provided opportunities to build personal relationships were highly valued.

Example

One of the difficulties with appreciative inquiry is that, despite its use, there have been, until recently, relatively few critiques of it as an approach and few evaluations of its impact. Recent reviews and articles that have begun to explore in depth the challenges of this approach are helpful. For example, Bushe (2011) provides a comprehensive review of the literature and recent critiques. However, we suggest that more challenging issues emerge from the assumptions about it as both a method and a process, such as:

- Given that appreciative inquiry starts from the assumption that a positive topic must be chosen and explorations of the organization are undertaken by examining its positive aspects, the decision about what counts as 'positive' and who decides this is inherently problematic, since we all see the world differently.
- The stance of not examining what is negative could be seen as ignoring valid concerns raised by people within the organization, which might be highly problematic.

Nevertheless, appreciative inquiry is proving a positive approach to analyzing and implementing organizational change and is a method worth considering for those researching change engagement processes (for example Ludema *et al.* 2001).

Deliberative inquiry

The idea of deliberative inquiry is to enable diverse groups to hear each other's points of view and to develop collective action – even if these groups do not necessarily agree with each other.

This research approach emerged from the theory of deliberative democracy and now deliberative inquiry itself is seen as a cornerstone of deliberative democracy. The premise of deliberative democracy is that there should be a shift or a rethinking about the relationship between governments and citizens, so that political decision making relies on consultation between government and people, rather than the imposition of policy by government on people.

> Deliberative inquiry is research that seeks to change policy and practice through consultation between people and political systems such as government and local power structures.

The overarching idea of deliberative inquiry is that deliberative democracy will enable the voices of citizens to be heard by taking an inclusive stance so that those of all races, classes and ages will be able to have an impact on decision making at government level. In many ways, it can be seen as an approach that has strong similarities with cooperative inquiry but, contrastingly, it is both highly collaborative and a much more public process than cooperative inquiry, as Kavanaugh *et al.* have argued:

> deliberation differs from participation in that it involves more public discussion, negotiation, prioritising, consensus building, and agenda setting. It is a multifaceted group process, one that typically occurs in public spaces, such as voluntary associations and public meetings.
>
> (Kavanaugh *et al.* 2005: 2)

Deliberative inquiry is defined as 'a policy and action-oriented form of inquiry which links the interrelated task of doing practical curriculum activity with conducting formal curriculum inquiry through a systematic structure of deliberation about curricular decisions' (Harris 1991: 285). According to Harris, typical questions of such concern are what to do in specific situations. For example, questions concerning how to deal with children using mobile phones or portable computer games in class. However, it is an approach that can be used in a wide variety of organizations, not just educational institutions.

Deliberative inquiry is an approach that seeks to explore multiple points of view in a sensitive way that shows respect for different views and the ways that different people make decisions about an issue. Harris argues that 'the claims reached are not claims for general knowledge but rather plans of action, grounded by justification' (Harris 1991: 286). Whilst appreciative inquiry begins with an appreciation of what is good and valued, deliberative inquiry invariably starts with the recognition of a conflicting state of affairs, and then proceeds into a search for data before finally searching for solutions (for example, Kelland and Kanuka 2007).

The focus in deliberative inquiry is in finding a means of enabling people to coordinate their actions through a form of consensus that is rational but not forced. Carcasson (2009) offers this helpful diagram and overview, shown in his Figure 1, our Figure 17.2.

Deliberative inquiry has been used by practitioners wanting to bring together people with diverse views. For example, Kakabadse *et al.* (2011) used it to campaign for and cause greater

Steps in deliberative inquiry tend to follow a pattern as follows:

1. Awareness, where a conflicting or unhelpful state of affairs stimulates motivation, discontent or an interest in change.
2. Data collection: the participants of a deliberative group collect data and look for evidences that tell them something about the issue. This includes:
   a. taking a critical stance as the first move towards shared searching
   b. using critique to guide constructive discussion and the bringing together of multiple viewpoints.
3. A practical outcome of the findings.

Deliberative issue analysis

Reporting ⟶ Action   Convening

Facilitating interactive communication

Figure 17.2 A model of deliberative inquiry (Carcasson 2009: 2)

integration of children's services across both government and non-government agencies. However, what Carcasson (2009) also points out is that deliberative inquiry additionally results in four discrete products:

(a) The identification and attempted resolution of *key obstacles* to collaborative problem-solving,
(b) The identification and working through of *tough choices* or tradeoffs,
(c) The identification and building upon of *common* ground,
(d) The identification and development of support for complementary action from a *broad and inclusive range of stakeholders.*

(Carcasson 2011: 1)

Deliberative inquiry thus enables those involved to voice their concerns in ways that acknowledge both individual participant's motivations and the demands of the contexts in which they work.

Example

1. *Deliberative issue analysis*: Involves researching issues from an impartial perspective to better understand the issue and to ultimately provide the community
   with material to structure productive deliberation. Deliberative events often utilize
   a 'backgrounder' or 'discussion guide' that provides an overall structure to the event.
   The terms 'naming' and 'framing' are sometimes used to describe the work often
   accomplished during this task.

2. *Convening*: High-quality deliberation relies on diverse audiences; thus, one of the
   key skills of deliberative practitioners is to develop and attract broad audiences to
   events to be part of the discussion. Individual meetings may call for particular
   audiences (such as experts or specific stakeholders) or for more of a general public
   audience.

3. *Facilitating interactive communication*: Deliberative inquiry relies on key communication processes that can get the most out of a group of diverse participants
   coming together to discuss a key issue and move the discussion forward. 'Interactive
   communication' here means communication that actually involves people going
   back and forth speaking and listening (unlike one-way communication that involves
   one side speaking and the other listening, such as through media or at certain
   public meetings where participants can approach the microphone one at a time to
   express their opinion to an audience without much, if any, interaction). Debate,
   deliberation and dialogue are all forms of interactive communication and, depending
   on the situation, each has the potential to improve the conversation. Once again,
   skilled, impartial facilitators and note takers are critical to achieving the potential
   of any interactive communication process.

4. *Reporting*: Lastly, deliberation needs skilled, impartial analysts to utilize the information captured at events to better inform the decision-making process, so that the
   hard work completed by the participants in the forum can be shared more broadly
   in the community. Those reports then feed back into the deliberative analysis, to
   improve the quality of any subsequent deliberative events on that topic.

(Carcasson n.d.)

Comparison of collaborative approaches

When identifying an issue, it is critical to outline the focus and scope of the research and the
problem or question to be examined (see Chapter 6 and 7). Given that collaborative approaches
are forms of applied research (for solving practical problems), the focus of the study (see Chapter
6) is likely to be an organization or process. The research question will probably partially or wholly
address gathering information necessary to solve or manage the issue. However, perhaps the
most important design consideration is deciding which approach to adopt in relation to the focus
of the study being undertaken. In Table 17.2 we offer some guidance.

DESIGNING AND DOING COLLABORATIVE APPROACHES

When using collaborative research, the researcher faces essential choices about philosophical
and personal position, framing the study, collecting data, working with data and writing about

Table 17.2 Types of collaborative research

Approach	Commonly adapted paradigms	Focus	Key features
Cooperative inquiry	Constructivism/ constructionism	To undertake research together that changes something for the better	Change is required by a group of people who want to cooperate together to ensure change Undertaking research with people who share similar concerns
Collaborative inquiry	Constructionism	To understand and transform practices in order to understand and improve them	Undertaking research in everyday life through reflecting on action Understanding how people see a particular action in everyday life
Appreciative inquiry	Constructivism	To examine what is positive in an organization and learn from this	Examining best practices to ensure such findings are used across an organization Making changes based on what is working (rather than what is not working)
Deliberative inquiry	Constructivism	To use the coordinated activity of a diverse group of people to change policy and practice	Enabling all voices to be heard so that everyone will have an impact on policy decisions Ensuring that multiple points of view are heard on a complex or conflictual issue

the results. In the next few paragraphs, we provide an overview of the choices researchers who use collaborative approaches often make. We follow this description by a summary of these common choices in Table 17.3. This table provides links to other parts and chapters in this book where we provide fuller descriptions and practical advice for doing qualitative research.

Philosophical and personal positioning

The philosophical positioning that collaborative researchers adopt tends to be either constructionism or constructivism (see Chapters 2 and 4). Collaborative researchers tend to be explicit about their personal position (see Chapter 5). Research tends to focus on problem solving and the expressed concept of change; there is always a strong sense of working with shared values in these approaches.

Focus of the study

Collaborative researchers focus on structures or processes (see Chapter 6) as the phenomenon of study, most often for the purpose of change. They sometimes, but not always, engage with the existing literature prior to beginning their studies and develop full literature reviews (see Chapter 8). They may choose to adopt a theoretical framework (Chapter 9) but it is not essential that they do so and, indeed, many researchers prefer to stay close to data and participants' perspectives.

Data collection

Researchers tend to approach fieldwork from an insider perspective (see Chapter 22) since, in collaborative research, insiders tend to come together to investigate an area of mutual interest. Collaborative research is based on cycles of action and reflection and therefore the data collection methods used within it tend to be flexible and emergent, shared, discussed and debated with all those involved. Researchers use a wide range of data, such as interviews, observations, and documents (see Chapters 23–26).

Working with data and findings

Data are gathered throughout the cycle and researchers and the stakeholders discuss them; thus data analysis and interpretation occur throughout the process. Researchers typically transcribe and code data according to what they hope to uncover (see Chapter 27). Researchers may analyze data through constant comparison or other basic analytical methods (see Chapter 28) and share information with the stakeholder(s).

Writing

Writing approach varies widely between researchers but writing is generally collaborative and shared with other researchers and stakeholders. However, as researchers here are operating from a constructionist or constructivist approach, they often choose creative approaches in writing about the results (Chapter 32).

Summary of choices when designing and doing collaborative research

In Table 17.3, we highlight key choices that researchers using collaborative research commonly make. Our intent is not to say how the approach must be done but rather to provide a description of the way that we have most often seen it in the literature. Thus, this table is intended to serve as a general guide that researchers may consider when they design and do their own action research studies.

ADVANTAGES AND CHALLENGES OF COLLABORATIVE APPROACHES

In the main, many of the advantages of this approach are also challenges; this is the experience of working collaboratively in an effective way and in ways that are honed, plausible and reflective of the community within which the researcher is working. Particular advantages and challenges are: issues of choice and power and the issue of authentic participation.

Issues of choice and power

There is an expectation by participants that primary researchers hold a level of experience and knowledge of participatory processes that can be initially offered to them. This needs to be carried out in an amenable manner. During the entire process, there is a need for the primary researcher to continually reflect on the delicate balance between incorporating and imposing knowledge. This openness to the inquiry process and equitable sharing of power and control demonstrates a respect for validating the experience of the participants, as well as the

Table 17.3 Designing collaborative approaches

Design	Specifics	Chapter
Philosophical stance	Constructivist and constructionist	4
Personal stance	High level of disclosure	5
Who or what of study	Structures and processes (groups and individuals)	6
Research questions	Focus on the practical	7
Literature review	Full literature review tends to be done	8
Theoretical/conceptual framework	May be used, but not always, since the focus is on exploring the practical with people	9
Time/place/participants	Single or multiple sites involving participants in the research	20
Ethics	Ethical design, treatment of individuals, processes, and presentation of products important; particular emphasis on treatment of individuals and respect for their opinions	21
Fieldwork	Collaborative, interview notes and field notes	22
Data collection methods	Structured and semi-structured interviewing, exploratory, or story line focus groups; observations, texts	23–26
Data handling	Coding of notes common	27
Analysis	Constant comparison or thematic analysis	28
Interpretation	Low levels of inference as researchers attempt to stay close to participant meaning.	29
Quality	View of quality, quality criteria and strategies to ensure quality important; particular emphasis on view of quality as it relates to the meaning of quality in co-inquirer research	30
Researcher voice	Ranges from outsider to insider voice depending upon goal of the report	31
Report	Creative methods or standard research report	32

understanding of how knowledge production can inform action (Rahman 1993). However, there is no guarantee that participants will take on the role of co-researcher and some, especially those who may be accustomed to more traditional research hierarchies, may well resist the sharing of power that is offered.

The issue of authentic participation

Although the aims of those using collaborative approaches are to ensure and maximize participation, sometimes this is not possible, however much energy is expended. There are issues of power and agency in any situation and on occasion these can be unresolvable. We suggest that mutual participation and true collaboration are rarely really possible, excepting between those of equal status. As Savin-Baden and Fisher state:

> It seems unacceptable to us to talk about collaborative inquiry when there is no evidence of collaboration; to advocate client-centred practice but leave the client voiceless in the reporting of the study; and to lay claim to an interpretive study but show no evidence of interpretation or, if this is done, not share those interpretations with participants. We believe that the way the research has evolved should be made explicit in the writing. This means describing how the strategies presented in the methodology have actually informed the process and making clear the ways in which meaning has been interpreted.
>
> (Savin-Baden and Fisher 2002: 191)

CONCLUSION

Collaborative approaches in qualitative research are many and varied, and what they have at their heart is an emphasis on transformation, change, participation and voice. Whilst some of these approaches might be seen as radical, problematic or impossible to evaluate, they are approaches that have in many communities and organizations both facilitated and brought about change. Perhaps one of the most poignant areas of change is in the use of appreciative inquiry in arenas that are more traditionally positivist, and yet appreciative inquiry has facilitated powerful changes and improved decision making in the area of patient safety. Many researchers have disregarded these approaches as being too difficult to use in complex settings but, certainly, colleagues in diverse settings show that this is not only possible but powerful in effecting change both personally and organizationally.

Reflective questions

Concept questions

■ What do you see as the difference between these four approaches?
■ In what setting would appreciative inquiry be most useful?

Application questions

■ As a researcher, how would you plan to manage issues of power in collaborative approaches?
■ Which approach would be the easiest to adopt for someone new to research and why?

Key resources

Reason, P. and Bradbury, H. (2006) (eds) *Handbook of action research: Participative inquiry and practice*, Thousand Oaks, CA: Sage.
This offers a wide range of different approaches to participatory research from a worldwide collection of authors.

Heron, J. (1996). *Co-operative inquiry: Research into the human condition*, London: Sage.
Although now quite an old text, it is well written and offers clear guidance on how to use this approach.

Torbert, W. (2001) The practice of action inquiry. *In*: P. Reason and H. Bradbury *Handbook of action research*. London: Sage. pp. 250–60.
This provides an overview of the use of collaborative inquiry and provides practical examples and illustrations.

Bushe, G. R. (2011) Appreciative inquiry: Theory and critique. *In*: D. Boje, B. Burnes, and J. Hassard, (eds) *The Routledge companion to organizational change*. Oxford: Routledge. pp. 87–103.

Chapter 18

Evaluation

INTRODUCTION

Some qualitative researchers regard **evaluation** simply as a process of ensuring a course or organization is effective. Evaluation therefore has been seen as something to just 'do': evaluate a course or a programme as if it were a simple and apolitical means of examining whether something is working or not. In this chapter, we unpack some of the myths about evaluation and show that there are many different approaches to evaluation. We begin by presenting some background to these approaches and then offer an overview of six types of evaluation. We introduce a more recent approach to evaluation, namely the linking of arts-based research and evaluation. In the last section, we explore the challenges of using evaluation and provide a practical overview of some of the issues that need to be considered.

ORIGINS OF EVALUATION

Evaluation has been used to study an organization or curriculum in such a way as to contribute to a review of policy and/or decision making within the organization. Originally, evaluation was an important part of enabling improvement to be made in educational curricula. Evaluators such as Cronbach (1963) and Scriven (1967), followed by Stufflebeam *et al.* (1971), developed the idea of evaluation as a service for administrators and managers in education. The work of Stake (1978), MacDonald (1971) and House (1980) was influential in developing different types of evaluation and pointing out that evaluation should be seen as both a political and ethical activity. However, Cronbach and Stufflebeam were also responsible for broadening the way evaluation was used for decision making, suggesting that evaluation should: '... draw attention to its full range of functions, we may define "evaluation" broadly as the collection and use of information to make decisions about an educational programme' (Cronbach 1963: 672).

During the 1960s and 1970s, evaluation involved collecting information to inform decision making. However, in the late 1970s and early 1980s, a shift occurred and evaluation came to be seen as something from which to learn and make changes, rather than a process of being judged. Simons suggests that this shift occurred due to:

> the realisation of the difficulty of informing particular decisions, evaluations forming only one small part of the data that is taken into account in coming to a decision; over-reliance on a model of decision making that has little correspondence with reality; and a reassessment of the responsibilities of evaluation.
>
> (Simons 1987: 20)

It was thus in the 1980s that evaluation moved away from being an act of judgment about the merits of a programme and moved toward being an exploration of what could be learned about a programme. At the same time as these changes, a breakaway group emerged in the form of the naturalistic school (Guba and Lincoln 1981), 'naturalistic' becoming a generic term that encompassed many of the alternative approaches to evaluation that developed. These alternative approaches were adopted by researchers as it was increasingly recognized that judgmental and quantitative forms of evaluation were not suitable for capturing the complexity of innovation and change. These early alternatives included illuminative evaluation, democratic evaluation and responsive evaluation. Hamilton suggested:

> Compared with the classical models, they tend to be more extensive (not necessarily centred on numerical data), more naturalistic (based on program activity, rather than program intent), and more adaptable (not constrained by experimental or preordinate design). In turn they are likely to be sensitive to the different values of program participants, to endorse empirical methods which incorporate ethnographic fieldwork, to develop feedback materials which are couched in the natural language of the participants, and to shift the locus of formal judgement from the evaluator to the participants.
>
> (Hamilton 1977: 339)

In many forms of evaluation, there is a sense that the process is concerned with learning about a situation, as well as trying to improve and change it (see, for example, Ryan and Cousins 2009).

> Evaluation is a process of studying an organization or activity in order to understand, improve or change it

Evaluation of the particular

Evaluation may focus on the particular, in the sense of a particular course, programme or organization. The shift towards this kind of evaluation, the idea of exploring the curriculum through story, was promoted by Stake (1967) but in the 1960s this appealed little to those in the American behavioural tradition. In the UK, other researchers were trying to make this shift too. What in fact occurred in the 1970s and 1980s was a move away from generalized quantitative evaluation towards evaluations that studied human action and experience. The primary purpose then became to clarify the values and effects of policies or programmes at a particular time and within a particular context.

Evaluation as a political persuasive activity

The fact that evaluation is always located in a political context brings with it both a sense of uneasiness and a demand for honesty. We suggest that the uneasiness emerges because values and morals are explicit and evident in evaluation in ways that are often less obvious in other forms of research which, in turn, brings to the fore the centrality of power in evaluation studies and implicit within any evaluation is the question of judgment. This then also means that honesty needs to be overt and central to any evaluation since the politics of evaluation is almost a public affair. As Vestman and Conner (2007) argue:

Politics takes place at every level of social interaction; it can be found within families and among small groups of friends just as much as among nations and on the global stage. What makes politics a distinctive activity, distinguishable from any other form of social behaviour, is that politics at its broadest concerns the production, distribution, and use of resources in the course of social existence. Politics is power: the ability to share desired outcome, through whatever means.

(Vestman and Conner 2007: 227)

Evaluation is political because it feeds into decision making. The programmes and organizations we evaluate are politically located and evaluation in itself is essentially a political tool and activity. MacDonald (1974) argued that evaluation is a distinct form of research; we argue further that the distinction depends on the type and purpose of the evaluation. However, Weiss (1991) suggested that politics and evaluation are connected in three main ways:

- programmes and policies are the result of political decisions
- evaluation reports enter the political arena because they are used to make decisions
- evaluation by its very nature has a political stance.

The discussion about evaluation as persuasion centres on the argument that research and evaluation should be seen as separate activities. The suggestion has been that evaluation can be nothing more than an act of persuasion, but we disagree with this stance. Authors who have argued that there needs to be this distinction have suggested that those who conceptualize evaluation as research may get caught 'in the restrictive tentacles of research responsibility' (MacDonald 1974: 15). Whilst in general there has been a shift away from this view, evaluation should be comprehensive and useful. Yet in these days where research needs to be used in practical ways, and to ensure that practices are evidence-informed, it is perhaps important that both research and evaluation are persuasive in their findings. We would therefore suggest, following Simons (1987), that the task of evaluation should be to contribute to dialogue and help shape understanding of social programmes and policy, rather than merely to help people decide between alternatives (Simons 1987: 20).

DESCRIPTION AND PURPOSE OF EVALUATION

In 2006, a number of global experts in the field came together to develop an evaluation manifesto based on their reflections of evaluation research over three decades (Elliott and Kushner 2007). The manifesto authors suggested a number of central points that need to be considered in evaluation methodology, the key ones being presented below:

Evaluation should be designed so as to provide insights into educational purposes and practice, including matters of curriculum, philosophy and social implication. In doing so, it will not solely concern itself with performances and its insights should be furthered by its own continuing debates about democracy, contractual conditions and other ideologies.

Evaluation should be a means by which both those engaged in the formation of policy (government agencies and other stakeholder groups) and the professional groups who are responsible for policy implementation are enabled to meet their accountability requirements to the citizenry and their representatives.

Evaluation should make explicit and proliferate rather than restrict the range of criteria for judging the merit, worth or significance of a programme. The aim should be to represent and open up for further deliberation pluralities of interests and values and to capture, not suppress, complexity.

Evaluation should be a means by which uncertainty and diversity in professional practice and community experience are recognized as conditions essential for democratic engagement and effective problem solving.

Evaluators should place high priority on the representation and analysis of outcomes and their relationship to processes and costs; not single outcomes but multiple, not mere correlates of outcomes, not goal-based impact only but also indirect effects as valued by various stakeholders.

Evaluation should contribute to theorising about conditions of change across as well as within programmes, and thereby create a critically reflective resource for programme and policy development.

(Elliott and Kushner 2007: 332–3)

For many years, evaluation was seen as a service activity that was predominantly quantitative in its approach. It was seen as a means of ensuring that programmes and organizations were meeting their goals and purposes. However, scholars began to see the importance of qualitative methods for evaluative purposes and the diversity of approaches has grown over time.

As we note later in this chapter, there are many different forms of evaluation. From a quantitative perspective, evaluation is usually adopted in order to reduce complacency and induce change. This kind of evaluation focuses on measuring outcomes, analyzing learning experiences and making more effective use of resources. However, in the 1960s, the evaluation landscape began to broaden so that evaluation began to be seen not just as a service but as a political and ethical activity. Thus from a qualitative perspective, evaluation should be chosen when a researcher wishes to help and improve decision making within an organization or programme or seek out understanding about why some issues or practice work better than others. Qualitative evaluation should also be chosen when the researcher needs to respond to a given audiences' requirement for information.

TYPES OF EVALUATION

There are diverse forms of evaluation that have different focuses and serve a wide number of purposes. What is at the heart of most of these approaches, however, is the desire to make knowledge public about curricula, organizations and practices, whilst at the same time ensuring honest and healthy professional development within them.

Traditional evaluation

This model was born out of the work of the educational psychologist Tyler (1969). Such evaluation involves stating goals and objectives in behavioural terms, developing measurement instruments, measuring achievement of goals and objectives, comparing objectives and achievements, interpreting findings and making recommendations (Stark and Lattuca 1997). This model has been criticized for its overt emphasis on behavioural objectives and mechanistic procedures for evaluation. However, it is a model frequently used today, often using both quantitative and qualitative approaches together.

Illuminative evaluation

This approach was designed by Parlett and Hamilton (1972; 1976), originally owing to concerns about traditional approaches to evaluation being used to examine innovations in education. The aims of illuminative evaluation are:

> to study the innovatory programme: how it operates; how it is influenced by the various school situations in which it is applied; what those most directly concerned regard as its advantages and disadvantages; and how students' intellectual tasks and academic experiences are most affected. It aims to discover and document what it is like to be participating in the scheme, whether as teacher or pupil; and, in addition, to discern and discuss the innovation's most significant features, recurring concomitants and critical processes. In short it seeks to illuminate a complex array of questions.
>
> (Parlett and Hamilton 1972: 144)

This move was away from psychology-based models of evaluation towards one that was based in sociology. This form of evaluation was designed to increase understanding of what was being evaluated. It focused on the explorations of the learning situation (Parlett and Dearden 1977). The idea is that the evaluation is conducted through the three stages of observation, inquiry and explanation. Therefore data collection involves:

- observation: the evaluator creates a portfolio of events that might at first appear to be on the edge of the study such as meetings, social events and seminars
- interviewing: the focus is to explore and examine the interviewee's perceptions from a clearly personal and storied perspective.

An illuminative evaluation would examine a course and look in depth at:

- how it is conducted
- the way in which the context affects the ways it is implemented
- what those involved see as its advantages and disadvantages
- the way students experience innovation and change
- participating in the process of innovation.

Tips

Responsive evaluation

The term responsive evaluation was coined by Stake (1983) and is a form of evaluation that emerged from those whose view it was that evaluations needed to be pragmatic in their approach. An example of this would be Simons' argument (see earlier in this chapter) for there being a focus on the particular (Simons 1987). In this type of evaluation, attention is given to the information and issues that those involved in the evaluation want to know about and the questions to which they want answers. Therefore, evaluation here is undertaken in relation to specific situations, contexts and questions.

This model takes into account the differences between what is supposed to happen and what actually happens. This form of evaluation is less concerned with the objectives of evaluation than with its effects in relation to the interests of relevant publics. Examples could be:

- the discrepancy between observed and intended antecedents
- observation of what goes on in a course
- a close look at outcomes of assessment methods that may distort the learning.

Responsive evaluation according to Stake (1983) is:

- reliant on natural communication
- focused on activities being undertaken rather than the intentions of those activities
- responsive to the stakeholder requirement for facts and knowledge
- considerate towards the different views and principles of those involved in the evaluation.

Tips

Naturalistic evaluation

This form of evaluation is generally seen as a generic term that was commonly used in the 1970s in response to the shift away from traditional forms of evaluation that used experimental design methods. The term 'naturalistic' emerged since the focus in these forms of evaluation was on ensuring that programmes and organizations were studied in their natural (social) contexts, using qualitative approaches to inquiry. Authors such as Stake (1978) and Lincoln and Guba (1985) argued for the use of direct observation, unstructured interviewing, reporting and dramatic reconstruction as useful means of gathering data. Wolf and Tymitz (1977) described this type of evaluation as:

> Actualities, social realities and human perceptions that exist untainted by the obtrusiveness of formal measurement or preconceived questions ... . Naturalistic inquiry attempts to present 'slice-of-life' episodes documented though natural language and representing as closely as possible how people feel, what they know, and what their concerns, beliefs, perceptions and understandings are.
>
> (Wolf and Tymitz 1977: 7–9)

MacDonald and Walker (1975) describe it in the following way:

> Ours is the task of the naturalist who wants to understand the variety and coherence of life in the pond, and its links with the world beyond.
>
> (MacDonald and Walker 1975: 2)

One of the strong arguments within this approach is that validity (the view that the evaluation must be honest and credible) must have a moral dimension. In practice, this means that there needs to be a participatory process so that power and control is in fact shared between the evaluator and the evaluated.

This form of evaluation involves gathering descriptive information regarding the evaluation object, setting, surrounding conditions, relevant issues and values and standards for worth and merit; determining, discovering and then later sharing information desired by relevant audiences; and negotiating decisions. This model, with its focus on collaboration and negotiation, involves collaboration with participants and is based upon their lived experiences. The researcher or evaluator interacts with the subjects who are being evaluated, who directly contribute both to the shaping of the research focus, and to drawing up conclusions. The researcher is a temporarily affiliated insider since he or she defines and shares with the subjects. This type of evaluation depends upon:

■ direct testimony: structured or semi-structured interviews
■ time, place, personalities involved.

Therefore the data collected need to be thick description characterized by richness and ambiguity. Thus practice is guided by personal 'knowings' based on personal experience and theory is informed by it.

Utilization-focused evaluation

This approach was developed by Patton (1982), who argued that evaluation should be focused on identifying relevant decision makers and information users in order to work with them in a collaborative way. The central distinction of this approach rests on the premise that 'utilisation-focused program evaluation is ... done for and with specific, intended primary users for specific, intended uses' (Patton 1997: 23). Therefore, the idea is that the importance of this approach is not just its utility but also that it must have impact. Patton notes that this approach begins with identifying stakeholders and working with them to understand, first, what it is they want to know as a result of the evaluation and, second, how they intend to use the results. Emphasis on the collaborative relationship between and among the evaluator and stakeholders empowers stakeholders to interact and learn from one another. Once the stakeholders are identified, Patton (1997) argues that the evaluator must ensure the evaluation is properly focused. He suggested that this should be undertaken through four main actions: focus on future decisions; focus on critical issues or concerns; focus on responsive approach; and focus on questions (Patton 1997: 184–5).

Thus, the utilization-focused approach sees utility and decision making being the most important parts of the evaluation. Although the idea is that this approach focuses on the content of an evaluation, the actual content or the design of the evaluation is not defined at the outset. Instead, this evaluation approach is seen as more of a strategy, as a means of making decisions so that the evaluation will be of value to those involved. Patton argued that the evaluator's role should be one that is both reactive and adaptive, so that evaluators should work with decision makers to design an evaluation that includes and provides data that will shed light on evaluation questions. For example, a manager may ask: 'Can you get me the answer to this question?' whereas an evaluator would ask 'How would the answer to that question enable you to improve and develop your organization?'.

In practice this type of evaluation:

■ allows for a crystallization of the purposes of the evaluation and by doing this then focuses explicitly on how the evaluation will be carried out
■ increases the possibility that the results will in fact be utilized; this is because key decision makers have been involved at the outset
■ encourages the exchange of ideas and sharing of information.

Tips

Democratic evaluation (now referred to as deliberative democratic evaluation)

This was developed and defined by MacDonald (1974), who took this stance arguing against two other types of evaluation. The first was bureaucratic evaluation, which he described as a form that was important in maintaining and extending managerial power. An example of this was Stufflebeam's model: the Context, Inputs, Process, Products (CIPP) model (Stufflebeam 1983), which argued that it was important to examine goals and inputs, as well as how an evaluation had been implemented. MacDonald was also concerned that it was not only the intended outcomes that needed to be analyzed but also the consequences that were not anticipated, essentially the unintended outcomes. The second type he stood against was one he termed 'power'. In practice, this meant that academics would legitimate public policy in exchange for compliance with the recommendations of the evaluation. Scriven's model is an example of how evaluation can be used as power in evaluating programmes and their improvement. Scriven (1972) suggests that misuse of power occurs when the evaluators are not cued into the programme's goals, which, according to MacDonald, exemplifies this type of evaluation. Instead of these models, MacDonald argues for democratic evaluation.

Example

DEMOCRATIC EVALUATION

- Provides information to the community.
- Values pluralism.
- Represents a range of perspectives and views.
- Allows the role of the evaluator to be that of a broker between differing groups.
- Enables data gathering and presentation to be accessible to non-specialist audiences.
- Ensures the evaluation is the collection of definitions and reactions.
- Offers informants confidentiality and control over the use of information.
- Provides a report that does not offer recommendations but seeks a 'best seller' status.
- Ensures that the key concepts are confidentiality, accessibility and negotiation.

(summarized from MacDonald 1974: 18)

This approach has gained considerable criticism from other evaluators, who have suggested that it is serving self-interested ends, largely it would seem because the stance of this approach is liberal. However, it is an approach that has been used successfully and, in many ways, has brought a strong challenge to those in the field of evaluation, as MacDonald argued:

> The fundamental issue, of course, is the impact of evaluation on the distribution of power, and this may come down in the end to the choice of discourse – a question of language. Evaluators who choose the discourse of technocratic management will empower the manager. Evaluators who choose the language of social science will empower themselves and their sector. Evaluators who choose a widely shared language may empower all of us. I'm a common language evaluator, how about you?

(MacDonald 1984)

Perhaps what is most important about this model is that the possibilities for its use relate to the context in which it is done. For example, corruption and trafficking are not areas where democratic evaluation is best used but programme evaluation and the exploration of classroom practices probably are.

Evaluation and arts-based inquiry

The interest in evaluation in the 2000s continues to grow, led by researchers such as Simons, who has linked evaluation and arts-based research. This form of evaluation takes the stance that arts-based media facilitates the portrayal of the process, learning and outcomes of evaluation. Simons and McCormack (2007) recognize others who are using the arts-based approach to inquiry alongside evaluation such as Cancienne and Snowber (2003), who used dance not only for evaluation but also to disseminate findings (Bagley and Cancienne 2001). However, they do point out that the specific use of creative arts for designing, interpreting and presenting an evaluation as a whole has yet to be undertaken. What they question is:

> How the creative arts can elicit and portray the essential values of a program to promote usable knowledge and understanding ... for example how to re-present artistic knowing, design an evaluation, document the values in the program, establish credibility, and communicate understandings that emerge through artistic expression.
>
> (Simons and McCormack 2007: 294)

Principles of using arts-based approaches and evaluation

There appear to be a number of central principles that can help to delineate this type of evaluation and we suggest they are as follows.

1. It moves away from traditional ideas of analyzing data (such as codes and categories) and instead begins with images and metaphors. Beginning with metaphors and images brings to the surface unconscious ideas and understandings, as well as helping to connect the experiences of participants.
2. It recognizes the importance of the creative process in helping to facilitate understanding of an issue by engaging with the whole person.
3. The values implicit in these kinds of evaluations become explicit through the creative process which, in turn, enables the evaluator to shape the evaluation. The evaluation then connects with participants, as well as shaping the design throughout the life of the evaluation.
4. Data are both documented and represented through artistic expression. As a result, the sense of peoples' experiences is realised through the creative process.
5. Interpretation is seen as an artistic process, so that the movement of different parts of data can be compared with a dance whereby the evaluator examines patterns, feelings and emotions of data in order to interpret them.
6. The concept of validity is broadened to incorporate understandings that emerge from artistic expression. For example, it should include criteria such as artistic substance, aesthetic form, engagement with the public and appropriateness of selection (Mullen and Finley 2003: 160).
7. Dissemination of findings occurs through artistic forms. For example: McCormack and Elliott (2003) presented *In Appreciation of Wisdom: The Voice of the Older Person*. This was dance set to music and intermingled with images of the ways in which caring for older people in nursing had changed over time.

This form of evaluation then uses the artistic process to undertake, represent and disseminate evaluation. In many ways, this is a new way of seeing and using evaluation which is strongly holistic, thereby shifting it firmly away from traditional forms of evaluation. As Simons and McCormack argue:

> Artistic knowing in evaluation creates new opportunities for evaluators to express their creativity, for participants to overcome barriers to participation, and for both to advance the sophistication of evaluation practice.
>
> (Simons and McCormack 2007: 308)

Table 18.1 summarizes and compares forms of evaluation.

Table 18.1 Comparison of forms of evaluation

Type	Commonly adapted paradigms	Focus	Key features
Traditional evaluation	Post-positivism Pragmatism	To measure achievement of goals and objectives	Establishing whether a programme or activity is effective and efficient
Illuminative evaluation	Pragmatism	To study an innovation to understand how it operates	Discovering and documenting what it is like to be part of an innovation or to illuminate issues
Responsive evaluation	Pragmatism	To answer the questions about the activity to which the stake holder(s) want(s) answers	Evaluating the effectiveness of activities that are being undertaken
Naturalistic evaluation	Constructivism	To understand how programmes and organizations operate in a natural context	Ensuring that programmes and organizations are studied in their natural (social) contexts
Utilization-focused approach	Pragmatism	To provide useful information that shows the impact of a change, intervention or programme to those involved in it	Identifying relevant decision makers and information users in order to work with them in a collaborative way
Democratic evaluation	Constructivism	To work with participants and to understand a range of perspectives and issues	Providing information in an accessible way to the community being evaluated
Evaluation and arts-based inquiry	Constructivism Constructionism	To use art to portray the learning and outcomes of evaluation	Recognising the importance of the creative process in helping to facilitate understanding of an issue by engaging with the whole person

DESIGNING AND DOING EVALUATION

When using evaluation, the researcher faces essential choices about philosophical and personal position, framing the study, collecting data, working with data and writing about the results. In the next few paragraphs, we provide an overview of the choices researchers who use evaluation often make. This description is followed by a summary of these common choices in Table 18.2 on page 285. This table provides links to other parts and chapters in this book where we provide fuller descriptions and practical advice for doing qualitative research.

Philosophical and personal positioning

The researcher's responsibility is to understand the essence of what is happening in the situation, as well as to consider how the participants work within the situation. Researchers choosing different types of evaluation, necessarily position themselves differently philosophically. As we have indicated, they have drawn from a range of paradigms, ranging from post-positivism to pragmatism, to constructionism to constructivism (see Chapters 2, 4 and 5).

Focus of the study

Researchers undertaking evaluation study a range of phenomena, including structures and processes. They should be clear about the issues we outline in Figure 18.1.

What is the evaluation for?	GOALS?
What means should be used?	METHOD?
What resources will be available?	FINANCE?
Why is it being undertaken?	FOCUS?
When is it to be undertaken?	TIMEFRAME?
How do we judge?	CRITERIA?
Where will the information be used?	APPLICATION?
Who undertakes it?	ORGANIZATION?
To whom will it be available?	DISSEMINATION?

Figure 18.1 Issues to consider when doing an evaluation

Researchers typically do not apply a conceptual or theoretical framework since they often are trying to generate new theory, rather than explore existing concepts or theories.

Data collection

Data may include anything that helps the researcher develop concepts that, in turn, lead to understanding. 'Anything' might include other research, newspaper articles, discussion boards, blog postings, lectures, seminars and television shows, or it might include more traditional data such as interviews, observations, and focus groups (see Chapters 23–26). However, evaluations can be complex and messy affairs. Yet, when beginning the process of evaluation, it is worth considering some of the ethical, moral and political decisions required at the outset, such as:

■ Who is the evaluation for?
■ Whose needs does the evaluation serve?
■ Who has access to the data?
■ Who owns the data?
■ Who controls the release of data?
■ What stays open and what remains hidden (and who decides)?

■   To whom is the researcher responsible (participants, sponsors, both)?
■   How is confidentiality managed?

Thus, ethical considerations often revolve around questions of design and processes (see Chapter 21).

Figure 18.2 demonstrates the different and styles and dimensions of evaluation.

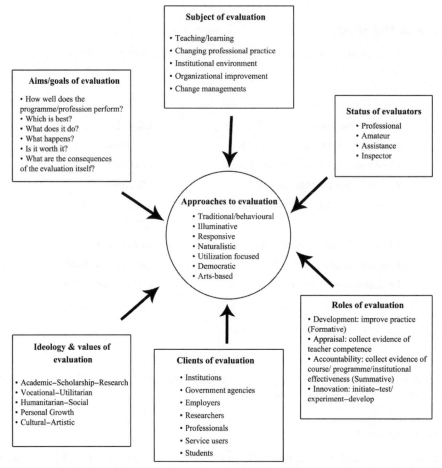

Figure 18.2 Styles and dimensions of evaluation (adapted from Savin-Baden and Major 2004: 144, originally adapted from Cox *et al.* 1981)

Working with data and findings

The researcher's aim is to understand the situation and to discover theory implicit in the data. Key phases in treating data are coding and sorting (see Chapter 27). Sorting is reading and re-reading notes in order to uncover categories and their interrelationships through a comparative and inductive process. From the process of sorting, the researcher then generates explanation and recommendations. Evaluators consider questions of quality ranging from how they view quality, to how to operationalize it, to how to strategize it; they place a particular emphasis on strategies (see Chapter 30).

Writing

While writing up can be done throughout the process, from the first point of data collection, these reports are generally initial reports. The final report tends to be in the form of a set of recommendations.

Summary of choices when designing and doing pragmatic qualitative research

In Table 18.2, we highlight key choices that researchers using evaluation research commonly make. Our intent is not to say how the approach must be done but rather to provide a description of the way that we have most often seen it in the literature. Thus, this table is intended to serve as a general guide that researchers may consider when they design and do their own evaluations.

Table 18.2 Designing evaluation

Design	Specifics	Chapter
Philosophical origins	Post-positivism, pragmatism, constructionism, constructivism	2
Philosophical stance	Outsider looking in	4
Personal stance	Low degree of disclosure of positionality in final report	5
Who or what of study	Most often processes and structures	6
Research questions	Research questions are constructed to understand practice.	7
Literature review	Not typically completed initially; literature may count as data	8
Theoretical/conceptual framework	Typically not used; goal is to understand practice not test it	9
Time/place/participants	Length of time in field varies by project Done in natural environment Purposeful sampling, frequently maximum variation	20
Ethics	Ethical design, treatment of individuals, processes and presentation of products important; particular emphasis on design and processes	21
Fieldwork	Extensive field notes taken throughout process	22
Data collection methods	Semi-structured interviews with individuals or focus groups Observations in context Review of documents or other pertinent materials Everything counts as data	23–26
Data handling	Open coding	27
Analysis	Constant comparison Thematic analysis	28
Interpretation	Highly interpretive	29
Quality	View of quality, quality criteria and strategies to ensure quality important; particular emphasis on strategies	30
Researcher voice	External or internal observer and reporter	31
Report	Data reported organized around recommendations, often in a traditional format	32

ADVANTAGES AND CHALLENGES OF EVALUATION

Whichever approach to evaluation is being adopted, all forms of evaluation include challenges. Challenges relate to issues such as who commissioned the evaluation and the identity of the stakeholders. Good evaluation should therefore:

- inform practice and not just be a summary of the past
- be collaborative, work from participants' perception of good practice
- enhance learning.

The most important issues to consider are:

- *Truth telling*: depending on what kind of evaluation being undertaken, the researcher needs to decide how the information gained will be managed and how to go about sharing findings that may be uncomfortable for others to hear.
- *Validity*: this is complex within evaluation and does vary markedly across forms of evaluation; however, the most important validity challenge is ensuring the researcher is as honest as possible about the findings and that credibility can be demonstrated to all audiences involved in the evaluation.
- *Data control*: when evaluations are funded by external organizations and involve gaining the perspectives of a variety of stakeholders, data control can be difficult. The researcher may be asked in the café or corridor about the findings so far, but it is important to be clear with those involved what will be shared and when that will be.
- *Protection of individual rights*: in most organizations, when an evaluation is going on, everyone knows about it. The researcher may be asked by one individual about the views of another individual but, however innocent the request, it is important to protect those spoken with and not purposely or inadvertently share views with others during the process of evaluation, unless that has been explicitly agreed.
- *Position and perspective of the evaluator*: it is important to be clear, as a researcher and with others, about the researcher role and make it clear how this will operate, what data will be collected, how findings are to be shared and the extent to which the researcher is able to be collaborative.

However, it is important to note that, despite the challenges and politics, there are many advantages to using this approach to research. Evaluation provides:

- *Feedback* about the way programmes, changes and new practices are working that can help improve practice further.
- *Improvement*, by helping to point out where changes need to be made to develop practice and also to improve innovations further.
- *Facilitation of change*. Evaluation can be a supportive force for change, as it can prompt consideration of new options within an organization, guide decision making and be inclusive of those involved in the change process.
- *Emphasis on positive as well as poor practice*. Evaluation can pinpoint areas of good practice that can be developed in other areas of an organization.
- *Transparency*, in terms of ensuring that values, morals and judgments within the organizations and practice are explicit.
- *Opportunity for voices to be heard* by those involved in the evaluation. Good evaluation should take the form of a consultation with stakeholders so that ideas can be exchanged and ways forward can be discussed. Fisher (2002) has suggested that user-led evaluation can result in stronger evidence, guarantee better quality data and ensure greater theoretical relevance can emerge from the data analysis.

CONCLUSION

Evaluation is a wide-ranging approach to research that stakeholders utilize with many different goals and methods in mind. Whilst quantitative evaluation is still undertaken within schools, universities and organizations, the difficulty with this form is that it focuses on improvement and accountability rather than learning from change. Evaluations with illuminative or arts-based approaches reflect the values of the broad base of qualitative inquiry more effectively than traditional forms of evaluation. However, evaluation can be used both as a form of research as well as an evaluation procedure, and it is important to decide on which of these it is before the researcher proceeds. Evaluation is an approach that is used to examine the value or worth of something and this itself makes such research complex and challenging whilst also bringing with it the need for clarity and honesty. The best forms of evaluation are those that include all stakeholders, encourage discussion of the purpose of the evaluation and ensure all those involved have a voice about what is undertaken, what is disclosed to the public, and the ways in which different voices within the evaluations are to be presented.

Concept questions

- What kinds of criteria should be used to decide which form of evaluation to use?
- Could any criteria be used across all forms of evaluation to judge the quality of the research (see Chapter 30)? If so, which?
- Are some forms of evaluation better suited to some disciplines and fields than others? Why or why not?

Application questions

- What are the goals of your research?
- Would an evaluation allow you to achieve your goals?
- What stakeholders would you include?
- What details would you share with stakeholders?

Reflective questions

Ryan, K. E. and Cousins, J. B. (2009) *The SAGE international handbook of educational evaluation*, Thousand Oaks, CA: Sage.
   This substantial handbook covers a wide number of evaluation approaches described by a diverse group of authors.

Elliott, J. and Kushner, S. (2007) The need for a manifesto for educational programme evaluation. *Cambridge Journal of Education*, 37 (3), 321–36.
   This offers a good history of evaluation and appraises the difficulties it has met over a period of time. It also suggests how evaluation should really be put into practice.

Shaw, I. F., Greene, J. C. and Mark, M. M. (2007) *Handbook of evaluation*, London: Sage.
   This provides overviews, examples and suggestions of good practice. Probably one of the best on the market in terms of the range of topics, focus and accessibility.

Key resources

Chapter 19

Arts-based approaches

INTRODUCTION

Arts-based research is gaining increasing attention from qualitative scholars. Many researchers see the spectrum of arts-based approaches as offering spaces to both interrupt and create space for discussions about dominant discourses in research and practice across a variety of disciplines. In this chapter, we begin by presenting the origins of these approaches and later explain that there are broadly three different types of arts-based research. We recognize that there are overlaps between the three types but we consider them separately to highlight key differences between them. In the last section of the chapter, we outline ways in which these approaches have been adopted and suggest too that such approaches need to be located more centre stage in the field of qualitative research.

ORIGINS OF ARTS-BASED APPROACHES

Arts-based approaches emerged from an educational event in 1993 at Stanford University, USA, that was funded by the American Educational Research Association. It brought together twenty-five researchers and practitioners to explore how research that was guided by arts in some way might be delineated (for example, Barone 2006; Barone and Eisner 2011; Finley 2000; 2003; Cahnmann-Taylor 2008; Rolling 2010). Arts-based approaches were later popularized by the work of McNiff (1998; 2008), who found that his students had begun to integrate their creative work with their research findings. What McNiff discovered was a strong (and possibly inseparable) link between the research and the artistic process, as his students began to integrate their personal creative expression with the production of a Master's thesis or doctoral dissertation. Before the popularization of arts-based approaches in the late 1990s, there had been a strong tradition of research in the area of performance, some of which was presented in Chapter 13. The subject areas of performance studies see *performance* as the object of inquiry and see reality as being constructed through action and events. Thus, in the context of this chapter, we argue that performance studies can be located as arts-based inquiry, since, as Schechner suggested:

> To treat any object, work or product 'as' performance — a painting, a novel, a shoe, or anything at all — means to investigate what the object does, how it interacts with other objects or beings, and how it relates to other objects or beings. Performances exist only as actions, interactions and relationships.

> (Schechner 2006: 24)

In the main, performance studies are seen as an intertwining of theory, method and event. Thus, as Conquergood (2002: 152) has suggested, it might be seen as 'a work of *imagination*, as an object of study. ... as a pragmatics of *inquiry* (both as model and method) ... as a tactics of *intervention*, an alternative space of struggle'. We suggest that this is a very specific form of research located very clearly in performance-based disciplines and, whilst important, it is something that is not readily used by most qualitative researchers. Instead, we suggest that arts-based approaches offer a broader stance and range of options from which a qualitative researcher may draw.

Arts-based research has emerged as a construction that occurs both across and between art and social science in order to reflect diverse human experience. Early studies in this field began with researchers using and following their creative process as their research method. Thus, arts-based research developed through the relationships that early artists/researchers had with their own creative processes and their beliefs that letting research and creativity unfold together would cause both art and research to emerge as outcomes. Although the focus of this approach began with the artistic process, arts-based approaches have changed and developed into a number of different forms, which cross the boundaries of other research approaches such as narrative inquiry, action research and evaluation. Arts-based research is therefore now used in a wide variety of ways, and examples of its use include performance, poetry, dance, drama, music and writing. These approaches involve creative expression in some way and in the main do not have a clear final outcome. The focus here is on exploration, understanding and meaning making.

DESCRIPTION AND PURPOSE OF ARTS-BASED APPROACHES

Arts-based approaches use arts, in the broadest sense, to explore, understand and represent human action and experience. The approaches within this genre use media to provoke questions in audiences; for example, by taking a stance on a social issue and/or political concern. Just as art is designed to challenge and prompt questions in the viewer or audience, so too does the arts-based researcher use the media to not only create artefacts but also to use these artefacts as a means of understanding and examining the experiences of the participants and researchers involved in the arts-based research. Thus, often, but not always, the artist is the researcher and the researcher the artist, with the position of the artist/researcher depending on the type of arts-based approach adopted. However, we recognize that arts-based approaches have been defined in a wide variety of ways and we include a number of these below:

> a research method in which the arts play a primary role in any or all of the steps of the research method. Art forms such as poetry, music, visual art, drama, and dance are essential to the research process itself and central in formulating the research question, generating data, analyzing data, and presenting the research results.
>
> (Austin and Forinash 2005: 460–1)

> First, there is the layer of the artistic performance itself – with a focus on the author's work with research-based drama. Then there is the layer of performance having to do with promoting the original artistic event. To best reveal the dangerous immediacy of this type of performance, the author includes in the body of the text a transcript from an interview with him conducted on national radio, about one of his dramas. Finally, there is the performance in everyday life of the arts-engaged researcher, revealed through descriptions of his responses prior to, during, and following the radio interview.
>
> (Gray 2003: 254)

arts-based methodologies bring both arts and social inquiry out of the elitist institutions of academe and art museums, and relocate inquiry within the realms of local, personal, everyday places and events.

(Finley 2008: 72)

Owing to the variety and range of perspectives about what constitutes an arts-based approach, it seems to us that arts-based research is located in the in between spaces, **liminal space**; for example, between public and private worlds, between political and social spaces and between imagination and action.

Liminal space

An in-between space or a space at the margins, often used to describe rites and ritual spaces (marriage, coming of age) where people are in transitions between states

Researchers who work in the arts-based field are often seen as taking up an opportunity to challenge the dominant discourses, not just in terms of social justice but also in relation to the nature and purpose of research itself. Examples of the use of arts to challenge the dominant discourses include writing blogs (Runte 2008), broadcasting radio (McKenzie 2008) and making quilts (Ball 2008) as research, and developing community arts as collaborative research (Barndt 2008). Indigenous story work can also be used (Archibald 2008), which is where arts-based approaches and narrative approaches overlap (see Chapter 15). As a result of the varieties of arts-based approaches available, many students and academics find the forms of arts-based inquiry presented here as troublesome and difficult.

Although we suggest there are three broad types of arts-based approaches, with further sub-types, there are some overarching principles that seem to apply across the different categories. These principles occur because, whilst these research approaches tend not to be prescriptive, there are characteristics that the different forms share. These six principles we have identified are drawn from the writings of a number of authors and would seem to reflect the general tenor of the arts-based research community.

Knowledge is generated through the work. It is not always initially clear to the artist/researcher in what ways knowledge might be generated. It might be in terms of what the work evokes for others or it might present a sociocultural change to those who encounter the work. At other times, knowledge might be generated by the artist/researcher for themselves through the work they are creating.

Example

CREATING KNOWLEDGE THROUGH WORK

An example of this is provided by Quinn and Calkin (2008) who provide dialogue in words and images between two artists doing arts-based educational research. An excerpt is presented below:

Jamie had used art in many ways. For example, he did many field sketches of Annette and the students; he collected the students' artwork and used their (and his) work as interview prompts, and he created visual metaphors as he and Annette discussed their work together in dialog journals. As we began our own dialog, the work that we decided to pursue was Jamie's use of drawings and paintings to represent each of the major phases of his study. Jamie had already created three large paintings, calling them 'methodological murals' because their subject matter focused in large part on methods at different phases of the study. Additionally, Jamie referred to these paintings as murals because they had eclectic compositions,

continued

since the goal of each was to try to represent 'everything' involved in each phase of the study. The first mural (see Figure 19.1) was done for Jamie's dissertation prospectus defence and represented (in visual language and metaphors) what he thought his dissertation study would be about and how it would be done.

Figure 19.1 The first mural Jamie created about his dissertation study (reprinted courtesy of the *International Journal of Education and the Arts*)

The second mural (see Figure 19.2) was done after his first unit, which was taught with Annette, and represented a major shift from a self-study to a collaborative study.

The third mural (see Figure 19.3) was created to represent the second unit that Jamie collaboratively taught.

Figure 19.2 The second mural Jamie created for his dissertation study (reprinted courtesy of the *International Journal of Education and the Arts*)

Figure 19.3 The third mural Jamie created for his dissertation study (reprinted courtesy of the *International Journal of Education and the Arts*)

Example

CREATING KNOWLEDGE THROUGH WORK

A colleague, Steve Dutton, an artist-scholar in the UK, explained to Maggi how knowledge and work was generated through his own struggles and cluelessness. What we understood from the information he shared is as follows:

He went to his study to create work; he didn't know what the work was, type or form. He fiddled and tried for days on different ideas and creations, just feeling clueless, lost, not knowing what he was doing. After a few more attempts, he began to photograph the pieces of work he had created as a record. Yet it was the photographs of the works in progress that became the work itself.

The research is guided by a moral commitment. For researchers in this field the work produced is expected to, as it were, 'take a stand'. Research and the related artefacts may, and often do, present and promote personal transformation both for the artist-researcher and the viewer (see Chapter 5).

There is a strong focus on reflexivity. In arts-based research, because of its very nature, the presence of the artist is evident through the work. However, because of the nature of arts-based disciplines and the critical and complex nature of art itself, the sense of reflexivity is heightened compared with other research approaches. Heightened reflexivity is not just a characteristic of this form of inquiry but is central to it, since arts-based research takes a critical stance towards itself and the world around. Therefore, for most arts-based researchers, the moral stance and sense of interruption through art is central to the research (see Chapter 5).

Accessibility is a firm focal point. A central stance in arts-based research is that the work does not only have the potential to challenge and transform but also that it is available and accessible to a wide and diverse audience. Such accessibility means not just that an audience can see or read the work but also that they can understand, engage and relate to it.

Diverse forms of quality are celebrated and brought together. Quality is difficult to define and manage in relation to arts-based research, particularly as some artist-researchers in this field suggest that the overarching purpose is knowledge advancement through the work that matters, rather than the work itself. Others suggest that good art is also good research. However, the art, as used, must support the research goals, whilst its quality, in terms of aesthetics, must hold meaning. Yet, at the same time, there also needs to be a quality of coherence that reflects the relationship between the purpose of the research and the means of undertaking it.

There is a sense of authenticity. The work and research must be intertwined and mutually shaping so there is sense of integrity about the art and the research. This is perhaps the most central of features in arts-based research, which is related to the idea of trustworthiness or plausibility in other forms of qualitative inquiry. This aspect is essential so that there is consistency and rigour characterizing the relationship between the research and the artwork (see Chapter 30).

Tips

Understanding your researcher stance is an important way of ensuring reflexivity in arts-based approaches to research.

Arts-based approaches should be adopted when the researchers, artists or participants want to use arts-based media to sha pe and explore meaning. For example, a group of people with learning disabilities may use ballet to present to an audience the difficulties they have in communicating in society. Alternatively, arts-based research may be used by the researcher-artist to examine the artistic process itself and how learning occurs through that process. A sculptor, teaching sculpting to students, may use the sculpting process as learning, research and reflection. Further, arts-based research may be used as a process of undertaking research using affect, intellect and physical movement, causing a mutual shaping of both the art and the research. For example, a group of teenagers may use performance to explore and research issues of sexual health, and may also choose to perform a play to the public to raise issues and concerns about oppression suffered by young parents.

TYPES OF ARTS-BASED RESEARCH

We suggest that there are three main types of arts-based research:

1. *Arts-based inquiry*: where the artistic process is used as research by artists, researchers and participants in order to understand the art itself or understand a phenomenon through the artistic process.
2. *Arts-informED inquiry*: that is of two types:
   a. where art is used to represent the findings of a study
   b. where art is used to represent a response to the findings of an issue or situation studied.
3. Arts-informING inquiry: where art is used in order to evoke a response from an audience (in the broadest sense) made to a situation or issue; the response may or may not be captured.

Arts-based inquiry

Arts-based inquiry not only involves the artist (of whichever type) but also those who are involved in the artwork in some way, including the participant and possible other researchers.

> Arts-based inquiry is the use of the artistic process, the making and doing of art as a means of understanding experience

Arts-based inquiry researchers might use sculpting, for example, to learn and understand more about a particular sculpting issue or a specific aspect of sculpting itself. This form of arts-based inquiry uses art for personal exploration to make sense of an issue, concern or medium. In this kind of arts-based research learning, research and personal exploration are seen as overlapping media and part of the artistic process and the research. For example, McNiff (2008) used twenty-six paintings and, through them, explored the use of imaginal dialogue. The idea of imaginal dialogue is valuable in arts-based research, since imagined dialogues can take several forms, including 'conversation between a self and an imaginal other(s), between aspects of the self . . . or between imaginal others with a self as audience to the imaginal scene' (Watkins 1986: 2). In arts-based research, imaginal dialogue involves the process of responding to art through movement, poetry and improvisation, as McNiff explained:

The focus of my research shifted away from experimenting with human subjects and toward the more direct examination of the artistic process. I want to emphasise how even though these artistic expressions may come from within me, I nevertheless attempt to study the art objects and the process of making them with as much objectivity as possible. I am intimately connected to what I make, and this relationship can further understanding, but it is still separate from me. The examination is both heuristic and empirical and thoroughly artistic.

(McNiff 2008: 31)

The idea in this kind of research is to create, examine and interpret art in ways that illustrate not only the artistic process but the impact of arts and issues on peoples' lives. In practice, the artist-researcher might bring together paintings, for example, created by different individuals and set up some kind of protocol that would include decisions about the types, size and colour of paintings to be included and the media and context that are used to respond to them. In practice, arts-based inquiry might involve choosing all paintings done over the last five years that relate to the subject of pain. The artist-researcher might choose to respond to these through movement and dialogue with a witness present who may take notes. Reflection and text created after the session by the artist-researchers helps them to examine how they have been affected and what new insights have been brought to bear. An example of this kind of study is illustrated by Reynolds and Vivat (2010), who explored the contributions of leisure-based art-making for helping to redevelop the identity for women living with chronic fatigue syndrome/myalgic encephalomyelitis. The findings indicated that half the woman saw their projects as being constrained by ill health whereas, for others, art-making offered more possibilities for identity reconstruction, despite continuing ill-health.

McNiff (2008) suggests that it is helpful to create a clear method that can be described and then implemented in a straightforward way. He also recommends that it is useful to design methods that can be replicated by other researchers. Further, he believes that despite being complex and difficult, it is essential to try to convey arts-based inquiry to others through text in order to reach a wide audience.

> When using an arts-based inquiry approach, there is often a tendency to try to do too much or to become lost in the process.

This type of arts-based inquiry supports the arguments of Denzin (2000), who argued for the need to bring emotional critique and political action to research. Thus, arts-based inquiry focuses on not just the end point or final representation but also on the process and expression of the work in a context.

Arts-informed inquiry

This form of inquiry broadly comprises two types: as a means of representing findings and as a means of representing a response to the situation being studied.

Arts-informed inquiry is perhaps one of the most well-known forms of arts-based research and comprises the process of using art to illustrate and represent findings. Some of the early ways of representing findings used photography. Walker, in the 1980s (discussed in Schratz and Walker 1995), argued that pictures were not to be used instead of words but as a means

Arts-informed inquiry comprises two types:

■ where art is used by artists and researchers to represent the findings of a study
■ where art is used by artists and researchers to represent a response to a situation studied

of enabling discussion to occur about the nature of context. More recently, photo story and digital storytelling have been used as a means of bringing together visual narratives, through the use of arts and images to represent narratives. Thus, overlap occurs between arts-based approaches and narrative approaches (see Chapter 15). Digital storytelling involves asking participants to present their point of view using images. It requires them to consider the use of their voice, the choice of music and the way the story is paced and presented (see Chapter 11). Many artist-researchers began using these new ways of representation by including narratives, poetry and photographs in traditional journal articles (for example, Park-Fuller 2003). More recently, the use of exhibitions has been used to represent findings, as have virtual worlds and virtual reality (for example Slater 2009; Benford *et al.* 1995). Some of the ways of representing data that are most common are poetry, painting, storytelling, music and dance. In many ways, these are a means of representation rather than necessarily a form of inquiry (see Chapter 31). What is significant here is that art is used to enhance understanding, reach multiple audiences and use media to make research findings accessible to a variety of people, as illustrated in the following examples.

Examples of representing findings

Saldaña (2010) uses ethnodrama, which employs the techniques of theatre production to produce a performance of participants' experiences. He argues:

> In theatre, the term for a play written to be read but not performed is a 'closet drama'. Researchers can certainly compose a field note-based script as a closet ethnodrama, but the next step and true test of a play's effectiveness come from its production mounting on stage. I encourage all researchers not only to develop written scripts, but to explore their realization through a staged reading or performance.
>
> (Saldaña 2010: 68)

In a different way, Lorenzo (2010) used storytelling and creative activities as both data triggers and for data representation. Her study involved using participatory research with disabled women living in informal settlements in Cape Town, South Africa, concerning their experience of poverty and discrimination in relation to race, gender and disability. The artwork in Figure 19.4 overleaf was used as both trigger and representation.

Lorenzo presents the interrelationship of arts-based media as both triggers for data collection and the data collection itself; then further as a means of representation in Table 19.1, overleaf on page 297.

Representing a response

This approach to arts-informed inquiry is not about representing findings per se but about representing a response to the findings. Invariably this kind of arts-based research is captured

Figure 19.4 A woman managing/happy with her load

as parts of a wider project and sometimes the responses are gained informally or through podcasts; therefore, in the main, they are published less than other forms of arts-based research. This is evident in Gray's works; we have highlighted where Gray mentions the 'response' to the findings:

> First, there is the layer of the artistic performance itself — with a focus on the author's work with research-based drama. Then there is the layer of performance having to do with promoting the original artistic event. To best reveal the dangerous immediacy of this type of performance, the author includes in the body of the text a transcript from an interview with him conducted on national radio, about one of his dramas. Finally, there is the performance in everyday life of the arts-engaged researcher, revealed through descriptions of his responses prior to, during, and following the radio interview.

(Gray 2003: 254)

Gray (2003) describes a performance about prostate cancer that included illness performances, treatment issues and care-giving performances presented by spouses. However, what is particularly noticeable is that Gray explains how it was not just evocative in terms of the art but in terms of how the performance itself created other performances.

Table 19.1 Data generation methods and processes (Lorenzo 2010: 132)

Data protection			
Data generation	*Data triggers*	*Facilitation techniques*	*Data capturing methods*
Storytelling groups	Drawings	Small group discussions	Videotaping Audiotaping Scribing
Narrative action reflection workshops	Drawings Clay work Clay sculptures Singing Music Movement Drama Critical incident stories Writing songs	Buzz groups Pairing Small group discussions (maximum of eight people in a group) Plenary groups Brainstorming	Field notes Photographs
Reflective journal	Writing poems		
Data: transcripts of video tapes, audiotapes, field notes and commentary on photographs			

Verification of data

Data analysis	Data interpretation
Six-step analysis of 'triggers' (Hope and Timmel 1995) Thematic analysis (Rubin and Rubin 1995) Reflective stance approach (Meulenberg-Buskens 1999)	Literature Consultative dialogues

Arts-informing inquiry

This form of inquiry is designed to evoke meaningful thought about art.

> Arts-informing inquiry is where art is used to evoke a response to a situation but the response may or may not be captured.

Perhaps one of the best examples of this is the work of Herman, who recognized that nonparticipants who viewed, heard or encountered evil acts responded to the telling of the stories related to these acts, and that this needed to be captured. She explained:

> I am interested in the images of evil events, in particular the images of genocide, and how they affect nonparticipants in these events. I want to know more about how and what researchers learn from other people's representations of our vast creative capacities for cruelty and what is our experience when we engage these images. How do they affect those of us who were not there? I believe we nonparticipants need to stay creatively engaged with this (fortunately) mediated experience to help prevent its continuing occurrence.
>
> (Herman 2005: 468)

What is significant here is that often the responses to experiences and data are disregarded and we do not recognize the value and importance of such responses. In practice, much of this arts-informed research occurs in hidden spaces, such as artists' studios and with community groups at art colleges and centres, and therefore it can be quite difficult to both discover and access this kind of inquiry. However, what is essential is that such research creates more data; additional content beyond what was initially presented, and therefore this adds new layers of meaning to studies. Herman explains:

> Those of us who are nonparticipants in the actual evil events find visceral information in liminal space. Whether we take direct accounts from survivors or gaze at a photo, we enter this space of mediated representation and we begin to form our own images. When researchers engage authentically with written testimony, photos, music, poems, and artifacts that have been generated by an evil event, we move into that same liminal space where writers, artists, theater, dance, and music performers access material to create their work. Here, in the space between the event and our imaginations, the images engage us and we are called to respond through a coherent sensibility and methodology: an arts-based response.
>
> (Herman 2005: 475)

This kind of response capturing has been used in a variety of ways. For example, following exhibitions of photographs and stories of holocaust victims, those who are survivors have been asked to retell their stores in response. Similarly, those visiting an exhibition of drawings and paintings of one woman's thirty-year story of long-term mental illness were asked to share their response to the work later. The power of the presentations of both the holocaust and the mental illness elicited often unexpected responses which in turn became data. A further example of the use of representation is presented by Salpeter (2005) in 'Telling tales with technology', who provides an overview of a number of projects that have used digital storytelling in the USA.

Those in the arena of arts-informing inquiry tend to focus on evoking meaning through the creation of complex, liquid and messy products or performances, ones that are oriented toward an 'evocative' epistemology (Denzin 1997). It is here that it is possible to see the overlap with performance studies. What Denzin means by an 'evocative' epistemology is that it offers a way of knowing that goes beyond vision, representation and mimicry, so that it is a way of knowing that performs rather than represents the world.

> Often, the most common type of this kind of arts-based research is through the use of performance.
>
> Performance in turn creates another performance – and it is important to recognize and acknowledge this as both data and findings.

This kind of performance creates powerful research spaces and is capable of exerting powerful influence on ways of 'doing' research. Yet some of these kinds of evocative epistemologies and forms of inquiry are problematic and almost too messy, and without any kind of text or interpretation the evocative epistemology is easily lost.

The three main types of arts-based research are summarized in Table 19.2.

Table 19.2 Types of arts-based approaches

Approach	Commonly adapted paradigms	Focus	Key features
Arts-based inquiry	Post-modernism Post-structuralism Constructivism	To understand the art or the phenomenon itself through the artistic process	Use of arts for personal exploration of concern or issue
Arts-informed inquiry	Post-modernism Post-structuralism Constructivism	To use arts to represent findings or represent a response to the findings	Use of art to enhance understanding, reach multiple audiences and make findings accessible
Arts-informing inquiry	Constructivism/ constructionism	To use art to evoke a response	Making meaning through complex and messy performances and products that have power and are evocative

DESIGNING AND DOING ARTS-BASED APPROACHES

In many ways issues of research design in arts-based approaches are no different from other studies. Currently, there is a dearth of literature in this area but we suggest that issues such as how the process of artistic knowing has emerged and how and if personal transformation is recorded, presented and understood are crucial. Further, validity and plausibility criteria need to be established, as well as sound reasoning for presenting art/research in the way it has been done.

When doing-arts based research, the researcher faces essential choices about philosophical and personal position, framing the study, collecting data, working with data and writing about the results. In the next few paragraphs, we provide an overview of the choices researchers who use arts-based approaches often make. We follow this description by a summary of these common choices in Table 19.3 on page 301. This table provides links to other parts and chapters in this book where we provide fuller descriptions and practical advice for doing qualitative research.

Philosophical and personal positioning

The arts-based researcher chooses from a range of philosophical positions depending on the type of study and often draws upon pragmatism, post-modernism, post-structuralism, social constructionism or constructivism (see Chapters 2 and 4). The researcher typically operates from an insider perspective and has a high level of disclosure about personal stance and gives attention to reflexivity (see Chapter 5).

Focus of the study

The phenomena of study in an arts-based study typically is an individual or an artefact (see Chapter 6). The main challenges in designing an arts-based approach lies in deciding:

- which type of arts-based approach to use
- the reasons for the approach adopted

- how methodological rigour will be ensured
- how art and research will be integrated creatively.

What is central to the development and design of the study is that the artist-researcher strives for egalitarianism (as far as possible) between those involved in the process and art and research, whether artist-researcher, performer, creator or bystander.

Data collection

Data collection in arts-based approaches is invariably elicited differently and often in less formal ways than activities such as interviewing and focus groups. For example, Bagnoli (2009) reflected on her move away from the use of interviews and has suggested that:

> The use of visual and creative methods can generally facilitate investigating layers of experience that cannot easily be put into words (Gauntlett 2007). Images are evocative and can allow access to different parts of human consciousness (Prosser and Loxley 2008): communicating more holistically, and through metaphors, they can enhance empathic understanding, capture the ineffable, and help us pay attention to reality in different ways, making the ordinary become extraordinary (Weber 2008).
>
> (Bagnoli 2009: 548)

Documents and visual data (see Chapter 26) provide some information that may be of use to those using arts-based approaches, particularly those driven by photographs and web-based media.

Working with data and findings

Many researchers see arts-based research as merely a means of representation and not research per se. Yet, by working with arts-based researchers, we have come to appreciate both the value of this kind of research, and its complexity as both method and product. However, it is important to consider what counts as data, how data might be analyzed and how these data will be presented. Arts-based approaches need to be used not just as someone's presentation of findings but to make a difference to people's lives. Furthermore data or 'product' and findings should represent and explore not only the process of a situation but also alternative possibilities and futures. Chapters 27 and 28 provide additional information on content analysis that may be used for visual products as well as text-based ones. The kinds (if any) of quality criteria that should be adopted are also an important consideration (see Chapter 30).

Summary of choices when designing and doing arts-based research

In Table 19.3, we highlight key choices that researchers using arts-based approaches commonly make. Our intent is not to say how the approach must be done but rather to provide a description of the way that we have most often seen it in the literature. Thus, this table is intended to serve as a general guide that researchers may consider when they design and do their own arts-based studies.

Table 19.3 Designing arts-based approaches

Design	Specifics	Chapter
Philosophical stance	Post-modernism and post-structuralism; constructivist and constructionist	4
Personal stance	High level of disclosure	5
Who or what of study	People and artefacts	6
Research questions	Focus on the practical	7
Literature review	Full literature review might or might not be done	8
Theoretical/conceptual framework	May be used but not always, since the focus is on exploration	9
Time/place/participants	Single or multiple sites and settings involving participants in the research	20
Ethics	Ethical design, treatment of individuals, processes and presentation of products important; particular emphasis on products	21
Fieldwork	Collaborative, interview notes and field notes	22
Data collection methods	Interviewing, exploration, arts, theatre, texts, focus groups; observations,	23–26
Data handling	Coding sometimes, more often move to analysis	27
Analysis	Constant comparison or thematic analysis	28
Interpretation	High levels of inference	29
Quality	View of quality, quality criterion and strategies to ensure quality important; particular emphasis on voicing the view of quality	30
Researcher voice	Ranges from outsider to insider voice depending upon type	31
Report	Creative methods and performance	32

ADVANTAGES AND CHALLENGES OF ARTS-BASED APPROACHES

Arts-based approaches have prompted considerable debate in the field of qualitative research both because are they different and diverse, and also because they introduce complexity and liquidity to the field of qualitative inquiry. The advantages of arts-based approaches are that they:

■ *Enable researchers to use art to explore, simulate and represent human action and experience.* They also provide a tangible product that evokes in ways that text alone cannot.
■ *Provide opportunities for researcher and participants to use and explore diverse media and explore and present new ways of knowing* thereby allowing researchers/artists to use diverse media to provoke questions in audiences on social issues and/or political concerns. Moreover, artefacts provide a means of understanding and examining the experiences of the participants and researchers involved in the arts-based research.

Just as there are advantages, challenges also exist with the use of arts-based approaches, which include:

■ *The difficulty of deciding which type to use and to think through the reasons and consequences of each approach.* Is for example the production of work, such as a sculpture, enough to explain the research question, the research itself and the findings without any text to explain and mediate it?

- *Knowing which type of arts-based inquiry will actually help to answer the specific research questions.* For example, is it better to explore evil practices as Herman (2005) did and respond through responsive art or is it better to undertake interviews and represent the findings through art?
- *Determining the kinds (if any) of quality criteria that should be used to evaluate the inquiry.* For instance, should quality criteria be developed by the researchers themselves for a given time and context, or should generic criteria be used across all arts-based research? There are some who believe that there should be quality criteria and others who argue against them, yet is it essential to worry about this or not? Richardson and Lockridge argued that to seek to develop such criteria begins to exert 'hegemonic control over what constitutes the beautiful' (Richardson and Lockridge 1998: 330).
- *The issue of representation.* At a time when there is an increased call for outcomes and outputs from most organizations, much arts-based inquiry is deposited as text in order to ensure publication in a respectable, high-ranked journal. Yet this shifts the focus away from the work being accessible and prevents the work from being seen and explored by others beyond the academic community. The dilemma for those in this field becomes how work is published so that it is not seen as art or research, but both.
- *How the interrelationship between art and research is to be managed.* For example, how are validity and quality to be dealt with and who decides what are data and what are not?

For many researchers in this area of inquiry, artworks and texts are expected to stand alone and be open to many and diverse interpretations. Yet this perspective seems to stand against many of the arguments that have been fostered in qualitative inquiry, whereby researchers should not leave the text to speak for itself, since it is mediated by time and context. Therefore, the role of the researcher is to interpret the text and explain it for those reading it. The question in arts-based approaches is: is this in fact enough, when the artwork itself introduces further questions and responses? There is a sense that if researchers wish to publish their findings, they need to exhibit high-quality writing skills in order to satisfy editors of research journals and succeed in achieving publication. However, in arts-based approaches, is this the case? Like good writing, must there also be artful representation of research? It would seem that some researchers in this field believe that good research must also be good art.

CONCLUSION

What is critical to remember about arts-based approaches is that they are essentially designed to introduce more questions than answers, both for the researchers and those viewing the 'findings'. What is at the heart of many forms of arts-based research is the desire to make radical statements about justice, equity and the control and prediction of knowledge. Although we have located a number of different types here, arts-based research remains difficult to define because of its wide ranges of forms and contexts. What makes it both challenging and interesting is that it is not prescriptive and often the 'rules' of qualitative inquiry cannot be applied easily. However, it is a form of inquiry that perhaps does put political, social and moral issues centre stage in ways that other qualitative approaches do not.

Concept questions

Reflective questions

■ What kinds (if any) of quality criteria should be used to evaluate arts-based approaches?

■ Could any criteria be used across all arts-based approaches to judge the quality of the research (see Chapter 30)? If so, which?

■ How may the production of a work, such as a sculpture, explain the research question, the research itself and the findings without any text to mediate it?

Application questions

■ Which type of arts-based inquiry will help to answer the research questions you are undertaking?

■ What will your philosophical positioning be?

■ How will you evaluate the research?

Key resources

Barone, T. and Eisner, E. W. (2011) *Arts-based research*, Thousand Oaks: CA: Sage.
This is a helpful and informative introductory text by two experienced authors. It is clear and helpful but it does not quite provide the breadth of the edited textbook by Knowles and Cole (2008).

Knowles J. G. and Cole A. L. (2008) *Handbook of the arts in qualitative research*, London: Sage.
This is a useful resource book that covers a wide range of arts-based approaches and from a number of different arts-based disciplines.

Qualitative Inquiry (2003) 9 (2)
This special issue covers a number of areas and provides interesting discussion points in particular.

Finley, S. (2003). Arts-based inquiry in QI: Seven years from crisis to guerilla warfare. *Qualitative Inquiry*, 9 (2), 281–96.

Savin-Baden, M. and Major, C. (2010) *New approaches to qualitative research: wisdom and uncertainty*, London: Routledge.
This provides several chapters that use different types of arts-based inquiry such as ethnodrama and the use of art to represent data.

Collecting data

Chapter 20

Time, place and participants

INTRODUCTION

Researchers face a series of choices related to the specifics of when and where to conduct their research, as well as the identities of their participants. What is at stake as a result of the choices that a researcher makes about these issues is the integrity of the study and the findings themselves. In making these choices, researchers set parameters that will ultimately frame what they will discover. In this chapter, we describe the influence of the time, place and participants on the study. We provide concrete advice about making good selections. Finally, we consider some of the practicalities involved in ensuring success in making these selections.

CHOOSING WHEN TO CONDUCT THE RESEARCH: TIME

As Miles and Huberman (1994: 110) suggest, 'Life is chronology' and as van Manen (1990: 10) suggests, 'a person cannot reflect on lived experience while living through the experience'. While life experiences are what qualitative researchers tend to study, Kelly and McGrath (1988) suggest that too few researchers consider the issue of time in their research, which can undermine the validity of the studies. Moreover, time can be a unique feature of qualitative research (Charmaz 1990: 1164; Sandelowski *et al.* 1992: 311), since the time during which the study is conducted may well influence participant responses and thus findings. Thus, time for conducting the research is a critical part of setting the focus of the study (Sandelowski 1998).

A researcher must use logic, and at times empathy, to determine when to conduct the study and how that time frame will influence the study itself.

CHOOSING THE RESEARCH SITE(S)

A research site is the space or place of the topic under study. However, the site is not simply where knowledge is uncovered; it is an integral part of the knowledge that is uncovered. Since the research site is indeed part of the meaning, a critical element of what is under study, it should be the most logical choice for the research being undertaken. Researchers can select a single site, multiple sites or virtual site.

Conducting research at a single site can have an advantage, as doing so typically allows a researcher to gain deeper information about a single institution. The disadvantages in relying

THE IMPORTANCE OF TIME

■ In studying the experiences of collegiate athletes, if the study is conducted during the season in which the sport takes place, it is a different study than if conducted during the off-season.

■ A researcher wishing to investigate patient experiences with critical illness has a time factor to consider. A patient who has been recently diagnosed may be in a good position to provide information about the initial sensations of learning about the diagnosis but he or she may feel stress, anxiety or depression that might influence responses to questions (there may also be an ethical issue, as we discuss in Chapter 21, with the timing of this data collection). Studying a recently diagnosed patient is a different study to investigating a patient who has had time to come to terms with the illness.

■ A researcher wishing to study socialization processes in organizations will end up with three different studies, depending on whether the participants chosen are interviewees for their first job, newly hired employees completing their orientation period or veteran workers with thirty years of service.

When selecting a site, it is important to choose one to which you will be able to gain access. Typically, knowing a gatekeeper can help with access (see Chapter 22).

Maggi Savin-Baden, Author

Choice of research sites

I chose to collect data within a field different from my own, from four curricula within higher education in Britain, where people believed themselves to be using a problem-based learning (PBL) approach. The reasons for making this choice about the initial data collection were:

■ By beginning with unfamiliar territory, I would be less likely to become waylaid by a familiar course and setting which might encourage me to make more than the usual amount of mistaken/unhelpful assumptions.

■ I believed an unfamiliar setting would force me to push the boundaries of my thinking and free me to 'begin with silence' (Psathas 1973).

■ I thought unfamiliarity would heighten my awareness about the ways in which the espoused values and intentions of using PBL differed from the reality of what was actually occurring in practice.

■ The research design was to be emergent (Lincoln and Guba 1985), which would mean that continual data analysis was both possible and desirable.

upon a single site are that findings will be limited to a single snapshot of a single place at a single time, so it will be essential to avoid unwarranted generalizations. Furthermore, participants may wish to protect the reputation of the site and so may not provide such full and honest responses as they might otherwise. Also, researchers may become so familiar with the site that they may be unable to generalize the findings clearly enough for applicability elsewhere.

There are advantages to selecting multiple sites. In particular, doing so allows for breadth of exposure and for comparisons across sites. Using multiple sites can have some disadvantages as well. In particular, it is possible to miss issues arising at later sites because researchers are already aware of and over familiar with them from earlier sites (because of 'hearing them all before'). A researcher also risks superficiality when moving from one site to another, as well as the possibility of not getting an in depth understanding of any one place.

Some researchers have also given attention to notions of space, what it is and how it matters in qualitative research (for example, Kuntz 2010; Hernes 2004). Hernes, for example, suggests that the following questions are important:

A main question is evidently what spaces matter, as the number is potentially infinite and any selection might seem about as viable as any other. Another question ... is how a space matters. A third question relates to the dynamics of the space; how and when does it appear, and how does it evolve?

(Hernes 2004: 66)

Writers such as Valentine (1992), Lefebvre (1991) and Olson (1987) have also begun to see space as more than just physical surroundings; they see it as a political container shaping and influencing people's thoughts and actions. Kuntz reflects on issues of space in the following researcher reflection.

Aaron M. Kuntz, University of Alabama, USA

Space as more than setting

All too often in qualitative research the material environment is overlooked, rendered an empty backdrop to meaning-making. That is, the places in which our research occur are given slight acknowledgement, most often named or described and then left behind and forgotten in our collective rush to find meaning that exists independent of the material environments in which they were uttered. There are, of course, consequences to such patterns of inquiry and my work seeks a more nuanced and interactive sense of space as a productive element in coming-to-know.

Most often, our material surroundings – the physical environments we encounter each and every day – are presented in our research as 'setting'. In this sense, traditional research articles present a quick overview of the 'research setting', offering a cursory description of the study's locale, for example, as well as the buildings and rooms in which the study takes place. In this sense, the setting is offered to orient the reader, to give a sense of place. From this point on, considerations of setting often drop away, coming to the fore only if participants remark on some physical characteristic of their environment. Throughout this process, space-as-setting remains entirely passive – it's

continued

just *there*. The material environment is represented as a fixed container-of-meaning: the a priori stage upon which the study takes place. In my own work, I strive to complicate this understanding, to consider the material environment as endlessly open and an active agent in how we make sense of the world in which we live.

If the material environment is more than setting, we might understand space as infused with, and an active contributor to, social meaning. In many ways, then, recognizing the intersection of material and social worlds becomes a methodological quandary – how are we to make sense of space as actively engaged in processes of meaning-making? How are we to critically engage with the spatial, and what are the implications for understanding space in newly dynamic ways?

Much as gender, race, and the body have been rendered within post-structural thought, space resists essentialized definition, never fully contained as a 'whole', 'organic', or 'static' entity. Thus, like other social entities that contribute to our identity, space is always incomplete, multiple, unbound, and shifting. We would do well in our methodological approaches to take such considerations of space seriously.

As a means for better engaging with the dynamic properties of space, I turn to materialist methodologies. Materialist analyses seek to understand and describe the influence of lived experience, embodiment and daily practices on larger cultural structures, as well as the effect of culture on materiality. From this materialist perspective, our physical environment acts upon us even as we act within and upon it. More simply, space is endlessly productive – it makes possible particular activities, encounters and ways of knowing. As an example, consider the role of the material environment on the most standard of qualitative research methods, the interview. Traditionally, conceptions of space-as-setting led researchers to limit the impact of the material environment on the interview itself. A researcher might, for example, seek a secluded setting to conduct the interview, away from 'distractions' or other material possibilities that might otherwise interfere with the intended conversation. As an alternative, consider the possibilities inherent in the walking interview, where participants negotiate a physical landscape together even as they discuss the issue at hand. Walking through a park might invoke new metaphors (of growth, perhaps or horizon?) thus making possible new ways of understanding key issues and insights. In this case, the material environment is far from passive, it continuously acts upon participants, opening new possibilities in ways that are all-too-infrequently examined.

Foregrounding the productive possibilities of space within qualitative research makes possible levels of analyses that attend to both the material and the social, the utterances we make and the multiple contexts from which they draw individual and collective meaning. Meaning-making is messy business, full of unexpected and overlapping processes of coming to know. By recognizing the implications of the spatial on our qualitative inquiry, we necessarily wrestle with the complexities inherent in living and reflecting upon material experiences in our daily lives. With each breath, space, time and the body intersect and are relationally productive, intersecting to contribute vast landscapes of meaning to the human condition.

Thus, researchers are beginning to understand that space and place are combined with time, participants and question, all of which are critical components of meaning and thus critical in the quest to discover of knowledge. Maggi provides an illustration of a study in which space and spatial practice were important.

SPACE AND SPATIAL PRACTICE STUDY

This study explored space and spatial practice in Second Life from the point of view of participants in higher education (lectures, developers and researchers) who had been Second Life residents for more than three years. It investigated uses of spaces, perception of space and participants' views of themselves in the Second Life space. The overarching research approach was narrative inquiry that was implemented since access to participants' stories and experiences of space seemed a helpful means of coming to understand space and spatial practice from users' perspectives. The first piece of data collection involved meeting key informants in the virtual world Second Life.

The focus of the meeting was to discuss understandings of 'space' in Second Life. What is worthy of note is that the space chosen was open with benches provided, as in the screen shot Figure 20.1, but during the discussions concerning space, those attending the meeting chose to change the space into something that they felt was a more comfortable space; this is shown in Figure 20.2.

Figure 20.1 The initial meeting space in Second Life

Figure 20.2 The space adapted by participants

Example

SELECTING PARTICIPANTS

Part of data collection preparation requires identifying participants, based upon who might best provide an answer to the research question. In Chapter 6, we defined the 'phenomenon of study' or the 'who' or 'what' that a researcher will study (the term phenomena of the study is related to the term *unit of analysis* used in quantitative research). As we indicated, phenomena may be individuals, groups, structures, processes, concepts or artefacts. It is the 'thing' that the researcher wants to talk about when the study is complete. Participants in the study, however, are different from the phenomenon of the study; participants are the individuals from whom researchers collect data (the term participants in the study is related to the term *unit of observation* in quantitative research). We offer the following examples of the differences between the two, in Table 20.1.

Table 20.1 Differences between phenomena and participants

Phenomena of the study		Participants in the study
Individuals	New working mothers	A sample of 25 new mothers working full time at AT&T
A group	Craft-makers	A sample of 30 quilt making women in Gee's Bend, Alabama
A structure	Organizational culture	A sample of 60 lecturers, students, and administrators studying or working at Davidson College
A process	Socialization	35 newly hired computer programmers in entry level positions at Google
A concept	Care	23 patients recently released from Druid Hills Hospital who received nursing care during their stay

Participants then are the specific group of individuals from whom the researcher collects data. The selection of participants necessarily will influence the findings. Sampling has been the subject of much attention in the literature (Trost 1986; Patton 1990; Strauss and Corbin 1990; Kuzel 1992; Miles and Huberman 1994; Stake 1994; Baxter and Eyles 1997). The literature indicates that researchers should consider several factors when deciding whether and how to sample.

Factors to consider when sampling

The first consideration for researchers to consider is whether to sample. In particular, the time, population and accessibility factors warrant attention when deciding upon whether to sample.

The time factor

Sampling can provide information quickly and there are many occasions when time is of the essence. For some researchers, a research project is bounded by a single semester or academic year, while others have longer windows of opportunity for engagement. The time factor may necessitate sampling and may provide indications about how large that sample should be.

The time factor

Qualitative research requires ample time for carrying out all the processes required, which probably will initially involve observations and interviewing as a minimum. Then, for each hour spent interviewing, time should be allocated for travel, setting up, debriefing, reflecting and writing memos and journals. Later, time for transcription, data analysis and data interpretation is also needed. Many researchers who believe they can do an extensive qualitative study within a single term or semester find that they cannot complete the work within that timeframe.

The population factor

There are instances in a researchers' career when the population for a study is simply too large for conducting a total population study. In the case of students in online classes in American universities, for example, approximately 3.9 million students are taking an online course. That number simply is unmanageable so, to study the population, it is necessary to work with a sample group.

The accessibility factor

There are some populations where the ability to gain access is fairly limited. Examples of such persons include prisoners, presidents and astronauts on assignments. The accessibility factor in such cases requires sampling, if sampling is even a possibility.

The accessibility factor

An important consideration is whether it is possible to gain access to the necessary information and in particular, access to participants who can provide it. We discuss this question more fully in Chapter 22, but it bears mentioning here, as having access to a gatekeeper who can facilitate entry to a site is critical and thus should be considered as part of the planning process. We note that site selection should not be entirely based upon sites to which an access point is readily available, but it should be at least one consideration when undertaking the site and subject selection process.

For these and other reasons, researchers must often choose a sample of participants to include, as frequently it simply is not feasible to conduct a qualitative research study on a whole population.

Method for participant selection/sampling

In most cases, sampling is desirable and making use of using good sampling approaches will help to ensure the study is robust. There are many ways to go about selecting participants for the study. The type of sampling done will depend upon both the question and the best approach for discovering its answer. There are two main schools of thought on how sampling should be done in qualitative research (Curtis *et al.* 2000): 'theoretical sampling' and 'purposeful sampling'. Theoretical sampling is designed to generate theory. It is carried out during data collection and grounded in data; as such, it is most frequently associated with grounded theory research (Glaser

Probabilistic sampling

When conducting research on a large population, it is often impractical to study every single member of the group. Instead, researchers attempt to determine a portion or sample of the population. Probability sampling refers to methods of selecting individuals to include in a study, where each member of the population has an equal chance of being selected (that is, they are randomly selected)

and Strauss 1967; Strauss and Corbin 1990). Purposeful sampling, on the other hand, is done a priori and is based upon the research tradition and research question. Purposeful sampling, in contrast to **probabilistic sampling**, is 'selecting information-rich cases for study in depth' (Patton 1999: 169) when the goal is to understand something and when generalization is unnecessary.

Most qualitative researchers, particularly those not doing grounded theory, use purposeful sampling (a sample is sometimes referred to as a panel; for example, Weiss 1994). Maxwell (2005: 88) suggests that purposeful sampling 'is a strategy in which particular settings, persons, or activities are selected deliberately in order to provide information that can't be gotten as well from other choices'. Creswell (2002) suggests that there are four goals for purposeful sampling: achieving representativeness of the context, capturing heterogeneity in the population, examining cases that are critical for the theories undergirding the study and establishing comparisons to illuminate the reasons for differences between settings or individuals. Curtis *et al.* (2000: 1002) identify the following key features of sampling in qualitative research.

- The method of drawing samples is not based on theories of the statistical probability of selection, but on other purposive or theoretical sampling criteria.
- Samples are small, are studied intensively, and each one typically generates a large amount of information.
- Samples are not usually wholly pre-specified, and instead selection is sequential (by a rolling process, interleafed with coding and analysis).
- Sample selection is conceptually driven, either by the theoretical framework that underpins the research question from the outset or by an evolving theory that is derived inductively from the data as the research proceeds.
- Qualitative research should be reflexive and explicit about the rationale for case selection, because there are ethical and theoretical implications arising from the choices which are made to include particular cases and exclude others.
- Qualitative samples are designed to make possible analytic generalizations (applied to wider theory on the basis of how selected cases 'fit' with general constructs) but not statistical generalizations (applied to wider populations on the basis of representative statistical samples).

A range of approaches to purposeful sampling has developed over time. In Table 20.2 we provide some approaches to purposeful sampling used by qualitative researchers.

Sampling strategies can and often should be combined. Researchers may wish to vary sampling strategies as needed or desired for different purposes, especially in large-scale and long term studies. Moreover, a researcher needs to be flexible in sampling, with the end goal being successful sampling, rather than rigid adherence to one particular sampling method.

Purposeful sampling, then, means careful selection of members of the community who are likely to provide the best information. It requires deep thought, planning and reflection about all aspects of the question and then to be creative when making decisions about who can provide the best information. If, for example, the research question is related to community attitudes and beliefs, then community leaders may not be the best choice for the sample as their opinions as leaders might not be representative of the community's views. Moreover, at times, the least obvious participants can provide the best information. The key is to have and provide a good rationale for the choice of selection that makes sense, given the research topic and questions.

Table 20.2 Purposeful sampling strategies (adapted from McMillan and Schumacher 1997; Miles and Huberman 1994; Creswell 1998)

Sampling strategy	Description	Example
Comprehensive or criterion sampling	Choose entire group by criteria	Female university leaders
Homogeneous sampling	Pick a small sample of individuals with a membership that has some similar and defining characteristics	First year students with IQs over 130
Maximum variation sampling	Select to obtain maximum differences of perceptions about a topic among information-rich informants or group	Persons of different ethnic groups and ages who are in favour of legalizing marijuana
Extreme-case sampling	Choose extreme cases after knowing the typical or average case	Individuals who have achieved outstanding success in long-distance running
Intense-case sampling	Select cases that are intense but not extreme illustrations	Participants who have had a family member murdered
Typical-case sampling	Know the typical characteristics, what is 'normal' or average of a group and sample by those	Group of first-year students at a specific institution that shows a typical gender balance
Unique-case sampling	Choice of the unusual or rare case of some dimension or event	Winners of the World Cup
Reputational-case sampling	Obtain the recommendation of knowledge-able experts for the best examples	Recommendations from the leading scientists in cancer research: the best examples of living life after beating cancer
Critical-case sampling	Identify the case that can illustrate some phenomenon dramatically	Lecturers who mentor students to achieve entry to prestigious graduate schools
Theoretical or concept sampling	Select persons or situations known to experience the concept/theory, to be attempting to implement the concept/theory or to be in different categories of the concept/theory	Two groups of students, one who appear to be deep learners and the other who appear to be surface learners, using Marton and Säljö (1984)
Opportunistic sampling	Takes place after the research begins, to take advantage of unfolding events that will help answer research questions	Subcultural group identified during initial research is then increased to gain an adequate number of its members.
Confirming and disconfirming sampling	Used to follow up on specific cases to test or explore further specific findings	Group of lecturers publishing articles about their teaching are increased in number to understand the extent of the practice

Some researchers use 'convenience sampling'. One form of convenience sampling is to simply select a group that is easily accessible. Another form is snowball or network sampling, in which each successive person or group is nominated by a prior person, who deems them an appropriate fit for the research. Convenience sampling is not a form of purposeful or theoretical sampling; so it presents a challenge for qualitative researchers, since the choice of participants by the researcher is compromised in some way.

Tips

How many participants are necessary?

The question of how many participants are necessary is commonly asked and it is one upon which scholars hold a range of opinions. We think that the answer, as is so commonly the case in qualitative research, is that it *depends*. It depends upon the answers to the following questions:

What does the research tradition call for? Some studies, such as auto-ethnographies, can be done with relatively few participants while others, such as a pragmatic qualitative research, require more.

What needs to be accomplished? Researchers should consider whether they are seeking in-depth responses, which would imply fewer participants, or breadth of opinion, which would imply more participants.

What type of sampling is to be done? At times, the sampling strategies themselves provide important clues about how many participants are necessary. Extreme-case sampling, for example, is just that – extreme cases – that might suggest a smaller number of participants. On the other hand, typical case sampling might imply striving for a larger number in order to get information from a range of individuals who meet the typical case.

How much quantity and detail of data will be collected from each individual? This question is related to the type of sampling. If the plan is to do lengthy interviews of individuals over an extended period of time, it is possible to have fewer participants. If on the other hand, the plan is for shorter interviews over an intensive time frame, it may be desirable to have more participants.

How many people possess the necessary characteristics? It is important to consider the total number of individuals in the group of interest. With a smaller population, it is possible to start with a larger percentage of the total population that could result in a smaller number than if a larger population is of interest. Studies have drawn on as few as two people up to many hundreds of participants. There is no one right answer to the question. The key is to make a good case for the number of participants selected for the sample.

Inviting participants

The challenge for (outsider) researchers is convincing potential interviewees that they should take the time and effort necessary to participate in the study. There are several ways to go about inviting potential participants to become involved in a research study. Some types of research site will have a 'gatekeeper' who, to varying degrees, will control the invitations to potential participants, make contact arrangements and provide the researcher with necessary information. At other sites, participants might be contacted face to face or by phone, letter or email. Invitations generally will provide information about the purpose of the session; the date, time and location of the session and details about how participants should signal willingness to participate. We provide a sample invitation to participate in a focus group on page 317, noting that conventions may vary by location and suggesting that researchers check with mentors, peers and the relevant ethics review board (see Chapter 21) for additional information about inviting participants.

When does sampling begin and end?

Usually, a researcher selects a sampling strategy and group of participants prior to data collection. There are at least four instances when sampling occurs after data collection starts. These are theoretical sampling (as in grounded theory research), snowballing, convenience sampling and confirmation/disconfirmation. If, having set the number of participants, researchers then find that they do not have enough information to identify recurring themes (if that is what they are seeking), it may be necessary to rethink the sampling approach or to add additional participants.

Dear Jane,

I'm writing to invite you to participate in a focus group designed to provide information about residents' experiences with the psychiatry clinical rotation. In the session, I will ask the group some general questions about what you have learned during your experiences with the clinic. I will tape and transcribe the session and will report the group's responses only, not individual responses to questions.

The focus group will take place on February 17 between 12:15 and 1:00. The group will be held at The Hospital Education Tower, Room 502. Pizza and drinks will be provided.

You are not required in any way to participate in the focus group, but I hope you will consider it, since your experiences will provide opportunities for improving the experience for future students. If you are willing to participate, please email me to let me know whether you will attend.

   Best wishes
      Claire Major

What is saturation and when is it reached?

Qualitative researchers continue to collect data from participants or from observations until they reach a point of *data saturation*, which theoretically occurs when the researcher is no longer hearing or seeing new information. Thus, sampling continues until the researcher reaches this point. However, for some researchers, the notion of saturation is misplaced, since the view is that this point can never be reached as there is always more to learn. This is particularly the case with approaches that have a constructivist or constructionist stance; for example, in participatory action approaches, narrative inquiry and arts-based inquiry.

> Miles and Huberman (1994) suggest that sampling strategy should be compatible with other aspects of the research design; this will involve deciding whether to use theoretical sampling (for example in a grounded theory study) or purposeful sampling (for other traditions). The strategy also should be likely to generate rich information, the kind necessary to answer the research question; and be extensive enough to produce believable explanations and descriptions. Finally, it should be ethical (see Chapter 21).

Tips

CONCLUSION

Choosing when, where and who to study requires concentrated effort by the researcher, who engages in an interrelated series of activities in order to do so. This process is what sets one research study apart from the next and is what makes qualitative research truly an investigation of the unique and the particular. In this chapter, we have offered some basic considerations for defining the focus of the study. These considerations have involved ideas about how to select who, where and when to study. These decisions all have direct implications on what the findings of a study will be, and as such, they should not be taken lightly.

Reflective questions

Concept questions

- What is the difference between area of knowledge and topic area?
- What is the difference between research purpose and research question?
- Why is space an important aspect of the scope of the study?
- Why is time an important aspect of scope?

Application questions

- What is your research topic?
- What is your research question?
- Is the setting you have selected the best one for answering your question?
- Are the participants you have selected the best ones to answer your questions?
- How can you justify your selection?

Key resources

In developing this chapter, we found the following chapters to be particularly informative:

Creswell, J. W. (1998) *Qualitative inquiry and research design: Choosing among five traditions*, Thousand Oaks, CA: Sage.
Creswell helpfully informed us for Table 20.2 on sampling techniques.

Kuntz, A. (2010) The politics of space in qualitative research. *In*: M. Savin-Baden and C. Major (eds) *New approaches to qualitative research: Wisdom and uncertainty*. London: Routledge.
This well-written chapter is one of the best at addressing issues of space.

Sandelowski, M. (1999) Time and qualitative research. *Research in Nursing & Health*, 22, 79–87.
Sandelowski's article provides one of the best overviews and analyses of the issue of time, a rarely treated topic; she stresses its importance throughout the research process.

Chapter 21

Ethics and ethical approval

INTRODUCTION

Ethical approval and ethical conduct of research are interrelated concepts. In this chapter, we describe reasons why paying attention to both are necessary. We begin by considering the current functions of ethical review boards and provide questions to help researchers think through the approval process. We next shift to a discussion of the some of the challenges of ethical approval for social science researchers. Finally, we advocate for moving beyond the minimal requirements of typical ethical approval processes towards the excellent treatment of people. We suggest in this chapter that, while ethical approval processes are typically fixed, researchers face a series of choices related to how they will situate their research and themselves ethically.

WHAT ARE ETHICS?

A basic definition of ethics, a variation of which is likely to be found in many dictionaries, is that ethics are the 'correctness' of particular behaviour. A related definition is that ethics are the moral principles that govern behaviour. Many have applied such definitions to ethics in social science research. Bogdan and Biklen (1992), for example, define ethics in research as the 'principles of right and wrong that a particular group accepts'. Ethics is also a branch of philosophy, however, that takes as a focus complex questions of morality, such as what is right and wrong or what is good and evil. The field of ethics has developed over the years and, today, many would argue that because the world is relational, questions of ethics are not simple, related to black and white answers as to what is right and what is wrong. Rather, ethics present complex questions often lacking clear answers. Moreover, some argue that ethics are not something that may be enforced, by codes or regulations; rather, there necessarily is an element of choice to them. Hoy (2004: 103) defines ethics as 'obligations that present themselves as necessarily to be fulfilled but are neither forced on one or are enforceable'. He suggests that ethical obligations and ethical actions are most evident in relationships with the powerless, for:

> The ethical resistance of the powerless others to our capacity to exert power over them is therefore what imposes unenforceable obligations on us. The obligations are unenforceable precisely because of the other's lack of power. That actions are at once obligatory and at the same time unenforceable is what put them in the category of the ethical. Obligations that were enforced would, by the virtue of the force behind them, not be freely undertaken and would not be in the realm of the ethical.
>
> (Hoy 2004: 184)

While social research is dynamic and, by its very nature, challenges researchers to be conscious of, to spot and to respond to ethical issues, even with the best (stated) intentions, social science researchers have not always honoured these obligations to individuals by choice, as may be seen through several ethical trials and transgressions of the past.

ETHICAL TRIALS AND TRANSGRESSIONS

A series of high profile incidents and scandals, largely in the USA and UK, have brought attention to and public outrage at the atrocities in the way that people have been treated during research studies. As Orb *et al.* (2001: 93) suggest 'Violations of human rights in the name of scientific research have been among the darkest events in history'. Such events, which ultimately led to the creation and entrenchment of the current ethics review process, include the Nuremberg trials, the Tuskegee syphilis study, the *Tearoom Trade*, the thalidomide scandal and the Alder Hey organs scandal.

Nuremberg trials

The Nuremberg trials were a series of military trials held after World War II that involved the prosecution of members of the Nazi party. During the subsequent trials (held after the major trial), judges delivered not only verdicts against several Nazi physicians who had performed experiments on inmates in concentration camps, but also their opinions on medical experimentation on human subjects. The result was the ten-point Nuremberg Code (1949):

1. Voluntary consent.
2. Potential of fruitful results that could not be obtained in another way.
3. Research plans based upon results of animal experimentation or knowledge of natural history that will justify experiment.
4. Avoidance of physical and mental suffering.
5. Avoidance of experiment if death or injury might result, perhaps unless experimenters also serve as subjects.
6. Risks taken that do not exceed importance of the problem.
7. Preparations and facilities that protect against even remote possibility of injury.
8. Experiments done only by qualified persons.
9. Subject ability to end the experiment during its course.
10. Scientist ability to end experiment if it is likely to result in injury, disability or death.

The code eventually was used to develop the Code of Federal Regulations that subsequently governed federally funded research in the USA (US Department of Health and Human Services 2009).

Tuskegee syphilis experiment

This research involved a clinical study carried out by the US Public Health Service designed to study the natural progression of untreated syphilis (Jones 1993). The study took place between 1932 and 1972 in Tuskegee, Macon County, Alabama. Subjects were 399 poor black rural men who had contracted syphilis before the experiment. The men were guaranteed to receive free health care, meals and burial insurance from the government for treatment for bad blood.

They were not told that they had contracted syphilis and they were not treated for it, even though penicillin was already proved to be an effective cure for syphilis. During the course of the experiment, many of the men died, their wives contracted syphilis from them and their children were born with congenital syphilis. This study and its attending outrage (Caplan 1992) led to several federal regulations requiring an institutional review board to protect human participants and ultimately to the development of the Belmont Report (1979), which is a statement of ethical principles as well as guidelines for resolving ethical issues, related to using human subjects in research. The report explains three fundamental ethical principles:

1. *Respect for persons.* This general ethical principle calls for treating people with respect, allowing informed consent and avoiding deception.
2. *Beneficence.* This principle requires treating people in an ethical way, so that they are protected from harm and an effort is made to secure their wellbeing.
3. *Justice.* This principle calls for a consideration of who should receive the benefit; the idea of 'fairness in distribution'.

These principles and the Belmont Report generally serve as a continued reference for ethics review boards.

Tearoom trade

This study was the subject of a 1970 PhD dissertation by Humphreys. He conducted an ethnographic study of anonymous homosexual encounters in public restrooms/lavatories (called 'tearooming' in the USA and 'cottaging' in the UK). He took the role of lookout for the participants, who did not know that they were under study. He also recorded their vehicle license/registration plate numbers and later interviewed them in the homes under false pretences, at which time he confirmed that over 50% of the men were outwardly heterosexual. This study raised ethical questions not only because of the researcher's deception and the lack of consent of the participants but also because identifying them placed them at risk of serious harm (since the behaviour under study was illegal).

Thalidomide scandal

During the late 1960s, thalidomide was a drug developed in Germany for use as a sedative and it was also prescribed to pregnant mothers as a treatment for morning sickness (Knightley *et al.* 1979). The drug was marketed as non-toxic and without side effects. It was used widely in several countries around the world, including UK, Japan, Australia and Africa, but the drug was not approved for use in the USA. It was administered to pregnant women with insufficient testing. Rigorous testing was not required in Germany at the time and the use of thalidomide led to massive birth defects in thousands of infants worldwide, including malformed or missing limbs, missing organs, deformed eyes or ears, blindness and cleft palette, as well as miscarriages and stillbirths. In January 2010, the British Government apologized to citizens who had suffered.

Alder Hey organs scandal

During the late 1990s, it was discovered that several hospitals, including the Alder Hey Children's Hospital, Liverpool, UK, were keeping children's organs, often hearts (this scandal is at times referred to as the 'stolen hearts scandal') without authorization. The practice was discovered when the mother of an infant who had died during open-heart surgery immediately after birth, began hearing rumours of a high mortality rate for infant heart surgery at the hospital and requested to see her deceased daughter's autopsy report. The report indicated that her heart had been retained without authorization; when the mother confronted the hospital staff, the heart was returned. This practice had been continuing for decades and, once discovered, word of it spread rapidly, raising concerns about scientific practices. Ultimately, the scandals led the UK to create the Human Tissue Authority and the Human Tissue Act 2004.

THE ETHICS REVIEW PROCESS IN QUALITATIVE RESEARCH

When compared with the experimental research used, particularly, in health settings, ethical questions in social sciences are arguably more nuanced (Orb *et al.* 2001). Qualitative researchers do not tend to conduct experiments on individuals but, rather are interested in answering questions that may well best be understood through gathering narrative and life stories, which seek understanding of lived experiences; these sometimes uncover complexities and innuendos related to individual ethics. This has led some scholars (such as Punch 1994) to question whether ethical issues are even a question in qualitative research. Moreover, scholars have questioned whether the formal ethics review process intended for experimental quantitative researchers is appropriate for qualitative research (Bresler 1996). Other researchers, such as Batchelor and Briggs (1994) have argued that failure to acknowledge and address the issues has left qualitative researchers unprepared. Dresser (1998) further argues that the protection of participants outweighs the administrative burdens of the ethical review process. We believe that, given the nature of our work, the question of ethics is one that is imperative for qualitative researchers to consider. We also acknowledge that, for the time being, the formal ethics review process governs both experimental quantitative and exploratory qualitative research and, thus, researchers need to be aware of the processes and procedures, which we describe more fully in this section.

What is an ethics review board?

An institutional review board, research ethics committee, human research ethics committee or related board or committee typically comprises a group of five or more lecturers, experts and administrators who review and potentially approve research proposals, as well as monitoring on-going studies to ensure the protection of human participants. In this chapter, we use the term 'ethics review board' to be inclusive of all such boards and committees. An ethics review board is most commonly in charge of reviewing studies both in social sciences, including anthropology, sociology and psychology, and also in applied professional fields, such as health, education and business. An ethics review board reviews research studies that range from clinical trials of drugs to investigations into attitudes or social behaviour. It primarily functions to protect human participants who are involved in a research study from psychological, physical, social or economic harm. It also reviews study proposals, research instruments (including surveys and interview protocols) and materials for participants (including requests for participation and **informed consent** forms).

Informed consent

Informed consent is the legal embodiment of the idea that a researcher should provide information to participants about the potential risks and benefits of participating in a study and should make clear their rights as participants so that they can make informed decisions about whether to take part.

Primary functions of an ethics review board

Ethics review boards typically have four primary responsibilities: assessing the risks and benefits of a proposed study, determining whether participants have given informed consent, ensuring the appropriate selection of participants and assessing the efficacy of privacy and confidentiality efforts.

Risks and benefits

One of the primary responsibilities of an ethics review board is to ensure that the potential for harm to participants is outweighed by the potential good of the study, or benefit, to participants or society (known as minimal risk). Risks may include *physical harm*, such as exposure to pain, injury or side effects; *psychological harm*, such as depression, guilt, embarrassment and loss of self-esteem, whether brief, recurrent or permanent; or *social and economic harm*, such as breach of confidentially resulting in embarrassment, loss of employment or criminal charges. Risks may be significant or minimal, although federal regulations typically only define **minimal risk**.

Minimal risk

Minimal risk means that the risk associated with the study is similar to that typically encountered in daily life or during the performance of routine physical or psychological examinations or tests.

One challenge occurs when assessing risk for vulnerable populations, a term that refers to groups who may not have the capacity to protect themselves, such as prisoners, children or pregnant women. In such cases, risk must be minimal.

When preparing the ethics review board application, consider the following questions:

- Have you articulated the risks and benefits?
- Have you proved that the risks outweigh the benefits?
- Have you proved that participants are not members of a vulnerable group? Have you taken reasonable care to protect them if they are?
- Have you exercised care to minimize risks and maximize benefits?
- Will participants receive compensation?
- Have you demonstrated how you will inform participants of the risks and benefits?
- Is there a process for regularly assessing whether an appropriate balance of risks and benefits is being maintained?

Tips

Informed consent

Another important duty of the ethics review board is to ensure that participants have given informed consent. This is an ethical consideration that involves demonstration of a respect for people. An ethics review board must consider whether adequate content concerning the potential risks and benefits of the research has been provided to participants and whether that content has been presented in a language that they can understand. Another consideration is whether researchers have engaged in an appropriate process to convey the risks and benefits to participants (they may even use audiovisuals, tests or advisors).

Finally, an ethics review board will consider whether the researcher has documented consent in some way, for example by providing an informed consent form with a counter signature facility. We provide a sample form in Table 21.1 but would caution researchers to follow the requirements of their own jurisdictions/institutions.

Table 21.1 Sample informed consent form

Lecturers experiences teaching online

Claire Major, Professor, The University of Alabama.
Professor, Higher Education Program
328C Graves Hall; Box 870302
The University of Alabama
Tuscaloosa, Alabama 35487

_____ (phone)
_____ (email)

You are being asked to take part in a research study. This study is called <u>Lecturers Experiences with Online Learning</u>. The study is being conducted by Claire Major, Professor at The University of Alabama.

What this study is about

This study is being conducted to explore lecturers' experiences with teaching online courses. Approximately 50 individuals who come from a range of institutional types and disciplines will participate in this study. The research will employ a basic qualitative design. You are being asked to participate in this study because of your current role as a designer and teacher of online courses, and therefore, your understanding of the online environment is significant to this study.

What you will be asked to do

If you decide to be in this study, you will be asked to do the following:

1. Participate in a recorded interview lasting between 45 minutes and I hour in length.
2. Possibly participate in follow up interviews.
3. Review and respond to transcription of interview.

Risks and benefits

Risks for participating in this study are minimal. There may be no direct benefits to you as a participant in this study. You will not be paid for the study, and the only cost to you is the cost of your time for participating. However, the information you provide may prove beneficial to the understanding and development of online learning as an instructional method in higher education. It should yield information about the changes that lecturers experience when teaching online. This information will help higher education leaders understand online learning from the lecturer's perspective. This information will help prepare lecturers for the experience and may lead to better teaching of these courses. Ultimately, students, parents, lecturers, and administrators may benefit if the information uncovered helps provide more efficient and effective lecturers' training to teach online.

Your participation is voluntary

Taking part in this study is completely voluntary. You may choose not to take part at all. You may refuse to answer any of the questions. If you start the study, you can stop at any time. Not participating or choosing to leave the study will not result in any penalty or loss of any benefits you would otherwise receive.

Your answers to questions will be confidential

The researcher will maintain confidentiality of study participants as a far as possible. Interviews will be conducted in a private setting and all interviews transcripts will be kept on the researcher's personal computer. Reports of the research will not name or otherwise identify individuals.

The University of Alabama Institutional Review Board is the committee that protects the rights of people in research studies. The Ethics Review Board may review study records from time to time to be sure that people in research studies are being treated fairly and that the study is being carried out as planned.

Contact information

If you have questions about the study right now, please ask them. If you have questions about the study later on, please call the investigator Claire Major at the contact information listed above. If you have any questions about your rights as a research participant, you may contact Ms. Tanta Myles, The University of Alabama Research Compliance Officer, at XXX-XXXX

I have read this consent form. The study has been explained to me. I understand what I will be asked to do. I freely agree to take part in it. I will receive a copy of this consent form to keep.

_____   _____ DATE
SIGNATURE OF RESEARCH PARTICIPANT

_____   _____ DATE
INVESTIGATOR

Informed consent is on-going and does not end when participants sign an informed consent form; rather, it is a process of continual negotiation (Field and Morse 1992; Kvale 1996; Munhall 1988). Informed consent may be achieved by full disclosure, adequate compensation and voluntary choice. In practice, it means striving for a balance between overinforming and underinforming (Kvale 1996).

Questions for the researcher to consider when developing the ethics review board application for informed consent include:

■ Does the plan involve members of vulnerable groups who may need special protection?
■ Is the language of the information appropriate to the population?
■ Is the explanation given in an appropriate time and place to allow for good decision making?
■ Who will explain the research to the participants? Should participants reaffirm consent periodically?

Tips

Selection of participants

The ethics review board has a responsibility to ensure that participants have been selected so that benefits and burdens have fair distribution. The underpinning idea is to best accomplish social justice. Thus, adults should be selected before children, competent individuals before incompetent individuals and non-institutionalized before institutionalized individuals. Those individuals considered already burdened should not have to accept burdens unless others cannot be found.

When preparing the ethics application for the selection of subjects, consider the following questions:

■ How will individuals be recruited?
■ Will the burdens fall on those most likely to benefit?
■ Will participant selection avoid burdening one group more than another?
■ Does the research require that the proposed population be studied?
■ Are there individuals who are more vulnerable to risks?
■ Will any characteristics of the group pose special risks?
■ Could the study be conducted with less vulnerable individuals?
■ Has the process overprotected any vulnerable groups so that they are denied a chance to participate?

Tips

Privacy and confidentiality

The ethics review board has the responsibility to ensure that the participants' privacy and confidentiality are respected. Privacy is being free from the view or attention of unauthorized others. It means having control over extent, timing and circumstance of sharing oneself (whether intellectually or behaviourally). Privacy is a special concern when conducting observational studies, when a researcher's presence is not known or when the researcher assumes a role in the group being studied. It is critical in such instances for a researcher to avoid being deceptive. Covert observation may be done of public behaviour (students walking around campus) but not private behaviour. Confidentiality involves the way in which data are handled. It ensures that the treatment of information that a subject has shared in trust will not be divulged in ways different to the permission already granted. Assuring privacy may involve limiting access to identifying data and ensuring records are stored in locked files.

Consider the following questions when preparing the ethics application:

■ Does the research involve observation when participants should expect privacy?
■ Will the researcher be collecting sensitive information? If so, what safeguards are in place to ensure data confidentiality?
■ Are the researcher's disclosures about confidentiality to participants adequate?
■ How will data be recorded and maintained?

Types of review

There are three primary types of review: full or high risk, expedited or medium risk and exempt or low risk.

Full or high-risk review

Full or high-risk review involves submitting a formal application to the board, waiting for the board to convene and hearing the outcomes. Many medical procedures or clinical trials require full board review. Many social science research projects may be exempt from review or qualify for expedited review; however, there are some social research subjects (for example, family and domestic violence) that require a high level of clearance and thus a full review.

Expedited or medium-risk review

When a researcher requests expedited or medium-risk review, the proposal may be reviewed on an individual basis. For expedited or medium-risk review, studies must pose no more than minimal risks that involve specific procedures determined by the ethics review board. Specific procedures include research involvement materials (such as data, documents, records); collection of data from voice, video and digital images; research on individual or group characteristics or behaviour, such as perception, cognition, motivation, identity, communication, cultural beliefs or practices; and the employment of survey, interview, oral history, focus group or programme evaluation.

Exempt or low-risk review

If the proposal qualifies for exempt or low-risk review, formal ethics review board approval is not required but it is the board that makes the decision. Several categories of research may be exempt, including normal educational practices, such as comparison of instructional techniques; educational tests, such as aptitude or achievement, unless it is possible that individual participants may be identified; evaluations of curricula, including surveys; and existing data, such as documents or records. These categories of research often, but not always, qualify for exempt review.

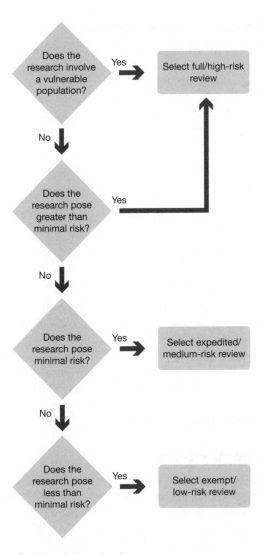

Figure 21.1 Decision tree for determining review type

The ethics review board full review process is conducted approximately monthly, while expedited reviews can occur on a rolling basis. In Figure 21.1, we offer the decision tree for determining where to submit an application initially (note that the ethics review board makes the final determination of which category of review the project fits).

SPECIAL ISSUES IN THE ETHICAL CONDUCT OF RESEARCH

There are many occasions in qualitative research that require a special consideration of ethics. Some of these times involve working with children and vulnerable groups, understanding the nature of consent, working in transnational settings, and researching online.

Ethics and children and vulnerable groups

Children or other vulnerable groups include those people who are not legally able to provide informed consent owing to age or incompetence, or who are in an unequal relationship with the researcher. This group also can include individuals with disability, who are members of a minority group or who have language difficulties. What counts as vulnerability is contested, since there are many reasons why research participants may be seen as vulnerable or disadvantaged. Issues to be aware of when doing research with these groups:

- reinforcement of stereotypes with particular groups
- exploitation of vulnerable participants
- causing of distress.

In most countries, before children can participate, consent is usually obtained from a parent or guardian based on information about what is involved and why, usually provided through an accessibly written information sheet.

The nature of informed consent

There is often an assumption made by researchers, once consent has been gained and a form signed, that this consent is both informed and lasts for the duration of the project. The question is whether individuals ever fully consent. We suggest that consent can never be something that is fully informed, as participants rarely completely understand what they have signed up for or indeed what is published as a result of what they have said, even if they have signed a form stating that they do. What is important, we believe, is that the ethical stance of a researcher is socially responsible. Such issues and concerns may make us uncomfortable but they also introduce questions that need to be considered.

Ethics in transnational settings

Researchers working internationally face a special set of challenges, since the review process and standards of ethical conduct of research may differ according to culture. What is ethical in one setting may not be ethical in another; what is considered ethical today may not be ethical tomorrow. Time and space matter. Often, there are multiple ethical layers. Some of these are culturally governed while others are more institutionalized. Palmer illustrates some of these complexities in her researcher reflection.

Researcher reflections

Associate Professor Betsy Palmer, Montana State University, USA

All research, both qualitative and quantitative, involves ethical considerations, but my 2011–12 fieldwork in a remote area of Nepal challenged me to consider new questions about conducting ethically responsible research. In preparation for my project, *Community Perspectives on Education in a Remote Region in Nepal*, I submitted an institutional review board application at my home institution.

continued

As an ethnographic study, I would not use the methods of qualitative research that I am accustomed to using – semi-structured interviews, focused observations using predesigned protocols, explicit gathering of paper or electronic documents. Instead, I anticipated largely observing naturally occurring behaviour by children, families and teachers as I struggled to understand the purpose of schooling in this community. Indeed, I was not sure that I would conduct a single interview but, if I did it, I might be interviewing individuals who could neither read nor write. To cover this eventuality, I created an informed consent protocol using the least technical language I could employ and that allowed individuals to consent verbally on an audio recorder. A larger question still loomed in the background: can the individuals in this study truly provide informed consent when they have no tangible, real-world experience to help them to comprehend the nuances of participating in social science research?

Informed consent is not limited to formal interviews, however. I needed to decide, while in the field, when I should inform individuals that I was a researcher; a decision complicated by my desire to observe individuals behaving naturally in their own community. If I began an observation by declaring that I was a researcher, people might modify their behaviour to respond to unstated expectations. Technically, I could observe 'public' behaviour without requesting formal consent but was this always the most ethical manner for conducting research? This led me to wrestle with another nuanced ethical consideration: when does my curiosity as a human being in a new environment end and my formal observation as a researcher begin?

My struggles with the ethics of my research were also complicated by my subjectivity in relation to the individuals I wanted to observe. I am married to a Nepali citizen from this village and so I entered the 'field' of my research as a family member to numerous villagers. Our two children travelled with us and I wanted them to experience the extended kinship networks that prevail there. As family members, we took many pictures and videos of our children as they experienced life in the village. If I have a video of my kids attending school with their cousins, can I use it in my study without first obtaining consent from the children, their parents and the teachers? Does my need to obtain consent apply only to visual artefacts that are made public? Conversely, is it honest to claim that I can analyze my data without having these visual representations influence my thinking?

The exotic environment of this study accentuated my struggles with ethical considerations but as I reflected on my circumstances, I realized that I face similar issues when conducting research closer to home. Can I truly turn off my observations as an educational researcher when I take my kids to school? Should I ask my sister, the kindergarten teacher, to sign a consent form before she relates a story about her classroom? My ethnographic research study in remote Nepal inspired me to reconsider many aspects of my identity as a researcher, my relationship to my participants and to re-evaluate how various methodological choices would affect not only the quality of the data I collected but my ethical responsibilities to the communities I hope to understand.

Ethics in online research

Ethics in online settings seems to cause considerable concern, even though the issues are at least somewhat related to those that occur in face-to-face research studies. Some of the areas that bear consideration include an exploration of what counts as consent in online spaces and who decides. Moreover, issues of privacy may have special importance in online settings, for reasons of security and availability for public scrutiny. However, issues of plausibility are also of concern in online research. It is worth considering whether you know who you are interviewing in an online setting and if this matters or not. For example, if your participants are unidentifiable, then does this mean your research lacks rigour because you neither know your population nor the demographics of those in your study? This, in turn, raises further questions about whether it is then possible for a researcher to acknowledge the complexities of managing 'truths' in research.

A summary of ethical considerations needed for online research is shown in Table 21.2.

Table 21.2 Ethical considerations when undertaking online research (adapted from McCleary 2007)

■ Be aware of causing harm
- Consider/reduce the level of vulnerability of group participants
- Consider/reduce the level of intrusiveness of the researcher's involvement
- Be careful not to ask for identifying information. If personal identifiers are necessary, record and store separately from research data as you would with face to face data
- Change all identifying information within email messages before storing data
- Use data encryption when available for sending sensitive data
■ Acknowledge the risks when entering certain online venues, such as chat rooms and online groups,
■ Be knowledgeable about the technology that you are using and the ways it can both harm and protect your research participants.

CHALLENGES OF THE ETHICS REVIEW BOARD FOR SOCIAL SCIENCE RESEARCHERS

While the ethics review board process is intended to protect human participants, social science researchers face several challenges when working within it. In particular, most of the regulations were developed for biomedical research and are only loosely related to social science research; for instance, qualitative research does not require experimenting on participants. Much of the language of the ethics review board reflects an emphasis on health fields, so other fields can find the process challenging. Furthermore, the contention is that biomedical ethics review boards have failed to understand social science research methods and that requirements for consent are overburdensome. In addition, the process has become more complicated in recent decades owing to legal risk. There are times, for example, in which confidentiality is not even an issue for participants and, indeed, they want to be recognized for their participation. Moreover, in some cases, ethics review boards have limited knowledge of vulnerable populations and thus may be overprotective; it can be useful for researchers to include an educative or explanatory element in their applications, which addresses issues specific to the research participants. This may help ethics review board members to consider the complex issues presented.

Ian Shaw, University of York

Ethics and decisions in qualitative research

I have sometimes been concerned that relying only on codes of research ethics risks compartmentalizing ethical aspects of research, and shutting them off into a preamble to research. For me, the practice of qualitative research ethics is presented afresh – and contextualized in distinct forms – at every stage of research. For example, the ethics of qualitative research *design* pose distinctive demands on principles of informed consent, confidentiality and privacy, social justice and research by practitioners. *Fieldwork* ethics raise special considerations regarding power, reciprocity and contextual relevance. Furthermore, the *analysis and uses* of qualitative inquiry evoke questions regarding, for example, the ethics of narrative research and the utilization of research.

To illustrate briefly, on matters of consent at the design stage, we can't always inform because we don't always know, since in qualitative methods responsiveness and adaptability are seen as *strengths* of the method. Eliot Eisner (1991) remarked that, if we embark upon a research study that we conceptualize, direct and write, we virtually assure that we will use others for our purpose. With the challenge of fieldwork in mind, John and Lyn Lofland (1995) ask if it is ethical to:

- see a severe need for help and not respond to it directly?
- take a calculated stance towards other human beings?
- take sides or avoid taking sides in a factionalized situation?
- 'pay' people with trade-offs for access to their lives and minds?

When it comes to analysis and writing, in narrative and life stories ethical issues are raised by the fact that as we encourage people to tell their stories, we become characters in those stories and, thus, change those stories. In presenting a life story, there develops a complex relationship between the biography of the research subject and the autobiography of the researcher (Mills 2002), with consequent ethical dilemmas. Consequently, a risk of betrayal arises, partly from the greater closeness and consequent trust that may develop between researcher and participant in qualitative research. In quantitative research, the greater distancing may make these issues less pointed. The risk of betrayal is increased because of the characteristic use of smaller samples and the emphasis on the details of how people live their lives.

The claim sometimes is made, that qualitative research is somehow more ethical than quantitative research. For me, no research strategies are especially privileged. To adapt a phrase from Ernest House (1980), qualitative researchers do not live in a state of methodological grace. Take for example, the 'delusion of alliance' in qualitative and feminist research. But none of this should paralyze us. Nor should it make us a soft touch for ethics committees that perceive ethical obstacles at every corner. Good qualitative research will be morally rich and ethically nuanced.

Further reading

Shaw, I. (2008) Ethics and the practice of qualitative research. *Qualitative Social Work* 7 (4), 400–14.

van den Hoonaard, W. C. (2002) (ed.) *Walking the tightrope: Ethical issues for qualitative researchers*, Toronto: University of Toronto Press.

BEYOND ETHICS REVIEW: TOWARD EXCELLENCE IN THE ETHICAL CONDUCT OF RESEARCH

While some scholars have suggested that there is a need for a code of ethics for qualitative researchers (see, for example, Berg 1989; Bogdan and Biklen 1992; Glesne and Peshkin 1992; Lancy 1993; Schratz 1993), currently, there is no one set way to achieve ethics in qualitative research. Guillemin and Gillam (2004) suggest that ethics are not a 'once only' event, a procedural thing to be overcome but instead suggest that there is a 'dailyness' of ethical work. Going with the notion of moving beyond the requirement of the ethical review and into the daily practice of ethics, in Figure 21.2 we offer some ethical issues to consider in the context of qualitative research, and we discuss them further in the sections following.

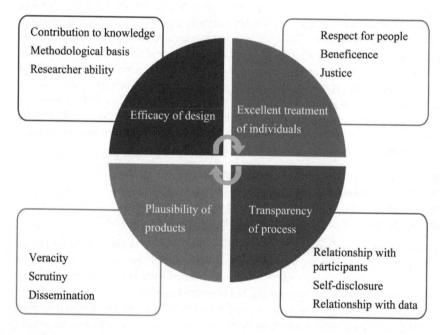

Figure 21.2 Ethical considerations

Efficacy of research design

Although it has not been given much attention in qualitative texts, some scholars have suggested that there are ethical considerations at play in the very design of a qualitative study. To us, it seems evident that studies should be designed with ethics in mind. Clearly, certain topics could have ethical implications (for example, to explore improper treatment of a marginalized group or to understand ways to better manage end-of-life care) and these topics in turn create questions of ethics in carrying out the studies (such as power issues in working with marginalized groups or risking stress of sick individuals). Beyond these obvious issues with sensitive topics, however, are more general issues in the design of qualitative studies. In particular, there is an ethical obligation to design research that may contribute to knowledge development, that has a sound methodological basis and that will be conducted by a researcher who possesses the knowledge, skills and ability to carry it out (Hammick 1996).

Contribution to knowledge

The underlying idea of this consideration is that researchers have an ethical responsibility to develop knowledge; thus, their studies should be designed so that they explore new concepts and ideas, and have a goal of moving research, theory and, arguably, practice forward. Qualitative researchers should carefully develop studies that have strong goals and objectives that are realistic and achievable. If the study will not add to knowledge or if the goals and objectives are not clear, then the study may not be ethical (Hammick 1996; Whiting and Vickers 2010).

Sound methodological basis

Hammick (1996) suggests that research should have a sound scientific basis. While we think *methodological basis* is a better term, we agree with the underlying idea that researchers should be able to defend the principles and procedures of their investigations. From an ethical standpoint, they should be able to provide a strong rationale for and theoretical analysis of the methods they have chosen.

methodology

Comprises the theoretical questions and issues related to a given body of methods and the principles that underlie the investigation

methods

are the procedures undertaken for carrying out the study. They are the tools of the investigation

Researcher ability

Researchers should possess the qualifications, knowledge and skills required to carry out the study. Knowledge in this sense includes both an appreciation of existing research and possessing adequate methodological understanding and facility with the methods to be applied. Knowingly lacking these while undertaking research could make the study unethical. A researcher should be at least minimally qualified to carry out the research and well (uniquely) positioned to do it. The researcher then should have or develop necessary abilities or not take on the study (Hammick 1996; Whiting and Vickers 2010).

Excellent treatment of individuals

The treatment of individuals is a consideration that has been well documented in the literature, since it stems directly from the trials and transgressions we described above. The question then is how to move beyond what is required to what is ethical. For us, research ethics comes down to a simple idea that a catch phrase from the film, *Bill and Ted's Excellent Adventure*, summarizes fairly well: 'be excellent to each other'. We think this phrase apt for several reasons. First, the phrase captures the idea that our participants are not different from us; they are us. Second, the phrase intimates the idea of the golden rule that we learn as children, 'do unto others as you would have them do unto you'; this rule still holds value for adults – and researchers. Third is the importance of the concept of excellence, which suggests that minimal standards are not enough; we should rather be unusually good. We believe that, to be excellent to each other, we must move beyond what is simply required; there must be an element of choice. The three principles we believe can help guide being excellent to each other are: respect for persons, beneficence and equal treatment or justice. The question is how to move beyond requirements to excellence.

Respect for persons

While this will no doubt be a requirement of the ethics review board, several scholars have explored further the notion of treating people with respect (Capron 1989; Hammick 1996) and we agree that ethical treatment requires moving beyond what is required into a consideration of what is excellent. We believe that respect may be accomplished in several ways beyond what is required. We are required for example, to provide individuals with *information* about the study, which may require the researcher to present general information about the study to participants and to avoid deception in research practices (Creswell 1998; Hammersley and Atkinson 1995). We believe it is important to consider not only whether adequate information about the study has been communicated but also whether that information has been really understood. Moreover, we find it essential to consider whether informed consent is continually assured and to weave ways for doing so into the research process. Participants also should have *autonomy* (Hammick 1996), meaning that they should be able to decide for themselves whether they will participate in a study; this often is achieved through informed consent (Hammick 1996; Whiting and Vickers 2010). We think it is critical to consider all aspects of this consent and what it really entails, bringing those considerations into the research design and methods. Another requirement is that individuals should have *privacy*, which may be accomplished when the researcher ensures confidentiality (Hammick 1996; Glesne and Peshkin 1992; Punch 1986; Creswell 1998). It also may be accomplished in how we choose to present findings, such as through case studies that are composites rather than representations of individuals that might give away identity (Creswell 1998). One additional consideration is that we believe that individuals should be honoured for being people with real lives and real responsibilities; they are *honoured* when a researcher is respectful of individuals' time and other responsibilities (Hammick 1996; Whiting and Vickers).

Beneficence

Several scholars call for protecting individuals from harm and for making every effort to ensure their wellbeing (see Capron 1989; Glesne and Peshkin 1992; Punch 1986). Researchers are required to accomplish this ethical consideration by balancing risk and benefit. This should be ensured by following codes of laws, such as the ethical review process (Hammick 1996). Beneficence is a requirement, however, and, for a real consideration of ethics, it is important to ask not what is merely required but rather how well it should be done. Is it possible to move beyond considerations of harm toward considerations of kindness and charity? A researcher might consider whether for example it is appropriate to take a stance of advocate for the participants to help assure their wellbeing.

Justice

This consideration requires treating individuals equally, by considering who should receive any benefit (Hammick 1996; Burns and Grove 2005; Capron 1989). Researchers are required to consider this issue when inviting participants, which should be done based only upon reasons related to the study (Whiting and Vickers 2010; Burns and Grove 2005). They also consider this issue when making a decision about whether to provide incentives, such as small gifts for participants. The term 'justice', however, is not synonymous with equal treatment. It is possible to do harm while making every effort to ensure equal treatment. Thus, while living in a relative world, a researcher should consider how 'doing right' by participants can be achieved.

Transparency of process

We believe that it is critical to be transparent, what Savin-Baden and Fisher (2002) and Major and Savin-Baden (2010a) call 'honesties' in research. Madill *et al.* (2000: 17) suggest that, 'Qualitative researchers have a responsibility to make their epistemological position clear, conduct

Maggi Savin-Baden, Author

At the outset of one study, I made the following decisions:

To protect identities:
- Anonymity was to extend to writing and verbal reporting.
- I would be careful about sharing information about others while in the field.

To treat people with respect and aim for collaborative research:
- People would be told of my research interests.
- I would not record/observe without consent.

To make my terms of agreement clear:
- I would use a consent form.
- I would negotiate the validity of my findings with those involved.

Researcher reflections

their research in a manner consistent with that position, and present their findings in a way that allows them to be evaluated properly'. There are a number of ways that transparency can be achieved in the research process (Savin-Baden and Fisher 2002; Major and Savin-Baden 2010a). For example, we can *situate ourselves in relation to participants*. Doing so requires an awareness of power relationships during interviews; the unique context of the researcher and the researched, and should lead to the researcher striving for a clear view of what participants mean while simultaneously seeking and acknowledging co-created meaning. We also may engage in *self-disclosure*, which involves the researcher in disclosing their positionality with participants, as well as voicing mistakes. To be transparent, we also may *situate ourselves in relation to the data*, which calls for a consideration of data ownership and how they are to be used. This requires taking a critical stance towards research, acknowledging the philosophical stance and the efforts toward criticality.

Plausibility of the research products

While there has been some discussion of ethical treatment of individuals in qualitative research, there has been far less consideration of ethics involved in creating the research product. We believe, however, that there are three primary ethical considerations related to the final research report and other forms of dissemination: scrutiny and accountability, veracity and dissemination.

Scrutiny and accountability

Scrutiny and accountability of the research is an ethical consideration. In the formal proposal of the study, individuals are required to complete the ethical review process (Hammick 1996; Whiting and Vickers 2010). Beyond this, however, there are other ways, such as peer examination and member checks, which can improve scrutiny and accountability of the work. These ways and others are detailed more fully in Chapter 30.

Veracity

The notion of veracity (Hammick 1996) suggests that the final narrative should have an element of authenticity or genuineness. We suggest striving for an honest and plausible accounting in the narrative (Major and Savin-Baden 2010a). Researchers should take people's stories into account when they propose and support arguments in their research texts and other media; it is critical to ensure that participant voices are portrayed honestly. Ways to accomplish this are described in Chapter 27.

Dissemination

A researcher should disseminate findings as widely as possible for the benefit of all interested parties, particularly ensuring that participants and the scholarly community are prime recipients (Hammick 1996; Nieswiadomy 2001; Polit and Beck 2006; MacNee 2004). It is to be hoped that the findings will contribute to knowledge, as already mentioned under efficacy of design (Nieswiadomy 2001).

Researcher reflections

Claire Howell Major

In considering ethics in my 2010 synthesis of nine existing qualitative studies, I made the following decisions:

■ Ethics in efficacy of research design:
  - I would take stock of existing knowledge in an effort to move the field forward.
  - I would conduct an extensive review of the quantitative studies that had been done previously.
  - I would learn more about the three ways Noblit and Hare (1988) suggest situating studies so that I could better undertake analysis.

■ Excellent treatment of individuals:
  - I would correspond with the authors of the original studies, since I did not have access to original participants.

■ Ethics in transparency of process:
  - I would include a positionality statement to describe my stance.

■ Ethics in plausibility of products:
  - I would conduct member checks with authors of the original studies for their review of my findings and interpretations.
  - I would disseminate my work to a broad and general audience to attempt to reach the most people.

CONCLUSION

In this chapter, we have considered the role of the ethics review board in protecting the rights of human participants. This is a requirement that researchers must complete prior to undertaking research. There are challenges with the ethical review process, however, in that in some senses it has become perfunctory. We recommend moving beyond protecting human participants to ensuring that one has maintained excellence in carrying out research with people.

Concept questions

■ What are ethics?
■ What do ethics mean in qualitative research?
■ Do you accept the proposition that ethical compliance is vital in all circumstances?

Application questions

■ What do you find to be the most compelling ways to achieve ethical excellence in:
   – design?
   – treatment of individuals?
   – process?

Reflective questions

Orb, A., Eisenhauer, L. and Wynaden, D. (2001) Ethics in qualitative research. *Journal of Nursing Scholarship*, 33 (1), 93–6.
This article provided some useful information about the history of scandals and trials and how these have shaped current practices.

Hammick, M. (1996) *Managing the ethical process in research*, Salisbury: Quay Books.
Hammick's research ethics wheel provided us with some useful ideas about the key issues that need to be addressed when considering ethics in qualitative research.

Guillemin, C. and Gillam, L. (2004) Ethics, reflexivity and 'ethically important moments' in research. *Qualitative Inquiry*, 10 (2), 261–80.
In this article, Guillemin and Gillam make important points about procedural ethics and a more everyday notion of ethics, which shaped our thinking about 'excellence' in ethics.

Ellis, C. (2009) Telling tales on neighbors: Ethics in two voices. *International Review of Qualitative Research*, 2 (1), 3–28.
A challenging article about both ethics and methods, in terms of the ethics of writing about others using ethnographic and auto-ethnographic methods.

Key resources

Chapter 22

Fieldwork

INTRODUCTION

Most qualitative researchers will at some point go to their research site(s) in order to collect data. This process sometimes is called fieldwork and at other times field research. Doing fieldwork requires a sense of artistry coupled with a practical approach. The artistry is related to reading situations, making sound but perhaps unusual decisions, following gut reactions and sometimes taking risks. The practice involves careful planning and preparation. In this chapter, we explore the concept and practice of fieldwork, identify its key characteristics and describe different types of fieldwork that researchers may choose to adopt. We suggest that thorough planning of practical matters aids and supports the artistry of fieldwork and is an essential component of most qualitative studies. In the latter sections of the chapter we describe some of the practical issues associated with doing fieldwork, such as specific issues to bear in mind while visiting the research site.

ORIGINS OF FIELDWORK

armchair fieldwork

In this type of fieldwork, the researcher does not travel to and stay at the research site but, rather, works with materials collected by others. In the past, examples of material collected by others included those acquired by traders, explorers and colonial officials. Today, materials include those such as documents and artefacts. (see Chapter 26).

Broadly speaking, fieldwork emerged from the work of early ethnographers, who moved away from being '**armchair**' anthropologists to becoming researchers who spent significant amounts of time in cultural settings in order to understand them.

This shift initially meant that researchers travelled overseas to study a particular (and often 'exotic') population. Thus, in the 1920s to 1930s, fieldwork involved visiting and living with 'other' cultures in order to observe them. Examples of such early fieldwork are seen in Malinowski's study of the social life of islanders in the Trobriand Islands (Malinowski 1922) and Mead's Samoan study concerning adolescence, childbearing and the influence of culture on personality (Mead 1928).

By mid-century, particularly during the 1960s, extensive fieldwork was being undertaken in local settings such as schools in ways that had not been done before. An example of such work was the SAFARI project, a project that sought to work *with* teachers in the UK in innovative ways to change teaching in schools. Projects such as this one prompted shifts in the 1970s and 1980s whereby researchers recognized that they should consider other issues related to fieldwork, such as the role of participants in shaping the research process during data collection (Simons 1987). Researchers now recognize that fieldwork is more than sitting in different cultures and reporting what they see. Instead, fieldwork requires an exploration of issues such as identity, reflexivity and positionality, as well as concerns about gender, power and spheres of influence. However, the concept of fieldwork remains complex and contested.

The advent of the twenty-first century has seen an expansion from early forms of fieldwork and to fieldwork practices that researchers have conceptualized in a whole host of ways. Since those early studies, for example, researchers have recognized that fieldwork is important not just for studying 'other' cultures but also for understanding what is taking place in local settings and in contexts and settings deemed to be familiar, including more formal sites such as businesses, hospitals and schools and more informal ones such as cafes (see the researcher reflection from Sebnem Cilesiz in Chapter 14 for an example). In such instances, the researcher attempts to 'make the familiar strange', which has required a new way of conceiving data collection, analysis and interpretation. Becker *et al.* (1977: 10) argued, for example, that when things are very familiar 'it becomes impossible to single out events that occur in the classroom as things that have occurred, even when they happen right in front of you ... it takes a tremendous effort of will and imagination to stop seeing the things that are conventionally "there" to be seen'.

DESCRIPTION AND PURPOSE

Fieldwork at a fundamental level is the process of collecting raw data from natural settings. Fieldwork often is taken up by qualitative researchers because of its wide capacity for letting them capture information about the ways in which individuals inhabit and experience their social worlds. As Bogdan and Biklen suggest in their text:

> Fieldwork sounds earthy. It is the way most qualitative researchers collect data. They go to the subjects and spend time with them in their territory – in their schools, their playgrounds, their hangouts, and their homes. These are the places where subjects do what they normally do, and it is these natural settings that the researcher wants to study.
>
> (Bogdan and Biklen 1982: 79)

Fieldwork

Some scholars use the term fieldwork interchangeably with observation. We use the term in a broader sense to refer to any data collection that happens in the field, or at the research site(s). In the next few chapters, we describe specific approaches to data collection that researchers might use when doing fieldwork: Chapter 23 Interviews, Chapter 24 Focus groups, Chapter 25 Observations and Chapter 26 Documents.

Tips

Fieldwork includes interviews of various sorts, natural conversations and unobtrusive methods (Bernard 1994). Fieldwork does not mean conducting a few fast interviews, sending out a pile of questionnaires or standing on a street corner asking any passer-by to answer some questions. Rather, fieldwork is a sustained process that requires careful planning and requires a sound research design and a clear rationale for data collection in place.

Fieldwork requires researcher awareness of the context, values and background of the site being studied. Fieldwork therefore involves researchers in a number of different activities. For example, researchers undertaking observation need to be there and watch people in their contexts whilst also staying long enough at a research site(s) so that they understand what is going on (often referred to as prolonged engagement). During this observation and prolonged engagement it is important that researchers recognize the roles that different people play within the research sites (for example gatekeeper, confidante, guide), whilst also accepting the practices and cultures of participants, which will in turn ensure quality in fieldwork by developing strong and sound relationships with those involved. The challenge of fieldwork for researchers is that it is demanding, tiring and exciting all at the same time.

Fieldwork can allow researchers to see what is really going on in a particular context and to understand how both formal and informal contexts are operating. Therefore researchers should choose fieldwork when they want to:

- gain thick description
- understand a particular culture, practice or setting
- get a first-hand view .
- collect primary data. *

TYPES OF FIELDWORK

Designing and doing fieldwork are exceedingly complicated tasks. The issues involve making choices about what its goals are, who will do it, from what perspective it will be done and how it will be done. These choices ultimately determine the type of fieldwork a researcher will take up. There are many different types of fieldwork, which we believe may be classified by goal, number of researchers involved, researcher perspective and level of disclosure.

The *goals* of fieldwork range from solving mysteries of interest to the researcher to examining the every-day existences of participants. Two types of fieldwork illustrate these goals: *detective fieldwork* and *ethnographic fieldwork*. Researchers undertake fieldwork in varying numbers, the common three types are: *solo, team, and collaborative fieldwork*. Researchers approach fieldwork in a variety of ways and they choose the approach and it is then their perspectives or vantage points that guides the selection of this type of fieldwork. They may be *outsiders, insiders or inside and outsiders*. There are varying degrees to which researchers in the field reveal themselves to the participants, or their *level of disclosure*. These range from providing full information to not providing any information at all. Two types of fieldwork on either side of this perspective illustrate the opposing ends of the continuum: *overt and covert fieldwork*. We provide overviews of these types of fieldwork in the following paragraphs, followed by a summary of them and advice for choosing from among them.

Detective fieldwork

This approach to fieldwork is based on the premise that everyone has a different point of view, and that some of these views may or may not overlap with other individuals' views on a number of issues. Detective fieldwork is hunting for clues and tracking down stories and perspectives from different people in order to make sense of a context, problem or issue. Seeing fieldwork as detection helps the researcher to recognize that different and diverse perspectives inform the truths and understandings of a setting; the researcher's role is to bring these together through some form of consensus. This developing consensus begins to provide answers to the research question being asked. The idea of seeing fieldwork as detection also helps the researcher to realize that fieldwork is a process of data collection, analysis in the field and writing both in and beyond the field. The activities (analysis, writing and so on) are often seen as separate but, in fact, they are interlinked and overlap. Austin and Farnsworth reflect:

> Latour (1996: 147) observes that "innovation studies are like detective stories", and it has been a connection he has himself traced and developed over a number of years. As a

metaphor, this fictional world is a productive one for social scientists because detective work illuminates much about the way innovation and investigation actually take place, along with the networks each mobilizes and assembles in the process. It also points to the unavoidably fabricated nature of the accounts that finally emerge – their provisional, representational, sometimes fictive characteristics.

(Austin and Farnsworth 2005: 147)

The kinds of innovative studies to which Latour is referring are those that take perhaps a more unusual approach to research (such as arts-based inquiry) or that tackle complex and new areas of research such as gun crime in playgrounds in remote rural villages. Thus, detective fieldwork should be seen as a process of tracking, tracing, assembling clues, revealing and reporting.

Ethnographic fieldwork

In this type of fieldwork, researchers seek to examine cultures and societies in order to reveal ways in which participants regularly live their lives and to recognize the value of difference and diversity in cultures different from the researchers' own. In short, this kind of fieldwork seeks to understand everyday lives and practices. A classic example of ethnographic fieldwork is found in the study by Becker *et al.* (1977), who investigated the students in medical schools to confirm and improve their understanding of the culture. The researchers who undertook this longitudinal study began exploring medical students as young people aspiring to be physicians and finished with them being actual skilled doctors; the researchers captured their idealism as well as their worries about becoming doctors. What became apparent in this study was that particular practices were used within the medical profession to induct students into that culture, and it was through this study that medical culture and practice became apparent to those outside it, possibly for the first time. As we mentioned in Chapter 13, ethnography involves studying a setting in depth over a period of time. Ethnographic fieldwork therefore requires the researcher to spend time with those they are studying. For example, researchers studying a student subculture on a university campus could choose to live as students staying in student accommodation and also attending lectures and even undertaking the required assessment. In ethnographic fieldwork, the researcher would live with a population for months or years. Nilan suggests that, in ethnographic fieldwork:

> The researcher tends to collect as much data as possible, in part because it is often not clear what may turn out to be relevant in the end. The methodological mandate to create ethnographic "thick description" (Geertz, 1973), and the fear of missing something which may later turn out to be important, usually results in the gathering of large amounts of data which cannot be easily categorized and analysed. The researcher may suffer from isolation, anxiety, stress and depression (Lee, 1995: 13), even in relatively straightforward fieldwork. The research accounts produced from ethnographic data can often seem like descriptive narratives, and inevitably, in the course of producing a research account which will be taken seriously by the academy, a lot of detail must be set aside.

(Nilan 2002: 365)

The three most important characteristics of ethnographic fieldwork are spending time in the setting, becoming immersed in the culture and developing strong and sound relationships with research participants.

Solo fieldwork

In solo fieldwork, a single researcher goes into the field to collect data. This is the most common type of fieldwork, yet it can be lonely and challenging because, as a solo researcher, there is relatively little support. If something occurs that is troublesome or disconcerting, there is no one to fall back on, as there is in team research. New researchers, however, often are accompanied by research supervisors prior to undertaking fieldwork alone. This is because planning fieldwork well requires that researchers understand its purpose and pitfalls. It requires careful conceptualization and design, as well as a sound plan. Thus, researchers need to develop their knowledge of fieldwork prior to entering the field, as Punch points out:

> Without adequate training and supervision, the neophyte researcher can unwittingly become an unguided projectile bringing turbulence to the field, fostering personal traumas (for researcher and researched) and even causing damage to the discipline.
>
> (Punch 1994: 83)

There have been discussions by researchers, such as Punch (1994), about whether novices should be well prepared for fieldwork or left to their own devices. We believe it is better to be prepared so that the researcher does not cause harm or offense and that ethical principles of research are adhered to.

Team fieldwork

In team fieldwork, a group of researchers comes together to work across a project but individuals work separately while collecting data. This type of fieldwork often is employed during a multiple-site study. The team meets regularly to share findings and to adapt the research design; however, they do not use explicit co-inquiry techniques but, rather, work independently to collect data which they then collate and discuss. This approach has the advantages of allowing for the development of large data sets but team research is complicated because it can result in unexpected tensions in the field, including issues about the different roles within the team, such as who is leading the team, how the team is expected to work together and who will be blamed if the fieldwork does not go well. When doing team fieldwork, roles should be clearly defined at the outset, junior staff should be supervized appropriately and there needs to be clarity about how, when and by whom the findings will be published.

Tips

One variety of team fieldwork is 'confrontational fieldwork', where the team undertakes fieldwork by, for example, asking provocative interview questions in order to reveal what it is that participants take for granted about everyday practices.

Collaborative fieldwork

In this form of fieldwork, which is usually used in approaches such as participatory action research and collaborative inquiry, researchers and participants work collaboratively as partners. The level of co-inquiry needed means that all those involved must be highly committed to this kind of research practice; otherwise the project is likely to fail. During fieldwork, the research team works together to share understandings, regardless of the kinds of data collected. In particular, they use explicit shared reflection methods about their own perspectives and their views about the collective dream and mission. Team fieldwork can become collaborative, although it typically does not begin that way. In their study that sought to examine collections of student writing for assessment and accountability purposes, Clark and Moss (1996) illustrate how collaborative fieldwork can involve not only other researchers but also participants as co-inquirers. Furthermore, in their study Moffit *et al.* (2009) explored how health research was used in rural and remote settings. What was significant in this study was the need for and use of networks to collect and manage data, and then analyze seventy-two qualitative transcripts jointly from different geographical areas. This meant that a high level of collaboration was required within the study. This resulted in opportunities to mentor undergraduate, masters and doctoral nursing students.

Outsider fieldwork

In outsider fieldwork, the researcher goes to a research setting to collect data in order to understand the unfamiliar or to make the familiar strange. A classic example of outsider research is Geertz's (1973) account of participating in a police raided cockfight in Bali. Geertz's involvement in the raid did ultimately open doors to Balinese culture and custom, which, before the raid, he was unable to accomplish since he and his wife were ignored by the Balinese men he sought to understand. Geertz reflected before the raid that he and his wife were 'non persons, spectres, invisible men' (Geertz 1973: 412). The challenge of outsider research is that the researcher is outside, sometimes feeling as if they are looking in, perhaps being voyeurs or even in the way. Ensuring that the researcher stays long enough in the field (prolonged engagement) helps the participants to become familiar with the presence of the researcher, and enables the researcher to become familiar with the setting and its cultures.

Insider fieldwork

Insider fieldwork is an approach in which researchers investigate the contexts in which they work, study or socialize. For example, a teacher may study classroom practices in his own school or a politician may examine the ethics of her own political party. The advantage of being an insider is that the researcher has considerable knowledge that an outsider does not. Tierney (1994) has suggested that interviewees are more likely to talk freely with an insider. A difficulty with insider research can be the blurring of boundaries between researcher and researched; for example, feminist research carried out by feminists. This means that there is potential for high levels of unhelpful bias, subjectivity and an inability to 'see' other points of view (Devault 2004). From the researchers' perspectives, they need to be aware that their insider knowledge may result in missing vital information, making false assumptions or misinterpreting data. The researcher will also need to be aware of conflicts of interests or whether their own political or moral perspectives may lead them to distort data. For example, Drake (2010) provides an example of the challenges of undertaking insider research where the project became problematic. The study examined postgraduate mathematics teaching in a UK university and compared research diary entries from two interviewees. Drake argued that, 'The validity of insider research requires reflexive consideration of the researcher's position, and this is especially pertinent in the case of research undertaken by practitioner researchers on professional doctorates' (Drake 2010: 85).

Insider and outsider fieldwork

This type of fieldwork is more unusual in that researchers are rarely both insiders and outsiders at the same time. However, Sherif (2001: 440) provides an interesting perspective on being both.

She explained how she felt torn 'between conflicting identities: the American graduate student, the Egyptian daughter, the single woman in her late 20s, and the trained anthropologist who was always observing and aware of the process as if from the outside'. What is evident in this work is that insider and outsider status is most likely to emerge when researchers are working within and across cultural contexts, as Sherif explained above. A further example is a study by Naples (2004), who examined a rural Iowan community in the USA. She describes herself as an outsider to the community because she has only recently moved there, yet, during data collection, she realized that other people also feel like outsiders to that particular community, owing to issues such as social inequalities and racial difference.

Overt fieldwork

This kind of fieldwork is done with the full knowledge of participants. It is the most common way in which research is carried out. A researcher who engages in overt fieldwork initially talks with gatekeepers and potential participants and, if engaging in observations, makes a conscious effort to let others know that.

Covert fieldwork

This kind of fieldwork typically is done secretly without consent. Issues, particularly ethical ones, attend this kind of fieldwork (see Chapter 21). A researcher might enrol as a student, get a job in a company or supermarket or lurk on street corners without alerting anyone that they have done so for the purpose of doing research. Covert research has been done perhaps more often than many of us know and there are some interesting and astonishing examples. One such example is a study by Cusick (1973), who became a participant-observer in a high school in order to understand how high school students dealt with issues within their school. Cusick sought to describe the student behaviour in high school, the way it affected the teachers, administrators and school organization as whole. Cusick attended classes, ate in the cafeteria and took part in the informal life of the school. However, perhaps one of the most famous and controversial forms of covert fieldwork (discussed in Chapter 21) was that undertaken by Humphreys (1970) entitled the *Tearoom trade: A study of homosexual encounters in public places*. Humphreys studied homosexual acts of men from diverse social backgrounds that took place in public toilets.

Comparison and choice of types of fieldwork

In the Table 22.1 we provide a summary and comparison of the different types of fieldwork.

Researchers typically do not select only one type of fieldwork; they choose one type of fieldwork in each category. Thus, they select a goal, a number, a perspective and a level of disclosure. We illustrate these choices in Table 22.2.

One researcher then may choose to take up detective, solo, outsider and covert fieldwork, while another might choose to take up ethnographic, collaborative, insider and overt fieldwork. The choices they make are dependent upon their philosophical stances, the norms of their research approaches, the research topic and question as well as the access they have to a particular community.

Table 22.1 Types of fieldwork

Type of fieldwork	Position of researcher	Form of data collection	Dilemmas
Ethnographic fieldwork	Outsider seeking to understand and engage with a particular culture	In-depth interviews and extensive observation	A tendency to become too familiar and involved with the culture being studied
Detective fieldwork	Tracing, checking, discovering	Collection of clues to bring together evidence	Managing wide ranging and often disparate evidence
Solo fieldwork	Working alone to collect data and managing complexities in the field	Interviews and observation	Loneliness, data collected seem to be obvious, inability to see strength of data collected
Team fieldwork	Collecting data individually but with reference to the team	Interviews, observation, focus groups	Collecting data differently so resulting in poor data set
Collaborative fieldwork	Working collaboratively and sharing findings in the field	Sharing findings in the field and focus groups	Disturbing cultures, as so many researchers are involved
Insider fieldwork	Researching a context from within	Interviews and observation	Overlooking what is obvious, causing offence
Outsider fieldwork	Researching a context from outside	Interviews and observation	Disturbing cultures, misunderstanding what is taking place
Insider/outsider	Working across roles and contexts	Interviews and observation	Role confusion for researcher and participants
Covert fieldwork	Hidden, clandestine	Secret observation	Largely seen as unethical because the researcher is not seeking to gain consent

Table 22.2 Fieldwork choices

Category	Choice	Summary
Fieldwork by goal	Detective	Solving mysteries
	Ethnographic	Exploring everyday life
Fieldwork by number of researchers	Solo	Sole researchers
	Teamwork	Multiple researchers
	Collaborative	Multiple researchers, co-inquiry
Fieldwork by perspective	Insider	In the study looking out
	Outsider	Outside the study looking in
	Insider and outsider	At the nexus of insider and outsider
Fieldwork by level of disclosure	Overt	Individuals informed of the research
	Covert	Individuals unaware of the research

DOING FIELDWORK

Once the researcher has considered and chosen the type of fieldwork to adopt, the practical aspects then have to be addressed. There are a number of issues that attend doing fieldwork. These include developing skills, preparing for the field and writing during data collection.

Developing skills

Bernard (1998) suggests that researchers should develop a set of skills and that this development occurs during the very process of fieldwork. These skills include learning the language, gaining explicit awareness, developing memory, retaining naïveté and building writing skills.

Learning the language

Participants have their own speech patterns, rhetoric and shared phrases that an observer will not share initially. The researcher will have to learn this language in order to engage with participants at the site. As Bernard (1994: 145) suggests, 'the most important thing you can do to stop being a freak is to speak the language of the people you're studying — and speak it well'. Like most immersion language learning, participants will initially talk down to participant observers and gradually elevate their communication, coinciding with observer readiness.

Gaining explicit awareness

It is easy to observe at a surface level; practically anyone can do it. Seeing the small details, however, takes concentrated awareness that can only be developed through prolonged exposure, after the observer has taken stock of and moved past the obvious.

Developing memory

The researcher has several responsibilities, including paying attention, seeing, learning and recording. It generally is not possible to record everything observed, so the researcher must develop memory for small things. Short notes can help but they do not replace seeing and remembering.

Retaining naïveté

As a researcher develops and learns during observation, it is possible to begin to take things for granted. Bernard suggests that it is important to maintain a position of novice or inexperienced member of the site so that the learning process continues.

Building writing skills

A researcher needs the ability to record what is going on and to write about the observation carefully. The researcher's field notes become the data, so it is critical for the writing to be clear. This is addressed in more detail later in the chapter.

Preparing for the field

There are many ways to prepare for fieldwork but the most important aspect is that researchers have a general sense of the research site prior to their visits to collect data. We offer practical advice about how to do this in the following sections.

Gaining access to the site: the gatekeeper

Gaining entry to a research site can be simple and straightforward with inside knowledge. Insiders have the unique luxury of having first-hand access to participants. However, if they are insiders, researchers need to be sure that they are not taking their access for granted. As an outsider, gaining access to a site without access to a gatekeeper can be challenging, and poor access can lead to poor data collection or even to having to select another site; therefore, finding an entry point is essential.

Most researchers have to determine a way to gain access to a site from the outside, as well as a way to make a connection with intended participants. A good gatekeeper is a highly ranking or regarded person who has access to most parts of the organization or environment. Examples of such gatekeepers are a head teacher, the leader of a tribe/community or a learning technologist. Without prior site knowledge, it is important to politely identify the correct decision maker(s), who can facilitate smooth and swift access to the correct individuals, groups and resources. Without access to a specific individual who can provide entry, it may be necessary to work with a group of individuals. Indeed, as Lincoln and Guba (1985: 253) suggest, 'the keys to access are almost always in the hands of multiple gatekeepers'. Gatekeepers will want to know about the research project prior to helping a researcher contact participants. As Creswell (1998) suggests, they will want to know:

- why the site was chosen and how it is important to the work
- what the research will accomplish and specifically how that will benefit them
- what time and resources are required for the research
- about the costs and potential risks of the research, whether political or productive
- how the results will be used.

Making preliminary visits, contacts and plans

Prior to the first official data collection, a researcher will need to make a preliminary visit to the field and contact individuals who can help with planning and scheduling the research. We see several ways in which this happens: scouting the site, selecting a time and finding a location for observations and interviews.

Scouting the site: A researcher will want to get a basic understanding of the layout of the research site. While maps can help if available, it is a good idea to visit the site ahead of formal observation or interviewing. Doing so provides researchers with an opportunity to get a feel for the site and to gather information that is vital for planning formal data collection. Such a visit allows for learning the way around the site, which will help him or her feel both more able to plan and more comfortable during data collection.

Selecting a time: Site visits should be made based upon when it is most critical for data collection and when participants are available, so initial searching for an appropriate time prior to the actual visit is essential. The research question may demand a certain time of year or even day and participants may be more readily available at certain times of the day that others. A good researcher will work to balance research needs with participant needs. When trying to determine a good time, it is important to consider the amount of time it will take participants to carry out the interview or focus group (generally between thirty minutes and two hours), including travelling to and from the interview location, as well as a few minutes of talking informally before and after the interview. Checking available schedules and working with a gatekeeper can help to accomplish this goal.

Finding a location for data collection: Data collection, whether interviews, focus groups or observation should be undertaken in as natural an environment as possible and should also be one that is easy for participants to find, access and in which to feel relaxed. A person's office might be a good choice for an individual interview, while a central location in an organization or community, such as a meeting or break room, would work well for a focus group interview. The size of the location also matters. An office would be appropriate for an individual interview, but focus groups require a room in which ten to twelve people can talk easily. Since it will probably be impossible to observe all areas of an organization or environment, particularly a large one, doing observations typically involves selecting a few key locations. How to go about making such a selection depends upon the purpose of and rationale for the research. The researcher may wish, for example, to try to spread out observations geographically to get a representative set of observations. On the other hand, a researcher may wish to purposefully select a few areas of observation, such as the busiest, the most representative of the topic or the ones with the most visual landmarks.

Ten things about fieldwork we wish someone had told us

Sometimes, stories about fieldwork feel like the stuff of legend. We offer the following pointers that we wish we had known prior to engaging in fieldwork.

1. You will be more nervous than you think you will be.
2. Observing is not easy.
3. Getting a good in-depth interview can make a researcher's heart soar – often out of all proportion.
4. Doing three interviews in a day is plenty and trying to do more usually results in mistakes.
5. When the digital recorder goes wrong (or you make a mistake turning it on) do not try and redo the interview. Instead, recognize the mistake, fix the technology, make some good notes and begin the interview from where you left off.
6. Sometimes, even with good planning, things go wrong, people get interview times wrong; two people (or none) turn up at the same time.
7. It is possible to become distracted in an interview and lose the thread – be honest if this happens. It is always better to be honest than pretend because people find you out.
8. Even people who have agreed to be interviewed sometimes say little or give one word answers and the interview then becomes difficult and challenging to manage.
9. Doing fieldwork is overwhelming and overstimulating and sometimes it is not possible to write fast enough to get the information down.
10. It is probably one of the most interesting explorations of humanity to engage in; first memories of doing fieldwork last for a long time.

Example of fieldwork

In the following researcher reflection, Betsy Palmer reflects upon her experiences in doing fieldwork.

Associate Professor Betsy Palmer, Montana State University, USA

Fieldwork

To conduct my ethnographic study of families and schooling, *Community Perspectives on Education in a Remote Region in Nepal*, I travelled to a village in Eastern Nepal, where I lived for two months. My husband was born in this village and I had previously visited there in 2006. I was eager to return to see how people in Pandok were faring with the political, social and economic changes that Nepal's democratic revolution had fostered. To reach the village, my family and I rode in a four-wheel-drive jeep over a deeply rutted dirt roads along steep cliffs into mud-clogged jungle for one and a half days. Then we walked, with porters carrying our supplies, through the rugged terrain of the Arun river valley for four and a half additional days.

This area is not part of the regular Nepal trekking routes, and I am one of only a handful of Westerners who have ever visited this village. The first few days after we arrived, the slopes near our home were covered in children watching every move I made. As a researcher, I longed to spend less time being observed and more time observing, so I worked quickly to align my visible daily behaviour with local routines. By taking on the many tasks of local women, I had less time to devote exclusively to my research work, consequently I learned to integrate field observations into every moment of my day.

Each morning, I woke up before the sun crept over the surrounding mountains. I dressed in my traditional dress, built a fire, brewed tea and started breakfast. On many days, relatives or friends would arrive by 7 a.m., necessitating a break from activities while we attended to our guests. While performing all these tasks, however, I was also able to observe people around me. Our house was located adjacent to the focus of my research, the village school, so as I washed dishes or laundry in the local stream, I could also observe children walking by on their way to school.

My predominant data collection method for this ethnographic study was observation. I used various strategies at different times to gain multiple perspectives on my target, the schooling of young children. In the most obvious strategy, I would walk to the school grounds with my smart pen and notebook, sit among the children on a bench and make specific notes about people and their behaviour. However, this method of direct observation often created a disruption in the children's natural behaviour, so I utilized less intrusive observation strategies as well. On certain days, I might walk to the hillside above the school and take notes from a distance. I also used a digital camera, a digital video camera and various audio recording devices to preserve particular scenes and sounds. I used these pictures and recordings later to refresh my memory and help me to accurately describe details of my field experience. I was somewhat limited in my

Researcher reflections

ability to use modern technology, however, because all my devices had to be charged via solar power and, when I used them in public, they distracted local individuals from their everyday activities. I had to therefore choose carefully how and when I would take pictures or record audio tracks.

I relied heavily on informants to help me to interpret various local behaviours. By asking a few simple questions in conversations around me, I could fill in details and gain valuable insights that helped me to deepen my understanding of the full context of schooling in the village. I used these opportunities to check my on-going interpretations of interactions that I observed and recorded in my field journal. I also made specific notes about my own subjective responses to conducting the study, reflecting on my values and behaviours and how my position in relation to my fieldwork was evolving over time.

Writing during data collection

Writing is part and parcel of the field experience. Such writing can range from note taking during interviews to field notes and journaling. We describe these forms of field writing in the following sections.

Note taking during interviews

It is the responsibility of the researcher to collect notes during the interview. Note taking is a key element in data collection. A researcher takes notes most often because it can allow him or her to jot down information about what's going on around him that can supplement the interview transcripts.

Note taking as sole means of recording data

While it is most common to use audio recording along with note taking of interviews, there are, at times, circumstances in which recorders or video cameras are not available or desirable (such as in informal interview). In these cases, paper and pencil alone will have to do. While this is a satisfactory method of data collection, it necessarily will limit the amount of information collected and, thus, the level of detail to which data analysis may be done. In these cases, note quality is critical. The researcher should strive for as full a transcript as possible. There are several approaches for taking notes without recording:

- *Word for word*: Those who know shorthand are in luck. They will likely be able to capture most of each interviewee's responses. However, most of us do not know shorthand, and for us, it is nearly impossible to record each and every word the participant utters.
- *Key phrases*: One technique for note taking is to write down the key phrases and points of each interview.
- *Summaries*: Some researchers try to summarize each participant's responses. They include direct quotes of interesting statements but generally record their own summaries of ideas. It is important to remember that, in doing so, it is your interpretation that you are summarizing, rather than the individual's words. It is challenging to stay true to the participant's

actual intent. Sometimes, summaries could take on a different meaning out of context and it is critical to avoid this. If the researcher is making summary notes only, he or she will need to treat the information with caution since it is his or her interpretation and as such is imperfect.

Note taking with other forms of recording

Recording the session as well as taking notes has distinct advantages and it changes the note taking approach. Recording the session will allow production of a full transcript later, so your notes will be taken to remind you (and your team) of what was said. Immediately after the session, the researcher reviews the notes and adds in detail to provide as full an account of the session as possible. Researchers should only include notes they are sure about. At this time, they should not make judgments about what participants meant; rather, they should indicate only what was said. If a researcher thinks judgment or interpretation is critical, then he or she can note it but the entry must make clear that it is a comment from the researcher, not the participant. There are several ways to record the session:

- *Audio*: Audio recording is one of the best methods of recording a session. Recording allows for developing a complete and accurate account, which can be useful when questions about responses or meanings arise. Using a digital recorder is ideal. A recording provides a documented account that can be reviewed, listened to or read again and again, particularly when there is confusion about the meaning of a participant's comment.
- *Video*: Video seems like an ideal way to capture interview and focus group sessions. In such recordings, it is possible not only to hear words and conversations but also to see facial expressions and to capture the surrounding environment on video. Yet video cameras may be distracting to individuals being interviewed, particularly if they have not had much exposure to being videoed. Self-consciousness can slow the free exchange of a natural conversation.
- *Online*: Online interviewing, done through chat or email, has the distinct advantage of producing full transcripts of the session. Still, note taking can be important, as it can allow the researcher to note time lapses.

Good interview notes help to 'transport' a researcher back to the site and they help during analysis and interpretation. A researcher takes notes to provide important and supplementary information about what else is going on during the whole interview period, that can supplement the interview transcript data.

Field notes

Prior to beginning observation, it is important to determine how they will be recorded. Researchers 'often experience deep ambivalence about whether, when, where and how to write jottings' (Emerson *et al.* 2001: 357). Most observers choose to use field notes of some kind or another. Field notes allow a researcher to record behaviour, events and surroundings of the research site. Field notes typically contain a date, time, location and details of what or who is being observed. What is recorded is driven by the research questions. The first notations tend to be jottings of the researcher: a few words or phrases to jog the researcher's memory later. Jottings are recorded so that they may be manipulated, arranged and rearranged, by category of interest, often on note cards. Jottings are later translated to field notes in which the researcher writes a detailed description of what was observed. It is advisable for a researcher to plan a regular time and place to write the field notes, which should be done as soon after the observation as possible to ensure accuracy. The researcher may also record thoughts about themes/interpretations but these should be clearly indicated. See Table 22.3 for a sample field note, contrasting overly vague notes and more appropriately detailed notes.

Table 22.3 Sample content of a field note (Baker and Sabo 2004: 38)

Vague and overgeneralized notes	Detailed notes
The new client was uneasy waiting for her intake interview. She fidgeted a lot and seemed nervous.	The client sat very stiffly on the chair next to the receptionist's desk. She picked up a magazine and let the pages flutter through her fingers very quickly without really looking at any of the pages. Then she set the magazine down, looked at her watch, pulled her skirt down and picked up the magazine again. This time she didn't look at the magazine. She set it down, took out a cigarette and began smoking. She watched the receptionist out of the corner of her eye, and then looked down at the magazine and back up at the two or three other people waiting in the room. Her eyes moved from people to the magazine to the cigarette to the people to the magazine in rapid succession. She avoided eye contact. When her name was called, she jumped like she was startled.
The patient was quite hostile towards the staff member.	When the staff member told her that she could not do what she wanted to do, the client began to yell at the staff member, telling her that she (the staff member) 'can't control (her) life', that she (the staff member) is 'nothing but on a power trip'. Then she yelled that she would like to 'beat the crap out of her'. She shook her fist in her face and stomped out of the room leaving the staff person standing there with her mouth open, looking amazed.

Memos

A memo can range from a scrawl on a Post-it® note indicating how codes relate to the literature, through to a drawing that indicates thoughts about relationships to categories, to a short essay which develops the theoretical implications of what the researcher is seeing. As Glaser suggests:

> Memos are the theorizing write-up of ideas about substantive codes and their theoretically coded relationships as they emerge during coding, collecting and analyzing data.
>
> (Glaser 1998: 177).

Memos allow researchers to document and refine ideas that occur when they first compare one incident to another and later concepts to earlier concepts, in search of a theory to explain their relationships. The researcher also seeks to indicate the relationships between concepts, often via tables, diagrams or figures. Theoretical memos allow the researcher to work on theories without working on the final paper. Final grounded theory is often developed by researchers using this approach by integrating several theoretical memos. Memoing enables the researcher to maintain creativity and flow, often by free writing, so eliminating the distractions that arise from grammar or style rules (Glaser 1998).

See Table 22.4 for a sample form for taking field notes, code notes and memos (or theoretical notes).

Table 22.4 Example form for note taking

Head notes (info about the participant)	

Sally, the receptionist, interviewed at her office on March 2, 2012.

Researcher field notes	Code notes
Sally is a very enthusiastic person. She seems perpetually upbeat and happy. She notes that the company is one that is good to the employees which in turn makes them want to work hard and to make a difference for their company to help the company meet their goals. Sally says she often works late or comes in early, without being asked and without requesting overtime.	Happy Hardworking

Memos/theoretical notes	

The concept of reciprocity may be at play here; the company gives to the employees and in turn the employees want to give something back to the company.

Not all researchers, however, take these detailed notes. We provide an example in a researcher reflection from Matt Mawer.

Matt Mawer, Coventry University, UK

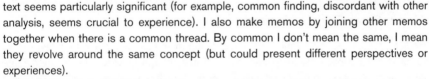

My notes look nothing like that, they're nowhere near as neatly organized for one thing! I don't code my observation field notes and reflections because they're already encoded (that is, not a verbatim transcript). To use this form you need someone doing grounded theory in a more formal fashion that includes all the procedural steps to the analysis.

Generally speaking, I attach notes to codes first and then make memos by transferring notes from codes if the text seems particularly significant (for example, common finding, discordant with other analysis, seems crucial to experience). I also make memos by joining other memos together when there is a common thread. By common I don't mean the same, I mean they revolve around the same concept (but could present different perspectives or experiences).

I think analytical writing is absolutely crucial to the process and codes are really just a way of getting the writing/thinking moving. They help, you see, but it is the writing that does the analysis for me. Other people, particularly those with more of an affinity for building code categories, will probably see it differently however.

Researcher reflections

Journaling during fieldwork

Journals allow for reflection upon the general research process as well as the researcher's behaviours, successes and struggles at the research site. Struggles might involve conflict, frustrations and fatigue, and invariably are about not only the practical aspects of data collection, but also the social, ethical and political issues a researcher faces in fieldwork settings.

Things to include in journals:

- depiction of activities – behaviour and acts
- researcher behaviour
- reconstructions of dialogue
- speculation, feelings, hunches
- confessions of mistakes, inadequacies, prejudices
- reflections on any frustrations.

Things to remember about journaling:

- Do not procrastinate – it is easy to avoid doing journal entries and feels sort of boring and inconsequential at the time
- Do not talk about it until it is written – talking with others can interrupt a researcher's thoughts
- Find a quiet place
- Allow adequate time
- Do it chronologically.

ADVANTAGES AND CHALLENGES OF FIELDWORK

In the past, it was easy to envision a researcher as a distant observer, often in a white lab coat, running experiments and then crunching the numbers. Today, particularly when conducting qualitative research in social science and professional fields, the picture that one might paint of a researcher is something quite different. Researchers may be seen entering sites, travelling across grounds; rushing to and from meetings and interviewing; spending hours upon hours in interviews, at times sympathizing and empathizing with participants and sharing their strife and struggles; and observing. Indeed, fieldwork is hard work. In the following author reflection, Maggi shares her perspective on the intensity of fieldwork.

Maggi Savin-Baden, Author

Before I did any real fieldwork – the actual going to an unknown place for a few weeks to meet the people I asked to interview – I just thought it would be fun and quite interesting. No one had ever said anything about how it really might be. I am not saying it was awful, just most of the time it was not how I thought it would be.

I assumed four interviews in a day would be fine, that I would easily get twenty interviews and four observations done in a week. I was wrong.

People told me things I felt they should not have and some were offended by what seemed to me quite straightforward questions. Some turned up late, others arrived early. People said they could spend thirty minutes with me and stayed for two hours.

Nothing prepared me for the sheer intensity of fieldwork; your nerves feel as if they are on fire. You can barely sleep some nights because your brain seems overloaded and overstimulated. The nights you do sleep you end up over sleeping and have to rush to get to the first interview the next morning. The excitement and the adrenalin, but also the questions and worry involved in fieldwork is something that is still, for me, a surprise.

The result of such intensity is that it can be easy for researchers to become overwhelmed by fieldwork; it is not always as easy for them to recognize or acknowledge this. When researchers have reached their limits, it can be a problem for the study, because what may emerge is a sense of irritation or impatience with participants or an inappropriate judgmental attitude during observations, which ultimately can affect both collection and interpretation of data. It is critical for a researcher to recognize human limitations and then to take steps to be realistic about the research process.

CONCLUSION

We have provided some information about the basic practicalities involved in doing fieldwork. Despite best planning, however, at times, fieldwork will not go as planned. Things will happen beyond the researcher's control and it is imperative to accept these things and to keep a sense of humour. The researcher will simply need to do the best job possible in order to get the best information possible from participants. That information will be data and a study is only as good as its data. However, what is central to sound fieldwork is good planning and organization, as well as being aware of the politics and agendas of those involved in the study.

Reflective questions

Concept questions

■ What is the purpose of fieldwork?
■ What are the particular challenges of a given type of fieldwork?

Application questions

■ What type of fieldwork would you use and why?
■ What are the issues and practicalities you need to consider before setting off to gain data from the field?

Key resources

De Laine, M. (2000) *Fieldwork, participation and practice ethics and dilemmas in qualitative research*, London: Sage.
   This covers a wide range of issues on fieldwork and explores many of the dilemmas faced by qualitative researchers.

Delmont, S. (2002) *Fieldwork in educational settings: Methods, pitfalls and perspectives*, London: Routledge.
   This is a down-to-earth practical book that examines sociological and anthropological approaches to qualitative research and provides a range of helpful examples.

Woodward, K. (2008) Hanging out and hanging about: Insider/outsider research in the sport of boxing. *Ethnography*, 9 (4), 536–60.

continued

Sherif, B. (2001) The ambiguity of boundaries in the fieldwork experience: Establishing rapport and negotiating insider/outsider status. *Qualitative Inquiry*, 7 (4), 436–47. These are two personal and interesting articles about the challenges and joys of fieldwork.

Chapter 23

Interviews

INTRODUCTION

Interviews are the mainstay of qualitative research and, within many research approaches (see Part 4), they are the central method of data collection. Designing and carrying out interviews is a demanding task that requires critical attention and time, and researchers face choices ranging from the type of interview to conduct, the medium in which to conduct them and the ways in which they will position themselves within them. In this chapter, we provide an overview of using interviews as a data collection approach, along with information about their advantages and disadvantages. We describe the range of different types of interviews used in qualitative research, as well as some of the different modes through which they may be accomplished. We also provide information about how to write effective interview questions and protocols. Finally, we provide tips for ensuring good interviews.

ORIGINS OF INTERVIEWS

The origins of interviews date from the early 1900s with anthropological studies and ethnographic approaches. Interviews developed simultaneously with observation as a method of data collection (see Chapter 24), as originally these two approaches were used together. Some of the early researchers, for example, entered a culture for the purpose of studying it and observed while also conducting interviews (Bernard 1988; 1994; Stocking 1983). Researchers originally used interviews to question meanings of experience and to provide access to the context of participants' behaviours (Seidman 1991: 4). Over the last century, interviews have evolved as a method of data collection; today, they are often paired with other forms of data collection rather than used as the central and sole method.

DESCRIPTION AND PURPOSE

Interviews are the most common method of gathering data for qualitative research and are an integral part of most of the research traditions (see Part 4). An interview in qualitative research is a conversation between two individuals in which the interviewer asks questions and the interviewee responds. When possible, the goal is to replicate in a research setting the elements of a natural conversation. The basic subject matter of the research interview is the meaningful perspectives conveyed by the participant. The participant's responsibility is to share something from his or her perspective or experience. The interviewer guides the conversation and strives to understand the participant's views as well as the meaning of what they say. To facilitate a conversation, the interviewer seeks to establish **rapport** with the interviewee.

Rapport
A close connection or relationship

Interviews enable the researcher to gain complex in-depth information from participants (Wengraf 2001). Although researchers may at times strive to uncover facts (Kvale 1996), the focus of most interviews is not about getting specific answers to questions but rather to develop understanding and interpretation of people and situations (Tierney and Dilley 2002; Warren 1988). Interviews are a central data collection method for exploring 'data on understandings, opinions, what people remember doing, attitudes, feelings and the like, that people have in common' (Arksey and Knight 1999: 2). In this way, the researcher can come to an understanding of the people and the cultures in which they live and work (Gubrium and Holstein 1995; 2001). Interviews are appropriate when a researcher wants to take advantage of the one-to-one communication form in order to probe deeply into a participant's experiences, and are ideal when the researcher wishes to follow up initial responses by probing for additional information that can help clarify or illuminate. Interviews are particularly appropriate when the information to be shared is sensitive or confidential.

The use and focus of qualitative interviewing is both broad and deep, and, as Schostak remarks, there are some challenges with using interviews to collect data:

> Don't be misled. The interview is not a simple tool with which to mine information. It is a place where views may clash, deceive, seduce, enchant. It is the inter-view. It is as much about seeing a world — mine, yours, ours, theirs — as about hearing accounts, opinions, arguments, reasons, declarations: words with views into different worlds.
>
> (Schostak 2006: 1)

What makes designing and doing interviews even more challenging is that their very nature is contingent upon the researcher's philosophical and methodological stance (see Chapter 4). In particular, someone who holds a pragmatist stance might well see the interview as the time during which meaning is to be 'found', whereas someone who holds a constructionist perspective might see the interview as the moment in which knowledge is (co)constructed. The difference is not trivial. Rather, it is essential to the meaning of the study. Moreover, the research approach taken up drives the type of interview the researcher chooses (see Part 4 for the kinds of interviews typically used in each approach). We advise researchers to consider their philosophical and methodological stances when developing and doing interviews.

TYPES OF INTERVIEWS

Researchers may select from a range of interview types (Rapley 2004). The type of interview they choose tends to be directly related to the research approach that is guiding the work. In this section, we consider the primary types of qualitative interviews as follows: structured, semi-structured, unstructured and informal.

Structured

In a structured interview, the researcher follows a preset script, asking each interviewee the same, closed questions using the same words in each interview, although sometimes the questions lean toward a more open-ended type. Standardized questions in which ordering and phrasing remains constant across interviews can allow for collecting some common information across participants. The interviewer typically is casual and friendly but refrains from inserting opinions. This type of interview can reduce the effect of the interviewer on the results. It may be used when the researcher has a well-developed understanding of the topic (for example, after conducting a research review in a well-established area or after the use of observations or less structured interviewing). This approach most often is used when it is important to minimize the variation in questions posed to interviewees; for instance, when the research is being conducted by a research team (see Chapter 22). A strength of this approach is that it makes it easier for others to replicate the study. In addition, a researcher's skills do not have to be as well developed as they do for some of the other interview forms; the interviewer simply has to follow the instructions. Moreover, these interviews tend to produce data that are consistent and that allow for comparison across many respondents. The limitation is that this interview form restricts the exploration of issues that were not anticipated when the questions were written. Because of their limitations, most qualitative researchers use semi-structured, unstructured or informal interviews (Bryman 2012).

Semi-structured

In a semi-structured interview, the researcher not only follows some preset questions but also includes additional questions in response to participant comments and reactions. The interviewer relies upon an interview protocol, asking questions and covering topics in a particular order, and from time to time strays from the guide as appropriate. The questions do not necessarily follow a set order as they do in structured interviews, but they are not as broad and free ranging as other forms of interviews. Rather, there is a tendency to move from the general to the specific, with gradual introduction to any sensitive issues or questions. The interviewer probes discussion and follows ideas. Semi-structured interviews are a good approach when the researcher has only one opportunity to interview someone, and are also an effective technique when several interviewers will be collecting data for the same project. A strength of this approach is that it allows the researcher to decide how best to use the limited time available and keeps the interaction focused. The questions tend to be open-ended enough to allow interviewees to express their perspectives on a topic or issue and also allow for comparable data that can be compared across respondents. A weakness of semi-structured interviews is that they do not always provide the interviewee with the opportunity to offer his or her own unique perspective. Semi-structured interviews are often used in qualitative research (Bryman 2012).

Unstructured

In an unstructured interview, the researcher has a goal and plan in mind but does not use a structured interview protocol. This type of interview relies upon the spontaneous generation of questions. Most questions arise from the context. The questions tend to be open-ended questions that require broad responses and that enable a conversation about a specific topic. An in-depth unstructured interview tends to take place as a conversation with a specific purpose. It is:

> a conversation between researcher and informant focussing on the informant's perception of self, life and experience, and expressed in his or her own words. It is the means by which the researcher can gain access to, and subsequently understand, the private interpretations of social reality that individuals hold.

> (Minichiello *et al.* 1990: 87)

Researchers use unstructured interviews when they have a deep understanding of the topic and the setting and possess a clear agenda, yet remain open to revising their ideas based upon their results. Unstructured interviews require speaking with interviewees, often on multiple occasions. The strength of this kind of approach is that it allows the interviewer to test preliminary understandings while remaining highly responsive. Unstructured interviews also can serve as a useful step toward developing more structured interview guides. A weakness is that they take considerable time (and multiple conversations over time). Another weakness is that the data gathered from each interview will be different and unlikely to be comparable with others. Creative interviews and post-modern interviews are a form of unstructured interviews.

CREATIVE AND POST-MODERN INTERVIEWING

In creative interviewing, the researcher seeks to use unconventional approaches to collect information from participants. Creative interviews are unconventional because they do not follow the rules of interviewing but, rather, require adapting to the situation of the interview (Douglas 1985).

Post-modern interviewing focuses on the way in which the interviewer co-constructs the meaning of experiences the interviewee shares. The methods may include polyphonic interviewing (recording participants' voices with minimal input from the interviewer) or focusing on moments in participant's lives that they describe as important and seeking to understand them as transformational experiences (Fontana and Frey 1994).

Informal

In an informal interview, the researcher talks with people in the field informally and without a structured protocol. The researcher does not record the interview but rather relies on memory and informal notes. The result is something resembling a casual conversation. Informal interviewing typically is part of the observation process (see Chapter 22). It tends to be done in the early stages of the research or when there is little literature on the research environment or topic; its strength is that it often uncovers new topics or issues. Informal interviews are often done to help develop more structured interview questions. Respondents may see the informal interview as a conversation, which may make them more open to discussion and able to speak more freely. It also is a good way to gain trust as well as understanding. Weaknesses are that data are not recorded and transcribed verbatim, the researcher's memory is imperfect and that data across respondents are unlikely to be comparable.

DESIGNING AND DOING INTERVIEWS

Choosing and doing interviews during a qualitative study means that researchers face several issues. Among them are assuming the roles and responsibilities of an interviewer, choosing appropriate media, developing strong questions and developing an interview protocol.

Interviewer roles and responsibilities

While interviewing, in addition to posing the questions and keeping the conversation flowing, the researcher will manage several responsibilities, each at various times and also simultaneously. Knowing these responsibilities ahead of time can make a researcher more aware and confident and also will help participants to feel confident and more inclined to take the session seriously. Ultimately, knowing and taking on board the researcher responsibilities will improve the quality of information gathered. We see two responsibilities as key: listening and observing.

Listening

As a researcher, it is imperative to be a good listener and this is a skill that researchers must develop (Rubin and Rubin 1995). Researchers should avoid talking too much, as it is important to hear from the participants. The researcher should encourage the individual to speak and then should listen to what is said in order to summarize comments and to check understanding. Researchers also much balance note taking with listening. A researcher should strive to remember comments and use them to introduce the next question, as it is only possible to ask good follow-up questions if participants' comments have been heard and understood. Interviewing requires intense concentration, most often for more than an hour, which in reality is very nearly impossible. There are several strategies, however, that can improve an interviewer's listening skills and attention:

- Practice before going into the field. If you are a novice researcher, try listening to a prior conversation and remembering the main points.
- Concentrate on what the speaker is saying. It is difficult to maintain full attention for more than 20 minutes at a time. If you are finding it difficult to concentrate, try repeating a participant's words mentally. It will help to reinforce their message in your mind and to direct your concentration.
- Avoid being judgmental about participant responses. The participant will not talk freely if they believe that you do not agree with them or are being judgmental. Try to keep an open mind. On the other hand, if you notice that you are reacting emotionally to what someone has said, say so and ask for additional information (for example, 'I'm not sure I understand you correctly, and I think I may be taking it personally. I thought you said . . . Is that what you meant?').

Tips

Observing participants during an interview

Observation is a method of data collection in its own right (see Chapter 25) but it also is an important part of the process of interviewing. Interviewees tend to send many messages through their body language and gestures. If researchers are to understand what participants mean, they should take note of these signals. While listening to participants' responses to questions, it is necessary to watch for anything that could indicate boredom, anxiety or impatience. A researcher will need to make adjustments quickly if this occurs. Researchers should observe both participant body language and the physical environment as well, to make notes about what is taking place during the interviews. Nonverbal messages to watch for include: facial expression, posture and eye contact.

Facial expression: Facial expressions provide information about how participants feel about what they are saying. While observing, a good researcher will write a list of expressions and include the message they might be sending.

Posture: The way in which people hold themselves during an interview provides important clues about how they are feeling about the discussion. Posture can convey such feelings as boredom, interest or anger.

Eye contact: Whether an individual maintains direct eye contact or not with an interviewer also can provide clues about meaning. If for example a participant looks down during an intense moment during the interview, it could indicate that he or she is not being completely honest, is embarrassed or does not want to think about it. It is the interviewer's job to be observant of these things and to try to give interpretation to their meaning.

Choosing appropriate interview media

Face-to-face interviews where the interviewer and the interviewee are in the same physical space at the same time remain by far the most common mode for conducting research. However, qualitative researchers more and more often are relying upon technology, such as telephones, instant messaging, email, computer conferencing and virtual worlds for collecting data. These methods offer new opportunities as well as new challenges that researchers should take into consideration when selecting a mode.

Telephone interviews

Telephone interviews take place on a telephone and offer a synchronous method for collecting data, although there is no visibility and, thus, no visual cues between the interviewer and the interviewees. Opdenakker (2006) suggests that telephone interviews are appropriate for data collection where:

- interviewee social cues are not critical information sources for the interviewer
- the interviewer has a small budget and little time for travel
- the research site has closed or limited access (such as hospitals, religious communities, prisons, the military, cults)
- standardization of the interview situation is not important
- anonymity is required or requested.

This approach is quick, inexpensive and effective with large groups of potential respondents. They are a good approach when the researcher does not have direct access to the participants.

Instant messaging interviews

Instant messaging interviewing uses synchronous computer communication such as chat or instant messaging. While it is synchronous, the lack of visibility between the researcher and interviewee prevents visual cues. Using instant messaging interviews for collecting information is appropriate when the conditions for using telephone interviews are met and as Opdenakker (2006) argues:

- both the interviewer and the interviewee are competent typists
- both the interviewer and the interviewee have access to computers.

This method is appealing to a tech-savvy generation and also is inexpensive.

Email interviews

Email interviews provide an approach to interviewing that is asynchronous, which can be an asset in some cases when it is otherwise difficult to gather information from interviewees. This method also does not allow for visibility between the interviewer and interviewee. Using email interviews to collect information is appropriate when the conditions for using telephone interviews and instant messaging interviews are met and as Opdenakker (2006) suggests:

- The interviewer and interviewee live in different parts of the world and are separated by several time zones so that synchronous interviewing for one party (interviewer or interviewee) is not possible or desirable.
- The interviewee will need or want to take time to respond to the developing dialogue.

This approach relies upon a commonly used, accepted and even mainstream technology and offers respondents time to think about questions prior to submitting their responses.

Computer conferencing/chat interviews

Computer conferencing is becoming an increasingly popular way to accomplish interviews, particularly when distance prevents face-to-face interviewing. This method allows for real-time, synchronous communication as well as visibility between interviewer and interviewee. Services such as Skype are helping the growth and development of this approach. Using computer conferencing is appropriate for collecting information when face-to-face interviewing is not possible and:

- social cues of the interviewee provide critical information to the interviewer
- both parties have access to computers and conferencing technology.

This approach mimics the face-to-face interview and has many of its advantages, such as being able to see facial expressions, read body language and get some insights from the interviewee's surroundings. It is also easier for the interviewee to participate in these sessions since they do not have to spend as much typing as they do with some of the other technologies; rather, a natural conversation can take place.

Interviews in online places and spaces

Researchers are showing increasing interest in interviewing in online places and spaces, including virtual worlds. Online spaces such as online courses and virtual environments allow for real-time communication. The twist is that, while there may be visibility between interviewer and interviewee, the visibility is of each other's graphically or virtually represented selves. Such representation of selves in the interview process opens a host of questions for the interviewer, such as whether the interview is gathering information about the user's perspective, and/or the avatar's, as well as whether the way in which the interviewee responds to the interviewer is based upon 'virtual' appearance. Using online and virtual world interviews is appropriate for collecting information when:

- the research question is related to the online virtual environment (such as, how does identity change in a virtual environment)

■ the research is being conducted on either an online or virtual population or an environment in which the interview is being conducted (for example, professors who teach in Second Life).

Figure 23.1 Interviewing in Second Life

Figure 23.1 provides an illustration of meeting space in Second Life.

When 'naturalistic' inquiry is desirable, engaging in research in the 'natural' or, in this case, 'technical' environment in which it occurs offers advantages.

Researcher reflections

Claire Howell Major, Author

The characteristic of conducting research in a natural setting seems like a fairly straightforward one that does not involve too many choices. Often, however, I find that there are choices related to what constitutes a natural environment. I am currently investigating tutor experiences teaching online. What is a 'natural' environment for online teachers? Is it their office where they work on their computers to teach the class or is it the online teaching environment itself (for example, the course management system, Second Life, Moodle or email)? The decision I have made is that the natural environment is the online environment in which the teaching occurs. This decision is giving me much to think about related to space and virtual space and how for me the technical has become the 'natural'.

Developing strong interview questions

Researchers using most interview types and modes will develop a question set. While some demographic questions may be necessary, interviewing questions often are open ended, although it may be necessary at times to ask a quick 'yes or no' question and then to explore the answer in more depth. Generally however, 'yes or no' questions do not encourage discussion. Questions tend to elicit information in the following areas, as King and Horrocks (2010) suggest:

- behaviours: what a person has done
- opinions/attitudes/values: what a person thinks
- feelings: what a person feels
- knowledge: what a person knows
- senses: what a person has seen, touched, heard, tasted, and smelled.

Questions may also be of several different types. We group them into initial questions, in-depth questions and follow-up questions.

Initial questions

Initial questions tend to be used at the beginning of the interview and researchers use these for obtaining background information and for laying a foundation for more probing questions later. Initial questions encourage participants to provide information in a low-risk way. Table 23.1 provides further information about these kinds of questions, in particular, highlighting their purposes and providing an example of each.

Table 23.1 Initial questions to ask

Type	Purpose	Example
Direct/descriptive/ linear questions	To elicit general often introductory information	Could you tell me what you do in your job?
Narrative questions	To elicit stories	How did you get your job?
Structural questions	To learn about basic processes needed to understand the participant's experiences	What are the stages involved in completing a sale?

Questions to gather in-depth data

After some initial questions, researchers typically begin probing for perspectives and experiences. These questions are the core of the research as they are intended to provide interviewees with an opportunity to share experiences from which meaning may be derived. In Table 23.2 we provide additional information about questions for gathering in-depth data.

Table 23.2 Questions to ask to get in-depth data

Type	Purpose	Example
Contrast questions	To encourage participants to think about extreme cases	What makes a day at work a good day or a bad day?
Evaluative questions	To enable participants to make a judgment	How do you feel after you have had a bad day at work?
Circular questions	To encourage meta-thinking	What do you consider your boss thinks about the way in which you do your job?
Comparative questions	To enable participants to put their own experiences in perspective	How do you think your professional life would differ if you were employed elsewhere?

Questions for following up

From time to time throughout the interview, the interviewee will need to ask questions to encourage participants to verify or expand an explanation that they have provided. Doing so helps to ensure that the interviewer understands the information correctly and that the interviewee has been given ample opportunity to share important information and perspectives. Table 23.3 shows more information about questions for following up on answers and explanations that participants have provided.

Table 23.3 Questions to ask as follow-up or response to participant questions

Type	Purpose	Example
Verification questions	To provide a paraphrase in order to check understanding	So you said that when you saw the advert for the job, you had a sense of what the position would entail? Is that accurate?
Prompts and probes	To enable participants to go deeper into an idea or example, to elaborate	Could you tell me a bit more about that? What do you mean when you say you are treated 'unfairly'?
Follow up questions	To elicit additional information in order to clarify confirm, or extend	You said your co-worker 'made you angry,' can you tell me some more about that? Could you give me an example?
Closure questions	To tie up a line of questioning or idea	'Did anything else happen that could help me understand your experience so far?'

Questions to avoid

While there are many questions to ask that can yield usable data, there also are questions that the interviewer should avoid. Novice or unskilled researchers can inadvertently use these questions when intending to probe respondents for additional information. Table 23.4 shows the kinds of questions interviewers should avoid.

Table 23.4 Types of question to avoid

Types	Reasons to avoid	Examples
Over-empathic questions	Ends up 'leading' the interviewee and may cause them to relate something that they would otherwise not	I can imagine that your job is quite difficult. Am I right?
Manipulative questions	Distorts data Directly leads a participant to a conclusion that they might not have come to	Your job sounds quite repetitive. Would you say that it is even worse than that?
Leading questions	Distorts and fabricates data Putting words into the participant's mouth	Given what you've told me so far, I don't suppose you'd say that you find your job to be rewarding?
'Why' questions	Tends to encourage intellectualization and can be threatening. Also implies that there is a simple answer	Why do you keep this job?

Question writing is not as simple as it might seem. Poorly written questions can confuse participants and, in turn, can lead to poor data and inaccurate interpretations. Questions should be written in simple language, which is roughly at the level of the participants. They should be short, direct and not contain multiple parts.

Developing interview protocols

Most researchers will use an interview protocol. An interview protocol is simply a written guide of the process to be followed during the interview. It consists of four main parts: the header, the script, the question set and the closing.

The header

The header is to record information about the session itself. The header typically contains the date, location and the names of the interviewee and interviewer. This facilitates working with data during analysis.

The script

The script contains essential information about the interview to share with the participant. It is common to provide an overview and purpose of the research. In addition, it is common to provide information about the way in which the interview will be recorded as well as an assurance about the confidentiality of the approach. Finally, it is common to include a reminder about informed consent.

Question set

The question set simply contains a list of the primary questions that will form the body of the interview. The questions are intended to be a flexible guide for the interview discussion. Researchers working within most research traditions tend to view them as prompts rather than scripts.

> It is a good idea to leave space between the questions for recording notes while keeping an eye on what question is to come next.

Tips

Closing

The closing of the interview protocol generally contains a few final comments about the research. It also provides a prompt to thank the participant and to provide contact information. See Table 23.5 for a sample interview protocol.

Table 23.5 Sample interview protocol

Interview protocol

Project: An investigation of lecturers learning through implementing problem-based learning (PBL)

Time of interview: _____

Date: _____   **Place**: _____

Interviewer: _____   **Interviewee**: _____

Interview procedure

You are being asked to participate in a research study investigating lecturers learning and thinking about teaching. The purpose of this study is to investigate what lecturers learn when they undertake innovative instructional strategies. During this interview, you will be asked to respond to several open-ended questions. You may choose not to answer any or all of the questions. The procedure will involve taping the interview, and the tape will be transcribed verbatim. Your results will be confidential, and you will not be identified individually.

Informed consent

Please sign the informed consent form signalling your willingness to participate.

Questions

1. What course or courses did you redesign to include PBL?

2. Describe the changes you made to the course(s) when you redesigned it to include PBL

    a. How much did you modify the existing course to include PBL?
    b. How did you modify it?
    c. Ask for copies of course syllabus and course materials.

3. How many times have you taught each course? Did the experience change over time?

4. What did you learn about teaching by implementing PBL (and how did you learn it)?

5. Did your experience as an instructor in a PBL course change the way you think about teaching? Your students? Your role as the instructor? Your content? How?

6. What did you learn about your discipline by implementing PBL (and how did you learn it)?

7. Describe your overall experience using PBL?

    a. What are the benefits?
    b. What are the challenges?

8. Are you still using PBL in the courses you teach? What has led you to that decision?

9. How have you shared your work with others?

    a. Written about it?
    b. Talked on campus?
    c. Talked at conferences?

Closing

Thank you for participating in this interview. We appreciate you taking the time to do this. We may contact you in the future for the purpose of follow up interviews. Again, let me assure you of the confidentiality of your responses. If you have any questions, please feel free to contact me by telephone at XXX-XXXX.

TIPS ON INTERVIEWING

There are many common questions that researchers ask about interviewing, which we address in this section. In addition, there are some important tips related to preparing for and reflecting upon interviews.

Common questions in designing interviews

Several questions related to planning interviews tend to come to the fore with some frequency. We provide responses to these questions below.

How many interviews should the researcher conduct?

The answer to this question greatly depends upon philosophical stance and the research approach being employed. Some researchers who are undertaking auto- or duo-ethnographic work, for example, have interviewed as few as two to four participants, although researchers who carry out studies of this size may face questions about the robustness of their studies. Other researchers have interviewed as many as 150 participants, although this high a number is difficult to justify because it is difficult to interview in depth. For a pragmatic qualitative study, typically around thirty participants is common. Researchers often carry out one main interview and then conduct follow-up interviews as well.

How long do interviews last?

The duration of the session is dependent upon a range of factors, including interviewer skill, suitability of interview questions and the level of engagement of the participant, among others. Typically, a one-on-one face-to-face interview will last for 60–90 minutes. If an interview only lasts 30–45 minutes when the desired length of engagement was an hour or more, a researcher may wish to review the questions to ensure that they are adequate to probe depth of meaning and should consider adding other probing questions to the list.

How many questions should the researcher ask in an interview session?

The answer to this question depends upon the type of interview being conducted, the types of questions being asked and the desired duration of the session. Generally, a semi-structured interview session, with a good set of ten to twelve semi-structured questions, with intent to follow up, should last about an hour.

Is it acceptable to change the questions after completing some interviews?

The answer to this question generally is yes; however, doing so may mean needing to have them reviewed by the ethics review board (see Chapter 21). After making an initial effort at drafting questions, they may require further development. One way to determine whether they need further refinement is to pre-test them. This process requires taking the question guide and trying it out with a person similar to individuals who will participate in the study. This allows a researcher to consider whether the stand-in participant understands the question in the way it is intended. Pre-testing may require a couple of iterations. The results of the bona fide interviews also will provide information about whether the questions are appropriate. With each new bit of information, questions may need refinement. This is normal and, unless the research tradition chosen requires strict adherence to a structured interview protocol, ongoing question development is part of the flexible and iterative process of data collection, ongoing analysis and feedback.

Practicalities when doing interviews

Bryman (2012) has several recommendations for preparing for interviews:

- Be familiar with the setting.
- Make sure equipment is ready and functioning.
- Make sure the setting is quiet.

After the interview, he recommends that interviewers should make notes about:

- How well the interview went (for example, was interviewee talkative, nervous, cooperative?)
- New ideas that the interview opened up.
- The setting (where it took place and how conducive the surroundings were to the interview).

Establishing rapport during interviews

Establishing rapport during an interview can be a challenge, particularly if the interviewer and the interviewee do not know each other well. A few simple practices, however, can help the interviewer establish rapport and build trust with the interviewee:

- Greet the participant.
- Introduce yourself.
- Smile.
- Shake hands.
- Comment about something likely to be of mutual interest (weather, the site, a news event).
- Provide initial information about the study and your purpose.
- Look at the speaker directly.
- Avoid being distracted by the environment.
- Nod occasionally.
- Smile and use other facial expressions.
- Pay attention to posture and make sure it is open (for example, do not sit with your arms folded while looking down).
- Encourage the speaker to continue with small verbal comments: 'yes', and 'right, right'.

ADVANTAGES AND CHALLENGES OF USING INTERVIEWS

Interviews have several distinct advantages as a method of qualitative data collection and are a personal form of research in which the interviewer speaks and relates directly to the interviewee. Interviews are a targeted form of data collection that can yield information to directly answer the research questions and also be used to probe and follow up. Interviews tend to yield in-depth information and be relatively easy for the interviewee to complete, particularly if they are done well, resemble a normal conversation and do not require the interviewee to complete any forms. In addition, interviews are well respected by most qualitative researchers, so they have credibility among those working in the field.

Qualitative interviews also have several disadvantages as they can be time consuming and resource intensive. They are dependent upon both the quality of the questions and the honesty of the participant. Yin (2009) suggests that sometimes participants may provide information they think the researcher wants to hear or casts themselves in a good light, rather than provide accurate information. Interviews also provide only the perspective of the interviewee, rather than the perspective of a group of individuals.

EXAMPLE

In the following researcher reflection, Karri Holley reflects upon using semi-structured interviews.

Associate Professor Karri Holley, University of Alabama, USA

Semi-structured interviews

Over the course of six months, I completed individual interviews with forty doctoral students enrolled in an interdisciplinary neuroscience programme. I met the students in a range of settings, including the campus coffee shop, the research laboratory and the university library. Some students spoke at length about their experiences in the programme, while others seemed hesitant and unsure about sharing their stories. We spoke across language barriers, given the high percentage of international students in the programme who spoke English as a second language, and disciplinary barriers, given my own training as a social scientist. But across these multiple settings and perspectives, I gained an understanding of what it meant to be a doctoral student in the programme. Even more than this understanding, however, I understood the programme from the students' point of view.

Using semi-structured interviews for this study allowed me to give cues to students as to my interests but also offered the students a sense of control over our time together. As I completed more interviews, I relied less on the interview protocol in front of me and more on the recurring stories emerging from the data. I consider the ability to actually engage in conversation with participants to be the hallmark of an effective interview. Rather than simply running through a laundry list of questions, the researcher makes a personal and very real connection. A shared characteristic among qualitative

Researcher reflections

continued

researchers, in my opinion, is a genuine curiosity about other people. Interviewing as a successful research technique depends on this interest.

The value of interviews is the opportunity to gain insight into how other people see and experience the world. I consider there to be few greater privileges than hearing someone tell me a story. The story is uniquely theirs. Even the acts of transcription and data analysis, labour-intensive as they might be, work to further unravel unique and compelling narratives.

CONCLUSION

Interviews are a staple of qualitative research data collection, but they should not be taken lightly. Researchers will make selections about the kinds of interviews to undertake as well as the ways in which to undertake them. We suggest that the type of interview that researchers use is dependent upon their philosophical and methodological positions; thus researchers should ensure that research framing, approach and data collection are congruent. The information in the research approaches chapters (Part 4) can provide a useful starting point for making these choices. In this chapter, we have reviewed some of the basics of designing and developing interviews with these issues in mind.

Reflective questions

Concept questions

- What is the primary reason to use interviews in qualitative research?
- What issues are important to consider when choosing the type of interview to use?
- What skills does a researcher need to conduct good interviews?

Application questions

- Which types of interviews are most appealing to you given your research approach?
- What kind of personal check list do you think might be useful for you to create as you prepare to collect data using interviews?

Key resources

Wengraf, T. (2001) *Qualitative research interviewing*, London: Sage.
This is a textbook that considers interviewing in-depth from a variety of perspectives and provides detail on how to manage interview data effectively.

Schostak, J. (2006) *Interviewing and representation in qualitative research*, Maidenhead: McGraw Hill.
This is short, sharp textbook that delves into the complexities behind using interviewing approaches by examining researchers' stance, reflexivity and issues of culture and language.

Seidman, I. E. (1991) *Interviewing as qualitative research: A guide for researchers in education and the social sciences*, New York: Teachers College Press.
This textbook concentrates upon the structure of the interview event and research project. It is grounded in the phenomenological tradition of three distinct, thematic interviews designed to question meanings of experience.

continued

Chapter 24

Focus group interviews

INTRODUCTION

While focus group interviews share some characteristics with individual interviews, they differ from them in both function and form. They allow researchers in particular to view social interactions in process and they require researchers to operate in a way that allows these to happen. For their practical utility, more and more often, qualitative researchers are choosing to adopt focus group interviews as a method of data collection. In this chapter, we describe what focus group interviews are and we consider the situations in which they are an effective method of data collection. We also provide some basic information about designing focus group interview questions and protocols, as well as practical advice for addressing the challenges that may arise during focus group interviews. Finally, we describe the advantages and challenges of this data collection method.

ORIGINS OF FOCUS GROUPS

Focus groups originated in the area of marketing in America during the early 1920s (Fern 2001). However, it was in the 1960s that focus groups became popular for collecting feedback in the forming and evaluating of television and television advertising. Marketing firms would pay small fees to members of the public to come to a focus group and express their views on the most appealing products and service. Focus groups became used more widely than surveys for gathering this kind of information because they enabled researchers to understand people's opinions and views more explicitly and so enabled the marketing profession to tailor marketing materials more effectively. Researchers have adapted these early forms of focus groups for their own ends and now researchers from myriad fields employ focus group interviews as a method of data collection.

DESCRIPTION AND PURPOSE

Understanding the difference between a *focus group* and a *group interview*, as well as an under-standing of the relationship of those two data collection forms, can help researchers to understand the focus group interview. A *focus group* is a gathering of a limited number of individuals, who through conversation with each other, provide information about a specific topic, issue or subject. Focus groups have been used in a range of settings to accomplish myriad goals; for example, evaluating products during marketing campaigns, providing political perspectives during elections and providing feedback on screenings of films and television programmes. These groups' function is to provide quick information about specified members' opinions. A *group interview* involves an interviewer who asks questions but, rather than asking them of a single interviewee, the interview is carried out with a group. In practice, in a group interview the interviewer asks a question and individuals respond in turn (Kitzinger 1994). It is a convenient way to collect data from multiple individuals at once (Kitzinger 1995). A *focus group interview* represents the nexus of the focus group and group interview, as we illustrate in Figure 24.1.

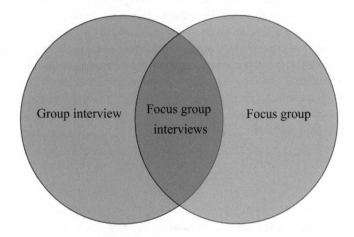

Figure 24.1 Nexus of focus groups and group interviews

A *focus group interview* at its most fundamental level is a qualitative data collection method that researchers have employed with a number of the research approaches that we described in Part 4, including pragmatic qualitative research, grounded theory and action research. It is a form of group interview but the primary difference between it and other group interviews is that interaction of the group members is encouraged, as it is in a focus group (Kitzinger 1995). In this way, focus groups can allow the researcher to view social processes in action. Thus, a focus group interview is a carefully planned and moderated interview.

Creswell suggests that:

A focus group interview can help a researcher to gather information about participants' perceptions related to a specific research area of interest. The general purpose of a focus group interview, then, is to provide a researcher with information about how a group thinks about a topic, to document the range of ideas and opinions held by members of a group and to highlight inconsistencies of beliefs among members in a particular community. Focus group interviews are particularly useful for understanding shared and common knowledge, which makes them an excellent approach for understanding cultures and subcultures and for doing cross cultural work (Hughes and Dumont 1993; Kitzinger 1995; Naish *et al.* 1994).

(Creswell 1998: 124)

See Claire's reflection about this below:

Researcher
reflections

Claire Howell Major, Author

I recently began working on a research project with a colleague who is a member of the faculty at our medical school's branch campus. The idea of the study was to help us understand medical residents' rotation experiences in a newly formed psychiatric clinic. We spent hours talking about the study design. We had a good idea of our philosophical stances, the research questions and the research approach that we wanted to employ but one of the issues that we struggled with most was the selection of the most appropriate approach for collecting data. We talked at length about the purpose of the study and what we wanted to accomplish. Ultimately, we decided that it was not individual experiences that were the phenomenon we wanted to study but, rather, the experiences of the residents as a group, a subculture in the medical school. We also wanted to understand the group's consensus and how their interactions were a part of that experience. This decision led us to select focus group interviews as our primary method of data collection, where we could observe their communication patterns and interactions in real time.

Focus group interviews are excellent for researchers who seek insight into a new area or to gain baseline information about a topic of interest. They also are useful for exploring an issue where opinions or attitudes have not been confirmed and where the researcher wants to understand group consensus, rather than individual meaning making. Focus group interviews can help a researcher to develop question guides for individual interviews as well as to verify data gathered from other methods. Creswell (1998) offers the following suggestions about when focus group interviews may be used most effectively:

> When the interaction among interviewees will likely yield the best information, when interviewees are similar and cooperative with each other, when time to collect information is limited, and when individuals interviewed one on one may be hesitant to provide information.
>
> (Creswell 1998: 124)

TYPES OF FOCUS GROUPS

There are a number of primary types of focus groups that have been differentiated by purpose (for example, Calder 1977; Folch-Lyon and Trost 1981) and are summarized in Table 24.1.

Table 24.1 Types of focus groups

Type	Purpose of the interview
Exploratory focus group	To increase researcher understanding of an issue, sometimes for the purpose of developing a research question. The group is assembled and asked some basic open-ended questions. This type of focus group typically is used in many of the research approaches we have described in Part 4 of this text, including pragmatic qualitative research and action research.
Phenomenological focus groups	To explore the respondent group's views and experiences. In this kind of focus group, a researcher seeks to understand, through group interaction, the essence of someone's experience, their consciousness and the essential features of someone's experience of a particular phenomenon. This type of focus group is often used in market research, as well as in phenomenological and phenomenographic research.
Clinical focus groups	To examine and unpack participants' hidden views to explore what might be affecting their predispositions or behaviours (Calder 1977). In practice, these types of focus groups can be very exploratory or focused on particular questions relating to, for example, someone's experiences of depression. These types of focus groups often are used in the health and medical professions, mostly when pragmatic and action research are being used.
Storyline focus groups	To enable researchers' understanding of what issues and concerns people find most important in a given situation. Participants are provided with a plot or storyline with missing components which they are asked to complete. This type of focus group often is used in action research and also with narrative approaches.
Issue development focus groups	To gain an overview of the reactions of the general populace. A presentation is made on either two or more competing or controversial topics and the group's responses are noted. This type is often used in marketing, advertising and media and it can be deployed for various qualitative research approaches.

Variations of focus groups

There also are variations of focus groups, which are more structured in approach, that some researchers use in qualitative studies. The Delphi technique and the nominal group technique are two variations of focus groups.

Delphi technique

The Delphi technique is a focus group method that is usually used to gain consensus on a particular issue. It is named after the ancient Greek oracle, Delphi, who was priestess at the temple of Apollo, the god of truth, sun and prophecy. This method is designed to gain what is termed 'opinion stability' through using iterative rounds of questioning, checking and feedback with experts. The Delphi technique became an accepted approach for gathering data from participants within their domain of expertise. Using the technique comprises undertaking three to four rounds of open-ended interview questions over a few months (at times a questionnaire is used), designed to elicit convergence of opinion on an issue. The purpose of using this approach is to seek out opinion, correlate informed judgment and expose underlying assumptions which are less likely to be found through survey questionnaires and interviews. This approach has been described as 'a method for structuring a group communication process so that the process is effective in allowing a group of individuals, as a whole, to deal with a complex problem' (Linstone and Turoff 1975: 3). It is an approach well suited to the exploration of complex areas and problems, as Hanafin *et al.* (2007) and Linstone (1978) have suggested, such as:

- Where ethical, political, legal, or social dilemmas dominate economic or technical ones.
- In situations where relevant experts are in different fields and not in direct communication.
- Where face-to-face contact is not possible or desirable owing to geographical factors.

The Delphi technique has the following characteristics:

- It is anonymous, in that expert views are used but the experts are not informed who else is being consulted.
- The process is structured so that responses are requested several times and these are funnelled and fed back so that experts can change or add to their opinions stated in the previous cycle.
- It is a reflexive approach so that experts are encouraged to be critical and self-reflexive throughout the cycles of data collection.

A researcher may choose to use this technique as it enables the collection of broad qualitative data from expert viewpoints and can include a research population from a wide and diverse background. However, it is also an approach that can be used when face-to-face meetings are not possible or when time differences and logistics also prevent frequent meetings; technology is a useful means for overcoming these limitations.

Nominal group technique

This approach tends to be more structured than focus groups and was originally developed by Delbecq and Van de Ven (1971); it comprises structured small-group discussion. The idea behind the technique is that the small-group process prevents the domination of discussion by a single person and at the same time encourages the more passive group members to participate. At the end of the discussion, people vote and a set of solutions and recommendations are compiled. The steps adopted in the process are:

- An idea or question is presented to the group by a researcher/moderator.
- Participants spend several minutes writing down their views about the topic in question.
- Each participant, in turn, contributes one idea to the facilitator, who records it on a flipchart.
- Similar suggestions are grouped together and then the group discusses and clarifies the ideas presented.
- Each participant privately ranks each idea.
- The ranking is tabulated and collated.
- The overall ranking is discussed and re-ranked (round 2).
- The votes are tallied to identify the ideas that are rated highest by the group as a whole and then the final rankings are tabulated and fed back to participants.

The advantage with nominal group technique is that voting is anonymous and everyone can participate equally in the decision making; however, a disadvantage is that opinions may not converge in the voting process and the process may seem too formal, structured and mechanical.

DESIGNING AND DOING FOCUS GROUPS

There are several issues involved in designing and doing focus groups. In particular, researchers choose roles and responsibilities, choose the medium in which they will be conducted and write focus group questions and moderating guides.

Researcher roles and responsibilities in focus group interviews

When choosing to employ focus group interviews, researchers must consider what role they will assume during the sessions. The researcher may take an active role in the discussions or choose to assume a more removed position from the group. The following are the most common researcher and moderator roles:

- *Researcher/moderator*: the researcher/moderator asks questions or prompts the group discussion.
- *Researcher observer*: the researcher observes and records, often with the following moderator roles in place:

    - *Trained moderator*: a moderator often selected by the researcher receives moderator training prior to facilitating a focus group session.
    - *Duelling moderators*: different moderators (typically not the researcher but selected and trained by the researcher) take opposite stances on the discussion topic or issue.
    - *Respondent/moderator*: one of the respondents acts as moderator.
    - *Two-way group moderators*: one focus group observes another and then discusses the discussions.

The decision of which role to assume depends upon the researcher's philosophical stance and beliefs about the researcher's place in the research (see Chapter 4 for further discussion of philosophical stance). However, most researchers choose to moderate focus group interviews themselves.

The moderator has several important responsibilities just as with individual interviews, including listening, observing and note taking. Moderating is more than just the role of being questioner and manager of responses. It requires a form of leadership of groups that can help maintain the flow of the discussion. In Table 24.2 overleaf we offer the suggestions for some of the roles and responsibilities a moderator assumes when facilitating an interview, and we provide example prompts they use to fulfil them.

Media for focus group interviews

In addition to face-to-face focus group interviews, three primary technologically enabled approaches seem to have particular utility. In *telephone focus group interviews*, the discussion is conducted over a telephone network, as in a conference call. In *computer conference or chat focus group interviews*, the discussion is conducted by way of computers connected to the Internet with instant response capability, which is essentially a computer-enabled text-based conference call. In *virtual world focus group interviews*, the discussion is accomplished in an immersive environment such as Second Life, with avatars meeting at a specific location in-world at an agreed time. See Chapter 23 for additional information about the advantages and disadvantages of these approaches.

Table 24.2 Moderator roles in focus group interviews

Role/responsibility	Prompt
Task master keeps the interview on track to accomplish the task at hand	Let's get back to the main point. I think we need to move on to the next question.
Encourager compliments individual group members on good ideas to encourage additional discussion	That's interesting. That's a great answer. I had never really thought about that before.
Probe presses individuals for deeper ideas and answers	Are you confident that that really works? Are we making a distinction between these two categories?
Clarifier ensures that the point is clear and that there is a clear understanding of what the participant has said	Let me make sure I understand what you are saying … Can you tell me a little bit more about that so I'm clear on what you mean? Let me restate this to make sure it's right. What I'm hearing is … Sounds like you are saying … What do you mean when you say … ? Is this what you mean?

Type and order of focus group interview questions

Focus group interview questions tend to follow the same categories that questions for individual interviews do: initial questions, in-depth questions and follow-up questions (see Chapter 23 for additional information about these question types). In addition to these primary types of questions, focus group interview questions may also be probes. Probes are short comments or questions to further stimulate discussion. In Table 24.3 we provide some sample questions and attending probes.

Table 24.3 Sample focus group interview questions and attending probes

Questions	Probes
How do you believe that technology is changing university culture?	
How is social media changing culture?	Facebook, blogs, Twitter?
How is instructional technology changing it?	Learning management systems, video lectures, Powerpoint?
How is information technology changing it?	Administrative tools? Library tools?

Ordering the questions can be particularly important in group discussion. Therefore, we offer the following guidelines for ordering the questions.

Move from general to specific questions

Beginning the session or topic area with the broadest questions tends to encourage interviewees to think about the topic. It also allows interviewees some room to explore ideas. This approach can help to elicit new information not yet considered. As the discussion progresses, more specific questions allow interviewees to provide more direct answers to the research questions. Structuring this way is particularly important in a group session to help the flow of the conversation.

Use behaviour questions before attitude questions

This technique allows interviewees to tell their own stories about what they have done. In addition, if respondents talk about their attitudes prior to discussing their behaviours, this may influence how they present their stories about behaviours in an effort to appear consistent with their previous statements, which is critical when they feel they may be judged by others.

Ask positive before negative questions

Beginning with positive questions sets a positive tone for the interview, which may in turn leave participants feeling more positive about their participation and, thus, more willing to participate. Starting with negative questions, on the other hand, presents too much opportunity for grousing at the outset, risking that it will become the focus of the conversation. Beginning with positives can help to keep the session balanced, which can be a challenge in a group setting.

Use unaided prior to aided questions

Unaided questions are broad or general questions that allow respondents to set the specifics themselves. Using these types of questions initially can help to reduce participant bias. For example, most often it would be more appropriate to ask what brands of smart phones they recognize, rather than beginning by asking them whether they have about the latest model of iPhone. The former allows the participants to supply information, while the latter is giving them the information. After using unaided questions, more detailed aided questions allow for gathering any specific information necessary.

The moderator's guide

A moderator's guide is a question guide with prompts and probes. It is much like the interview protocol (discussed in Chapter 23), yet it also contains information to help keep group discussion on track. The guide should be flexible enough to allow the discussion to move in different directions, yet avoid moving completely away from the topic of interest. The moderator's guide may be developed by the researcher with or without input from stakeholders. The guide typically contains several specific categories of information, including the following:

- *Logistics*: reminds the moderator about information related to the date, location and participants; also useful in data analysis.
- *Research goals*: gives the moderator the purpose of the research.
- *Respondent profile*: reminds the moderator of the interviewee's characteristics and backgrounds.
- *Topics*: helps the moderator recall the specific topics to address.
- *Timing guide*: provides a general estimate of how long respondents should spend discussing each topic.
- *Purpose of the session*: sets tone and helps build trust.
- *Disclosures*: reminds the moderator to make the necessary informational statements and to gather required consent forms.
- *Introduction*: allows the moderator to associate names and faces, and for participants to meet each other if they do not know one another already.

- *Questions and activities*: contains the question set along with any specific group activities the researcher might choose to use (such as debate, paired responses)
- *Closing*: reminds the moderator to thank participants and to provide them with researcher contact information.

In Table 24.4 (opposite) we provide a sample moderator's guide.

Planning ground rules for focus group interviews

When holding a focus group interview, it is sensible to have ground rules in place for participation and to let interviewees know these in advance. The following are some sample ground rules:

- Only one person talks at a time (if appropriate; this is usually a good idea for taping and transcription purposes).
- Confidentiality is assured.
- Keep the conversation 'in the group', since side conversations can distract the conversation flow.
- *All* should plan to participate, since everyone has important ideas and opinions.
- Anything someone wants to say is important.
- There are no right or wrong answers to questions.
- The goal is to hear all sides of an issue, positive and negative.

In addition to researcher-established ground rules, participants may be invited to establish their own ground rules for discussion. Ground rules may be posted so that they are visible to the participants during the session (for example, on flipchart paper positioned where all can see).

Managing focus groups

As focus group interviews comprise a relatively large number of individuals to interview, some problems may arise during a session.

Someone is dominating the conversation

As with any group, in a focus group discussion there may be a tendency for one or two people to dominate the conversation. Researchers should avoid letting this behaviour go completely unchecked, so that all participants have the opportunity to speak their minds. In addition, the participants who are not dominating verbally are often the most thoughtful ones and so can provide some compelling information. Moreover, women and minorities tend to be less dominating in such situations than alpha males (Aries 1976; Thomas-Hunt and Phillips 2004), so developing a plan to curb dominant behaviour can help to avoid losing important information from the whole representative group.

No one responds to a question

There are times when a researcher asks a question and participants immediately and enthusiastically begin providing important information related to the topic. There are other times when they do not. There are a host of possible reasons for a delayed response, including participants processing the question, formulating a response or being uncomfortable either with

Table 24.4 Sample focus group moderator's guide

Logistics	• Date of interview: _____ • Location of interview: _____ • Potential participants for the session: _____
Research goals	• Determine participant attitudes toward the psychiatric clinic • Determine the educational value of student participation in the clinic • Learn about the benefits and barriers of student participation
Respondent profile	Second and third year medical residents who have direct experience in referring patients to the psychiatric clinic.
Topics to cover	• Participant experience referring clinics • Participant experience seeing patients
Timing guide	• Introduction 5 minutes • Referral process 15 minutes • Educational value of referral 20 minutes • Clinic experience 20 minutes • Educational value of clinic 20 minutes • Close 10 minutes • Total 90 minutes

Purpose of the session	Thank you for joining our focus group discussion. My name is _____ and I will be facilitating our discussion today.
	    Have any of you ever participated in a focus group? We're going to be talking about the clinic today. We want to hear about your experiences with it. It's a way for you to provide us with information about this program for the purpose of improving it. Our session should last for about an hour and a half.
	    Right now, I want to let you know a few things about what we're doing today.

Disclosure	• Audio taping • Consent • Observers helping to listen/take notes • Consent forms • Plans for reporting
Procedures	• There are no right or wrong answers; we want to hear your personal perspectives; • Be honest; want to know what you really think about the clinic; • We want to hear from everyone – so don't be shy; on the other hand be considerate of others if you notice that you are talking too much and others are contributing less; • One person should talk at a time, but there is no need to raise your hand to contribute; try to let the conversation to flow naturally; • No official breaks – restrooms are located…
Participant introductions	• First name; • Year of residency; • When did you participate in the clinic?

QUESTION GUIDE

Process of referring patients to the clinic
1. Describe the reason for which you referred a patient to the consultation clinic?
2. How did the referral process go?
3. What happened after you referred the patient?

Educational influence of referring patients to the clinic
4. Did the process of referring a patient change you in any way as a doctor?
   • Probe: How?
5. Since receiving the consult, has your attitude changed towards mental health assessment and treatment for your patient?
   • Probe: How?

Experience seeing patients in the clinic
6. Tell me about the clinic.
7. In working in the clinic, how did you evaluate each patient?
8. What did you evaluate them for?
9. Was the supervision provided by the attending physician appropriate?
   • Probe: How?

Educational influence of seeing patients in the clinic
10. How do you rate your interviewing skills and assessment skills when evaluating for mental health issues in a patient in the following areas?
11. Since the consult, has your attitude changed towards mental health assessment and treatment for your patients?
    • Probe: How?

What additional resources or skills do you need, in order to be able to appropriately assess and treat patients like the one you saw in the consultation clinic, in a family medicine clinic instead?

Conclusion	Does anyone have anything else they want to add to our discussion today? What is the most important question that we have discussed?

Thank you for your help today. This session was informative. If you have any questions after the session, you may reach me by phone at XXX-XXXX.

the topic itself or responding to it in front of others. The researcher should make an effort to determine the possible reason for silence in order to devise an effective plan for moving the conversation forward.

Group veers off task

Sometimes even the most receptive and engaged group can veer off the task. Indeed, an enthusiastic group is more likely to veer off task than a less interested group. The moderator's responsibility is to keep the group on topic, even when excitement leads them in a different direction. An effective moderator's guide can help a researcher to avoid the rogue group but, at times, participants will simply need to be led back to the subject at hand.

People are having side conversations

Particularly in larger focus group interviews, it is possible for a couple of individuals to pull away from the main group and to begin a private conversation. Often these will be well-intentioned individuals who simply are discussing the issue with each other. However, when they do this, it may mean losing important data that they could have provided and it also may be distracting for other group members, as well as complicating note taking and causing 'babble' on recording mechanisms.

Respondent skips ahead

Even with the best planned moderator's guide, there will be times when an interviewee jumps ahead a question or two. If it is an important question, it may be appropriate to allow it. However, at some point researchers should address all of the questions, since they were critical enough to be a part of the question set.

People start to leave

If the focus group goes on for a long time, then it is possible that participants will decide that they must leave. The participants may well have another engagement or they simply may feel that they have contributed as much as they can. Whatever the potential reason, typically it is not possible or desirable to stop someone from leaving.

People start to check their mobile phones

Busy individuals can begin to feel the call of work during focus group sessions, particularly during a lull or after the interview has run on for a while. Participants can begin to feel distracted and desire to 'check in' for a few minutes. It is a good idea to pre-empt such problems by having a ground rule of turning off phones and keeping them off during the session.

Dealing with problems in focus groups

Try the following techniques to curb undesired behaviour:

- Pre-empt it by asking interviewees to think for one full minute before responding. This technique gives more introverted individuals time to compose their thoughts and makes them more likely to participate.
- Use body language to discourage the behaviour:
  - Turn away from the individual to discourage talking.
  - Stand behind the individual so that he or she cannot make eye contact.
- Send a short but direct verbal message:
  - Tell the interviewee that he or she has made some interesting points and that it would be beneficial to hear from some of the other participants.

If a question appears to fall flat, consider the following techniques:

- Wait. Sometimes people need time to process the question prior to responding. Silence can be difficult, but sometimes the wait is worth it.
- Rephrase the question. If after waiting there still is no response, ask whether interviewees understand the question.
- Skip it, move on, and try to return to it later.

If the group veers too far from the topic, try the following:

- Thank them for their enthusiasm and ask them to reconsider the current question.
- Remind them that the time is limited and restate the question.

If a small number of participants are having a side conversation, try the following:

- Use body language. If possible, move toward the individuals talking. Standing near them generally discourages side conversations.
- Try to make eye contact with them; this also tends to discourage side conversations.
- Ask them to share what they are talking about with the rest of the group, as it could provide some important ideas worth considering.

If it is important to focus on the question at hand before moving ahead to the area that the interviewee is discussing, try the following:

- Let the respondent finish in order to avoid losing data; the participant might not be as inclined to discuss it when the question recurs.
- Thank the respondent and ask if she/he would be prepared to provide an additional response later to a preceding question that has been omitted in error.

If it is close to the end of the session and someone is preparing to leave, try the following:

- Let the group know that there are only a few more questions that will take only a few more minutes of their time.
- Reiterate how much their participation is appreciated and stress how important their responses are to the research.

If a few participants have begun to check their mobile phones, consider the following:

- Ask the group for their full attention.
- Use body language by physically moving nearer to the phone users.
- If it is distracting others, ask them to turn their phones off.

Example

In this researcher reflection, Kamberelis describes his experience using focus groups as a form of data.

Researcher reflections

George Kamberelis, University of Wyoming

Focus groups: contingent, synergistic articulations of inquiry, politics and pedagogy

Latent in all focus group research is the potential for contingent, synergistic articulations of three functions: inquiry, politics and pedagogy. Reflecting upon how these articulations have surfaced in my own work, several key principles for facilitating effective focus groups have emerged. In what follows, I share some of these principles in relation to a study of how immigrant women from Mexico responded to the exigencies of their new life in the Midwestern United States.

First, one should expect (even celebrate) contingent group dynamics, conflict and even contradiction during focus group sessions, especially early on in any study. In this study, several highly contested discussions occurred around work and marriage that led to rich, productive discussions and even political activism about gender roles and relations and working conditions at manufacturing plants, some of which I discuss in some detail below.

Finding or creating safe, comfortable, communal meeting spaces for the participants is also very important. We mostly held our meetings in participants' homes and community sites where they got together anyway (for example, churches, community centres). Our meetings also always involved sharing meals. Most popular were potluck dinners, where each participant could bring something to share with others. These kinds of spaces and activities helped us all develop relationships that were increasingly comfortable, trusting, caring and mutually rewarding.

Exploiting pre-existing social networks also contributes to the success of focus group work. We asked our first few participants about the social settings most important to them (such as church, the Latino Coalition, work, the community centre) and to invite others from those settings to participate in our focus groups. Participants who joined our groups via such invitations were usually the ones to attend most often, to share most fully and to assume leadership roles.

Creating opportunities for building solidarity relations is also crucial to focus group work. We always allowed time for participants to mingle, share experiences, and develop friendships during our meetings. They often talked about shared problems and how to solve them. For example, they discussed how frustrating many aspects of their lives were because they didn't speak English well. These were mostly 'gripe' sessions with little talk about how to solve this problem. As an increasing sense of solidarity developed among them, however, they surfaced hidden, macro-level factors such as linguistic and cultural imperialism.

Using maximally open-ended prompts that allow participants to take over discussions almost always results in richer and more complex conversations that often surface serious issues. We once asked our participants what would make their daily lives easier. They began talking about scarce and unreliable transportation in the city.

We asked what they thought they could do to resolve the problem. Instead of answering our question, they began talking about underground car services run by entrepreneurial Mexican American men. This conversation surfaced even more serious problems such as sexism (for example, husbands who would not allow their wives to get driver's licences). Within weeks of this discussion, a group of women created a cooperative ride sharing system that eventually forced mercenary car services to lower their fees. In about a year, women who had licenses began to teach women who didn't have licenses how to drive and arranged for them to take their driving tests.

Listening for and responding to subtexts that emerge during focus group sessions often excavates important but sensitive topics for discussion. By subtexts, I mean comments that are glib but seem to index a surplus of meaning, emotional weight or some kind of root cause. For example, talk about their concerns for their children's school success and gender roles within their marriages surfaced only occasionally and in glib ways in our study. We intentionally asked them to talk more about the issues. Floodgates opened, ushering in rich discussions about macro-level problems such as sexism and financial stressors.

Finally, listening for and responding to emotional, cognitive and pragmatic breakdowns opens up kinds and amounts of talk that are easily left behind unless researchers notice and ask about them. By breakdowns, I mean occurrences such as crying, uncomfortable silences, anger and response cries such as 'I am at the end of my rope and just don't know what to do'. Responding to breakdowns turned out to be extremely important in a series of discussions about our participants' educational experiences and histories. During our initial discussion, many women shared colourful stories both of positive and negative school experiences in Mexico. We noticed one woman, however, who kept silent but seemed on the verge of tears. We revisited the topic of school experiences during our next gathering. The woman who had been silent earlier revealed that she had a learning disability, that teachers and fellow students alike had called her 'stupid' throughout school, that she still bore scars of shame from these experiences and that she feared her children might suffer the same fate. Her story led many other women to share more powerful and painful stories of negative school experiences. The group also talked about various biological, psychological and social structures and forces that can 'damage' students and they shared strategies for protecting their own children against potentially negative school experiences.

Operating according to the principles I have discussed helps to surface synergistic linkages among inquiry, politics and pedagogy that are always latent within focus group work. This potential often discloses complexities, nuances and contradictions embodied in 'lived experience'. It also indexes social and economic forces that often get glossed or explained away by one or another cultural logic. Exploiting this potential is thus particularly effective for making the invisible visible.

continued

TIPS FOR USING FOCUS GROUPS

The aim of a focus group conversation is to achieve as near as possible a natural discussion that elicits useful information about the group's consensus. The discussion should be focused on a single topic, facilitated by a moderator who keeps the group focused on that topic. The interview type tends to be semi-structured (see Chapter 23 for more information about semi-structured interviews), with some standardization of questions. Participants most often share common characteristics (such as age, gender, education, religion), intended to allow group members to be more comfortable with each other and thus to share ideas and opinions more freely, without fear of being judged. There are several practical considerations when using focus groups, which we discuss in the following sections.

Who should participate in a focus group interview?

Focus group participants should share some common characteristics, since they will talk more openly if they do. Having people with backgrounds that are too varied may restrict their openness. Researchers should consider both the research topic and the participants' characteristics (age, gender, culture) or statuses that might restrict discussion. At the same time, researchers should avoid having participants who are too familiar with one another (such as friends and family) participate, as this situation may also have a limiting effect. Grouping types of people together is important as well. For example, if conducting research on cheating on a university campus, grouping tutors and students together would deter the openness of student responses to questions. The selection process should not be overly complicated, however. Too much diversity will result in too many different groups, some of which will be meaningless. Finding an appropriate balance requires common sense.

How many focus group interviews should a researcher plan to hold?

There is no set answer to this question. It depends upon the different stratifications (such as age, educational level, socioeconomic status, health status) that the researcher deems important to the research. It also depends upon the topic. Finally, it may depend upon the variability of the responses that the researcher receives in the first iterations of a first session. Thus, a researcher should hold enough groups to ensure that participants can provide adequate information. Typical focus group studies have a minimum of three focus group interviews and a maximum of several dozen groups. Once the focus group interviews are no longer providing new information, then it is unnecessary to conduct more. This may occur after as few as three sessions.

How many individuals should be invited to participate?

The answer to this question depends largely upon the length of time available for discussion, the number of questions that should be asked, and the depth of the responses desired. Focus group interviews typically comprise six to twelve people, although many researchers consider groups of eight to be about the right size to encourage a good group conversation. There are reasons, however, to have slightly smaller or larger groups (Morgan 1996). In particular, mini-focus groups often are used; typically, these are composed of four to five members, a size that allows for diversity of opinion yet avoids having so many people involved that conversation becomes challenging. Ultimately, how many groups to have depends on how many total participants are possible and what variations exist naturally in the community.

Tips

Invite a few more people than desirable in case a few do not show up. Avoid inviting too many, in case potential participants have to be turned away.

How long do focus group interviews last?

How long the focus group session lasts varies widely and depends in part on the topic and the size of the group. A typical session lasts for around an hour and a half.

How many questions should one ask in a focus group session?

Usually ten to twelve well-developed questions will result in a one-and-a-half to two-hour group.

ADVANTAGES AND CHALLENGES OF FOCUS GROUP INTERVIEWS

Focus group interviews offer a number of advantages and challenges for qualitative researchers. For example, they are a socially oriented procedure that can encourage responses as individuals rehearse ideas with each other which results in 'a kind of "chaining" or "cascading" effect; talk links to, or tumbles out of, the topics and expressions preceding it' (Lindlof and Taylor 2002: 182). Focus group interviews mimic group discussion, which is a form of communication that occurs naturally in most communities. Focus group interviews also lead participants to engage in many different forms of everyday communication, including jokes, teasing and arguing, that can provide useful data not captured in other forms of data collection (Kitzinger 1995). In this way, they allow for in-depth discussion and for development of broad insights. Focus group interviews tend to result in information being generated more quickly than from individual interviews, since they allow the collection of opinions of more than one person in one session. Thus, they also tend to be less expensive and time intensive than individual interviews. Furthermore, they also have longevity as an approach; Merton and Kendall (1946) pioneered their use with their classic article. Focus group interviews are often well accepted by research community members and have a high face validity. In addition, increasing sample size does not require additional time or resources when using focus group interviews.

There also are a number of challenges with using focus group interviews. They are not effective in all situations. For example, they are not a good method for collecting data when the researcher wants to know how common the expressed opinions are in a community, to document behaviours or to gain a detailed picture of specific or complex beliefs. While they may be useful for uncovering information about sensitive topics, they may not be the best approach to use when the discussion has the potential to become emotionally charged. The potential for participants to influence each other exists. At times, an individual may feel silenced by the presence of others (Kitzinger 1995). In addition, participants may discuss what is socially acceptable, rather than what is really going on in the environment. They are not an appropriate substitute for individual interviews, as the two have very different purposes (individual interviews serve to explore how individuals make meaning, whereas focus groups serve to gain understanding about group consensus).

There are some practical challenges as well. They are time consuming and, given the number of participants typically involved, the number of questions that may be asked is limited. Groups may be difficult to assemble and may vary considerably in composition and responses; indeed, the quality of the data is dependent upon the willingness of the participants and the group dynamics of the conversation. Discussion should occur in an environment that is conducive to conversation, which may not be readily available. In addition, data from focus groups generally are more difficult to analyze than are data from individual interviews, because multiple voices and perspectives are present and often there is little in-depth description. Moreover, results cannot generally be used to make statements about the larger community as the sample sizes are often small and discrete.

CONCLUSION

Focus groups are appealing for researchers who seek to study the interactions and communication dynamics of groups. Those interested in natural conversations and discourse may find focus groups particularly useful. In this chapter, we have described focus group interviews and the processes that are involved in planning for them. In particular, we explored how to use focus groups and provided practical advice for employing them.

Reflective questions

Concept questions

■ What is the primary reason to use focus groups?
■ What types of focus groups are there?

Application questions

■ Would focus groups yield good information for your study?
■ What kind of focus group would you choose?
■ How would you respond if the members are not participating?

Key resources

Kitzinger, J. (1994) The methodology of focus groups: The importance of interactions between research participants. *Sociology of Health and Illness*, 16, 103–21.

Kitzinger, J. (1995) Qualitative research: Introducing focus groups. *British Medical Journal*, 311, 299–302.
Although older sources, these articles provided useful practical information about focus groups.

Creswell, J. W. (1998) *Qualitative inquiry and research design: Choosing among five traditions*. Thousand Oaks, CA: Sage.
Creswell provides some solid overview information about focus groups.

Lindlof, T. R. and Taylor, B. C. (2002). *Qualitative communication research methods (2nd edn.)*, Thousand Oaks, CA: Sage.
In this text, the authors provide useful information about the advantages and challenges of focus groups.

Chapter 25

Observation

INTRODUCTION

One of the hallmarks of qualitative approaches is that they involve investigation within a natural rather than controlled setting. Context is considered to not only be important but also central to the understanding of meaning. One of the best ways to develop understanding of context is observation. In this chapter, we describe observation as a data collection approach and its different types. We describe the different roles that researchers take on when doing observations. We offer practical suggestions for carrying out and evaluating observation in a qualitative study and finally we outline the advantages and disadvantages of this data collective method.

ORIGINS OF OBSERVATION

Observation has long been a staple of ethnographic work and so has been a method of data collection for over a century (Kawulich 2005). One early instance of a researcher using observation as a data collection approach was Cushing's four and a half year study of the Zuni people, around 1879. Cushing learned the language, participated in the customs and become clearly accepted, for which he was criticized by the establishment in losing his objectivity and 'going native', since he did not publish this work extensively. As another example, around 1888, Webb studied poor neighbourhoods, taking a job as a rent collector and later as a seamstress, although she had independent financial means. In the early 1900s, Malinowski (1922/1984) and Mead (1928), mentioned previously in Chapter 22, also used observation but they did not participate in the cultures (Bernard 1988; 1994; Stocking 1983). By the 1940s, observation was a widely used method of data collection (Kawulich 2005).

DESCRIPTION AND PURPOSE OF OBSERVATION

Observation is a form of qualitative data collection that is fundamental to understanding a culture (Silverman 2001). It is the 'fundamental base of all research methods' (Adler and Adler 1994: 389). As Marshall and Rossman (1989/1995: 79) suggest, it involves 'the systematic description of events, behaviours, and artefacts in the social setting chosen for study'. Observation is a data collection method that illustrates the larger picture or context of the research:

Observation captures the whole social setting in which people function, by recording the context in which they work. The analogy of a jigsaw is useful here. Interviews with individuals provide the pieces of the jigsaw and these pieces are then fitted into the 'picture on the box' which is gained through observation. Observation is also an on-going dynamic activity that is more likely than interviews to provide evidence for process – something that is continually moving and evolving.

(Mulhall 2002: 308)

Observation is a method for understanding how individuals construct their realities. As Mulhall (2002: 307) indicates, 'the way people move, dress, interact and use space is very much a part of how particular social settings are constructed. Observation is the key method for collecting data about such matters'. Observation is a way for a researcher to document everyday practices of participants and to better understand their experiences. It is more, however, than looking for visual cues and making notes about them. In fact, observation is usually more complex than it first appears because it involves researcher feelings and emotions about themselves, those they observe, what they observe, where they observe and the decisions they make during the process of observation.

DeWalt and DeWalt (2002: 92) suggest that 'the goal for design of research using participant observation as a method is to develop a holistic understanding of the phenomena under study that is as objective and accurate as possible given the limitations of the method'. They also suggest that it can help the researcher to develop an understanding of the context around the phenomenon of study. Observation has wide uses as it can help to answer descriptive questions, build theory or generate or test hypotheses (DeWalt and DeWalt 2002). Indeed, observation has been used with a number of the research approaches that we describe in Part 4, including pragmatic qualitative research, grounded theory, ethnography, narrative inquiry and action research.

Observation should be used if and when it serves a specific purpose in the research. This approach is particularly useful for understanding how or why something occurs within a natural setting. Schensul et al. (1999: 91) suggest that observation may be used to accomplish the following goals:

- To identify and guide relationships with informants.
- To help researchers get the feel for how things are organized and prioritized, how people interrelate, and the cultural parameters.
- To show the researcher what the cultural members deem to be important in manners, leadership, politics, social interaction and taboos.
- To help the researcher become known to the cultural members, thereby easing facilitation of the research process.
- To provide the researcher with a source of questions to be addressed with participants.

Bernard adds that observations help to improve the validity of a study (Bernard 1994). Observation also provides information about the physical environment's influence on the researched. Moreover, observation may be used to examine nonverbal expressions, to determine who interacts with whom and how, to evaluate how participants interact with each other and to gauge the degree to which they do certain things (for instance, how much time they spend in certain activities (Schmuck 1997). In addition, observation may be an effective data collection approach when self-reported information (what people say) is likely to be different from actual information (what people really do).

USES OF OBSERVATION

By way of example, asking university students directly about their social drinking behaviours could lead students to misreport information. The students might under-report or over-report their behaviours for a number of reasons. Observing students in a social setting, however, could yield more realistic information. Depending upon the research question, the researcher might wish to collect both self-reported information (gathered through interviews or focus groups) as well as take a bird's eye view of actual behaviour through attending bars used by the students.

Example

TYPES OF OBSERVATION

There are several different ways to categorize observation. The first involves the extent of the observation. Observation may be *exhaustive*, in which one observes anything and everything. The researcher assumes no base knowledge and thus tries to collect everything. An advantage is being comprehensive in coverage; the obvious disadvantage is collecting information that may not be relevant. Observation may be *focused*; in this case participants' responses from interviews then guide researcher decisions about future observation. Here an advantage is not having to collect minutiae; a disadvantage is that researchers might not uncover everything of importance during interviews and thus might miss something. Observation also may be *selective*, in which the researchers focus on various types of activities to seek out differences among them (Angrosino and Mays de Perez 2000: 677); selective observation has similar advantages and disadvantages to focused observation but is homed in more on actions of importance to the research.

Another categorization of observation is the way in which it is conducted. Observation may be *structured*, which requires predetermined observation protocols derived from theory or research. In this approach, researchers may use a template to record their observations. Templates may be developed from core concepts derived from the literature or after informal preliminary observation, and can help to provide standardized information gathered over time and systematic and focused data collection. Using this approach, however, can result in the problem of ignoring any categories or themes initially missed, so we recommend using them in conjunction with other approaches to recording. Observation may also be *unstructured*, in that what is observed is not pre-structured, but rather is based upon what stands out to the researcher at the time of the observation (Mulhall 2002). Most often qualitative researchers employ a combination of these two forms of observation.

Finally, duration is a way of categorizing observation. Observation may be long term, lasting years in the field as in the case of ethnographic research on a given culture. It may also be *short term*, lasting for a few months or weeks, depending upon the norms of the research approach.

DESIGNING AND DOING OBSERVATION

Researchers who have decided to use observation face a number of issues when designing and doing it. They necessarily make decisions, for example, about what stance to take during observation and what to observe.

Researcher stance during observation

Conducting observation requires the researcher to engage in a systematic process of planning, watching, seeing, listening, hearing, understanding and documenting. The researcher strives to maintain awareness of how participants react to research presence as well as to record any personal bias. When they use observation, researchers must engage five senses, seeking a 'written photography' of the research situation (Erlandson *et al.* 1993).

Some researchers draw distinctions between two main stances toward observation: participant and direct, which implies that it is possible for a researcher to be a 'non-participant' in some cases. We find this distinction problematic and instead would rather make distinctions about the *levels of participation* that a researcher assumes at the research site. Maggi offers the following reflection:

Researcher reflections

Maggi Savin-Baden, Author

As a young researcher I could never quite understand the difference between direct and participant fieldwork. To me if you were doing fieldwork you had to be participating. Yet I had peers, PhD students like me mainly, who seemed to feel that you could observe objectively, tick boxes and stand outside the situation. I found this troublesome – and still do. Yet what I have come to realize is that we can do fieldwork in a whole host of ways; however, I still believe that you cannot simply leave your identity at the door when engaged in fieldwork.

Sociological researchers have frequently described their roles in observation; for example, Gold's (1958) typology of participant roles as well as Alder and Alder's (1987) typology of membership roles. Although not all researchers identify with these (Angrosino and Rosenberg 2011), knowing about them can help researchers to consider how their philosophical stance necessarily positions them, and so make more considered choices about how to undertake observation. Such observation roles may be viewed on a continuum, as we indicate in Figure 25.1. The five roles mentioned are then summarized on the following pages.

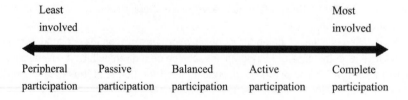

Figure 25.1 Continuum of observation roles

Amy Bender offers the following reflection on observation:

Associate Professor Amy Bender, University of Toronto, Canada

Observation raises interesting methodological and ethical questions for me as a qualitative researcher in nursing. From my interpretivist perspective, there is no such thing as 'non-participant' observation of human beings. For this reason, reflexivity in the form of journaling and debriefing within the research team is, for me, at the heart of this type of data collection. Patricia Benner (1994) argues that when the non-reflective aspects of life are the focus of inquiry, dialogue *and* observation are required. Taken-for-granted ways of being or doing things are so much a part of the participant's everyday world that interview discussions alone (a reflective exercise) will never be enough. So, observation has been valuable in my research, precisely because I am interested in getting at the taken-for-grantedness of phenomena such as nurses' relational work, tuberculosis (TB) patients' experiences of stigma and mental health and peer support.

As an observer, I take in not only what participants are doing and saying but also aspects of the setting – the ways that places and spaces themselves give meaning to participants' behaviours, ideas and beliefs. On the surface, observations include the physical environment, the people and their activities, and they have specifically identified beginning and end points. On a deeper level, observation, and all the related writing, is infused with the observer's biases, reactions, and over- and under-identification with the participants and the setting itself.

In my own study of TB nurses' relational work (Bender *et al.* 2011), I approached my role as observer by following what seemed to be straightforward procedural steps. I also explained these steps to participants as part of the informed consent process. But then it came time for the actual nursing home visits that I was observing, and my presence as observer was far from straightforward. I was part of the very relationships I wanted to study. How could I not be? So here came also reflexivity – as part of a quality interpretive analysis of observation 'data' and as part of living research ethics beyond protocols. In this study, my presence was necessarily considered within the flow of a typical home visit and I dutifully informed both nurse and client that I was only there to observe; that they should carry on as usual and 'pretend I'm not here'. But the absurdity of such was pointed out to me by the participants themselves.

In fact, trying to stand back and remain silent became a distraction and an impediment to the natural flow of the 'usual' visits. Several times, clients asked me to sit closer and, after shifting my physical positioning while still attempting to remain a silent observer, I would be then invited into the conversations. It was soon apparent that some participation on my part was not only necessary but, in fact, preferable in terms of allowing for a natural flow of conversation to happen. Yet, as a nurse researcher studying nurses, I caught myself filtering what was actually happening with questions of what *I* would do in the situation, what *I* would say if that was *my* client. Even when I could relax a little into natural conversation, the reflexive examination continued. It was an important sorting out, in the moment, of who I was as an observer and deciding how I would respond to (and record) what I observed. How would my presence in the relationships that I was also trying to observe become part of the process, the interpretations? How would I keep myself and my attitudes about nursing separate? And, now, as I continue on into other projects, how am I to participate without participating, and yet still remain authentic as my 'self'? Such is the challenge and the intrigue of observation in qualitative research.

Peripheral participation

In peripheral participation, the researcher is on the periphery and observes situations by way of web cameras or two-way mirrors. This role is the most marginal and the researcher strives to maintain a detached point of view about the site and participants, the goal being to remain as unbiased as possible. Some will argue that this form of participation is direct and non-participatory; we simply see it as the lowest level of participation; even though a peripheral actor in the site, the researcher is, in our view, always a participant in it.

Passive participation

For passive participation, the researcher is on the scene and has only minimal involvement in it. In this way, the researcher often functions as a spectator or bystander and does not interact directly with others. In this kind of participation the researcher seeks to be detached, observing rather than engaging. The researcher attempts to be as unobtrusive as possible to avoid potentially biasing the observation. This form of observation can be done relatively quickly, particularly when compared to more active forms of participation. In this kind of participation, some of the observation may happen unobtrusively (for example, on a college campus, observing the greatest traffic areas by watching for worn paths in the grass). Alternately, a researcher may select an out of the way post to assume during observation. For example, an observer seeking to understand college culture might find a corner in a student building or dining hall to watch the interactions. As with peripheral participation, passive participation does not provide detailed information about the social context being studied, which can be gained by more active participation.

Balanced participation

In balanced participation, the researcher strives to find a balance between the role of insider and outsider, participating occasionally but not fully. For balanced participation, the researcher joins in any activities that others do but not all of them. The researcher 'combines participation in the lives of the people being studied with maintenance of a professional distance that allows adequate observation and recording of data' (Fetterman 1998: 34–5). It requires the researcher to remain aware of the balance to be achieved as insider and outsider simultaneously. It also at times requires withdrawal from the site to retain the outsider role.

Active participation

In active participation, the researcher claims a central place in the site or setting, by functioning within it as well as observing it. This role is dependent upon acceptance by participants. This type of participation requires longer engagement than others: often, months to years of work in order to be accepted as part of the culture. Extensive time spent at the research site also helps to ensure that the researcher is seeing the natural phenomenon.

Complete participation

Complete participation means that the researcher is fully immersed and is an active participant; it also means that the researcher is an accepted member of the community at the research site and is engaged in insider fieldwork (see Chapter 22). The researcher often has begun the research as an insider participant and thus has a natural reason for being part of the setting. The researcher functions as part of the group being studied. The complete participant seeks to avoid changing the research environment, whether observing overtly or covertly.

Claire Howell Major, Author

Researcher
reflections

In the research project that I have described elsewhere in this book, I was investigating tutor experiences with problem-based learning. It was the first time, during my research career, that I assumed the role of complete participant. In the past, I had always tried to function as a passive or balanced participant, so adopting this research project meant taking on a completely different role. I worked on the site and the participants were my friends and colleagues. I had a vested interest in the project's success, particularly since I was serving as a project leader. I wondered whether I could even do research as such an involved member of the community. That was when I began to consider that a researcher is never neutral and bias free. It occurred to me that I never had been, nor ever would be, neutral as a researcher. I realized, rather, that there are degrees of neutrality and that, in this case, I was at the extreme end (for me) of not being neutral. I decided that the story of the participants needed to be told and that I could do it because I understood nuances that no one else would about the site. I involved a co-researcher, who had no connection to the site, because I thought she could help me see things that I was too immersed to notice or grasp as being important. It was a great experience and a significant point of change for me in my thinking as a researcher.

How to choose a role

Atkinson and Hammersley (1994: 249) suggest four dimensions of participant observation that should be considered when selecting a role:

■ Whether the researcher will be known to be a researcher by all those being studied, or only by some or none.
■ How much, and what, will be known about the research by whom.
■ What sorts of activities the researcher will carry out in the field and how this will locate her or him in relation to the various conceptions of category and group membership used by participants.
■ What the orientations of the researcher are; how completely and consciously the researcher will be able to adopt the orientation of insider or outsider.

Atkinson and Hammersley suggest several additional factors to consider when selecting a role:

■ Conditions of the site.
■ Researcher abilities, philosophical perspectives, demographic characteristics.
■ Potential changes during the research process that may occur in the researcher, the researched or the site.

We see it as the researcher responsibility to provide a strong rationale for the selection of their role.

WHAT TO OBSERVE

Merriam (1998) suggests making sure that observation fits with the purpose of the study and the research question. Wolcott (2001) similarly suggests that researchers ask themselves to consider what they want to know and what information they can gather to best answer that. Creswell (1998) provides some specific details, suggesting that the observer may wish to focus on several points: physical setting, participants, activities, interactions, information delivery, 'subtle factors'. Since these can be useful items for including on a template, we provide additional details about these sources of observational data.

Physical setting

Observing the physical setting provides critical contextual information about the research environment that frequently is overlooked. The layout of a site and its architecture and pathways can provide researchers with a sense of how space is used, as well as a general sense of the flow of activity. Art plays a critical role in understanding a site, as paintings, pottery and sculpture provide important clues about how participants see the world and what they deem beautiful, useful or representational. On a college campus, for example, one could examine the layout of the grounds, the style of architecture, the art that is displayed, the graffiti, bumper stickers on cars and so on to provide information about the context.

Participants

Observing participants on site can provide information about the participants themselves. What are they wearing (formal or casual)? How quickly do they move? Do they smile or frown? All of these things can provide important contextual cues. On the college campus, one might observe students, lecturers, administrators and service personnel to get a general sense of who they are and how they feel about being there.

Activities

A researcher may also choose to observe activities that take place on a research site. Activities provide important information about a culture, in that they show what participants enjoy or feel that they need. On the college campus for example, a researcher could observe that there are extra-curricular classes, plays and concerts, which may signal that the institution values knowledge, learning and culture.

Interactions

A researcher may also choose to observe interactions. These may include whether and how participants come together. Do they stay isolated from each other? Partner? Form small groups? Are there interactions taking place in the form of face-to-face communications? Are they spending time texting instead of conversing? Answers to these questions provide important contextual clues. In the case of the college campus, the researcher may observe groups of students, groups of tutors, tutor and student interactions, the use of mobile phones, and so on. The researcher may consider who is included in interactions and who is (at times choosing to be) left out.

Delivery of information

An observer at a site may wish to observe how information is delivered, which may happen in a number of ways, from informal discussions to more formal meetings to communities of practice. In the case of the college campus, a researcher might notice that a campus tour, for example, is a way that knowledge of the institution is delivered to outsiders or newcomers.

'Subtle factors'

An observer will want to pay careful attention to what Creswell (1998) refers to as 'subtle factors'. These include nonverbal or symbolic communication. This could include paying attention to participant's talk (including intonation) and body language. The researcher seeks to observe these things and considers their relevance and significance, particularly in light of the research questions.

TIPS FOR CONDUCTING OBSERVATION

We offer the following tips for conducting observation.

- *Have a plan.* A researcher generally begins with an expressed plan, although this is not always the case. The plan typically requires **prolonged engagement** in the field with indications of when observation will be standardized and when it will be improvised. The plan also specifies what to record (and what to leave out). When observing, the researcher carefully watches individuals as they are engaged in natural settings and situations. The researcher makes clear notations and detailed recordings of how observation occurred, as well as clear notations of exactly what happened (typically without interpretation at this stage).

> **Prolonged engagement**
> Staying in the research context long enough to understand what is taking place in terms of language, cultures and interactions

- *Positionality matters.* What a researcher brings in terms of prior experiences and beliefs necessarily influences the way research is conducted, which in turn influences results.
- *Place matters.* Where a researcher chooses to conduct observation is a direct result of the view of the researcher's role in observation; it also will influence the participant's view of the researcher. This, in turn, will influence the findings of the observation. Finding an unobtrusive place can allow for more natural action on the part of the participants to unfold.
- *View matters.* It is possible to observe at least two different levels. Merriam (1998) suggests moving from a wide to a narrow-angle perspective, focusing on a single person, activity or interaction before returning to the overall situation.
- *Presence matters.* The presence of the researcher necessarily influences the situation, regardless of how much distance is desired. (*Much is made of this in writings about research, but it is unavoidable and therefore, although it needs to be acknowledged, making too much of it can be a mistake.*)
- *Ethics matter.* While some researchers have argued that, at times, covert observation is warranted (see Mays and Pope 1995; Clark and Moss 1996; Johnson 1992; Mulhall 2002), we believe that one should avoid observing people without their consent if at all possible. It is important to respect their rights to privacy and to respect them as individuals (see Chapter 21). It is also important to remember that people rarely know to what they are consenting, so their agreement is provisional upon seeing how they will be portrayed. It is

difficult at times, however, to obtain consent from everyone being observed. DeWalt *et al.* (1998) recommend that the researcher take some field notes publically to reinforce what the researcher is doing; collecting data for research purposes. It is also important to understand cultural norms and to address issues such as potential exploitation and inaccuracy of findings (Marshall and Batten 2004).

EVALUATING THE QUALITY OF OBSERVATION

Observation is a difficult thing to evaluate, since it is contingent upon the researcher's position, focus, research question and choice of method. As a data collection approach, it is also dependent upon what role the researcher assumes. Thus, assessing a peripheral observation or a passive observation would be very different from observing an active or complete participant observation. We offer the following general considerations:

- Has the researcher identified a clear role as observer?
- Is this role consistent with the researcher's philosophical position?
- Is the role appropriate given the research question and method?
- Has the researcher maintained the role throughout the study, or provided justification for changing roles?
- Has the researcher spent sufficient time immersed in the field?
- Has the researcher gathered the information needed to answer the question?

ADVANTAGES AND CHALLENGES OF USING OBSERVATION

Observation can provide a researcher with nuanced contextual information about the research and the participants within a natural environment, which could not be derived from another data collection approach. It can allow researchers to access the 'backstage culture' (de Munck and Sobo 1998: 43). A researcher invariably will see things that those who are routinely involved may not notice, as well as gain information that people may not be willing to share in interviews. Being on the scene in context can improve rapport with participants and encourage free or freer exchange of information. And it can allow them to view or participate in unscheduled events (de Munck and Sobo 1998).

One of the greatest disadvantages of observation, however, is that a researcher's presence might have an effect on the situation, although Frankenberg (1980: 51) states that, 'I do not think that a single observer in, say, a village or tribe is going to change custom and practice built up over years or even centuries'. Researchers also must face their own subjectivity; Mulhall provides her perspective:

> In my view observational data, rather more than interview data, are subject to interpretation by the researcher. I say this because observers have a great degree of freedom and autonomy regarding what they choose to observe, how they filter that information, and how it is analysed.

> (Mulhall 2002: 308)

Moreover, a researcher's participation in a community might cause him or her to develop favourable or unfavourable interpretations of participants or to have an emotional response to the participation, although this too may be used to advantage. Jorgensen offers the following illustrative account:

> In seeing a setting from my (1989) study of occult claims to knowledge, I planned to find a particular group ... I found participation with most groups to be unpleasant. As a scientist, these beliefs and practices, though very entertaining, were difficult to take seriously, especially during sustained periods of intimate interaction with members of a group. I began to question whether or not it would be possible to conduct the study as planned. Fortunately, I resolved this difficulty by performing a series of roles (seeker, client, occult practitioner) that placed me in direct contact with the occult milieu — eventually as a fully participating insider — and did not require ongoing involvement with a particular cultic group. Though entirely unplanned at the outset, this adaptation to the conditions of the field of study actually facilitated detailed study of a larger set of phenomena (networks of occultists) than would have been possible had I found and remained involved with one group.
>
> (Jorgensen 1989: 41–2)

Further, it is possible that a researcher simply is not interested in what happens out of the public eye. It simply will not provide information they need about their phenomenon of interest (de Munck and Sobo 1998); for example, if they are interested in the subjective life experiences of participants. Finally, it can lead to erroneous description, since researchers may find some subjects simply more interesting subjects of observation than others; they might, for example, be more interested in observing political or religious activity than eating and sleeping (Johnson and Sackett 1998).

A researcher should consider whether potential advantages outweigh disadvantages when making a decision about whether to employ observation as a method of data collection.

CONCLUSION

Conducting observation within the environment under investigation can yield essential information about it, yet all too frequently researchers do not employ this data collection approach when it could add value to the study or they are not as systematic about the processes as they might be. In this chapter, then, we describe observation as a systematic approach for data collection that may be used in qualitative research. Observation can be a powerful way to collect qualitative data. It is easy to take observation lightly, yet observation is truly a challenging data collection approach. If it is to be done at all, it should be done well, and this requires time, patience and skill.

Reflective questions

Concept questions

■ What is a good reason to use observation?
■ What information can you ascertain by using observation?

Application questions

■ What role is most suitable to you given your philosophical stance and research approach?
■ What should you take with you when you observe?
■ How can you signal your purpose to those whom you are observing?

Key resources

Kawulich, B. (2005) Participant observation as a data collection method. *Forum Qualitative Sozialforschung/Forum: Qualitative Social Research*, 6(2), Article 43. This article provided us with a useful overview of observation. In particular it contained some information about the origins of observation that is not readily available in other sources.

DeWalt, K. M. and DeWalt, B. R. (2002) *Participant observation: A guide for fieldworkers*. Walnut Creek, CA: AltaMira Press. This book provides useful practical information for carrying out observation. It informed our thinking about several aspects of observation, in particular the tips for carrying out observation.

Chapter 26

Documents

INTRODUCTION

People inhabit worlds that are increasingly documented. They journal, tweet or blog their experiences; record their conversations through emails and through Twitter; participate in virtual communities in which their interactions are captured; and take photos to preserve images of events. They increasingly are using computers to document their experiences through a combination of text and images, such as through video smart phones, video sharing (such as Flickr) and image sharing or social network sites (such as Facebook). Organizations of varying types have their own documents, which include strategic plans, mission statements and logos. They too are increasingly using computers to display and communicate such information; for example, through websites and blogs. These **documents** can provide a researcher with a rich and often readily accessible source of information for understanding participants and the research context. Many qualitative researchers choose to use documents as a form of data, whether as the sole form of data or in combination with other forms of data. In this chapter, we discuss forms of documents that researchers may choose to use in their studies. We describe the opportunities and challenges that using documents present researchers.

Documents
Written, printed, visual or electronic matter that provides information or evidence or that serves as an official record

ORIGINS OF USING DOCUMENTS

The disciplinary origins of using documents to gain understanding are many and varied. Aristotle's work on interpretation, for example, provides groundwork for much of contemporary interpretation. He states that:

> But the mental affections themselves, of which these words are primarily signs (semeia), are the same for the whole of mankind, as are also the objects (pragmata) of which those affections are representations or likenesses, images, copies (homoiomata).
>
> (Aristotle, De Interp. i. 16a4).

Scholars, prior to the 1900s, used a special form of hermeneutics to examine biblical passages and, after the 1900s, largely influenced by the work of Heidegger (see Chapter 2), the work changed toward a more interpretive reading of any text. Humanists such as historians, for example, have long used analysis documents, such as diaries, in their work. English scholars have long examined texts along with authors' personal correspondences and diaries. Anthropologists also have used documents, most often to supplement interviews and observations. Sociologists similarly have used historical document analysis to supplement their work.

Likewise, visual documents have long been a part of arts and humanities research. Historians, for example, have used images in their work, particularly photographs. In the 1960s, with the development of culture studies, researchers began to consider kinds of images, modes of production and contexts of dissemination. During the last decade, visual data have gained acceptance in a range of disciplines and fields in which qualitative researchers work (Prosser 2011). In particular, the advent of personal computers and online environments have led to the creation of myriad documents that can be useful to qualitative researchers. Documents, then, whether textual, visual or electronic, have over time become an increasingly common form of qualitative data.

DESCRIPTION AND PURPOSE OF DOCUMENTS AS DATA

Documents are records of things that may take written, photographic, electronic or other forms. The underlying intent of a document is to convey a message or information to individuals or groups who will consume it. Thus documents are 'constructed in particular contexts, by particular people, with particular purposes, and with consequences – intended and unintended' (Mason 2002: 110). Documents can provide important clues for a researcher about the research context.

Using documents frequently is associated with several of the research approaches we described in Part 4, such as pragmatic qualitative research, grounded theory, ethnography and narrative approaches. Qualitative researchers choose to include documents as data in such studies for a number of reasons. Using them, for example, can provide qualitative researchers with information that they might not be able to gain through other data collection approaches. These data also are invaluable when the research context emphasizes the value of them (for example, online community or organization with prominent branding). Documents, then, provide information about the image that individuals or members of an environment or organization actively seek to convey to others. They are particularly useful for providing historical context and background information of a research environment. According to Silverman:

> qualitative researchers use text to understand the participants' categories and see how these are used in concrete activities like telling stories (Propp 1968; Sacks 1974), assembling files (Gubrium and Buckholdt 1982) or describing 'family life' (Gubrium 1992). The constructionist orientation of many qualitative researchers thus means that they are more concerned with the process through which texts depict 'reality' than with whether such texts contain true or false statements.
>
> (Silverman 2005: 160)

Moreover, documents both contain content and are agents that may be mobilized by others (Prior 2003).

TYPES OF DOCUMENTS

Documents are a representation of information with the intent to communicate. Typically, documents provide written information. Documents may be primary sources, developed directly by those who are part of the environment or culture, or secondary sources, developed by others who are outsiders, separated by time, place or another factor. There are many different types of documents that qualitative researchers may be interested in collecting, and the different types of documents represent different genres of communication (Orlikowski and Yates 1994). Some of these types include:

- Textual documents, such as the following:
    - *Public documents.* Public documents are items that are accessible by anyone using fairly standard and accessible means of retrieval. Examples of such documents include articles, documentaries, books, newspapers, novels, speech transcripts and published strategic plans.
    - *Practical documents.* Practical documents are not often as readily available as public documents but, rather, include those written products that are used regularly by members of a community. Examples of such documents include training manuals, procedure manuals, newsletters and flow charts.
    - *Files.* Files are generally of historic interest, as they preserve records of members of a community. They may include statistical records, meeting minutes and memos and computer files.
    - *Personal documents.* Personal documents are those that an individual creates and uses. Examples of personal documents include letters, journal entries, portfolios, case notes and even flipchart/blackboard/whiteboard notes.
- Visual documents. There also are many visual documents that may be of interest to researchers, including photographs or logos.

LOGOS AND HOW THEY CAN COMMUNICATE

Cousin (2005: 121) has pointed out that virtual learning environments are fraught with images that are deeply problematic, such as 'a little white male professor' that adorned Web CT (Blackboard) as its premier logo. Such images of scaffolding, structure and safety can, we suggest, indicate stability and control.

Example

- Audio visual documents. This category includes media such as videos or narrated slideshows.
- Electronic documents. While there is some overlap between electronic documents and textual and visual documents, as those may be put online, increasingly individuals are living their lives online and some documents reside online or in virtual space. These documents are of growing interest to researchers. We provide an example of an electronic document in the following example on page 406 overleaf.

ONLINE GAMING ENVIRONMENT AS DOCUMENT

Bennerstedt (2008) undertook a study of gamers' practices in the game, World of Warcraft™ and drew situated activity systems, which is:

how participants deploy the diverse resources provided by talk [. . .], sequential organization, posture, gaze, gesture, and consequential phenomena in the environment that is the focus of their work in order to accomplish the courses of action that constitute their life world.

(Goodwin 2000: 1519).

Bennerstedt examined semiotic fields present in the game and used video recording to analyze participants' discourse using interactional analysis in order to understand cues used by players.

DESIGNING AND DOING STUDIES USING DOCUMENTS

Researchers have a range of issues to consider when choosing documents. They must determine whether they have the necessary skills, identify a specific purpose for the use of documents, determine systems for collecting and classifying them and examine their quality.

Skills required of a researcher using documents

Using documents may seem like a simple undertaking but, in fact, it is a rather complex task that requires a high level of skill on the part of the researcher. A researcher will need the skill of categorization in order to be able to make an initial assessment of the kind of document under consideration. This skill requires a high level of attention to detail as well as a high level of organizational skills to deal with a vast amount of content and visual information. The researcher also will need the skill of contextualization to consider its significance to the larger culture and environment. Researchers should possess the skill of criticality, which requires interrogating a document on a number of levels, from the level of intent with which its creator developed it, its purpose, its level of depiction of reality or its staged reality. The researcher should be able to consider the creators' perspective and distance from the document or object and the framing of it.

Collecting, organizing and recording documents

Collecting and organizing documents requires collecting as many relevant documents as possible. Those that cannot be directly collected may be copied, photographed or saved to a computer; the keyword is relevant. Researchers must cull through documents and save only those that are

Organizing

A simple physical or digital filing system can be a useful way to store and organize information. Separate files may be created for the different kinds of data, which may be organized alphabetically. Manila folders with labels or their digital equivalent are appropriate for this purpose. Software programs, such as Nvivo, allow for managing electronic documents and visual data. Items should be filed immediately so that they do not accumulate into a pile that must be later sorted; stacking is not a good substitute for filing, since stacks can be intimidating and inefficient.

relevant; although it is tempting to retain all possible information, extraneous information can be simultaneously distracting and misleading. Often, a collection of documents can become unwieldy.

Assessing the quality of documents

Scott (1990) proposed a set of criteria for evaluating the quality of documents. These criteria require asking a set of questions about the document:

- Is it authentic?
- Is it credible?
- Is it representative?
- What does it mean?

Attending each of these questions are some issues that researchers should consider when evaluating the quality of the source.

Is the document authentic?

The question of whether the document is authentic may be considered in the light of two key questions:

- Is the source genuine?
- Was it developed by an individual or group with authorized credentials?

Researchers may consider Platt's (1981) suggestions to determine when a document is genuine or when its authenticity requires close scrutiny. According to Mogalakwe (2006: 225), close scrutiny is required when:

- it does not make sense logically or has obvious errors
- there are internal inconsistencies in terms of style and content
- there are different versions of the same product
- the version available is derived from a dubious, suspicious or unreliable secondary source
- it has been in the hands of a person or persons with vested interest in a particular reading of it.

The researcher should strive to ensure that the document is genuine and has integrity. In addition to authenticating the product itself, a researcher also should authenticate authorship of the document, since some documents might be forged or falsified, such as letters, diaries or photos used on websites.

By way of an example of determining the authenticity of a document, a researcher might determine a need to examine the contents that an academic dean submits for an annual report. The researcher might consider the questions above to determine whether it is genuine: are there obvious errors in the report? Are there style inconsistencies? Do different versions of the document appear in different contexts (for example, one sent to the provost, one to external constituents)? The researcher might also consider the authorship of the document. The dean is generally an expert who can report on such matters, but can the researcher assume that the dean, rather than a public relations or communications office, drafted the statement? Does it matter who created it? These are important considerations when determining authenticity, and they are particularly important to the researcher who has not recorded the information directly.

Is the document credible?

The question of whether a document is credible is related to whether it is authentic. The answer may depend upon whether the document is error or distortion free, which in turn may be related to the purpose of the document. Credibility is related to whether the creator had a sincere viewpoint. Credibility may be enhanced by the fact that documents tend to be created independently and prior to the research, but the perspective and purpose of the works are still in question. In the example about the annual academic report, the question becomes whether the statement is intended to be accurate and unbiased or whether it is designed to promote the College, enlist gifts from donors, or attract potential students. The answer might have implications for whether the document is error or distortion free and thus credible.

Is the document representative?

The question of whether the document is characteristic of others involves a consideration of whether it is like the full population of potential articles. A researcher might consider whether recording has been selective (for example, only successes) in the documents and what members have preserved (for instance, meeting minutes) as against what has not been recorded and retained. A researcher should consider the degree of confidence in the data set and its integrity. In the example of the annual report, a researcher might consider whether the document is similar or dissimilar to those in the past. A researcher might think about what information has been reported and what has been left out.

What does the document mean?

The question of what the document means is related to whether it is clear and comprehensible. Researchers might ask what the content means or what it might mean to its author or its intended audience? What is its significance? Is it a statement of current conventions? Or is it a statement of projections or intentions? Scott (1990) suggests that documents may have both a literal and a face value from which the audience may reconstruct significance. Interpretive understanding, on the other hand, occurs when the research relates the literal meaning to the context in which documents were created or produced (Mogalakwe 2006). Thus, the representations should be considered as a whole. In the example of the dean's annual report, the dean may choose to report faculty members' grant funding from external grants only or from both internal and external grants. Both reports might be technically accurate, but they present a different emphasis on the work that faculty members have done and may be considered in the context of a larger picture (for example, whether the college is seeking increased prestige). These are critical considerations for a qualitative researcher who has determined to use documents.

Analyzing documents

To begin analyzing documents, the author in a sense engages with the author of the document being studied (ten Have 2004). As Scott (1990) suggests:

> Analysis involves mediation *between the frame of reference of the researcher and those who produced the text. The aim of this* dialogue is to move within the 'hermeneutic circle' in which we comprehend a text by understanding that frame of reference from which it was produced, and appreciate that frame of reference by understanding the text. The researcher's

frame of reference becomes the spring board from which the circle is entered, and so the circle reaches back to encompass the dialogue between the researcher and the text.

(Scott 1990: 31)

Scott recommends a consideration of the movement of content from author to recipient: intended content, received content and internal meaning.

Practically, when analyzing documents, the researcher tends to focus on how and for whom the document was created. Researchers should consider what was and was not included in the document. Finally, a researcher may ask some of the following questions:

- Who created the document?
- How was the document presented?
- What illustrations and examples did the creator use?
- What was the general format of the document?
- For what purpose was it created?
- Who was the intended recipient?
- How was the document used?
- On which occasions was the documents used?
- In what places was the document used?
- Who used it?
- What behaviours or rituals accompanied its use?
- What do members of the community say about it?
- How do individuals and groups judge it?

These questions provide an initial consideration of how researchers may begin to analyze documents. Content analysis is an analytic approach frequently employed with documents. Keyword analysis, constant comparison and semiotic analysis has also been frequently used with documents. We describe specific approaches to data analysis further in Chapters 27 and 28.

TIPS FOR USING DOCUMENTS

While documents can play an important role in data collection, there are several practical points to take into consideration when planning to use them. Among these are the following:

- Provide a strong rationale for using documents. For example, they often are well suited to be paired with other data collection techniques, and using only documents requires using a compatible research tradition as well as a good reason for excluding other forms of evidence.
- Ensure that document use is appropriate and within the bounds of the researcher's philosophical stance and research method. As Atkinson and Coffey suggest:

> In paying due attention to such materials, however, one must be quite clear about what they can and cannot be used for. Documents are 'social facts', in that they are produced, shared and used in socially organized ways. They are not, however, transparent representations of organizational routines, decisions-making processes, or professional diagnoses. They construct particular kinds of representations with their own conventions.

(Atkinson and Coffey 2004: 58)

■ Ensure that the material provides evidence that addresses the research question. If it does not, it should be excluded.

■ Ensure the purpose is clear. Haw and Hadfield (2011: 2) suggest some important considerations for using video in social science research, which we suggest are important for considering how to use any document. Researchers should consider whether they are using visual data for:

- extraction – to examine an interaction or issue to study in depth, such as an interaction between client and counsellor in therapy.
- reflection – to encourage those in the research to reflect upon their practices; therefore, sessions are recorded in order to discuss what took place and examine particular practices, such as how to improve teaching practice.
- projection – to help participants to understand and unpack issues such as power, racism and stereotyping.
- participation – to enable participants to display and voice their views in order that they can help shape the design, process and product of the research.
- articulation – to enable participants to represent and communicate their view to others by visual means.

Taking these practical considerations into account can help a researcher to make a decision about whether and how to use documents and can ensure that the appropriate steps have been taken to use them legally.

ADVANTAGES AND CHALLENGES OF USING DOCUMENTS

Using documents has unique advantages and disadvantages. While they provide further evidence to help a researcher understand a research environment or culture which is useful in and of itself, there are several additional advantages to using documents. The behaviour that documents capture occurs in a natural setting, generally prior to the research project and generally without the intention of serving as data, so it tends to have a strong face validity. Documents tend to reveal what people do or did as well as what they value. These representations are tangible examples of social meaning-making. There are also some disadvantages attending the use of documents. A focus on documents is fairly new in qualitative research, so there may be resistance from those who may perceive the research to be less scientific or empirical than other data forms. Visual documents also tend to be created for a specific purpose (such as promoting a person or an organization), so in some ways documents can be 'staged'; thus, they tend to reveal what the cultural group wants others to know about it.

In the following author reflection, Claire provides an example of a study using documents.

Claire Howell Major, Author

In a study designed to investigate changes attending faculty adoption of problem-based learning (Major and Palmer 2006), my colleague Betsy Palmer and I decided to do a case study of faculty teaching at a comprehensive university that was undertaking a grant-funded project to incorporate problem-based learning across the undergraduate curriculum. We used a range of data collection approaches but we relied most heavily on individual interviews with faculty members.

In addition to the interviews, however, we deemed it important to collect documents to support and explain findings from interviews. To learn more about the courses, for example, we collected syllabi from the faculty members who had elected to use problem-based learning in their courses. We elected to examine syllabi since they tend to serve as blueprints for the course. Syllabi tend to contain some standardized information typical to the institution but also information that differs from course to course, depending on the instructor, discipline and course level.

Analyzing what the syllabi emphasized provided us with important information about what each instructor was trying to accomplish in a specific course. When analyzing data, we considered the following questions:

- Who created the syllabus?
- Who used the syllabus?
- How was the syllabus used?

Some faculty members, for example, heavily emphasized the learning outcomes they hoped students would achieve, while others emphasized the problem and related assignments.

There were several other important differences as well. Many syllabi, for example, were created by a team of faculty members who worked together for the grant project, indicating the emphasis the institution had on collaboration. Not only did the faculty members and students use the syllabi, but also grant project staff used the syllabi, which evidenced that more individuals were paying attention to the course than the usual students and faculty members. The syllabi were used by project staff to document evidence of problem-based learning in interim and final reports, thus demonstrating an emphasis of the project on accountability. All of these were indicators that problem-based learning was a larger phenomenon on campus than an individual faculty member or student might have conveyed. They provided important information that the researchers could address in interviews with faculty members, project staff and administrators. The differences the researchers found in syllabi, taken together with other data, were telling. We found that the syllabi provided insights into education processes, the values of the institution, and the meaning of education as members constructed it. Leaving them out of data collection and analysis could have had a detrimental effect on our understanding.

EXAMPLES

In the following researcher reflection, Eric Laurier describes his ethnographic study in which he used video transcripts.

Researcher reflections

Eric Laurier, University of Edinburgh, UK

Habitable cars: the organization of collective private transport

The world's inhabitants are spending more of their lives inside the car than ever before. Sustainable transport requires people to try and travel together whenever possible, rather than the current situation where the majority of cars that can carry multiple travellers only carry one. Much of existing research on car transport has been based either in modelling the causes of accidents or doing cost–benefit analysis of modal choice or route selection.

My colleagues and I undertook an ethnographic project, first to describe the social activities that have emerged in, been displaced or translated into the space of the car, its journey and related sites and, second, to investigate the arrangements of travelling together and car sharing.

Our approach was aimed at a better understanding of the perspectives of the car travellers and what they actually do during their journeys. While the overall activity might be travelling, within that activity, there are numerous other practices, some of them driving-related and the majority unrelated to driving, if woven through it. The ethnography was concerned with the practical reasoning of drivers and passengers exhibited in their language, gestures, use of objects and orientation to the road environment.

Approximately fifty participants consisting of drivers and passengers of fifteen vehicles were recruited for the study; we selected them to provide a contrasting mix of vehicle type, relationships (such as families, co-workers, friends) social classes, ages and gender mixes. What was also of importance was catching a variety of journey types such as school-runs, commuting and shopping trips.

During data collection, I spent one week travelling in each car getting to know its occupants and their journeys and then handing over a pair of video cameras to the car travellers. The cameras were consumer-level cameras and their placement in the car was decided by the travellers, though a view of the road and the car interior was the aim. The travellers were asked to record six typical journeys, although in practice they often recorded more. By the close of the data collection, there were 240 hours of video recordings of car journeys. A corpus of selected clips that were consented to by the travellers was then assembled for ongoing analysis; these have been used by other research projects on car travel.

Data analysis was carried out through the data session format that has been developed in conversation analysis and ethnomethodology. The project team, with a number of visiting experts, would regularly spend two hours slots examining short fragments of the recordings in great detail. The ambition being both to identify recurrent

continued

methods utilized by car travellers and to describe the lived work of whatever practices were then being accomplished. Figure 26.1 is a fragment of a longer transcript used to examine how the two passengers assess the driver cornering around a roundabout:

In the first frame, the front-seat passenger is replying briefly to an earlier comment by the passenger in the rear who's been discussing trying out various kinds of mountain bikes. The interest is not so much on the topic of the conversation as how their speaking becomes adapted to the occupants' shared awareness of the road situation. What is

Figure 26.1 Video transcript from an ethnographic study investigating car sharing (Laurier *et al.* 2012).

continued

particularly visible in this part of the transcript is the passengers' monitoring oncoming cars until they make it on to the roundabout. The rear seat passenger disengages first to return to describing her difficulties with one mountain bike (frame 3) then we see the front seat passenger also disengage her attention and look out of the side window (frame 5). Later in the transcript, the driver throws the passengers around in their seats as he exits the roundabout and this leads to the assessments of his driving and an account from him that he is driving a hire car that is smaller than his own car.

The asymmetries of the tasks undertaken by and incumbent upon driver and passenger were an abiding feature of travelling together. Where much of existing research on the role of passengers treated them as a distraction, our ethnography demonstrated they have a number of roles in supporting the driver (for example, navigating, noticing hazards). A hint of this can be garnered from the figure where both passengers turn to watch the approaching vehicles on entering the roundabout. Cars turned out to be key sites for relationships of caring between most obviously families but also co-workers and friends.

My colleagues and I have published a number of articles about this research; one citation is as follows:

Laurier, E., Brown, B., and Lorimer, H. (2012) What it means to change lanes: Actions, emotions and wayfinding in the family car. *Semiotica*, 191 (4), 117–36.

There is also a website detailing more about the project, which is available at:

http://web2.ges.gla.ac.uk/~elaurier/habitable_cars/

CONCLUSION

People increasingly are documenting their lives and, as such, they are creating important information that can help researchers to understand both them as individuals and also the various spaces and places that they inhabit. Such documents can provide researchers with useful information that can help them to understand the research context and the ways in which researchers develop, maintain and store information that they deem valuable. The key is ensuring that the documents serve an important role in the research.

Reflective questions

Concept questions

■ What is a primary reason for using documents as data?
■ What types of documents do qualitative researchers typically use?
■ What are the challenges of using documents?

Application questions

■ Do documents have a place in your study as data?
■ Do you have the skills necessary to successfully use them?

Haw, K. and Hadfield, M. (2011) *Video in social science research*, London: Routledge. This text provided us with some ideas about how and why documents might be used in a qualitative study.

Atkinson, P. and Coffey, A. (2004) Analysing documentary realities. *In*: D. Silverman (ed.) *Qualitative research: Theory, method and practice*. London: Sage. pp. 56–75. This text also provides useful information about how documents may and may not be used.

Scott, J. (1990) *A matter of record: Documentary sources in social research*, Cambridge: Polity.
Although an older resource, this text provided some useful practical information.

Key resources

Working with data and findings

PART SIX

Chapter 27

Data handling and coding

INTRODUCTION

There comes a time during the research process when researchers must face their data. Sometimes, it appears as if there is a mountain of them to deal with and researchers must choose how they will handle them. Researchers go about it in a variety of ways, some of which we describe in this chapter. When beginning qualitative data analysis, most qualitative researchers engage in some combination of the following phases: characterizing, cutting, coding, categorizing, converting and creating. In this chapter we present these phases and then suggest some ways of doing preliminary data analysis.

CHARACTERIZE

One of the first steps in the process of data analysis is characterizing the data, and researchers choose how they will go about this. Words may be recorded and transcribed '**verbatim**' for example.

Verbatim

To express in exactly the same words originally used

The term 'verbatim', however, is a somewhat slippery one because, in reality, the process requires analysis and interpretation (Roberts 2004; Green *et al.* 1997). Indeed, the goals of the research study and the philosophical and methodological assumptions of the researcher have implications for the form and content of transcripts, since different features of data will be of analytical interest (Bailey 2008; Roberts 2004). Indicating which data are significant, for example, reflects a researcher's assumptions about what counts as data for a particular project. One researcher may decide that the social talk at the beginning and end of an interview is important while another may not. A third researcher may decide that verbal tics (ah, um) are important to record, while a fourth may not. Meaning, for many qualitative researchers, resides not only in what a participant says but also the way in which it is said (Bailey 2008; Heritage *et al.* 2006). Thus, some transcripts will simply record the words, while others will record other aspects, including the speaker's tone, pacing, timing and pauses, which can be important elements for data interpretation.

The initial characterization of the data reflects what the researcher thinks is important and because of this, we consider it to be one of the first steps in data analysis. The following transcriptions illustrate differences in interpretation of what is important.

EXAMPLE 1: VERBATIM TRANSCRIPT

Claire: OK, so now that you've used it for a semester, how would you describe your experiences with problem-based learning?

Linda: I think problem-based learning is great. I mean for students, it's a real challenge for them. They have to really work when they've been used to being given the information. It seems to motivate them to work on a problem that they might actually run into when they are on the job. It really gets them going. But I always wonder, way down deep, whether I'm covering the content they need to pass boards, you know? What if I'm not giving them what they need? What if they don't pass? It makes it difficult for them and for me to buy into it completely.

EXAMPLE 2: VERBATIM TRANSCRIPT

Claire: OK. So . . . Now that you've used it . . . for a semester . . . (um), how would you describe your experiences with problem-based learning?

Linda: I think problem-based learning is great . . . I mean for students, it's a real challenge for them. (laughs) . . . They have to really work (um) when they've been used to being given the information. It seems to motivate them to work on a problem that they might actually run into when they are on the job. It really gets them going. But (um) I always wonder . . . way down deep (appears to be concentrating) . . . whether I'm covering the content they need . . . to pass boards . . . you know? . . . (pauses, and frowns) What if I'm not giving them (um) what they need? What if they don't pass? (pause). It makes it difficult for them and for me to (um) buy into it completely.

In the second representation of this interaction, the pacing of the conversation is more apparent, the speaker's hesitation is a bit more evident and the body language provides clues to meaning.

As human interaction is complex, the process of transcription in turn requires data reduction and characterization. Researchers must make choices about which features of interaction to transcribe, as well as about the level of detail to include. Their decisions necessarily rest upon their philosophical stances, the research approaches and the aims of a research project. They must strike a balance between usability and accuracy of a transcript (Bailey 2008; Tilley 2003).

Immersion in the data

Tips

Once they have characterized their data, researchers typically immerse themselves in it. In order to accomplish this, they read, listen or view it over and over again. The underlying idea of doing this is so that they begin to understand it at both a gut level and as a whole, before they begin to analyze it. Analyze, at a fundamental level, means to break apart, so researchers need to understand and be able to sense the whole, before beginning this process.

CUT

In most approaches to qualitative data analysis, an initial step involves cutting the data into meaningful segments. We call this phase 'cutting' because this approach has involved and sometimes still involves actually cutting data apart with scissors. Cutting can occur at the level of word, phrase, sentence or full transcript. Cutting now happens in many ways, however, whether through writing text segments on note cards or simply highlighting meaningful chunks in a word processing file or by marking the chunks in a data analysis software package. Sandelowski (1995: 373) suggests beginning data analysis by simply underlining key phrases 'because they make some as yet inchoate sense'.

The idea is to simply break apart or reduce the information for close examination.

We provide an example of cutting from the data we shared above, using the briefer version of the interaction for ease of readability (we use this version in the remainder of the chapter as well). Table 27.1 demonstrates the sample text cut in a word processing file.

Table 27.1 Cut text

I think problem-based learning is great.
I mean for students, it's a real challenge for them.
They have to really work when
they've been used to being given the information.
It seems to motivate them to work
on a problem that they might actually run into when they are on the job.
It really gets them going.
But I always wonder, way down deep,
whether I'm covering the content they need to pass boards, you know?
What if I'm not giving them what they need?
What if they don't pass?
It makes it difficult for them and for me to buy into it completely.

We note that not all research approaches or data analytical approaches (see Chapter 28) call for cutting the text at this level; indeed, some approaches call for reading the text more holistically.

CODE

When researchers engage in an examination of their data, they generally begin to notice things that stand out in the data set, such as behaviours, events, activities, strategies, states of mind, meanings, patterns, relationships, interactions or consequences. Often, they assign a descriptive label that captures the meaning of each data segment. These labels often are nouns but may also include both adjectives and adverbs; these can convey underlying properties of these concepts. Researchers normally repeat this process with all their relevant data, with similar segments of data being marked with the same label. This process is called coding. Coding allows for noting details and implications of data chunks. It also makes it easier to search data, make comparisons and identify patterns worthy of further investigation. Coding allows for a close study of data, whether the close reading of text, critical listening to an audio or marking of a visual image.

Coding generally is done to accomplish one of two things: description or analysis. Descriptive coding is simply a process of summarizing or describing the text and it tends to involve deriving codes from the actual language of the text. Analytical coding, on the other hand, means deriving codes based upon what the researcher believes is going on. Charmaz (2006), for example, suggests asking the following questions about the data when engaged in analytical coding:

- What is going on?
- What are people doing?
- What is the person saying?
- What do these actions and statements take for granted?
- How do structure and context serve to support, maintain, impede or change these actions and statements?

A code in the context of qualitative research is a system of symbols (such as letters or short words) that is used to represent and label a theme. A code should be a meaningful name that provides an indication of the idea contained in the data segment. Codes tend to be based upon themes, topics, ideas, terms, phrases and keywords. They also may be based upon theory and explanations from outside the data (such as a paradigm or theoretical framework). Codes that come directly from the data (as with grounded theory) are called *inductive codes*. Those codes based upon prior theory or literature are called *a priori codes*. If the same segment of data gets more than one code, which does happen on occasion, these are called *co-occurring codes*. In addition to using codes for content, it is possible to use additional codes based upon the characteristics of the participants (for example, age or gender may be coded). These additional codes are called *facesheet codes* and they tend to be used in tandem with other codes.

Johnny Saldaña offers his reflection on coding on the facing page. Saldaña's book (Saldaña 2012) is a useful resource, given its specific focus on and practical advice about coding.

Examples of codes

In Saldaña's text, he describes first-cycle coding and second-cycle coding. An example of first-cycle coding is open coding. An example of second-cycle coding is axial coding. Glaser and Strauss (1967) initially developed these approaches to coding when they developed their grounded theory method but many qualitative researchers working with a range of other research approaches have adopted these two forms of coding.

Open coding

In open or initial coding, the researcher conceptualizes the data (often field notes) line by line (Charmaz 2006). Coding is often placed in the margins of field notes. Open coding can be a tedious process, since it requires conceptualizing all related incidents in order to yield many concepts.

Johnny Saldaña, Arizona State University, USA

Coding qualitative data

The Coding manual for qualitative researchers (2nd edn., London: Sage Publications, 2012) is a resource that profiles thirty-two different methods for coding and analyzing qualitative data. These methods range from simple descriptive topical indexing to evocative ways of capturing a participant's values, attitudes and beliefs, to more complex methods for discerning causation and cultural categories of meaning. The general purpose of coding is to develop a series of researcher-generated constructs that symbolize and thus attribute interpreted meaning to each individual datum for later purposes of pattern detection, categorization, theme and concept development, assertion-building, theorizing, and other analytical processes.

As an example, a passage of data from a male PhD student interviewed during the second year of his programme of study reads: 'I'm 27 years old and I've got over $50,000 in student loans that I have to pay off, and that scares the hell out of me. I've got to finish my dissertation next year because I can't afford to keep going to school. I've got to get a job and start working'.

The specific coding methods you choose are based on several factors such as your research questions, projected outcomes, the conceptual framework and methodology you've adopted, the types of data you've collected, and even your personal experiences and preferences as an analyst. Thus, each coder brings not only an analytical lens but different analytical *filters* to the enterprise. One researcher might decide on a *descriptive code* for this interview passage and labels it in a straightforward way: STUDENT DEBT. A second researcher who prioritizes the emotional dilemmas of the participant might label the datum with an *emotion code*: DESPERATION. And a third researcher might use a phrase that the participant himself said which stood out and thus codes the passage, 'I'VE GOT TO' – a code placed in quotation marks to identify this as an *in vivo code*. (You may have read the passage above and came up with a fourth possible label for the datum.)

Quantitative research's precision rests with numeric accuracy. In qualitative research, our precision rests with our word choices. So, is one of these three codes 'better' than the others? No, because each research study is unique and so are its analytical methods. There is no one 'right' way to code qualitative data but the thirty-two different methods outlined in *the Coding manual for qualitative researchers* do suggest that some choices are more appropriate than others. Coding qualitative data is not a precise science; it's primarily an interpretive act. And as frustrating as that may seem to you, don't think of it as ambiguous guidance – think of it as having flexible options.

Most important is to acknowledge that coding is just *one* way of analyzing qualitative data, not *the* way. As you've been learning in this book, there is a spectrum of approaches to analysis. There are times when coding the data is absolutely necessary and times when it's most inappropriate for the study at hand.

Axial coding

Although Glaser and Holton (2004) disagree with this approach on the basis that it imposes structure and thus stifles creativity, Strauss and Corbin (1990; 1998) proposed an axial coding phase in addition to open coding. Axial coding involves 'a set of procedures whereby data are put back together in new ways after open coding, by making connections between categories'. The authors proposed the use of a 'coding paradigm' (Kelle 2005) that involves 'conditions, context, action/interactional strategies and consequences' (Strauss and Corbin 1990: 96). The coding paradigm requires focusing on causal relationships and seeking to categorize incidents into a frame that structures generic relationships. Using our text, we provide an example of open and axial coding in Table 27.2.

Table 27.2 Example of open and axial coding

Text segment	Open coding	Axial coding
I think problem-based learning is great	Positive feeling	Motivator
I mean for students, it's a real challenge for them	Challenge	Barrier
They have to really work when	Challenge	Barrier
they've been used to being given the information	Passive	Barrier
It seems to motivate them to work	Motivation	Motivator
On a problem that they might actually run into when they are on the job	Real world	Motivator
It really gets them going	Motivation	Motivator
But I always wonder, way down deep	Uncertainty	Barrier
Whether I'm covering the content they need to pass boards, you know	Coverage	Barrier
What if I'm not giving them what they need?	Coverage	Barrier
What if they don't pass?	Outcomes	Barrier
It makes it difficult for them and for me to buy into it completely	Uncertainty	Barrier

These coding approaches may be used for coding visual documents as well as text, as Eric Margolis demonstrates in his researcher reflection.

Researcher reflections

Eric Margolis, Arizona State University, USA

The studying of visual data produced by cultures

The mainstream of the social sciences and humanities is remarkable in the way that it has privileged the written word over all else. Not only the founding fathers, but generally everyone who has come after, spends almost all their professional time engaged in word play. Social scientists do little more than, in the words of Bob Dylan, 'Read books, repeat quotations, draw conclusions on the wall'. Ethnographers pay more attention than most to verbal (as opposed to written) information. But here, too, the decided prejudice is in favour of self-report and words. Yet, modern culture is composed of jillions of nonverbal images.

continued

I employ critical visual theory in attempts to study visual images produced as part of culture. Visual images are primary evidence of human productive activity; they are worked matter. Their use and understanding is governed by socially established symbolic codes. Visual images are constructed and may be deconstructed; that is, given a number of different readings. They can be analyzed with techniques developed in diverse fields of literary criticism, art theory and criticism, content analysis, semiotics, deconstructionism or the tools of ethnography.

My work has focused on the interpretation of historic photographs, mostly in two areas: coal mining and schools. My approach has been to collect large numbers of images, and to investigate and interpret them using the basic tools of grounded theory: for example, careful description, constant comparison, initial coding and axial coding – eventually leading to theoretical understanding. In this I 'borrow' additional techniques from the above mentioned fields; for instance, I have examined photographic images for their iconic, indexical and symbolic meanings.

Two recent articles provide good examples. In Margolis and Rowe (2011), Jeremy and I explored the use of two different approaches to the study of historical photographs. In his analysis of a photograph of 'Kaloma', sometimes referred to as the wife of Wyatt Earp, he relied on post-positivist techniques, which he termed 'photo forensics', to trace the history of the image. I used interpretivist approaches to examine possible symbolic meanings in a photograph of what may be a class of future teachers teasing their professor.

Figure 27.1 A class teasing their professor

In a second article, written with two former students, we examined a large number of school photographs, coding for ceremonies and rituals enacted in grade school. Of perhaps 10,000 images from many time periods and countries, the grounded theory approach yielded the following categories: rituals of the habitual, coming of age ceremonies, patriotic rituals and ceremonies, and degradation rituals and ceremonies.

Some of my articles may be found at: http://margolis.faculty.asu.edu/Articles.html.

While many qualitative researchers use these forms of coding, they are not the only way to code text; indeed, as Saldaña notes in his reflection on p. 323, his text describes thirty-two different forms of coding, so qualitative researchers have many options for choosing how they will code data. As we have indicated, the researcher's philosophical stance (see Chapter 4; also Creswell 2007; Mason 2002) influences coding, as do a number of other features such as the norms of the research approach (see Part 4), the research question and topic (Kvale 1996), the way in which fieldwork is undertaken and field notes are developed (see Chapter 22) and the analytical approach to be adopted (see Chapter 28).

Saldaña also raises the question of whether coding and data analysis are synonymous. As he indicates, several scholars suggest that they are related but not the same (Baist 2003; Richards and Morse 2007; Charmaz 2006). Where Saldaña ultimately falls on the issue is this:

> I advocate that qualitative codes are essence-capturing and essential elements of the research story that, when clustered together according to similarity and regularity — a pattern — they actively facilitate the development of categories and thus analysis of their connections. Ultimately, I like one of Charmaz's (2006) metaphors for the process when she states that coding 'generates the bones of your analysis . . . [I]ntegration will assemble those working bones into a skeleton'.
>
> (Saldaña 2012: 45)

Coding and analysis are not the same and indeed many qualitative researchers do not code. However, coding can provide clues to meaning and these clues and the connections between them may ultimately be analyzed. This can count as preliminary analysis, which may be developed further during final data analysis (see Chapter 28).

CATEGORIZE

As researchers accumulate codes, they frequently seek a way to organize or categorize them. This phase involves movement from seeking the particular (individual codes) to seeking the general (patterns within those codes). Categories tend to be non-hierarchal or flat (a general list) or instead hierarchical (a list of categories, or sub-codes). An example of this is given in Figure 27.2.

Categorizing this information may suggest new ways of thinking or new codes that the researcher had not thought of previously. Categories can become a critical component of data analysis. Categories must 'be responsive to the research question(s) and:

- Be as *sensitive* to the data as possible
- Be *exhaustive* (enough categories to encompass all relevant data)
- Be *mutually exclusive* (a relevant unit of data can be placed in only one category)
- Be *conceptually congruent* (all categories are at the same conceptual level)'.

(Merriam 2009: 186)

- Flat coding categories:
    - o PBL as challenge
    - o PBL as catalyst
    - o PBL as motivator
    - o PBL as authentic approach
- Hierarchical coding categories:
    - o PBL Advantages (as seen by the professors in the study)
        - – Challenge
        - – Catalyst
        - – Motivator
        - – Authenticity
    - o PBL Disadvantages (as seen by the professors in the study)
        - – Coverage
        - – Acceptance

Figure 27.2 Categories of coding

CONVERT (INTO THEMES)

Once codes and categories have been developed, these tend to be converted into themes. A theme is a unifying or dominant idea in the data and finding themes is the heart of the data analysis process. The art and science of developing themes has challenged qualitative researchers over time. This stage of analysis marks a movement from description, categorization and preliminary analysis toward interpretation (see Chapter 29). Here is a basic example of themes that were found in our sample text.

PRIMARY THEMES

- Lecturer opinion of problem-based learning as a teaching approach.
- Lecturer perceptions of benefits of problem-based learning to enhance student learning outcomes.
- Lecturer doubts concerning the fulfilment of all her teaching responsibilities when she uses this approach.
- Lecturer's incomplete buy-in to the approach.

Example

CREATE

Many researchers create visual displays of their data findings, which can be particularly useful during data analysis. Miles and Huberman (1994) also call this phase 'data display'. The most common ways of going about this typically involve some sort of visual representation of the data. The most common approaches for characterizing data include comparison matrices, tables and figures.

Comparison matrices

A matrix is a table with both rows and columns. When a cell is selected, it indicates an occurrence of a finding at the junction of the row and column. Using a matrix allows a researcher to demonstrate how findings compare across participants. A comparison matrix is shown in Table 27.3.

Table 27.3 Example of a comparison matrix

Themes	Motivational	Challenging	Authentic	Catalyzing
Linda	•	•	•	•
George	•			•
Diane		•	•	
Charles	•			•
Max	•			•

Descriptive tables

Descriptive tables simply contain a base-level description of the data and allow a researcher to summarize a general overview of the findings quickly. A descriptive table is shown in Table 27.4.

Table 27.4 Example of a descriptive table

Overarching themes	Description of categories within overarching themes
Lecturer enjoyment	Approbations • Positive comments • Descriptions of successes
Perception of benefits to student	Outcomes • Improved skills • Improved knowledge Affective: • Enthusiasm • Satisfaction
Lecturer doubts	Expressions of uncertainty • Coverage • Centrality
Lecturer partial acceptance	Plans to use again Descriptions of a more piecemeal approach

Integrative figures and diagrams

These involve making a sketch or drawing to illustrate how something works or to otherwise clarify the relationship between the parts of a whole. They are used to pull detail together in order to make sense of the data, particularly with respect to emerging theory. The figures might be concept maps or network graphs or even simple illustrations. In Figure 27.3 we provide a

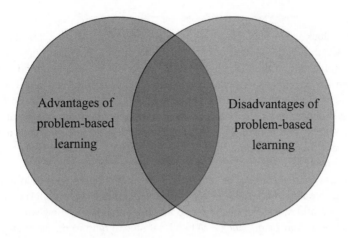

Figure 27.3 Example of using a Venn diagram for coding

Venn diagram documenting the extremes in tutor experiences with problem-based learning; those who enjoyed it, those who disliked it and, in between, those who struggled to reconcile the difficulties they experienced over the advantages they felt students received.

DOING PRELIMINARY DATA ANALYSIS

There are several issues that researchers may wish to consider in conjunction with preliminary data analysis. In particular, they should consider how to proceed when meeting coding difficulties, determine whether to use computer programs for preliminary analysis and determine how they will document the process.

Overcoming coding

Not all research approaches require or even value the cutting, coding, converting and creating processes of data analysis. Even those using approaches that do value these treatments of data recognize that there are periods when it is possible to be overcome with codes and categories to the point of being paralyzed. In her researcher reflection, Gina Wisker describes how this might happen and provides a useful description of how she moved past such a moment.

Professor Gina Wisker, University of Brighton, UK

Writing my way out of a shed-load of data

When carrying out qualitative research that uses triangulation (that is, at least two methods to collect the data), it is almost inevitable that there comes a moment when there is so much data, from so many different sources, that a researcher can get drowned in data, and stuck.

Researcher reflections

continued

I became stuck when managing data from a piece of action research that used (i) interviews with a large number of doctoral students and (ii) focus groups with some of those students and then (iii) attempted to turn some of the interpreted results into illustrative based studies. Everything seemed fascinating and relevant, I wanted to quote everything, and I had no idea about how I would select and manage the data.

Over-labelling and categorizing – some of us can get embroiled in categorizing, sub-categorizing and finding there are thousands of sub-categories with tiny bits of interview and focus group data in each, all neatly labelled but not actually contributing to an argument.

Overwhelmed – some of us feel so snowed under by the shed-load of data that attempting to categorize would be impossible and, either way, the feeling is of being overwhelmed and stuck. For me, this also led to a stuck place in my writing.

Moving beyond being stuck – When I get stuck I tend to do other things, clean the house, walk the dog on the seafront or round the garden. Actually, this releases thinking energies and helps me to return to the task of focusing, analyzing and writing. Walking about clears my mind and then I decide to focus and get on with the analysis.

What am I looking for really? I reminded myself of my research question, which helped to narrow the wide range of data I'd generated, so that I could, on the one hand, take an overview or helicopter view of the landscape of the data and then identify the hot spots which related directly to, or at least marginally to, my question.

Selecting and highlighting themes – I had underlined and started to annotate and identify themes – so I returned to this task and drew a small mind map of the central question and three or four major emerging themes, then returned to the data and focused on what parts of the highlighted and annotated elements of this vast mass of data could fit in with these themes, which had emerged from my thorough reading of theory and critical work on the topic.

Theorizing and arguing – As I selected out the informative and factual data which related to the themes, I also annotated with comments; informative, analytical and reflective. With these three kinds of writing response, I found that the theories that underpinned the work started to enable me to focus more on developing an argument that was conceptual. I had reflected and theorized and understood something from the emerging patterns in relation to the overall question and the theories that helped me ask that question. I realized then that I had selected examples of the data which enabled me to make the arguments and to carry the thread through the analysis and discussion.

It needed a lot of rewriting, checking, cutting quotations, ensuring nothing relevant was hiding under less immediately obvious language. But then I could write it through – thematically discussing the data from two sources. Finally, I was ruthless and developed a couple of cases from the synthesis, the overview and the tight focus of data, on answering the question and developing an argument.

Choosing to use (or not) computer programs

Traditionally, qualitative data have been analyzed 'by hand' and some researchers (including the authors of this text) still prefer this hands-on approach. Sorting by hand allows researchers to actually be 'hands on' during the process. They work with the data enough to know it extensively and to develop an intuitive sense of its essential features and elements. It allows them to begin to feel the patterns in the data and to physically shift and sort until findings do, as we tend to say, 'emerge' from out of the chaos.

Several computer packages, however, have been designed for qualitative data analysis and, increasingly, qualitative researchers are using these to help with the process of data analysis. Currently, the most popular packages are:

- ATLAS – http://atlasti.de
- Ethnograph – http://qualisresearch.com
- HyperResearch – http://researchware.com
- Nvivo – www.qsrinternational.com
- NUD-IST – www.qsrinternational.com

Creswell (1998; 2007), Silverman (2005) and Merriam (2009) all offer descriptions of the ways in which such computer packages may be used in qualitative research. We agree with these researchers that such packages offer some advantages. In particular, they help researchers to manage large volumes of text in ways that provide quick counts and displays of information. They also can be helpful when multiple researchers from different locations are working on a project together; they allow for data sharing.

In our view, however, researchers would be well served to do a few studies with the old-fashioned 'by hand' method before using the computer packages. We think that doing so will help them better understand the processes involved and therefore make them better users of the technological tools.

Claire Howell Major, Author

The dissertation students I encounter typically have solid computer skills and frequently they ask me about using a computer to process data. I have found, however, that sometimes, if students have not had direct experience with analyzing data by hand, they can risk 'missing the forest for the trees'. I believe that it helps students to understand the underlying processes of analysis if they try it by hand first. So I encourage them to try hand coding and analysis on several transcripts, at least, before trying it with the computer. I expect this seems old-fashioned to many of them, but then again I have had several students say that they are glad that they did analysis by hand first and that it greatly helped their interpretation process later to have done so.

Researcher reflections

We also believe that it is important for a researcher to consider whether the computer package is appropriate for the particular study. A researcher should first determine the norms of the research approach before making a decision about whether to use a technology tool during analysis, and if so, which tool. These tools may well be useful for coding some of the larger data sets but may not be as useful for other tasks. However, it may be more difficult to use them with some of the more holistic, intuitive or specialized data analysis approaches (see Chapter 28).

Keeping logs and records during data analysis

Many researchers keep a list of codes and categories, so that they can keep track of the codes and their meanings. A code list may suggest why the researcher has created the code, details of what the code comprises, what should fit into the code and what should be left out, and general thoughts about the analysis. In Table 27.5, we provide an example of a code list.

Table 27.5 Sample code list

Acceptance	About accepting the challenge to use problem-based learning (PBL)
Authenticity	About making the experience an authentic one for students
Challenge	About finding (positive) challenge in using the approach
Coercion	About being coerced into trying it
Conversion	About conversion of course materials to PBL
Coverage	About ability to 'cover' knowledge in PBL
Scaffolding	About providing students with mental structures to help them through the experience
Student readiness	About student ability to take up the challenge of PBL
Tinkering	About tinkering around the edges of a course to 'try' PBL before diving in

Another way to accomplish logging during the process of data analysis is through *enumeration*. Enumeration calls for taking account of qualitative elements for the purpose of allowing a researcher to better describe them later when presenting the text. While some researchers merely do word counts for enumeration, more useful methods may be to examine how many times a code appears and is associated with a particular participant. Doing so allows a researcher later to choose more precise language when talking about the themes. For example, it can generate numerically accurate descriptions of 'most', 'a few', 'one' and so on. A matrix similar to that in Table 27.3 on page 428 may be particularly useful for this task.

Finally, researchers may choose to create analytical memos. Analytical memos are notes that researchers take about the coding process. These can help researchers remember how they have coded things a certain way and why, and they also help ensure the quality of a study (see Chapter 30).

Researcher reflections

Claire Howell Major, Author

Sample analytical memo

I really empathize with Linda. When I initially decided to try problem-based learning, writing the problem was not the most difficult problem for me. One of the biggest challenges was feeling confident that students were still really learning, without me controlling that. What I see in the data is that Linda is uncertain about the student learning. Thus uncertainty should be a code. Ultimately, I think that uncertainty could have been a barrier for me continuing to use it, and I think that's going on for Linda here as well. The motivators may eventually win out, but that is an important meaning unit to consider as well.

CONCLUSION

Preliminary data analysis is a key component in the qualitative research process, and researchers must choose from several different options in deciding how to go about it. Typically, they employ a combination of the approaches that we have explored in this chapter. All too frequently, however, researchers end analysis with a description and display of their codes and categories and do not go on to more in-depth analysis. We now encourage researchers to read Chapter 28 for an overview of the various forms of analysis that researchers employ.

Reflective questions

Concept questions

■ What are the basic processes involved in pre-analysis of data?
■ What are the benefits and challenges of using a computer to analyze data?

Application questions

■ What is your view of the utility of coding?
■ What is the best way to display your data?

Key resources

Saldaña, J. (2012) *The coding manual for qualitative researchers (2nd edn.)*, Thousand Oaks, CA: Sage.
    Saldaña's text is a useful overview that provides a description, purpose and practical advice about coding.

Sandelowski, M. (1995) Qualitative analysis: What it is and how to begin. *Research in Nursing & Health*, 18, 371–5.
    Sandelowski's work provided us with a useful overview and introduction into beginning qualitative data analysis.

Bailey, J. (2008) First steps in qualitative data analysis: Transcribing. *Family Practice*, 25 (2), 127–31.
    Bailey provides useful information about data transcription and helped us to conceive of it as an early form of data analysis.

Chapter 28

Data analysis

INTRODUCTION

In a search to uncover meaning, qualitative researchers analyze data derived from many sources including interview transcripts, field notes, journals, photographs and videos. The analytical method they choose necessarily influences the results or themes that they discover. Data analysis is one of the most critical phases in the qualitative research process, yet researchers all too frequently fail to give it the attention necessary to ensure sound results. Indeed, researchers often state that themes 'emerged' from the data, as if by magic; rarely do they indicate or even intimate the complex analytical process involved and that the researcher is indeed active during this process.

In this chapter, we explore a number of key methods of data analysis. We initially describe five primary methods of analyzing data to uncover thematic analysis. These serve as a useful introduction to data analysis and have been used by researchers who both hold various stances and use different research approaches. More specialized methods of data analysis can be used by researchers adopting particular research approaches (for example, researchers using phenomenology might choose phenomenological analysis). Next, we describe eight specialized methods of data analysis which are analytical induction, heuristic/phenomenological analysis, hermeneutical analysis, ethnographic analysis, narrative analysis, discourse analysis, semiotic analysis and event analysis. These basic and specialized methods certainly are not the only methods of data analysis that a qualitative researcher could employ; others exist. In our opinion, however, these are the approaches that are most frequently used by those undertaking qualitative research studies and many of them may be used with a number of different kinds of data. For these reasons, we believe that the approaches we have selected warrant the attention they receive in this chapter.

WHAT IS DATA ANALYSIS?

Qualitative data analysis is an ongoing process that involves breaking data into meaningful parts for the purpose of examining them. The ultimate goal of qualitative data analysis is 'to make sense out of the data' (Merriam 2009: 203), with an intentional effort toward answering the research questions; thus, when researchers break data apart, as we described in Chapter 27, they must also examine them and put them back together in a way that makes sense. Hatch describes it this way:

Data analysis is a systematic search for meaning. It is a way to process qualitative data so that what has been learned can be communicated to others. Analysis means organising and interrogating data in ways that allow researchers to see patterns, identify themes, discover relationships, develop explanations, make interpretations, mount critiques, or generate theories. It often involves synthesis, evaluation, interpretation, categorisation, hypothesising, comparison, and pattern finding. It always involves what Wolcott calls 'mindwork' ... Researchers always engage their own intellectual capacities to make sense of qualitative data.

(Hatch 2002: 148)

In qualitative research, data analysis begins as soon the project begins and continues through to the submission of the final report. The process in qualitative research usually is an *inductive* process, of moving from small units of information to uncover the larger picture that emerges from them, rather than *deductive*, of moving from the larger to the smaller. It also tends to be **iterative** and cyclical.

Iterative
Repeating again and again

Yin (2009) offers several suggestions about the process of data analysis, indicating that it should answer the research questions, address all possible interpretations, reflect the existing literature on the topic and be informed by the work of other scholars. It is data analysis that ties together each aspect of the research project.

PRIMARY METHODS OF DATA ANALYSIS

There are a number of analytical approaches from which qualitative researchers may choose. Which method to choose is a critical decision, because the method invariably influences the focus of data analysis and thus the results. In this section, we describe some of the primary methods used for qualitative data analysis. We provide examples of coding using the following example. It is an interview response from a lecturer who had long taught traditionally, using lecture and discussion, about switching to a problem-based learning format:

I don't know how to put it, you don't see yourself as a teacher, you don't see yourself as a lecturer, yours is a different role. You have expertise in the area that you work, but it's not teaching, you are not really here to do teaching, you are here teaching outside the frame. I find it rewarding in the way that you know you see the student moving on, you see the student buzzing, you know, but in terms of me giving, that's one thing I don't know, what do I give?

(Savin-Baden and Major 2007: 845)

Keyword analysis

A keyword analysis is exactly what it sounds like. It involves searching out words that have some sort of meaning in the larger context of the data. The idea is that, in order to understand what the participants say, it is important to look at the words with which they communicate. Bernard and Ryan (2010) suggest several ways to analyse keywords, including:

- *Frequent repetition of terms*: researchers note words or synonyms that people frequently use.
- *Unusual use of terms*: researchers note use of words in an unusual way, which may reflect local usage. Patton (1990: 306, 393–400) calls these terms 'indigenous categories' and contrasts them with 'analyst-constructed typologies'.

■ *Words used in context (keywords-in-context)*: the researcher looks at keywords and the words immediately surrounding them. Then they sort phrases into groups with similar meaning.

Here, we provide an example of keyword analysis in which we have underlined the keywords.

Example

I don't know how to put it, you don't see yourself as a teacher, you don't see yourself as a lecturer, yours is a different role. You have expertise in the area that you work, but it's not teaching, you are not really here to do teaching, you are here teaching outside the frame. I find it rewarding in the way that you know you see the student moving on, you see the student buzzing, you know, but in terms of me giving, that's one thing I don't know, what do I give?

While the sample text is short it is still possible see the following keywords:

■ Frequent repetition: I/you, don't, teaching.
■ Unusual terms: moving, buzzing.
■ Words in context: 'not teaching'.

This primary method allows a researcher to focus on the words themselves. The analysis demonstrates the lecturer's uncertainty about the new problem-based learning approach; it is not teaching, yet students are moving and buzzing. Recent computer technology, in the form of qualitative software, allows for quick counting of keywords; it is further possible to create a visual display of how different words are emphasized, and are thus 'key' (see Figure 28.1).

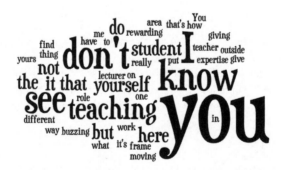

Figure 28.1 Wordle of text that illustrates keywords

Constant comparison

Constant comparison is an analytical method that researchers use to develop themes and ultimately generate theory. While Glaser and Strauss (1967) developed constant comparison along with grounded theory and it is strongly linked with that research approach, this method has since been adapted and adopted with a range of different qualitative research approaches.

Indeed, it is one of the most frequently used analytical methods of qualitative data analysis. The constant comparison process involves the following basic steps:

- Identify categories in events and behaviour.
- Name indicators in passage and code them (open coding).
- Continually compare codes and passages to those already coded to find consistencies and differences.
- Examine consistencies or patterns between codes to reveal categories.
- Continue the process until the category 'saturates' and no new codes related to it are identified.
- Determine which categories are the central focus (axial categories) and, thus, form the core category.

According to Charmaz (2005: 515), the constant comparative method of grounded theory means:

- comparing different people (such as their views, situations, actions, accounts and experiences)
- comparing data from the same individuals with themselves at different points in time
- comparing incident with incident
- comparing data with category
- comparing one category with another.

Constant comparison, constant modification and constant sharpening of emerging theory occurs during a grounded theory study. Table 28.1 shows how a typical constant comparison analysis might be applied to our example text.

Table 28.1 Emergent codes from constant comparison analysis

I don't know how to put it	Uncertainty
You don't see yourself as a teacher	Different teaching role
You don't see yourself as a lecturer	Different teaching role
Yours is a different role	Different teaching role
You have expertise in the area that you work	Teacher expertise
But it's not teaching	Different teaching role
You are not really here to do teaching	Different teaching role
You are here teaching outside the frame.	Different teaching role
I find it rewarding in the way that	Rewards
You know you see the student moving on	Student role
You see the student buzzing, you know	Student role
But in terms of me giving	Uncertainty
That's one thing I don't know, what do I give?	Uncertainty

Content analysis

Content analysis is the process of examining a text at its most fundamental level: the content. It is an analysis of the frequency and patterns of use of terms or phrases and has been applied to a range of research approaches. While content analysis typically has been applied to print/text, it also has been adapted to analyze visual artefacts. Over time, this method of qualitative data analysis has taken two primary forms: classical content analysis and ethnographic content analysis.

Classical content analysis

Classical content analysis strives to make 'replicable and valid inferences from data to their context' (Krippendorf 1980: 21) as well as to make 'objective, systematic, and quantitative descriptions of the manifest content of communication' (Berelson 1952: 489). It also seeks to 'make inferences by systematically and objectively identifying specified characteristics within text' (Stone *et al.* 1966: 5). Classical content analysis involves the following steps:

- examine the text or artefact
- peruse it in its entirety
- determine the properties of the text/artefact
- examine overt and latent emphases
- determine rules for categorizing:
    - determine how much data will be analyzed at any one time (whether a line of text, a sentence, a phrase, part of the artefact)
    - determine categories
    - they must be inclusive (all examples fit within a category)
    - they must be mutually exclusive (no examples fit within more than one category)
    - determine themes that emerge from the categories.

We provide an example of classical content analysis in Table 28.2.

Table 28.2 Classical content analysis

Rewards	1
Student Role	2
Teacher Expertise	1
Different Teacher Role	6
Uncertainty	3

Domain analysis

Spradley defines a domain as 'any symbolic category that includes other categories' (Spradley 1979: 100). It is a collection of categories that are related. For example, the domain of chocolate would include sweet, bitter and semisweet (and some would argue white, although others would disagree). These share a relationship because they are kinds of chocolate. Spradley (1979: 185) suggests that there are several potential relationships in the data, as follows:

1. Strict inclusion (X is a kind of Y).
2. Spatial (X is a place in Y, X is a part of Y).
3. Cause–effect (X is a result of Y, X is a cause of Y).
4. Rationale (X is a reason for doing Y).
5. Location for action (X is a place for doing Y).
6. Function (X is used for Y).
7. Means–end (X is a way to do Y).
8. Sequence (X is a step or stage in Y).
9. Attribution (X is an attribute, or characteristic, of Y).

The process of domain analysis is as follows:

■ Select the semantic relationship (from above list).
■ Prepare a domain analysis worksheet, listing all of the terms that fit the semantic relationship.
■ Select a sample of field notes.
■ Seek terms to describe the semantic relationship.
■ Formulate questions about the relationship (for example, are there different kinds of chocolate?).
■ Repeat the process for each different semantic relationship.
■ List all of the domains discovered.

We provide our example of domain analysis in Figure 28.2.

Using domain analysis, we identified the following terms and relationships:

(a) Possible cover terms: teaching roles

(b) Possible included terms: uncertainty, different, rewards

(c) Possible semantic relationships: X is an attribute (characteristic) of Y

For the semantic relationship above, 'X' is the included term (e.g. uncertainty) and 'Y' is the cover term of teaching role. From these terms and relationships, the researcher can construct questions; for example:

'How do teacher roles change?'

or

'How do student roles change?'

Figure 28.2 Domain analysis coding

Thematic analysis

Thematic analysis is a method of identifying, analyzing and reporting patterns in the data (Braun and Clarke 2006). There is no clear agreement for what thematic analysis is or how one does it, although it appears that much of what qualitative researchers do when analyzing data under the generalist term of qualitative data analysis is actually thematic analysis (Braun and Wilkinson 2003). At other times, researchers who appear to be doing thematic analysis are actually calling it something else, such as narrative analysis or discourse analysis.

Researcher reflections

Claire Howell Major, Author

I have a background in English literature and, during my first experiences with social science/qualitative research, I was naturally drawn to thematic analysis. It was well in keeping with my humanist mind-set and allowed me to use the skills that I had gained in examining texts for examining life experiences instead. While we have it listed as a 'basic approach' because it can be used across so many different research traditions, I still find it to be one of the most complex and compelling approaches to data analysis.

Thematic analysis at a fundamental level is 'the process of recovering the theme or themes that are embodied and dramatized in the evolving meanings and imagery of the work' (van Manen 1990: 78). Thematic analysis is not necessarily wedded to any pre-existing philosophical stance or theoretical framework and can be used across many of them:

> It can be a method which both works to reflect reality, and to unpick or unravel the surface of 'reality'. However it is important that the theoretical position of a thematic analysis is made clear, as this is all too often left unspoken (and is then typically a realist account). Any theoretical framework carries with it a number of assumptions about the nature of data, what they represent in terms of 'the world,' 'reality', and so forth. A good thematic analysis will make this transparent.
>
> (Braun and Clarke 2006: 8)

This method provides a general sense of the information through repeated handling of the data. The idea is to get a feel for the whole text by living with it prior to any cutting or coding. It is not the most scientific sounding method but we believe it to be one of the best. The researcher can rely on intuition and sensing, rather than being bound by hard and fast rules of analysis. Braun and Clarke (2006) recommend doing the following when conducting thematic analysis:

- familiarize yourself with your data
- generate initial codes
- search for themes
- review themes
- define and name themes
- produce the report.

What is unique about thematic analysis is that it acknowledges that analysis happens at an intuitive level. It is through the process of immersion in data and considering connections and interconnections between codes, concepts and themes that an 'aha' moment happens, as we have described elsewhere in this text (see Chapters 5 and 29). Figure 28.3 shows our early phase of thematic analysis.

SPECIALIZED METHODS OF DATA ANALYSIS

The five methods described thus far are primary tools for data analysis that may be applied across various research approaches. Qualitative researchers, however, also have an array of more

EXAMPLE OF CODED TEXT

Note: Not a teacher

Note: Not a lecturer

I don't know how to put it, you <u>don't see yourself as a teacher</u>, you <u>don't see yourself as a lecturer</u>, yours is a <u>different role</u>. You have expertise in the area that you work, but it's not teaching, you are not really here to do teaching, you are here teaching outside the frame. I find it <u>rewarding</u> in the way that you know you see the <u>student moving on</u>, you see the <u>student buzzing,</u> you know, but in terms of me giving, that's one thing I don't know, <u>what do I give</u>?

Analysis:

The key phrases that seem to hold meaning indicate that the speaker believes he is not functioning in a traditional teaching role. He sees some rewards in terms of student learning but is uncertain about what he is adding to that process.

Figure 28.3 Text coded using thematic analysis

specialized methods of data analysis that tend to be paired with a specific philosophical position and one or two research approaches. These analytical methods tend to require a high level of skill on the part of the analyst, extensive reading to develop knowledge of the method and, at times, expert guidance. We provide a broad overview of some of these methods in this section.

Analytical induction

The process of analytical induction requires an examination of similarities between phenomena or events for the purpose of developing basic concepts of understanding. Analytical induction proceeds with an investigation of broad categories of understanding and then it moves on to developing sub-categories. It has been one of the classic research methods associated with ethnography. The basic process is as follows:

- Examine an event.
- Develop a hypothetical statement of what happened during the event.
- Examine a different but similar event to determine whether the new event fits the hypothesis.
- If the event does not fit the hypothesis, revise the hypothesis.
- Repeat the process and revise the hypothesis until it explains all examples encountered.
- Develop a hypothesis that accounts for all cases.

This process often is used in ethnography. In addition, a modified version of this inductive method can be used in conjunction with most qualitative data analysis methods. The concept was developed by Znaniecki (1934) and refined by Lindesmith (1952), Becker (1958), and Katz (1983).

Heuristic or phenomenological analysis

The word *heuristics* comes from the Greek *heuriskein*, meaning 'to find, to discover'. This approach goes hand in hand with phenomenography (see Chapter 14) and requires an attempt to discover how an individual in a context makes sense of a particular phenomenon. It needs a combination of psychology and interpretation and generally may be viewed as a problem-solving approach to data analysis. Phenomena are considered generally to relate to an occasion of individual significance, such as a major life event. It is the researcher's experience as part of the data which may be analyzed. The idea is that the researcher's experience and understanding is all that can be known (see, for example, Lofland and Lofland 1995: 14). Creswell (1998: 147–8), describing an approach by Moustakas (1994), who followed in the Husserlian tradition, suggests that the process involves responding to interview data in the following way:

- The researcher writes his or her own description; some researchers following Husserl do this in order to bracket out their experiences.
- The researcher lists statements related to how the individuals experience the topic, striving for a non-repetitive and non-overlapping list.
- The researcher groups the statements into 'meaning units' and writes a description of the experience.
- The researcher compares his or her description to the new description and develops a composite.

This approach is one of the most structured of the specialized data methods.

Interpretive phenomenological analysis

Data can also be organized using *interpretive phenomenological analysis*, which was developed by Smith (for example, Smith *et al.* 1995), following Heidegger. Although it takes a strong epistemological stance, it acknowledges that the researcher's engagement with the participant's text has an interpretative element. Using *interpretive phenomenological analysis* involves close reading of the text, initial bracketing of ideas and the creation of codes and structures to then arrive at a group of themes. Ranked categories are then identified so that it is possible to suggest a hierarchical relationship between them. See the example on facing page 443.

Hermeneutical analysis

The term hermeneutic comes from the Greek *hermeneuein*, which means 'to interpret'. This method is commonly used in Biblical studies to assess text but, in the social science context, it involves the analysis and interpretation of social events and their meanings to participants. This method also has been most often paired with phenomenology/phenomenography. The emphasis is on context and behaviour, the purpose being to interpret the general meaning in the context in which it occurs. It is a consideration of the relationship of the whole to the parts and the parts to the whole. Meaning is thought to reside in author intent/purpose, the context and the encounter between author and reader. Themes are related to the dialectical context. The process involves:

- seeking the meaning of text for people in the situation
- telling the participant's story

The aim of interpretative phenomenological analysis (IPA) is to explore in detail how participants are making sense of their personal and social world, and the main currency for an IPA study is the meanings that particular experiences, events and states hold for participants. The approach is phenomenological, in that it involves detailed examination of the participant's life world; it attempts to explore personal experience and is concerned with an individual's personal perception or account of an object or event, as opposed to an attempt to produce an objective statement of the object or event itself.

Examples of psychological research questions addressed in IPA studies:

- How do gay men think about sex and sexuality? (Flowers *et al.* 1997)
- How do people with genetic conditions view changing medical technologies? (Chapman 2002)
- What is the relationship between delusions and personal goals? (Rhodes and Jakes 2000)
- How do people come to terms with the death of a partner? (Golsworthy and Coyle 1999; 2001)
- How does a woman's sense of identity change during the transition to motherhood? (Smith 1999)
- What model of the person do priests have? (Vignoles *et al.* 2004)
- How do people in the early stage of Alzheimer's disease perceive and manage the impact on their sense of self? (Clare 2003)
- What influences the decision to stop therapy? (Wilson and Sperlinger 2004)
- What forms of social support are helpful to people in pain? (Warwick *et al.* 2004)
- How does being HIV positive impact on personal relationships? (Jarman *et al.* 2005)

(Smith and Osborn 2003: 54–5)

- bracketing the self out in analysis (to avoid telling the researcher story rather than the researched story)
- seeking to interpret different layers of text
- constructing knowledge by using context to understand and create.

Influenced by a number of other scholars working in the field, van Manen (1990) developed this method.

Ethnographic analysis

Ethnographic analysis, true to its name, goes hand in hand with ethnography (see Chapter 13 for additional information about ethnography). There is no one method of ethnographic analysis but, rather, there is a set of general strategies that ethnographic researchers tend to use. According to Merriam (2009), the ethnographer uses a classification scheme, either based upon concepts typically found in culture (emic perspective) or developed by the researcher (etic perspective). A researcher using the emic perspective would draw from an existing cultural classification scheme, such as Lofland and Lofland's (1995) four categories: 1) the economy; 2) demographics (including race, gender, ethnicity, class); 3) basic human experiences in everyday life; and 4) the environment. A researcher using the etic perspective begins with the data; frequently, the etic approach resembles the thematic approach described above but it is done specifically to examine a given culture in an effort to find data patterns. Wolcott (1990) suggests that analysis ultimately requires sorting in a quantitative way, often involving tables, figures and charts and, at times, leads to typologies or taxonomies.

When working with documents, some researchers use *ethnographic content analysis*, which requires 'the reflexive analysis of documents' (Altheide 1987: 65). It also is 'used to document and understand the communication of meaning, as well as to verify theoretical relationships' (Altheide 1987: 68). Altheide's description of ethnographic content analysis positions it as something of a cross between constant comparison and content analysis, a mixture of narrative and numerical analysis that allows researchers to identify themes during the process of coding.

Narrative analysis

Narrative analysis is not one specific method but rather is a range of methods that frequently are used with the narrative approaches that we describe in Chapter 15. At times, narrative analysis is characterized as a form of discourse analysis and, at other times, it is considered its own collection of methods (for example, Murray 2003; Riessman 1993). In qualitative research, narrative analysis requires the researcher to focus on the ways in which participants use stories to interpret the world. It treats stories as interpretive, 'storied', social products that individuals produce in unique contexts, to represent themselves or their worlds, rather than as facts to be assessed for 'truthfulness'. Interviews are thus viewed as 'storied' and necessarily biased. Three key ways to analyze narrative influence are:

- structural analysis, which focuses on core events (see Labov 1973)
- sociology of stories, which focuses on cultural, historical and political contexts (for example, Plummer 2001)
- functional analysis (Bruner 1990), which focuses on what work stories do in participants' lives.

Discourse analysis

Discourse analysis is not a specific method but rather is a term that describes a range of methods of analyzing language, whether through text, speech or sign (Burman and Parker 1993; Potter and Wetherell 1987; Willig 2003). It has been at times paired with ethnography, narrative approaches and case studies, as well as action research approaches. It involves the 'linguistic analysis of naturally occurring connected spoken or written discourse' (Stubbs 1983: 1) and provides 'insight into the forms and mechanisms of human communication and verbal interaction' (van Dijk 1985: 4). The purpose is for the construction and negotiation of power and meaning in discourse and interaction. The object of analysis is any communication event. The event is described as a set of speech acts, such as sentences, rhetorical devices, turn taking, conflicts, truth claims or propositions. The preference is to analyze language as it occurs in natural text, although focus groups interviews are often analyzed too. Moreover, discourse analysts have analyzed doctor–patient interaction, police interactions, court proceedings and a host of other interactions. The general process involves:

■ a search for patterns (questions and answers, who dominates the discourse and how, or any other observable patterns of interaction)
■ an attempt to 'map out' discourse structure and function as well as the relationships between participating individuals
■ engagement in close analysis of language.

Some of the most influential developers of these approaches include Gee (2005) and Halliday and Matthiessen (2004). An example of an approach that falls within the category of domain analysis is *corpus analysis*. Corpus studies are often seen as counting and categorizing constructions occurring in a corpus, yet they facilitate testing ideas by exploring language as a tool of communication. Some theorists, such as Halliday and Matthiessen (2004), in the theory of systemic functional linguistics, imply that choice is inherent in the use of language; that is, not that this is conscious but, for example, if one is using 'I' one is not using 'we'. Further, the speaker is to a certain extent constrained by what the language and register requires of them. However, others such as Hoey (2005; 2006) suggest that choice is problematic, arguing that individuals do not choose but are primed to use language in particular ways. Thus, corpus analysis, for example, can be used to explore the extent to which students were primed to talk about assessment in particular ways in two different contexts.

Semiotic analysis

Semiotic analysis involves a study of signs and symbols as well as how their meaning is constructed within a culture. It has been paired with arts-based approaches, narrative approaches and ethnography. This kind of analysis involves a broad view of cultural products including popular media, such as digital and visual artefacts. This method assumes that meaning is not inherent in the products; rather, their meaning is derived through their relationships with other things. There are three critical factors that warrant consideration: the **sign vehicle**, **sense** and **referent**.

Sign vehicle
The form of the sign

Sense
The sense made of the sign

Referent
What the sign 'stands for'

Semiotic analysis involves the following:

■ identification of the text or object
■ examination of the researcher's purpose in selecting the text or object
■ clarification of the sign vehicle
■ description of modality (reality claims)
■ analysis of paradigm (for example, genre, theme)
■ consideration of what is termed the syntagmatic structure of the text (such as narrative, argument)
■ examination of rhetorical tropes (such as metaphors or metonyms)
■ examination of intertextuality (for example, does it allude to other texts or genres)
■ analysis of semiotic codes (representations).

Manning (1987) is a leader in the development of this approach.

Event analysis

The purpose of an event analysis is to examine and represent the chronological series of events in an actual or folkloristic accounting as logical structures (Tesch 1990). The idea is that people cause or prevent events from occurring, which can provide important evidence. It begins with identification of a specific starting point and a specific end point. An abstract logical structure of the event is developed and then compared with the actual event. The analysis examines elements and the connection of elements, including boundaries, as well as the assumptions that govern the connections. The goal is to develop an explanatory model (Heise 1988). This method is often used with video, where events can be watched again and again.

A related method is critical event analysis, which involves presenting participants with typical scenarios of behaviour. The researcher solicits the following from participants:

- opinions about the cause, structure and outcome of an incident
- information about participant feelings and perceptions
- description by participants of actions that were (or should have been) taken during the incident
- resultant changes they might see in their own future behaviour.

CHOOSING AN APPROACH FOR QUALITATIVE DATA ANALYSIS

With so many possible methods of data analysis, it is difficult to know which one to choose. The researcher needs to first and foremost consider the purpose of the analysis. As we demonstrated with our sample text in the primary approaches, different analyses yield different interpretations, and so the one chosen depends on what one hopes to learn. In particular, a researcher may consider:

- important terms, as in keywords?
- frequently used terms and phrases, as in content analysis?
- a comparison of key concepts, as in constant comparison?
- the relationships among ideas, as in domain analysis?
- a general sense of what the speaker is saying, the meaning of the whole in context, as in thematic analysis?

A further consideration is what research approach has been used. In many cases, there is a direct match between the research approach and the analytical method. A final consideration in determining what kind of analysis to adopt depends upon the type of data the researcher possesses. Text, visual data and documents often require different methods of analysis. The decision tree in Figure 28.4 is adapted from one developed by Bernard and Ryan (2010) for use with some of the primary methods described earlier in this chapter.

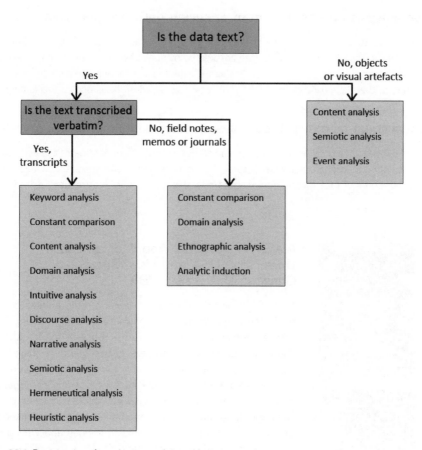

Figure 28.4 Decision tree for selecting a data analysis approach

PRACTICALITIES OF DATA ANALYSIS

Data analysis is often both a new task that requires a new way of thinking for researchers and complicated in parts. We offer the following thoughts and suggestions about data analysis.

Data analysis is an ongoing process

Data analysis is incorrectly seen as something that is only commenced after the data collection is completed. However, analysis starts during data collection (Bogdan and Biklen 2007), when a researcher begins by exploring the literature before and during data collection. It also begins early, when a researcher makes research decisions that narrow the study, and develops analytical questions. The process also begins during data collection sessions that have been developed from information from previous observations. Writing memos and testing out ideas and themes on participants is another way to ensure that data analysis is ongoing as is use of metaphors, analogies and concepts as well as visual devices (Bogdan and Biklen 2007).

Data analysis can be a form of ensuring data are plausible

Ultimately, we recommend using more than one method of data analysis. Doing so allows for a form of plausibility, a form that is not often considered by qualitative researchers. If the researcher does two or three kinds of analysis on the same data and the results complement each other, this lends to the plausibility of the findings. It may also broaden the scope of the findings.

A theoretical framework can play an integral role in data analysis

While we have indicated that philosophical stance is critical during data analysis, when a complementary theory is used (see Chapter 4), it can be a critical component in data analysis. Alecia Jackson and Lisa Mazzei demonstrate how this happens in their researcher reflection.

Researcher reflections

Alecia Y. Jackson, Appalachian State University, USA and Lisa Mazzei, Gonzaga University, USA

Alecia Y. Jackson and Lisa A. Mazzei are the authors of the book, *Thinking with theory in qualitative research: viewing data across multiple perspectives*. The purpose of the book is to challenge qualitative researchers to use theory to think *with* their data (or use data to think *with* theory) in order to accomplish a reading of data that is both *within and against interpretivism*. Alecia and Lisa's work is couched in an argument that if qualitative data interpretation and analysis are limited to mechanistic coding, reducing data to themes and writing up transparent narratives, then they do little to critique the complexities of social life; such simplistic approaches preclude dense and multi-layered treatment of data. Furthermore, Alecia and Lisa's analytical frameworks challenge simplistic treatments of data and data analysis in qualitative research that, for example, beckon voices to 'speak for themselves' or that reduce complicated and conflicting voices and data to thematic 'chunks' that can be interpreted free of context and circumstance.

In the context of qualitative research, specifically qualitative research that concerns itself with an analysis of speech and conversations, good methodologists are taught to organize data in order to make sense of and represent what they have learned. Well-trained methodologists are carefully taught to be attentive to their field notes and transcription data in order to sort and sift and identify the codes and categories that emerge from the data. However, Alecia and Lisa's methodological aims are against interpretive imperatives that limit so-called 'analysis' and inhibits the inclusion of previously unthought of 'data'. It is such a rethinking of an interpretive methodology that gets qualitative researchers out of the representational trap of trying to figure out what the participants in a study 'mean' and helps to avoid being seduced by the desire to create a coherent and interesting narrative that is bound by themes and patterns.

Alecia and Lisa adapt a little phrase from Deleuze and Guattari (1987b: 4) that captures their 'thinking with theory in qualitative research'. That little phrase is 'plugging in'. They first encountered 'plugging in' on page four of Deleuze and Guattari's (1987a) *A thousand plateaus*: '. . . When one writes, the only question is which other machine the literary machine can be plugged into, must be plugged into in order to work'. In thinking with theory, multiple texts (or literary machines) are confronted: interview data, tomes of theory, conventional qualitative research methods books, things previously written, traces of data, reviewer comments, and so on, *ad infinitum*. Engaging 'plugging in' as a *process* rather than a *concept*, is a constant, continuous process of making and unmaking, a process of arranging, organizing, fitting together. So to see it at work, researchers must ask not only how things are connected but also what territory is claimed in that connection. The figuration of 'the threshold' is a way to situate a 'plugging in' or how to put the data and theory to work in the threshold to create new analytical questions. In the space of the threshold, theory and data constitute or make one another and the divisions among and definitions of theory and data collapse. In 'thinking with theory' (or 'plugging in'), data are not centred or stabilized but used as brief stopping points and continually transformed and exceeded; theory is used to turn data into something different and data is used to push theory to its limit. Plugging in creates a different relationship among texts: they *constitute* one another and in doing so create something new. By refusing a closed system for fixed meaning (that is, transferable patterns and themes generated from coding data with reductive language), a 'plugging in' focuses on the generative aspects of texts and keeps meaning on the move. Alecia and Lisa present three manoeuvres that are involved in an analytical 'plugging in':

1. Putting philosophical concepts to work via disrupting the theory/practice binary by decentring each and instead showing how they *constitute or make one another*;
2. Being deliberate and transparent in what analytical questions are made possible by a specific theoretical concept and how analytical questions that are used to think with *emerged in the middle* of 'plugging in'; and
3. Working the same data repeatedly to 'deform [them], to make [them] groan and protest' (Foucault 1980: 22–3) with an overabundance of meaning, which in turn not only creates new knowledge but also shows the *suppleness of each when plugged in*.

continued

CONCLUSION

Data analysis is one of the most critical phases in a qualitative research study and, all too frequently, researchers give it short shrift. In this chapter, we have provided an overview of some of what we see as the most common steps researchers use when undertaking qualitative data analysis. We have provided readers with information about both primary methods of qualitative data analysis and specialized methods. We have argued that the analytical method adopted will necessarily influence the results. We also have suggested that using more than one approach can increase understanding and can provide an additional layer of triangulation. Finally, we have provided information to help guide readers through choosing an analytical method.

Concept questions

- What are the primary differences between primary forms of data analysis and specialized data analysis?
- What is the rationale for using more than one analytical method?

Application questions

- What analytical method will you choose?
- How will you justify the selection?
- Does the section fit naturally with your philosophical position, research tradition and research focus and questions?

Leech, N. L. and Onwuegbuzie, A. J. (2007) An array of qualitative data analysis tools: A call for data analysis triangulation. *School Psychology Quarterly*, 22 (4), 557–84.
Leech and Onwuegbuzie's article was particularly influential to us in developing this chapter. We found their demonstration of their analytical approaches with actual data to be particularly useful, which is why we have quoted their work in this chapter.

Bernard, H. R. and Ryan, G. W. (2010) *Analyzing qualitative data: Systematic approaches*, Los Angeles, CA: Sage.
Bernard and Ryan's book provides a useful overview of many analytical methods used in qualitative data in an accessible way; we have cited their work in this chapter and adapted a flow chart.

Sandelowski, M. (1995) Qualitative analysis: What it is and how to begin. *Research in Nursing & Health*, 18, 371–5.
Sandelowski's work provided us with a useful overview and introduction into beginning qualitative data analysis.

Chapter 29

Data interpretation

INTRODUCTION

Data interpretation can be a complex and confusing part of the research process, largely because it is difficult to identify a precise set of processes that underlies it, as well as to follow a specific set of steps to achieve it. Even the language that qualitative researchers frequently use to describe interpretation lacks precision and clarity. Many researchers, for example, use the phrase 'the findings emerged' to describe interpretation, a phrase that seems to intimate an almost magical process rather than to describe what actually happens during interpretation. On the other hand, the phrase also seems simple and straightforward, almost as if by leaving data lying around for a few days it will all make sense. It seems to us, however, that moving from analysis to interpretation is one of the greatest challenges that a qualitative researcher faces. In this chapter, we begin by defining the term 'interpretation' and examine the relationship between analysis and interpretation. In the remainder of the chapter, we suggest ways of undertaking data interpretation, although we acknowledge that data interpretation is a complex iterative process, not bound by rules and easily defined strategies.

WHAT IS INTERPRETATION?

While few qualitative texts treat the topic of interpretation specifically, those that do offer useful definitions of interpretation. These texts suggest to us three central questions that need to be addressed to begin an answer to the question of 'what is interpretation'? These three questions are:

- Is it a process or a product?
- How is it different from analysis?
- When does it happen?

A process or a product?

The short answer to this question is that it is both. Interpretation is the act of explication, explanation and elucidation. The process requires a mix of logic and intuition. A leader in the field of qualitative research whose work on interpretation has been particularly informative, Peshkin (1993: 24) suggests that interpretation allows for several sub-categories of outcomes or products: explaining and creating generalizations; elaborating on existing concepts; developing new concepts; providing insights that change behaviour, refining knowledge and identifying problems; clarifying and understanding complexity; and developing theory. The tension between these two co-existing forms of interpretation is evident in Denzin's description of thick interpretation, in which he argues that it:

> attempts to unravel and record these multiple meaning structures that flow away from interactional experience. It assumes that multiple meanings will always be present in any situation. No experience has the same meaning for two individuals. This is so because meaning is emotional and biographical.
>
> (Denzin 1989a: 102)

Such work, then, requires the process (unravelling) and the product (recording). Both of these require not only logic but also hunch, creativity and personal investment, and necessitate ordering and structuring to find the logic as well as creativity to find and document the emerging narrative or story.

What is the difference between analysis and interpretation?

While analysis (see Chapters 27 and 28) requires breaking apart data to produce concepts and themes, interpretation involves translation of those concepts and themes. Analysis describes what was said, whereas interpretation attempts an explanation or translation of what underlies what was said. Put simply, analysis involves uncovering patterns in data and interpretation involves uncovering meaning, so analysis aids interpretation (Hatch 2002; Leech and Onwuegbuzie 2007). As Wolcott (1994: 36) suggests, 'the term interpretation is well suited to mark a threshold in thinking and writing at which the researcher transcends factual data and cautious analysis and begins to probe into what is to be made of them'.

What is difficult when beginning the move from analysis, which can be quite ordered and structured, towards interpretation, which is messy, is the necessity of managing multiple meanings and (sometimes) competing ideas and views that emerge in data. In Figure 29.1, we provide an example of the move from analysis to interpretation.

While it is easy to define differences between analysis and interpretation, in reality there is a fine line between where analysis ends and interpretation begins. It is perhaps for this reason that many researchers present explanations but stop short of interpretation.

When does interpretation occur?

Interpretation begins during conceptualization of the study, during data collection, when the researcher also must determine what is important and what is not. Moreover, interpretation is done during and after analysis, when a researcher moves from processing data to understanding and interpreting them. Indeed 'all interpretations are unfinished, provisional, and incomplete' (Denzin 1989b: 64). Interpretation also, we believe, is something that is done during the act of reading and understanding.

An example

In an article entitled, 'The nature of interpretation in qualitative research', Peshkin (2000) describes a research project investigating a Native American youth population, in which he documents his

Statement: **We love the traditional red London bus**

Analysis	Interpretation
• *Key terms appear to relate the symbolism attached to 'London bus', 'red', 'traditional'*	• *The London bus represents what it means to be English. They are symbolic of London and all that is associated with its history and culture*

Figure 29.1 Example: London Routemaster bus (image © Getty Images)

attempt to make sense of the data through a description of selected crossroads (that he calls problematics) during the process of interpretation. In the following example, we share a quote from Peshkin's work, in which he describes how he views interpretation.

PESHKIN'S PROCESS OF INTERPRETATION

I have been engaged in the process of interpretation from the very beginning of my research process. I do so in order to create my starting point – a conception of what my inquiry will be about. This conception is mutable. It must be if I am to exploit the opportunities for learning that my fieldwork makes possible. I select what will come into and affect my conception. Such selection, together with ordering, associating and meaning making, is an element of interpretation. Stated otherwise, interpretation is an act of imagination and logic. It entails perceiving importance, order and form in what one is learning that relates to the argument, story, narrative that is continually undergoing creation.

Interpretation has to do with the confluence of questions, images and ideas that are the starting point of my inquiry, or the conceptualizing of my study.

Interpretation has to do with where I choose to look to see that something is going on with regard to my conceptualization, or the situating of my study.

Example

continued

Interpretation has to do with the judgment of what to collect that provides documentation for what I think is going on, or the instantiating of my study and the further focusing of its field of inquiry.

Interpretation has to do with what to select for writing that establishes or affirms what I have identified that has gone on, or the composing of the elements of my research story.

Finally, interpretation has to do with a perspectival accounting for what I have learned, or the shaping of the meanings and understandings of what has gone on from some point of view, an issue of the crisis of representation for some observers (see Gubrium and Holstein 1995). It is inconceivable to me that I can conduct any aspect of my research except from some point of view, which is to say that other interpretations, other meanings and understandings, are imaginable. Indeed, they may offer sturdy competition to my own. For everyone's work, however, there is a court, not of last resort, but of public discourse. It comes into session when our work is published.

... I have intended to clarify the intersection of my subjectivity and what I incorporated in my interpretation. I do this not for the sake of confession or self-indulgence but to clarify the sources of my imagination that underpin my interpretation and, ultimately, my representation of what I learned about academic underachievement.

I conclude my work with the best constructions I can create, trusting that I have steered clear of such self-deception and self-delusion that would undermine my commitment to the reason, logic, coherence, and the like that I strive for.

(Peshkin 2000: 9)

STRATEGIES FOR DOING INTERPRETATION

Some researchers find data interpretation easier than others yet, for many, interpretation is a challenge because it is not just about using particular devices or strategies; it is instead connected to understanding data in context and examining the values and perspectives of all those involved in the study. There are, however, several strategies that can help researchers move toward interpretation. We offer the following strategies to assist with data interpretation that can provide researchers with options for developing interpretations. We do not advocate that the researcher employs all of these strategies in a given study. Rather, we believe that the particular study will suggest which of these are the most appropriate. We suggest the following strategies as options: noticing meaning signals, framing interpretations, working with the research approach and writing to reveal interpretations.

Noticing signals of meaning

When researchers review data and analyses, it is imperative that they watch for unobtrusive signals of meaning. We believe that researchers should look for several key aspects of data to help them interpret meaning: organizing principles, oppositional talk, subtext and metonymy and metaphor, since these aspects can inform interpretation in important ways.

Recognizing organizing principles

Organizing principles are defined here as the categories used by people to justify, explain, defend and define themselves. So another way of interpreting data is to explore how people choose to categorize themselves, how they talk about themselves in relation to the issues under study. Take, for example, a group of lecturers in a health sciences faculty: some will define themselves as physiotherapists or nurses but others will define themselves instead as teachers, lecturers or researchers. The ways in which people talk about themselves, how they define themselves, can help us to see their values and how they see themselves in relation to one another, their organization and their profession. Thus, when interpreting data by moving away from themes about 'learning' or 'assessment' in an interview or trying to identify the common meanings in these categories across all participants, the use of organizing principles would explore how notions of learning and assessment are used by different participants, in different contexts, to argue a point or take up a particular stance.

Recognizing oppositional talk

Oppositional talk often occurs when people define something by saying what it is not. The aim of using this device is to 'prevent the listener interpreting the talk in terms of this noxious identity by acknowledging the possible interpretation and then denying it' (Potter and Wetherell 1987: 77). As Potter and Wetherell have argued, an example of such an explicit disclaimer would be 'I'm no sexist but . . .'. During data interpretation it is possible to identify oppositional talk more subtly in terms of participants defining themselves and their positions in opposition to others and their stances. By exploring such perspectives, it becomes possible to understand how participants see and define themselves. For example, someone might say 'I'm not an evangelistic qualitative researcher like Claire and Maggi, who believe that you need to have a conceptual framework, but I do qualitative work'. In this situation, the participant defines and defends his or her position 'in relation' to others. In examining such a statement, it is possible to see how participants in research make sense of themselves, what they believe in and how they see other people's values in relation to their own, which informs a researcher's interpretation.

Examining subtext

Subtext is an underlying but distinct theme that may be found in an act of communication and that often signals its implicit meaning. Uncovering subtext requires understanding the language that participants are using in order to understand what is being said. It also requires searching for thoughts not expressed directly in the words or statements; it rather may be found in elements such as emotion, enunciation, body language and tension. Uncovering subtext may emerge as with a consideration of the following questions: 'What is this person really arguing for? What does the person actually believe about the issue under study?' It is easy for a researcher to misconstrue what a participant means if the researcher is not paying attention to subtext. We illustrate the importance of subtext to interpretation in the example overleaf on page 456.

Exploring metonymy and metaphor

The use of figurative terms and imagery such as metonymy and metaphor, is something that is also a useful means of interpreting data. Both metonymy and metaphor may be found in data and unpacking what is meant by their use is a way of exploring the subtext. Metonymy is where

UNCOVERING SUBTEXT

Consider the following phrase:

'I can't do that here.'

Where the participant places emphasis, a signal of subtext, indicates the meaning of the statement:

'*I* can't do that here.'

'I can't *do that* here.'

'I can't do that *here*.'

someone substitutes for the name of the thing the name of an attribute of it. An obvious example of metonymy would be that we refer to the American presidency as 'the White House', 'the stage' for the theatre or 'the City' to refer to the British financial and banking industry. Individuals tend to be relatively unaware of the use of metonymy in speech and often adopt new forms through the power of media, such as the press and radio. Metaphor involves making a comparison between two things that seem unlike each other but actually have something in common. An example of a metaphor is: 'He created a storm of controversy'. Thus, examining metonymy and metaphor can promote insight into researchers' and participants' tacit assumptions by exploring how such figurative terms are used. Exploring the ways in which participants use metonymy and metaphor can be an effective means of understanding how participants see and theorize their world and can help researchers to see the influences of class and culture in their lives.

Robin Jarrett, University of Illinois, USA

Metaphor: community-bridging parenting

The question of why some low-income, African American youths succeed against the odds of neighbourhood and family poverty has guided my work for well over two decades. I wanted to better understand processes of resilience than deficits. In high-risk neighbourhoods characterized by rampant joblessness, crime, delinquency, gang violence, drugs and premature parenting, the result of economic downturns, neighbourhood disinvestment and other structural factors, it is not surprising that some youths do not develop in conventional ways. What is surprising is that some youths do, despite the neighbourhood context in which they live. These are the youths who, graduated from high school, if not college, are engaged in prosocial behaviours, and, more generally, go on to become socially and economically productive members of society. I had read the descriptive qualitative work of others and in my own ethnographic explored this question. Parents whose children who succeeded against the odds seemed to share common behaviours.

Resilient parents typically have limited education yet they exhibited strong parenting skills to promote positive youth development. Low-income African American parents raising teens in high-risk neighbourhoods closely monitored their teens. These parents know where their teens are at all times. They make sure that their teens' time is spent in adult-controlled institutions and forbid friendships with street-oriented young people. Instead, they encourage relationships with other socially mobile youth. They also exhibited strong resource seeking skills. These parents seek out effective schools, youth programmes, tutoring activities and other institutionally based opportunities and make certain their young people take advantage of them. Parents' behaviours are both protective and promotional in nature.

Miles and Huberman (1994) detail the many functions of metaphors, including data reduction devices, pattern-making devices and connecting findings to theory. In particular, they note that metaphors can help the researcher move beyond simple description to higher inferential or analytical levels. While I was able to identify and describe a repertoire of effective parenting behaviours, I needed to go further in making sense of parents' activities. I needed to move to a higher level of abstraction. As I tried to make sense of what I was seeing, hearing and reading about, I began to ask myself what is this thing like? Can I somehow link this complex of parenting behaviours to something that I am already familiar with? Is there an analogy that I can use that will give deeper meaning to my description of parenting behaviours? To aid my use of metaphors, I was intrigued by anthropologist Ulf Hannerz's notion of 'ghetto specific' lifestyles and behaviours. He saw them as behaviours and practices that were geared to the local community. Yet, I thought that parents who raised successful youth were doing just the opposite. They were preparing their teens for the world beyond the local 'ghetto' community. The metaphor of bridge seemed to capture this complex of parenting behaviours. When we think metaphorically, bridges are said to connect, link and span. Bridges by definition can also be thought of as conduits, passages and crossings. One formal definition of bridge is 'a structure spanning and providing passage over a gap or barrier'. Indeed, neighbourhood poverty and its attendant risks can be a barrier. With this metaphor in mind, I used the term community-bridging parenting. These were parenting behaviours that connected low-income African American children to middle-class worlds beyond the local impoverished community.

continued

Using frameworks

When researchers 'do' interpretation, they can use prior theory and research literature as framing guides for their interpretations. In particular, interpretations may be made using the theoretical or conceptual framework, or even the literature review, as a guide. The key is to ensure that these frameworks do not force interpretations but serve rather as a way to view them, making judgments about whether the theories or concepts are useful, and if so in what ways.

Contextualize findings with literature

Using existing literature can help a researcher to draw connections or support interpretations and can highlight unique contributions to a topic (Mills 2006). Using prior findings to frame interpretations also can help the field to advance. Doing so can provide critical context for the researcher's findings. Drawing upon a conceptual framework in particular can help researchers organize their thoughts and seek out meaning that proves or disproves the existing literature base.

Using theory as a guide

A theory also can inform interpretation and often researchers use their theoretical frameworks as a guide or lens for interpretation. A theory can provide researchers with a focus, a signal of what may be important and what might be excluded. The important aspect of the theory is the way in which it helps researchers understand meaning, contextualizing it by prior work.

Working within a research approach to guide the search for meaning

In Part 4, we describe a range of commonly adopted qualitative research approaches. Working within a given approach often provides a researcher with a framework or guideline that can help the meaning-making process, which is shown in Table 29.1.

Table 29.1 Interpretation guided by research approach

Pragmatic qualitative research	The focus of interpretation is a basic description of the issue under study. Interpretation is guided by themes that emerge during data analysis. Interpretation happens when interconnections are noted.
Grounded theory	The focus of the interpretation is to develop a new theory. Interpretations are guided by concepts and theories that emerge during data analysis. Interpretation happens when a central concept is identified and explained and others are noted (Strauss and Corbin 1990). The central concept is intended to explain the issue under study.
Phenomenology	The focus of the interpretation is to understand a phenomena or experience. Interpretation is guided by the notion of the search for essence, during which the researcher presents the meaning and context of the phenomenon to the wider research community. Free imaginative variation is a technique (Husserl 1962/1977). In practice, free imaginative variation means that the researcher freely changes some aspect of the phenomenon being studied and then sees what change has taken place.
Case study	Interpretation is centred upon the focus or unit of study. Interpretation happens when the researcher considers different interpretations (Yin 1994).
Ethnography	The focus of the interpretation is the culture itself; researchers strive to avoid bias and imposing their own beliefs. Interpretation focuses on identifying behaviours that others would find credible.

In addition to these approaches, there are several others from which researchers might draw in order to develop their studies and frame their interpretations. Indeed, researchers have been creative in their application of different research approaches. In the following examples we describe three additional approaches that researchers have adopted during the course of qualitative work: interpretive anthropology, interpretive interactionism and symbolic interactionism. After a brief description of each, we then provide a published example of how applying these approaches have helped researchers shape interpretations.

INTERPRETIVE ANTHROPOLOGY

Interpretive anthropology, sometimes called symbolic anthropology, is a tradition that has been strongly championed by philosophers such as Geertz (1973), who believed that the world and facts associated with it were not just out there waiting to be discovered. Interpretive anthropology requires studying cultural symbols to understand how those symbols might be interpreted in context, which can help a researcher to better understand a particular society. It is the role of the researchers, then, to make meaning; thus, researchers discover the meaning of events or concepts rather than observing the event or concept itself. In interpretive anthropology, the researcher's focus is on understanding the symbols participants use in context, thus interpretations are guided by that focus. For example, Geertz, using interpretive anthropology to guide his efforts, explained how he tried to understand and interpret the concept of self-hood:

> I have tried to get at this most intimate of notions not by imagining myself someone else, a rice peasant or tribal sheikh, and then seeing what I thought, but by searching out and analysing the symbolic forms – words, images, institutions, behaviours.
>
> (Geertz 1983: 58)

Example

INTERPRETIVE INTERACTIONISM

This tradition, developed by Denzin (1989b), appears to be a reaction against the behavioural approach of symbolic interactionism. Essentially, what Denzin suggests is a more critical stance towards meaning making, which takes account of cultural representation, gender, issues of class and biography. He argues:

> You must interact with significant selected others in your ministry context to uncover local theories of interpretation ... When the researcher has done so, he or she will have uncovered the conceptual structures that inform the subject's actions. Unless the researcher accomplishes this, he or she will be ignoring the subject's point of view.
>
> (Denzin 1989b: 125)

Denzin is suggesting that through understanding how participants interpret it is possible to uncover the structure of meaning, which in turn guides the researcher's interpretations. In interpretive interactionism, the researcher's focus is on understanding the logical structures of participant meaning making, which provides a focus for the interpretation.

Loo *et al.* (2006) sought to trace behavioural patterns of management accountants, comprising activities and courses of action. They used interpretive interaction to enable them to depict observable, recurrent activities and patterns of interaction characteristic for a group of persons. The researchers reported on the behaviour of management accountants and controllers in shaping, maintaining and exerting control.

Example

SYMBOLIC INTERACTIONISM

Symbolic interactionism is a sociological tradition that is concerned with small-scale, everyday human interaction and communication. Blumer (1969) claimed that symbolic interactionism is based on three assumptions:

1. Humans respond to objects on the basis of the meanings the objects possess for them. For example, using a stick to aid walking versus using it as a tool to get coconuts out of a tree.
2. These meanings come from communication between people (such as my mother showing me how to use a stick to get coconuts out of a tree).
3. These meanings are modified through communication, discussion and interpretation.

Some authors (Denzin in particular) suggest that such an approach is behavioural, since it studies behaviour and attempts to enter the worlds of those being studied in order to observe how people see the situations in which they find themselves.

In symbolic interactionism, the researcher's focus is on understanding how participants construct meaning through communication, which in turn guides interpretation.

Vrasidas (2001) used this tradition for a study on distance education to examine the nature of interaction in an online course offered partly online and partly face-to-face. Using a symbolic interactionist approach, Vrasidas defined interaction as the process consisting of the reciprocal actions of two or more actors within a given context and sought to uncover the meaning making accomplished by participants in online courses.

Writing as a process of uncovering interpretation

In addition to locating signals, framing interpretations and relying on a research tradition, there are several writing strategies that can inform interpretations, including writing stories and biographies, speaking for ourselves, using and writing poetry and reading the writing.

Writing stories and biographies of the participants

Writing a biographical account of participants enables a researcher to interpret data through focusing on an individual in context. This process demands that researchers locate people in a context and community and describe both what they do and how they see themselves. We provide a sample biography in the author reflection on the facing page.

Writing these kinds of accounts helps researchers begin to analyze how they view research participants and to engage with the judgments and perspectives they have brought to the research. The process demands reflexive interpretation and from there, it is possible for most researchers to write an interpretative biographical account that they can discuss with the relevant participant. This process facilitates interpretation, by not only enabling researchers to see how they have come to know participants but also to review their own biases – to see how they have imposed value judgments upon participants. It is through examining such biases that researchers may learn, through self-critique, to develop a better set of biases. It also helps them to see that

Maggi Savin-Baden, Author

During my research into problem-based learning, I began a biography of one of the nursing students who I interviewed like this:

Sally's belief that her learning was someone else's responsibility stemmed from her uncompromising experiences in life: brought up in a Catholic family, Sally believed that there were clear guidelines and right answers. Her low self-esteem – she described herself as being 'not particularly intelligent' – had emerged from her position in the family as one of the few who had not achieved high grades at 'A' level. This meant that she not only wanted to be told what to learn but also needed to be affirmed in the choices she had made: Sally expected not only that the tutors would provide her with the knowledge and skills that she needed to become a nurse, but that they would also show her how to make connections between herself and the learning. On clinical practice, she received clear instructions about the right way to undertake tasks; in lectures she was given a body of knowledge, but during problem-based learning days at university she was expected to take responsibility for her own learning.

Researcher reflections

they have already begun interpreting data: what they know about the participants and their contexts. It is possible, then, to begin to explore how participants' stories overlap and interlock and to examine the ways in which such accounts relate to the overarching issue under study.

Speaking for ourselves

When researchers write in the first person, they speak for themselves; this approach helps researchers to break through one of the barriers in qualitative interpretation, that of 'voicelessness'. What we mean is that many of us do not know how to begin to position ourselves as researchers and, thus, how to speak when presenting data. The result is that we try to attribute our perspectives and views to the participants instead of making it clear what is their interpretation and what is our reflection upon their interpretations. Through writing in the first person it becomes possible to see one's own interpretations. It is important to acknowledge and recognize that we also use multiple voices and hold multiple perspectives and that these change and move over time. Managing such shifts can become somewhat complicated when writing up our research, remembering how we position(ed) ourselves then, as we write now and how our position might change again in the future as we rewrite and reflect. As our personal, professional and researcher identities change, so does our data interpretation and of how 'honest' we have been in the research process.

Using and writing poetry

The use of poetry for interpretation is also a helpful approach and it is used to understand not only the data but also the place of the researcher in relation to the data. As much of what is researched is linked to people's biography, the use of poetry as a vehicle for reflexive interpretation becomes a means of juxtaposing the researcher's autobiography with the biographical accounts of the participants. This approach has been used in particular by Harvey (2004) in his exploration of the influence of organizations on the work life of employees. By juxtaposing a poem he has written about his own experience within an organization, with those he has written on behalf of participants, he has been able to explore the ways in which different conceptions of 'organization' impact on organizational behaviour and notions of life-long learning. For example, Harvey's poem 'Lifeskills' depicts the clash of personal and organizational values; seeing it portrayed through sharp imagery in poetic form helped participants to share their narratives and images (see Figure 29.2).

Lifeskills

Hidebound

Locked-in

Got to develop

That second skin

Drop the lot

Shut up shop

Pump up the muscle

Prepare to fight

Wearied

Spent

In the red

Of the mental tank

Lost the battle

Odds too tight

Taken to the cleaners

By the corporate might

Figure 29.2 *Lifeskills* poem by Harvey

Reading the writing

Reading the preliminary drafts of interpretations, whether field notes or early drafts of the paper, can also be a way of refining interpretations. Researchers may strive to develop an internal dialogue with what they are reading that helps them to analyze what they really think about the research. Moreover, Lea (1999) has argued that it is important to understand that there needs to be a dialogue between the reader and the text, so reading the writing as a potential member of the intended audience can help the researcher assume the role of tentative reader and to explore the interpretations. Being aware of one's own position as a writer – whether being stuck, in full flow or at any point in between – that is part of the process of being a clear and effective writer. Sometimes it is vital to write in one way in order to move on to a new stage of writing and a new level of consciousness:

> the ability to 'unfocus' from the person or group or data we are studying and to allow a kind of communion to emerge, such that we are at one and the same time in touch with our own process and with the other.
>
> (Reason and Rowan 1981: 113)

GOOD PRACTICES IN DATA INTERPRETATION

Interpretation is not an easy task. There are, however, some practices that we believe can help researchers develop better interpretations.

Acknowledgement of subjectivity

As Peshkin (2000: 6) noted 'we are not indifferent to the subject matter of our inquiries'. Pope (2007), in turn, identified this issue as problematic for new researchers, suggesting that subjectivity begins with the naming of a topic. Pope argues that researchers need to acknowledge this subjectivity if they are to learn anything new about what they are studying. One way that she has her students make such acknowledgements is through a 'subjectivity audit' (Pope 2007: 174) in which they write about themselves and their subjectivity at different phases of the research (before, during, and after data collection).

Demonstration of the tentative nature of interpretation

One of the real concerns that all qualitative researchers face is the question of whether participants are telling the 'truth' or even 'their truth'. As Peshkin notes, 'my interpretation assumes the authenticity of [my participants'] assessments' (Peshkin 2000: 8). Thus, a burden rests with researchers to ensure that they have gained the best available information. This goal may be accomplished by multiple interviews with the same participants, collection of observational data, and working with other researchers (Pope 2007).

Openness to negotiation and renegotiation of meaning

Part of the process of interpretation demands that, as researchers begin to make sense of the language used by participants and engage with the subtext, they begin to see the gaps in the interpretation and the flaws in what they are seeking to present. It is often the case that researcher accounts do not coincide with the perspectives of the participants. For some researchers, it seems acceptable to censor their own interpretations if participants do not agree with them. For other researchers, reaching some kind of agreement is seen as a vital part of the reflexive process. This situation is often where data interpretation feels messier and less organized than perhaps desirable. Researchers should determine then whether they are comfortable with disagreement or whether they will need to renegotiate meaning with participants.

Recognition of the role of shared 'truth'

The options about how interpretations are managed are complex and multifaceted, so that decisions about power over, and ownership of, data (and interpretation thereof) tend to relate to the nature of the research topic and the type of data, as well as those involved. It is through the negotiation of what would be a more honest account that we begin to make the shift away from description and analysis towards an interpretative account. Yet, with some topics, the nature of honesties and truths may remain contested ground. It is only by realizing that both researcher and participants' perspectives are complex and contested that we can come to know our own shifting stances and realize that our beliefs and values are relative. Thus, we believe that shared truths are achieved most often through dialogue.

APPROACHES TO DOCUMENTING INTERPRETATIONS

While interpretation can be a complex challenge for a researcher to understand, articulating how it happened can be an even greater challenge. Increasingly, however, researchers are being called upon to explain how their interpretations occurred and to prove the value of the interpretations to journal editors, reviewers, dissertation committees, and so forth. Suggestions for explaining and documenting how interpretation might occur follow.

Documenting theoretical perspective adopted for interpretation

Acknowledging one's views of how the process happens, supported with a theoretical perspective, can help a reader feel confident in the quality of interpretations. Such acknowledgement frequently is done by presenting a theoretical or conceptual framework (see Chapter 9) early in the study, probably at the end of the literature review; and then by describing how it will be used in the methods section of the work, or was used during the discussion of the results. A researcher, might for example, acknowledge that the framework will provide an initial structure for examining themes, whether compatible with or contrary to the framework.

Demonstrating the move from analysis to interpretation

With our example of the London buses (Figure 29.1), we demonstrated the move from analysis to interpretation. While we do not believe that a researcher needs to justify every interpretation made, providing an example or two of how it happened in practice in the particular study in question can be useful. In our 2007 qualitative synthesis (Savin-Baden and Major 2007), for example, we included a table that demonstrated analysis, first-order interpretation and second-order interpretation.

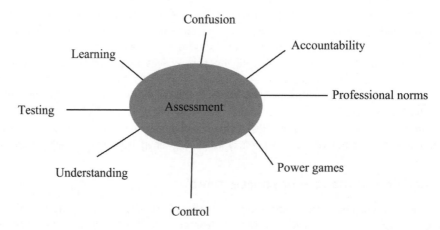

Figure 29.3 Linking interpretations

Mapping the interpretive process

One way of documenting interpretations is to use maps and show links. Illustrations can be simple, as in Figure 29.3, or, for more complex, as in Tombs's illustration, see Figure 29.4, where she has shown links, ideas and connections between interpretations.

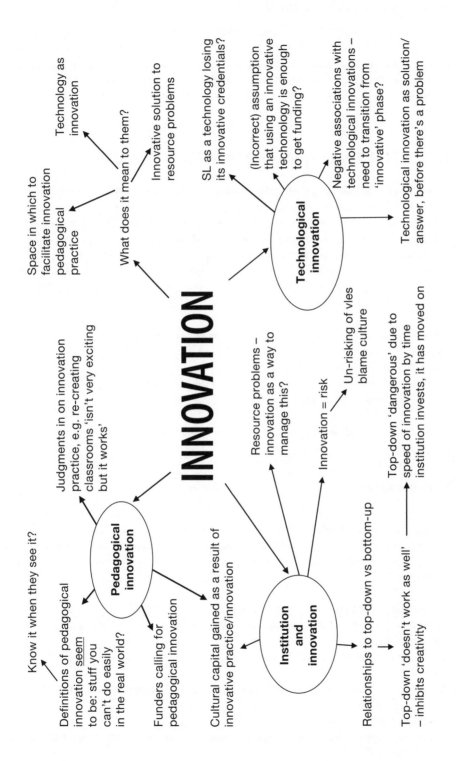

Figure 29.4 Complex mapping of interpretations by Gemma Tombs, Researcher, Coventry University

Identifying the strategies used

At an earlier point in the chapter, we provided several examples of strategies for interpretation, including watching for meaning signals, framing interpretations, working with the research approach and writing for revealing interpretations. Articulating the kinds of strategies used to develop interpretation, often in the methods section after a description of the analytical techniques (see Chapters 27 and 28), can be useful for helping a reader to understand how interpretations happened.

CRITERIA FOR EVALUATING DATA INTERPRETATION

One of the other challenges of interpretation is demonstrating how plausible the interpretations are. Data interpretation needs to be firmly based in the experience and perspectives of the participants. It is a process whereby we seek to represent and understand people's perspectives of themselves and how others shape the contexts in which they live and work. However, it is vital to ensure that we also situate ourselves honestly in relation to the whole of the data set. This should not be in any kind of rule bound way connected with class, gender or race but by recognizing our biases, values and beliefs and how they affect the way we see the data. Therefore we need to consider:

- What is being argued for in the ways these data are presented?
- How are people's biographies included?
- What are the values being portrayed?
- What are the interpretations saying about those who are part of the study?
- How is the context being represented?

Below we offer some criteria to apply when considering whether the interpretive process yielded plausible results.

Is it reasonable?

Interpretations are only plausible to the extent that they are true to their objects. As Peskin (2000) suggests, 'my credibility rests on others seeing and accepting the relationship between my facts and my reasoning' (p. 6) . . . 'Clearly if my assumptions are unwarranted, my interpretation is seriously flawed' (p. 8). We offer the following questions for gauging whether interpretations are reasonable:

- Do the interpretations provide a good overview of the situations?
- Is there a sense that what is being argued is plausible, reasonable and worthy of being included?
- Do the interpretations appear to help to explain and represent participants' views and voices?
- Do interpretations appear to reflect the perspectives of the participants and the context in which they live and or work?
- Do the stories seem logical and coherent?
- Are there different explanations or negative cases that would suggest that the interpretations are not credible?

Does it lead to understanding?

Interpretations of qualitative data are also plausible to the extent that they lead to understanding, rather than just knowledge. The aim of interpretation is to take the reader to the next level. We offer the following questions for gauging whether interpretations are understandable:

- Do the interpretations move beyond analysis to illuminating meaning?
- Have complex forces at play such as power, difference and culture been acknowledged?
- Do interpretations clarify and build upon what participants have said through the interpretation of subtext?

Is it useful?

Interpretation is good only to the extent that it is useful to the intended audience. Thus, the interpretation should be something that will benefit the intended audience. We offer the following questions for gauging the usefulness of the interpretations.

- Is the interpretation described at a suitable level for the intended audience?
- Will the reader be able to gauge the accuracy of the proposition?
- Will the interpretations clarify the meaning of their object to the intended reader?

ISSUES TO BE AWARE OF IN DATA INTERPRETATION

Oversimplification

Oversimplification is the process of just taking what is said at face value, and expecting those reading the data to necessarily understand what is being said without it being explained (expecting the data to speak for itself). This can be compounded by the use of computer packages that tend to break things down into detailed themes and words, that result in deconstruction rather than reconstruction of the data. By listing themes we then tend to fit what people said to these, rather than actually letting complexity emerge. What happens to many new researchers when trying to analyze data is that they become stuck in long lists of categories, data seem disparate and unconnected, and then there arises a huge reluctance to let go of initial categories, because somehow they seem safe and logical. Managing such unwieldy themes, helped along by bumper packs of felt tip pens, is something many of us have tried, often. In the process of data analysis we try to round off the rough edges of data, resisting material that will not fit into neat categories and ignoring the issues that we do not understand.

Negotiation and renegotiation of meaning

When we, as researchers, write accounts of the settings and people who are part of the research there is a need to negotiate meaning. After we have begun to get at the subtext we then need to share our interpretations with those involved. This is often where data interpretation feels messier and less organized than perhaps we would like.

CONCLUSION

The nature of the process of interpretation often is hidden in qualitative studies, yet it is important to consider how it happens. The actual process of the interpretation is difficult to express in a transparent way. Ensuring transparency in interpretation means that the negotiation of meaning must go beyond the mere recycling and description of transcription. Meaning should be negotiated beyond just checking that researcher interpretation coincides with participants' intentions and actions. Interpretation instead should be negotiated through discussion of concepts, language, understandings and experience. Transparency requires engaging with the issue of ownership of interpretation, so there is a sense that the interpretations presented are shared truths and shared values, and that peoples' norms and values, including the researcher's, are evident in the way data are presented and portrayed.

Reflective questions

Concept questions

■ What is interpretation and who decides?
■ How is it possible to know when analysis ends and interpretation begins?

Application questions

■ What are the best approaches by which to accomplish data interpretation?
■ How will you justify the selection?
■ Does the selection fit naturally with your philosophical position, research tradition, and research focus and questions?

Key resources

In writing this chapter, we found the following sources to be particularly useful:

Peshkin, A. (2000) The nature of interpretation in qualitative research. *Educational Researcher*, 29 (9), 5–9.
Peshkin's piece on interpretation is one of our favourites, as he illustrates the complexity of interpretation and describes his own struggles with text juxtaposed with meta-narrative.

Pope, D. (2007) Peshkin's problematics: Teaching the nature of interpretation in qualitative research. *Qualitative Research Journal*, 6 (2), 173–82.
Pope's excellent reflective essay about Peshkin's article informed much of our thinking about key challenges associated with interpretation.

Wisker, G and Savin-Baden, M. (2009) Priceless conceptual thresholds: beyond the 'stuck place' in writing. *London Review of Education*, 7 (3), 235–47.
This article also informed our thinking, and a few sections of this chapter were adapted from the article.

Chapter 30

Quality

INTRODUCTION

This chapter is about what many writers in both Europe, particularly the UK, and the USA refer to as quality (see Silverman 2005; Creswell 1998; Flick 2009; Mays and Pope 2000a; 2000b). While we recognize that the term is a value-laden one, we have chosen to use it as it seems to us to be an overarching term that encompasses many different views and perspectives. The literature abounds with debates about what quality is, how to recognize it and what strategies to use to accomplish it when carrying out a study. In this chapter, we attempt not only to acknowledge these but also to cut through some of them to get to the essence of quality. We begin by posing the main questions a researcher should consider when deciding how to ensure and document the quality of a study, and then go on to describe a range of goals, criteria and techniques for answering them. Researchers should not be bound to a specific viewpoint or set of criteria; instead, they should have a range of options through which they may establish and communicate their own perspectives and approaches to naming, knowing, and engaging the quality of a study.

CRITICAL QUESTIONS FOR ENSURING AND DOCUMENTING QUALITY OF QUALITATIVE RESEARCH

There are several critical questions that cut across many attempts at outlining terms, criteria and strategies related to quality. Understanding such questions can help a researcher think through processes related to ensuring and documenting quality. We illustrate these questions in Figure 30.1.

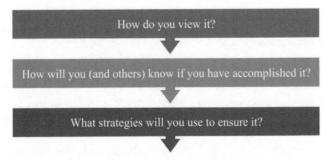

Figure 30.1 Questions for documenting the quality of a qualitative study

Too often, researchers will give much more attention to one of the questions and less to the others, which diminishes their efforts to establish and document the quality of the research. It is important for researchers to describe decisions related to all three questions when ensuring and documenting the quality of the study.

By presenting these questions, we do not intend to bind researchers to a single definition, concept or strategy; rather, we believe that the answers to the questions are and should be unique to individual researchers in different research studies. The questions instead serve as a model for thinking about how researchers define, know and operationalize the quality of a given study. Researchers have the freedom to choose terms and approaches that are most appropriate and important for them given the circumstances of the research. The decisions that a researcher makes should be consistent and relate to one another.

HOW DO YOU VIEW QUALITY?

Many scholars have developed and advanced what they believe to be appropriate terms for describing what they mean by quality. These terms provide insight into what researchers see as the core quality concept for a qualitative study (see Davies and Dodd 2002; Mishler 2000; Seale 1999a; Stenbacka 2001). Table 30.1 demonstrates some of these core concepts.

Table 30.1 Core quality concepts for a qualitative study

Core concept	Authors
Truth value	Guba and Lincoln 1981; Guba and Lincoln 1989
Trustworthiness	Lincoln and Guba 1985
Authenticity	Guba and Lincoln 1989
Goodness	Emden and Sandelowski 1998
Relevance	Hammersley 1990
Rigour	Sandelowski 1986, 1993
Epistemological and methodological adequacy	Calderón 2009
Plausibility	Major and Savin-Baden 2010a

What all of these terms share is an attempt to break free from positivist notions of quality and to embrace a broader conception of quality for a qualitative study.

We do not advocate that the qualitative research community agree to take up one view or another; we argue that a one-goal-fits-all approach would be inappropriate. Indeed, some terms themselves seem more compatible with specific philosophical paradigms (see Chapter 4). The term researchers choose ultimately communicates a philosophical view of the nature of being and it signals an implicit research goal. For example, to us, the term:

■ 'Truth value' appears compatible with a post-positivist perspective, which asserts that though there is a reality, it is imperfectly understandable.
■ Trustworthiness seems congruent with ideas that fit a critical rational perspective, which holds with the position that we cannot separate ourselves from what we know in our search for 'objectivity'.
■ Authenticity seems congruent with interpretivist philosophical positioning, which asserts that reality is constructed intersubjectively through socially and experientially developed meanings.

- *Goodness* appears to be allied with notions of post-modernism and critical theory, which hold that reality is created through commonly held political, cultural, economic, ethnic and gender values and that research can be a way to expose those.
- *Relevance* gives emphasis to the importance of the research in context and is allied with a constructivism paradigm which holds that realities are locally constructed.
- *Rigour* intimates that if researchers are sufficiently diligent, then they will be able to uncover some version of the truth.
- *Plausibility* emphasizes the idea of ensuring quality with a reader, being compatible with the constructionism paradigm, which holds that the knower and the known are interlinked and truth is negotiated through dialogue.

We believe that researchers should choose and use a core term that is compatible with their philosophical world views, and should define it both for themselves and their readers in order to express how they see their primary goals in qualitative research. Calderón's (2009) notion of *epistemological and methodological adequacy* addresses this issue. Researchers should consider what best matches a specific philosophical stance (see Chapter 4) and a specific research approach (see Part 4). When this process is completed and then quality has been addressed, researchers will finally have to consider whether they have accomplished quality.

HOW WILL YOU (AND OTHERS) KNOW IF YOU HAVE ACCOMPLISHED QUALITY?

Once researchers have a general sense of what they are trying to accomplish (whether rigour, trustworthiness, plausibility), the next consideration is how to detail it so that they (and others) will be able to tell whether they have accomplished it. This process typically means identifying criteria that articulate clear goals that ultimately may be assessed. There are great disagreements in the literature about what criteria are the most appropriate and fitting. As Sandelowski and Barroso have suggested:

> Scholars across the practice and social science disciplines have sought to define what a good, valid, and/or trustworthy qualitative study is, to chart the history of and to categorise efforts to accomplish such a definition, and to describe and codify techniques for both ensuring and recognising good studies ... [but] after all this effort, we seem to be no closer to establishing a consensus on quality criteria.
>
> (Sandelowski and Barroso 2002: 2)

There are many arguments for why this lack of agreement remains, ranging from the notion that we have not quite 'cracked it' yet, to the notion that developing a single concept or criteria set is contrary to the subjective nature of qualitative research and inappropriate considering the range of research approaches, a view with which we are sympathetic.

The lack of agreement about how to assess quality ultimately stems from a fundamental disagreement about what 'it' is. Some scholars believe that 'it' should be a process of verification (see Creswell 1998; Morse *et al.* 2002; Miles and Huberman 1994). Morse *et al.* (2002) describe verification as 'the process of checking, confirming, making sure, and being certain'. Verification, however, is not a rote process, but the notion that a researcher may evaluate quality in a variety of ways during the process of research. Other scholars describe 'it' as an evaluative process, being a documentation of quality for consumption by a reader (Lincoln and Guba 1985).

Documentation is the process demonstrating that quality can be confirmed by supporting evidence. It is critical for researchers to consider whether they believe the purpose of ensuring quality is verification or documentation or a combination, as this will drive decisions about the approaches they adopt.

A range of approaches

Perhaps not surprisingly, the growth in the number and kind of approaches to verification and documentation in the past three decades has been remarkable. We document just a few of these in Table 30.2.

Table 30.2 Approaches to verification and documentation

Researchers	Criteria
LeCompte and Goetz (1982)	Internal validity, external validity, reliability, objectivity
Lincoln and Guba (1985)	Credibility, transferability, dependability, confirmability
Sandelowski (1986; 1993)	Credibility, fittingness, auditability, confirmability, creativity, artfulness
Eisenhart and Howe (1992)	Completeness, appropriateness, comprehensiveness, credibility, and significance
Miles and Huberman (1994)	Objectivity/confirmability; reliability/dependability/auditability; internal validity/credibility/authenticity; external validity/transferability/fittingness; utilization/application/action orientation
Thorne (1997)	Methodological integrity, representative credibility, analytic logic, interpretive authority
Yardley (2000)	Sensitivity to context; completeness of data collection, analysis and interpretation; reflexivity; practical and theoretical utility
Malterud (2001b)	Reflexivity, transferability (external validity) and thorough consideration of sampling issues
Whittemore et al. (2001)	Primary: credibility, authenticity, integrity; Secondary: explicitness, vividness, creativity, thoroughness, congruence, and sensitivity
Calderón (2009)	After epistemological and methodological adequacy: relevance, validity and reflexivity
Major and Savin-Baden (2010a)	Verisimilitude, reflexivity, criticality, honesties

Such growth has the advantage of providing researchers with a number of options to consider when identifying a set of criteria with which to evaluate their work. The growth in approaches, however, has the disadvantage that the terms have become something of a confusing mess. As Morse et al. (2002) put it, 'the literature on validity has become muddled to the point of making it unrecognisable' (Morse et al. 2002: 4).

Whatever validity is, I apparently 'have' or 'get' or 'satisfy' or 'demonstrate' or 'establish' it.
(Wolcott 1990: 121)

Researchers should choose criteria that appear most fitting to their work from the outset and be clear about them throughout the research process.

Traditional approaches to ensuring quality of process: validity and reliability

In quantitative research, the gold standard for demonstrating quality of process has been **'validity'**. Validity, at its most fundamental level, means that a researcher should be able to lay claim to the strength of the findings, to demonstrate that they are 'true'. As Cook and Campbell (1979: 37) put it, validity is the 'best available approximation to the truth or falsity of a given inference, proposition or conclusion'. As Joppe explains:

> Validity determines whether the research truly measures that which it was intended to measure or how truthful the research results are. In other words, does the research instrument allow you to hit 'the bull's eye' of your research object? Researchers generally determine validity by asking a series of questions, and will often look for the answers in the research of others.
>
> (Joppe 2000)

In establishing validity, a researcher seeks to answer the question: 'was I right?'. In this sense, the term has application for both quantitative and qualitative researchers. There are several kinds of validity in both qualitative and quantitative research; qualitative researchers most frequently use the terms **internal validity** and **external validity**.

Reliability is another 'gold standard' for ensuring the quality of the process in quantitative research. Reliability suggests that measurements should be consistent and repeatable; in other words, an instrument should measure the same thing each time it is used with the same subjects in similar conditions. Joppe defines reliability as:

> The extent to which results are consistent over time and an accurate representation of the total population under study is referred to as reliability and if the results of a study can be reproduced under a similar methodology, then the research instrument is considered to be reliable.
>
> (Joppe 2000)

Kirk and Miller (1986: 41–2) identify three types of reliability used in quantitative research, which relate to: (1) the degree to which a measurement, given repeatedly, remains the same; (2) the stability of a measurement over time; and (3) the similarity of measurements within a given time period.

Validity
Ensuring that the experiment is designed effectively to measure the subject variables

Reliability
Ensuring that the experiments can repeatedly measure these variables accurately

Internal validity
The true causes of the results you uncovered; in short, how do findings match reality?

External validity
An evaluation of the extent to which results may be assumed true for other cases

The applicability of validity and reliability to qualitative research

There has been hot debate about whether validity and reliability are appropriate criteria for application in qualitative research. Researchers in Europe and particularly the UK have argued that they can be applied to qualitative research (Rolfe 2006; Morse *et al.* 2002). Such researchers argue that the goal of finding plausible and credible outcome explanations is critical to all research. Morse *et al.* (2002) suggest that 'reliability and validity remain pertinent in qualitative inquiry and should be maintained'. Long and Johnson (2000: 30) explain the underlying sentiment that 'there is nothing to be gained from the use of alternative terms which, on analysis, often prove to be identical to the traditional terms of reliability and validity'.

Others argue that the terms are appropriate but that they need to be reworked and fitted to qualitative research (Patton 1990; Morse *et al.* 2002). Winter (2000: 1) suggests that the current definition of validity is inappropriate for qualitative research and, instead, should be 'a contingent construct, inescapably grounded in the processes and intentions of particular research methodologies and projects'. Strauss and Corbin (1990: 250) similarly explain that the 'usual canons of "good science" . . . require redefinition in order to fit the realities of qualitative research'.

Another group of qualitative scholars believe that a tension exists between embracing subjectivity while establishing 'objective' criteria for demonstrating quality. In America, the majority of qualitative researchers do not apply the terms validity and reliability (Hammersley 1992; Kuzel and Engel 2001; Yin 1994). These researchers believe that the research community has been dominated for too long by positivist claims to knowledge (truth), quality assurance and the paths by which to document and prove their discovery (validity and reliability), which are not compatible with the goals of qualitative research. Moreover, traditional notions of validity and reliability are much easier to apply to an instrument, rather than a broad based approach; qualitative researchers most often rely upon themselves as the instrument of data collection and are rather guided by a self-created protocol; thus, the terms simply are not a good fit. Ely et al. (1991: 95) suggest that 'the language of positivist research is not congruent with or adequate to qualitative work'. Davies and Dodd (2002: 281) similarly argue that conceptions of rigour used in qualitative research should differ from those used in quantitative research by 'accepting that there is a quantitative bias in the concept of rigor, we now move on to develop our reconception of rigor by exploring subjectivity, reflexivity, and the social interaction of interviewing'.

Our view of the answer to this question is that it depends upon the researcher's philosophical stance. Those researchers who hold a pragmatic philosophical stance may choose to adopt validity and reliability as their criteria since they fall closer to realism than idealism on the continuum (see Chapter 5). Those researchers who fall closer to idealism, for example constructivists, may find that they are too grounded in positivist and post-positivist philosophies for these to be adequate criteria for their work.

Contemporary criteria for ensuring quality related to the research process

A range of criteria has been used to ensure the quality of the research process in qualitative research (Major and Savin-Baden 2010a: 79–84). In particular, these criteria seem to be aimed at serving as guides for researcher responsiveness.

Criticality

Criticality is the behaviour of those who are engaged in research and the complex cognitive functions that they must perform to complete it. Researchers should strive for and demonstrate critical analysis and awareness while engaged in research. In conceptions of criticality, too, scholars have indicated the need to position findings in ways that affirm negations as well as truth. In discussing criticality, Marshall (1990), for example, indicated the need to search for alternative hypotheses and negative instances and to examine biases; we suggest that criticality helps in the process of developing a better set of biases.

Reflexivity

Reflexivity as a concept suggests that the position or perspective of the researcher shapes everything (see Chapter 5). As Malterud (2001b: 483–4) suggests, 'a researcher's background and position will affect what they choose to investigate, the angle of investigation, the methods judged most adequate for this purpose, the findings considered most appropriate, and the framing and communication of conclusions'.

Honesties

Honesties (following Stronach *et al.* 2002) as a concept requires researchers to acknowledge not only the cyclical nature of 'truths' but also that the nature of honesties is defined by people and contexts, and helps us to avoid the prejudice for similarity and against difference in data interpretation. Furthermore, data about ethics, conduct and accountability can be distinguished by differences of theory and practical action, but they can never actually be isolated from one another. Issues such as these in both research and practice demand that we engage with deceptions – our own and those involved in the research – and this in turn forces us to consider how we deal with such (benevolent) deception.

Integrity

Researcher integrity is a concept that identifies the researcher as a person who will necessarily enable a unique interpretation of a data set (Johnson 1999; Whittemore *et al.* 2001). Therefore the researcher must strive for integrity, which may be accomplished, for example, by ensuring that interpretations are grounded within the data and reflected in the text. Maintaining integrity is a complex activity, partly because our perspectives change and move as we undertake the research and partly because the research and the researched change and move as well.

Verisimilitude

Verisimilitude, although an unwieldy term, simply argues for seeking truth-likeness, or the quality of seeming to be true, by examining more and more truths for the purpose of excluding those that ultimately prove not to be truth. In this way, the researcher then comes closer to discovering plausible truths. The concept of verisimilitude thus can be used as a vehicle through which an analysis framework may be scrutinized and findings examined in more depth.

Criteria for ensuring quality related to the research product

The gold standard for criteria related to the research manuscript has been Lincoln and Guba's (1985) classic text. The authors recommended four main criteria to help researchers think through issues related to quality in qualitative research:

- *Credibility* rests on the notion that study results should be convincing and, therefore, are to be believed. Credibility implies that findings represent some sense of reality. In the qualitative researcher's case, the 'reality' is the participants' reality.
- *Transferability* infers that findings may have applications in similar situations elsewhere. The responsibility of demonstrating transferability is believed to rest with the one who wishes to apply the results to different situations.
- *Dependability* suggests that research findings will endure over time. This concept requires the researcher to document the research context, making clear the changes that occur while the research is ongoing.
- *Confirmability* is a term that suggests that the researcher has remained neutral during data analysis and interpretation. The term leaves open a space for interpretation on the part of

the researcher, yet the interpretation must be confirmed by others, which many scholars, including the authors, see as problematic. The term implies that the researcher should demonstrate that results could or should be confirmed or corroborated by others.

The challenges of relying too heavily on criteria for ensuring quality

The problem with relying solely upon describing the criteria by which the quality of a study may be known or assessed is that researchers can at times over-rely on these criteria, which can obscure what efforts actually occurred to ensure quality. As Whittemore *et al.* argue:

> The problem with [reliance on Lincoln and Guba's conception] is that investigators rely on the theoretical assurance of validity at the expense of the practical application ... validity claims often appear as standardised language from methods books without evidence that the investigator went through the application of strategies in a specific study.
>
> (Whittemore *et al.* 2001: 527)

Over-reliance on criteria has obscured actual attempts toward ensuring quality that take place within the studies themselves; these attempts are lost in a sea of theoretical conceptions. Describing the criteria at the expense of meaningful documentation of how a researcher actually carried out research in our view is detrimental, not only to the research and the researcher, but also to the reader.

WHAT STRATEGIES WILL YOU USE TO ENSURE QUALITY?

There is a range of strategies that researchers can use to help operationalize their quality criteria during the course of the study, suggested by Lincoln and Guba (1985), Creswell (1998) and others (see, for example, Britten *et al.* 1995; Creswell 1998; Elder and Miller 1995; Giacomini and Cook 2000; Hammersley 1990; Lincoln and Guba 1985; Major and Savin-Baden 2010a: 77; Malterud 2001b; Mays and Pope 2000a; 2000b; Miles and Huberman 1994; Morse *et al.* 2002; Patton 1999; Popay *et al.* 1998; Yardley 2000). There are a handful of techniques that seem to have gained acceptance and prevalence within the qualitative research community. The strategies researchers choose drive what they do during the research process, both during engagement in the process and in creating the final research product. These strategies offer researchers easy opportunities to engage in good research practice, but there also are inherent challenges with their use, which should be taken into account if researchers decide to use them. Thinking through the challenges ahead before employing the strategies can help researchers to maximize advantages and minimize challenges.

Strategies used to ensure quality during the research process

Several strategies that scholars have mentioned deal with ensuring quality during the research process itself. These strategies then tend to provide formative information for a researcher so that changes may be made to the research prior to developing the final product. Researchers should select which ones to use based upon the needs of the research, what they have identified as their core goal for ensuring quality (whether rigour or plausibility) and their criteria (whether validity or trustworthiness).

Methodological coherence

This technique involves ensuring congruence between the research question, methods, data and analytical processes. Researchers make the case that they have accomplished this in their methods sections. The challenge of this approach is that qualitative research is not linear: the research question may change and methods may be modified as the situation demands; this may be accounted for in the narrative.

Experience over time

This method involves staying in the field for an extended period of time. Longer periods in the field allows the researcher to gain as much exposure as possible to the researched and gives the reader some confidence that the researcher has done due diligence. However, it is important to remember that dramatic events can cause changes that will affect data even within an extended timeframe.

Triangulation

In triangulation or cross-examination at multiple points, the idea is that the research is more credible. Triangulation may be of data (time, space and persons), investigators (multiple researchers), theory (more than one scheme applied), method (using more than one method) (Denzin 1978) or analysis (Leech and Onwuegbuzie 2007). Triangulation means that the researcher has multiple data points that can broaden their understanding of the subject of their research. However, triangulation tends to encourage the cleaning up of data, tidying data into themes and ignoring those data that do not fit. There is an assumption that data, people, contexts and methods can be triangulated and that taking up such an approach will necessarily result in some kind of validity.

Audit trail

This requirement involves developing a description of the entire research process, from the start to the final reporting. It needs sound record keeping of raw data, analysis products (such as condensed and theoretical notes), reconstruction and analysis products (for example, structure of themes and categories, findings, final report), process notes (methods, trustworthiness notes), intentions and dispositions (personal diaries or journals) and instrument development information (protocols, schedules) (Lincoln and Guba 1985: 319–20). This approach can help a researcher to remember important events and retrace steps if necessary. It is a time-consuming process; it is difficult to do well and does not 'verify' the quality of a manuscript, but rather produces the whole timetable and record of the research process, enabling easy referral back to anything uncertain or feared to have been omitted.

Member checking

This strategy involves checking with participants for feedback or verification of interpretation. As a result, research is thought to be more credible. This approach allows participants a voice in what the findings say and the opportunity to correct any possible misinterpretations on the part of the researcher. Since they have not read the other studies, however, participants may see things differently from the researcher. Members thus may argue that the interpretation is incorrect from their perspectives, whether rightly or wrongly, and thus can negatively affect data transformation. Claire's author reflection expands on this theme overleaf.

Researcher
reflections

Claire Howell Major, Author

In working with dissertation students, when we turn to discussions about quality, most students will say that they are going to do member checks to ensure it. My immediate response is almost always 'why?'. I confess that member checks are not a quality strategy that I often employ, because I generally find other techniques more compatible with both my philosophical paradigm and the research approaches that I most frequently use. I have, however, used member checks when they were appropriate for the study (such as my 2010 qualitative synthesis, during which I checked with the authors of the original studies to ask them whether my interpretations were consistent with their own). My position, then, is that the quality strategy employed should be consistent with the philosophical stance, the research goals and the research tradition employed. Thus, by asking students 'why?', I hope to move them away from simply choosing a few techniques in order to get the job done and toward thinking critically and strategically about their approaches to quality. The goal then is to have the selection of the ways to ensure quality to be a meaningful process that informs the study and the findings, and not a checklist to be marked.

Peer examination/external audit

This technique involves peers reviewing various phases of the research to confirm suitability. In an external audit, an expert not involved in the process examines the processes and products. The 'expert' checks accuracy and ensures findings and interpretations are supported by data. This approach allows the reader to feel confident, since an 'expert' and 'outsider' who is (theoretically) 'objective' has conferred a judgment about the worth of the research. However, a caution is that an external expert may not have the same nuanced understanding of the data as the researcher and may come to different conclusions. This approach then can lead to the question of whose opinion counts or is more valid, which can be harmful to research findings. Often, qualitative researchers are expected to prove interrater reliability. This is a positivist perspective that threatens the interpretive nature of the undertaking.

Negative case analysis

Negative case analysis requires searching out data elements that do not support or actually contradict findings emerging during data analysis. This approach requires that the researcher think critically. The goal of negative case analysis is to refine the analysis until it explains the majority of cases, which if a researcher is not careful can result in 'forcing' data into themes and categories.

Strategies frequently used to document quality in the product

We have over time come to view the *reader* of the research manuscript as a critical component of the research itself. A researcher, without doubt, has the reader in mind throughout the research process, particularly when developing the final manuscript, with good reason. The reader imparts existence and meaning to the research through reading the research manuscript. Research is then a process of production and response. The research manuscript is 'a dynamic vehicle that mediates between researcher/writer and reviewer/reader, rather than a factual account of events after the fact' (Sandelowski and Barroso 2002: 3).

As Rolfe suggests:

> judgements can only be made about the way that the research is presented to the reader rather than directly about the research itself ... such judgements are predominantly aesthetic rather than epistemological. This prompts a shift to the criteria and language of literary criticism.
>
> (Rolfe 2006: 308)

Sandelowski and Barroso (2002: 8) similarly argue that 'the only site for evaluating research studies – whether they are qualitative or quantitative – is the report itself'. The manuscript then is an effect to which a reader will respond. This is an important point to take into account when considering how to ensure and document the quality of a study.

Part of ensuring and demonstrating the quality of a qualitative study necessarily 'happens' during the writing *and* reading of the research manuscript. This idea is consistent with many of the criteria by which to evaluate quality (such as trustworthiness, credibility, authenticity), including our notion of plausibility (Major and Savin-Baden 2010a). As we see it, researchers need to present a plausible case of research contexts, participants' stories or participants' experiences of phenomena. Plausibility involves creating meaning with a reader by appearing worthy of belief in terms of philosophical framing, tradition, methods, analysis and interpretation. Thus, form, content and meaning become one and criteria become largely aesthetic. Such criteria have been described by Whittemore *et al.* 2001; Sandelowski 1993; 2002; Major and Savin-Baden 2010a). These approaches include writing with explicitness, vividness, creativity, thoroughness, congruence and sensitivity. Several specific strategies aid in demonstrating the quality of a research product at an aesthetic level.

Dense description of methods

In this technique, the researcher describes various approaches that the researchers employed. Doing so allows a reader to consider whether the researcher has made a good attempt during the research process and to consider whether the findings are transferrable. Often, researchers reduce methods sections and use imprecise terminology. Such imprecision should be avoided by providing sufficient information about methods.

Researcher positionality statement

This statement (see Chapter 5) enables the reader to establish the researcher's role in the process. Owing to the inherent nature of the interpretive process, there is a sense that what is being sought is not a stance against bias, but a view that the research process will enable a 'better set' of biases to be created – that occurs through a deeper understanding of the issue under study. Making positionality clear can provide the reader with the ability to determine whether bias has unnecessarily influenced the results. Positionality statements have become almost rote in some instances, however, and at times they add little and in fact detract from the overall research. Moreover, researchers tend to align themselves in classes of bias (I am this or that, I like this or that) and often they miss the very things that could influence them; in these cases, positionality statements become worth little and may even become a liability.

Dense description of context

This technique involves providing sufficient information about the culture and context within which the research is situated. Doing so allows the reader to consider whether the findings might be the same in similar contexts. Relying too heavily on context, rather than viewing the unified data set, however, can lead the researcher to make inferences that may or may not be accurate.

Dense description of findings

In this description, the researcher presents a sufficient number of strings of data (often in the form of quotations or extracts from field notes). This approach provides 'proof' to the reader that the researcher has made good decisions. It also provides additional information about whether the research might be transferable. Relying too heavily on thick description, however, can lead to laziness on the part of the researcher, who may not be doing due diligence in interpretation. Furthermore, most dissemination outlets have space and word count limitations that can limit dense sampling of data.

Strategies used in the different research approaches

Many scholars have pointed out that there is no 'monolithic' qualitative research approach; rather, there is a range of approaches (see Part 4) and a group of strategies. In Table 30.3, adapted from Creswell (1998), we outline the strategies frequently used in the five basic research approaches (see Chapters 10–14).

Table 30.3 A comparison of approaches (adapted from Cresswell 1998: 219)

Tradition	Author	Terms/criteria	Strategies
Basic qualitative	Caelli *et al.* (2003)	Rigour	Articulating a knowledgeable, theoretically informed choice regarding their approach to rigour Selecting an approach to document it that is philosophically and methodologically congruent with their inquiry
Grounded theory	Strauss and Corbin (1990)	Verification/validity; Supplemental validity	Relating data to categories Comparing findings to literature
Phenomenology	Moustakas (1994)	Truth Intersubjective validity	Articulating individual perceptions Testing out with others
Ethnography	Hammersley and Atkinson (1995)	Triangulation Respondent validity	Triangulation (multiple forms) Member checking
Case study	Stake (1995)	Validity	Triangulation Member checking

PUTTING IT ALL TOGETHER

Individual researchers or research teams should define what quality means to them. Initially, they should clearly define their goal criteria and measure their finished product against these criteria. They also can apply strategies to help them ensure quality. In the following researcher reflection,

Calderón illustrates the importance of relying upon a philosophical position (see Chapter 4) to frame questions related to quality. He also illustrates the importance of moving from criteria to research process, to operationalizing quality in the written research report.

Carlos Calderón, Centro de Salud de Alza, Donostia, San Sebastián, Spain

Quality assessment in qualitative research must be understood as an open and dynamic approach. Qualitative research is located at the crossroads of different theoretical trends and disciplines and, therefore, we should not look for any one size or closed standard. On the other hand, everything is not of the same value in qualitative studies, particularly in fields such as healthcare research. Researchers, funding institutions, journal editors and, above all, the beneficiaries of qualitative research results, need to know what is better or worse and why. If we delimited a 'good research area' that linked the substantive components of qualitative research with their methodological and procedural requirements, we would be able to distinguish three interconnected dimensions of quality to be taken into account (Calderón 2009).

The first one is related to the *criteria* or the basic theoretical–methodological references. Beyond their labels – many proposals have been made – researchers need to inform their *theoretical–methodological approach* and its *adequacy* with regard to the research question. To that end, it will also be necessary that researchers adopt a *reflexive* attitude about their roles and ethical commitments, as well as the *relevance* (for what and for who) and *validity* (what and how) of the research. The dimension of criteria is fundamental because of its theoretical–methodological anchorage, plural in its diversity of trends and necessary to assess the coherence of the research as a whole, that is, in the dimensions of *process* and *writing* too.

The *process* as a dimension has to do with the development of the research work. Therefore, it includes the different steps or stages – justification, bibliographic review, data generation, analysis and discussion of findings – which need to be informed with transparency and honesty, both in its procedural and in the more theoretical and interpretive facets. In this case, practices, models and methods are also plural but the openness and flexibility in their use should not collide with the coherence we claimed with regard to the baseline criteria.

The dimension of *writing* represents, on the one hand, the synthesis and final phase of the research process and, on the other, the principal means of communication with the audiences and the intermediaries of such communication (editors, scientific committees). It entails some elements of restrictive formalization and also of rhetorical and aesthetic expression, all of them to be pondered and properly managed.

A good example of the lack of coherence among the aforementioned dimensions can be found in Sandelowski and Barroso's metasynthesis of sixty-two qualitative studies conducted in the United States with women who are HIV positive (Sandelowski and Barroso 2003). According to the authors, thirty-eight of these reports had no explicit methodological orientation and the other twenty-four were presented as grounded theory, phenomenological, ethnographic, narrative and/or feminist works. However – they underline – the findings in twelve of these twenty-four reports were produced

Researcher reflections

continued

based on some form of relatively manifest content analysis. From my viewpoint, this type of divergence is fairly common. Theoretical options should not remain reduced to a simple label regarding the final article appearance. Ethnographies require observational work and exhaustive behaviour description and interpretation; phenomenological studies demand in-depth approaches to individuals' meanings; grounded theory-based projects must inform the category coding and construction process, and so on; and, in general, qualitative researchers should try to offer both sound and creative explanations about their research questions. From this perspective, the different strategies and techniques applied within the *process* or *writing* dimensions (triangulation, member checking, thick description, and so on) cannot, by themselves, ensure the quality of qualitative research. They rather need to be based on the elements of the *criteria* dimension.

Consequently, *criteria*, *process* and *writing* do not mean any new standard or closed checklist. Their justification as dimensions to be considered will, in any case, derive from their usefulness for better grounding our assessments and for improving the quality of qualitative research.

Thinking through all these steps in the process can help a researcher achieve quality and we offer the following example of how the process works in practice.

Example

Sarah was undertaking a qualitative study that intended to investigate the lived experiences of lecturers teaching in immersive environments. In particular, she was interested in how they constructed identities when stripped of physical markers of age, gender, race, and so forth, and instead created avatars to represent the person they wished to portray online. She decided to use the research tradition of virtual ethnography, using online interviewing as the method of data collection. Feeling strongly the importance of the readers' role in the research, Sarah felt that the concept of plausibility best expressed her personal views related to what quality should mean in qualitative research.

Sarah spent hours upon hours before beginning data collection on thinking through a plan for ensuring and documenting the quality of the study. She thought two concepts outlined important and attainable goals for her in her work: criticality and credibility. Thinking about criticality, she knew she needed to demonstrate analytical thinking and critical thinking during analysis. Thinking about credibility, she knew she should strive to document a believable account of the experience of lecturers she interviewed.

Sarah knew that there were several strategies she could employ to demonstrate criticality and credibility. For criticality, she decided to employ triangulation of analytical methods; she would use ethnographic content analysis and intuitive analysis. She also would employ negative case analysis to ensure her results. To demonstrate credibility, she would include dense description of her findings, particularly through strings of quotations from participants. In addition, she provided ample details about the lecturers and their lives to support the quotations. She also decided to use dense description of her methods so that readers had ample evidence about her research approach.

A diagrammatic portrayal of Sarah's example is shown in Figure 30.2.

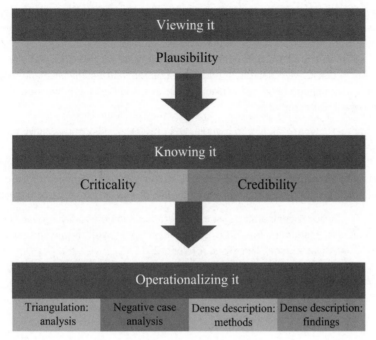

Figure 30.2 Sarah's approach to achieving and documenting quality

CONCLUSION

In this chapter, we have considered some of the key issues in ensuring and documenting the quality of a qualitative study. We have asserted that researchers have a range of options to consider when determining how to establish quality in a study. We have outlined the questions that researchers should consider when making decisions about how they will ensure and document quality of a given study. We encourage researchers to make decisions about how best to establish the quality of their studies, based upon their philosophical perspectives, the research approaches that they are employing, and the needs and demands of their individual studies.

Concept questions

- What is quality?
- Should quality considerations be formative, summative or both?
- Why is quality such a highly debated topic in qualitative research circles?

Application questions

- How will you define quality?
- How will you and others know if you have ensured it?
- How will you present evidence of it in the final manuscript?

Reflective questions

Key resources

Morse, J. M., Barrett, M., Mayan, M., Olson, K. and Spiers, J. (2002) Verification strategies for establishing reliability and validity in qualitative research. *International Journal of Qualitative Methods*, 1 (2), 1–19. [www.ualberta.ca/~iiqm/backissues/1_2Final/html/morse.html#note3]. Accessed 11 June 2012.
Morse *et al.*'s article provides an excellent overview of the various strategies for quality in qualitative research. In particular, their notion of summative and formative evaluation helped shape our thinking about this issue, although we view it as not necessarily an either or.

Whittemore, R., Chase, S. K. and Mandle, C. L. (2001) Validity in qualitative research. *Qualitative Health Research*, 11, 522–37.
Whittemore *et al.*'s article contains an overview of some of the various approaches to quality and makes a concerted effort to synthesize them. The criteria they discuss prompted our thinking about writing strategies to ensure and document quality.

Winter, G. (2000) A comparative discussion of the notion of validity in qualitative and quantitative research. *The Qualitative Report*, 4 (3&4). [www.nova.edu/ssss/QR/QR4-3/winter.html]. Accessed 11 June 2012.
This article provided a useful overview of the basics of validity and reliability and it contained an overview of some of the issues associated with the concepts.

Writing about the research

PART SEVEN

Chapter 31

Researcher voice

INTRODUCTION

Along with the myriad ways in which researchers may report the results of their studies, there are many linked considerations about how the researcher will tell the story of the research within the chosen manuscript structure. In particular, there are some choices researchers will necessarily make about the identity they portray in this report. Lincoln (1997) suggests, for example, that a researcher should consider the following questions: In what voice will I speak? What character am I? In this chapter, we offer some considerations about how researchers develop their voice, as well as about how they characterize and position themselves in the research report. We indicate that such characterizations typically are and should be compatible with the philosophical frames and research approaches undergirding the study. We recognize that there are differences in researcher position in the written report across the different research approaches, so we describe how these differences may come across in reality.

WRITER VOICE

Writer voice is a term that refers to authorial style or what makes the person's writing unique and conveys attitude, personality and character. Writers should attempt to speak in a voice that both reflects their individualities and also locates them within the research and that is philosophically and methodologically appropriate. Doing so adds to the plausibility of the written report and so contributes to the quality of the study (see Chapter 30). It is critical for researchers to develop and convey their own unique writing voices that are well suited to the research.

Qualitative scientific results must be written and presented in the accepted way, portraying a post-positivist leaning and thus writing style. So, in many journals, writers' voices sound similar and imitate the voices of those working in natural sciences. This standard form of the research report may be appropriate in some instances but not in others. Moreover, qualitative researchers strive diligently to present the voices of the participants and, in so doing, can oftentimes privilege them to the extent that their own voices become lost or severely backgrounded. This may be appropriate for some studies (for example those done from a pragmatic perspective) but not as appropriate for others (for example those done from a constructionist approach). St. Pierre describes her approach to writing in her researcher reflection overleaf.

Researcher reflections

Elizabeth St. Pierre

Writing as thinking

As academics, we write all the time; but the kind of writing I most enjoy is adventurous – it's writing to think, to move, to travel. In this writing, words appear on the page, one after the other – 'ideas, theories I had not thought before I wrote them'. Sometimes I've written 'something so marvellous it startled me. *I doubt I could have thought such a thought by thinking alone*' (Richardson and St. Pierre 2005: 970). For me, writing is thinking.

In addition, writing is always imbricated in *reading*; and, during the course of a research project, I collect data to write/think with as I read; for example, a book by Foucault, an interview transcript, a film, a novel, an article in the *New Yorker*, field notes from an observation. I long for words as I write. When I'm tired or have run out of words, I often stand over my big unabridged dictionary and turn its pages looking for a word, any word, that might give me energy and initiate a line of flight. I know I can open any book by Deleuze and Guattari and find more words than I could use in a dozen lifetimes. In writing texts that are almost beyond me, I've learned that, in order to write the next sentence I cannot yet think, I may have to stop writing and read for a week, a month, a year, maybe a lifetime. That is the pleasure of writing – all that reading.

I use post-structural theories of subjectivity to think with and, thus, I don't subscribe to expressivist writing theories' romance with *voice* (see St. Pierre 2008). Such theories rely on an essentialist subject, one with a unique, authentic voice that has been alienated and silenced, perhaps by a bad English teacher, but can be liberated and *expressed*. On the contrary, I find nothing wrong with the rhetorical strategy of *not* expressing oneself too directly, of being less present in the text, just out of reach. We write, of course, for different purposes and audiences that require different approaches, but I do not believe I have a voice that exists in advance of writing. Rather, subjectivity is produced *in the writing*. There was no writer before this text. And there is no reader before you read. Whatever you make here was/is produced as I wrote and you read. Together we move in this assemblage, this entanglement of reading and writing. My advice is to read, read, read and write, write, write. Anything can happen and will.

Conveying voice requires the writer to own their philosophical and personal stances and to choose how much information about those to convey to a reader (see Chapter 5), as well as to consider the positions of the participants. Mitchell explains in a researcher reflection.

Associate Professor Roland Mitchell, Louisiana State University, USA

Finding a writing voice, one that is authentic/genuine/your own, but that is also compatible with and does not overshadow the voices of participants

The first step in finding a writing voice is to recognize that you have something to say and then start the arduous work of convincing yourself/others that it is worthy to be heard.

Titles like writer, researcher and scholar seem foreign to our everyday experience. Further, they bring to mind historic figures like John Dewey, Madame Curie or Audre Lorde, whose achievements seem well beyond the average person's ability. Despite the fact that these are monumental individuals, we all have distinct voices and, in the end, great ideas come from ordinary folks. I personally remember as a graduate of a small historically black college when I started a doctoral programme at a large historically white university, I was under the impression that the ideas that I studied during my undergraduate education would be useless. However, as I worked to develop my own voice as a researcher, I found that the differences between the two environments actually afforded opportunities to infuse unique insights about both.

The next step is to guard against being so deeply entrenched in your own personal discovery/development of a voice, that it becomes difficult to engage competing epistemologies or areas of literature. In short, get over yourself or risk the title that all qualitative researchers dread: 'Navel Gazer'. Either end of this precarious spectrum (attempting to disappear behind the cloak of researcher objectivity or being so deeply ensconced in personal experience that you cannot relate to others) is a tell-tale sign of short-sided research. I personally consider that a remedy to both of these researcher afflictions is to highlight the relational aspect inherent to qualitative research. In these regards the following questions guide my own thinking:

- What is your relationship to the literature/theories for which you are situating your study?
- What is your relationship to your participants?
- How knowledgeable are you about the epistemologies and discursive communities that are important to your participant(s)?

Good researchers fluctuate between knowledge of self and knowledge of community. Qualitative researchers refer to these sensibilities as reflexivity but I personally believe that more is needed. The dialogical relationship that I am aiming for is a relationship that is constantly in the making. Researchers must not only be students of specific research paradigms but they must also become students of the participants' discursive communities. This stance is difficult because we are often guilty of believing that proof of our competence means that we are all-knowing.

Hence, I am calling for a sense of vulnerability for the researcher that mirrors the position that the participants (regardless of whether we admit it or not) occupy. In my chapter in *Voice in qualitative inquiry* (Mitchell 2009: 93), I discuss this position as researchers being trained to listen with soft ears, or 'ears that have been primed ...

continued

absorbent, keenly tuned to the discourses that made the voice possible (p. 77)'. This approach to research destabilizes the privileged position of the researcher, but it affords the possibility of hearing and representing the cacophony of expected/unexpected experience inherent to human communities, and as a result provides more fully developed representations.

Despite the fact that writing about qualitative research demands some evidence of writer voice, since the researcher is the instrument of data collection, there is a tendency for many academics to never really present themselves, to consider who they are in relation to other writers and the research report. Two concrete choices can help researchers make conscious decisions about how to convey their writing voices: whether to use active or passive voice and whether to use direct or indirect writing.

Active or passive voice

Researchers choose, whether intentionally or unintentionally, to write in an active or passive voice, although sometimes they mix the two. In the active voice, the subject of the sentence (for example, the participant Jane) is or does the verb (for example, says). An example of an active sentence then is: 'The committee approved the changes'. In passive voice, the subject is acted upon by something unknown, for example: 'The changes were approved'. In the passive voice example, it is unclear who has done the approving. Generally, passive voice is less clear and precise than active (although passive voice is a traditional choice in research from a positivist or post-positivist perspective).

Tips

When possible, use active rather than being verbs

Being verbs include the following: am, is, are, was, were, be, been, being, has, have, had, do, does, did, may, must, might, can, could, shall, should, will, would.

Using active verbs, which show direct action by the subject of the sentence, tends to make writing stronger; they are more efficient and powerful.

- *Example sentence with being verb*: John would like to participate in the study.
- *Example sentence with active verb*: John volunteered to participate in the study.

Both sentences convey similar ideas but the sentence with the active verb is more specific and it eliminates an extra word from the sentence. Moreover, using active verbs eliminates the tendency to use passive voice.

Direct or indirect writing approaches

One way that researchers strive to establish a specific writing voice is to make a distinction between direct and indirect writing. Knowing the difference between these two is particularly important when deciding how to present data produced from research participants. With *direct speech*, researchers quote the actual words of the participants. With indirect speech, researchers report what the participant said without quoting the exact words.

DIRECT AND INDIRECT SPEECH

Direct speech: She said, 'I don't know'.

Indirect speech: She said she didn't know.

While both forms of speech are conveying similar ideas, the direct speech is giving voice to the participant while the indirect speech is giving voice to the researcher. Researchers who have adopted particular research approaches are likely to choose the type of speech that is most compatible with their perspectives. A first-person participant researcher would adopt direct speech when possible, while a third-person limited omniscient researcher, trying to convey distance, would use indirect speech.

RESEARCHER PLACE IN THE TEXT

Developing the research report (see Chapter 32) offers researchers a chance to think and write about themselves, since they typically, whether intentionally or unintentionally, assume the role of narrator in the report. When researchers think about the role that they will play in the research process (see Chapter 5), they should also begin to consider what role they will take in the final research report and strive to ensure that these are congruent. It is in the report that researchers tell the stories of who they were in the process of the research, situating themselves in the writing, while simultaneously unfolding the story of the research. They, in essence, construct a writing persona.

We define writer persona as the character or personality of the writer as it is revealed in the writing. Indeed, in the report, researchers construct persona that Jung suggests:

> is nothing real: it is a compromise between individual and society as to what a man should appear to be. He takes a name, earns a title, represents an office, he is this or that. In a certain sense all this is real, yet in relation to the essential individuality of the person concerned it is only a secondary reality, a product of compromise, in making which others often have a greater share than he.
>
> (Jung 1953: 156)

The persona a researcher creates is the 'implied author'. Real, physical authors create different personas at different times and different places, making the implied author a fictional construct who influences the relationship with the reader: 'The author creates, in short, an image of himself and another image of his reader; he makes his reader, as he makes his second self' (Booth 1961: 138). In the case of the qualitative research report, the persona is an intentional character that the researcher constructs *with* an intended audience.

We believe that qualitative researchers should make clear choices about their places in the text, including the three key components of point of view, level of insight and degree of distance.

Point of view

There are three points of view researchers may choose from which to present the research: first person, second person narrator and third person. We believe that researchers should choose the view that has been the most consistent with the role they have assumed during the research and, likewise, they should assume a role during the research that is compatible with the way they plan to tell the story. Both first- and third-person points of view are used regularly, while second-person narrator is hardly used at all.

First person

A researcher writing in *first person* presents the findings from his or her perspective. It is indeed common for qualitative researchers to use first-person self-references (I, me, us, we) when describing the research processes; doing so directly positions them in the report. The advantage of a first-person point of view is that it makes the implied author accessible to the audience, since they are in effect situated as a character in the report and the research (Bowler 2006). A disadvantage of using first person is that the audience perceives that the researcher does not possess any extra information that is not directly observed. Thus, researchers can only convey what they know directly, and have to avoid inference. Researchers using this point of view draw attention to themselves as direct actors; attention is shifted in some ways away from the story and the reader, giving some prominence to the researcher's role. This focus of attention is more fitting in some paradigms than others (a researcher using interpretive phenomenology, for example, might draw attention to their own ideas and perspectives, while those using a post-positivist pragmatic approach would be unlikely to position themselves as direct actors). The researcher's reliability also is judged by the reader based upon what he or she knows about the researcher's positionality (see chapter 5) and the degree to which the readers find the research trustworthy (see Chapter 30). Researchers at times switch between first and third person, as we describe below.

Second person

Very few qualitative researchers use *second-person* narrative voice. Doing so requires the use of 'you' as the pronoun in an attempt to draw the reader in as a de facto character. While in theory this is a legitimate point of view to take up, the difficulty with this grammatical position lies in how difficult or easy it is for the readers to imagine themselves in the story (Bowler 2006). This mode shifts emphasis away from the researcher and from the story toward the reader, in an attempt to draw the reader in as a pseudo-character or participant. While doing so sounds good in theory, it is difficult to sustain. The reader often begins to feel that the 'you' of the research is not him or her at all. Moreover, views may be foisted on to the reader that he or she does not share and does not agree with, which can cause resistance. This mode is still experimental and infrequently used in qualitative research.

Third person

In *third person*, the researcher is superimposed upon the story being relayed through the research (Bowler 2006). The third-person researcher is a teller of the story but as a non-character who is a separate entity from the participants. A researcher choosing this point of view is limited to describing, observing and commenting and, necessarily, is prohibited from participating. The third-person point of view has a long history in positivist research and scientific inquiry; a researcher would self-reference as 'the researcher found' rather than say 'I found'. Some qualitative researchers criticize this point of view as loss of the self in research (Richardson 1998). As we see it, using third person is simply more appropriate in some paradigms than others (a researcher using pragmatic grounded theory might be more inclined to use third person and simple description than someone using critical ethnography). Using third-person can give the researcher freedom to convey any piece of information required to tell the complete story of the research; in this role, the researcher speaks with the voice of authority. At times, researchers will switch between first and third person. In particular, they often use first person when describing the research process but third person when talking about the findings.

Level of insight about the researched

The level of insight portrayed relates to how much knowledge the researcher claims to hold about the inner workings of participants' minds. The researcher may assume one of three levels of knowledge: **delimited**, limited or omniscient.

Delimit
To determine the limits or boundaries of

Researchers who claim a *delimited* perspective assume the level of simply seeing, hearing and recording, much as if they are viewing a scene through a video camera. They choose what they will know about and what they will not consider. First- or third-person researchers may present themselves as simply reporters of all that they have seen and heard. Researchers assuming a *limited* position present themselves in the text as if they only know what one person thinks; this stance is not unusual in first-person narratives, where the researcher only claims full knowledge of his or her own views. An *omniscient* position is one in which the researcher intimates knowledge of everything and describes actual events and true motives of participants. This position is more common with a third-person grammatical person and with positivist and post-positivist perspectives as well as some pragmatic positions (see Chapter 4). Some scholars lament the overlay of the positivist research position on qualitative research. As Richardson explains:

> our sense of self is diminished as we are homogenised through professional socialisation, through rewards and punishments. Homogenisation occurs through the suppression of individual voices. We have been encouraged to take on the omniscient voice of science, the view from everywhere. How do we put ourselves in our own texts, and with what consequences? How do we nurture our own individuality and at the same time lay claim to "knowing" something?
>
> (Richardson 1998: 347)

While we are sympathetic to this view, we acknowledge that it is more philosophically appropriate in some paradigms than others.

Degree of distance from the research

Researchers should position themselves in the research reports as either *major participants*, *observer participants* or *reporters*, depending upon the degree of distance they are trying to achieve. *Major participants* are directly involved in the phenomena under study. *Observer participants* are balanced participants who try to accurately convey what they have heard and seen. *Reporters* attempt to present themselves as neutral, passive observers and recorders of information. These positions correlate to some of the observation roles we describe in Chapter 25.

Summary: researcher point of view

When deciding how to position themselves in the research report, researchers should consider three key issues: point of view, level of insight and degree of distance. We illustrate these in Figure 31.1.

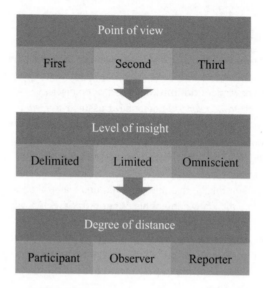

Figure 31.1 Creating a researcher persona

Some combinations are more common than others. It is common for a first-person researcher to use a delimited level of insight and to function as a participant. It is also common for a third-person researcher to claim a limited or omniscient level of insight and function as an observer or reporter. Thinking through these issues during the early design phase of research can help researchers to understand more about themselves, their views of reality and the future roles they should adopt in the research process. Also, it will enable them to prepare for writing the research report and to be more successful in the final accounting of the research.

RESEARCHER POSITION IN THE TEXT ACROSS RESEARCH APPROACHES

While the format of the report varies across approaches, so too does researcher position and voice, for good reason. As Richardson advises:

> Language, then, is a constitute force, creating a particular view of reality and of the Self. Producing "things" always involves value — what to produce, what to name the productions, and what the relationship between the producers and the named things will be. Writing "things" is no exception. No textual staging is ever innocent (including this one). Styles of writing are neither fixed nor neutral but reflect the historically shifting domination of particular schools or paradigms.

> (Richardson 1998: 350)

The various researcher positions adopted across approaches become apparent a variety of ways; in the research approach which has been chosen (see Chapters 10–19), in the topic and question (see Chapter 6), in the data collected (see Chapters 23–26) and in the report structures adopted. In the following section, we describe and illustrate the differences that might occur when writing up having used particular approaches.

Writing pragmatic qualitative research

When writing about pragmatic qualitative research, researchers typically choose the traditional research report format (see Chapter 32). In so doing, they rely heavily on description to communicate meaning to their intended audience, often adopting a third-person point of view and often choosing a limited or omniscient perspective. They tend to remain remote, expressing the degree of distance from the research as observers or reporters. Writing often is indirect and intended to convey information, although direct quotations may be interspersed. In the following sample text by Thorne *et al.* (2004a), the authors present findings from a pragmatic study, which they call 'interpretive description'. The researchers remain in the background while broadly describing and highlighting the participants' experiences. The researchers use sample quotes to support their ideas and prove their point.

SAMPLE TEXT

Managing fear

Fear was a prominent theme in the findings, particularly within the participants' accounts of the prediagnostic and diagnostic phases of the illness trajectory. In the weeks and months prior to diagnosis, fear was related to uncertainty about the cause of vague, intermittent, and troubling symptoms. Fear tended to escalate when the participants began to doubt the legitimacy of their symptoms and to question their own competency. When the diagnosis was finally confirmed, consideration of the possible illness trajectory could precipitate another wave of fear. In the words of one participant,

> You start as a normal human being going through emotions of shock and fear because of the not knowing what the future holds . . . having [my physician] talk to me for an hour or so at my diagnosis wasn't enough. I remember a couple of days later when I was all alone and had this, this huge massive fear wash over me, thinking, . . . what's going to happen to me? Am I going to be able to work? Am I going to be in a wheelchair?

The participants invested a great amount of time and energy into managing their fear. Foremost among the strategies the participants used to assuage fear was engagement in a quest for knowledge about what their symptoms might mean (prior to diagnosis) and then to understand what [the illness] might mean (both prior to diagnosis and subsequent to confirmation of the diagnosis).

(Thorne *et al.* 2004a: 10)

Writing grounded theory

In traditional grounded theory, the pragmatic origins of the approach are readily seen, as the research report often resembles the traditional social science report (see Chapter 32). Often researchers will refer to themselves in the third person and take a limited perspective as an observer. Writing tends to be generally indirect, although direct quotes may be interspersed.

There are other forms of grounded theory, such as constructivist grounded theory, post-modern grounded theory and discursive grounded theory (see Chapter 12), which require a different voice and researcher persona. The following sample text is from an article by Pitney and Ehlers (2004), who took a classic grounded theory approach to researching the mentoring processes of athletics students. The writing is formal, almost scientific in nature, and shares findings crisply and concisely, punctuated with strings of data. The sample text documents one of their findings about prerequisites for mentoring.

SAMPLE TEXT

Grounded theory (mentoring prerequisites)

Several prerequisites for an effective mentoring relationship were identified. Mentoring prerequisites refers to the 3 aspects of an early affiliation that allowed for the mentoring process to initiate: accessibility, approachability, and protégé initiative.

The participants suggested that a potential mentor needs to be accessible for a mentoring relationship to evolve. When asked what characteristics she would look for when attempting to find a mentor, Karen stated, "Well, accessibility is . . . kind of a big thing for me. If I . . . ever need questions answered or need any ideas, [I need] for [my mentor] to be there [for me]." Sandy reflected this same concept when she discussed why she was not involved in a mentoring relationship: "A lot of times I felt like we were . . . really busy . . . more time constraints really, it seems like everything was . . . rushed . . . and we didn't usually have easy access to people." Our data suggest effective mentors are able to balance their time so that they are available to the students.

The second important subcategory of the mentoring prerequisites category is approachability. Student participants suggested when individuals were accessible, approachability was important for a mentoring relationship to develop. From the students' perspective, approachability hinged on feeling respected by the CI and not being made to feel demoralized during a personal interaction. For example, Jenny stated,

> I think that for me . . . [my mentor is] someone that I could go up and ask [a] question to and feel like they could give me the right answer. Somebody that would not try to [make me feel like] I'm so stupid. . . . Someone that would talk to me on a personal basis, not [indicating] that "I'm smarter than you." I wouldn't want to feel intimidated.

Some evidence suggested that aspects of a person's personality and attitude mediated the level of approachability. Students were less likely to approach a potential mentor if they were treated in a brusque and demeaning manner and more likely to approach a mentor if they felt respected.

The last prerequisite indicated by our data involved the student's responsibility. Indeed, our data suggest that mentoring relationships emerge not only because of a mentor's action but also because of a student's initiative. Thus, a mentoring relationship is truly a 2-way street. The participants stated that protégés should "ask questions," "be good listeners," "be patient," "be inquisitive," "be willing to actively learn," and "show extra effort." Tim voiced the following:

> Don't sit back . . . and think everything's going to come to you. Go and ask questions, go and do things. Don't expect [your mentor] to give you everything in the world. It's on a 2-way basis, you help them, and they help you back. Don't expect a 1-way road and have them do everything for you and you do nothing for them because down the line they'll sit back and think about it and wonder what they really taught you.

(Pitney and Ehlers 2004: 376)

Writing ethnography

Shakespeare (2009) argues that ethnography demonstrates the analytical journey of the researcher, who is a part of the environment being studied. She argues that writing should demonstrate the messiness of the journey in the quest for understanding. Uses of figures of speech, such as metaphors, synecdoche or irony are common (Creswell 1998). Writing in this genre tends to be done both with the intent to describe the culture under study and also with a literary sense of storytelling about the culture. Writers either choose first or third person and they describe differing levels of insight, typically striving for a delimited perspective. They also vary in their degree of involvement, often choosing the observer role but, at times, acknowledging a stronger participant role. In the following text, Fine (1991) presents information from a study about a minority school-aged population who were having troubles with attrition. Her approach was critical, in that she was advocating for the culture as well as exploring it. In the following sample text, the storied-ness of ethnographic writing is evident. Fine pulls the reader into the story of these inner-city students and immediately conveys their struggles. The text is rich and layered and gives ample description to provide the reader with the cultural and political context necessary to situate and understand Fine's findings.

SAMPLE TEXT

Ethnography

> Mr Stein, at the first Parent-Teacher Association Meeting: "Welcome to CHS. I am proud to say that 80 percent of our graduates go on to college."
>
> Mr Stein failed to mention that only 20 percent of CHS ninth graders ever graduate.

Over the past three decades a splendid series of federal and state decisions have secured the privilege of public schooling for all children. Indeed, in the 1980s, public education can be considered fully legally accessible throughout the United States. Today questions of equity must focus not on educational access, but on educational outcomes. . .

> *CHS: A context of equal opportunities and unequal outcomes*
>
> Ronald: Every time I get on the subway I see this drunk and I think "not me." But then I think, "Bet he has a high school degree."

A comprehensive high school in upper Manhattan, CHS was available to any adolescent in the designated sending region of the borough. The student body was predominantly African-American and Latino, largely lower income and working class. This school was, by reputation, *good* – according to representatives of the Board of Education and teachers as well as administrators throughout the city. To some this meant *safe*. The school ranked well in the board's analysis of disciplinary incidents in the city schools. To others this meant *stable*. The principal was one of the senior principals in the city and had been at CHS for twenty-five years. To many this meant *pleasant*. The school was situated in a newly gentrifying, largely white upper-middle-class section of the city, although a pocket of lower-income tenements still stood in the immediate vicinity. The clear message was that these students and their households, located primarily in central Harlem, would never survive the local scenes of "urban renewal."

(Fine 1991: 13–14)

Writing phenomenologically

While writing is a clear form of the phenomenological process, researchers who employ this research approach also should think about how they may present findings phenomenologically. Grace *et al.* (2009) suggest that writing phenomenologically means evoking empathy with an audience. Phenomenology according to them is 'much more than simple descriptive text. It captures the essence or deep meaning of a phenomenon' (Grace *et al.* 2009: 115). They also suggest that writing tends to be straightforward, concrete and tonal. Researchers often write from a first- or third-person perspective and typically approach it from a delimited or limited point of view. This goal is evident in the following sample text of a phenomenography by Ferguson (cited in Grace *et al.* 2009: 115). In this text, Ferguson writes as a first person with a (de)limited level of insight and as a major participant. This phenomenological text deals with the issue of fear, as did the basic qualitative text by Thorne *et al.* (2004a) presented earlier in this chapter. The former text is descriptive of the findings, while this one strives to convey the emotion at a personal and deep level, intending to evoke empathy in the reader.

SAMPLE TEXT

Phenomenology

It's a long walk, these five blocks to the doctor's office and yet not really long enough. My feet are moving and the surroundings are passing, but I have little awareness. My mind is numb with fear. I am aware of little else than the lump in my neck and the appointment I am about to keep ... When I called Dr. Robb's office on December 29, the receptionist said, "Oh, yes, Mrs. Ferguson, just a moment." She obviously went off to talk with Dr. Robb, returning to say, "Dr. Robb wants to see you. Could you come to the office today?" At that moment I knew. All the fear I had been struggling to hold at bay over the Christmas season came tumbling down on me. My mind raced. I felt panic, dread, terror. I ran immediately to my husband who tried to calm me by persuading me there might be many reasons why Dr. Robb would want to see me. But I would not be persuaded. And now, as I walk to my appointment, I hope upon hope that I am wrong.

(Ferguson 1991)

Writing narrative

Gannon (2009) argues that writing narrative revolves around interpreting life stories for understanding by a readership. She further states that 'narrative can be intensely pleasurable because storytelling is central to human existence. Narratives are deeply affective, engaging and consequently also potentially painful' (Gannon 2009: 72). Narrative appeals to audience emotions. Narrative may be written by the researcher or collaboratively with the participants. This form of inquiry typically is presented in narrative form, with characters, plotlines and story arcs. The researcher may be a central figure or may be in the background. Narrative may also be intact, if it is told as transcribed from recorded media, (see Gannon 2009) in the following sample text:

SAMPLE TEXT

Narrative: (not) belonging

I started school the February when I was five. When I was in Grade One, the teacher taught the meaning of two words: adopted and abundance...

Well, it was only very shortly afterwards. I think all the kids in the country were down at our place and up came this fellow. He lived further up the street than we did. He came up and Dad was out there with us. Our house was fairly close to the picket fence. This fellow, Hughie Coke, looked through the fence and said, rather drearily, "... Are these all yours?"

Dad said, "Yes Hughie. They're all mine", talking about us kids.

He just peered through and pointed at me and said, "I bet she's not."

That afternoon, I started to think. I got a clip for something. I was always getting the clip. Dad said I grew up "like a devil untied". Anyway, I didn't think I was chastised rightly. I thought about "adopted", then I thought about the "redhead". I was the only redhead there and neither my mother or father had red hair. I didn't have sense enough to go back to my grandmother. All Mum's family didn't have red hair.

It just went on from there. At different times I'd think, "Yes, that's right. Mum'll hit me but she won't hit her own kids!" I was really upset about it though I didn't even know if I was adopted. Well, this went on 'til I was about ten, I supposed. I used to look up the papers to see what kind of work I could do, though I had made my mind up that I wanted to be a milliner. But I wasn't happy, not really happy...

Anyway, I went right on like this until my youngest brother was born. What do you think? He came to light with red hair. He saved my bacon really. He was born at home. The nurse came out and said, "Well, you've got another little redhead." Oh, I was that pleased. I felt like I belonged after that.

I kept this as a secret, deep down. I never told Mum till I was about eighteen what my childhood was like from when I was five till when I was ten, when Lyn was born. It was silly really but it just happened that way. If old Hughie hadn't come and pointed me out, "She doesn't. She doesn't belong to you", but that was all right. I belonged to the family then.

(Gannon 2009: 79)

Writing about action research

Writing about action research is done for the specific purpose of presenting information that can help solve a problem or make an improvement. Researchers often take on a third-person objective role and seek to report findings. For this reason, at times the writing is indirect but pointed (however, those who take more critical approaches to applied research, such as in Frierian participatory action research, tend to adopt a more layered, descriptive and critical style). Baskerville (1999) for example, describes an information systems action research project focused on sematic database prototyping, specifically completing a systems analysis. Two organizations were involved, a division of a consortium of universities and a military-related government organization. The organization had been unsuccessful in two former attempts of their systems analysis. Here, we provide a sample of the text.

SAMPLE TEXT

Action research (intervention diagnosis)

The initial diagnosis discovered that the early projects were defeated by the large set of data classes, the large volume of data, and the high degree of volatility in the organisational environment. The team closely attended the need for highly flexible applications, and turned to information engineering theory. According to this theory, such organisations should center their requirements on the data model, because of the inherent stability of the data relationships compared to the volatility of processes. However, the team realised that there were practical problems with the adoption of information engineering. First, there were no trained, experienced database designers available, and database design is rather esoteric in nature.

Higher government or consortium management was not committed because of the earlier failures. Information engineering requires a large interval of initial database analysis, which would not prove acceptable to either organisation. Relief from neither problem was predicted by the team. Management of both organisations wanted quick, measurable and highly visible results. The inability of previous database specialists to communicate with the users had created user alienation. Further, a tight budget and the temporary nature of the project prevented assimilation of database specialists into the team, or extended training of the existing team.

(Baskerville 1999: 22)

Tips

Avoid meta-discourse

Meta-discourse is writing about writing and it is almost always unnecessary.

Examples of meta-discourse include: 'it is important to note that the participants shared their time and energy'; 'I would like to point out that this required effort on their parts'; or 'I would like to take the opportunity to thank my participants'.

Instead 'participants shared their time and energy'; 'this required effort'; and 'thank you' are all simple, clear and direct.

WRITING ACROSS A STUDY

We believe that it is important to have a congruent research design, in which paradigms and beliefs match design and methods. In this chapter, we have argued that congruence extends to the written product. Paradigms should be congruent with research approach, which, in turn, should be congruent with research focus, and congruency should follow on through research methods, analytical strategy and interpretation techniques. Written product should be the final consequential part of the seamless process. We outline this relationship in the Figure 31.2.

Position > Frame > Approach > Data > Analytic strategy > Written product

Figure 31.2 The congruent research design

When considering the writing process in particular, researchers should be aware of their paradigms so that they know how they view 'reality' and how to apprehend it. Doing so will affect their choices of wording and syntax. They should consider their frame; all too often, researchers lose track of the research phenomenon or question, leading to rambling text that adds little value to the knowledge base. They should be aware of their research approaches, as the conventions for writing in each are different. They need to consider their data collection methods and be sensitive to how these methods are described in the final report, as well as to their processes of analysis. They need to be aware of the different ways to construct a final report, to give voice to conventions of the field, to their participants and equally importantly, to themselves. Holliday explains in this researcher reflection.

Adrian Holliday

Writer voice

Writing qualitative research is very far from a straightforward process, because researchers need to take responsibility both for being the sole author of what they write, while at the same time being as faithful as they can to representing what they hear and see. Even when the data comprise verbatim what their informants say in interview, the way in which these words  are selected, arranged and interpreted is of their own framing and agenda. Good research is when, and perhaps only when, researchers are taken to unexpected places by their data, and have to adjust their voices accordingly.

The following description of the different types or layers of researcher voice is edited and updated from Holliday (2007: 133–4). The *first voice* is in fact the personal narrative because this is about what happened to stimulate the research or to help the researcher get into the data. The *second voice* comprises the data (descriptions, artefacts, transcripts, recordings, documents, and so on). In this sense, separated pieces of personal narrative (reconstructed memories) are also data. The *third voice* comments on the data at the time of collection. At the time of writing, this can also act as data – about how the researcher felt when she or he was collecting the data – and can in itself appear as another personal narrative about the experience of doing the research.

Researcher reflections

continued

The *fourth voice* comments on the first three voices at the time of writing. This voice has the critical role of directing the reader to the specific aspects of the data which is extracted from the corpus into the written study. In this voice, researchers must take immense care to make sure that any assumptions about the data are properly grounded in the data itself. The *fifth voice* is the final overarching argument that connects and pulls together all the others, and that speaks about the whole research process and takes the final responsibility. Voices 1–3, voice 4 and then voice 5 thus correspond to the distinction between *data*, *commentary* (taking carefully about each data extract) and *argument* (saying what it all means).

It is not easy to be too specific about these voices, which can overlap and swirl around each other. It is easy, however, for writers of research to become stuck in any one of them. Studies that become rambling, formless personal statements are stuck in the first voice; and those that find it difficult to stand back and give interpretive space to their data may be stuck in the second voice. Written studies that are not clear in how they are dealing with the research and the data have not succeeded in getting into the fifth voice. *Thick description* is built from all the data in voices 1 through 3; and it is the fourth voice that speaks the description. It is the rigorous way in which this thick description is crafted, through a thorough and detailed interconnecting of data, which will provides the validity for the research.

CONCLUSION

In this chapter, we have showed the importance of researchers placing their own character and voice in the report. We have suggested that they create a persona or intended author by way of choosing a point of view, a level of insight and a degree of distance. We have argued that researchers can support their characters by choosing writing conventions, such as a passive or active voice and a direct or indirect style. Finally, we have described diverse conventions of writing across different research approaches. The central message of this chapter is that readers should think about these issues while in the early design stages of their studies so that they may plan for them accordingly.

Reflective questions

Concept questions

■ Why are there so many different approaches to writing qualitative research?
■ Why are there different writing conventions associated with the different research approaches?
■ What are the conventions that are most prominent in each of the research approaches (basic qualitative, grounded theory, case study, ethnography, phenomenology, arts-based, narrative and applied qualitative research)?

Reflective questions

■ What considerations related to writing voice are most salient to the write up of your study?
■ How will you position yourself as a character within your research report?

Higgs, J., Horsfall, D., and Grace, S. (2009) *Writing qualitative research on practice*, Rotterdam, The Netherlands: Sense Publishers.
This edited volume provided us with one of the most comprehensive resources of information about writing across different qualitative genres that we could find. It has useful examples to highlight different writing practices.

Lincoln, Y. (1997) Self, subject, audience, text: Living at the edge, writing in the margins. *In*: W. G. Tierney and Y. S. Lincoln (eds) *Representation and the text: Re-framing the narrative voice*. Albany, NY: State University of New York Press. pp. 37–56.
Lincoln provided us with critical questions for thinking about how researchers should develop their writing voices.

Merriam, S. B. (1998) *Qualitative research and case study applications in education*, San Francisco: Jossey-Bass.
Merriam provides useful information about writing case studies.

Key resources

Chapter 32

The research report

INTRODUCTION

An often overlooked and yet critical part of the research process is planning for the final report. We believe that an important consideration even during the research design phase is the intended audience and how the report will be presented to them. The report should reflect the research process itself, suggesting philosophical underpinnings while telling a story about the research process and its discoveries. While some researchers choose to adopt a more traditional reporting form, others choose to adopt alternative forms for conveying meaning; in addition, report format often varies according to the research approach employed. We believe that such differences are appropriate and desirable and require advanced thinking and planning. In this chapter, then, we present a rationale for identifying an **intended audience** and describe both more traditional and alternative research reporting forms. Developing the report should be a seamless part of the research process; design, conduct, and product are inextricably linked. For these reasons, we believe that researchers should keep the final product in mind throughout the research process and to plan for it while undertaking the research.

Intended audience

The group of readers that the researcher is specifically targeting

WHAT IS A QUALITATIVE RESEARCH REPORT?

A research report is a text that presents and describes findings from an empirical research study (Barzun and Graff 2004). Beyond simple presentation and description, however, a report explains, interprets and defends positions and findings. The researcher may also use the research report to suggest ways forward and implications for practice. In the case of qualitative research, developing a research report means telling the story of the entire research so that it describes the researchers' rationale for taking it on: the ideas and concepts that underpinned the study. It should also include the methods that were used to gather information, the analytical processes that were used to discover new knowledge and the resulting interpretations. Reports may appear in many different dissemination formats including dissertations, theses, monographs, books, book chapters, journal articles and online sources.

LOCATING THE INTENDED AUDIENCE

As Merriam (1998: 229) suggests 'the first and one of the most important considerations in preparing to write your final report is deciding whom the report is for'. Indeed, the audience is a critical factor when framing the research report. Marshall and Rossman (2006) suggest that the usefulness of the research report to its intended audience may be more important than the study's methodological rigour. Similarly, Wolcott (2009: 6) argues that 'there is little point to writing up qualitative research if we cannot get anyone to read what we have to report, and no point at all to research without reporting'.

The intended audience is important and should be considered fully in the research planning and design process, rather than only being considered when the research has been conducted, almost as an afterthought. Furthermore, it is critical from the outset to make a distinction between the intended audience and the **reader** (Major and Savin-Baden 2010a).

Reader
Anyone who comes across the report and reads it for any number of purposes

Having a writing plan will enable researchers to communicate with an intended audience from the outset and ensure that the correct kind and quantity of data are collected in order to develop the report. It also will ensure they make sound decisions about how to analyze and interpret those data so that an audience will be open and able to make meaning from them, since the audience co-creates meaning with the reader. As Richardson suggests:

> Unlike quantitative work, which can carry its meaning in tables and summaries, qualitative work depends upon people's reading it. Just as a piece of literature is not equivalent to its 'plot summary', qualitative research is not contained in its abstracts. Qualitative research has to be read, not scanned; its meaning is in the reading.
>
> (Richardson 1998: 346)

Indeed, a research report is a dialogue between the researcher and the reader. Thus, being aware of and trying to communicate with an intended audience helps researchers to ensure that they are thinking about the details that will be essential to convey to a reader. This distinction is necessary because research texts have meaning when they are read and understood by a reader and the focus can be sharper when having a particular readership in mind. As Schatzman and Strauss state:

> Since one can hardly write or say anything without there being some real or imagined audience to receive it, any description necessarily will vary according to the audience to which it is directed. Audiences 'tell' what substances to include, what to emphasise, and the level and complexity of the abstractions needed to convey essential facts and ideas.
>
> (Schatzman and Strauss 1973: 118)

There are several ways in which the audience offers the researcher indications about what to include, which should be taken into account during the design process.

WAYS THAT THE AUDIENCE 'TELLS' WHAT TO INCLUDE IN THE RESEARCH REPORT

Understanding the intended audience for the study will influence the kind of information that a researcher will present to set the context of the study, through the introduction of the paper and the literature review (Major and Savin-Baden 2010a). Some of the issues to consider are:

- *Different audiences will have different levels of knowledge about a topic.* Researchers who are writing for novice audiences have a duty to provide adequate background information for them. Some audiences will need more persuasion about the value of the topic than others, which can influence the amount of detail and information that a researcher will need to include.
- *Different audiences will also have different preconceptions or misconceptions about the subject.* The amount of text that researchers will have to use in establishing the information required to counter misconceptions or to lay the foundation necessary to understand the findings is also determined by the intended audience. This 'telling' requires that a researcher spend time evaluating the value of potential research, situating it within the broader research context from the outset (see Chapter 8) and considering its dissemination and publication.
- *The audience also affects the way that the researcher presents methods and findings.* In particular, different stakeholder groups tend to want different levels of detail and different presentation formats (Major and Savin-Baden 2010a). Policy makers may want short and succinct as well as visually appealing overviews. Teachers, nurses, doctors and researchers might prefer to have less of an overview, but rather more detail for providing guidance for specific actions that they might then take in practice or research. Knowing the intended audience can help researchers present the findings to their best effect. This 'telling' that the audience does requires a researcher to consider the focus of the work, which in turn influences the unit of analysis, as well as the scope of the study (see Chapter 6).
- *The audience affects what recommendations are likely to be of interest.* University leaders might be more concerned with knowing about how to affect change on campus or how to conduct staff development workshops, while a teacher might appreciate tips for applying a pedagogical approach in the classroom. What researchers say about the process, the findings and the future should be directed to the intended audience, since they are the ones who will make meaning of them. Targeting a specific group can allow for clarity of focus as well as economy of language.
- *Knowing the intended audience will affect the format a researcher will choose* (Major and Savin-Baden 2010a). Indeed, as some scholars have suggested, 'We have to approach it as an analytical task, in which the form of our reports and representations is as powerful and significant as their content' (Coffee and Atkinson 1996: 109). The format of the report is part of the meaning of the research (form is meaning and meaning is form). Indeed, White *et al.* (2003) suggest that the report is a continuation of the interpretation (see Chapter 29). Since the audience are participants in the meaning-making process, it is critical to identify the form that will best enable them to make meaning.

FORMS OF REPORTING

There really is no one unique way that a researcher must 'write up' a research report. Many social science research papers, however, tend to follow a fairly standard and widely accepted format.

They do so largely because social science research reporting has been done this way for decades, originating with positivist research and the scientific method and shifting over time to reflect the social science disciplines; hence, it is what social science researchers know. Moreover, this somewhat conventional format in many ways mirrors the research design and process and, thus, it is a logical way to present and share information. It is a particularly effective form for those operating from a pragmatic paradigm (see Chapter 4). Yet many researchers who have adopted other stances have modified this format for their own use, changing and adapting the format to suit their own needs or have rejected and subverted it outright. As it is so widely used and it reflects the research process itself, we believe that it is important for a researcher to know this conventional format even if (and perhaps especially so) a researcher eventually makes the decision not to follow it. There are many texts that describe the reporting form of social research, specifically qualitative, with good effect (for example, Hammersley and Atkinson 1995; Holloway and Wheeler 1996; Patton 2002; Rubin and Rubin 1995; Seale 1999b; Strauss and Corbin 1998; Wolcott 2009). In Table 32.1 we outline what many see as the main elements of a social science research report.

Table 32.1 Elements of a social science research paper (adapted from Major and Savin-Baden 2010)

Element	Description
Introduction	Outlines the need for the study, often indicating a need for change in policy and practice
Literature review	Describes the key literature related to the research; often argues for filling a knowledge gap
Research methods	Contains a description and justification of the research approach (see Part 4) selected as well as a description of the process(es) of data collection (see Part 5) and approaches to data analysis and interpretation (see Part 6)
Findings	Presents findings of the study, generally done in both report and visual form
Discussion	Translates knowledge into useful and consumable information for a specific audience, often attempting to appeal to both researchers and decision makers. Typically makes suggestions for practice as well as for future research
Conclusion	Briefly summarizes the key findings, highlights their relevance and argues for the importance of having undertaken the research

In the next few sections, we highlight the purpose of each of these various sections in a traditionally formatted research report.

Claire Howell Major, Author

When working with students who are writing dissertation proposals, I tell them that, in chapter 1, they should *argue* that the study should be done. In chapter 2, they should *argue* for how the proposed study builds, extends or problematizes the existing literature. In chapter 3, they should *argue* for why the methods they have selected are the most appropriate for the study. I tell them that the dissertation proposal is not simply a recounting of information; it is an argument for why and how the study should be done. It is my impression that those students who make the strongest arguments are the ones who have the most collegial and productive dissertation proposal meetings.

Researcher reflections

The introduction

The introduction to a research report is intended both to draw reader attention and interest and also to serve as the reader's orientation to various elements of the study (Major and Savin-Baden 2010a). It lays out a clear rationale for why the research is important to undertake (see Chapter 6). As such, the introduction is the first signal of the research problem, questions or issues to be investigated (Creswell 1994). The introduction also lays critical groundwork to develop the reader's knowledge of the topic and important contextual considerations. Finally, the introduction establishes the research question and the method of investigation (Creswell 1994; Calabrese 2006). The focus of the introduction is to guide readers in, to tell them what you are going to tell them. It is both important to outline this initial information in the introduction and it is also essential for the researcher to acknowledge the presence of the reader, whether implicitly or explicitly, thereby helping to gain attention and support for the work. Researchers should strive to address the audience directly as they work through the different elements of the introduction.

The literature review

In Chapter 8, we described the processes involved in conducting a literature review. Below, we provide information about what is required when writing this section for a report (Major and Savin-Baden 2010a).

Description of the processes undertaken

Generally, a researcher documents the processes taken to identify previous studies, to evaluate them and to select them for inclusion in the literature review. All too frequently, researchers fail to provide any information about their biases in selecting and evaluating studies, which gives a reader inadequate information to determine whether the author has done an appropriate review. At times, search terms and protocols for inclusion and exclusion are appropriate to include, as they provide an audience with clues about what has been included and what might have been overlooked.

Thematic overview of related research

Normally, a researcher will present the prior research (and other literature if being included) thematically (Calabrese 2006). Doing so provides the reader with information about the kinds of research that have already been done. It also helps to set the stage for the future study by moving toward the creation of a conceptual framework.

Tips

When writing up the literature review, think about four or five main themes that become apparent from that literature. Highlighting these main themes will help the reader understand how you are positioning your research in relation to this information.

There are instances, however, when the prior research may be best presented chronologically or study-by-study if the particular research warrants it, although we find that such instances are rare.

Description of specific studies

It is useful to provide detail about the studies included for a reader to be able to judge their merit or worth. This means providing some details about methods, numbers in the study and the type of research undertaken, as this is invaluable for helping readers understand what took place in the study. Moreover, choosing appropriate verbs for precision of meaning can also be valuable (for example, the researcher 'found' if describing a finding, the researcher 'argued' if presenting an argument, or the researcher 'concluded' if the researcher has gone beyond findings into a discussion or consideration of the work).

Providing orienting concepts

Some research approaches do not require a full literature review prior to collecting and analyzing data (classic grounded theory, for example). However, excluding prior literature from a report can leave a reader feeling mystified and without adequate information necessary to understand the study. One approach to using literature in a qualitative research study is to provide an overview or highlight the chief bodies of knowledge that the audience will be expected to understand, in order to be able to appreciate the findings and interpretations of the studies. This approach works particularly well when the research is not well known or when it is doubtful that an audience has had much access or exposure to it.

Orienting concepts

In Savin-Baden and Major (2007) for example, the study was about how using problem-based learning changed staff teaching knowledge and practice. For their literature review, the authors provided an overview of three key areas of literature:

- teacher knowledge
- pedagogical content knowledge/discipline-based pedagogy
- staff experience of problem-based learning.

Without information about these framing concepts, audience members who were unfamiliar with the knowledge bases would have had more difficulty understanding what staff may know about teaching and learning, and thus how staff knowledge may change with time and experience.

Example

Description of the theoretical or conceptual framework, if used

The literature review section can be the place in which researchers present the theoretical or conceptual framework (or both) used in the study (Creswell 1994). Other researchers may position frameworks in the approaches chapter. Typically, this section involves a general description of the framework, an outline of its essential features and elements, and a model or figure of some kind to illustrate it. Researchers also may wish to include information about who else has used a similar model and how, if appropriate.

Research methods

The methods section serves several purposes. It involves presenting the argument for conducting a study (Major and Savin-Baden 2010a). It also outlines the specific steps that the researchers took throughout the research process (Creswell 1994; Calabrese 2006). The overarching goal in this section is to make the study process transparent to the intended audience, and to explain why the study should have been carried out in the way that it was actually done. Generally, the following subsections are included in the methods section:

- *Statement of and rationale for overall research tradition.* In this section, the researcher states that the research will be qualitative and offers a rationale for why that is the best approach to answering the overarching research question.
- *Proposed research approach.* This section identifies the specific research approach (case study, ethnography, grounded theory) and argues why it is the most appropriate choice.
- *Main research question and potential sub-questions.* The researcher states the research questions (how, what, why) and sub-questions.
- *Site selection and rationale.* This section describes the site of the research, in terms specific enough for the reader to understand the context (but usually not specific enough to identify the institution/s) and articulates why the site is the best one for the research.
- *Participant selection and rationale.* In this section, the researcher describes the participants. This section generally indicates the number of participants and often provides information about demographic characteristics as well as any characteristics that are distinctive and important to the study.
- *Ethics section.* This section indicates what the ethical implications of the study were and how they were dealt with, and it outlines the way the researcher tackled issues such as bias, ethics, informed consent and plausibility.
- *Data collection procedures.* In this section, researchers discuss the ways in which data collection occurred, including how access to the site was gained, how participants were invited, and how data were stored. Researchers also describe the data collection methods, such as interviews and observations (see Part 5).
- *Data analysis procedures.* In this section, which all too frequently is given short shrift in qualitative studies, researchers provide information about what methods were used to analyze the data (see Chapters 27 and 28).
- *Data interpretation processes.* In this section, a researcher provides information about the interpretive process, most often citing a philosophical paradigm as well as a theoretical or conceptual framework that guides thinking (see Chapter 29).

The findings

The purpose of the findings section provides an opportunity to present what has been discovered through the process of study. At the heart of the findings section should be a presentation of the discoveries made (Major and Savin-Baden 2010a). This aspect is the researchers' opportunity to tell the story that they found contained in the data (Calabrese 2006). The process involves constructing a logical report designed to weave the information together in a way that makes sense and that is plausible to the audience. Researchers typically present the report by plotting themes in a logical order, presenting exemplars and indicating the transitions. We believe that it is possible to accomplish these goals by choosing a logical structure, relying on thick description and using visual displays, which we discuss in the next few sections.

Selecting an organizational structure

The findings sections of qualitative research studies may take a number of forms. While we do not wish to prescribe any one structure, there are a number of structures that can be particularly helpful in organizing a qualitative research study (Major and Savin-Baden 2010a). These are:

1. *Narrative logic.* The idea behind a narrative ordering of a study is that there is an overarching story implicit in the data that should be told. This story is unfolded and presented with an eye toward the artistic and creative elements of storytelling. Chronology often is the device used to order the narrative.
2. *Natural presentation.* This organizational structure often is suited to presentation of findings from a study that demonstrates a process. The findings are arranged in a way that mirrors the process, so that it is a natural sequencing of events or actions. The process may or may not be a linear one and the key elements are identified and presented in sequence.
3. *Central concept.* If the study uncovered a central or umbrella concept, the content of the report may be organized around it. In this approach the central concept is generally treated initially and sub-concepts are introduced while demonstrating how they support the central concept.
4. *Most important to least important.* We find that in qualitative studies, some themes and concepts are more prevalent than others but, often, the presentation treats them as if they are of equal weight. Presenting them from most important to least important provides the reader with a sense of scale.
5. *Most simple to most complex.* This approach is useful for presenting complicated findings, particularly to busy readers who would appreciate a scaffolding effect. The findings are arranged from simple ideas building to more complex concepts, which require more unpacking.
6. *Theory guided.* As we noted above, researchers may wish to use a conceptual or theoretical frame to guide interpretations. If this is done, then the theory may provide a logical structure for sequencing themes and concepts.
7. *Thematic presentation.* This is where the findings are presented as three to five overarching themes that researchers have discovered in the data. Together they are used to frame the data for the whole study, comprising thick description and in-depth interpretation of data.

These strategies are logical ways to structure findings but they are only effective if exemplars demonstrate their efficacy as devices. Exemplars are often events, observations, actions, details or examples that illustrate the researcher's accuracy in interpreting the data. They are best conveyed through use of thick description.

The discussion

In developing a discussion section, researchers go beyond the presentation of findings and are able to spend time providing a rationale for them, as they articulate ways in which the interpretations are supported. The discussion is a place to stand – a place to get your message across about what it is that you have found. This section typically comprises three key areas: connecting the findings to theory and literature; recommendations for research; and recommendations for practice and policy (Major and Savin-Baden 2010a), which we describe more fully in the next few sections.

Connecting the findings to theory and literature

A discussion section generally begins by reflecting on the findings of the study in terms of the key themes. Researchers illuminate both the themes and their significance to the overall study; they also connect themes to other literature and make connections to a theoretical body of knowledge and in some cases to quantitative literature, showing how the study extends those findings. Links may also be made with qualitative literature, showing how the findings support, refute or build a bridge to connect related concepts. The general discussion can tie together large bodies of knowledge for the reader, showing important connections that the findings have demonstrated.

Recommendations for research

In making recommendations for further research, researchers have an opportunity to drive the development of a field of study or discipline, by saying where the research has led and what it has shown. Furthermore, researchers often have a sense of the location of problematic areas in the literature and can indicate how the research should be improved or expanded. Several key areas for researchers to consider include whether in future studies:

- There are different people/stakeholders who should be interviewed.
- There are different environments that should be examined.
- There are similar conditions/events/processes/subjects that should be studied.
- There are methodological gaps that are apparent.
- New questions have emerged as a result of the study that need to be researched.

Such considerations can drive the development of future research and thus knowledge production. This review, however, must be done with grace and caution. It is equally important for researchers to indicate what has been done well in the research as it is to point out what should be done in the future.

Recommendations for policy and practice

The findings generally are intended both to prompt conversations and debates and also to inform policy and practice. The section on recommendations for policy and practice is often the section most read by policy makers and busy academics. They are also often the most difficult to write, because they represent a shift in the way researchers think about findings, and also because of the confusion over the aims of existing policies and lack of information about how to make recommendations for them. We recommend thinking about the differences between policies, procedures and guidelines, which we define below:

- Policies are strategies, rules and principles intended to guide actions.
- Procedures involve an action or set of actions that are necessary to implement policies.
- Guidelines are statements of procedures required to carry out policies, usually written in abridged form and made widely available.

Researchers can focus on any or all of these for making recommendations for policy. To illustrate our point, we offer an example here.

Example

Policy, procedure and guideline

In Major's article (2010) about lecturer experiences online, her intended audience was university administrators. She found that lecturers who participate in distance learning change their views of their roles. Thus, she made several recommendations, which may be thought of as influencing policy, procedure and guidelines as follows:

Table 32.2 Recommendations for influencing policy, procedure and guidelines

Policy	Lecturers who are planning to teach online should be prepared for a change in roles
Procedure	Lecturers who are planning to use distance learning will participate in staff development workshops describing how roles may change online
Guideline	The university requires that lecturers who teach online will participate in a professional development orientation workshop, as outlined in the online handbook

In recommendations for future policy and practice, researchers have the opportunity to discuss how their findings can contribute to important changes in these areas, as well as to outline specific steps or actions that should be taken.

The conclusion

The conclusion is an opportunity for a final word to the reader and thus is a space to argue for the importance of the study. There are several strategies that researchers can employ when developing a conclusion. We offer a few suggestions for consideration:

- Conclude by returning to the ideas, concepts, examples, facts or themes presented in the introduction. While it is important to steer away from introducing new concepts, it also is important to provide a sense of completeness of the study. Returning to initial concepts can help the reader feel that the study has been tied together and provide a sense of closure.
- Summarize the key points or findings from the paper. Researchers should not rely on the conclusion to summarize the important points by repeating them verbatim. A brief summary can help reiterate and reinforce the 'take away' points.
- Acknowledge the lack of conclusion to the study itself. Often, researchers feel like they have assumed a position of knowing 'the answers'. However, it is just as important to acknowledge when there is no definite conclusion to be made. Indeed, often what is found during a study is that there are more questions to be asked; this is a valid concluding point as well.
- Ensure that the 'so what' questions are answered. In short, show what the implications are and illustrate that it is not a utopian study with no consequences. The study should take care to make sure that it has some implication, and this can be accomplished by ensuring its importance and implications are presented clearly.
- Speculate on the future of the topic and make inferences for the direction it will develop. Researchers have assumed the role of authority (in a manner of speaking) on a given topic and thus have the important task of discussing where the future of the work lies.

■ Consider the methodological implications of the work. While the subject matter is important, the process of qualitative research study is always being developed. Thus, researchers will want to spend time discussing the methodological issues that arose during the work, to provide future researchers with sound advice.

While these are among a range of suggestions, ultimately, what is included in a conclusion is dependent upon study goals, the intended audience, the findings, their implications and the methodological issues that arose during the study. At its heart, though, the conclusion should function to provide a sense of closure and leave the reader with a lasting impression of the study. Jones and Vitullo have the following researcher reflection.

Researcher reflections

Photograph by Michael Branscom

Elizabeth Jones and Elizabeth Vitullo, Holy Family University, USA and West Virginia University, USA

Adopting the typical structure for a social science research paper

The typical structure of a social science research paper can help researchers demonstrate that qualitative research is a viable method to investigate real issues or problems in the field of study. In our article in the *Journal of General Education* (Vitullo and Jones 2010), we used this structure to good advantage.

We began the article with a short problem statement that discussed the key assessment issues in higher education. This problem statement was necessary and set the context for issues facing college faculty and administrators. The purpose of our study was to investigate the current learning outcomes and assessment practices in selected schools of business. We wanted to find what types of general education learning outcomes (such as critical thinking, information literacy, or communication) were important in schools of business. We stated four open-ended research questions that closely tied back to the purpose of our study.

We presented a short literature review that was directly tied to the purpose of the study and the research questions. We utilized recent literature that focused on our research questions. Such literature was mainly from refereed journals and books. Using these types of literature sources strengthened the overall research. We also described how we selected certain schools of business to be part of this study and identified the criteria we used to make these selections. Our intent was to find accredited schools of business that had a history of doing assessment and were considered models in terms of their practices. An advantage to formally reviewing models of good practice was that we could find important information to share with others who seek to strengthen their own practices. We described our analytical techniques for reviewing the information in the assessment documents and stated the limitations.

We reported major findings including themes that emerged. We compared these results with literature that called for ideal assessment practices and we determined through our study in reality how certain schools of business did follow best practices. As we concluded our study, we discussed the implications for future research and practice.

The organization of this research study followed a typical, traditional structure for reporting a qualitative research study. This organization facilitated our concise reporting of best practices for conducting and making assessment meaningful across our sites that could be implemented at similar colleges.

continued

RETHINKING THE TRADITIONAL RESEARCH REPORT: CREATIVITY AND PLAY IN THE RESEARCH REPORT

Some qualitative researchers follow the traditional format of a researcher report (indeed, in some of the research approaches it is generally accepted practice to do so). Other researchers have begun to rethink what counts as a 'text' and what it means in the context of qualitative research and thus have taken liberties with the traditional report format or have reacted against it. Franzosi (1998: 547) argues that 'Texts do not just index a relation between words and between texts, but between text and social reality'. Higgs *et al.* (2009) have a similar view of text, as evident in Figure 32.1.

a text is

not just about writing

rather it refers to

the communication of meaning in many forms

a text expresses experimental, emotional,

biographical and cultural meanings

and makes them open to interpretation.

(Higgs *et al.* 2009: 37)

Figure 32.1 What is text?

Barone and Eisner (2011) have stated that researchers use a variety of written texts to present their research, some of which include poetry (Sullivan 2000), the novel (Coulter 2003; Dunlop 1999; Sellito 1991), the novella and short story (Kilbourne 1998), the ethnodrama (Saldaña and Wolcott 2001) and sonata form case study (Sconiers and Rosiek 2000). Weaver-Hightower presents a researcher reflection, based on his use of comics to re-present research on pages 516–517.

Researcher reflections

Marcus Weaver-Hightower, University of North Dakota, USA

Sequential art for qualitative research

Background

In 2006, my wife's and my first daughter, Matilda, died; she was stillborn at full term (recounted in Weaver-Hightower 2012). As part of working through my grief, I began attending support groups with my wife and looking for materials that would speak to my experience as a father. Finding very little – most was about and for mothers – I began research that would hopefully represent the experiences of fathers who have suffered stillbirths and other infant deaths.

Purpose

My original intention was to conduct phenomenology in the mode of Moustakas (1994), presenting the essence of the experience for a range of fathers. Yet one of the first fathers interviewed, Paul (a pseudonym), had a story that was so compelling, I felt it needed to be the focus of a narrative inquiry on its own (Connelly and Clandinin 1990). His experience of losing twins shared similarities with other fathers' stories but the double impact of two children lost also made his story unique. Yet I couldn't seem to construct the story in a way that conveyed in text alone the tragedy that he wrenchingly expressed in person. After reflecting on it, it hit me: I had to show, not just tell. Taking inspiration from my long time love of comic books and graphic novels, I decided that telling Paul's story in 'sequential art' (Eisner 1990) – panelled pages of drawings and text – could convey visual experience that would supplement the text by conveying mood and motion.

Methods

To construct Paul's story as sequential art, I took the verbatim transcript of our two-hour, semi-structured interview (supplemented with knowledge gained from years of knowing and interacting with him) and converted it into a script suited to a graphic novel-style presentation. This involved 're-storying' his narrative to create a chronological and thematic sequence suitable for panel-to-panel presentation. I was able to compress Paul's answers by showing graphically the things he spoke of (such as reported speech and setting). Though the story remained text heavy – words are still the currency of qualitative research, after all – I cut down the story to only significant statements and eschewed the repetitions typical of extemporaneous stories.

Constructing the text script was the first phase of the analytical process. The next was putting the words together with images. Using McCloud's (2006) heuristic decisions for sequential artists, I chose the moments to show, the way to frame them, the mood and style, the words to mutually enhance the images and the ways the pages would flow. These choices required a different, visual analysis of the data, forcing me to consider the lived experience through chronology, motion, setting, expression and more – all things we value in qualitative research but have a hard time conveying to readers in words alone.

continued

Findings and conclusion

Much like other qualitative approaches, reporting research through sequential art seeks to represent – to voice – others' life worlds and the richness and diversity of human experience. Ultimately, I find, the arts-based, sequential art approach adds an ineffable 'something' beyond the textualization of experience. Seeing and showing images gives the researcher and readers more access, more senses to use, in coming to understand an experience.

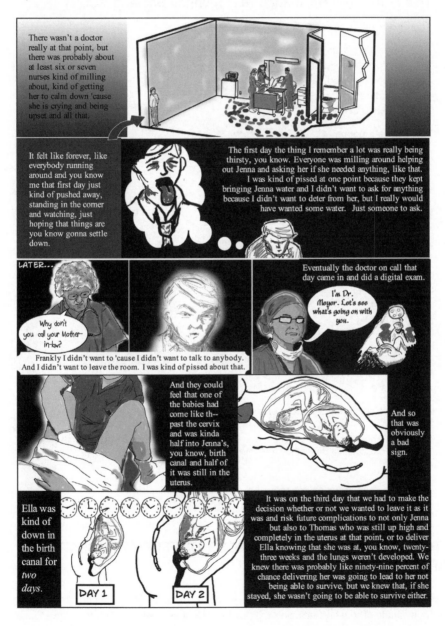

Researchers also have begun to experiment with a range of other media, such as music, dance, drama, images and verse, paintings and photographs (Higgs *et al.* 2009). Some of these are fixed in time and place, such as images or paintings. Others are deemed to exist as texts only in the moment and temporally, such as dance and drama. Saldaña explains this point of view poetically.

This is not a performance text (Johnny Saldaña 2006)

This is not a performance text.

These are words on printed paper
(or projected on a monitor
Depending upon your subscription format)
in poetic form
published in a journal.

This is a poem.

This is not a performance text.

You are not hearing me
speak these words aloud to you
as I recite them from memory.

You are not seeing me
on a raised platform
with bright lights focused
on my body.

You are not sitting down
in darkness
watching me
read or act or perform.

You are reading a poem—
You are reading a printed artefact.

This is not a performance text

Saldaña, J. This is not a performance text. *Qualitative Inquiry* 12 (6), 1091–8, copyright © 2006 by SAGE Publications. Reprinted by Permission of SAGE Publications.

Arts-based approaches are more fully explained in Chapter 19.

THE RESEARCH REPORT ACROSS DIFFERENT RESEARCH APPROACHES

Researchers consciously or unconsciously respond to the traditional report structure. They do so for a variety of reasons including their philosophical perspectives and the conventions which they have taken up. Often researchers *adopt* the traditional format, using the existing structures and conventions to guide their work, which has its place in qualitative research reporting. At other times, they *rework* the traditional format to suit their own needs and ends, which additionally moves the field forward. They may also *subvert* the traditional format, overthrowing it for a more fluid, temporal and creative account, which we celebrate for how it evokes understanding at a different level. Reactions to the traditional format are highlighted below.

The writing and reporting conventions of published studies differ according to research approach. Basic qualitative and grounded theory researchers, using paradigms that grow out of a post-positivist perspective, often seem to adopt the more traditional format, as do researchers using action research and evaluation (except those adopting a critical perspective, who then tend to take on more adapted or subverted approaches). Phenomenology and ethnography researchers, stemming from interpretive traditions, often tend to rework and adapt the traditional format to their own ends (again, unless coming to these approaches from a more critical perspective). Arts-based and narrative researchers, along with those from other reflexive traditions that blend humanities and arts with social research, usually rework or subvert the format, carving a new path. Case study researchers, who normally use a second research approach (see Chapter 10), tend to adopt or adapt whatever form is traditional to this second research tradition.

These differences are apparent in published studies. Indeed, Creswell (1998: 173–89) describes the writing forms typically used across five research traditions that he identifies. He discusses overall rhetorical structures (the basic sections included in a research report) and embedded rhetorical structures (devices or techniques that are used within the narrative). Table 32.3 on p. 521 summarizes Creswell's structures and adapts and extends his ideas to the other research approaches we have identified, such as basic qualitative method, narrative inquiry, arts-based inquiry and applied research studies (for example, action research, collaborative research and evaluative inquiry).

PUBLISHING THE RESEARCH REPORT

There are a number of outlets for qualitative research, including books, articles, book chapters, white papers and conference proceedings. The path to getting a paper published can be an interesting one, as Wimpenny describes in her researcher reflection.

Dr Katherine Wimpenny, Research Fellow, Coventry University, UK

Getting qualitative research published: an example of collaborative writing

In my experience, writing up qualitative research has often been a collaborative endeavour, working with a team of researchers and, where possible, with participants as co-researchers and co-writers. This is not a straightforward process but nonetheless a worthy and important pursuit which can provide great satisfaction. One example of collaborative writing I have recently been involved in sought to present a new methodology developed to examine findings from data synthesized across three PhD studies. The paper was written following an invitation

Researcher reflections

continued

for articles to be included in a special edition of the *Australasian Journal of Educational Technology* (AJET) looking at virtual worlds in tertiary education. As a team of five qualitative researchers, we viewed this as an exciting and valuable opportunity to present our work from the field.

One of the early challenges experienced in the writing process was agreeing the main focus for the paper, ensuring that it represented individuals' work whilst demonstrating coherence across the piece. Presenting a collation of the rich findings from across three data sets within word count limitations, whilst providing the reader with adequate opportunity to examine what was being claimed in light of the particulars of the inquiry was challenging. As Chenail (1995) contends, trust needs to be built between the researcher and the reader. This was especially pertinent as we had subjected the three distinct but interrelated studies, each using different methodologies which remained soundly qualitative, to a new participatory action synthesis process (Wimpenny and Savin-Baden 2012). The overarching study explored the socio-political impact of virtual world learning on higher education and the three studies were part of this.

Whilst the team writing process proved fruitful at many levels of learning, our experience was not devoid of tension and unearthed a considerable range of issues and perspectives. For example, whilst it felt supportive to share the workload and divide up writing tasks within agreed timeframes, the presentation, analysis, synthesis and interpretation of the data and how it would be best presented resulted in frequent team meetings, challenging us all as individuals to review our ideological influences, which give rise to beliefs and understandings. To help negotiate the process I was nominated early on as first author to take responsibility for coordinating meetings, keeping notes, managing version control on the redrafting of our writing and working with individuals to 'smooth' writing styles to make the piece work as a whole, as well as preparing the manuscript for final submission.

We received comments back from the AJET editors and five reviewers ranging from 'accepted', to 'minor amendments', and 'major revisions'! Whilst the review process provided a valuable means of developing our paper to best effect, managing team members' contributions and responding to reviewers' comments required careful handling in order to defend our respective positions, whilst not risking further amendments or potential rejection. Writing for publication takes commitment and effort to see the process through; it can be disheartening to receive criticism when so much work has gone into a paper but, as qualitative researchers, we need to be persistent and resilient, as we experienced. After a period of over twelve months, we received confirmation that our paper had finally been accepted and was deemed by the editors as making a very worthy contribution (Wimpenny et al. 2012). Onwards!

Table 32.3 Forms of writing across research traditions and approaches

Tradition	Overall rhetorical structures	Embedded rhetorical structures
Pragmatic qualitative research	Traditional five sections.	Presentation of findings by themes. Use of a combination of thin and thick description.
Grounded theory	Often adopts a structure similar to the traditional one: • Major research questions. • Literature review, which does not present key concepts or suggest hypotheses but rather demonstrates gap or bias in knowledge. • Methods, done early in the study. • Findings with a theoretical scheme. • Relationship of the new theory to other theory.	Structures depend upon the purpose. Findings often are stated as propositions. A diagram or figure of the new theory often is provided.
Phenomenology	Five sections typically included in a research report; the 'research report'.	Presenting the 'essence' of an experience for participants. This involves including a short paragraph in the narrative or as a figure. Discussion about the philosophy that underlies phenomenology. Creative closing.
Ethnography	Introduction to engage the reader's attention and focus the study then links researcher's interpretation to wider disciplinary issues. Setting and methods. Analytical claims and at times 'excerpt commentary units' in which an author includes an analytical point, provides orientation about the point, presents an excerpt or direct quote, then provides commentary about the quote that is related to the point. Conclusion, relation and elaboration on thesis advanced at the beginning.	Depiction of scenes, in which writers use thick description. Dialogue written in the dialect and natural language of the culture. Presentation of 'scenes' from the culture.
Narrative approaches	Telling the life story or stories of individual(s). Chronological sequencing of events.	Story set with plot lines. Traditionally exposition, rising action climax, falling action and denouement.
Action research/ participatory action approaches	Often adopts a structure similar to the action research process (which we describe more fully in Chapter 16), which may include identification of a problem, planning, implementing, and evaluating.	Structures depend upon the purpose. Findings are descriptive, and conclusions may be presented as action items.
Arts-based inquiry	Dependent upon the form of arts-based inquiry, may be any of the following: • Traditional reporting format with the use of artistic form in findings. • Dramatization of findings and presentation in a written artistic form such as poetry or drama. • Rejection of traditional structures in favour of more temporal and performance 'texts'.	Visual, pictorial, evocative.

CONCLUSION

Qualitative researchers face an array of choices when deciding how to present their work. They intentionally or unintentionally speak to a specific audience and we suggest that they benefit by being intentional about to whom they want to speak. Researchers may choose to use a more traditional format, experiment with the format or use more alternative approaches to conveying the processes and products of the research. Whatever approach researchers choose, we argue that it is critical for them to ensure that philosophical lenses, the research processes and the final report are congruent, and to find an appropriate way to communicate this with their intended audience.

Reflective questions

Concept questions

■ Why is writing focused on the intended audience so important?
■ When is the traditional format more appropriate?
■ When may non-traditional approaches to text be used with good effect?

Application questions

■ Who is your intended audience?
■ Is a more traditional format appropriate for your work or would a better choice be to rework or subvert the traditional structure?

Key resources

Major, C. H. and Savin-Baden, M. (2010a) *An introduction to qualitative research synthesis: Managing the information explosion in social science research*, London: Routledge.
Our existing work on qualitative research synthesis obviously informed us greatly. Indeed, parts of this chapter were adapted from this book, particularly the chapter on writing about the research synthesis.

Creswell, J. (1998) *Qualitative inquiry and research design: Choosing among five traditions*, Thousand Oaks, CA: Sage.
Creswell's work provides insightful and useful information about key differences in the presentation of the five different traditions that he identifies.

Merriam, S. B. (1998) *Qualitative research and case study applications in education*, San Francisco: Jossey-Bass.
Merriam's chapter about writing provides some useful information that helped us to consider the role of the audience and the different report sections.

GLOSSARY

Anti-positivism   Anti-positivism is the perspective that the social realm should not be subject to the same methods of investigation as the natural world; that academics should reject empiricism/positivism in favour of more interpretive, constructivist and critical perspectives.

Armchair fieldwork   In this type of fieldwork, the researcher does not travel to and stay at the research site but, rather, works with materials collected by others. In the past, examples of material collected by others included those acquired by traders, explorers and colonial officials. Today, materials include those such as documents and artefacts. (see Chapter 26).

Cartesian   Those things that are of or related to René Descartes, his mathematical methods, or his philosophy, especially in regards to an emphasis on logical analysis and mechanistic interpretation of physical nature.

Case   The bounded case.

Case narrative   The written description of the case.

Case study method   The approach to data collection and analysis.

Choice   An act of making a selection among options.

Choosing   A process of examining available options and making a decision about the best amongst them, given a particular set of circumstances.

Coding paradigm   A coding paradigm is a generic structure used to guide coding (see Chapter 27).

Collaboration   Sharing the work between individuals who then come together to solve or manage a problem.

Cooperation   Mutual engagement of participants in a coordinated effort to solve the problem together.

Deconstructionism   A form of criticism (usually of literature or art) that seeks to expose hidden contradictions in a work by delving below its surface meaning; it is often associated with post-structuralism.

Delimit   To determine the limits or boundaries of.

Documents   Written, printed, visual or electronic matter that provides information or evidence or that serves as an official record.

Duo-ethnography   Duo-ethnography uses conversation with another to explore how cultural influences have shaped a person's beliefs and decisions.

E-science   The activity of undertaking large-scale science projects through distributed global collaborations enabled by the Internet, which require access to very large data collections and large scale computing resources.

Empiricism   Empiricism is a philosophy about the nature of knowledge that suggests that experience, especially of the senses, is the only source of knowledge. This term is closely related to positivism, and at times the terms are used interchangeably.

Evaluation   The process of studying an organization or activity in order to understand, improve or change it.

External validity   External validity is an evaluation of the extent to which results may be assumed true for other cases.

Free imaginative variation   This is when researchers believe they have a sense of the essential characteristic of a phenomenon and then ask themselves what they can change without losing the phenomenon. The researcher changes this aspect of it and evaluates what alteration then takes place.

Grey literature   'Grey' literature comprises unpublished studies, such as conference presentations and dissertations.

Ideographic   Methods which highlight the unique elements of the individual phenomenon–the historically particular.

Iterative   Repeating again and again.

Incident   In grounded theory, an incident is a selection of the data, whether a word, line or paragraph, that the researcher has labelled.

Informed consent   Informed consent is the legal embodiment of the idea that a researcher should provide information to participants about the potential risks and benefits of participating in a study and should make clear their rights as participants so that they can make informed decisions about whether to take part.

Intended audience   The intended audience is the group of readers that the researcher is specifically targeting.

Internal validity   Internal validity refers to the true causes of the results you uncovered; in short, how do findings match reality?

Knowledge   The body of 'truths', information or awareness that humans have acquired or constructed.

Liminal   A threshold or a sense of being on a threshold in an in between space.

Liminal space   A liminal space is an in between space or a space at the margins, often used to describe rites and ritual spaces (marriage, coming of age) where people are in transitions between states.

Liminality   A state of being in between two positions, so that there a sense of being a 'transitional being' (Turner 1967) for which confusion and ambiguity becomes the norm.

Metaphysics   A branch of philosophy concerned with explaining the fundamental nature of being. Metaphysics attempts to answer two questions: 'What is there?' and 'What is it like?'.

Minimal risk   Minimal risk means that the risk associated with the study is similar to that typically encountered in daily life or during the performance of routine physical or psychological examinations or tests.

Nomothetic   Methods that call for the formulation of general or universal laws.

Paradigm   A paradigm is a belief system or world view that guides the researcher and the research process (Guba and Lincoln 1994).

Participation   Taking part, sharing something, often in a group who are involved in shaping and implementing research.

Philosophical mashups   We define philosophical mashups as the integration of two different philosophies, often within a single study. We encourage novice researchers to be aware of philosophical mashups in principle, so that they can recognize these mashups when they occur. However, we believe it is best initially for new researchers to identify, stay within and fully comprehend one philosophical tradition, before trying a mashup themselves.

Philosophy   The term philosophy, broadly conceived, means the study of both knowledge and the nature of reality and existence. Qualitative researchers tend to choose from interpretive, constructivist and critical philosophical stances.

Pragmatic   Concerned with practical results.

Probabilistic sampling   When conducting research on a large population, it is often impractical to study every single member of the group. Instead, researchers attempt to determine a portion or sample of the population. Probability sampling refers to methods of selecting individuals to include in a study, where each member of the population has an equal chance of being selected (that is, it is randomly selected).

Problem   The reason the study should be done.

Prolonged engagement   Prolonged engagement means staying in the research context long enough to understand what is taking place in terms of language, cultures and interactions.

Purpose   What the research will accomplish, what its intent is.

Qualitative research   Social research that is aimed at investigating the way in which people make sense of their ideas and experience.

Quantitative research   The systematic collection and analysis of numerical data used to prove or disprove a hypothesis. It is based on the premise that something is meaningful only if it can be observed or counted.

Rapport   A close connection or relationship.

Reader   The reader might be anyone who comes across the report and reads it for any number of purposes.

Referent   What the sign 'stands for'.

Reliability   Ensuring that the experiments can repeatedly measure these variables accurately.

Research question   An interrogative sentence that highlights the phenomenon to be studied and indicates what the researcher wishes to know about it.

Saturation   Saturation is a point at which no new themes are being uncovered.

Sense   The sense made of the sign.

Sign vehicle   The form of the sign.

Socialization   Socialization is a process by which individuals acquire the habits, beliefs and accumulated knowledge of society through education and training for membership in a group or organization.

Subject   The general field or area.

Topic   The specific matter of interest.

Unit of analysis   Unit of analysis simply means the specific element that the researcher will be able to say something about at the end of the study; the unit then drives the analysis (see Chapter 6).

Validation   In educational research, validation refers to the process of ensuring that the instrument in question will gather the information that it intends to gather (see Chapter 30 for additional information about validity).

Validity   Ensuring that the experiment is designed effectively to measure the subject variables.

Verbatim   To express in exactly the same words originally used.

BIBLIOGRAPHY

Abbott, A. (2004) *Methods of discovery: Heuristics for the social sciences*, New York: Norton.

Adams, R. G. and Sardiello, R. (2000) *Deadhead social science: 'You ain't gonna learn what you don't want to know'*, Walnut Creek, CA: Altamira.

Adelman, C., Jenkins, D. and Kemmis, S. (1980) Rethinking case study: Notes from the second Cambridge conference. *In:* H. Simons (ed.) *Towards a science of the singular.* Norwich: Centre for Applied Research in Education, University of East Anglia.

Adler, P. A. and Adler, P. (1987) *Membership roles in field research*, Newbury Park, CA: Sage Publications.

–––– (1994) Observational techniques. *In:* N. K. Denzin and Y. S. Lincoln (eds) *Handbook of qualitative research.* London: Sage. pp. 377–92.

Agger, B. (1991) Critical theory, poststructuralism, post-modernism: Their sociological relevance. *Annual Review of Sociology*, 17, 105–31.

Alexander, C. (1979) *The timeless way of building*, New York: Oxford University Press.

Alexander, C., Ishikawa, S., Silverstein, M., Jacobson, M., Fiksdahl-King, I. and Angel, S. (1977) *A pattern language: Towns, buildings, construction*, New York: Oxford University Press.

Altheide, D. L. (1987) Ethnographic content analysis. *Qualitative Sociology*, 10 (1), 65–77.

Altman, D. G. and Bland, M. J. (1997) Statistical notes: Units of analysis. *BMJ*, 314, 1874.

Alvesson, M. and Sandberg, J. (2011) Generating research questions through problematization. *Academy of Management Review*, 36 (2), 247–71.

–––– (2013) *Constructing research questions*, London: Sage.

Alvesson, M. and Sköldberg, K. (2009) *Reflective methodology (2nd edn.)*, London: Sage.

Ancona, D., Kochan, T., Scully, M., Van Maanen, J. and Westney, E. (1999) *Managing for the future: Organizational behavior and processes (2nd edn.)*, Cincinnati, OH: South-Western.

Angrosino, M. and Mays de Perez, K. (2000) Rethinking observation: From methods to context. *In:* N. K. Denzin and Y. S. Lincoln (eds) *Handbook of qualitative research (2nd edn.).* Thousand Oaks, CA: Sage. pp. 637–707.

Angrosino, M. and Rosenberg, J. (2011) Observations on observation: Continuities and challenges. *In:* N. K. Denzin and Y. S. Lincoln (eds) *Handbook of qualitative research.* Thousand Oaks, CA: Sage.

Annells, M. (1996) Grounded theory method: Philosophical perspectives, paradigms of inquiry and post-modernism. *Qualitative Health Research*, 6 (3), 379–93.

Anthony, S. E. and Jack, S. M. (2009) Qualitative case study methodology in nursing research: An integrative review. *Journal of Advanced Nursing*, 65 (6), 1171–81.

Archibald, J. (2008) An indigenous storywork methodology. *In:* J. G. Knowles and A. L. Cole (eds) *Handbook of the arts in qualitative research.* London: Sage.

Aries, E. (1976) Interaction patterns and themes of male, female, and mixed groups. *Small Group Behavior*, 7 (1), 7–18.

Arksey, H. and Knight, P. (1999) *Interviewing for social scientists*, London: Sage.

Ary, D., Jacobs, L. C. and Razavieh, A. (1990) *Introduction to research in education*, Philadelphia, PA: Hold, Rinehart and Winston.

Atkinson, P. (1995) Some perils of paradigms. *Qualitative Health Research*, 5 (1), 117–24.

Atkinson, P. and Coffey, A. (2004) Analysing documentary realities. *In:* D. Silverman (ed.) *Qualitative research: Theory, method and practice.* London: Sage. pp. 56–75.

Atkinson, P. and Hammersley, M. (1994) Ethnography and participant observation. *In:* N. K. Denzin and Y. S. Lincoln (eds) *Handbook of qualitative research.* Thousand Oaks, CA: Sage.

Atkinson, S. and Burden, K. (2007) Virtuality, veracity and values: Exploring between virtual and real worlds using the 3v model. *Proceedings Ascilite, 2007 Singapore 2007.* [www.ascilite.org.au/conferences/singapore07/procs/atkinson.pdf].

Austin, D. and Forinash, M. (2005) Arts-based inquiry. *In:* B. Wheeler (ed.) *Music therapy research (2nd edn.).* Gilsum, NH: Barcelona.

Austrin, T. and Farnsworth, J. (2005) Hybrid genres: Fieldwork, detection and the method of Bruno Latour. *Qualitative Research*, 5 (2), 147–65.

Ausubel, D. P., Novak, J. S. and Hanesian, H. (1978) *Educational psychology: A cognitive view*, New York: Holt, Rinehart and Winston.

Bagley, C. and Cancienne, M. (2001) Educational research and intertextual forms of (re)presentation: The case for dancing the data. *Qualitative Inquiry*, 7 (2), 221–37.

Bagnoli, A. (2009) Beyond the standard interview: the use of graphic elicitation and arts-based methods. *Qualitative Research*, 9, 547.

Bailey, J. (2008) First steps in qualitative data analysis: Transcribing. *Family Practice*, 25 (2), 127–31.

Bain, A. (1897) *Education as a science*, New York: D. Appleton and Company.

Baist, T. N. (2003) Manual or electronic? The role of coding in qualitative data analysis. *Education Research*, 45 (2), 143–54.

Bales, R. (1970) *Personality and interpersonal behaviour*, New York: Holt, Rinehart and Winston.

Ball, H. K. (2008) Quilts. *In:* J. G. Knowles and A. L. Cole (eds) *Handbook of the arts in qualitative research.* London: Sage.

Banning, J. H. (2000) Bumper sticker ethnography: A study of campus culture. *Journal of Student Affairs*, 9, 11–17.

Barndt, D. (2008) Touching minds and hearts: Community arts as collaborative research. *In:* J. G. Knowles and A. L. Cole (eds) *Handbook of the arts in qualitative research.* London: Sage.

Barone, T. (2001) *Touching eternity: The enduring outcomes of teaching*, New York: Teachers College Press.

–––– (2006) Arts-based educational research then, now, and later. *Studies in Art Education*, 48 (1), 4–8.

Barone, T. and Eisner, E. W. (2011) *Arts-based research*, Thousand Oaks, CA: Sage.

Barrett, M. and Walsham, G. (2004) Making contributions from interpretive case studies: Examining processes of construction and use. *In:* B. Kaplan, D. P. Truex III, D. Wastell, A. T. Wood-Harper and J. I. Degross (eds) *Information systems research: Relevant theory and informed practice.* Boston, MA: Kluwer Academic.

Barthes, R. (1977) Introduction to the structural analysis of narrative. *In:* S. Sontag (ed.) *A Roland Barthes reader.* London: Vintage.

Barzun, J. and Graff, H. F. (2004) *The modern researcher (6th edn.)*, Belmont, CA: Thomson/Wadsworth.

Baskerville, R. (1999) Investigating information systems with action research. *Communications for the Association for Information Systems*, 2 (19), 1–32.

Batchelor, J. A. and Briggs, C. M. (1994) Subject, project or self? Thoughts on ethical dilemmas for social and medical researchers. *Social Science & Medicine*, 39 (7), 949–54.

Bateson, G. (1978) Afterword. *In:* J. Brockman (ed.) *About Bateson.* London: Wildwood House.

Bateson, M. C. (1990) *Composing a life,* New York: Atlantic Monthly Press.

Baumbusch, J. L. (2010) Conducting critical ethnography in long-term residential care: Experiences of a novice researcher in the field. *Journal of Advanced Nursing,* 67 (1), 184–92.

Baxter, J. and Eyles, J. (1997) Evaluating qualitative research in social geography: Establishing" 'rigour' in interview analysis. *Transactions of the Institute of British Geographers,* 22 (4), 515–25.

Baxter, L. A. (1991) Content analysis. *In:* B. M. Montgomery and S. Duck (eds) *Studying interpersonal interaction.* New York: The Guilford Press.

Becker, H. S. (1958) Problems of inference and proof in participant observation. *American Sociological Review,* 23, 652–60.

–––– (1967) Whose side are we on? *Social Problems,* 14, 239–47.

Becker, H. S., Greer, B., Hughes, E. and Strauss, A. L. (1961) *Boys in white: Student culture in medical school,* New Brunswick, NI: University of Chicago Press.

–––– (1977) *Boys in white: Student culture in medical school* (reprint edn.), New Brunswick, NJ: Transaction Books.

Belenky, M., Clinchy, B., Goldberger, N. and Tarule, J. (1986) *Women's ways of knowing: The the development of self, voice, and mind,* New York: Basic Books.

Belmont Report (1979) National Commission for the Protection of Human Subjects of Biomedical and Behavioral Research Regulations and ethical guidelines. The Belmont report: Ethical principles and guidelines for the protection of human subjects of research, Washington DC: US Department of Health and Human Services. [www.hhs.gov/ohrp/humansubjects/guidance/belmont.html].

Benbow, J. (1994) *Coming to know: A phenomenological study of individuals actively committed to social change.* Unpublished doctoral dissertation, Graduate School of Education, University of Massachusetts Amherst.

Bender, A., Peter, E., Wynn, F., Andrews, G. and Pringle, D. (2011) Welcome intrusions: An interpretive phenomenological study of TB nurses' relational work. *International Journal of Nursing Studies,* 48 (11), 1409–19.

Benford, S., Bowers, J., Fahlén, L. E., Greenhalgh, C. and Snowdon, D. (1995) User embodiment in collaborative virtual environments. *In: CHI '95 proceedings of the SIGCHI conference on human factors in computing systems.* New York: ACM Press/Addison-Wesley.

Benner, P. (ed.) (1994) *Interpretive phenomenology: Embodiment, caring, and ethics in health and illness,* Thousand Oaks, CA: Sage.

Bennerstedt, U. (2008) Welcome to the digital puppet show: Positioning work and make-believe methods in role play MMORPG servers. *In:* O. Leino, G. Calleja and S. Mosberg Iversen (eds) *Proceedings of The [Player] Conference, 2008 Denmark, August 26 to 29.* Copenhagen. pp. 53–86.

Berelson, B. (1952) *Content analysis in communications research,* New York: Free Press.

Berg, B. (1989) *Qualitative research methods for the social sciences,* Needham Heights, MA: Allyn and Bacon.

Berger, P. L. and Luckmann, T. (1966) *The social construction of reality: A treatise in the sociology of knowledge,* Garden City, NY: Anchor Books.

Bernard, H. R. (1988) *Research methods in cultural anthropology,* Newbury Park, CA: Sage.

–––– (1994) *Research methods in anthropology: Qualitative and quantitative approaches (2nd edn.),* Walnut Creek, CA: AltaMira Press.

–––– (1998) *Handbook of methods in cultural anthropology,* Walnut Creek, CA: AltaMira Press.

Bernard, H. R. and Ryan, G. W. (2010) *Analyzing qualitative data: Systematic approaches,* Los Angeles, CA: Sage.

Best, J. W. and Kahn, J. V. (1993) *Research in education (7th edn.)*, San Francisco, CA: Jossey Bass.

Bhaskar, R. (1989) *Reclaiming reality: A critical introduction to contemporary philosophy*, London: Verso.

Biddix, J. P. (2010) Relational leadership and technology: A study of activist college women leaders. *NASPA Journal about Women in Higher Education*, 3 (1), 25–47.

Black, D. (2000) Dreams of pure sociology. *Sociological Theory*, 18, 343–67.

Blumer, H. (1969) *Symbolic interactionism: Perspective and method*, Englewood Cliffs, NJ: Prentice Hall.

Bogdan, R. C. and Biklen, S. K. (1982) *Qualitative research for education. An introduction to theory and methods*, Boston: Allyn and Bacon.

–––– (1992) *Qualitative research for education*, Needham Heights, MA: Allyn and Bacon.

–––– (2007) *Qualitative research for education: An introduction to theories and methods (5th edn.)*, Boston: Pearson.

Boone, R. G. (1904) *Science of education*, New York: Scribner's Sons.

Booth, W. C. (1961) *The rhetoric of fiction*, Chicago, IL: University of Chicago Press.

Bormann, E. (1972) Fantasy and rhetorical vision. The rhetorical criticism of social reality. *Quarterly Journal of Speech*, 58, 396–407.

Boud, D., Cohen, R. and Walker, D. (1993) Introduction: Understanding learning from experience. *In:* D. Boud, R. Cohen and D. Walker (eds) *Using experience for learning*. Buckingham: Open University Press.

Boud, D., Keogh, R. and Walker, D. (1985) *Reflection: Turning experience into learning*, London: Kogan Page.

Bowler, B. (2006) Narration and point of view. *Bewildering stories*. [www.bewilderingstories.com/issue212/narration1.html]. Accessed 16 June 2012.

Braun, V. and Clarke, V. (2006) Using thematic analysis in psychology. *Qualitative Research in Psychology*, 3 (2), 77–101.

Braun, V. and Wilkinson, S. (2003) Liability or asset? Women talk about the vagina. *Psychology of Women Section Review*, 5 (2), 28–42.

Brentano, F. (1874) *Psychology from an empirical standpoint*, London: Routledge.

Bresler, L. (1996) Ethical issues in the conduct and communication of ethnographic classroom research. *Studies in Art Education: A Journal of Issues and Research National Art Education Association*, 37 (3), 133–44.

Brickell, E. (2002) What I am. *The Ultimate Collection*. Hip-O Records.

Britten, N., Jones, R., Murphy, E. and Stacy, R. (1995) Qualitative research methods in general practice and primary care. *Family Practice*, 12 (1), 104–14.

Brodrick, K. and Mandisa, M. (2005) Effectiveness of the non-profit organisation 'grandmothers against poverty and aids' – a study. *Southern African Journal of HIV Medicine*, (19), 37–41.

Bruner, J. S. (1986) *Actual minds, possible worlds*, Cambridge, MA: Harvard University Press.

–––– (1990) *Acts of meaning*, Cambridge, MA: Harvard University Press.

–––– (1996) *The culture of education*, Cambridge, MA: Harvard University Press.

–––– (2002) *Making stories: Law, literature, life*, New York: Farrar, Straus and Giroux.

–––– (2004) Life as narrative. *Social Research*, 71 (3), 691–710.

Bryant, A. and Charmaz, K. (eds) (2007) *The SAGE handbook of grounded theory*, London: Sage.

Brydon-Miller, M. and Maguire, P. (2009) Participatory action research: Contributions to the development of practitioner inquiry in education. *Educational Action Research*, 17 (1), 79–93.

Bryman, A. (2004) *Quantity and quality in social research*, London: Routledge.

–––– (2008) *Social research methods (3rd edn.)*, Oxford: Oxford University Press.

–––– (2012) *Social research methods (4th edn.)*, Oxford: Oxford University Press.

Bryman, A. and Bell, E. (2003) *Business research methods*, Cape Town: Oxford University Press.

Buckingham, B. R. (1876) *Research for teachers*, New York: Silver, Burdette and Co.

Bullough, R. V. and Pinnegar, S. (2001) Guidelines for quality in autobiographical forms of self-study research. *Educational Researcher*, 30 (3), 13–21.

Burgess, J. E. (2006) Hearing ordinary voices: Cultural studies, vernacular creativity and digital storytelling. *Continuum: Journal of Media and Cultural Studies*, 20 (2), 201–14.

Burman, E. and Parker, I. (1993) *Discourse analytic research: Repertoires and readings of texts in action*, London: Routledge.

Burns, E. and Bell, S. (2011) Narrative construction of professional teacher identity of teachers with dyslexia. *Teaching and Teacher Education: An International Journal of Research and Studies*, 27 (5), 952–60.

Burns, N. and Grove, S. K. (2005) *The practice of nursing research. Conduct, critique and utilization (5th edn.)*, Philadelphia: WB Saunders.

Burr, V. (1995) *An introduction to social constructionism*, London: Routledge.

Burrell, G. and Morgan, G. (1979) *Sociological paradigms and organizational analysis*, London: Heineman Educational.

Bushe, G. R. (2011) Appreciative inquiry: Theory and critique. *In:* D. Boje, B. Burnes and J. Hassard (eds) *The Routledge companion to organizational change*. London: Routledge. pp. 87–103.

Caelli, K., Ray, L. and Mill, J. (2003) 'Clear as mud': Toward greater clarity in generic qualitative research. *International Journal of Qualitative Methods*, 2 (2), 1–13.

Cahnmann-Taylor, M. (2008) Arts-based research: Histories and new directions. *In:* M. Cahnmann-Taylor and R. Siegesmund (eds) *Arts-based research in education: Foundations for practice*. New York: Routledge.

Calabrese, R. L. (2006) *The elements of an effective dissertation and thesis: A step-by-step guide to getting it right the first time*, Lanham, MD: Rowman & Littlefield Education.

Calder, B. J. (1977) Focus groups and the nature of qualitative marketing research. *Journal of Marketing Research*, 14, 353–64.

Calderón, C. (2009) Assessing the quality of qualitative health research: Criteria, process and writing. *Forum Qualitative Sozialforschung / Forum: Qualitative Social Research*, 10 (2), Article 17.

Camp, W. G. (2000) Formulating and evaluating theoretical frameworks for career and technical education research. *Journal of Vocational Education Research*, 26 (1), 4–25.

Caplan, A. L. (1992) Twenty years after. The legacy of the Tuskegee syphilis study. *Hastings Center Report*, 22 (6), 29.

Capron, A. M. (1989) Human experimentation. *In:* R. M. Veatch (ed.) *Medical ethics*. Boston: Jones and Bartlett.

Carcasson, M. (n.d) *The Cycle of Deliberative Inquiry: The Four Key Tasks of Deliberative Practice.* Colorado State University. Available www.cwi.colostate.edu/.../The_Cycle_of_Deliberative_Inquiry.docx

–––– (2009) *The cycle of deliberative inquiry. Completed as part of a learning agreement with the Kettering foundation: Re-conceptualizing the work of public deliberation*, Fort Collins, CO: Colorado State University.

–––– (2011) *The four distinct products of deliberation and deliberative inquiry spring 2011 SPCM 207 coursebook*, Fort Collins, CO: Colorado State University.

Carnwell, R. and Daly, W. (2001) Strategies for the construction of a critical review of the literature. *Nurse Education in Practice*, 1, 57–63.

Carr, W. and Kemmis, S. (1986) *Becoming critical: Education, knowledge and action research*, London: Falmer.

Castellani, B. (1999) Michel Foucault and symbolic interactionism: The making of a new theory of interaction. *Studies in Symbolic Interaction*, 22, 247–72.

Chapman, E. (2002) The social and ethical implications of changing medical technologies: The views of people living with genetic conditions. *Journal of Health Psychology*, 7, 195–206.

Charmaz, K. (1990) 'Discovering' chronic illness: Using grounded theory. *Social Science and Medicine*, 30, 1161–72.

—— (2000) Grounded theory: Objectivist and constructivist methods. *In:* N. K. Denzin and Y. S. Lincoln (eds) *Handbook of qualitative research (2nd edn.)*. London: Sage.

—— (2005) *Grounded theory: Methods for the 21st century*, London: Sage.

—— (2006) *Constructing grounded theory: A practical guide through qualitative analysis*, London: Sage.

Chase, S. E. (2010) *Learning to speak, learning to listen: How diversity works on campus*, Ithaca, NY: Cornell University Press.

Chenail, R. J. (1995) Presenting qualitative data. *The Qualitative Report*, 2 (3), 1–8.

Chinn, P. L. and Jacobs, M. K. (1983) *Theory and nursing: A systematic approach*, St Louis: Mosby.

Clandinin, D. J. (ed.) (2007) *Handbook of narrative inquiry: Mapping a methodology*, Thousand Oaks, CA: Sage.

Clandinin, D. J. and Connelly, F. M. (2000) *Narrative inquiry*, San Francisco, CA: Jossey-Bass.

Clandinin, D. J. and Huber, J. (2010) Narrative inquiry. *In:* P. Peterson, E. Baker and B. McGaw (eds) *The international encyclopedia of education (3rd edn.)*. Oxford: Elsevier.

Clandinin, D. J. and Rosiek, J. (2007) Mapping a landscape of narrative inquiry: Borderland spaces and tensions. *In:* D. J. Clandinin (ed.) *Handbook of narrative inquiry: Mapping methodology*. London: Sage.

Clare, L. (2003) Managing threats to self: Awareness in early stage Alzheimer's disease. *Social Science and Medicine*, 57, 1017–29.

Clark, C. T. and Moss, A. P. (1996) Researching with: Ethical and epistemological implications of doing collaborative, change-oriented research with teachers and students. *Teachers College Record*, 97 (4), 518–48.

Clarke, A. E. (2003) Situational analyses: Grounded theory mapping after the post-modern turn. *Symbolic Interaction*, 26, 553–76.

—— (2005) *Situational analyses: Grounded theory after the post-modern turn*, Thousand Oaks, CA: Sage.

Clifford, J. and Marcus, G. E. (eds) (1986) *Writing culture. The poetics and politics of ethnography*, Berkeley, CA: University of California Press.

Coffee, A. and Atkinson, P. (1996) *Making sense of qualitative data*, Thousand Oaks, CA: Sage.

Cohen, L. and Manion, L. (1994) *Research methods in education (4th edn.)*, London: Routledge.

Cohen, L., Manion, L. and Morrison, K. (2000) *Research methods in education (5th edn.)*, London: Routledge.

Cole, M. and Wertsch, J. V. (1996) Beyond the individual – social antimony in discussion of Piaget and Vygotsky. *Human Development*, 39, 250–6.

Collier, J. (1945) United States Indian administration as a laboratory of ethnic relations. *Social Research*, 12 (3), 265–303.

Colyar, J. and Holley, K. A. (2010) Narrative theory and the construction of qualitative texts. *In:* M. Savin-Baden and C. Major (eds) *New approaches to qualitative research: Wisdom and uncertainty*. New York: Routledge.

Comte, A. (1968–1970) *Œuvres*, Paris: Anthropos (11 vols).

Conceição, S. C. O. (2006) Faculty lived experiences in the online environment. *Adult Education Quarterly*, 57 (1), 26–45.

Connelly, F. M. and Clandinin, D. J. (1990) Stories of experience and narrative inquiry. *Educational Researcher*, 19 (5), 2–14.

Conquergood, D. (2002) Performance studies: Interventions and radical research. *Drama Review: A Journal of Performative Studies*, 46, 145–56.

Cook, T. D. and Campbell, D. T. (1979) *Quasi-experimentation: Design and analysis for field settings*, Chicago, IL: Rand McNally.

Cooke, B. and Kothari, U. (2001) *Participation: The new tyranny?*, London: Zed.

Cooper, S. (2005) Contemporary UK para-medical training and education; how do we train? How should we educate? *Emergency Medicine Journal*, 22, 375–9.

Cooper, S. and Endacott, R. (2007) Generic qualitative research: A design for qualitative research in emergency care? *Emergency Medicine Journal*, 24 (12), 816–19.

Cooperrider, D. L. and Srivastva, S. (1987) Appreciative inquiry in organizational life. *In:* W. Pasmore and R. Woodman (eds) *Research in organization change and development.* Greenwich, CT: JAI Press.

Cooperrider, D. L., Whitney, D. and Stavros, J. M. (2008) *Appreciative inquiry handbook (2nd edn.)*, Brunswick, OH: Crown Custom Publishing.

Coppola, N. W., Hiltz, S. R. and Rotter, N. (2002) Becoming a virtual professor: Pedagogical roles and asynchronous learning networks. *Journal of Management Information Systems*, 18 (4), 169–90.

Corey, S. (1953) *Action research to improve school practice*, New York: Teachers College, Columbia University.

Coulter, C. (2003) *Growing up immigrant in an American high school.* Unpublished doctoral dissertation, Arizona State University Tempe.

Cousin, G. (2005) Learning from cyberspace. *In:* R. Land and S. Bayne (eds) *Education in cyberspace.* Abingdon: RoutledgeFalmer.

Cox, R., Kontianien, S., Rea, N. and Robinson, S. (1981) *Learning teaching: An evaluation of a course for teachers in general practice*, London: University Teaching Methods Unit, Institute of Education.

Crenshaw, K. (1994) Mapping at the margins: Intersectionality, identity politics, and violence against women of color. *In:* M. A. Fineman and R. Mykitiuk (eds) *The public nature of private violence: The discovery of domestic abuse.* New York: Routledge.

Creswell, J. W. (1994) *Research design: Qualitative and quantitative approaches*, Thousand Oaks, CA: Sage.

—— (1998) *Qualitative inquiry and research design: Choosing among five traditions*, Thousand Oaks, CA: Sage.

—— (2002) *Educational research: Planning, conducting, and evaluating quantitative and qualitative research*, Upper Saddle River, NJ: Merrill Prentice Hall.

—— (2003) *Research design: Qualitative, quantitative, and mixed methods approaches (2nd edn.)*, Thousand Oaks, CA: Sage.

—— (2007) *Qualitative inquiry and research design: Choosing among five approaches (2nd edn.)*, Thousand Oaks, CA: Sage.

Cronbach, L. J. (1963) Course improvement through evaluation. *Teachers College Record*, 64 (8), 672–83.

Cronin, P., Ryan, F. and Coughlan, M. (2008) Undertaking a literature review: A step-by-step approach. *British Journal of Nursing*, 17 (1), 38–43.

Crooks, T. J. (1988) The impact of classroom evaluation practices. *Review of Educational Research*, 58 (4), 438–81.

Curtis, S., Gesler, W., Smith, G. and Washburn, S. (2000) Approaches to sampling and case selection in qualitative research: Examples in the geography of health. *Social Science and Medicine*, 50, 1001–14.

Cusick, P. A. (1973) *Inside high school: The student's world view*, New York: Holt, Rinehart and Winston.

Cutliffe, J. R. (2005) Adapt or adopt: Developing and transgressing the methodological boundaries of grounded theory. *Journal of Advanced Nursing*, 51 (4), 421–8.

D'Andrade, R. G. (1992) Schemas and motivation. *In:* R. G. D'Andrade and C. Strauss (eds) *Human motives and cultural models.* Cambridge, UK: Cambridge University Press.

Davies, D. and Dodd, J. (2002) Qualitative research and the question of rigor. *Qualitative Health Research,* 12 (2), 279–89.

Davis, M. S. (1986) That's classic! The phenomenology and rhetoric of successful social theories. *Philosophy of Social Sciences,* 16, 285–301.

Dawn, M. (2010) *The writing on the wall: High art, popular culture and the Bible,* London: Hodder and Stoughton.

De Laine, M. (2000) *Fieldwork, participation and practice ethics and dilemmas in qualitative research,* London: Sage.

De Venney-Tiernan, M., Goldband, A., Rackham, L. and Reilly, N. (1994) Creating collaborative relationships in a co-operative inquiry group. *In:* P. Reason (ed.) *Participation in human inquiry.* London: Sage.

Delbecq, A. L. and Van de Ven, A. H. (1971) A group process model for problem identification and program planning. *Journal of Applied Behavioral Science,* VII, 466–92.

Deleuze, G. and Guattari, F. (1987a) *A thousand plateaus: Capitalism and schizophrenia,* trans. B. Massumi, Minneapolis, MN: University of Minnesota Press.

—— (1987b) *On the Line,* trans. John Johnston, New York: Semiotexte.

Delmont, S. (2002) *Fieldwork in educational settings: Methods, pitfalls and perspectives,* London: Routledge.

De Munck, V. C. and Sobo, E. J. (1998) *Using methods in the field: A practical introduction and casebook,* Walnut Creek, CA: AltaMira Press.

Denzin, N. K. (1978) *The research act: A theoretical introduction to sociological methods,* New York: McGraw Hill.

—— (1989a) *Interpretative biography,* London: Sage.

—— (1989b) *Interpretive interactionism,* Newbury Park, CA: Sage.

—— (1997) *Interpretive ethnography: Ethnographic practices for the 21st century,* Thousand Oaks, CA: Sage.

—— (2000) Aesthetics and the practices of qualitative inquiry. *Qualitative Inquiry,* 6 (2), 256–65.

Denzin, N. K. and Lincoln, Y. S. (1994) Introduction: Entering the field of qualitative research. *In:* N. K. Denzin and Y. S. Lincoln (eds) *Handbook of qualitative research.* Thousand Oaks: Sage.

—— (1998) *Collecting and interpreting qualitative materials,* Thousand Oaks, CA: Sage.

—— (2005) *The SAGE handbook of qualitative research,* Thousand Oaks, CA: Sage.

—— (2011) *The SAGE handbook of qualitative research (4th edn.),* Thousand Oaks, CA: Sage.

Denzin, N. K., Lincoln, Y. S. and Smith, L. T. (2008) *Handbook of critical and indigenous methodologies,* Thousand Oaks, CA: Sage.

Derrida, J. (1986) *Glas,* Lincoln, NE: University of Nebraska Press.

—— (1988) *Limit inc,* Evanston, IL: Northwestern University Press.

Descartes, R. (1979/1641) *Meditations in first philosophy,* Cambridge: Hackett Publishing Company.

Devault, M. L. (2004) Talking and listening from women's standpoint. *In:* S. Nage Hesse-Biber and M. L. Yaiser (eds) *Feminist perspectives on social research.* New York: Oxford University Press.

a*In:Participation in human inquiry.*

DeWalt, K. M. and DeWalt, B. R. (2002) *Participant observation: A guide for fieldworkers,* Walnut Creek, CA: Alta Mira Press.

DeWalt, K. M., DeWalt, B. R. and Wayland, C. B. (1998) Participant observation. *In:* H. R. Bernard (ed.) *Handbook of methods in cultural anthropology.* Walnut Creek, CA: AltaMira Press.

Dewey, J. (1931) *Philosophy and civilization*, New York: Minton Balch. http://faculty.uml.edu/rinnis/45.301%20Ways%20of%20Knowing/Qualitative%20Thought.htm

———— (1938) *Experience and education*, New York: Collier Books. http://faculty.uml.edu/rinnis/45.301%20Ways%20of%20Knowing/Qualitative%20Thought.htm

Dickens, L. and Watkins, K. (1999) Action research: Rethinking Lewin. *Management Learning*, 30 (2), 127–40.

Dilthey, W. (1900/1996) The rise of hermeneutics. *In:* R. A. Makkreel and F. Rodi (eds) *Hermeneutics and the study of history*. Princeton, NJ: Princeton University Press.

Dixon-Woods, M., Bonas, S., Booth, A., Jones, D. R., Miller, T., Shaw, R. L., Smith, J., Sutton, A. and Young, B. (2006) How can systematic reviews incorporate qualitative research? A critical perspective. *Qualitative Research*, 6, 27–44.

Dooley, K. E. (2007) Viewing agricultural education research through a qualitative lens. *Journal of Agricultural Education*, 48 (4), 32–42.

Dougiamas, M. (1998) A journey into constructivism. [http://dougiamas.com/writing/constructivism.html]. Accessed 16 June 2012.

Douglas, J. (1985) *Creative interviewing*, Beverly Hills, CA: Sage.

Downe-Wamboldt, B. (1992) Content analysis: Method, applications, and issues. *Health Care for Women International*, 13 (3), 313–21.

Doyle, L. H. (2003) Synthesis through meta-ethnography: Paradoxes, enhancements, and possibilities. *Qualitative Research*, 3 (3), 321–44.

Drake, P. (2010) Grasping at methodological understanding: A cautionary tale from insider research. *International Journal of Research and Method in Education*, 33 (1), 85–99.

Dresser, R. (1998) Time for new rules on human subjects research? *Hastings Center Report*, 28 (6), 23–4.

Dunlop, R. (1999) *Boundary bay: A novel*. Unpublished doctoral dissertation, University of British Columbia, Vancouver.

Duran, J. (2001) A holistically Deweyan feminism. *Metaphilosophy*, 32, 279–92.

Eisenhardt, K. M. (1989) Building theories from case study research. *The Academy of Management Review*, 14 (4), 532–50.

Eisenhart, M. and Howe, K. (1992). Validity in educational research. *In*: M. LeCompte, W. Millroy and J. Preissle (eds) *The handbook of qualitative research in education*. San Diego, CA: Academic Press. pp. 642–80.

Eisner, E. W. (1990) *Comics and sequential art*, Parasmus, NJ: Poorhouse Press.

———— (1991) *The enlightened eye: Qualitative inquiry and the enhancement of educational practice*, New York: Macmillan.

Elbaz, F. (1991) Research on teacher's knowledge: The evolution of a discourse. *Journal of Curriculum Studies*, 23, 1–19.

Elder, N. C. and Miller, W. L. (1995) Reading and evaluating qualitative research studies. *Family Practice*, 41 (3), 279–85.

Ellingson, L. L. and Ellis, C. (2008) Autoethnography as constructionist project. *In:* J. A. Holstein and J. F. Gubrium (eds) *Handbook of constructionist research*. New York: Guilford Press.

Elliott, J. (1991) *Action research for educational change*, Buckingham: Open University Press.

Elliott, J. and Kushner, S. (2007) The need for a manifesto for educational programme evaluation. *Cambridge Journal of Education*, 37 (3), 321–36.

Elliott, J. A. and Olver, I. N. (2009) Hope, life, and death: A qualitative analysis of dying cancer patients' talk about hope. *Death Studies*, 33 (7), 609–38.

Ellis, C. (2004) *The ethnographic LI: A methodological novel about autoethnography*, Walnut Creek, CA: AltaMira Press.

———— (2009) Telling tales on neighbors: Ethics in two voices. *International Review of Qualitative Research*, 2 (1), 3–28.

Ellis, C. and Bochner, A. P. (eds) (1996) *Composing ethnography: Alternative forms of qualitative writing*, Walnut Creek, CA: AltaMira Press.

Ely, M., Anzul, M., Friedman, T., Garner, D. and Steinmetz, A. M. (1991) *Doing qualitative research: Circles within circles*, London: Routledge.

Emden, C. and Sandelowski, M. (1998) The good, the bad, and the relative, part 2: Goodness and the criterion problem in qualitative research. *International Journal of Nursing Practice*, 5, 2–7.

Emerson, R. M., Fretz, R. I. and Shaw, L. L. (2001) Participant observation and fieldnotes. *In:* P. Atkinson, A. Coffey, S. Delamont, J. Lofland and L. Lofland (eds) *Handbook of ethnography*. London: Sage.

Endacott, R., Scholes, J., Cooper, S., Mcconnell-Henry, T., Porter, J., Missen, K., Kinsman, L. and Champion, R. (2011) Identifying patient deterioration: Using simulation and reflective review to examine decision making skills in a rural hospital. *International Journal of Nursing Studies*, 49 (6), 710–17.

England, R. (2008) Getting personal: Reflexivity, positionality, and feminist research. *In:* Bauder, H. and Maurio, S. E. (eds) *Critical geographies: A collection of readings*, Kelowna, B.C., Canada. Praxis (e) press. http://www.praxis-epress.org/CGR/18-England.pdf

Eriksson, P. and Kovalainen, A. (2008) *Qualitative methods in business research*, Thousand Oaks, CA: Sage.

Erlandson, D. A., Harris, E. L., Skipper, B. L. and Allen, S. D. (1993) *Doing naturalistic inquiry: A guide to methods*, Newbury Park, CA: Sage.

Etherington, K. (2009) Life story research: A relevant methodology for counselors and psychotherapists. *Counselling and Psychotherapy Research*, 9 (4), 225–33.

Evans, M. (2005) Auto/biographical methods. *In:* G. Griffon (ed.) *Research methods for English studies.* Edinburgh, UK: Edinburgh University Press.

Falk Rafael, A. R. (1996) Power and caring: A dialectic in nursing. *Advances in Nursing Science*, 19 (1), 3–17.

Fals-Borda, O. (1991) Some basic ingredients. *In:* O. Fals-Borda and A. Rahman (eds) *Action and knowledge: Breaking the monopoly with participatory action research.* New York: Apex Press.

—— (1992) Evolution and convergence in participatory action-research. *In:* J. Frideres (ed.) *A world of communities: Participatory research perspectives.* Toronto: Captus University Publications.

—— (2001) Participatory (action) research in social theory: Origins and challenges. *In:* P. Reason and H. Bradbury (eds) *Handbook of action research.* London: Sage.

Faris, R. E. L. (1967) *Chicago sociology 1920–1932*, Chicago IL: University of Chicago Press.

Featherstone, M. (1991) *Consumer culture and post-modernisms*, London: Sage.

Feeley, N. and Gottlieb, L. N. (1998) Classification systems for health concerns, nursing strategies, and client outcomes: Nursing practice with families who have a child with chronic illness. *Canadian Journal of Nursing Research*, 30 (1), 45–59.

Ferguson, F. (1991) Awaiting the diagnosis. *Phenomenology & Pedagogy*, 9, 312–18.

Fern, E. F. (2001) *Advanced focus group research*, Thousand Oaks, CA: Sage.

Fetterman, D. M. (1998) *Ethnography: Step by step. Applied Social Research Methods Series.* Thousand Oaks, CA: Sage.

Field, P. A. and Morse, J. M. (1992) *Nursing research. The application of qualitative approaches*, London: Chapman and Hall.

Fine, M. (1991) *Framing dropouts: Notes on the politics of an urban public high school*, Albany, NY: SUNY Press.

Fine, M., Weis, L., Weseen, S. and Wong, M. (2000) For whom? Qualitative research, representations and social responsibilities. *In:* N. K. Denzin and Y. S. Lincoln (eds) *Handbook of qualitative research.* Thousand Oaks, CA: Sage.

Finlay, L. (2002) Negotiating the swamp: The opportunity and challenge of reflexivity in research practice. *Qualitative Research*, 2 (2), 209–30.

–––– (2011) *Phenomenology for therapists*, Oxford: Wiley-Blackwell.

Finley, S. (2000) Dream child. *Qualitative Inquiry*, 6 (3), 432–4.

–––– (2003) Arts-based inquiry in QI: Seven years from crisis to guerilla warfare. *Qualitative Inquiry*, 9 (2), 281–96.

–––– (2008) Arts-based research. *In:* J. G. Knowles and A. L. Cole (eds) *Handbook of the arts in qualitative research*. London: Sage.

Fisher, M. (2002) The role of service users in problem formulation and technical aspects of social research. *Social Work Education*, 21 (3), 305–12.

Flaskerud, J. H. and Nyamathi, A. M. (2000) Collaborative inquiry with low-income latina women. *Journal of Health Care for the Poor and Underserved*, 11 (3), 326–42.

Flew, A. (ed.) (1984) *A dictionary of philosophy*, London: Pan.

Flick, U. (2009) *An introduction to qualitative research*, (4th edn.) London: Sage.

Flick, U. (2006) *An introduction to qualitative research*, (3rd edn.) London: Sage.

Flowers, P., Smith, J. A., Sheeran, P. and Beail, N. (1997) Health and romance: Understanding unprotected sex in relationships between gay men. *British Journal of Health Psychology*, 2, 73–86.

Flyvbjerg, B. (2011) Case study research. *In:* N. K. Denzin and Y. S. Lincoln (eds) *The SAGE handbook of qualitative research*. London: Sage.

Folch-Lyon, E. and Trost, J. (1981) Conducting focus group sessions. *Studies in Family Planning*, 12 (12), 443–9.

Foley, D. E. (2002) Critical ethnography: The reflexive turn. *Qualitative Studies in Education*, 15 (5), 469–90.

Fontana, A. and Frey, J. H. (1994) Interviewing: The art of science. *In:* N. K. Denzin and Y. S. Lincoln (eds) *Handbook of qualitative research*. Thousand Oaks, CA: Sage.

Foss, S. (1989) *Rhetorical criticism*, Prospect Heights, IL: Waveland Press.

Foucault, M. (1979) *Discipline and punish: The birth of the prison*, Harmondsworth: Penguin Books.

–––– (1980) *Power/knowledge: Selected interviews and other writings: 1972–1977*, trans. L. Marshall, C. Gordon, J. Mepham, K. Soper, ed. Colin Gordon, New York: Pantheon Books.

Frankel, R. M. and Devers, K. J. (2000) Study design in qualitative research: Developing sampling and data collections strategies. *Education for Health*, 13 (2), 263–71.

Frankenberg, R. (1980) Participant observers. *In:* R. Burgess (ed.) *Field research: A sourcebook and field manual*. London: Allen and Unwin.

Franzosi, R. (1998) Narrative analysis – or why (and how) sociologists should be interested in narrative. *Annual Review of Sociology*, 24, 517–54.

Freire, P. (1970) *Pedagogy of the oppressed*, New York: Continuum.

–––– (1973) *The pedagogy of the oppressed*, New York: Seabury.

Frideres, J. (1992) Participatory research: An illusionary perspective. *In:* J. Frideres (ed.) *A world of communities: Participatory research perspectives*. York, Ontario: Captus University Publications.

Frye, N. (1957) *The anatomy of criticism*, Princeton, NJ: Princeton University Press.

Gabrielian, V. (1999) Qualitative research methods: An overview. *In:* G. J. Miller and M. L. Whicker (eds) *Handbook of research methods in public administration*. New York: Marcel Dekker.

Gadamer, H. G. (1960/1975) *Truth and method*, London: Sheed and Ward.

Gallagher, S. (1992) *Hermeneutics and education*, Albany, NY: State University of New York Press.

Gannon, S. (2009) Writing narrative. *In:* J. Higgs, D. Horsfall and S. Grace (eds) *Writing qualitative research on practices*. Rotterdam, The Netherlands: Sense Publishers.

Gardner, N. (1974) Action training and research: Something old and something new. *Public Administration Review*, 34, 106–15.

Gardner, S. K. (2010) Contrasting the socialization experiences of doctoral students in high- and low-completing departments: A qualitative analysis of disciplinary contexts at one institution. *Journal of Higher Education*, 81 (1), 61–81.

Gauntlett, D. (2007) *Creative explorations. New approaches to identities and audiences*, London: Routledge.

Gaventa, J. and Cornwall, A. (2001) Power and knowledge. *In:* P. Reason and H. Bradbury (eds) *Handbook of action research. Participative inquiry and practice.* London: Sage.

Gee, J. P. (2005) *An introduction to discourse analysis: Theory and method*, London: Routledge.

Geertz, C. (1973) *The interpretation of cultures*, New York: Basic Books.

–––– (1983) *Local knowledge: Further essays in interpretive anthropology*, New York: Basic Books.

–––– (1988) *Works and lives: The anthropologist as author*, Stanford, CA: Stanford University Press.

Gergen, K. J. (1978) Toward generative theory. *Journal of Personality and Social Psychology*, 36 (11), 1344–60.

–––– (2001) Psychological science in a post-modern context. *American Psychologist*, 56, 803–13.

–––– (2009) *An invitation to social construction (2nd edn.)*, Thousand Oaks, CA: Sage.

Gergen, K. J. and Gergen, M. M. (1991) Towards reflexive methodologies. *In:* F. Steier (ed.) *Method and reflexivity: Knowing as systemic social construction.* London: Sage.

Giacomini, M. K. and Cook, D. J. (2000) Users' guides to the medical literature: Xxiii. Qualitative research in health care. A. Are the result of the study valid? *JAMA*, 284 (3), 357–62.

Giddens, A. (1984) *The constitution of society*, Cambridge: Polity Press.

–––– (1992) *The transformation of intimacy*, Cambridge, UK: Polity Press.

Giele, J. Z. and Elder, G. H. (1998) *Methods of life course research: Qualitative and quantitative approaches*, Thousand Oaks, CA: Sage.

Giorgi, A. (1989) One type of analysis of descriptive data: Procedures involved in following a phenomenological method. *Methods*, 1, 39–61.

–––– (1997) The theory, practice, and evaluation of the phenomenological method as a qualitative research. *Journal of Phenomenological Psychology*, 28 (2), 235–260.

Gitlin, A. D., Siegel, M. and Boru, K. (1989) The politics of method: From leftist ethnography to educative research. *International Journal of Qualitative Studies in Education*, 2 (3), 237–53.

Glaser, B. G. (1978) *Theoretical sensitivity: Advances in the methodology of grounded theory*, Mill Valley, CA: Sociology Press.

–––– (1992) *Basics of grounded theory analysis: Emergence vs forcing*, Mill Valley, CA: Sociology Press.

–––– (1998) *Doing grounded theory: Issues and discussions*, Mill Valley, CA: Sociology Press.

–––– (2001) *The grounded theory perspective: Conceptualization contrasted with description*, Mill Valley, CA: Sociology Press.

–––– (2003) *The grounded theory perspective 11: Description's remodeling of grounded theory*, Mill Valley, CA: Sociology Press.

–––– (2004) Naturalistic inquiry and grounded theory. *Forum Qualitative Socialforschung/ Forum: Qualitative Social Research*, 5 (1), Article 7.

Glaser, B. G. and Holton, J. (2004) Remodeling grounded theory. *Forum Qualitative Socialforschung/Forum: Qualitative Social Research*, 5 (2).

Glaser, B. G. and Strauss, A. L. (1967) *Discovery of grounded theory: Strategies for qualitative research*, New York: Aldine De Gruyter.

Glesne, C. and Peshkin, A. (1992) *Becoming qualitative researchers: An introduction*, New York: Longman Publishing Group.

Goetz, J.P. and LeCompte, M.D. (1984) *Ethnography and qualitative design in educational research*, New York: Academic Press.

Gold, R. (1958) Roles in sociological field observation. *Social Forces*, 36, 217–13.

Golsworthy, R. and Coyle, A. (1999) Spiritual beliefs and the search for meaning following partner loss among older adults. *Mortality*, 4, 21-40.

———— (2001) Practitioners accounts of religious and spiritual dimensions in bereavement therapy. *Counselling Psychology Quarterly*, 14, 183–202.

Goodley, D. and Parker, I. (2000) Critical psychology and action research. *Annual Review of Critical Psychology*, 2, 3–18.

Goodwin, C. (2000) Action and embodiment within situated human interaction. *Journal of Pragmatics*, 32, 1489–522.

Gough, D. and Elbourne, D. (2002) Systematic research synthesis to inform policy, practice, and democratic debate. *Social Policy & Society*, 1 (3), 225–36.

Grace, S., Higgs, J. and Ajjawi, R. (2009) Writing phenomenologically. *In:* J. Higgs, D. Horsfall and S. Grace (eds) *Writing qualitative research on practices.* Rotterdam: Sense Publishers.

Gramsci, A. (1971) *Prison notebooks*. New York: International Publishers.

Graneheim, U. H. and Lundman, B. (2004) Qualitative content analysis in nursing research: Concepts, procedures and measures to achieve trustworthiness. *Nursing Today*, 24, 105–12.

Gray, R. E. (2003) Performing on and off the stage: The place(s) of performance in arts-based approaches to qualitative inquiry. *Qualitative Inquiry*, 9 (2), 254–67.

Green, J. C. (2007) *Mixed methods in social inquiry*, San Francisco, CA: Jossey Bass.

Green, J. C. and Caracelli, V. J. (1997) Defining and describing the paradigm issue in mixed-method evaluation. *In:* J. C. Green and V. J. Caracelli (eds) *Advances in mixed-method evaluation: The challenges and benefits of integrating diverse paradigms.* San Francisco CA: Jossey Bass.

Green, J. C., Franquiz, M. and Dixon, C. (1997) The myth of the objective transcript: Transcribing as a situated act. *Tesol Q*, 31, 172–6.

Green, J., Green, S. W. and Cushing, F. H. (1990) *Cushing at Zuni: The correspondence and journals of Frank Hamilton Cushing, 1879–1884*, Albuquerque: University of New Mexico Press.

Greenbank, P. (2003) The role of values in educational research: The case for reflexivity' *British Educational Research Journal*, 29 (6), 791–801.

Grundy, S. (1987) *Curriculum: Product or praxis*, London: Falmer.

Guba, E. G. and Lincoln, Y. S. (1981) *Effective evaluation*, San Francisco, CA: Jossey Bass.

———— (1989) *Fourth generation evaluation*, Newbury Park, CA: Sage.

———— (1994) Competing paradigms in qualitative research. *In:* N. K. Denzin and Y. S. Lincoln (eds) *Handbook of qualitative research.* Thousand Oaks, CA: Sage.

———— (2005) Paradigmatic controversies, contradictions, and emerging confluences. *In:* N. K. Denzin and Y. S. Lincoln (eds) *The SAGE handbook of qualitative research (3rd edn.).* Thousand Oaks, CA: Sage.

Guba, E. G., Lynham, S. and Lincoln, Y. S. (2011) Paradigmatic controversies, contradictions, and emerging confluences revisited. *In:* N. K. Denzin and Y. S. Lincoln (eds) *The SAGE handbook of qualitative research (3rd edn.).* Thousand Oaks, CA: Sage.

Gubrium, J. (1992) *Out of control: Family therapy and domestic order*, Newbury Park, CA: Sage.

Gubrium, J. and Buckholdt, D. (1982) *Describing care: Image and practice in rehabilitation*, Cambridge, MA: Oelschlager, Gunn & Hain.

Gubrium, J. F. and Holstein, J. A. (1995) *The active interview*, Thousand Oaks, CA: Sage.

––– (2001) *Handbook of interview research*, London: Sage.

Guha, M. L., Druin, A. and Fails, J. A. (2011) How children can design the future. *Human Computer Interaction, Users and Applications: Lecture Notes in Computer Science*, 6764, 559–69.

Guillemin, C. and Gillam, L. (2004) Ethics, reflexivity and "ethically important moments" in research. *Qualitative Inquiry*, 10 (2), 261–80.

Habermas, J. (1971) *Knowledge and human interests,* Boston: Beacon Press.

Halliday, M. A. K. and Matthiessen, C. M. I. M. (2004) *An introduction to functional grammar (3rd edn.)*, London: Arnold.

Hamel, J., Dufour, S. and Fortin, D. (1993) *Case study methods*, Newbury Park, CA: Sage.

Hamilton, D. (1977) Making sense of curriculum evaluation: Continuities and discontinuities in an educational idea. *Review of Research in Education*, 5 (1), 318–47.

Hammersley, M. (1990) *Reading ethnographic research: A critical guide*, New York: Longman.

––– (1992) Some reflections on ethnography and validity. *International Journal of Qualitative Studies in Education*, 5 (3), 195–203.

––– (2009) Why critical realism fails to justify critical social research. *Methodological Innovations Online*, 4 (2), 1–11.

Hammersley, M. and Atkinson, P. (1995) *Ethnography: Principles in practice (2nd edn.)*, London: Routledge.

––– (2007) *Ethnography: Principles in practice (3rd edn.)*, London: Routledge.

Hammersley, M. and Gomm, R. (1997) Bias in social research. *Sociological Research Online*, 2 (1).

Hammick, M. (1996) *Managing the ethical process in research*, Salisbury: Quay Books.

Hanafin, S., Brooks, A. M., Carroll, E., Fitzgerald, E., Gabhainn, S. N. and Sixsmith, J. (2007) Achieving consensus in developing a national set of child well-being indicators. *Social Indicators Research*, 80, 79–104.

Harding, S. (1987) Introduction: Is there a feminist method? *In:* S. Harding (ed.) *Feminism and methodology.* Bloomington, IN: Indiana University Press.

Hargens, L. L. (2000) Using the literature: Reference networks, reference contexts, and the social structure of scholarship. *American Sociological Review*, 65, 846–65.

Harris, I. (1991) Deliberative inquiry: The arts of planning. *In:* E. C. Short (ed.) *Forms of curriculum inquiry.* New York: State University of New York Press.

Harris, M. S. and Hartley, M. (2011) Witch-hunting at crucible university: The power and peril of competing organizational ideologies. *The Journal of Higher Education*, 82 (6), 691–719.

Hart, C. (1998) *Doing a literature review: Releasing the social science imagination*, London: Sage.

Hartley, J. and McWilliam, K. (eds) (2009) *Story circle: Digital storytelling around the world*, Chichester: Wiley-Blackwell.

Harvey, B. (2004) *The impact of the commodification of relationship on lifelong learning.* PhD Thesis, University of Leicester.

Hatch, J. A. (2002) *Doing qualitative research in education settings*, Albany, NY: SUNY Press.

Haw, K. and Hadfield, M. (2011) *Video in social science research*, London: Routledge.

Healy, M. E. (1947) Le Play's contribution to sociology: His method. *The American Catholic Sociological Review*, 8 (2), 97–110.

Heidegger, M. (1927/1962) *Being and time*, New York: Harper.

Heinze, A. (2008) *Blended learning: An interpretive action research study.* PhD thesis, University of Salford.

Heise, D. R. (1988) Computer analysis of cultural structures. *Social Science Computer Review*, 6 (1), 183–97.

Hendry, P. (2010) Narrative as inquiry. *The Journal of Educational Research*, 103 (2), 72–80.

Heritage, J., Maynard, D. W. and Robinson, J. (2006) Soliciting patients' presenting concerns. *In:* J. Heritage and D. W. Maynard (eds) *Communication in medical care: Interaction between primary care physicians and patients.* Cambridge: Cambridge University Press.

Herman, L. (2005) Researching the images of evil events: An arts-based methodology in liminal space. *Qualitative Inquiry,* 11 (3), 468–80.

Hernes, T. (2004) *The spatial construction of organization,* Amsterdam: John Benjamins.

Heron, J. (1971) Experience and method: An inquiry into the concept of experiential research. [www.human-inquiry.com/Experience%20And%20Method.pdf]. Accessed 10 March 2012.

—— (1981) Experiential research methodology. *In:* P. Reason and H. Bradbury (eds) *Human inquiry: A sourcebook of new paradigm research.* Chichester: Wiley.

—— (1996) *Co-operative inquiry: Research into the human condition,* London: Sage.

Heron, J. and Bradbury, H. (2008) Extending epistemology within a cooperative inquiry. *In:* P. Reason and H. Bradbury (eds) *Handbook of action research: Participative inquiry and practice (2nd edn.).* London: Sage.

Heron, J. and Reason, P. (1997) A participatory inquiry paradigm. *Qualitative Inquiry,* 3 (3), 274–94.

—— (2006) The practice of cooperative inquiry: Research 'with' rather than 'on' people. *In:* P. Reason and H. Bradbury (eds) *Handbook of action research: Participative inquiry and practice.* London: Sage.

Higgs, J. and Cherry, N. (2009) Doing qualitative research on practice. *In:* J. Higgs, D. Horsfall and C. Grace (eds) *Writing qualitative research on practice.* Rotterdam, The Netherlands: Sense Publishers.

Higgs, J., Horsfall, D. and Grace, S. (2009) *Writing qualitative research on practice,* Rotterdam, The Netherlands: Sense Publishers.

Hine, C. (2000) *Virtual ethnography,* London: Sage.

—— (2007) Connective ethnography for the exploration of escience. *Journal of Computer-Mediated Communication,* 12 (2).

Hitchcock, G. and Hughes, D. (1995) *Research and the teacher: A qualitative introduction to school-based research (2nd edn.),* London: Routledge.

Hoey, M. (2005) *Lexical priming: A new theory of words and language,* Oxon: Routledge.

—— (2006) Language as choice: What is chosen? *In:* S. Hunston and G. Thompson (eds) *System and corpus: Exploring connections.* London: Equinox.

Holden, M. T. and Lynch, P. (2004) Choosing the appropriate methodology: Understanding research philosophy. *Marketing Review,* 4, 397–409.

Hollan, J., Hutchins, E. and Kirsh, D. (2000) Distributed cognition: Toward a new foundation for human–computer interaction research. *ACM Transactions on Computer–Human Interaction,* 7 (2), 174–96.

Holley, K. A. and Taylor, B. J. (2009) Undergraduate student socialization and learning in an online professional curriculum. *Innovative Higher Education,* 33 (4), 257–69.

Holliday, A. R. (2007) *Doing and writing qualitative research (2nd edn.),* London: Sage.

Holligan, C. (2011) Feudalism and academia: UK academics' accounts of research culture. *International Journal of Qualitative Studies in Education,* 24 (1), 55–75.

Holloway, I. (1997) *Basic concepts for qualitative research,* Oxford: Blackwell Science.

Holloway, I. and Wheeler, S. (1996) *Qualitative research for nurses,* Oxford: Blackwell Science.

Holt, N. L. (2003) Representation, legitimation, and autoethnography: An autoethnographic writing story. *International Journal of Qualitative Methods,* 2 (1), Article 2. [www.ualberta.ca/~iiqm/backissues/2_1/html/holt.html]. Accessed 13 June 2012.

Holter, I. M. and Schwartz-Barcott, D. (1993) Action research: What is it? How has it been used and how can it be used in nursing? *Journal of Advanced Nursing,* 128, 298–304.

Honderich, T. (ed.) (1995) *The Oxford companion to philosophy,* New York: Oxford University Press.

Hope, A. and Timmel, S. (1995) *Training for transformation: A handbook for community workers*, revised edition, Zimbabwe: Mambo Press.

Horkheimer, M. (1982) *Critical theory*, New York: Seabury Press.

———— (1993) *Between philosophy and social science*, Cambridge, MA: MIT Press.

Horkheimer, M. and Adorno, T. W. (1972) *Dialectic of enlightenment*, New York: Herder and Herder.

House, E. R. (1980) *Evaluating with validity*, Beverly Hills, CA: Sage.

Hoy, D. (2004) *Critical resistance: From poststructuralism to post-critique*, Cambridge: MIT Press.

Hughes, D. and Dumont, K. (1993) Using focus groups to facilitate culturally-anchored research. *American Journal of Community Psychology*, 21 (4), 775–806.

Human Tissue Act 2004 (c. **30**) London: HMSO http://www.legislation.gov.uk/ukpga/2004/30/contents

Humphreys, L. (1970) *Tearoom trade: A study of homosexual encounters in public places*, London: Duckworth.

Husserl, E. (1907/1964) *The idea of phenomenology*, The Hague: Nijhoff.

———— (1962/1977) *Phenomenological psychology*, The Hague: Nijhoff.

Hussey, J. and Hussey, R. (1997) *Business research: A practical guide for undergraduate and postgraduate students*, Basingstoke: Palgrave.

Hutchins, E. (1995) *Cognition in the wild*, Cambridge, MA: MIT Press.

Iyengar, S. (2010) *The art of choosing*, New York: Twelve.

Jackson, A. Y. and Mazzei, L. A. (2011) *Thinking with theory in qualitative research: Using epistemological frameworks in the production of meaning*, London: Routledge.

Jarman, M., Walsh, S. and DeLacey, G. (2005) Keeping safe, keeping connected: A qualitative study of HIV-positive women's experience of partner relationships, *Psychology and Health*, 20, 533–53.

Jenner, B. and Titscher, S. (2000) *Methods of text and discourse analysis*, London: Sage.

Jensen, L. A. and Allen, M. N. (1996) Meta-synthesis of qualitative findings. *Qualitative Health Research*, 6, 553–60.

Johnson, A. and Sackett, R. (1998) Direct systematic observation of behavior. *In:* H. Russell Bernard (ed.) *Handbook of methods in cultural anthropology*. Walnut Creek, CA: AltaMira Press.

Johnson, M. (1992) A silent conspiracy? Some ethical issues of participant observation in nursing research. *International Journal of Nursing Studies*, 29, 213–23.

———— (1999) Communication in healthcare: A review of some key issues. *Journal of Research in Nursing*, 4, 18–30.

Jonassen, D. H. (1991) Objectivism versus constructivism, do we need a new philosophical paradigm? *Educational technology research and development*, 39 (3), 5–14.

Jones, J. H. (1993) *Bad blood: The Tuskegee syphilis experiment*, New York: Free Press.

Joppe, M. (2000) The research process. [www.ryerson.ca/~mjoppe/rp.htm]. Accessed 25 February 1998.

Jorgensen, D. L. (1989) *Participant observation: A methodology for human studies*, Newbury Park, CA: Sage.

Jung, C. (1953) *Two essays on analytical psychology*, New York: Pantheon Books.

Kakabadse, N. K., Kakabadse, A., Lee-Davies, L. and Johnson, N. (2011) Deliberative inquiry: Integrated ways of working in children services. *Systemic Practice and Action Research*, 24 (1), 67–84. [https://dspace.lib.cranfield.ac.uk/bitstream/1826/5269/1/Deliberative_inquiry.pdf]. Accessed 12 June 2012.

Katz, J. (1983) A theory of qualitative methodology. *In:* R. M. Emerson (ed.) *Contemporary field research: A collection of readings*. Prospect Heights, IL: Waveland.

Kavanaugh, A. L., Isenhour, P. L., Cooper, M., Carroll, J. M. and Rosson, M. B. (2005) Information technology in support of public deliberation. *Communities and Technologies*, Part 1, 19–40.

Kawulich, B. (2005) Participant observation as a data collection method. *Forum Qualitative Sozialforschung / Forum: Qualitative Social Research*, 6 (2), Article 43.

Kazubowski-Houston, M. (2010) *Staging strife: Lessons from performing ethnography with Polish Roma women*, Montreal: McGill-Queens University Press.

–––– (2011a) Thwarting binarisms: Performing racism in postsocialist Poland. *Text and Performance Quarterly*, 31 (2), 169–89.

–––– (2011b) Don't tell me how to dance! Negotiating collaboration, empowerment apoliticization in the ethnographic theatre project 'hope'. *Anthropologica*, 53 (2), 229–4.

Keith, H. (1999) Feminism and pragmatism: George Herbert Mead's ethics of care. *Transactions of the Charles S. Peirce Society*, 35, 328–44.

Kelland, J. H. and Kanuka, H. (2007) 'We just disagree': Using deliberative inquiry to seek consensus about the effects of e-learning on higher education. *Canadian Journal of Learning and Technology*, 33 (3).

Kelle, U. (2005) Computer-assisted qualitative data analysis. *In:* C. Seale, G. Gobo, J. F. Gubrium and D. Silverman (eds) *Qualitative research practice*. London: Sage.

Kelly, J. R. and McGrath, J. E. (1988) *On time and method*, Newbury Park, CA: Sage.

Kemmis, S. (1980) The imagination of the case and the invention of the study. *In:* H. Simons (ed.) *Towards a science of the singular.* Norwich: CARE.

–––– (2010) What is to be done? The place of action research. *Educational Action Research*, 18 (4), 417–27.

Kemmis, S. and McTaggart, R. (1988) *The action research planner*, Geelong, Victoria: Deakin University Press.

–––– (2005) *Participatory action research: Communicative action and the public sphere (3rd edn.)*, Beverly Hills, CA: Sage.

Kerlinger, F. N. (1979) *Behavioral research: A conceptual approach*, Philadelphia, PA: Holt, Rinehart and Winston.

Kestenbaum, V. (1977) *The phenomenological sense of John Dewey: Habit and meaning*, Atlantic Highlands, NJ: Humanities Press.

Khanna, R. E. (2011) *The journal of course approval: Hitting the target but missing the point.* PhD Thesis, Coventry University.

Kidd, S. A. and Kral, M. J. (2005) Practicing participatory action research. *Journal of Counseling Psychology*, 52 (2), 187–95.

Kilbourne, B. (1998) *For the love of teaching*, London, Ontario: Althouse Press.

Kim, J. H. and Latta, M. M. (2010) Narrative inquiry: Seeking relations as modes of interactions. *Journal of Educational Research*, 103, 69–71.

Kincheloe, J. L. and McLaren, P. (2005) Rethinking critical theory and qualitative research. *In:* N. K. Denzin and Y. S. Lincoln (eds) *The sage handbook of qualitative research (3rd edn.).* Thousand Oaks, CA: Sage.

King, K. E. (1995) Method and methodology in feminist research: What is the difference? *Journal of Advanced Nursing*, 20, 19–22.

King, N. and Horrocks, C. (2010) *Interviews in qualitative research*, London: Sage.

Kirk, J. and Miller, M. L. (1986) *Reliability and validity in qualitative research*, Beverly Hills, CA: Sage.

Kitzinger, J. (1994) The methodology of focus groups: The importance of interactions between research participants. *Sociology of Health and Illness*, 16, 103–21.

–––– (1995) Qualitative research: Introducing focus groups. *British Medical Journal*, 311, 299–302.

Klenke, K. (2008) *Qualitative research in the study of leadership studies*, Bingley, UK: Emerald Group.

Knafo, S. (2008) *Critical approaches and the problem of social construction. Reassessing the legacy of the agent/structure debate in IR, Working Paper No. 3*, Brighton: Centre for Global Political Economy, University of Sussex.. [www.sussex.ac.uk/cgpe/documents/cgpe-wp03-samuel-knafo.pd]. Accessed 16 June 2012.

Knightley, P., Potter, E. and Wallace, M. (1979) *Suffer the children: The story of thalidomide*, New York: Viking Press.

Knowles, J. G. and Cole, A. L. (2008) *Handbook of the arts in qualitative research*, London: Sage.

Kobayashi, A. (2003) GPC ten years on: Is self-reflexivity enough? *Gender, Place and Culture*, 10 (4), 345–9.

Kovach, C. R. (1991) Content analysis of reminiscences of elderly women. *Research in Nursing & Health*, 14 (4), 287–95.

Krippendorff, K. (1980) *Content analysis. An introduction to its methodology*. Thousand Oaks, CA: Sage.

Ku, H. B. (2011) Happiness being like a blooming flower: An action research of rural social work in an ethnic minority community of Yunnan province, PRC. *Action Research*, 9 (4), 344–69.

Ku, H. B. and Ip, D. (2011) Designing development: A case study of community economy in Pingzhai, Yunnan province, in PRC. *China Journal of Social Work*, 4 (3), 235–54.

Kuhn, T. S. (1962; 2nd edn 1970) *The structure of scientific revolutions*, Chicago, IL: University of Chicago UP.

Kuntz, A. (2010) The politics of space in qualitative research. *In:* M. Savin-Baden and C. Major (eds) *New approaches to qualitative research: Wisdom and uncertainty*. London: Routledge.

Kuzel, A. (1992) Sampling in qualitative inquiry. *In:* B. Crabtree and W. L. Miller (eds) *Doing qualitative research*. Newbury Park, CA: Sage.

Kuzel, A. and Engel, J. D. (2001) Some pragmatic thoughts about evaluating qualitative health research. *In:* J. M. Morse, L. Swanson and A. Kuzel (eds) *The nature of qualitative evidence*. London: Sage.

Kvale, S. (1996) *Interviews: An introduction to qualitative research interviewing*, London: Sage.

Labov, W. (1973) The boundaries of words and their meanings. *In:* J. Bailey and R. W. Shuy (eds) *New ways of analysing variation in English*. Washington, DC: Georgetown University Press.

Labov, W. and Waletsky, J. (1967) Narrative analysis. *In:* J. Helm (ed.) *Essays on the verbal and visual arts*. Seattle, WA: University of Washington Press.

Lancy, D. F. (1993) *Qualitative research in education: An introduction to the major traditions*, New York: Longman.

Lather, P. (1991). *Getting smart: Feminist research and pedagogy with/in the postmodern*, New York: Routledge.

Latour, B. (1996) *Aramis or The Love of Technology*. Cambridge, MA: Harvard University Press.

Laurier, E., Brown, B. and Lorimer, H. (2012) What it means to change lanes: Actions, emotions and wayfinding in the family car. *Semiotica*, 191 (4), 117–36.

Laverty, S. M. (2003) Hermeneutic phenomenology and phenomenology: A comparison of historical and methodological considerations. *International Journal of Qualitative Methods*, 2 (3), 1–29.

Lawrence-Lightfoot, S. and Davis, J. H. (1997) *The art and science of portraiture*, San Francisco, CA: Jossey Bass.

Lea, M. R. (1999) Academic literacies and learning in higher education. Constructing knowledge through texts and experience. *In:* C. Jones, J. Turner and B. V. Street (eds) *Students writing in the university: Cultural and epistemological issues*. Philadelphia, PA: John Benjamin's Publishing Company.

Leander, K. M. and McKim, K. K. (2003) Tracing the everyday 'sitings' of adolescents on the internet: A strategic adaptation of ethnography across online and offline spaces. *Education, Communication and Information*, 3 (2), 211–40.

Leca, N. and Naccache, P. (2006) A critical realist approach to institutional entrepreneurship. *Organization*, 13 (5), 627–51.

LeCompte, M. D. and Goetz, J. P. (1982) Problems of reliability and validity in educational research. *Review of Educational Research*, 52 (2), 31–60.

Lee, R. M. (1995) *Dangerous fieldwork*. Qualitative research methods series 34. London: Sage Publications.

Leech, N. L. and Onwuegbuzie, A. J. (2007) An array of qualitative data analysis tools: A call for data analysis triangulation. *School Psychology Quarterly*, 22 (4), 557–84.

Lefebvre, H. (1991) *The production of social space*, London: Blackwell.

Leggo, C. (2008) Narrative inquiry: Attending to the art of discourse. *Language & Literacy*, 10 (1), 21. http://www.langandlit.ualberta.ca/Spring2008/Leggo.htm

Le Play, F. 1982/1879. Les ouvriers europeens. (Tours: Mame, 1879), vol. 8. *In:* C. B. Silver (ed.). *Frederic Le Play on family, work and social change*, Chicago: The University of Chicago Press.

Leshem, S. and Trafford, V. (2007) Overlooking the conceptual framework. *Innovations in Education and Training International*, 44 (1), 93–105.

Lewin, K. (1946) Action research and minority problems. *Journal of Social Issues*, 2 (4), 34–46.

–––– (1947) Group decisions and social change. *In:* T. M. H. Newcomb, E. L. Hartley (eds) *Readings in social psychology*. New York: Henry Holt.

–––– (1948) *Resolving social conflict*, London: Harper and Row.

Lincoln, Y. S. (1997) Self, subject, audience, text: Living at the edge, writing in the margins. *In:* W. G. Tierney and Y. S. Lincoln (eds) *Representation and the text: Re-framing the narrative voice*. Albany, NY: State University of New York Press. pp. 37–56.

Lincoln, Y. S. and Guba, E. G. (1985) *Naturalistic inquiry*, Newbury Park, CA: Sage.

–––– (1990) *The paradigm dialogue*, Newbury Park, CA: Sage.

Lindesmith, A. R. (1952) Two comments on W. S. Robinson's 'the logical structure of analytic induction'. *American Sociological Review*, 17, 492–93.

Lindlof, T. R. and Taylor, B. C. (2002) *Qualitative communication research methods (2nd edn.)*, Thousand Oaks, CA: Sage.

Linstone, H. A. (1978) The Delphi technique. *In:* H. Fowles (ed.) *Handbook of futures research*. London: Greenwood Place.

Linstone, H. A. and Turoff, M. (1975) *The Delphi method: Techniques and applications*. Reading, MA: Addison Wesley.

Lippitt, R. and Radke, M. (1946) New trends in the investigation of prejudice. *Annals*, 244, 167–76.

Livingstone, T. (2005) *Child of our time*, London: Random House.

Locke, L. F., Spirduso, W. W. and Silverman, S. J. (1987) *Proposals that work: A guide for planning dissertations and grant proposals (2nd edn.)*, Newbury Park, CA: Sage.

Lofland, J. and Lofland, L. (1995) *Analysing social settings*, Belmont, CA: Wadsworth.

Lombardo, T. J. (1987) *The reciprocity of perceive and environment: The evolution of James J. Gibson's ecological psychology*, Hillsdale, NJ: Lawrence Erlbaum Associates.

Long, T. and Johnson, M. (2000) Rigour, reliability and validity in qualitative research. *Clinical Effectiveness in Nursing*, 4, 30–7.

Loo, I. D., Nederlof, P. and Verstegen, B. (2006) Detecting behavioural patterns of Dutch controller graduates through interpretive interactionism principles. *Qualitative Research in Accounting and Management*, 3 (1), 46–66.

Lorenzo, T. (2010) Listening spaces: Connecting diverse voices for social action and change. *In:* M. Savin-Baden and C. Major (eds) *New approaches to qualitative research: Wisdom and uncertainty*. London: Routledge.

Loseke, D. R. (2007) The study of narrative identity. *Sociological Quarterly*, 48, 661–88.

Ludema, J. D., Cooperrider, D. L. and Barrett, F. J. (2001) Appreciative inquiry: The power of the unconditional positive question. *In:* P. Reason and H. Bradbury (eds) *Handbook of action research.* London: Sage.

Lundeberg, M. A., Bergland, M., Klyczek, K. and Hoffman, D. (2003) Using action research to develop preservice teachers' beliefs, knowledge and confidence about technology. *Journal of Interactive Online Learning*, 1 (4).

Lyotard, J. F. (1979) *The post-modern condition: A report on knowledge,* Manchester: Manchester University Press.

McCarthy, C., Durham, A. S., Engel, L. C., Giardina, M. D. and Malagreca, M. A. (2007) *Globalizing cultural studies,* New York: Peter Lang.

McCleary, R. (2007) Ethical issues in online social work research. *Journal of Social Work Values and Ethics*, 4, 6–26.

McCloud, S. (2006) *Making comics: Storytelling secrets of comics, manga, and graphic novels,* New York: Harper.

McCormack, B. and Elliott, J. (2003) In appreciation of wisdom: The voice of the older person. *Inaugural professorial lecture.* University of Ulster, Northern Island.

McCreaddie, M. and Payne, S. (2010) Evolving grounded theory methodology: Towards a discursive approach. *International Journal of Nursing Studies*, 47 (6), 781–93.

McCutcheon, G. and Jurg, B. (1990) Alternative perspectives on action research. *Theory into Practice*, 24 (3), 144–51.

MacDonald, B. (1971) The evaluation of the humanities curriculum project: A holistic approach. *Theory into Practice*, 10 (3), 163–7.

–––– (1974) Evaluation and the control of education. *In:* B. MacDonald and R. Walker (eds) *Innovation, evaluation, research and the problem of control.* Norwich: University of East Anglia.

–––– (1984) *Democratic evaluation in practice,* Paper presented at the Second National Evaluation Conference 26–27 July, Melbourne, Victoria, Australia.

–––– (1994) *Values, power and strategy in evaluation design – some preliminary considerations. Evaluating Innovation in environmental Education,* Paris: OECD/CERI.

MacDonald, B. and Walker, R. (1975) Case study and the social philosophy of educational research. *Cambridge Journal of Education*, 5 (1), 2–11.

MacKay, N. (1997) Constructivism and the logic of explanation. *Journal of Constructivist Psychology.*, 10 (4), 339–61.

McKenna, H. (1997) *Nursing theory and models,* Abingdon: Routledge.

McKenzie, C. (2008) Radio in/for research: Creating knowledge waves. *In:* J. G. Knowles and A. L. Cole (eds) *Handbook of the arts in qualitative research.* London: Sage.

MacKenzie, N. and Knipe, S. (2006) Research dilemmas: Paradigms, method and methodology. *Issues in Educational Research*, 16 (2), 1–13.

McKernan, J. (1991) *Curriculum action research. A handbook of methods and resources for the reflective practitioner,* London: Kogan Page.

–––– (1996) *Curriculum action research. A handbook of methods and resources for the reflective practitioner,* London: Kogan Page.

McMillan, J. H. and Schumacher, S. S. (1997) *Research in education: A conceptual introduction,* New York: Longman.

MacNee, C. L. (2004) *Understanding nursing research: Reading and using research in practice.* Philadelphia, PA: Lippincott Williams and Wilkins.

McNiff, S. (1998) *Arts-based research,* London: Jessica Kingsley Publisher.

–––– (2008) Arts-based research. *In:* J. G. Knowles and A. L. Cole (eds) *Handbook of the arts in qualitative research.* London: Sage.

McTaggart, R. (1991) Principles for participatory action research. *Adult Education Quarterly*, 41, 168–87.

Madill, A., Jordan, A. and Shirley, C. (2000) Objectivity and reliability in qualitative analysis: Realist, contextualist and radical constructionist epistemologies. *British Journal of Psychology*, 91, 1–20.

Madison, D. S. (2005) *Critical ethnography: Method, ethics, and performance*, London: Sage.

Major, C. and Palmer, B. (2006) Reshaping teaching and learning: Changing faculty pedagogical content knowledge. *Higher Education*, 51 (4), 619–47.

Major, C. H. (2010) Do virtual professors dream of electric students? College faculty experiences with online distance education. *Teachers College Record*, 112 (8), 2154–208.

Major, C. H. and Savin-Baden, M. (2010a) *An introduction to qualitative research synthesis: Managing the information explosion in social science research*, London: Routledge.

––––– (2010b) Exploring the relevance of qualitative research synthesis to higher education research and practice. *London Review of Education*, 8 (2), 127–40.

Malinowski, B. (1922/1984) *Argonauts of the Western Pacific*, Long Grove: Waveland Press.

––––– (1967) *Giornale di un antropologo (a diary in the strict sense of the term)*, Roma: Armando.

Malterud, K. (2001a) The art of science of clinical knowledge: Evidence beyond measures and numbers. *The Lancet*, 358, 397–400.

––––– (2001b) Qualitative research: Standards, challenges and guidelines. *The Lancet*, 358, 483–8.

Manning, P. K. (1987) *Semiotics and fieldwork*, Newbury Park, CA: Sage.

Manning, P. K. and Cullum-Swan, B. (1994) Narrative, content, and semiotic analysis. *In:* N. K. Denzin and Y. S. Lincoln (eds) *Handbook of qualitative research*. Thousand Oaks, CA: Sage.

Margolis, E. and Rowe, J. (2011) Disclosing historical photograph. *In:* E. Margolis and L. Pauwels (eds) *Handbook of visual research methods*. London: Sage.

Marshall, A. and Batten, S. (2004) Researching across cultures: Issues of ethics and power. *Forum Qualitative Sozialforschung / Forum: Qualitative Social Research*, 5 (3), Article 39.

Marshall, C. (1990) Goodness criteria: Are they objective or judgement calls? *In:* E. G. Guba (ed.) *The paradigm dialog*. Newbury Park, CA: Sage.

Marshall, C. and Rossman, G. B. (1989/1995) *Designing qualitative research*, Newbury Park, CA: Sage.

––––– (2006) *Designing qualitative research*, Thousand Oaks, CA: Sage.

––––– (1999) *Designing qualitative research*, Thousand Oaks, CA: Sage Publications.

Martin, V. (2008) *A narrative inquiry into the effects of serious illness and major surgery on conceptions of self and life story*. PhD Thesis, University of Bristol.

Marton, F. (1994) Phenomenography. *In:* T. Husén and T. N. Postlethwaite (eds) *The international encyclopedia of education (2nd edn.)*. Oxford: Pergamon.

Marton, F. and Säljö, R. (1984) Approaches to learning. *In:* F. Marton, D. Hounsell and N.J. Entwistle (eds) *The experience of learning*. Edinburgh: Scottish Academic Press.

Mason, J. (2002) *Qualitative researching (2nd edn.)*, London: Sage.

Mason, J. and Waywood, A. (1996) The role of theory in mathematics education and research. *In:* A. J. Bishop, K. Clements, C. Keitel, J. Kilpatrick and C. Laborde (eds) *International handbook of mathematics education*. Dordrecht: Kluwer Academic. pp. 1055–89.

Masters, J. (1995) The history of action research. *In:* I. Hughes (ed.) *Action Research Electronic Reader, The University of Sydney*. The University of Sydney.

Maxwell, J. (2005) *Qualitative research design*, London: Sage.

May, T. (1993) *Social research: Issues, methods and process*, Buckingham: Open University Press.

––––– (1998) Reflexivity in the age of reconstructive social science. *International Journal of Social Research Methodology, Theory and Practice*, 1 (1), 7–24.

―――― (1999) Reflexivity and sociological practice. *Sociological Research Online*, 4 (3).

Mays, N. and Pope, C. (1995) Qualitative research: Observational methods in health care settings. *British Medical Journal*, 311, 182–184.

―――― (2000a) Qualitative research in health care: Assessing quality in qualitative research. *BMJ*, 320 (7226), 50–52.

―――― (2000b) Quality in qualitative health research. *In:* N. Mays and C. Pope (eds) *Qualitative research in health care (2nd edn.)*. London: BMJ Books.

Mead, M. (1928) *Coming of age in Samoa: A psychological study of primitive youth for Western civilisation*, New York: William Morrow and Company.

Meleis, A. I. (1991) *Theoretical nursing: Development and progress (2nd edn.)*, Philadelphia PA: Lippincott.

Merleau-Ponty, M. (1962/1945) *Phenomenology of perception*, London: Routledge.

―――― (1964/1998) The visible and the invisible. *In:* W. McNeill and K. S. Feldman (eds) *Continental philosophy: An anthology*. Oxford: Blackwell Publishers.

Merriam, S. B. (1988) *Case study research in education*, San Francisco, CA: Jossey Bass.

―――― (1998) *Qualitative research and case study applications in education*, San Francisco: Jossey-Bass.

―――― (2009) *Qualitative research: A guide to design and implementation*, San Francisco, CA: Jossey-Bass.

Mertens, D. M. (1998) *Research methods in education and psychology. Integrating diversity with quantitative and qualitative approaches*, Thousand Oaks, CA: Sage.

―――― (2005) *Research methods in education and psychology: Integrating diversity with quantitative and qualitative approaches (2nd edn.)*, Thousand Oaks, CA: Sage.

Merton, R. K. and Kendall, P. L. (1946) The focused interview. *American Journal of Sociology*, 51, 541–57.

Meulenberg-Buskens, E. (1999) *Leadership and facilitation in participatory research and action*, Cape Town: Research for the Future.

Meyer, J. H. F. and Land, R. (eds) (2006) *Overcoming barriers to student understanding: Threshold concepts and troublesome knowledge*, London: Routledge.

Mezirow, J. (1981) A critical theory of adult learning and education. *Adult Education*, 32, 3–24.

―――― (1991) *Transformative dimensions of adult learning*, San Francisco, CA: Jossey Bass.

―――― (2000) *Learning as transformation: Critical perspectives on a theory in progress*, San Francisco, CA: Jossey Bass.

Miles, M. B. and Huberman, A. M. (1994) *Qualitative data analysis (2nd edn.)*, Thousand Oaks, CA: Sage.

Mills, E. (2002) Hazel the dental assistant and the research dilemma of (re)presenting a life story. *In:* W. C. Van Den Hoonaard (ed.) *Walking the tightrope: Ethical issues for qualitative researchers*. Toronto: University of Toronto Press.

Mills, G. E. (2006) *Action research: A guide for the teacher researcher (3rd edn.)*, Upper Saddle River, NJ: Merrill.

Minichiello, V., Aroni, R., Timewell, E. and Alexander, L. (1990) *In-depth interviewing: Researching people*, Hong Kong: Longman Cheshire.

Mishler, E. G. (2000) Validation in inquiry-guided research: The role of exemplars in narrative studies. *In:* B. M. Brizuela, J. P. Stewart, R. G. Carrillo and J. G. Berger (eds) *Acts of inquiry in qualitative research*. Cambridge, MA: Harvard Educational Review.

Mishra, P. and Koehler, M. J. (2006) Technological pedagogical content knowledge: A framework for integrating technology in teacher knowledge. *Teachers College Record*, 108 (6), 1017–54.

Mitchell, R. (2009) 'Soft ears' and hard topics: Race, disciplinarity, and voice in higher education. *In:* L. Mazzei and A. Jackson (eds) *Voice in qualitative inquiry: Challenging conventional, interpretive, and critical conceptions in qualitative research*. New York: Routledge. pp. 77–97.

Moffitt, P. M., Mordoch, E., Wells, C., Martin Misener, R., McDonagh, M. K. and Edge, D. S. (2009) From sea to shining sea: Making collaborative rural research work. *Rural and Remote Health*, 9 (1156).

Mogalakwe, M. (2006) The use of documents in social research. *African Sociological Review*, 10 (1), 221–30.

Montoya, M. E. (2003) Máscaras, trenzas, y grenas. *In:* A. K. Wing (ed.) *Critical race feminism: A reader* (2nd edn.). New York: New York University Press. pp. 70–7.

Morgan, D. L. (1996) Focus groups. *Annual Review of Sociology*, 22, 129–52.

Morgan, G. and Smircich, L. (1980) The case of qualitative research. *Academy of Management Review*, 5, 491–500.

Morse, J. M., Barrett, M., Mayan, M., Olson, K. and Spiers, J. (2002) Verification strategies for establishing reliability and validity in qualitative research. *International Journal of Qualitative Methods*, 1 (2), 1–19.

Moustakas, C. (1994) *Phenomenological research methods*, Thousand Oaks, CA: Sage.

Mulhall, A. (2002) Methodological issues in nursing research. In the field: Notes on observation in qualitative research. *Journal of Advanced Nursing*, 41 (3), 306–13.

Munhall, P. (1988) Ethical considerations in qualitative research. *Western Journal of Nursing Research*, 10 (2), 150–62.

Mullen, C. A. (2003) A self-fashioned gallery of aesthetic practice, *Qualitative Inquiry*, 9, 165–181.

Murray, M. (2003) Narrative psychology. *In:* J. A. Smith (ed.) *Qualitative psychology: A practical guide to research methods.* London: Sage.

Naish, J., Brown, J. and Denton, B. (1994) Intercultural consultations: Investigation of factors that deter non-English speaking women from attending their general practitioners for cervical screening. *BMJ*, 309, 1126.

Naples, N. A. (2004) The outsider phenomenon. *In:* S. Nage Hesse-Biber and M. L. Yaiser (eds) *Feminist perspectives on social research.* New York: Oxford University Press.

Neergaard, M. A., Olesen, F., Andersen, R. S. and Sondergaard, J. (2009) Qualitative description – the poor cousin of health research? *BMC Medical Research Methodology*, 9 (52).

Nicholson, L. J. (1990) *Feminism/post-modernism*, London: Routledge.

Nieswiadomy, R. M. (2001) *Foundations of nursing research (4th edn.)*, New Jersey: Pearson Education Inc.

Nightingale, D. J. and Cromby, J. (eds) (1999) *Social constructionist psychology: A critical analysis of theory and practice*, Buckingham: Open University Press.

Niglas, K. (2000) Combining quantitative and qualitative approaches. Paper presented at the European Conference on Educational Research, Edinburgh, 20–23 September. [www.leeds.ac.uk/educol/documents/00001544.htm]. Accessed 17 June 2012.

Nilan, P. (2002) Dangerous fieldwork re-examined: The question of researcher subject position. *Qualitative Research*, 2 (3), 363–86.

Nimmon, L. E. (2007) ESL-speaking immigrant women's disillusions: Voices of health care in Canada: An ethnodrama. *Health Care for Women International*, 28, 381–96.

Noblit, G. W. and Hare, R. D. (1988) *Meta-ethnography: Synthesizing qualitative studies*, Newbury Park, CA: Sage.

Norrick, N. (2005) The dark side of tellability. *Narrative Inquiry*, 15 (2), 323–43.

Nuremberg Code. (1949) *Trials of war criminals before the Nuremberg military tribunals under Control Council Law 10(2) No. 10, Nuremberg, October 1946–1949*, Washington, DC: U.S. Government Printing Office, *1949*. Volume 2, pp. 181–2. [http://history.nih.gov/research/downloads/nuremberg.pdf].

O'Brien, R. (2001) Um exame da abordagem metodológica da pesquisa ação [an overview of the methodological approach of action research]. *In:* R. Richardson (ed.) *Teoria e prática da pesquisa ação [theory and practice of action research].* João Pessoa, Brazil: Universidade Federal da Paraíba.

Olson, G. (1987) The social space of silence. *Environment and Planning D. Society and Space*, 5 (3), 249–62.

Onwuegbuzie, A. J. and Leech, N. L. (2005) Taking the "Q" out of research: Teaching research methodology courses without the divide between quantitative and qualitative paradigms. *Quality & Quantity*, 39, 267–95.

Opdenakker, R. (2006) Advantages and disadvantages of four interview techniques in qualitative research. *Forum Qualitative Sozialforschung / Forum: Qualitative Social Research*, 7 (4).

Orb, A., Eisenhauer, L. and Wynaden, D. (2001) Ethics in qualitative research. *Journal of Nursing Scholarship*, 33 (1), 93–6.

Orlikowski, W. J. and Yates, J. (1994) Genre repertoire: Examining the structuring of communicative practices in organizations. *Administrative Science Quarterly*, 39, 541–74.

Outhwaite, W. (1975) *Understanding social life*, London: Allen and Unwin.

———— (2009) *Habermas: Key contemporary thinkers (2nd edn.)*, Cambridge, UK: Polity Press.

Owen, I. R. (1994) Phenomenology – what is it? And what does it do? *The Newsletter of the History and Philosophy Section of the British Psychological Society*, 19, 18–24.

Palmer, B. and Major, C. (2007) Engendering the scholarship of teaching: A case study. *International Journal for the Scholarship of Teaching*, 1 (2), 1–15.

Pan, L. (2009) *Preparing literature reviews: Qualitative and quantitative approaches (3rd edn.)*, Glendale, CA: Pyrczak.

Papert, S. (1990) Introduction. *In:* I. Harel (ed.) *Constructivist learning.* Boston, MA: MIT.

Park, P. (1993) What is participatory research? A theoretical and methodological perspective. *In:* P. Park, M. Brydon-Miller, B. Hall and T. Jackson (eds) *Voices of change: Participatory research in the United States and Canada.* Westport, CT: Bergin and Garvey.

Park-Fuller, L. (2003) Audiencing the audience: Playback theatre, performative writing, and social activism. *Text and Performance Quarterly*, 23 (3), 288–310.

Parlett, M. and Dearden, G. (1977) *Introduction to illuminative evaluation: Studies in higher education*, Sacramento, CA: Pacific Soundings Press.

Parlett, M. and Hamilton, D. (1972) Evaluation as illumination: A new approach to the study of innovatory programmes. *In:* D. Hamilton, D. Jenkins, C. King, B. Macdonald and M. Parlett (eds) *Beyond the numbers game: A reader in education evaluation.* London: Macmillan.

———— (1976) Evaluation as illumination: A new approach to the study of innovatory programs. *In:* G. V. Glass (ed.) *Evaluation studies review annual, volume 1.* Beverly Hills, CA: Sage.

Patton, M. Q. (1982) *Practical evaluation*, Beverly Hills, CA: Sage.

———— (1990) *Qualitative evaluation and research methods (2nd edn.)*, Newbury Park, CA: Sage.

———— (1997) *Utilization focused evaluation: The new century text (3rd edn.)*, London: Sage.

———— (1999) Enhancing the quality and credibility of qualitative analysis. *Health Services Research*, 34 (5), 1189–208.

———— (2001) *Qualitative research and evaluation methods*, Thousand Oaks, CA: Sage.

———— (2002) *Qualitative research and evaluation methods (3rd edn.)*, Thousand Oaks, CA: Sage.

Peach, C. (2002) Social geography: New religion and ethnoburbs – contrasts with cultural geography. *Progress in Human Geography*, 26 (2), 252–60.

Perkins, D. (2006) Constructivism and troublesome knowledge. *In:* J. H. F. Meyer and R. Land (eds) *Overcoming barriers to student understanding: Threshold concepts and troublesome knowledge.* Abingdon: Routledge.

Peshkin, A. (1993) The goodness of qualitative research. *Educational Researcher*, 22 (2), 24–30.

———— (2000) The nature of interpretation in qualitative research. *Educational Researcher*, 29 (9), 5–9.

Piaget, J. (1951) *The child's conception of the world*, London: Routledge.

———— (1969) *The mechanisms of perception: Translated [from French] by G. N. Seagrim*, London: Routledge.

Pitney, W. A. and Ehlers, G. (2004) A grounded theory study of the mentoring processes involved with undergraduate athletic training students. *Journal of Athletic Training*, 39 (4), 344–51.

Platt, J. (1981) Evidence and proof in documentary research. *Sociological Review*, 29 (1), 31–52.

Plummer, K. (2001) The call of life stories in ethnographic research. *In:* P. Atkinson, A. Coffey, S. Delamont, J. Lofland and L. Lofland (eds) *Handbook of ethnography.* London: Sage.

Polit, D. and Beck, C. (2006) *Essentials of nursing care: Methods, appraisal and utilization (6th edn.),* Philadelphia, PA: Lippincott Williams and Wilkins.

Polkinghorne, D. (1983) *Methodology for the human sciences: Systems of inquiry,* Albany: State University of New York Press.

———— (1989) Phenomenological research methods. *In:* R. S. Valle and S. Halling (eds) *Existential-phenemenological perspectives in psychology.* New York: Plenum. pp. 41–60.

———— (1995) Narrative configuration in qualitative analysis. *In:* J. A. Hatch and R. Wisniewski (eds) *Life history and narrative.* London: Falmer Press.

Popay, J., Rogers, A. and Williams, G. (1998) Rationale and standards for the systematic review of qualitative literature in health services research. *Qualitative Health Research*, 8 (3), 341–51.

Pope, D. (2007) Peshkin's problematics: Teaching the nature of interpretation in qualitative research. *Qualitative Research Journal*, 6 (2), 173–82.

Popoviciu, L., Haywood, C. and Mac an Ghaill, M. (2006) The promise of post-structuralist methodology: Ethnographic representation of education and masculinity. *Ethnography and Education*, 1 (3), 393–412.

Popper, K. (1959) *The logic of scientific discovery,* London: Hutchinson.

———— (1968) *Conjectures and refutations,* New York: Harper.

———— (1972) *Objective knowledge: An evolutionary approach,* Oxford: Clarendon Press.

Potter, J. and Wetherell, M. (1987) *Discourse and social psychology: Beyond attitudes and behaviour,* London: Sage.

Potter, W. J. (1996) *An analysis of thinking and research about qualitative methods,* New Jersey: Lawrence Erlbaum Associates Publishers.

Price, J. N. (2001) Action research, pedagogy and change: The transformative potential of action research in pre-service teacher education. *Journal of Curriculum Studies*, 33 (1), 43–74.

Prior, L. (2003) *Using documents in social research using documents in social research,* London: Sage.

Prokop, T. McKay, S. and Gough, P. (2007) *An example of Appreciative Inquiry as a methodology for child welfare research in Saskatchewan Aboriginal communities.* CECW Information Sheet #51E. Toronto, ON: University of Toronto, Faculty of Social Work. http://www.cecw-cepb.ca/sites/default/files/publications/en/TransmissionofValues51E.pdf.

Propp, V. (1968) *Morphology of the folktale,* Baltimore, MD: Port City Press. pp. 19–65.

Prosser, J. (2011) Visual methodology: Toward a more seeing research. In: N. K. Denizen and Y. S. Lincoln (eds) *The Sage Handbook of qualitative research* (4th edn). Thousand Oaks, CA: Sage.

Prosser, J. and Loxley, A. (2008) *Introducing visual methods.* ESRC National Centre for Research Methods Review Papers, NCRM/010. [http://eprints.ncrm.ac.uk/420/]. Accessed 17 June 2012.

Prosser, M. and Trigwell, K. (1999) *Understanding learning and teaching,* Buckingham: Open University Press.

Prosser, M., Trigwell, K. and Taylor, P. (1994) A phenomenographic study of academics' conceptions of science teaching and learning. *Learning and Instruction*, 4, 217–31.

Psathas, G. (1973) *Phenomenological sociology: Issues and applications,* New York: Wiley.

Punch, M. (1986) *The politics and ethics of fieldwork,* Newbury Park, CA: Sage.

———— (1994) Politics and ethics in qualitative research. *In:* N. K. Denzin and Y. S. Lincoln (eds) *Handbook of qualitative research.* Newbury Park, CA: Sage.

Quinn, R. D. and Calkin, J. (2008) A dialogue in words and images between two artists doing arts-based educational research. *International Journal of Education and the Arts,* 9 (5).

Rahman, A. (1993) *People's self-development: Perspectives on participatory action research: A journey through experience,* London: Zed Books.

Ramsden, V. R. (2003) Learning with the community. Evolution to transformative action research. *Canadian Family Physician,* 49, 195–97.

Rapaport, R. (1970) Three dilemmas in action research. *Kidd,* 23, 499–513.

Rapley, T. (2004) Interviews. *In:* C. Seale (ed.) *Qualitative research practice.* London: Sage.

Raskin, J. D. (2002) Constructivism in psychology: Personal construct psychology, radical constructivism, and social constructivism. *In:* J. D. Raskin and S. K. Bridges (eds) *Studies in meaning: Exploring constructivist psychology.* New York: Pace University Press.

Rawnsley, M. M. (1998) Ontology, epistemology, and methodology: A clarification. *Nursing Science Quarterly,* 11 (1), 2–4.

Reason, P. (1988) *Human inquiry in action,* London: Sage.

———— (2002) The practice of cooperative inquiry. *Systemic Practice and Action Research,* 15 (3), 169–76.

Reason, P. and Bradbury, H. (2006) Introduction: Inquiry and participation in search of a world worthy of human aspiration. *In:* P. Reason and H. Bradbury (eds) *Handbook of action research: Participative inquiry and practice.* Thousand Oaks, CA: Sage.

Reason, P. and Heron, J. (1995) Co-operative inquiry. *In:* J. A. Smith, R. Harre and L. Van Langenhove (eds) *Rethinking methods in psychology.* London: Sage.

Reason, P. and Rowan, J. (eds) (1981) *Human inquiry: A sourcebook of new paradigm research,* Chicester: Wiley.

Reber, A. S. (1995) *The Penguin dictionary of psychology,* New York: Penguin Books.

Reed-Danahay, D. E. (1997) *Auto/ethnography: Rewriting the self and the social,* Oxford: Berg.

Reeves, S., Albert, M., Kuper, A. and Hodges, B. (2008) Why use theories in qualitative research. *BMJ,* 337 (949).

Reichardt, C. S. and Cook, T. D. (1979) Beyond qualitative versus quantitative methods. *In:* T. D. Cook and C. S. Reichardt (eds) *Qualitative and quantitative methods in evaluation research.* Beverly Hills, CA: Sage.

Reynolds, F. and Vivat, B. (2010) Art-making and identity work: A qualitative study of women living with chronic fatigue syndrome/myalgic encephalomyelitis (CFS/ME). *Arts and Health,* 2 (1), 67–80.

Rhodes, J. E. and Jakes, S. (2000) Correspondence between delusions and personal goals: a qualitative analysis. *British Journal of Medical Psychology,* 73, 211–25.

Richards, L. and Morse, J. M. (2007) *Readme first for a user's guide to qualitative methods (2nd edn.),* Thousand Oaks, CA: Sage.

Richardson, L. (1997) *Fields of play: Constructing an academic life,* New Brunswick, NJ: Rutgers University Press.

———— (1998) Writing: A method of inquiry. *In:* N. K. Denzin and Y. S. Lincoln (eds) *Collecting and interpreting qualitative materials.* Thousand Oaks, CA: Sage.

———— (2000) Evaluating ethnography. *Qualitative Inquiry,* 6 (2), 253–55.

Richardson, L. and Lockridge, E. (1998) Fiction and ethnography: A conversation. *Qualitative Inquiry,* 4 (3), 328–36.

Richardson, L. and St. Pierre, E. A. (2005) Writing: A method of inquiry. *In:* N. K. Denzin and Y. S. Lincoln (eds) *Handbook of qualitative research (3rd edn.).* Thousand Oaks, CA: Sage.

Riessman, C. K. (1993) *Narrative analysis,* Newbury Park, CA: Sage.

Ritchie, J. and Lewis, J. (2003) (eds) *Qualitative research practice: A guide for social science researchers*, London: Sage.

Rittel, H. and Webber, M. (1973) Dilemmas in a general theory of planning. *Policy Sciences*, 4, 155–69.

Ritzer, G. and Goodman, D. J. (2007) *Classical sociological theory*, Maidenhead: McGraw Hill.

Roberts, C. (2004) Qualitative data analysis. Transcribing spoken discourse. *FDTL Data Project 2004*, London: King's College University of London.

Robson, C. (2002) *Real world research (2nd edn.)*, Oxford: Blackwell.

Rolfe, G. (2006) Validity, trustworthiness and rigour: Quality and the idea of qualitative research. *Journal of Advanced Nursing*, 53 (3), 304–10.

Rolling, J. H. (2010) A paradigm analysis of arts-based research and implications for education. *Studies in Art Education*, 51 (2), 102–11.

Ropers-Huilman, R. and Winters, K. Y. (2011) Imagining intersectionality and the spaces in between: Theories and processes of socially transformative knowing. *In:* M. Savin-Baden and C. Howell Major (eds) *New approaches to qualitative research: Wisdom and uncertainty.* London: Routledge.

Rorty, R. (1979) *Philosophy and the mirror of nature*, Princeton, NJ: Princeton University Press.

———— (1991) *Objectivity, relativism, and truth: Philosophical papers (volume 1)*, Cambridge, UK: Cambridge University Press.

Rubin, H. and Rubin, I. (1995) *Qualitative interviewing: The art of hearing data*, Thousand Oaks, CA: Sage.

Rudestam, K. E. and Newton, R. R. (1992) *Surviving your dissertation*, London: Sage.

Runte, R. (2008) Blogs. *In:* J. G. Knowles and A. L. Cole (eds) *Handbook of the arts in qualitative research.* London: Sage.

Ryan, A. B. (2006) Post-positivist approaches to research. *In*: Antonesa, M., Fallon, H., Ryan, A. B., Ryan, A., Walsh, T. and Borys, L. *Researching and writing your thesis: a guide for postgraduate students.* Maynooth, Ireland: MACE Maynooth Adult and Community Education. pp. 12–26 [http://eprints.nuim.ie/archive/00000874/].

Ryan, K. E. and Cousins, J. B. (2009) *The SAGE international handbook of educational evaluation*, Thousands Oaks, CA: Sage.

Ryle, G. (1971) *Collected papers. Volume II collected essays, 1929–1968*, London: Hutchinson.

Sabo, K. and Baker, A. (2004) *Participatory evaluation essentials: A guide for non-profit organizations and their evaluation partners.* The Bruner Foundation, http://www.bruner foundation.org.

Sacks, H. (1974) On the analysability of stories by children. *In*: R. Turner (ed.) *Ethnomethodology: Selected readings.* Harmondsworth: Penguin Education.

St. Pierre, E. A. (2008) Decentering voice in qualitative inquiry. *International Review of Qualitative Research*, 1 (3), 319–36.

Saldaña, J. (2005) *Ethnodrama: An anthology of reality theatre*, Walnut Creek, CA: AltaMira Press.

———— (2006) This is not a performance text. *Qualitative Inquiry*, 12 (6), 1091–8.

———— (2010) Writing ethnodrama: A sampler from educational research. *In:* M. Savin-Baden and C. Major (eds) *New approaches to qualitative research.* London: Sage.

———— (2012) *The coding manual for qualitative researchers (2nd edn.)*, Thousand Oaks, CA: Sage.

Saldaña, J. and Wolcott, H. F. (2001) *Finding my place: The Brad trilogy.* A play adapted by Johnny Saldaña from the works of, and in collaboration with, Harry F. Wolcott. Tempe, AZ: Arizona State University Department of Theatre.

Salmon, P. (1989) Personal stances in learning. *In:* S. W. Weil and I. McGill (eds) *Making sense of experiential learning: Diversity in theory and practice.* Buckingham: Open University Press.

Salpeter, J. (2005) Telling tales with technology, *Tech & Learning* 15 February. [www.tech learning.com/showArticle.jhtml?articleID=60300276] Accessed 17 June 2012.

Sandberg, J. and Alvesson, M. (2011) Ways of constructing research questions: Gap-spotting or problematization? *Organization*, 18 (1), 23–44.

Sandelowski, M. (1986) The problem of rigor in qualitative research. *Advances in Nursing Science*, 8 (3), 27–37.

—— (1993) Rigor or rigor mortis: The problem of rigor in qualitative research revisited. *Advances in Nursing Science*, 16 (2), 1–8.

—— (1995) Qualitative analysis: What it is and how to begin. *Research in Nursing & Health*, 18, 371–5.

—— (1998) Writing a good read: Strategies for re-presenting qualitative data. *Research in Nursing & Health*, 21, 375–82.

—— (1999) Time and qualitative research. *Research in Nursing & Health*, 22, 79–87.

—— (2000) Focus on research methods: Whatever happened to qualitative description? *Research in Nursing & Health*, 23, 334–40.

—— (2002) Reembodying qualitative inquiry. *Qualitative Health Research*, 12 (1), 104–15.

Sandelowski, M. and Barroso, J. (2002) Reading qualitative studies. *International Journal of Qualitative Methods*, 1 (1), Article 5.

—— (2003) Classifying the findings in qualitative studies. *Qualitative Health Research*, 13 (7), 905–23.

—— (2007) *Handbook for synthesizing qualitative research*, New York: Springer.

Sandelowski, M., Holditch-Davis, D. and Harris, B. G. (1992) Using qualitative and quantitative methods: The transition to parenthood of infertile couples. *In:* J. F. Gilgun, K. Daly and G. Handel (eds) *Qualitative methods in family research*. Newbury Park, CA: Sage.

Sandelowski, M., Voils, C. I., Leeman, J. and Crandell, J. M. (2011) Mapping the mixed methods–mixed research synthesis terrain. *Journal of Mixed Methods Research*, 28 (4), doi:10.1177/1558689811427913.

Sarbin, T. R. (ed.) (1986) *Narrative psychology: The storied nature of human conduct*, New York: Praeger.

Savin-Baden, M. (2004) Achieving reflexivity: Moving researchers from analysis to interpretation in collaborative inquiry. *Journal of Social Work Practice*, 18 (3) 365–78.

Savin-Baden, M. (2010) *A Practical Guide to Using Second Life in higher education*. Maidenhead: McGraw Hill.

Savin-Baden, M. and Fisher, A. (2002) Negotiating 'honesties' in the research process. *British Journal of Occupational Therapy*, 65 (4), 191–3.

Savin-Baden, M. and Major, C. H. (2004) *Foundations of problem-based learning*. Buckingham: Society for Research in Higher Education and Open University Press.

Savin-Baden, M. and Major, C. (2007) Using interpretive meta-ethnography to explore the relationship between innovative approaches to learning and innovative methods of pedagogical research. *Higher Education*, 54 (6), 833–52.

Savin-Baden, M. and Wimpenny, K. (2007) Exploring and implementing participatory action research. *Journal of Geography in Higher Education*, 31 (2), 331–43.

Schatzman, L. and Strauss, A. L. (1973) *Fieldwork research: Strategies for a natural sociology*, Englewood Cliffs, NJ: Prentice-Hall.

Schechner, R. (2006) *Performance studies: An introduction*, London: Routledge.

Schensul, S. L., Schensul, J. J. and LeCompte, M. (eds) (1999) *Essential ethnographic methods: Observations, interviews, and questionnaires*, Walnut Creek: Rowman & Littlefield Publishers.

Schlick, M. (1918; 2nd edn. 1925) *Allgemeine erkenntnislehre*, Berlin: Springer.

Schmuck, R. (1997) *Practical action research for change*, Arlington Heights, IL: IRI/Skylight Training and Publishing.

Schostak, J. (2006) *Interviewing and representation in qualitative research*, Maidenhead: McGraw Hill.

Schratz, M. (1993) Qualitative voices in educational research. *Social Research and Educational Studies*, Series 9, 1–7.

Schratz, M. and Walker, R. (1995) *Research as a social change: New opportunities for qualitative research*, London: Routledge.

Schuh, K. L. and Barab, S. A. (2008) Philosophical perspective. *In:* J. M. Spector, M. D. Merrill, J. V. Merrienboer and M. P. Driscoll (eds) *Handbook of research on educational communications and technology (3rd edn.)*. New York: Lawrence Erlbaum Associates.

Schwandt, T. A. (1994) Constructivist, interpretivist approaches to human inquiry. *In:* N. K. Denzin and Y. S. Lincoln (eds) *Handbook of qualitative research.* Thousand Oaks, CA: Sage.

———— (2000) Three epistemological stances for qualitative inquiry: Interpretivism, hermeneutics and social constructionism. *In:* N. K. Denzin and Y. S. Lincoln (eds) *Handbook of qualitative research (2nd edn.)*. Newbury Park, CA: Sage.

Sconiers, Z. and Rosiek, J. (2000) Voices inside schools – Historical perspective as an important element of teachers' knowledge: A sonata-form case study of equity issues in a chemistry classroom. *Harvard Educational Review*, 70 (3).

Scott, J. (1990) *A matter of record: Documentary sources in social research*, Cambridge: Polity.

Scriven, M. (1967) The methodology of evaluation. *In:* R. Tyler, M. Gagne and M. Scriven (eds) *Perspectives of curriculum evaluation: Vol. 1. Aera monograph series on curriculum evaluation.* Chicago: Rand McNally.

———— (1972) Pros and cons about goal-free evaluation. *Evaluation Comment*, 3 (4), 1–4.

Seale, C. (1999a) Quality in qualitative research. *Qualitative Inquiry*, 5 (4), 465–78.

Seale, C. (1999b) *The quality of qualitative research*, Oxford: Blackwell.

Seidman, I. (1991) *Interviewing as qualitative research: A guide for researchers in education and the social sciences*, New York: Teachers College Press.

———— (1998) *Interviewing as qualitative research: A guide for researchers in education and the social sciences (2nd edn.)*, New York: Teachers College Press.

Sellito, P. (1991) *Balancing acts: A novel.* Unpublished doctoral dissertation, Hofstra University, New York/Rotterdam.

Shakespeare, P. (2009) Writing ethnography. *In:* J. Higgs, D. Horsfall and S. Grace (eds) *Writing qualitative research on practice.* The Netherlands: Sense Publishers. pp. 95–104.

Shaw, I. F. (2008) Ethics and the practice of qualitative research. *Qualitative Social Work*, 7 (4), 400–14.

Shaw, I. F., Greene, J. C. and Mark, M. M. (2007) *Handbook of evaluation*, London: Sage.

Sherif, B. (2001) The ambiguity of boundaries in the fieldwork experience: Establishing rapport and negotiating insider/outsider status. *Qualitative Inquiry*, 7 (4), 436–47.

Shulman, L. S. (1986) Those who understand: Knowledge growth in teaching. *Educational Researcher*, 15 (2), 4–14.

Silverman, D. (2001) *Interpreting qualitative data (2nd edn.)*, Thousand Oaks, CA: Sage.

———— (2005) *Doing qualitative research: A practical handbook (2nd edn.)*, London: Sage.

Simons, H. (1980) Towards a science of the singular: Essays about case study in educational research and evaluation. *Occasional Publication*, 10, 262.

———— (1987) *Getting to know schools in a democracy: The politics and process of evaluation*, Lewes: Falmer Press.

———— (1996) The paradox of case study. *Cambridge Journal of Education*, 26 (2), 225–40.

———— (2009) *Case study research in practice*, London: Sage.

Simons, H. and McCormack, B. (2007) Opportunities and challenges integrating arts-based inquiry in evaluation methodology. *Qualitative Inquiry*, 13, 292–311.

Slater, M. (2009) Place illusion and plausibility can lead to realistic behaviour in immersive virtual environments. *Philosophical Transactions of the Royal Society of London. Series B: Biological Sciences*, 364 (1535), 3549–57.

Small, S. A. (1995) Action-oriented research: Models and methods. *Journal of Marriage & the Family*, 57 (4), 941–55.

Smith, J. A. (1999) Towards a relational self: Social engagement during pregnancy and psychological preparation for motherhood. *British Journal of Social Psychology*, 38, 409–26.

Smith, J. A. and Osborn, M. (2003) Interpretative phenomenological analysis. *In:* J. A. Smith (ed.) *Qualitative psychology: A practical guide to research methods.* London: Sage.

Smith, J. A., Harré, R. and Van Langenhove, L. (1995) Idiography and the case study. *In:* J. A. Smith, R. Harre and L. Van Langenhove (eds) *Rethinking psychology.* London: Sage.

Smyth, R. (2004) Exploring the usefulness of a conceptual framework as a research tool: A researcher's reflections. *Issues in Educational Research*, 14 (2), 167–80.

Snape, D. and Spencer, L. (2003) Foundations of qualitative research. *In:* J. Ritchie and J. Lewis (eds) *Qualitative research practice: A guide for social science researchers.* London: Sage.

Snowber, C. N. and Cancienne, M. B. (April 2003) Writing rhythm: Movement as method. *Qualitative Inquiry*, 9 (2), 237–53.

Somekh, B. and Lewin, C. (2005) *Research methods in social sciences*, London: Sage.

Sparkes, A. C. (2009) Novel ethnographic representations and the dilemmas of judgment. *Ethnography and Education*, 4 (3), 303–21.

Sparkes, A. C. and Smith, B. (2005) When narratives matter: Men, sport, and spinal cord injury. *Medical Humanities*, 31 (2) 81–8.

Spiegelberg, H. (1960) *The phenomenological movement (2nd edn.)*, The Hague: Nijhoff.

Spradley, J. P. (1979) *The ethnographic interview*, New York: Holt, Rinehart & Winston.

Srivastva, S. and Cooperrider, D. L. (1986) The emergence of the egalitarian organization. *Human Relations*, 39 (8), 683–724.

Stake, R. (1967) Toward a technology for the evaluation of educational programs. *In:* R. Tyler, M. Gagne and M. Scriven (eds) *Perspectives of curriculum evaluation: Vol. 1. Aera monograph series on curriculum evaluation* Chicago, IL: Rand McNally.

—— (1978) The case study method in social inquiry. *Educational Researcher*, 7 (2), 5–8.

—— (1983) Responsive evaluation. *In:* T. Husén and T. N. Postlethwaite (eds) *International encyclopedia of education: Research and studies.* New York: Pergamon Press.

—— (1994) Case studies. *In:* N. K. Denzin and Y. S. Lincoln (eds) *Handbook of qualitative research.* London: Sage.

—— (1995) *The art of case research*, Thousand Oaks, CA: Sage.

—— (2002) Program evaluation, particularly responsive evaluation. *Evaluation in Education and Human Services*, 49 (IV), 343–62.

—— (2005) Case studies. *In:* N. K. Denzin and Y. S. Lincoln (eds) *The Sage handbook of qualitative research.* London: Sage.

—— (2010) *Qualitative research: Studying how things work*, New York: Guilford.

Stark, J. S. and Lattuca, L. R. (1997) *Shaping the college curriculum: Academic plans in action*, London: Allyn and Bacon.

Stenbacka, C. (2001) Qualitative research requires quality concepts of its own. *Management Decision*, 39 (7), 551–5.

Stenhouse, L. (1975) *An introduction to curriculum research and development*, London: Heinemann.

—— (1988) Case methods. *In:* J. P. Keeves (ed.) *Educational research, methodology and measurement: An international handbook.* Oxford: Pergamon.

Stewart, D. and Mickunas, A. (1990) *Exploring phenomenology: A guide to the field and its texts (2nd edn.)*, Athens, OH: Ohio University Press.

Stocking, G. W. (1983) The ethnographer's magic: Fieldwork in British anthropology from Tylor to Malinowski. *In:* G. W. Stocking (ed.) *Observers observed: Essays on ethnographic fieldwork.* Madison, WI: University of Wisconsin Press.

Stoller, P. and Olkes, C. (1987) *In sorcery's shadow: A memoir of apprenticeship among the songhay Songhay of Niger,* Chicago, IL: University of Chicago Press.

Stone, P. J., Dunphy, D. C. and Smith, M. S. (1966) *E general inquirer. A computer approach to content analysis,* Cambridge, MA: The MIT Press.

Strauss, A. L (1987) *Qualitative analysis for social scientists,* Cambridge: Cambridge University Press.

Strauss, A. L. and Corbin, J. (1990) *Basics of qualitative research: Grounded theory procedures and techniques,* Newbury Park, CA: Sage.

―――― (1994) Grounded theory methodology: An overview. *In:* N. K. Denzin and Y. S. Lincoln (eds) *Handbook of qualitative research.* Thousand Oaks, CA: Sage.

―――― (1998) *Basics of qualitative research: Techniques and procedures for developing grounded theory (2nd edn.),* Thousand Oaks, CA: Sage.

Stronach, I., Corbin, B., McNamara, O., Stark, S. and Warne, T. (2002) Towards an uncertain politics of professionalism: Teacher and nurse identities in flux. *Journal of Educational Policy,* 17 (1), 109–38.

Stubbs, M. (1983) *Discourse analysis: The sociolinguistic analysis of natural language,* Chicago, IL: University of Chicago Press.

Stufflebeam, D. L. (1983) The CIPP model for program evaluation. *In:* G. F. Madaus, M. Scriven and D. L. Stufflebeam (eds) *Evaluation models: Viewpoints on educational and human services evaluation.* Boston, MA: Kluwer Nijhoff.

Stufflebeam, D. L., Foley, W. L., Gephart, W. J., Guba, E. G., Hammond, R. E., Merriam, H. O. and Provus, M. M. (1971) *Educational evaluation and decision making.* Itasca, IL: F. E. Peacock Publishers.

Sullivan, A. M. (2000) Notes from a marine biologist's daughter: On the art and science of attention. *Harvard Educational Review,* 70 (2), 211–27.

Swanson, L. (2009) Complicating the 'soccer mom': The cultural politics of forming class-based identity, distinction, and necessity. *Research Quarterly for Exercise and Sport,* 80 (2), 345–54.

Taba, H. and Noel, E. (1957) *Action research: A case study,* Washington, DC: Association for Supervision and Curriculum Development.

Tashakkori, A. and Teddlie, C. (2003) *Handbook of mixed methods in social and behavioural research,* London: Cassell.

Tellis, W. (1997) Introduction to case study. *The Qualitative Report,* 3 (2).

ten Have, P. (2004) *Understanding qualitative research and ethnomethodology,* London: Sage.

Tesch, R. (1990) *Qualitative research: Analysis types and software tools (vol. 337),* Philadelphia, PA: RoutledgeFalmer.

Thomas, G. and James, D. (2006) Re-inventing grounded theory: Some questions about theory, ground and discovery. *British Educational Research Journal,* 32 (6), 767–95.

Thomas, W. and Zaniecki, F. (1927) *The Polish peasant in Europe and America,* Knopf: New York.

Thomas-Hunt, M. C. and Phillips, K. W. (2004) When what you know is not enough: Expertise and gender dynamics in task groups. *Personality and Social Psychology Bulletin,* 30 (12), 1585–98.

Thornberg, R., Halldin, K., Bolmsjö, N. and Petersson, A. (2011) Victimising of school bullying: A grounded theory. *Research Papers in Education.* DOI: 10.1080/02671522.2011.64 1999.

Thorne, S. (1997) The art (and science) of critiquing qualitative research. *In:* J. M. Morse (ed.) *Completing a qualitative project: Details and dialogue.* Thousand Oaks, CA: Sage. pp. 117–32.

Thorne, S. E., Con, A., Mcguinness, G., Mcpherson, G. and Harris, R. (2004a) Health care communication issues in multiple sclerosis. An interpretive description. *Qualitative Health Research*, 14 (5), 5–22.

Thorne, S. E., Jensen, L. A., Kearney, M. H., Noblit, G. and Sandelowski, M. (2004b) Qualitative metasynthesis: Reflections on methodological orientation and ideological agenda. *Qualitative Health Research*, 14, 1342–65.

Thorne, S. E., Kirkham, S. R. and Henderson, A. (1999) Ideological implications of the paradigm discourse. *Nursing Inquiry*, 4, 1–2.

Thorne, S. E., Kirkham, S. R. and MacDonald-Emes, J. (1997) Interpretive description: A noncategorical qualitative alternative for developing nursing knowledge. *Research in Nursing & Health*, 20, 169–77.

Tierney, M. (1994) On method and hope. *In:* A. Gitlin (ed.) *Power and method.* London: Routledge.

Tierney, M. and Dilley, P. (2002) Interviewing in education. *In:* J. F. Gubrium and J. A. Holstein (eds) *Handbook of interview research: Context & method.* Thousand Oaks, CA: Sage.

Tilley, S. A. (2003) Challenging research practices: Turning a critical lens on the work of transcription. *Qualitative Inquiry*, 9, 750–73.

Torbert, W. (1981) Why educational research has been so uneducational: The case for a new model of social science based on collaborative inquiry. *In:* P. Reason and J. Rowan (eds) *Human inquiry: A sourcebook of new paradigm research.* London: Wiley.

–––– (2001) The practice of action inquiry. *In:* P. Reason and H. Bradbury (eds) *Handbook of action research.* London: Sage. pp. 250–60.

Trafford, V. and Leshem, S. (2008) *Stepping stones to achieving your doctorate*, Maidenhead: Open University Press.

Traylen, H. (1994) Confronting hidden agendas: Cooperative inquiry with health visitors. *In:* P. Reason (ed.) *Participation in human inquiry.* London: Sage.

Trede, F. and Higgs, J. (2009) Framing research questions and writing philosophically: The role of framing research questions. *In:* J. Higgs, D. Harsfall and S. Graces (eds) *Writing qualitative research on practice.* Rotterdam, The Netherlands: Sense Publishers.

Treleaven, L. (1994) Making a space: A collaborative inquiry with women as staff development. *In:* P. Reason (ed.) *Participation in human inquiry.* London: Sage.

Trigwell, K., Prosser, M. and Lyons, F. (1999) Relations between teachers' approaches to teaching and students' approaches to learning. *Higher Education*, 37, 57–70.

Trigwell, K., Prosser, M. and Taylor, P. (1994) Qualitative differences in approaches to teaching first year university science courses. *Higher Education*, 27, 74–84.

Trost, J. (1986) Research note: Statistically nonrepresentative stratified sampling: A sampling technique for qualitative studies. *Qualitative Sociology*, 9 (1), 54–7.

Turner, V. (1967) *The forest of symbols: Aspects of Ndembu ritual*, Ithaca, NY: Cornell University Press.

–––– (1982) *From ritual to theatre*, New York: PAJ Publications.

Tyler, R. W. (1969) *Basic principles of curriculum and instruction*, Chicago, IL: University of Chicago Press.

Urquhart, C. (2001) An encounter with grounded theory: Tackling the practical and philosophical issues. *In:* E. M. Trauth (ed.) *Qualitative research in IS: Issues and trends.* Hershey, PA: Idea Group Publishing.

US Department of Health and Human Services (2009) *Code of Federal regulations, Title 45 Public welfare Part 46 Protection of human subjects*, Washington DC.

Valentine, G. (1992) Images of danger: Women's sources of information about the spatial distribution of male violence. *Area*, 24 (1), 22–9.

Valle, R., King, M. and Halling, S. (1989) An introduction to existential-phenomenological though in psychology. *In:* R. Valle and S. Halling (eds) *Existential-phenomenological perspective in psychology*. New York: Plenum Press.

van den Hoonaard, W. C. (2002) *Walking the tightrope: Ethical issues for qualitative researchers*, Toronto: University of Toronto Press.

van Dijk, T. (1985) Introduction: The role of discourse analysis in society. *In:* T. van Dijk (ed.) *Handbook of discourse analysis*. Orlando, FL: Academic Press.

Van Maanen, J. (1996) Ethnography. *In:* A. Kuper and J. Kuper (eds) *The social science encyclopedia (2nd edn.)*. London: Routledge.

———— (1998) *Tales of the field. On writing ethnography*, Chicago: University of Chicago Press.

van Manen, M. (1990) *Researching lived experience: Human science for an action sensitive pedagogy*, Albany, NY: State University of New York Press.

———— (1997) *Researching lived experience: Human science for an action sensitive pedagogy (2nd edn.)*, London, Canada: The Althhouse Press.

Van Niekerk, L. and Savin-Baden, M. (2011) Re-locating truths in the qualitative research paradigm. *In:* M. Savin-Baden and C. Major (eds) *New approaches to qualitative research: Wisdom and uncertainty*. London: Routledge.

Vasconcelos, A. C. (2007) The use of grounded theory and of arenas/social worlds theory in discourse studies: A case study on the discursive adaptation of information systems. *The Electronic Journal of Business Research Methods*, 5 (2), 125–36.

Vestman, O. K. and Conner, R. F. (2007) The relationship between evaluation and politics. *In:* I. F. Shaw, J. C. Greene and M. M. Mark (eds) *Handbook of evaluation*. London: Sage.

Vidich, A. J. and Lyman, S. M. (2000) Qualitative methods: Their history in sociology and anthropology. *In:* N. K. Denzin and Y. S. Lincoln (eds) *Handbook of qualitative research. (2nd edn.)*, Thousand Oaks: Sage.

Vignoles, V. L., Chryssochoou, X., and Breakwell, G. M. (2004) Combining individuality and relatedness: Representations of the person among the Anglican clergy. *British Journal of Social Psychology*, 43, 113–32.

Vitullo, E. and Jones. E. (2010) An exploratory investigation of the assessment practices of selected association to advance collegiate schools of business – accredited business programs and linkages with general education outcomes. *Journal of General Education*, 59 (2), 85–104.

Vrasidas, C. (2001) Interpretivism and symbolic interactionism: 'Making the familiar strange and interesting again' in educational technology research. *In:* W. Heinecke and J. Willis (eds) *Research methods in educational technology*. Greenwich, CT: Information Age Publishing Inc.

Walker, R. (1983) Three good reasons for not doing case studies in curriculum research. *Journal of Curriculum Studies*, 15 (2), 155–65.

Wallerstein, N. and Duran, B. (2003) The conceptual, historical and practice roots of community based participatory research and related participatory traditions. *In:* M. Minkler and N. Wallerstein (eds) *Community-based participatory research for health*. San Francisco, CA: Jossey-Bass/Wiley. pp. 27–52.

Warren, C. (1988) *Gender issues in field research*, Newbury Park, CA: Sage.

Warwick, R., Joseph, S., Cordle, C. and Ashworth, P. (2004) Social support for people with chronic pain: What is helpful for whom? *Psychology of Health*, 19,117–34.

Watkins, J. M. (1986) *Invisible guests. The development of imaginal dialogues*, Hillsdale, NJ: Analytic Press.

Watkins, J. M. and Mohr, B. (2001) *Appreciative inquiry: Change at the speed of imagination*, San Francisco, CA: Jossey Bass.

Weaver-Hart, A. (1988) Framing an innocent concept and getting away with it. *UCEA Review*, 24 (2), 11–12.

Weaver-Hightower, M. B. (2012) Waltzing Matilda: An autoethnography of a father's stillbirth. *Journal of Contemporary Ethnography.* DOI: 10.1177/0891241611429302.

Weber, R. P. (1990) *Basic content analysis (2nd edn.)*, London: Sage.

Weber, S. (2008) Visual images in research. *In:* J. G. Knowles and A. L. Cole (eds) *Handbook of the arts in qualitative research: Perspectives, methodologies, examples, and issues.* London: Sage.

Weiss, C. H. (1991) Evaluation research in the political context: Sixteen years and four administrations later. *In:* M. W. Mclaughlin and D. C. Phillips (eds) *Evaluation and education: At quarter century.* Chicago, IL: The University Press.

Weiss, R. S. (1994) *Learning from strangers: The art and method of qualitative interviewing*, New York: Free Press.

Wengraf, T. (2001) *Qualitative research interviewing: Biographic narrative and semi-structured method*, London: Sage.

Wheeler, B. (2005) Developing a topic. *In:* B. Wheeler (ed.) *Music therapy research.* Gilsum, NH: Barcelona Publishers.

Whipps, J. D. (2004) Jane Addams social thought as a model for a pragmatist–feminist communitarianism. *Hypatia*, 19, 118–13.

White, C., Woodfield, K. and Ritchie, J. (2003) Reporting and presenting qualitative data. *In:* J. Ritchie and J. Lewis (eds) *Qualitative research practice: A guide for social science students and researchers.* London: Sage.

Whiting, L. S. and Vickers, P. S. (2010) Conducting qualitative research with palliative care patients: Applying Hammick's research ethics wheel. *International Journal of Palliative Nursing*, 16 (2), 58, 60–2, 64–6, 68.

Whitmore, K. F. and Laurich, L. (2010) What happens in the arcade shouldn't stay in the arcade: Lessons in classroom design. *Language Arts*, 88 (10), 21–31.

Whittemore, R., Chase, S. K. and Mandle, C. L. (2001) Validity in qualitative research. *Qualitative Health Research*, 11, 522–37.

Williams, R. F. (2006) Using cognitive ethnography to study instruction. *Proceedings of the 7th International Conference of the Learning Sciences.* Mahwah, NJ: Lawrence Erlbaum. [http://hci.ucsd.edu/102b/readings/williams-cogethno.pdf]. Accessed 17 June 2012.

Willig, C. (2001) *Qualitative research in psychology: A practical guide to theory and method*, Buckingham: Open University Press.

–––– (2003) Discourse analysis. *In:* J. A. Smith (ed.) *Qualitative psychology: A practical guide to research methods.* London: Sage.

Willis, P. and Smith, T. (2000) Coming to being, seeking and telling. *In:* P. Willis, T. Smith and E. Collins (eds) *Being, seeking, telling: Expressive approaches to qualitative adult education research.* Adelaide: Post Pressed.

Wilson, E. O. (1998) *Consilience: The unity of knowledge*, New York: Knopf.

Wilson, M. and Sperlinger, D. (2004) Dropping out or dropping in? A re-examination of the concept of dropouts using qualitative methodology. *Psychoanalytic Psychotherapy*, 18, 220–37.

Wimpenny, K. (2010) Participatory action research: An integrated approach towards practice development. *In:* M. Savin-Baden and C. Major (eds) *New approaches to qualitative research: Wisdom and uncertainty.* London: Routledge.

Wimpenny, K. and Savin-Baden, M. (2012) Exploring and implementing participatory action synthesis. *Qualitative Inquiry*, 18 (8) 689–98.

Wimpenny, K., Savin-Baden, M., Mawer, M., Steils, N. and Tombs, G. (2012) Unpacking frames of reference to inform the design of virtual world learning in higher education. *Australasian Journal of Educational Technology*, 28 (Special issue, 3), 522–45.

Winter, G. (2000) A comparative discussion of the notion of validity in qualitative and quantitative research. *The Qualitative Report*, 4 (384).

Wisker, G. and Savin-Baden, M. (2009) Priceless conceptual thresholds: Beyond the 'stuck place' in writing. *London Review of Education*, 7 (3), 235–47.

Wolcott, H. F. (1990) *Writing up qualitative research*, London: Sage.

–––– (1992) Posturing in qualitative inquiry. *In:* M. D. LeCompte, W. L. Millroy and J. Preissle (eds) *The handbook of qualitative research in education*. New York: Academic Press.

–––– (1994) *Transforming qualitative data*, London: Sage.

–––– (2001) *Writing up qualitative research*, California: Sage.

–––– (2009) *Writing up qualitative research (2nd edn.)*, Newbury Park, CA: Sage.

Wolf, R. L. and Tymitz, B. L. (1977) Toward more natural inquiry in education. *CEDR Quarterly*, 10 (3), 7–9.

Woodward, K. (2008) Hanging out and hanging about: Insider/outsider research in the sport of boxing. *Ethnography*, 9 (4), 536–60.

Yardley, L. (2000) Dilemmas in qualitative health research. *Psychology and Health*, 15, 215–28.

Yin, R. K. (1984) *Case study research: Design and methods (1st edn.)*, Beverly Hills, CA: Sage.

–––– (1993) *Applications of case study research*, Beverly Hills, CA: Sage.

–––– (1994) *Case study research. Design and methods (2nd edn.)*, Thousand Oaks, CA: Sage.

–––– (2002) *Case study research. Design and methods (3rd edn.)*, Newbury Park: Sage.

–––– (2009) *Case study research. Design and methods (4th edn.)*, Thousand Oaks, CA: Sage.

Youdell, D. (2006) *Impossible bodies, impossible selves: Exclusions and student subjectivities. Cross Cultural Perspectives, Volume 3*. Dordrecht: Springer.

Znaniecki, F. (1934) *The method of sociology*, New York: Farrar and Rinehart.

Zuber-Skerritt, O. (1996) *New directions in action research*, London: The Falmer Press.

Zuboff, S. (1984) *In the age of the smart machine: The future of work and power*, New York: Basic Books.

INDEX